APL

An Interactive Approach

Third Edition

Leonard Gilman
International Business Machines Corporation

Allen J. Rose
Allen Rose Associates

JOHN WILEY & SONS, Inc.   New York · Chichester · Brisbane · Toronto · Singapore

Library of Congress Cataloging in Publication Data

Gilman, Leonard, 1930-
    APL : an interactive approach.

    Includes index.
    1. **APL** (Computer program language) I. Rose,
Allen J. II. Title. III. Title: A.P.L.

QA76.73.A27G54   1983   001.64'24   83-14716

Printed in the United States of America

10 9 8 7 6 5 4

Foreword

APL is both a programming language and a system that supports the writing, editing, using, saving and sharing of programs. It is appropriate to think of them as one since all use of APL involves both in an integrated way.

The two are interactive and mediated from terminals so that personal involvement is continual and natural and—for computer systems—relatively effortless. As this book so admirably illustrates, one can 'sneak up' on the mastery of APL starting from an almost negligible investment in language and system techniques. At the other extreme, once one has mastered APL one has accomplished something of permanent value and benefit: programs of great value and interest can be written by one person that in other languages would require a team!

The power of the APL language comes from its direct manipulation of aggregates of data in the form of arrays. Everyone recognizes that computers excel where aggregates are manipulated, where the descriptive details of a function do not grow with the size of the aggregates being manipulated, and where one description suffices to cover a large population of aggregates. Most other languages require their programs to penetrate these structures, manipulate the components individually even in order to achieve a uniform effort. It is not surprising that APL programs are significantly shorter and more lucid than programs in most other languages. In programming, clarity is not a consequence of discursiveness or low information density in the program text.

Because of its power in aggregate and component manipulation, APL has many more primitive functions than other languages. Rather than adding to complexity, this multiplicity actually simplifies. When a typical processing need arises, APL has a primitive function that naturally performs it. Learning the properties and uses of these primitives adds but a little to the labor of APL mastery. Shortly after encountering a function one sees how it 'falls:in' with others already understood and soon it begins to participate in program constructions in a natural way.

Programmers are surprised and pleased to discover that all APL primitive functions get used and that none are arcane and of questionable utility. Even more, one soon acquires skill in combining these functions artfully into phrases commonly called 'idioms', that are frequently used and that extend every programmer's arsenal of programming constructions. No other language supports such a rich development of idioms, or even permits one to think idiomatically.

It is often said of APL that it provides too much choice for programmers—there are too many ways to perform desired functions, and among a group of APL programmers the same task will often lead them to create quite different programs. Consequently, reading APL programs is not trivial. Considering that APL text is often one-third to one-fifth the size of equivalent text in another language, APL programs turn out to be as understandable as those in other languages. The very richness of the set of APL functions that makes its mastery so challenging makes the learning of other languages much easier once APL is learned.

APL has its own operating system and thus use of APL is much the same (but alas not identical) on all computers, from the smallest and cheapest to the largest and most expensive. Unlike BASIC, for which each computer has its own idiosyncratic version, APL is a paragon of constancy between machines.

The workspace in which the user's APL traffic is organized is a natural, simple and friendly environment in which to compute. Its permanence is set by the individual user and can comfortably be thought of as an immense personal blackboard. Indeed, each user has a large number of such blackboards identified by chosen names and between which the user can flit and transfer data and function. Best of all, a workspace can be frozen, suspended in time, saved and resumed in the future as though no time had passed. A collection of workspaces forms a library and the user has access to both public and private libraries to which he has been granted access.

More idiosyncratic than the workspace, APL supports large files—but differently on most machines. A recent development in APL is heterogeneous nested arrays. Their value is unquestioned, but the permanence of their definition and form within the APL language is still under study. Like all living languages APL changes, but more slowly and carefully than most others. Unlike most other languages APL affects the way one thinks about programming: familiarity with BASIC or PASCAL does not automatically translate over to expertise in APL.

This is not a book on programming or even programming in APL. Instead it is a carefully organized journey through the APL language and system. The journey is amazingly smooth and painless. The book reads very well. One does not have to be a computer specialist to understand the material. The exercises are by and large elementary, though a few difficult problems are scattered throughout. No book on APL can present a complete specification of the APL language and system and still be readable. However, this book, in conjunction with an APL system, provides the basic spectrum of insights into APL behavior:

(a) Read the material on issue X.

(b) Do a sample of the exercises.

(c) Execute some obvious instances of X at the terminal.

(d) Pose questions about X of the form 'What if... .' Execute them at the terminal. Between the results obtained and a re-reading of the text one will soon say, 'Ah, that is why this happened and I now understand issue X.'

By the time one has read the book, the details of APL behavior will have become so engraved in one's skull that one will think naturally at the programming level but perform at the primitive function level. One will have become an APL programmer.

Alan J. Perlis
New Haven, Conn.
August 1983

Preface

Today's APL systems are substantially more powerful than the APL described in the first edition of 'Interactive Approach' in 1970. During that time APL has evolved from a language with 'funny looking symbols' used as a novel calculator of small scientific problems into a full-featured general purpose programming system.

The community of APL users has grown also—over 250,000 copies of the previous editions of this work have been circulated worldwide. Well-attended international APL conferences are regularly sponsored by major computing societies.

The interests of APL users are as varied as people themselves, and we are still surprised and impressed by the breadth and sophistication of applications of APL that we see. We believe the next few years will yield an even more rapid rate of growth for APL, largely due to its availability on low cost, individual processors such as the IBM Personal Computer.

It has not been easy for us to keep current with all the changes in APL and its uses. We wanted to retain in this edition the informality and readability that our readers told us were in the previous editions, and yet include the important language extensions and their application. All this for an audience that ranges from high school to MBA candidates, and includes casual do-it-yourselfers, educators and professional programmers.

This edition emphasizes practical information-processing applications somewhat more than scientific examples. Engineering and mathematical material is included, but we indicate what may be skipped without loss of continuity. Our guide is the rule 'what you don't know shouldn't hurt you.'

At the suggestion of nearly everyone, we take up elementary function definition (programming) quite early—most readers will be able to write simple programs in their first session on the computer. Advanced topics such as report formatting, generalized arrays, files, and interacting with the operating system are deferred and can be read in any sequence, or skipped entirely. All of the programs and examples displayed in the book can be entered from the keyboard, or may be purchased in machine readable form for popular systems. See inside the back cover for details.

Like the previous editions, this book has been designed and tested for use in formal courses as well as for self study. In either case we recommend that Chapters 1 through 16 be read in sequence, and that the reader have access to an APL system to try things out (after all, the subtitle is *An Interactive Approach*). It isn't necessary to memorize the details in these chapters because the index (prepared by an APL program, of course) is thorough enough that the book serves as a reference manual as well as a text.

We hope you enjoy this book as much as we have enjoyed writing it for you. It is the interaction with our readers that helps us keep a pulse on APL usage. We encourage you to correspond with either or both of us.

Many people have contributed to this book indirectly through their efforts on the previous editions, where they are cited. For this edition, we are grateful for the good work of Ms. Jillian Wade, an author in her own right and an accomplished APL programmer and instructor. She entered, edited, criticized, and verified much of the text and provided ideas which were significant improvements over our own. We thank Mr. Alan Graham for his guidance and the problem set for the chapter on nested arrays, as well as for many other suggestions that have been incorporated into this edition.

Leonard Gilman
19 Horseshoe Road
Mt. Kisco, NY 10549

Allen J. Rose
Box 58, Kinue Road
Captain Cook, Hawaii 96704

September, 1983

CONTENTS

APL

An Interactive Approach

Chapter 1: Getting started

Imagine having a mindless assistant at your beck and call who will readily and accurately carry out your every instruction. However, he requires that you be extremely precise in your instructions: that you neither leave out any detail nor give him conflicting instructions. Your communication with this faithful person would become very precise. In contrast, natural languages are filled with inherent ambiguities. For example, a telegram reading 'STRIKE AT MINE. COME AT ONCE' means one thing to a mining engineer, and quite another thing to a shop steward from the miners' union. Hence, you and he might develop and adopt some artificial language which is (1) well suited to the type of instructions being communicated; (2) easily learned and remembered by you and your assistant; (3) not prone to ambiguities; (4) extendable to cope with future unanticipated needs; and (5) terse, so that no time is wasted in idle conversation.

Assuming that the tasks put to this assistant are mostly record keeping and arithmetic in nature, it is likely that the language would readily lend itself to expressing instructions. If this faithful assistant does nothing other than what you direct, and if you direct him to do only work that you would have done otherwise, isn't he being used as a *tool*? A special type of tool to be sure—one that we *communicate* with rather than just push, pull or turn.

Now no one wants to be thought of as a tool. And no one has to, at least as far as record keeping and calculations are concerned. Computers do that type of work better, cheaper, faster and more accurately than any human. But like our faithful assistant (and unlike other tools), we communicate with a computer to get it to work.

A *programming language* is the means through which we tell the computer what to do and it tells us what it has done. It would be desirable to use a language well suited to the tasks to be done. *Natural* languages such as English, French or German are simply too ambiguous and too verbose for the task.

As a result of the development of time-sharing, in which regular telephone lines are used to connect inexpensive remote typewriters and display screens equipped for teleprocessing ('terminals') to a single central computer, and the more recent availability of low cost personal computers, a number of specialized languages have appeared with features adapted to this environment. Among them is APL, the name being an acronym for *A Programming Language*, which is the title of a book by Dr. K. E. Iverson (New York, John Wiley, 1962) defining a notation for mathematics which has evolved to the APL that is presented in this book.

Not only is APL similar in many respects to algebraic notation, but it also contains many useful functions not expressible concisely with conventional symbols. It has been proven to be very efficient for describing algorithms (problem-solving procedures). And because of the ease with which complicated problems can be expressed in APL, it has been very useful where fast answers are needed for one-time problems (so-called 'quick-and-dirty' solutions) or to model applications, particularly where the application itself is expected to undergo frequent change.

The text will therefore concentrate on the use of APL for problem-solving on a computer. This detailed exposition will begin soon, but first we will give a brief introduction to the operation of the computer or terminal and the establishment of the telephone connection. In this introduction, little consideration will be given to the characteristics and operation of any of the other parts of the APL system, since the user of a time-sharing system is removed from the immediate vicinity of the computer and usually need not worry about anything other than his terminal and his problem needing solution. The user of a personal computer should consult his owner's manual for instructions specific to his computer.

What the APL system does

The following is an example of a user interacting with an APL computer. First, he can enter arithmetic problems and the computer will display the answers:

    2+2

```
      3÷4
0.75

      3.1×5
15.5
```

As the examples show, APL can be used much like a hand calculator. Instructions and data are entered by the user through the keyboard beginning six spaces to the right of the margin, and shown in boldface in this book. After each line is entered, the RETURN key is pressed to signal the computer that the entry is complete. The computer's response begins on the next line, at the left margin.

We can assign (store) a string of numbers to a variable called X, and ask the computer to execute the instruction shown, $+/X$ (read as 'sum over X'), with a response of 17.1:

```
      X←3  4  1.1  3  6
      +/X
17.1
```

The variable X can be used repeatedly as, for example,

```
      2+X
5 6 3.1 5 8
```

And we have the ability to call on programs previously stored in the computer. Here is one that carries out statistical calculations on data that we enter. The following examples were obtained from a terminal with access to programs that probably aren't available to the reader at this point. Hence, attempts to duplicate these results may not be successful.

```
      STATISTICS
ENTER DATA
☐:
      4  3  4.4  5  1  6.2
6 OBSERVATIONS ENTERED
AVERAGE IS 3.933333333
RANGE IS 5.2
STANDARD DEVIATION IS 1.787363048

☐:
      8  9  7.8  6.4
4 OBSERVATIONS ENTERED
AVERAGE IS 7.8
RANGE IS 2.6
STANDARD DEVIATION IS 1.070825227
☐:
      STOP
```

As the instructions indicated, we terminated execution by typing $STOP$.

The hardware

Let's take a brief look at the terminal and telephone and associated equipment. It will be assumed in the remainder of this book that the communications terminal you will be using is equipped with the APL character set and capable of corresponding with an APL computer system.

APL KEYBOARD

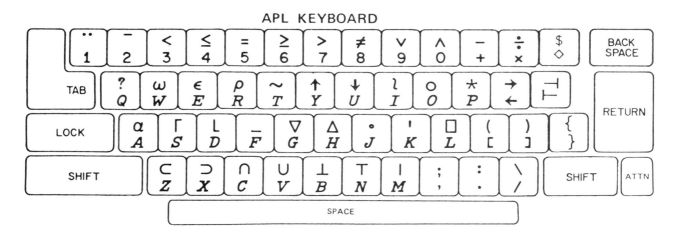

The space bar is at the bottom of the keyboard and the alphabetic and numeric characters are in the conventional typewriter positions. But you will find some of the other symbols unfamiliar, and some of the familiar symbols may not be located where you might expect them. There may also be minor differences in the number and arrangement of the keys, depending on the terminal manufacturer.

The SHIFT key is used in the usual manner for upper shift characters, and the RETURN key (or EXECUTE or ENTER on some terminals) on the right is used to tell the system that you are finished with whatever you are entering, and are now ready for the terminal to respond.

Somewhere on the terminal is an ON-OFF switch, which is the main power control. Also located on the terminal may be a switch marked LOCAL-REMOTE or ONLINE-OFFLINE. When the switch is in the LOCAL or OFFLINE position the terminal can be used as an ordinary electric typewriter. The REMOTE or ONLINE position is the correct one for APL.

Besides the typewriter-like terminals, another type features a video display instead of a printer. An example of this type is the IBM 3278 display terminal, with this keyboard

IBM 3270 APL Data Analysis Feature Keyboard

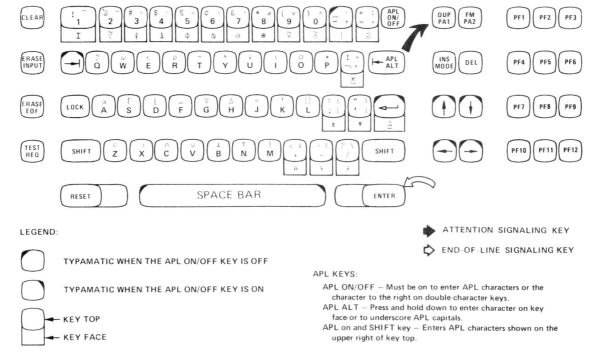

LEGEND:

⬭ TYPAMATIC WHEN THE APL ON/OFF KEY IS OFF

▭ TYPAMATIC WHEN THE APL ON/OFF KEY IS ON

◀ KEY TOP

◀ KEY FACE

▶ ATTENTION SIGNALING KEY

▷ END-OF-LINE SIGNALING KEY

APL KEYS:

APL ON/OFF — Must be on to enter APL characters or the character to the right on double-character keys.

APL ALT — Press and hold down to enter character on key face or to underscore APL capitals.

APL on and SHIFT key — Enters APL characters shown on the upper right of key top.

There are three shifts on this keyboard. The regular APL characters on the tops of the keys are obtained in the same manner as on other terminals, that is, by using the shift keys. The compound characters on the front of some keys and all the underscored alphabetic characters are produced by holding down the APL ALT key along with the desired character.

These display terminals are usually 'hardwired' to a computer. Turning on the power is all you need to establish the connection. They are capable of producing all the characters shown, both EBCDIC and text. To sign on APL, press the ENTER and APL ON/OFF keys, and follow the instructions below for entering your personal ID.

The keyboard of the IBM Personal Computer equipped with STSC's APL*PLUS software is similar to that of the IBM 3278. The APL*PLUS PC System has two principal modes of operation: it can be used as a stand-alone APL system in the usual sense, and it can also be used as a dial-up or hardwired terminal connected to a time-shared computer. In fact, it can even operate in both modes simultaneously (see page 241), but for now you can switch it from stand-alone to time-sharing or back by pressing both the ALT and F8 keys.

Turn on your terminal or computer and set the LOCAL-REMOTE switch (if there is one) to LOCAL. Practice entering your sign-on identification in the form) *usernumber* : *password*. The sign-on for user 1500 with the password *DGIL* would be entered as

)1500:*DGIL*

The use of the password is optional, but strongly recommended for security reasons. If a password is not used, the sign-on command is simply of the form) *usernumber*.

Should you forget to hold down the shift key, you will get] instead of). That is an incorrect entry and you would not be able to sign on. Repeat the above exercise. When you are finished practicing, set the LOCAL-REMOTE switch to REMOTE and leave the power switch on.

If you are using a stand-alone APL system such as for the IBM Personal Computer, you are both the user and the computer manager. As a user, you only need to know how to use APL as presented in this book. However, because it is a personal system, there isn't any central staff (other than yourself) to run backups, install system upgrades, etc. Hence, if you value the continuity of your data and programs, follow the vendor's system management advice.

Those of you using a time-sharing system will need to know the telephone access number, how to set the switches on your terminal and dataset, modem or accoustic coupler, and the particular sequence of network control codes to get you properly connected. There are so many variants possible that we can't begin to help you here. Moreover, most of the system and equipment manuals are difficult for the novice to decipher. Your best bet is to ask someone on the staff of your vendor or information center to help you get connected. After the first few tries things will work smoothly, and by experimentation you may even be able to understand the manuals.

Some APL systems will conceal the sign-on by overprinting random characters (on print terminals) or blanking it out (on display terminals). These features may be automatically invoked at sign-on or triggered by a command like a simple right parenthesis or) *BLOT*. They are intended to protect your user number from unauthorized use, and should be used if available.

A typical sign-on with the terminal response looks like this:

)1500:*DGIL*
OPR: *SYSTEM AVAILABLE TO* 10 *PM TONIGHT*
057) 9.44.03 10/25/82 *LGILMAN*

     WELCOME TO APL

057) tells which port (telephone line) connects you to the computer, and it is followed by the time in hours, minutes, and seconds, the date and the user's name. The next line identifies the system. Sometimes there may also be a message from the computer operations center with news for all users.

Having signed on, we are ready to do some simple calculations:

     3+5
8
     2+2
4

There may well be variations in the above sign-on procedure in different APL systems and with different terminals. For example, when using an ASCII terminal at 30 characters per second on many commercial time-sharing systems, you must enter ○ (shift *O*) before the right parenthesis. You should consult your computer center for specific sign-on instructions and hints. For stand-alone small computers that can also be used as terminals, consult the manufacturer's reference manual for more detailed sign-on instructions. Likewise, VS APL running under various environments requires a sign-on sequence that may differ from one installation to another.

Sign-off

At this point let's assume you have successfully signed onto an APL system and are ready to try it out. However, before we get into how you use it, we want to mention how you sign off. Don't actually sign off now, if you want to try out APL.

Here is the sign-off procedure: enter)*OFF*, press RETURN and wait for the computer's response. After that, turn the power switch off. If you are using an acoustic coupler, turn it off and hang up the telephone.

```
      )OFF
057   10.04.15 10/25/82  LGI
CONNECTED 0.20.12 TO DATE    4.19.26
CPU TIME  0.00.01 TO DATE    0.01.03
```

Sign-on and sign-off are APL *system commands*. They tell the computer to do something for you. There are many such commands, like)*ERASE*,)*CLEAR*,)*LOAD*,)*COPY* that will be introduced as needed.

All times shown are in hours, minutes and seconds. The cumulative connect time for this user in this billing period is 4 hours, 19 minutes and 26 seconds. The cumulative computer usage time is 1 minute and 3 seconds.

Different APL systems may use accounting displays other than the one shown here. In any case it is wise to make sure you understand how you're being charged or budgeted. Contact your sales representative if you are using a commercial system, or the computer center management otherwise.

To change the password, or include one for the first time, the sign-off command is modified to be)*OFF*: new password, while to remove the password enter)*OFF*:. Some systems may also have a special command for this,)*PASSWORD* old password:new password. Passwords may be any combination of letters and numbers, only the first eight of which are recognized by APL. To ensure security and privacy they should be randomly chosen and not be too short. Your computer center management may have further instructions for their proper use.

From now on we assume you are seated at an active terminal or have ready access to one. Many of the chapters will have instructions to get you into a special workspace, which is a block of internal storage (called 'memory'), and in which there are programs and exercises for your use. More about this later.

In the early chapters try to get as much finger practice as you can. Remember that the slowest part of the APL system is you, the user. You are limited by the speed with which you can enter information at the keyboard. If you are a typist, learn to touch-type your APL rather than use the 'two-finger' method.

Elementary arithmetic operations

We'll begin with the simple arithmetic operations, + × − ÷, the symbols for which are in the upper right portion of the keyboard. The decimal point is in the lower right part of the keyboard. All the symbols are used in the conventional manner.

In many places in this book, when there are a few short examples in sequence, we will place them across rather than down the page, to save space.

Addition

```
       3+4                .5+.6              1.45+5.99
7                  1.1                7.44
```

You've just barely started, but already there is one error you are free to make. Suppose you enter

```
   3+
```

You ask '3+ what?' It isn't a meaningful statement because you haven't indicated a second value for the plus symbol to operate on. The computer responds by displaying

```
SYNTAX ERROR
   3+
    ∧
```

This error message tells you that the statement has been improperly formulated in APL, i.e., is 'ungrammatical' in the sense that we are using perfectly good symbols, but using them incorrectly. The caret (∧) marks where the error was detected. The exact form of the error display, including the position and number of carets, may vary slightly with different versions of APL.

Multiplication

```
         5.1×7.9              3×6
40.29                  18
```

The symbol for multiplication is ×. It must always be explicitly used in APL. In conventional notation expressions like A(B) or even AB mean multiply A by B; however, in APL it must be written $A \times B$.

Subtraction

```
       5-2              2-5
3                  ‾3
```

Notice the overbar (‾) in the last response. The symbol means 'negative.' In a way it is a description, like the decimal point, attached to the number that follows it. It is *not* an indication of an operation to be performed. For that, the subtraction sign (−) is used.

Let's try some more examples using the negative sign (upper shift 2):

```
     3+‾2              ‾2+3              −2+3
1              1              ‾5
```

If you think there's something peculiar about the last example, where a subtraction sign was used in place of the negative sign, relax; the distinction will be made in Chapter 7.

Division

```
       3÷5              5÷3
0.6              1.666666667
```

By now you have probably noticed in your own practice with the arithmetic operations that at most ten significant figures will be displayed in the response. Most APL systems carry out calculations to approximately sixteen figures and round off to ten figures in the display. Trailing zeros are not displayed. In Chapter 17 a command will be introduced that will allow the number of places displayed to vary from 1 to 16.

So far so good. But how about

```
      5÷0
DOMAIN ERROR
      5÷0
       ∧
```

Here we see a different type of error. The operation is a valid one, but we tried to divide by 0, which is not in the *domain* of possible divisors. This seems reasonable enough, until you try 0÷0: you get a 1. The version of APL used here follows the rule that any real number divided by itself is 1.

Corrections and comments

Now suppose we have to enter numbers that are a little harder to type than what we have been using thus far, and (heaven forbid) we made a mistake. Specifically, suppose we entered 2×3.14169 and really meant 2×3.14159, but haven't yet pressed the RETURN key.

The error can easily be corrected. On print terminals, strike the BACKSPACE key (gently, because it may be a 'repeating' key on some terminals) to move the cursor, or position indicator, over to where the error begins. Then press the LINEFEED key. The cursor will move down. This signifies that everything above and to the right has been wiped out from the memory of the system and won't be seen by the computer:

```
      10÷3.14159
           2
13.142
```

In the following examples we want 23×506 but actually enter 3×506. All we need do is to backspace just before the 3 and type 2 as shown, provided, of course, that RETURN hasn't yet been pressed:

```
      23×506
11638
      3×506
1518
```

```
      3×506
      2
11638
```

The fact that the 2 is shown on another line is immaterial, since the system doesn't know that we moved the roller and paper manually for illustrative purposes here. We can also glean from this example that the order in which characters are entered at the keyboard is immaterial. What you see on the paper or screen is what you get with APL.

You have undoubtedly concluded by this time that the way to get rid of a whole line is to backspace all the way to the left margin and press ATTN:

```
      1234567×12345678
∨
```

On most APL systems using ASCII terminals, BREAK will get rid of the line without having to backspace. If you are using a display terminal like the IBM 3278, corrections are made by entering new characters in place of the old after moving the cursor to the appropriate position. Furthermore, you may use the DELETE and INSERT keys to change the entry, or the ERASE INPUT key to erase the characters in the input area of the screen, or the CLEAR key to clear the entire screen.

The combination of upper shift *C* (∩) and the small circle (upper shift *J*, ○) overstruck means that a comment follows. Comments may contain any APL symbols and call for no response from the system.

```
      ⍝ THIS IS HOW TO MAKE A COMMENT
```

This doesn't mean that all combinations of overstruck characters are possible in APL. The times and divide signs have been overstruck in the example below, with a resulting *ENTRY ERROR* (*CHARACTER ERROR* on some systems). Allowable overstrikes will be taken up as needed in succeeding chapters.

```
      34*73
ENTRY ERROR
      34▨        (The display is moved forward one line here for illustrative purposes.)
        ×73
2482
```

Note that the original input is reproduced only up to the first illegal character, here indicated by the ▨, where the cursor comes to rest. At the same time the keyboard is unlocked and ready to accept the correct characters for processing and display, as though you had entered the entire line at once.

Occasionally the computer will report an error even when you haven't made one. At other times there may be misprints not traceable to mechanical or electrical problems in the terminal itself. This happens when there is a faulty telephone connection. If errors are reported frequently, hang up the phone and dial in again. At times transmission difficulties may result in a *RESEND* message. When this happens, the input line is lost and must be reentered.

An introduction to vectors

Imagine a store which, following a disastrous fire, is left with just three items for sale, A, B, C. Here is the sales record of the number of items sold over a two-week period:

```
         |   A      B      C
  -------+--------------------
  WEEK 1 |   9      7      8
  WEEK 2 |   3      4      5
```

Before the store goes out of business, what are the total sales for each item? The obvious answer is to add the weekly totals for each item separately as

```
      9+3              7+4              8+5
12                 11               13
```

In APL there is a much more compact way to do this:

```
      9 7 8+3 4 5
12 11 13
```

This leads us into a unique and time-saving feature of APL: its ability to process arrays of numbers. In the previous example the array was one-dimensional, with the elements all arranged in a single string, called a *vector*. We'll see later that APL can handle multidimensional arrays as well.

Let's now change the problem:

```
         |   A      B      C
  -------+--------------------
  WEEK 1 |   9      7      8
  WEEK 2 |   5      5      5
```

Treating this as a problem involving vectors, we enter

```
      9 7 8+5 5 5
14 12 13
```

To save still more entry time, where all the elements of one of the vectors are identical, just enter that value once, and APL will extend it automatically to match the other vector in length:

```
      9 7 8+5
14 12 13
```

Now for some do's and don'ts. First, suppose we run all the numbers together:

```
      978+555
1533
```

The absence of space between the digits causes the system to interpret the series as a single number. Again, what you see is what you get. Does this mean that the numbers or the operation symbol must be separated by any fixed number of blanks? The following example makes clear that one blank is sufficient as a separator, but extra blanks don't hurt:

```
      9    7 8+    5
14  12  13
```

What if the two vectors don't have the same number of elements?

```
      9  7  8  +  5  3
LENGTH ERROR
      9  7  8  +  5  3
            ^
```

We get an error message because the computer doesn't know which number goes with which. The only exception to this is where all the elements are identical, in which case only one of them need be entered, as in the example 9 7 8 + 5 above.

Some people have felt that in a problem like 9 7 8 + 5 3, APL should supply a trailing zero. However, other people feel it should supply the zero on the left side (0 5 3 versus 5 3 0). In general, where there's no unambiguous best way to do it, APL simply doesn't take short cuts.

This *parallel processing* of vectors, to give it a name, works equally well with other arithmetic operations:

```
      1  2  3  4×2
2  4  6  8
```

If, for example, a cookie recipe required 6, 4 and 2 cups respectively of three ingredients, and we wished to make only one-third of a batch, then the required amounts are

```
      6  4  2÷3
2  1.333333333  0.6666666667
```

Again, suppose that the above three ingredients cost respectively 1, 5 and 7 cents per cup. What is the total cost for each ingredient?

```
      6  4  2×.01  .05  .07
0.06  0.2  0.14
```

As we shall see soon, there are many operations that can be used with vectors. We will also be able to invent functions that behave just like our ordinary arithmetic operations in that they can be used with vectors.

PROBLEMS

1. DRILL. (Some of the drill problems in this chapter and others may result in error messages.)

```
6  8  2  4+3  9  1  1        5  4  3×6            1  2  8÷1  2  0
1  0  9  8-4  2  2  3        10÷10  5  2  1        ¯2  0  .81+15  6  ¯5
3-¯1  ¯56.7  0  ¯.19         3  4×1  2  3          2¯¯3
```

2. Additional finger exercises. (What happens if you leave out the comment symbol?)

   ```
   ⍝NOW IS THE TIME FOR ALL GOOD MEN TO COME TO THE AID
   ⍝IF AT FIRST YOU DON'T SUCCEED, TRY AGAIN
   ⍝HOW NOW BROWN COW
   ⍝PRACTICE MAKES PERFECT
   ⍝THE SLOWEST PART OF THE APL SYSTEM IS USUALLY THE USER
   ```

3. At a basketball game a ticket seller sold 155 adult tickets at $1.25 each, 89 student tickets at .50 each, and accepted 45 courtesy passes at .25 each. Write an APL expression which gives the income from each class of tickets.

4. A taxi fleet owner recorded mileages of 1263, 1997 and 3028 for his three cars. Operating expenses for each car during the same period were $59.50, 79.88 and 83.00, respectively. What was his cost per mile for each car?

5. An inept salesperson sells four radios for $47, $18, $68 and $10 but forgets to collect the 5% sales tax. How much was lost on each radio?

6. A car dealer illegally resets the odometers of some used cars on his lot. If the odometers read 45201, 64677, 52468 and 68893 miles *after* setting each one back 15000 miles, what is the true mileage for each car?

7. Four hundred responses to a survey were received. For the five questions on the survey there were 356, 205, 189, 322 and 257 'yes' answers. What fraction of the respondents gave positive answers to each question?

8. (For terminals with a backspace key.) Type 3 − 2. Backspace and overstrike the subtract sign with a plus sign (without using ATTN or LINEFEED). Then press RETURN and explain the result.

Chapter 2: Useful tools

All of our work so far has been done in hand calculator or *immediate execution* mode. This has the disadvantage that once we enter the numbers and the operation symbol to be used and then press RETURN, execution proceeds and we get an answer (unless we tried something illegal). But the work is lost. It is no longer available to us for any future calculation, except on some display terminals where we can 'page' or 'scroll' back.

You will now be introduced to the data storage feature of APL. This will permit reusing data without having to reenter it. Then, as an extension of the concept of a vector, two-dimensional arrays will be examined in the latter part of the chapter.

Assignment

Any good calculator has the ability to store constant factors so that they can be used over and over again without having to be reentered each time. For instance, suppose we are given a series of problems all involving the constant 0.75:

```
      2×.75              4+.75              .75×.75
1.5                 4.75                 0.5625
```

As it stands, .75 has to be typed each time. What we'd like is some way to save this number and have it available for reuse. It may seem trivial at this point because our repeated factor, .75, doesn't take many keystrokes, but what if the expression you had to repeat had a large number of digits in it?

In APL, the term *assignment* is used to describe the placing of the results of an expression in storage. It works this way:

```
   A←.75
```

The expression above is read as '*A* is assigned the value .75'. From this point on, unless the contents of our *workspace* (the place in the computer where our work is being done) are destroyed or a different value is assigned to *A*, entering *A* will be equivalent to entering .75. Since *A* is a name to which we are free to assign any value we want, even though we chose a specific one here, it and other names used in a similar manner are called *variables*.

Here are some calculations you can do with *A*:

```
     2×A                4+A                A×A
1.5                 4.75                 0.5625
```

Flushed with success, you ought to be ready to try your hand at another assignment:

```
   B←1 2 3 4 5               2×B
                       2 4 6 8 10
```

A, like death and taxes, is still with us. So try

```
   A+B                        B×B
1.75 2.75 3.75 4.75 5.75    1 4 9 16 25
```

If we keep this up, sooner or later we will run out of letters of the alphabet. What then? The next logical step is to use multiple letter names:

```
   PI←3.14159               PI×PI
                       9.869587728
```

The name in the example above wasn't chosen haphazardly. Subject to restrictions on length and usable characters (to be discussed later in this chapter), you have a wide choice of possible names for objects in APL. We suggest as a general rule that names be chosen for their mnemonic utility. This simplifies identification and enhances consistency, making it easier for you and others to follow what has been done.

You may have noticed above that when an assignment is made, the terminal doesn't display its result. This is reasonable enough, since all we are asking when we make an assignment is for something to be placed in storage. And if we don't tell it where to go, it goes on the paper, like a well-trained house pet.

A is still in storage. Here it is again:

      A
0.75

What happens if we mistakenly or otherwise use *A* for a second assignment? For instance,

      A←2+*B*

If we display *A* now, we get

      A   2+*B*
3 4 5 6 7   3 4 5 6 7

The new values of *A* replace the old, which are lost. Moral of the story: if you want to save the values stored in a variable name, don't override the assignment. Use a different name instead.

There are several ways to extend the number of possibilities for variable names. Underlining (upper shift *F*) is one way:

     A̲←3.2   *A̲*+5   *A̲*
             8.2   3.2

A̲ is clearly different from *A*, which still has its last assigned value. In effect this gives us 52 letters to choose from, alone or in multiple character names like

     DATA←5 2 7 8

Most major APL systems allow up to 77 characters in a variable name, but it doesn't pay to make it too long. Remember, *you* are the one who will have to enter it. Numbers can also be included in any position except the first, as shown by

     X3Y2←20   *3XY2*←20
                    SYNTAX ERROR
                      3 *XY2*←20
                        ^

but special symbols for operations, spaces and punctuation marks may not be used in a name. Exceptions: the symbols Δ (upper shift *H*) and Δ̲ are treated as alphabetic characters, and some systems allow the characters _ and ‾ (shift *F* and shift 2) to be used in names, but not in the first position. Incidentally, APL did put the value 20 (see above) in storage under the name *XY2*:

     XY2
20

You can make multiple assignments in the same statement. In certain cases this is a handy timesaver. Here is an example:

     A←2+*B*←3 1 5   *A*   *B*
                    3 1 5   5 3 7

However, don't use multiple assignments unless there is a clear and obvious relation among the variables; it can cause more confusion than it's worth.

Now let's try

     A+*W*
VALUE ERROR
     A+*W*
       ^

It should be obvious what's wrong. The computer didn't recognize the variable name W because there hasn't been any value assigned to that name. A is still a valid variable, but not W:

```
      A                    W
5  3  7            VALUE ERROR
                       W
                       ∧
```

This raises another question: how can you find out what variable names you already have in storage? The command $)VARS$ (for 'variables') produces an alphabetized listing of the variables in storage:

```
      )VARS
A         B        DATA     PI      X        XY2      X3Y2     A̲
```

A partial listing of the variable names beginning with a given letter or letters, say PE, to the end of the alphabet can be obtained with:

```
      )VARS PE
PI        X        XY2      X3Y2     A̲
```

and in APL2 $)VARS\ PE\ ST$ lists alphabetically all variables from PE through ST.

Underlined letters such as $A̲$ come after all nonunderlined letters, so far as their display order is concerned. For a long listing, if you don't want to continue the display, press ATTN (BREAK on an ASCII terminal, or CLEAR on the IBM 3278) to stop it. This technique can be used to interrupt execution of any expression currently being processed.

Expressions starting with a right parenthesis are known as *system commands*. You have already used two of them, sign-on and sign-off, and $)VARS$ is another. More will be introduced as the need arises.

Getting back to our $VALUE\ ERROR$, if we give W a value and then call for $A+W$, we no longer get an error message,

```
      W←0.1                A                    A+W
                     5  3  7            5.1  3.1  7.1
```

and not only is execution successful, but W is added to the list of variables in storage:

```
      )VARS
A         B        DATA     PI      W        X        XY2      X3Y2     A̲
```

Now W behaves just like the other variables and can be reassigned:

```
      W                    W←2×W                W
0.1                                       0.2
```

Suppose that you want to get rid of one or more variables while still actively working in APL. Entering

```
      A←
```

buys you nothing since the response of the system is

```
SYNTAX ERROR
      A←
        ∧
```

and entering $A←0$ also gets you nowhere, since the only thing that happens is that the value 0 is assigned to A.

Another system command, $)ERASE$, is useful here. This command is followed by the name(s) of the variables to be erased. Its execution elicits no response from the system other than the cursor moving over 6 spaces:

```
      )ERASE A B DATA
      )VARS
PI        W        X        XY2      X3Y2     A̲
```

An introduction to matrices

While useful in and of itself, the concept of a vector, introduced at the end of the first chapter, is far too limited in the real world. We would certainly stand accused of myopic vision if, like the strange inhabitants of Flatland, we didn't recognize the need for arrays which are multidimensional.

The sales record table on **page 8**

```
            |   A       B       C
------------+-------------------------
WEEK  1  |   9       7       8
WEEK  2  |   3       4       5
```

is an obvious case in point. For tabulating data or correlating information which purports to relate two quantities or more, an array of two dimensions, called a *matrix*, is necessary.

We could continue this discussion and come up into a general n-dimensional array, but our finite minds are likely to boggle at the conception of any array beyond three dimensions. Also, since the great majority of users of arrays don't normally require more than two dimensions, we'll stick with two dimensions until much later in the text, after a firm foundation has been laid.

Now for the goodies. Before using matrices we have to know how to create them. Unlike vectors, which can be created in APL by simply typing the elements in a single line, matrices require two more pieces of information: how many rows and how many columns. Incidentally, the words *dimension* and *axis* are frequently used to refer to a direction along which an array extends in space. Loosely speaking, they are somewhat interchangeable with the word *dimension* as we used it previously. Put another way, we need to state how big the array will be in each direction, that is, how many rows and columns. More specifically, the example matrix

```
1   2   3   4
5   6   7   8
9  10  11  12
```

has 3 rows and 4 columns, i.e., its *shape* is 3 4. The first dimension, which gives the number of *rows*, is of length 3, which corresponds to the size of one column, while the second dimension, of length 4, gives the number of *columns*, and corresponds to the size of one row.

If you're still with us, let's now take a look at how we can build these matrices. The symbol ρ (upper shift *R*) is employed for array construction. In use, the numbers on the left specify the shape of the resulting matrix, and consist of two integers detailing the number of rows and columns, in that order. The numbers on the right are the elements to be included in the array, with these elements ordered by rows. Here are some examples:

```
      2 3ρ4 7 8 2 4 6
4  7  8
2  4  6
```

```
      A←4 2ρ7 8 4                    B←3 4ρ1 2 3 4 5 6 7 8 9 10 11 12 13 14
      A                              B
7  8                               1   2   3   4
4  7                               5   6   7   8
8  4                               9  10  11  12
7  8
```

Two pertinent comments need to be made at this point. First, if there aren't enough elements to make up the array, APL goes back to the beginning of the 'storage pile' on the right and starts over as in *A* above. Second, if there are too many elements, only those needed are used and the rest ignored, as in *B*.

The symbol ρ used in this manner is called *reshape*. It takes what is on the right, which could be a single number, vector, matrix, three-dimensional or higher array, and reshapes it according to the numbers on the left. The following example is illustrative:

```
      2 3ρB                    10ρB
1  2  3                        1  2  3  4  5  6  7  8  9  10
4  5  6
```

The shape of the result is dependent on the number and magnitude of the elements on the left:

```
        8ρ3 0 1                       3 2ρ100                    2 3 4ρ7 8 2 2 3
3 0 1 3 0 1 3 0                       100 100                7 8 2 2
                                      100 100                3 7 8 2
                                      100 100                2 3 7 8

                                                             2 2 3 7
                                                             8 2 2 3
                                                             7 8 2 2
```

If there is one element on the left, the result is a vector; two elements form a matrix; three elements form a three-dimensional array, etc. Don't be alarmed by the last example, which is three-dimensional, consisting of 2 planes (or pages) each of which contains 3 rows and 4 columns. It is included at this point only for illustrative purposes.

How large an array can be defined? Every APL system limits the numbers of elements an array can have. The limit is based on such factors as the size of the workspace, the amount of other data already stored in the workspace, and certain characteristics of the data itself (an integer usually takes less space than a mixed fraction, for example). We'll cover this matter in more detail later. But for now, if you get the message *WS FULL* you'll know that you have tried to deal with more data than your system allows.

Operations with matrices

Now that you know how to build and store matrices, there are many things you can do to manipulate their elements. We begin by defining two matrices M and N:

```
M←4 3ρ1 2 0 1 3 2 3 4 2 3 3 0
N←4 3ρ2 3 7 8 1 4 2 5 0 0 7 6

        M                    N
1 2 0                2 3 7
1 3 2                8 1 4
3 4 2                2 5 0
3 3 0                0 7 6
```

As an extension of our earlier work with vectors in the last chapter, we can add 2 to each element of M, or divide each element by 3:

```
    2+M                  M÷3
3 4 2            0.3333333333    0.6666666667    0
3 5 4            0.3333333333    1               0.6666666667
5 6 4            1               1.333333333     0.6666666667
5 5 2            1               1               0
```

We can multiply two matrices together element-by-element, or subtract one matrix from another:

```
    M×N                    M−N
 2   6   0       ‾1  ‾1  ‾7
 8   3   8       ‾7   2  ‾2
 6  20   0        1  ‾1   2
 0  21   0        3  ‾4  ‾6
```

PROBLEMS

1. Assign the vector 3 4 5 6 7 to the name A and make B equal to two times A.

2. Which of the following are valid variable names in APL?

   SPACEMAN   *B+ALPHA*   *SIXTY-FOUR*
   X SQUARED   *Δ3X*   *4BY5*

3. Construct **A** matrix M with 5 rows and 3 columns, consisting entirely of the number 7, and **B** matrix Q of the same size as M, each of whose rows contains 4 9 11.

4. Convert the matrix M from problem 3 into a matrix N of all 1's in at least two different ways.

5. A store sells 3 items, A, B, C. Over a one-week period, the amounts sold are respectively 8, 15, 7. The following week's sales record is 12, 4, 0. Put this data in a matrix S, each of whose rows represents a week's sales. The prices of A, B, C the first week are respectively \$3.10, 2.00, 4.17, but because of rapid inflation, these prices increase to 3.50, 2.75, 4.35 in the second week. Put this data in a matrix P and use it to construct a table of total sales revenue by item over the two-week period.

6. The base pay for shipping clerks in a warehouse is \$4.50 per hour, with time-and-a-half after 40 hours. If in a certain week the 5 clerks working put in 40, 55, 46, 40 and 40 hours respectively, compute their gross pay for the week. (What if someone worked less than 40 hours? We'll see how to handle that problem in the next chapter.)

7. The year of birth of each member of a family is stored in a vector $BIRTH$. Compute for each member of the family **A** age, **B** year of retirement (at age 65), **C** number of years left until retirement. Assume the present year is YR.

8. Using the data from problem 7, Chapter 1, what fraction of the respondents gave 'no' answers to each question?

9. A company charges a flat fee PH for postage and handling on all orders, plus the applicable sales tax. If the day's sales are stored in the vector $SALES$ and the tax rates in the vector TAX (one element for each element in $SALES$), what is the total cost to each customer?

Chapter 3: Additional operations and tools

In the previous chapters we dealt with individual numbers, which we will now call *scalars*; strands of numbers, for which the term *vectors* was used; and two-dimensional arrays, which we called *matrices*. Left partly unanswered at that time was the question of what combinations of these are allowed in APL, as well as what the shape of the result might be. Let's now direct our attention to the question by formulating a few simple rules and giving appropriate names for the concepts to be considered.

Primitive scalar dyadic functions

There are seven rules that govern the ways in which vectors, scalars and matrices can be combined. In what follows, the letter f stands for any of the arithmetic operations that we have already introduced. Later in this section we'll further classify and categorize these operations to make it easier for you to relate them to others that are yet to come.

rule	result		arguments
1	$SCALAR$	←	$SCALAR$ f $SCALAR$
2	$VECTOR$	←	$SCALAR$ f $VECTOR$
3	$VECTOR$	←	$VECTOR$ f $SCALAR$
4	$VECTOR$	←	$VECTOR$ f $VECTOR$
5	$MATRIX$	←	$SCALAR$ f $MATRIX$
6	$MATRIX$	←	$MATRIX$ f $SCALAR$
7	$MATRIX$	←	$MATRIX$ f $MATRIX$

The terms under 'result' tell us the shape of the result when the function is performed on various combinations of argument shapes.

In some newer versions of APL, these rules have been extended so that, for example, it is now possible to add a vector to each column of a matrix. The vector, of course, would still have to match the length of the column. This extension is discussed in more detail on page 211.

This is as good a place as any to introduce a little additional terminology. Why? you ask. Naming something doesn't tell us any more about it and it might even mislead us by making it easy for us to talk glibly of things we may not know much about. But mathematicians especially, being the perverse creatures that they are, insist on more formal names for the tools and concepts they work with. And having a name for something does have the advantage of letting the namer identify without ambiguity (we hope!) that which is under discussion.

First, if F stands for an operation to be performed, the things it is to operate on will be called *arguments*. In support of our previous comment we quote here (out of context) Samuel Johnson: 'I have found you an argument, but I am not obliged to find you an understanding.'

Thus, in the expression 5 × 6, the left argument is 5, and the right argument is 6. Both arguments can be scalars (rule 1),

```
      3+5
8
```

or one can be a vector, either on the right or the left (rules 2 and 3), or both arguments can be vectors (rule 4).

```
      2+3 5 7                    5 6 8×3                    3 6 8÷2 1 4
5 7 9                    15 18 24                    1.5 6 2
```

The only stipulation is that both arguments be the same length. As an obvious corollary, the lengths of the resulting vectors in the above two examples are the same as those of the vector arguments.

By substituting the words *size* or *shape* for *length* in the last two sentences, the same reasoning can be shown to hold for various combinations of matrices and scalars (rules 5, 6, 7). In fact, an inspection of the seven rules and the examples will convince you that they can all be boiled down into a single rule for operations on n-dimensional arrays (n=0,1,2, with 0 being associated with scalars), provided that appropriate size restrictions in the arguments are observed. Can you state this rule?

The operators that we have been working with are more properly called *functions*, because a result is obtained as a consequence of the function operating on its argument(s). (One of the dictionary meanings of 'function' is 'performance' or 'execution.')

Furthermore, the word *dyadic* is associated with these functions, since they require *two* arguments (at least as we have been using them thus far). They are also called *primitive* because they are immediately available on the APL keyboard. And finally (at long last!), they are referred to as *scalar* because functions of this type are defined first for scalars and then extended element by element to vectors, matrices and other arrays. In summary, the operations + − × ÷ are called *primitive scalar dyadic functions*.

Operation tables for the arithmetic functions

For each of the functions thus far introduced, we can construct an *operation table*, with the left argument down the vertical column on the left and the right argument across the top. To save space, only the integers 1 2 3 4 will be used as arguments:

```
+| 1 2 3 4        -| 1   2   3   4      ×| 1  2   3   4      ÷| 1   2    3    4
-+--------        -+-------------       -+-----------        -+---------------
1| 2 3 4 5        1| 0  ¯1  ¯2  ¯3       1| 1  2   3   4      1| 1  1÷2  1÷3  1÷4
2| 3 4 5 6        2| 1   0  ¯1  ¯2       2| 2  4   6   8      2| 2   1   2÷3  2÷4
3| 4 5 6 7        3| 2   1   0  ¯1       3| 3  6   9  12      3| 3  3÷2   1   3÷4
4| 5 6 7 8        4| 3   2   1   0       4| 4  8  12  16      4| 4   2   4÷3   1
```

Since it is a downright nuisance to construct these operation tables by hand, let's use this opportunity to introduce a new APL feature which behaves somewhat differently from the simple arithmetic functions used so far, but which, nevertheless, will be a great timesaver for us in the future.

We'll begin by introducing a problem that involves a large number of multiplications. It asks that we compute the taxes to be paid for items costing varying amounts and taxed at different rates:

```
TAX       |   TAX RATES
TABLE     | .01   .02   .05
----------+----------------
        1 | .01   .02   .05
COST    2 | .02   .04   .10
OF      3 | .03   .06   .15
ITEM    4 | .04   .08   .20
        5 | .05   .10   .25
```

The result desired is the matrix which is obtained by getting all possible products of costs and rates. You can see that if the cost and tax rate vectors had large numbers of noninteger elements, this procedure could involve a lot of work.

Outer product

APL has an *operator*[1] which may be applied to arrays in precisely the way needed to fill in the table above. It is called the *outer product* or *outer result*. To illustrate it, let the left argument be the vector of costs *A* and the right argument the tax rates *B*:

```
A←1 2 3 4 5              B←.01×1 2 5
```

---

[1]Formally speaking, an APL operator is something which works on a function to change in some systematic way the result that would normally be obtained from that function.

The outer product is

    A∘.×B

0.01	0.02	0.05
0.02	0.04	0.1
0.03	0.06	0.15
0.04	0.08	0.2
0.05	0.1	0.25

which is read '*A* jot dot times *B*.' The little circle, called *jot*, is the upper shift *J*. Clearly, the outer product in this case gives all possible multiplications of the left and right arguments, i.e., a modified 'times' table.

Any primitive scalar dyadic function can be used after the period in place of ×, as for instance,

    A∘.+B

1.01	1.02	1.05
2.01	2.02	2.05
3.01	3.02	3.05
4.01	4.02	4.05
5.01	5.02	5.05

Notice that the shape of the result is the catenation (chaining together) of the shapes of the two arguments. In this case it is a matrix with five rows and three columns.

The outer product lets us do a wide variety of things. For example, here we produce an addition table and a subtraction table:

    A∘.+A

2	3	4	5	6
3	4	5	6	7
4	5	6	7	8
5	6	7	8	9
6	7	8	9	10

    A∘.−A

0	¯1	¯2	¯3	¯4
1	0	¯1	¯2	¯3
2	1	0	¯1	¯2
3	2	1	0	¯1
4	3	2	1	0

The other operation tables can be obtained in the same way. We'll have more to say about outer product in Chapter 21.

In the meantime, to continue our story, here is an operation table for which no function is specified. Can you guess what it is?

```
   | 1    2    3    4
---+----------------
 1 | 1    1    1    1
 2 | 2    4    8   16
 3 | 3    9   27   81
 4 | 4   16   64  256
```

Power function

You should be able to see that the previous table represents raising to powers. The left argument values are raised to the powers indicated by the right argument. This power function exhibits the characteristics we would expect from a primitive scalar dyadic function. All we need is a symbol for it. This brings up an interesting aspect (or failing, if you prefer) of conventional mathematical notation, and one which will become even more apparent as we go along.

Notice how we write the four arithmetic functions:

$$2 + 3$$
$$2 - 3$$
$$2 \times 3$$
$$2 \div 3$$

And then we come along and write for the power function

$$2^3$$

The operation to be performed is specified not by a symbol but by position, which is not only inconsistent but potentially dangerous since it is very easy sometimes to miss the elevated position of the power in writing or reading.

In APL the symbol `*` (upper shift *P*) is used to represent raising to a power, as in

```
      2*3
8
```

Like the other primitive scalar dyadic functions, it extends to vectors and matrices as well:

```
      2 4 3*2
4  16  9
      A←2 3ρ1 2 3 4 5 6
```

```
      A                     A*3
  1  2  3              1    8    27
  4  5  6             64  125   216
```

In algebra, roots are shown to be the same as fractional powers, e.g., finding the square root of a number is the same as raising it to the one-half power. So instead of writing $\sqrt{2}$ to mean the square root of 2, in APL this is

```
      2*.5              9 64*.5
1.414213562          3 8
```

The power function is the key to compound interest calculations. If you were to start a savings account with a $500 deposit (principal) and your banker offers you 6% interest for a year's use of the money, you would have $530 at the end of the first year. Now if that sum were saved for another year at the 6% rate, you would then have $561.80 (`530+.06×530`). The general formula to compute the future value F of P dollars saved for N years with an annual interest rate of R in conventional notation is

$$F = P \times (1+R)^n$$

Thus, the future value of $500 over 8 years at .06 annual interest rate is

```
      RN←1.06*8              500×RN
                        796.9240373
```

Or, you can watch your money grow each year by doing

```
      RN←1.06*1 2 3 4 5 6 7 8
      500×RN
530 561.8 595.508 631.23848 669.1127888 709.2595561 751.8151295 796.9240373
```

On the other hand, if the same annual interest rate, 6%, were offered by another bank, but here the compounding were done quarterly, the future worth of $500 over 8 years would be

$$500 \times \left(1 + \frac{.06}{4}\right)^{4 \times 8}$$

yielding

```
      RN←1.015*32              500×RN
                        805.1621601
```

Negative powers, which are the equivalent of the reciprocal of the number raised to the corresponding positive power, are also available to the APL user, as in the following:

```
      2*¯2
0.25
```

And now that we have the power function at our disposal, it can be used to generate very large numbers, as, for instance,

```
      100*8
1E16
```

which raises the question of whether there is any largest number in APL. You may want to experiment on the terminal to determine what, if any, it is.

Scaled or exponential notation

In the last example you saw a new notation, which some of you may recognize as being similar to what is used in other higher level programming languages and many 'scientific' hand calculators. It is intended to avoid writing a monster like 10,000,000,000,000,000. The E may be interpreted as 'times ten to the ... power.'

This notation is equally convenient for very small numbers,

```
      .01*9
1E¯18
```

and can be employed in many different ways to express the same number, say, 530:

```
      530      =      53×10
      5.3E2           5.3×100
      .0053E5         .0053×100000
      530E0           530×1
      5300E¯1         5300×.1
```

APL not only produces results in scaled notation, but lets you enter data this way also:

```
      1+33              1+3.3E1              1+.33E2              1+330E¯1
34                34                   34                   34
```

Users have considerable freedom in formatting their inputs, although the common practice of using commas to separate groups of digits isn't allowed because the comma itself is an APL function, to be discussed later. The results generated by the APL system are somewhat more restricted. Problems 1 and 2 at the end of the chapter will give you some clues as to these limitations.

The rest of this chapter and the next will introduce more primitive dyadic functions. Some of these will be employed frequently by most APL users; others, like logarithms and combinations, will be of value to a more specialized fraternity, nonmembers of which should feel free to study them with no more than passing interest, or for that matter, ignore them completely.

Logarithms

The logarithm function is an inverse of the power function. The logarithm of a number N to the base B is that power to which B must be raised to equal N. In APL this is written $B \circledast N$, the symbol being that for power ($*$) overstruck with the large circle (upper shift O).

Thus, since it is true that $10*3$ is 1000, then the base-10 log (to use the usual abbreviation) of 1000 is written as $10 \circledast 1000$. Of course, this function also works with vector and matrix arguments:

```
      10⊛1000                           2 2 10⊛4 8 1000
3                                 2 3 3

      X←2 3ρ1 2 3 4 5
      X                                 2⊛X
1 2 3                             0         1           1.584962501
4 5 1                             2         2.321928095 0
```

Notice that the base is the left argument and the number whose log is being found is the right argument.

Logarithms, like powers, are often used in financial calculations involving compound interest. For example, to find how many years it would take for your savings to double at 5, 6, 7, 8, 9 or 10 percent annual compound interest,

```
      RATES←.01×5 6 7 8 9 10
      RATES←1+RATES
      RATES
1.05 1.06 1.07 1.08 1.09 1.1
      RATES⊛2
14.20669908 11.89566105 10.24476835 9.006468342 8.043231727 7.272540897
```

We admit that powers and logarithms are a bit tougher to grasp than our old friends $+$ $-$ $\times$ $\div$. But they are so useful in helping to solve money-related problems that we felt you should be exposed to them early in this book. To give you a breather, we're now going to end this chapter with two uncomplicated but very useful new functions.

Maximum and minimum

Try the following exercises, exploring the working of the symbol ⌈ (upper shift *S*):

      3⌈5   **5⌈3**   **5⌈5**
5   5   5

Lest you be tempted to think that ⌈ always generates a 5, look at

      3⌈1
3

If you experiment with this function for a while, you will see that it selects the larger of the left and right arguments and is appropriately named the *maximum* function. Its operation table looks like this:

```
      1 2 3 4 5∘.⌈1 2 3 4 5
  1   1 2 3 4 5
  2   2 2 3 4 5
  3   3 3 3 4 5
  4   4 4 4 4 5
  5   5 5 5 5 5
```

Since there's a maximum function, you would expect a companion *minimum* function. It is found on the upper shift *D* key, and it selects the smaller of the two arguments:

      3⌊5   **5⌊3**   ¯**5⌊3**   ¯**5⌊**¯**3**
3   3   ¯5   ¯5

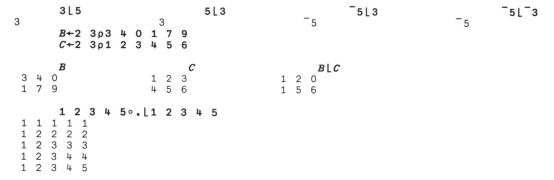

```
      B←2 3ρ3 4 0 1 7 9
      C←2 3ρ1 2 3 4 5 6

      B                C              B⌊C
  3 4 0            1 2 3          1 2 0
  1 7 9            4 5 6          1 5 6

      1 2 3 4 5∘.⌊1 2 3 4 5
  1   1 1 1 1 1
  2   1 2 2 2 2
  3   1 2 3 3 3
  4   1 2 3 4 4
  5   1 2 3 4 5
```

'Smaller' and 'larger' are relative terms, and, indeed, the mathematician defines them according to position on the real number line:

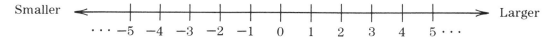

Thus, the smaller of two numbers is that one which is farther to the left, and the larger one, farther to the right. That's why ¯5 is a smaller value than ¯3 or 3.

Let's consider a couple of simple problems. There are three students who got grades of 90, 80 and 55 in an exam, and on a retest received 70, 80 and 75, respectively. Their kind-hearted instructor wishes to record for each student only the larger of the two grades received. How can he do it? The right answers are 90 for the first student, 80 for the second, and 75 for the third. In APL this is obtained by

      90 80 55⌈70 80 75
90 80 75

A second problem: we have purchased an odd lot of lumber consisting of four boards of lengths 5, 8.1, 10 and 7.9 feet. Unfortunately, our truck can carry boards no longer than 8 feet without running afoul of the law. Boards longer than 8 feet have to be trimmed to 8 feet. The 'trimming' is done in APL by

```
        8⌊5 8.1 10 7.9
5 8 8 7.9
```

and the second and third boards are the ones which get cut down. These are two trivial examples, but here are some with great practicality.

The 1983 rules for U. S. Social Security withholding state that the employee pays 6.70% of the lesser of his annual salary or $35,700. The equivalent expression in APL is $BASE \leftarrow SALARY \lfloor 35700$ followed by $WHOLD \leftarrow .0670 \times BASE$.

Remember problem 10 of Chapter 2? It awarded time-and-a-half for all hours worked over 40. When we left it, we still didn't have a way to calculate wages if someone worked less than 40 hours. That can now be fixed by following $OT \leftarrow HOURS - 40$ with $OT \leftarrow 0 \lceil OT$. This changes any 'negative' overtime to zero overtime.

Of all the primitive scalar dyadic functions learned so far ($+ \ - \ \times \ \div \ * \ \circledast \ \lceil \ \lfloor$), maximum and minimum are different from all the others in one significant respect: no knowledge of an operation table is needed to use them—only the ability to distinguish larger and smaller. They are inherently simpler than even addition and subtraction. In fact, very young children can conceptualize $\lceil$ and $\lfloor$ before they can + and −.

User-defined functions

Up to now you've worked only with some of the primitive APL functions available directly to you on the keyboard. If you wanted to solve the same problem several times with different arguments, your knowledge of APL thus far would dictate that the instructions would have to be repeated for each set of arguments.

In common with other higher level programming languages, APL offers users the ability to define their own functions (within limits) using names instead of symbols. We will give you a bare-bones look at this feature, with a fuller treatment to start in Chapter 8. There will be a minimum of explanations at this time, since we are reserving our detailed commentary for later.

Let's use as an example the compound interest problem on **page 20**. Assume our principal is $1. If we had a special function, call it ▨, available to us on the keyboard to do the calculation, then we could write $FV \leftarrow R▨Y$, where FV is the future value of $1 at $R\%$ for Y years. The symbol ▨ would have to have been so defined by the implementors of the APL system that whenever it was encountered, it would add 1 to .01 times the left argument and raise that number to the power represented by the right argument.

Needless to say, no such symbol exists since the APL system is a general one, not specifically designed for financial analysis. The primitive functions that are provided, however, can be combined to do just about anything.

Enough said. To define a function to compute future value, enter the following:

    $\nabla Z \leftarrow L \ FV \ R$ (RETURN)

∇ (called *del*) is the symbol that tells APL you are about to define a function. The $Z \leftarrow$ (any variable name will do) will make your function behave like a primitive. L and R are arbitrary variable names for the arguments, and FV is the name chosen for the function. The system responds with a [1], ▨ indicating where the cursor is, waiting for some instruction(s) on line 1.

[1]   ▨

Enter

[1] $L \leftarrow .01 \times L$

followed by a return to indicate you are through with the line. The system responds with [2] and the remaining instruction is now entered:

[2] $Z \leftarrow (1+L) * R$ (RETURN)
[3]   ▨

To tell the system that you are finished defining this function, enter a second ∇. The cursor comes to rest in its usual position, outside the function:

```
[3]    ∇
       △
```

Now we can use FV to compute future values:

```
       FUT1←10 FV 8
       FUT1
2.14358881
       500×FUT1                 ⍝ FUTURE VALUE OF $500
1071.794405
       10 FV 1 2 3 4 5 6  ⍝ FUTURE VALUE OF $1 FOR EACH YEAR UP TO 6
1.1 1.21 1.331 1.4641 1.61051 1.771561
```

To define and use even simple functions you need to know a little more than what we've said so far. First, the arguments are subject to the same rules as the primitives (page 17). Second, the result, like the primitives, may be stored in a variable. Third, multiple line instructions are executed sequentially. And last, that line of the function that produces the final result (here, line 2) must begin in the same way as the *header* (top line with all the names), in this case, $Z←$, for the result to be storable.

What happens if you make a mistake? APL provides excellent editing capability (Chapter 10), but only a few simple commands will be introduced now.

To display the list of defined functions, enter $)FNS$, while the command $∇FUNCTIONNAME[□]∇$ displays the function itself:

```
       )FNS
FV
       ∇FV[□]∇
    ∇  Z←L FV R
[1]    L←0.01×L
[2]    Z←(1+L)*R
    ∇
```

A function may be erased with $)ERASE$, or a line replaced by the command $∇FUNCTIONNAME$ $[LINENUMBER]$ *new instructions* $∇$. For example, if we wanted to change the instruction on line 2 of FV to $(1+L)×R$ (that's wrong, of course, but who cares?), we would enter $∇FV[2]Z←(1+L)×R∇$. To get rid of a line, enter $∇FUNCTIONNAME[△linenumber]∇$.

Some systems offer other ways to define functions. In particular, a method called *direct definition* is gaining popularity among academic users. If that's your calling, you may want to take a peek at page 298.

PROBLEMS

1. DRILL

```
¯2*.5                    1 10⍟1                 10⍟0
3*4 3 2 1 0 ¯5           2*.5 .333 .25 .2       1 9 ¯5 ¯2⌊0 6 4 3
21.268E1+4.56E¯2         1*0 1 10 100 1000      ¯8*.3333333333333
5 0 ¯22 15⌈3 7 ¯10.8 2   8.3E0×7.9E¯3 56        ¯7.11E4÷9.45E¯3
2 3 4 5⍟2                ¯2⍟25                  346×2E3.7
```

2. Key in $1E0$, $1E1$, etc. to $1E11$. Do likewise for $1E¯1$ through $1E¯6$. Note where the break point is in APL for the display on large and small numbers in E-notation.

3. Given a cube each of whose edges have length L. Write the APL steps needed to find its surface area. Execute for $L←3$ 7 15 2.7.

4. Assign $A←1$ 2 3 4 and $D←3×A$. Execute $A∘.×D$ and $D∘.*A$.

5. Use the outer product to generate a table of squares and square roots of the integers 1 through 5.

6. Express the number of seconds in the year (365 days) in scaled notation.

7. A journeyman snail finishing his apprenticeship is now allowed by the union to travel at a snail's pace (12 ft. per day). Express this in miles per hour.

8. Execute ⁻8*.5. Why the error message?

9. An astronomical unit (AU) is approximately 93,000,000 miles, the distance from Earth to Sun. Using scaled notation, find the distance in AU's of an object that is 1,500,000,000 miles away.

10. Store A sells 4 kinds of vegetable for 15, 20, 32 and 29 cents a pound. At store B the prices are 18, 20, 10 and 49 cents a pound, respectively. The policy of a third store, C, is to meet the competition's prices. Write an APL expression to determine store C's selling prices for the 4 items.

11. The pH of a solution is a measure of its acidity or basicity, and is defined as the logarithm (base 10) of the reciprocal of the hydrogen ion concentration in moles/liter of solution. Use APL to express the pH of a solution whose concentration is C.

12. You are given two matrices of prices, A and B. Define a new matrix C such that each element of C is the smaller of the corresponding elements of A and B.

13. **A** What is the future value of $1000 in ten and one half years if it earns 8% annual interest, compounded monthly? **B** Is this better than a 7.9% annual interest compounded daily? Use 360 as the number of days in a year.

14. Fold a piece of paper. It's now twice as thick as it was before. If the paper is .01 cm thick, how many times do you have to fold it to make it at least a kilometer thick?

15. A certain bacterium is known to grow 15% in a day. How long does it take for it to be 1000 times its starting size?

16. As I was going to St. Ives, I met a man with 7 wives. Each wife had 7 sacks. Each sack held 7 cats. How many cats? How many sacks? How many wives? How many were going to St. Ives?

17. Using the outer product, show the future value of $1 compounded annually at 0, 2, 4, 6, 8 and 10 percent for 1 through 10 years.

18. If inflation reduces the purchasing power of saved cash by 10% per year compounded, how long will it take for a dollar saved today to be worth only one fourth as much in real purchasing power?

Chapter 4: More primitive dyadic functions

This chapter introduces the remaining primitive dyadic functions, which will complete the set begun with + − × ÷ ⋆ ⊛ ⌈ ⌊ . While we will be discussing 13 new ones, it really won't be very difficult; after we struggle through the first two individually, the remaining ones fall into two simple categories that are easy to learn and remember.

Combinations

A relatively simple combinatorial problem in mathematics is to find the number of ways one can group 2 things out of a population of 4. Let's solve the problem by brute force, with 4 objects, A, B, C, D. The possible combinations are AB AC AD BC BD and CD. We'll assume the order isn't significant, so that CA and AC, for example, will be considered to be the same. Thus, there are 6 ways of grouping 2 things out of a population of 4.

In combinatorial theory it is shown that the formula (in conventional notation)

$$\frac{m!}{n!(m-n)!}$$

gives the number of ways of grouping m objects n at a time. For the case above, this would be (in conventional notation)

$$\frac{4!}{2!(4-2)!}$$

or 6. To remind those of you whose math is rusty, m! means $m \times (m-1) \times (m-2) \times ... \times 1$, so that 4! is the same as $4 \times 3 \times 2 \times 1$.

As you might hope, the process is somewhat easier in APL. It is done with the same symbol !, called *binomial* or *combinations*. The symbol is formed by striking the period, BACKSPACE and the quote symbol (upper shift *K*) so that the two characters line up. Of course, if your keyboard has the ! symbol, use it directly.

```
      2!4
6
```

When formed by overstriking, the symbols ' and . *must* be lined up. If they aren't, different things (none of them good) happen, depending on which APL system you use. Some will admonish you with *SYNTAX ERROR* or *OPEN QUOTE*, others will both admonish you and supply a second quote, and yet others will act dead regardless of what you do, until you figure out that you have to enter another quote. More about the use of quotes in Chapter 13.

The primitive scalar dyadic function ! can take both vector and matrix arguments:

```
      0 1 2 3 4!4
1 4 6 4 1

      X←2 3ρ0 1 2 3 4 5
      2!X
0  0  1
3  6 10
```

Its operation table looks like this:

```
        0 1 2 3 4∘.!0 1 2 3 4
    1 1 1 1 1
    0 1 2 3 4
    0 0 1 3 6
    0 0 0 1 4
    0 0 0 0 1
```

That portion of the table consisting of the nonzero integers can be removed to form what in mathematics is called Pascal's triangle,

```
              1
           1     1
        1     2     1
     1     3     3     1
  1     4     6     4     1
```

which, if you're interested, is a way to calculate and display the coefficients generated in the expansion of an expression of the form $(A+B)^n$ by the Binomial Theorem.

Finally, to complete the picture, our arguments don't have to be integers:

```
    2.1!5.6
13.48487115
```

For the benefit of the more mathematically sophisticated, this is related to the complete beta-function of probability theory. Don't panic. It won't be mentioned again!

Residue

The next primitive scalar dyadic function to learn is called *residue*. We can illustrate it with a trivial example. Assume that we are at the zoo with only 8 peanuts and 3 children who are to share the wealth evenly. We aren't able to cut up a single peanut. How many do we have left?

The simple-minded way to do this would be to start with 8 and take away 3, leaving 5. Then take 3 more away, with 2 remaining, too few to distribute to the children. In formal language, the 3-residue of 8 is 2. This isn't, of course, the only way to solve the problem. We could also divide 8 by 3, see that it goes in twice and get a remainder of 2.

The symbol for residue is |, which is the upper shift *M* . In APL, the 3-residue of 8 is entered as 3 | 8.

Our peanut problem can be enlarged by considering the distribution of varying amounts of peanuts to the 3 children:

```
    3|0 1 2 3 4 5 6 7 8
0 1 2 0 1 2 0 1 2
```

Here is another problem in which 5 peanuts are distributed among 1, 2 and 3 children:

```
    1 2 3|5
0 1 2
```

The residue function is a handy one for generating all kinds of useful results. For instance, asking for the 1-residue of a number is a convenient way to get the fractional part of the number:

```
    1|2.5 31.23
0.5 0.23
```

Now what about the residues of negative numbers, say 3 | ¯4? Previously we saw that a recurring pattern was generated by

```
    3|0 1 2 3 4 5 6 7 8
0 1 2 0 1 2 0 1 2
```

So when we try

```
        3|¯4 ¯3 ¯2 ¯1 0 1 2 3 4 5 6 7 8
2 0 1 2 0 1 2 0 1 2 0 1 2
```

we expect, and get, a continuation of the recurring pattern. If you think about it a bit, you will see another way to obtain the residue of a negative number. For our example above, add 3 to ¯4 to get ¯1. Then add 3 again to get 2. In general, the rule is to keep adding until the result is zero or positive.

Suppose the left argument is negative. Then the result is also negative, or 0 if the right argument is a multiple of the left argument:

```
        ¯8 3 ¯3 ¯2|¯4
¯4 2 ¯1 0
```

Applications requiring negative left arguments are few and far between. However, if you insist on pursuing this, try a few examples. Observe that the residue always lies between 0 and the value of the left argument. More formally, the result of $L \mid R$ is R if L is zero; otherwise it equals $R - (N \times L)$ for some integer N.

There is one residue class of particular interest in the computing industry, the 2-residues of the integers:

```
        2|0 1 2 3 4 5
0 1 0 1 0 1
```

Here we have a continuing pattern with 0 and 1 as its only elements. If we so choose, we can let 0 represent the state of a circuit with the switch open (no current) and 1 with the switch closed. Data that has values of 0 or 1 only is often called *bit* data. We'll have more to say about this soon.

Relational functions

In APL there are six *relational* functions, $< \leq = \geq > \neq$, which are found on the keyboard as the upper shift 3 through 8. They have the usual mathematical meanings, *less than, not greater than, equal, not less than, greater than* and *not equal*, respectively. The reason they are called *relational* is that they inquire about the truth or falsity of the relationship between two quantities.

For example, consider the statement A<B. It is really a question asked of the computer: 'Is A less than B?' It calls for a response of 'yes' or 'no', because either A is less than B or it isn't. Let's try this on the terminal:

```
        3<5                 5<3                 3<3
1                 0                 0
```

Clearly, a 1 response means the statement is true, and 0 false. Indeed, the only two values you ever get from any of the relational functions are 0 and 1.

```
        3<1 2 3 4 5                 A←2 3ρ1 2 3 4 5 6
0 0 0 1 1                 2<A
                              0 0 1
                              1 1 1
```

We can now use this function to help us in a selection problem. Suppose as store owners we have a number of accounts, with $3, $¯2, $0, $2 and $¯3 as balances, and we want to flag or mark those accounts which are overdrawn (represented by negative values). The *less than* function will solve our problem.

```
        3 ¯2 0 2 ¯3<0
0 1 0 0 1
```

Does < have all the qualities of a primitive scalar dyadic function? Here is its operation table:

```
        1 2 3 4∘.<1 2 3 4
0 1 1 1
0 0 1 1
0 0 0 1
0 0 0 0
```

By this time you ought to be able to convince yourself that *less than* meets our criteria for a primitive scalar dyadic function, as do indeed the rest of the relationals. We won't go through them all, but let's explore just one more, =. Entering

```
        3 ‾2 0 2 ‾3=0
0 0 1 0 0
```

generates a listing of those accounts from the previous example whose balance is 0. You should be able to see many other possibilities. For instance, to get vectors of all 1's or all 0's, try

```
        0 1 2 3=0 1 2 3              0 1 2 3=3 2 1 0
1 1 1 1                          0 0 0 0
```

Logical functions

Not all the juice has yet been squeezed out of the subset 0 1 of the real numbers. Here is a function ∧ (upper shift 0), called *and*, whose entire operation table is

```
     0 1∘.∧0 1
0 0
0 1
```

The result is 1 if and only if both arguments are 1, otherwise it is 0.

You have probably noticed that only 0 and 1 were used as arguments for *and*. Notice what happens when we try

```
     2∧0
DOMAIN ERROR
     2∧0
       ∧
```

Just as zero is not in the domain for division, all values other than 0 and 1 are not in the domain for ∧; and attempts to use them result in *DOMAIN ERROR*s.

For those who have some background in mathematical logic, the analogy between 0 and 1 and the true-false entries in the truth table for *and* will be apparent. In any event, this function provides yet another means of generating 0's and 1's, and will be useful in writing programs later on. The *and* function is an example of a class of functions called *logical* or *Boolean*.

Some of you will no doubt immediately see uses for this function. Others may be encountering it for the first time. For those of you in the latter category we offer the following example.

You have two vectors containing respectively the prices and amounts in inventory of each item sold. You want to generate a vector of 0's and 1's showing which items have to be reordered (less than 5 in inventory) and which at the same time sell for $50 or more. The following function will do the job:

```
      ∇RESULT←PRICE REORD INVENTORY
[1]      PRICES50←PRICE≥50
[2]      INVENTORY5←INVENTORY<5
[3]      RESULT←PRICES50∧INVENTORY5
[4]   ∇
```

Another logical function is ∨ (upper shift 9), called *or*. The result is 1 if either or both of the arguments are 1:

```
     0 1∘.∨0 1
0 1
1 1
```

Referring to the inventory example above, suppose now you want to identify those items the orders for which exceed the number in inventory or for which there are less than 5 in stock.

```
      ∇RESULT←ORDERS IDENT INVENTORY
[1]      ORDERS←ORDERS>INVENTORY
[2]      RESULT←ORDERS∨INVENTORY
[3]   ∇
```

There are yet two more functions in this class, ⍲ and ⍱, (*nand* and *nor*). You may have guessed already that *nand* stands for 'not and' and *nor* for 'not or.' The overstruck character ∼ (upper shift T) implies negation. Below are their operation tables:

```
      0 1∘.⍲0 1              0 1∘.⍱0 1
  1 1                      1 0
  1 0                      0 0
```

You can see that everywhere 0 appears in the table for ∧, a 1 appears for ⍲, and vice versa. The same holds for ∨ and ⍱.

Logical functions are used in programming to test a set of conditions (true and false usually being represented by 1 and 0 respectively), and then to take actions based on the outcome of the tests. Logical functions are also widely used to represent or simulate switching circuits.

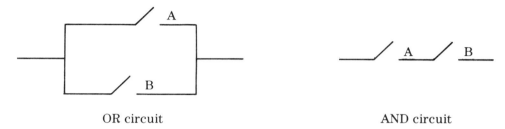

OR circuit   AND circuit

In the left figure electricity flows if either switch A or switch B is on, while in the right figure electricity flows only if both A and B are on. Read '0' for off and '1' for on, and the figures correspond to the *or* and *and* tables respectively. Keep in mind that it is a short step to go from simple electrical circuits like these to the fundamentals of digital computer design.

There are 16 possible logical connectives, although we have taken up only 4 of them. To illustrate how others can be generated, let's assume we need a function that gives us an *exclusive or*, with operation table

```
    | 0 1
 ---+-----
  0 | 0 1
  1 | 1 0
```

the result being 0 if and only if both arguments are 0 or both are 1. Can we produce this table in APL?

The answer is yes. It is that part of the operation table for ≠ where both arguments are 0 or 1. A similar approach yields many of the other logical connectives.

```
      0 1 2 3∘.≠0 1 2 3
      ⧄ 1 1
      ⧄ 1 1
  1 1 0 1
  1 1 1 0
```

Summary

We have now introduced and illustrated almost all of the primitive scalar dyadic functions. Before going on, here is a brief recapitulation:

$A+B$	sum of A and B	$A<B$	
$A-B$	B subtracted from A	$A\leq B$	Relationals all yield
$A\times B$	product of A and B	$A=B$	1 if true
$A\div B$	A divided by B	$A\geq B$	0 if false
$A*B$	A raised to the power B	$A>B$	
$A\circledast B$	base-A logarithm of B	$A\neq B$	
$A\lceil B$	larger of A and B	$A\vee B$	logical or of A and B
$A\lfloor B$	smaller of A and B	$A\wedge B$	logical and of A and B
$A\mid B$	A residue of B	$A\⍱B$	logical nor of A and B
$A!B$	combinations of B items taken A at a time	$A\⍲B$	logical nand of A and B

Any of these functions can be used to replace the character f in the rules (**page 17**) for combining scalars, vectors and matrices.

PROBLEMS

1. DRILL

```
1  9  8|3  4  6                    1|3.4  ¯2.2  .019
0  1  2  3  4!3  4  5  6  7         0|1  2  3
3|¯3  ¯1  0  1  2  3               ¯2  4  ¯5|8  13  3.78
0  0  1  1∨0  1  0  1               2  3  0<5  ¯1  4
1  0  1  0∧1  0  0  1               3  1  2≠1  2  3
2  4  7  ¯2>6  ¯1  0  4             0  1  2  3=0  1  3  2
4  ¯5  ¯1  ¯6.8≥4  1  ¯1  2         0  0  1  1⍱0  1  0  1
8  7  6  5  4  3  2  1≤1  2  3  4  5  6  7  8    1  0  1  0⍲1  0  0  1
```

2. How can the functions = and | be used in APL to identify the factors of an integer N?

3. A is a vector of accounts, with the negative values representing those overdrawn. Use one or more of the relational functions to flag those accounts *not* overdrawn.

4. Write an APL expression to return a 1 if either condition A is true or condition B is false.

5. Execute 0 1∘.=0 1. Contrast this with the operation table on page 30. What name would be appropriate to assign to this logical connective?

6. You happen to have in storage a vector S of four positive elements. Use S to generate each of the following in at least five different ways: **A** a vector Z of four zeros, and **B** a vector Y of four ones.

7. Write APL statements which will produce a logical vector C with 1's corresponding to the even numbers in a vector $A \leftarrow ¯6\ 7\ 2\ 4\ ¯21$.

8. Obtain as many of the remaining logical connectives as you can from the functions introduced so far.

9. Execute the following outer products for $A \leftarrow 0\ 1$: $A \circ .\times A$ $A \circ .\lfloor A$ $A \circ .\lceil A$ $A \circ .*A$ $A \circ .|A$ $A \circ .!A$. What logical or relational function is each equivalent to?

10. How can the residue function be used to tell whether one number A is exactly divisible by another number B?

11. Write an APL expression to tell what clock time it is, given the number of elapsed hours H since midnight.

12. How many quadrilaterals can be formed by joining groups of 4 points in a collection of 30 points in a plane.

13. If $1 | N$ produces the fractional part of N, how can the residue function be used to get the integral part of the number?

14. Write an expression to get the fractional part of a negative number.

15. A student's answers (0 for no, 1 for yes) to a survey are stored in a vector $RESP1$. Six months later the student again takes the same survey. His latest answers are stored in $RESP2$. Show how to identify the questions **A** to which the responses both times were 'yes' and **B** which were answered differently in the two surveys.

16. (For lovers of FORTRAN or BASIC.) In other programming languages you may run across statements like I=I+1, where I is a counter for some iterative procedure. There is, of course, no finite real number that equals itself when 1 is added to it. This statement is to be interpreted as 'increment I by 1 and *store* the result in I'. What is its APL equivalent?

Chapter 5: Algorithms, reduction and scanning

We now introduce the concept of an *algorithm*, which is nothing but a series of steps that together comprise a prescription for defining a function or solving a problem. Two examples will be given. The first, taken from plane geometry, will involve no new APL functions and will be used solely as an illustration of an algorithm. The second example, although very useful in its own right, quite frankly, is an excuse to introduce one of the most widely used APL operations, *reduction*, which allows us to compute among the elements of a single vector or matrix. Finally, *scan*, which can be thought of as a powerful extension of reduction, will be introduced.

Algorithms

Here is the example referred to above, which everyone should recognize as the butt of numerous jokes and misspellings of its name. The problem is to calculate the hypotenuse of a right triangle, given the sides as shown:

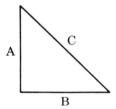

A convenient and time-honored rule for finding C is the Pythagorean Theorem. It states that to get C we have to square A, add it to the square of B, and then find the square root of this sum.

Here is how this sequence of steps can be executed in APL:

```
A←3
B←4
A2←A*2
A2
```
9
```
B2←B*2
S←A2+B2
S
```
25
```
C←S*.5
C
```
5

Of course, if we didn't want to save the result by storing it in C, we could have eliminated its assignment and displayed the result directly by entering $S*.5$.

Now think about this: we had to assign A and B initially in the sequence; otherwise, when we called for the values of $A2$, $B2$ and S along the way as checks on our work, we would have gotten *VALUE ERROR*s, or perhaps some previously assigned value. We'll see later, when we learn how to store instructions (programming), that this assignment of values for the variables need not be done beforehand.

Let's assign new values to A and B, this time solving two triangles simultaneously:

```
        A←1  3
        B←1  4
        C
5
```

What happened? Why did we get the same value for C even though A and B changed? We answer this question by asking another: when we assign a quantity like $A2+B2$ to some variable S, what is it that is stored? Not the *instruction* $A2+B2$, but the result of executing that instruction with the numbers stored in $A2$ and $B2$. Thus, assignment can't ordinarily be used to store instructions; only *values* can be stored this way.

```
        A2←A*2                    B2←B*2                  S←A2+B2
        A2                        B2                      S*.5
1  9                        1  16                   1.414213562  5
```

However, instructions *can* be stored in a user-defined function:

```
        ∇C←A HYP B
[1]     A2←A*2                         1  3 HYP 1  4
[2]     B2←B*2                    1.414213562  5
[3]     S←A2+B2
[4]     C←S*.5
[5]     ∇
```

A set of instructions like the above, that collectively represents a prescription for solving a particular problem, is called an *algorithm*. Defined functions in APL, therefore, are a mechanism for saving and calling algorithms.

Finally, we can check on the variables in storage in the usual manner,

```
        )VARS
A       A2        B       B2        C       M       N       PI
RATES   RN        S       W         X       XY2     X3Y2    A
```

and the new variables specified in our right triangle algorithm are now included. Of course, your listing may differ from this if you happen to have defined additional variables in the current terminal session. However, it should contain at least these names.

Reduction

You saw how working with vectors and matrices allowed us to do *parallel processing* of data, with a resulting saving in time and number of keystrokes required. We now extend this concept to show how meaningful operations can be effectively performed on the elements of a single vector or matrix. Continuing with the analogy with electrical circuits, we may call such work *series processing*.

Let's begin with a common business calculation, an invoice extension. Assume that several different items have been purchased. We'll use Q and C to represent the quantities and the costs, respectively.

```
        Q←6  2  3  1  0              C←2  4  3  5  10
```

To get the vector of total costs, we execute

```
        X←Q×C                           X
                               12  8  9  5  0
```

But now, to obtain the grand total, we have to add up all the elements of this vector. In conventional notation, the mathematician indicates the sum of the elements of a vector by writing

$$\sum_{i=1}^{n} x_i$$

$\sum$ means 'sum' while i is a running variable from 1 to n, identifying the individual elements of the vector. The total number of elements is n, 5 in the invoice extension problem we are working on. If this seems potentially like a lot of work, don't be too concerned. In what follows we will show how to carry out the summation in APL with minimal effort.

Getting back to the problem at hand, our objective is to sum across the elements of a vector. We do this in APL with $+/X$. This is read as 'plus reducing X,' or 'the plus reduction of X.' The symbol / (lower right corner of the keyboard) is called *reduce*, because it reduces the vector to a single element:

```
      +/X
34
```

How this operator works is worth discussing in more detail. The APL system inserts the function symbol which appears to the left of the / between each pair of elements of the vector, and groups them so that the order of execution is $12+(8+(9+(5+0)))$.

The reason for the grouping is that each function operates on everything to the right of it. If you think about what this means, you will see that this is equivalent to operating on the rightmost pair of elements first, taking that answer together with the next element to the left, and so on. Following this through step by step, we obtain

```
      12+(8+(9+(5+0)))
      12+(8+(9+  5   ))
      12+(8+  14      )
      12+  22
        34
```

You may be inclined to argue that we are making a big to-do about nothing, since with addition it doesn't really matter whether we work from right to left or left to right. We'll see later, however, that arbitrary order of execution (called *commutativity*) is not general. For the time being, just remember that in APL reduction proceeds from right to left.

Times reduction

Now consider still another problem. A rectangular box has the dimensions 2 by 3 by 4 centimeters. What is its volume? To answer the question we obviously want

```
      2×3×4
24
```

If we assign the vector of the dimensions to Z, then $×/Z$ should give us our answer:

```
      Z←2 3 4
      ×/Z
24
```

In this case, × is planted between each neighboring pair of elements, and the internal calculation is carried out in this sequence:

```
      2×(3×4)
      2×  12
        24
```

Since raising to integer powers is the same as repeated multiplication, then a clumsy alternative to $1.06\star4$ (future value of a dollar compounded annually for 4 years at a constant rate of 6%) is $×/1.06\ 1.06\ 1.06\ 1.06$. That's not very exciting itself, but it does lead to methods for dealing with varying interest rates. For example, the future value of a dollar compounded for 4 years with annual interest rates of 5%, 7%, 6% and 5.5% for each of the years in turn is simply $×/1.05\ 1.07\ 1.06\ 1.055$.

Reduction on matrices

A matrix has two dimensions to be concerned about, and that makes reducing matrices a little harder than reducing vectors. Suppose we have sales information by weeks showing the numbers sold of each of five items, as in the table below:

```
            |      ITEMS
      SALES |  1   2   3   4   5
      ------+-------------------
      W  1  | 15  18   9   2   7
      E  2  |  4  15   1   8   6
      E  3  |  0   4   0   8   3
      K  4  | 12  10  13   7   9
```

It is reasonable to ask what the sales record is by item for the month (i.e., over the 4-week period). This involves a summation along the columns, or, put another way, across the *first* dimension of the matrix.

To show this operation in APL, we first put the matrix in storage:

```
      S←4 5ρ15 18 9 2 7 4 15 1 8 6 0 4 0 8 3 12 10 13 7 9
      S
15 18  9  2  7
 4 15  1  8  6
 0  4  0  8  3
12 10 13  7  9
```

The desired summation is obtained by

```
      +⌿S
31 47 23 25 25
```

$⌿$ is the symbol for reduction overstruck with the subtract sign. It is used for summing the elements in each *column* of a matrix. The result is a vector with as many elements as there are *columns* in the matrix.

If in the above example we wanted gross sales records by weeks, we would obtain it by entering

```
      +/S
51 34 15 51
```

This sums the elements in each *row* of the matrix, that is, across the *last* dimension. The result is a vector with as many elements as there are *rows* in the matrix.

In summary, $+⌿$ causes a reduction across the *first dimension* of any array, and $+/$ reduces across the *last dimension* of any array. A vector has only one dimension, so that $+⌿$ and $+/$ will have the same effect.

The word 'reduce' was selected because it does indeed reduce the number of dimensions. A matrix reduces to a vector, and a vector reduces to a scalar.

Algorithms for averaging and counting

We can now profitably talk about an algorithm to get the average of the elements of a vector such as

```
      X←2 4 3 3 2.5 2
```

To get an average we need two things: the sum of all the elements in the vector we are averaging, and the number of elements. The first is easy: $+/X$ is 16.5. We could then get the average by dividing this sum by the number of elements obtained by manually counting them. One way to 'count' the number of elements using APL is

```
      X=X
1 1 1 1 1 1
```

The result of all 1's is no surprise, since each element of X is equal to itself. As you can see, this generates a vector consisting of as many 1's as there are elements in X. But where does that lead us? Now all we have to do is add up those 1's to find the number of elements:

```
      M←X=X                    N←+/M                       N
                                           6
```

We can now complete the calculation of the average of 2 4 3 3 2.5 2:

```
      T←+/X                    T                           T÷N
                   16.5                     2.75
```

The expression $+/X=X$ is a rather awkward way to obtain a count of the number of elements in a vector. As a reward for your patience, we'll now introduce the *shape* function, $ρ$. Its job is to return the size of the array to its right.[1]

---

[1]Since $ρ$ in this context has only a single argument (as opposed to $A⊕B$, which has a left and right argument), it is called a *monadic* (rather than dyadic) function. More about this in Chapter 7.

Our algorithm for averaging can now be more succinctly expressed as

```
T←+/X                    N←ρX                    T÷N
                                    2.75
```

or even more usefully as a defined monadic function:

```
        ∇ T←AVERAGE X
[1]     T←+/X ⋀ NOTE USE OF T FOR STORING INTERMEDIATE RESULT.
[2]     T←T÷ρX
[3]     ∇
        AVERAGE X
2.75
```

When you apply *shape* to a matrix, the result isn't simply a count of elements, but rather is a vector holding the numbers of rows and the number of columns.

```
    A←2 3ρ1 4 5 6 8 9            B←1 2 3∘.⌈1 2 3 4
    A                           B
1 4 5                       1 2 3 4
6 8 9                       2 2 3 4
    ρA                      3 3 3 4
2 3                             ρB
                        3 4
```

Maximum, minimum and logical reduction

Plus reduction and minus reduction are very common in APL. But reduction isn't limited to just + and ×. Any primitive scalar dyadic function can be used. Here is an illustration using the maximum function. Remember Z, the vector of dimensions of the rectangular box we introduced earlier?

```
    Z
2 3 4
```

Suppose we wanted to get the longest dimension in Z, i.e., pick out the maximum value. Then by analogy, just as we had

```
    2+(3+4) is2+7 or 9
    2×(3×4) is 2×12 or 24
```

for +/Z and ×/Z, respectively,

```
    2⌈(3⌈4) is 2⌈4 or 4
```

represents ⌈/Z, and returns the largest value in Z.

On the terminal, try

```
    ⌈/Z                 ⌊/Z
4                   2
```

The last example, minimum reduction, is carried out like this:

```
    2⌊(3⌊4) is 2⌊3 or 2
```

Note that the symbol before the reduction operator is again placed between each pair of neighboring elements, and the groupings are the same as before.

Yet another simple application involves the logical functions in an accounts identification problem. Let X be a vector of balances:

```
    X←3 4 2 ‾2 1
```

Our job is to see if any of the balances are overdrawn (negative). The first step is to assign a vector of the same length as X, containing a 1 in each place where X is less than 0. Then use *or* reduction:

```
    LZ←X<0              LZ              ∨/LZ
                   0 0 0 1 0            1
```

(Remember that *or* returns a 1 if either or both arguments are 1.) Our answer can be interpreted as follows: if 1, then at least one account is negative; if 0, then no accounts are negative.

Let's reset X and repeat the problem to illustrate the other possibility:

```
    X←3 6 1 0 3         LZ←X<0          ∨/LZ
                                         0
```

Can you tell what the significance of the answers might be if we had used ∧/LZ in the algorithm instead of ∨/LZ?

Minus reduction

This use of reduction is only for those of a mathematical persuasion. All others should skip this section.

```
      −/3  2  1  4
 ¯2
```

Because of the right-to-left sequence of execution of APL, −/3 2 1 4 is equivalent to 3−2+1−4 in conventional notation—in other words, it produces the *alternating sum*. You can view it as 3−(2−(1−4)).

Here is a somewhat messy example, an expression to calculate π:

$$\pi = 4 \times \left(\frac{1}{1} - \frac{1}{3} + \frac{1}{5} - \frac{1}{7} + \frac{1}{9} - \cdots + \cdots \right)$$

Let's translate this into APL. Our first step is to get the vector of denominators, stopping after 10 terms. Next, we take their reciprocals, find the alternating sum and multiply it by 4.

Practically speaking, this isn't a very good way to get π because the series converges so slowly that a very large number of terms is needed to obtain an accurate value. However, it's dandy for illustrative purposes. First, we generate the vector 1 3 5 ... 19 from the vector 1 2 3 ... 10:

```
      N←1 2 3 4 5 6 7 8 9 10
      N←2×N
      N
2 4 6 8 10 12 14 16 18 20
      N←N−1
      N
1 3 5 7 9 11 13 15 17 19
```

The reassignment of N and 2×N and N−1 destroys the previously assigned values of N, as discussed on page 12.

The reciprocals can be obtained by assigning

```
      R←1÷N
      R
1 0.3333333333 0.2 0.1428571429 0.1111111111 0.09090909091 0.07692307692
      0.06666666667 0.05882352941 0.05263157895
```

and the alternating sum by

```
      T←−/R
```

Our answer for π (at last!) is

```
      4×T
3.041839619
```

which is about 0.1 off because we used too few terms for such a slowly converging series. However, after all this work, you will be pleased to hear that APL provides a primitive function for π, that it is alive and well, and is discussed in Chapter 7.

A defined function to compute π with this algorithm would look like this:

```
       ∇Z←PICALC N
[1]    Z←2×N
[2]    Z←Z-1
[3]    Z←1÷Z
[4]    Z←-/Z
[5]    Z←4×Z
[6]    ∇
       PICALC 1 2 3 4 5 6 7 8 9 10
3.041839619
```

If $-/$ is the alternating sum, then $\div/$ is the alternating product, which you can verify for yourself on the terminal.

Scanning

There are many instances when you may want to operate on the elements of an array one at a time and cumulatively with some primitive dyadic function, i.e., do a series of 'partial reductions' as you 'scan' the array. The simple example which follows illustrates the use of APL's scan operator.

Suppose you opened a bank account. You deposit $100 the first week, and in weeks two, three and four you write checks for $25, $50 and $33 respectively. In the fifth week you deposit $80, and then withdraw $40 and $10 during the following two weeks. If you store the data in a vector M, using negative values to represent outgoing funds,

```
    M←100 ¯25 ¯50 ¯33 80 ¯40 ¯10
```

then the balance at the close of the seventh week is $+/M$ or $22. More interesting yet is keeping track of the balance on hand each week. Using reduction, you could find this by executing

```
       +/100
100
       +/100 ¯25
75
       +/100 ¯25 ¯50
25
       +/100 ¯25 ¯50 ¯33 ⍝ WHAT IS THE SIGNIFICANCE OF A NEGATIVE RESULT?
¯8
       +/100 ¯25 ¯50 ¯33 80
72
       +/100 ¯25 ¯50 ¯33 80 ¯40
32
       +/100 ¯25 ¯50 ¯33 80 ¯40 ¯10
22
```

The plus-scan, which uses the symbol \, found on the same key as /, does it all at once:

```
       +\100 ¯25 ¯50 ¯33 80 ¯40 ¯10
100 75 25 ¯8 72 32 22
```

The shape of the result is the same as the shape of the argument. The last element is what would have been obtained had you performed a reduction instead of a scan.

Using the matrix S entered earlier in this chapter, you can scan across the second dimension or across the first dimension:

```
       S                    +\S                   +⍀S
15 18  9  2  7        15 33 42 44 51        15 18  9  2  7
 4 15  1  8  6         4 19 20 28 34        19 33 10 10 13
 0  4  0  8  3         0  4  4 12 15        19 37 10 18 16
12 10 13  7  9        12 22 35 42 51        31 47 23 25 25
```

In the examples above, the last column or row is the same as what would have been obtained by reduction along the same dimension.

Any of the primitive dyadic functions can be used with scan, just as with reduction. Here is our π-finding algorithm using scan instead of reduction. You can see how the accuracy of the result improves as the number of terms increases:

```
      R←1÷1  3  5  7  9  11  13  15  17  19
      T←−\R
      4×T
4  2.666666667  3.466666667  2.895238095  3.33968254  2.976046176  3.283738484
      3.017071817  3.252365935  3.041839619
```

Logical scans

Scans of arrays that consist only of zeros and ones are particularly interesting. $\wedge\backslash$ applied to a logical vector LV results in a vector of ones up to the first zero of LV and zeros thereafter. It is often used to count the number of elements until some condition changes, such as a space character following a word. A common expression in APL is $+/\wedge\backslash LV$, which returns a count of the number of leading ones in LV.

Other useful logical scans are $\vee\backslash LV$, which returns zeros up to the first one in LV, and $<\backslash LV$, which returns a vector of all zeros except for a one in the position corresponding to the first one in LV. $\neq\backslash LV$ can be used for parity indication. The result is one if the sum of the number of ones encountered so far is odd, and zero if even. An equivalent expression is $2\,|\,+\backslash LV$.

PROBLEMS

1. DRILL

+/3 7 ¯10 15 22	−/2 4 6 8 10	×/2 4 6 8 10
÷/3 5 2	∗/3 2 1	∧/1 0 1 1
∧/1 1 1	∨/0 1 0 1	∨/0 0 0
=/3 2 2	>/1 ¯2 ¯4	⌊/¯2 4 0 ¯8
⌈/1 ¯14.7 22 6	×\3 2 7 9	⌈\4 12 7 14

2. State in words what tests are represented by ∧/, ∨/ and =/.

3. For $AV \leftarrow 3\ 6\ 8\ 2\ 4$, evaluate $+/3 \times AV$.

4. Write a one-line APL expression to assign Q as the vector 1 7 ¯2 ¯3 and find the largest element in Q.

5. Set up an algorithm in APL to calculate the area of a triangle by Hero's formula, Area = $\sqrt{S(S-A)(S-B)(S-C)}$. A, B and C are the lengths of the sides of the triangle, and S is the semiperimeter. In your algorithm use L as the vector of sides of the triangle.

6. Write an APL expression to give the slope of the line passing through the points with coordinates (X_1, Y_1) and (X_2, Y_2). By definition, the slope of a straight line is the difference in the values of the vertical coordinates of two points on the line divided by the difference in the values of the corresponding horizontal coordinates.

7. Each row of a matrix S represents sales by weeks of some item over a two-month period. Create a new matrix SR which gives a running tally of cumulative sales over this time period.

8. Explain the action of each of the following on a logical vector LV: ∧\$LV$, <\$LV$, ∨\$LV$.

9. You are given a vector of sales transactions $SALES$, with taxes not included. Write expressions to determine **A** the number of transactions, **B** the highest and lowest sales, **C** the total sales, **D** the amount due on each transaction including a 4% sales tax, **E** the average sale.

10. Incredible Charlie, a used car dealer sold 6, 2, 1, 8, 4 and 3 cars during successive days of a sale-a-thon. **A** How many did he sell altogether? **B** If 15 customers traded in their cars, and 4 of those were immediately wholesaled to another dealer, by how much did the inventory of cars in stock change? **C** What is the average profit per sale if total profit is $6300? **D** How much was paid out in sales commissions if they average $75 per car sold?

11. Execute $T \leftarrow 10 \rho 1$ and then $+\backslash T$. The result is not surprising; however, would you have thought to use scan to generate a sequence like this?

Chapter 6: Order of execution

In the last chapter we saw that in reduction the effective order of execution was from right to left, since each functional symbol operated on everything to the right of it. It was as a result of this rule that $-/$ gave us the alternating sum. Does this order of execution concept apply to all functions of APL? You should make up some examples to convince yourself at this point that it does.

One good illustration is the problem on page 37 that calculates a value for π. There we used a large number of steps to get the result; but a much neater and more elegant way to write the algorithm is

```
       ∇Z←PI1 N
[1]    Z←4×-/1÷ ¯1+2×N
[2]    ∇
       PI1 1 2 3 4 5 6 7 8 9 10
3.041839619
```

Here, working from right to left, first the computer produces the sequence 2 4 6 ... by multiplying 1 2 3 ... by 2. Then ¯1 is added, which gives us the odd numbers 1 3 5 ... These are divided into 1, yielding the reciprocals. After $-/$ makes an alternating sum out of the reciprocals, the result is multiplied by 4 to give π.

The same approach can be taken with our old friend the invoice extension problem (page 33). In this case the total cost of the products Q with individual costs C can be written as $+/Q×C$. Numerically it can be expressed as

```
       +/6 2 3 1 0×2 4 3 5 10
34
```

Changing the order of execution

Don't be tempted by these examples into thinking that all problems can be solved this neatly. A case in point is the calculation of the hypotenuse. See what happens as we foolishly enter the following sequence:

```
       A←3
       B←4
       A*2+B*2*.5
22041.01477
```

Why this result? Working from right to left, $2*.5$ is 1.414223562, and 4 is raised to the 1.41413562 power, giving 7.102993301. Then 2 is added, giving 9.102993301. Lastly, 3 is raised to that power, giving the (undesired) result 22041.01477.

The correct way to carry out the hypotenuse algorithm on one line follows. You should study the sequence in which things are calculated in it:

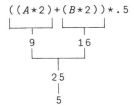

This is a good place to make three observations: (1) pairs of parentheses are used in APL in exactly the same way as in conventional mathematical notation, that is, the normal order of execution is interrupted and expressions within parentheses are evaluated separately; (2) aside from the above use of parentheses, there is no hierarchy of functions specifying the order of execution in APL; and (3) a single right parenthesis is used in APL to denote system commands, as contrasted to their use in calculations, where a pair is required.

Having said this much, we now hedge a bit to point out that APL2 treats order of execution in a slightly different way; although there still is no hierarchy of functions, nor of operators, operators take precedence over functions.

Getting back to the hypotenuse example, A and B are squared, then added, and finally this sum is raised to the .5 power. Let's executed this for specific values of A and B:

```
      A←3
      B←4
      ((A*2)+(B*2)).5
SYNTAX ERROR
      ((A*2)+(B*2)) 0.5
                  ^
```

The omission of the symbol $*$ before the .5 was deliberate. We needed an excuse once again to call a subtle point to your attention. In conventional notation you were able to get away with expressions like A(B+C) because tradition allowed it. But in APL there is no such assumption. If some function f is meant, then f must be explicitly used. It certainly helps to keep the language concise and free of ambiguities.

Reentering the line correctly produces the hypotenuse:

```
      ((A*2)+(B*2))*.5
5
```

As you can see in the following example, which omits the parentheses around $B*2$, parentheses aren't always needed. (Why not in this example?)

```
      ∇C←A HYP1 B
[1]   C←((A*2)+B*2)*.5
[2]   ∇
      3 HYP1 4
5
```

Now one more rehash of an old problem, the calculation of averages. We saw that it was necessary to get the sum of the elements of the vector X and divide this by the number of elements in X:

```
      ∇Z←AVERAGE1 X
[1]   Z←(+/X)÷ρX
[2]   ∇
```

From right to left, ρX yields the number of elements of X, which in turn is divided into the sum of the three elements of X.

Parentheses aren't needed around the expression $+/X$ on the extreme left, but for a reason different from what you might expect. This can be shown by looking at $+/1\ \ 2\ \ 3÷3$, which is arithmetically equivalent to $(1÷3)+(2÷3)+(3÷3)$, or 2. This is exactly the same as $(1+2+3)÷3$. It doesn't make one bit of difference if we divide the elements of the vector by 3 before summing or after, since, of course, the divisor (here 3) is the same for all elements. However, it does make a difference *computationally* because it is a matter of three divisions and three additions in one case as compared to one division and three additions in the other.

A natural extension of this algorithm can be used to get row and column averages for a matrix. For example, let the matrix M be the number of units sold for 4 products (across) during 3 weeks (down):

```
      M←3 4ρ6 7 9 10 4 0 4 8 3 1 9 7
      M
6  7  9 10
4  0  4  8
3  1  9  7
```

The average number of units sold per week over the 4 products is

```
      (+/M)÷4
8 4 5
```

and the average number of units of each product sold per week over the three weeks is

```
      (+⌿M)÷3
4.333333333 2.666666667 7.333333333 8.333333333
```

Can you write a one-line expression to get the grand average of all the elements of the array? And while you're at it, can you think of a way to get the APL system to generate the number of elements in the rows and columns?

The elegant simplicity of APL's right-to-left sequence of execution means that we don't have to remember arbitrary rules of precedence as found in conventional notations. This is particularly advantageous because APL has many more primitive functions. Having to pay attention to arbitrary rules of precedence would just make life harder.

However, we predict that you will have trouble breaking away from one part of conventional notation: what does 3×2+4 mean to you? If you said 10, you're still doing your multiplications before your additions, as in conventional notation. In APL, $3 \times 2 + 4$ is 18, because in the strict right-to-left sequence, $2 + 4$ is 6, and then 3×6 is 18. If you are uncomfortable with this departure with tradition, we suggest that you use parentheses liberally to give your statements clarity. For example, if you really wanted to calculate (3 × 2) + 4, then enter it that way. Note, however, that the experienced APL'er would probably express it as 4 + 3 × 2, because that takes less time to enter on the terminal.

As you begin to exercise your skills building expressions with many functions, don't hesitate to over-parenthesize. When you are more at home in your understanding of the APL language, you can experiment with omitting nonessential parentheses.

A polynomial illustration

An elegant demonstration of the order of execution rule and the power and versatility of APL can be seen in the following example showing how polynomials can be written and evaluated. Consider the typical algebraic polynomial expression $3-2X+9X^2+4 \times X^3$ (conventional notation) which we want to evaluate for X, say 10. How can this be represented in APL?

We'll start with the most obvious, a direct transliteration from the conventional notation:

```
X←10
3+(¯2×X)+(9×X*2)+4×X*3
4883
```

A little better version, which eliminates the parentheses, is

```
3+X×¯2+X×9+X×4
4883
```

Observe the sequence of steps APL takes to obtain the result.

$$3 \quad + \quad 10 \quad \times \quad ^-2 \quad + \quad 10 \quad \times \quad 9 \quad + \quad 10 \quad \times \quad 4$$

$$\longleftarrow 40 \longrightarrow$$
$$\longleftarrow 49 \longrightarrow$$
$$\longleftarrow 490 \longrightarrow$$
$$\longleftarrow 488 \longrightarrow$$
$$\longleftarrow 4880 \longrightarrow$$
$$\longleftarrow 4883 \longrightarrow$$

But you can't really appreciate the economy of the APL notation until you have taken advantage of its ability to handle arrays. Here is the *pièce de résistance* of our polynomial example:

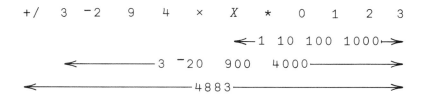

Lines and statements

Now that you can express complete formulas on one line, you may be tempted to pack as much on a single line as possible. An exercise of this sort has its good and bad points. First the good news: it has the effect of forcing you to review all the APL you know while looking for the proper combination of symbols and order that solves the problem. And now the bad news: lines of APL so written are frequently difficult for others to read and understand. To show that you really do have sympathy for others, as well as to enhance the concepts involved, you should arrange your lines so that each one represents a distinct part of the algorithm and can stand more or less on its own feet.

Every APL author has his or her own stable of favorite horror stories in this connection. One of ours is the following, which happens to be a one-line representation of the calculation of the correlation coefficient from statistics. If you're not mathematically inclined, don't worry. This isn't designed to scare you out of several days' growth, but rather to cause you to swear off such activity in the future. Here it is:

$$R \leftarrow (+/X \times Y) \div ((+/(X \leftarrow X-(+/X) \div \rho X) \ast 2) \times +/(Y \leftarrow Y-(+/Y) \div \rho Y) \ast 2) \ast .5$$

In the above line, aside from the fact that it's almost impossible to read, there is the latent risk that in some future APL implementation it might not work at all and indeed is pornographic! Pornography is as elusive and hard to define in APL as it is in the courts. Most experienced APL users will agree that they know it when they see it, but refuse to be pinned down to a definition.

A better arrangement for the correlation algorithm is

$$X \leftarrow X-(+/X) \div \rho X$$
$$Y \leftarrow Y-(+/Y) \div \rho Y$$
$$R \leftarrow (+/X \ast 2) \times +/Y \ast 2$$
$$R \leftarrow (+/X \times Y) \div R \ast .5$$

On some APL systems, the economy of the one-liner can be achieved by employing the diamond ◇. It lets you put related statements on the same line, without sacrificing brevity or clarity. Each statement is separated by diamonds; and the system executes the first statement on the left, then the next, and so on until the last (rightmost) statement on the line is executed. The usual order of execution rules apply within each statement. Here is one way to write the above algorithm with the diamond:

$$X \leftarrow X-(+/X) \div \rho X \quad ◇ \quad Y \leftarrow Y-(+/Y) \div \rho Y$$
$$R \leftarrow (+/X \ast 2) \times +/Y \ast 2 \quad ◇ \quad R \leftarrow (+/X \times Y) \div R \ast .5$$

The two lines above could have been pushed into one long one with another diamond, but that might look too formidable. In the final analysis, how much you put on one line is a matter of personal taste, but you should avoid constructing long lines (without the diamond) which might be hard for others to follow.

Another feature of many newer systems is that a comment can be placed on any line. The rule is that all characters to the right of the ⍝ symbol are ignored by the computer:

$$X \leftarrow X-(+/X) \div \rho X \quad ◇ \quad Y \leftarrow Y-(+/Y) \div \rho Y \quad ⍝ \text{ CENTER X AND Y}$$
$$R \leftarrow (+/X \ast 2) \times +/Y \ast 2 \quad ⍝ \text{ CALCULATE DIVISOR - SQUARED}$$
$$R \leftarrow (+/X \times Y) \div R \ast .5 \quad ⍝ \text{ FINAL RESULT R IS CORRELATION}$$

PROBLEMS

1. DRILL

    ```
    4*3⌈3*4            5*3×5               76÷+/2+3×1 2 3 4
    (4*3)⌈3*4          1÷2+¯5 6 0 8 ¯6     6÷2−4*3
    ```

2. Which of the following six expressions have the same value?

    ```
    (B*2)−4×A×C         B*2−4×A×C           B×B−(4×A)×C
    ((B*2)−4×(A×C))     (B×B)−(4×A)×C       (A×¯4×C)+B*2
    ```

3. Construct **APL** expressions for each of the following: **A** three-fourths plus five-sixths minus seven-eighths; **B** the quotient of the two differences, nine-sevenths minus eight-tenths, and one-third minus two-fifths.

4. The geometric mean of a set of N positive numbers X is the Nth root of their product. Write an APL expression to calculate this for $X←1$ 7 4 2.5 51 19.

5. What is wrong with the expression $A+B=B+A$ to show that the operation of addition is commutative, i.e., the order of the arguments is immaterial?

6. The Gregorian calendar provides that all years from 1582 to about 20,000 that are divisible by 4 are leap years, with the adjustment that of the centesimal years (1600, 1700, etc.) only those divisible by 400 are leap years, and of the millenial years those divisible by 4000 are not. Write a one-line APL expression to determine whether a given year Y is a leap year.

7. Why is this APL expression, $(X*2)−(2×X×Y)+Y*2$, wrong for $X^2−2XY+Y^2$ (conventional notation)? Correct it.

8. Rewrite the polynomial APL expression $(¯3×X*4)+(2×X*2)−8$ without parentheses. Do *not* use reduction.

9. Write an APL expression to compute the root-mean-square of the elements of a vector. (This is the square root of the average of the squares.)

10. What is a possible interpretation of the following?

    $$PROPOSE←RING∧WEATHER∧(JILL<JACK)∧JACK<AGELIMIT$$

11. Rewrite as a single expression the future value algorithm (page 20) to calculate the interest on P dollars at R percent compounded annually for T years. How would you change the expression to provide for compounding quarterly?

12. You are required to assign 5 to C if A is greater than B; otherwise, C is assigned the value 4. Similarly, if A is greater than B, and D is less than E, then C is 10. Otherwise, C is 8.

13. Without executing it on the terminal, what is $2+2$ $2+2$?

14. You are an industrial spy working for a bank, and have managed to steal a vector from a rival bank. The APL vector V contains all their accounts. Find: **A** how many accounts they have; **B** the average value of the accounts; **C** how many accounts are in the red; **D** how many are exactly zero; **E** the values of the largest and smallest accounts; **F** the percentage of accounts above \$100; **G** the number of accounts between \$100 and \$200 inclusive; **H** how many of the nonnegative accounts are exact multiples of \$100.

15. Construct an APL expression that will yield a value A if A is greater than B, otherwise zero.

16. The Sharp-as-a-Tack Company offers to sell one square inch of Klondike land for \$0.25. Compute the gross income per acre (an acre is 160 square rods and one rod is 16.5 feet).

17. A resort hotel charges \$235 per person double occupancy for seven days, six nights (Modified American Plan). Extra nights are \$39 per person. Children under 12 are half-price. With a service charge of \$3.20 per person per day and \$4 daily tax on the M.A.P. rate, what is the cost for a family of 5 (2 under 12) staying 10 days, 9 nights?

18. Carry out the following instructions and explain the results.

```
A←15.8                    A←15.8
B←(A←4)×A                 B←(A←4)×0⌈A
B                         B
```
16   63.2

19. The matrix $FUND$ (shape 3 by 10) records the shares a broker sold of each of 10 stocks during the first three trading hours of the day. If the vector $COMM$ contains the per share brokerage fee for each of the stocks, find the total commission earned during the three hours.

20. A customer paid for three kinds of dried fruit at a health food store: $5 for apricots at $2.75/pound, $4.50 for banana chips at $1.80/pound and $7.25 for papayas at $3/pound. What was the largest quantity purchased?

21. Write an expression to determine whether a given matrix A consists of all 0's and 1's.

22. A store has a vector of the current year's transactions called $BILLS$. There is a parallel vector in the same order called $DATE$, which contains the Julian dates of the transactions (days are numbered consecutively from 1 to 365). Write an instruction to update $BILLS$ by adding 1.5% to those bills over 30 days. The current Julian date is the variable $TODAY$.

23. You own three cars:

car	year	price	cumulative gas cost	cumulative miles driven
Chevy	1975	$5200	$9660	98,730
Ford	1981	$8100	$8556	84,000
Lincoln	1980	$8450	$3080	28,000

If gas prices averaged $1.35/gallon for the Chevy, $1.30 for the Ford, and $1.47 for the Lincoln during the entire period of ownership, and the sales tax on each was 4% of the prices shown, calculate: **A** gallons of gas used for each car and all three; **B** tax paid for each car and all three; **C** average number of miles per year for each car; **D** average miles per gallon for each car; **E** average gas cost per year for each car; **F** average gas cost per mile for each car and for all three; **G** total gas cost; **H** total number of miles; **I** average number of miles per year driven.

24. Compute the net pay for each of a group of workers if R is the hourly rate, H the number of hours worked and S, $I1$ and $I2$ are the current percentage deductions for social security, Federal and State income taxes.

25. An office equipment salesperson sold 2, 4, 0, 1 and 3 typewriters (stored in the vector $SALES$) during a five-day period. **A** Was the sales quota for the week (6) made? **B** If there is a commission of $50 on each unit sold, how much was earned in commissions each day? **C** For 5 of the typewriters trade-ins were taken at an average value of $75 each. If the units sold for $600 each, what is the net revenue to the company after payment of commission?

26. A store creates its own special assortment of mixed nuts from cashews (30% by weight), pecans (10%), almonds (10%), walnuts (10%), Brazil nuts (5%) and peanuts (35%). A batch of 10 pounds is to be made up. However, the person doing the mixing is crazy about pecans and eats half as much as goes into the mixture. If the nuts cost wholesale $2, $2, $1.50, $1.25, $1.80 and $.40 a pound respectively, and the store has to make a profit of $1 per pound sold, what should be the minimum selling price?

27. Telegrams (remember them?) between two cities are $2.50 for the first 15 words or fewer and $.10 per additional word. Write an expression to give the cost of any telegram based on the number of words.

28. You are given the following vectors for a group of employees: M (marital status, 0 for single and 1 for married), S (sex, 0 for male and 1 for female), A (age in years), L (amount of group life insurance carried). Write an expression to pick out those employees who are at the same time married, male, younger than 55, and carry more than $50,000 of life insurance.

Chapter 7: Monadic and circular functions

Primitive scalar monadic functions

Just as on page 18 we introduced the term *dyadic* to describe functions which require two arguments, so we will use the term *monadic* where only a single argument is needed. Let's now take a look at how some monadic functions are represented in conventional mathematical notation:

$$-x \quad \text{arithmetic negation}$$
$$x! \quad \text{factorial}$$
$$|x| \quad \text{absolute value}$$
$$x^{-1} \text{ or } 1/x \quad \text{reciprocal}$$
$$e^x \quad \text{exponential}$$
$$\ln x \quad \text{natural logarithm}$$
$$\sqrt{x} \quad \text{square root (dyadic)}$$
$$\bar{x} \quad \text{logical negation}$$

Whatever other merits this mishmash has, consistency certainly isn't one of them; for the symbol which is the functional indicator may appear on the left, the right, both sides, on top, or be in a special position, or be represented by an alphabetical name!

These same functions are represented in APL as follows:

$$-X \quad \text{arithmetic negation}$$
$$!X \quad \text{factorial}$$
$$|X \quad \text{absolute value}$$
$$\div X \quad \text{reciprocal}$$
$$\star X \quad \text{exponential}$$
$$\circledast X \quad \text{natural logarithm}$$
$$X \star .5 \quad \text{square root (dyadic)}$$
$$\sim X \quad \text{logical negation}$$

Notice that for all the monadic functions in this list, the symbol comes before the argument. Many of the symbols are also used for dyadic functions, but the meanings may not always be closely related.

Let's explore some of them on the terminal. For any of them, you can use scalars, vectors and matrices as arguments. The more mathematical of these functions, such as factorial, exponential, logarithm and the circular functions (to be discussed later in this chapter) may be omitted from your study without loss of continuity if you won't be using them in your later work.

Arithmetic negation

This function, also called *negative* and additive inverse, simply negates the argument that follows it:

```
      -3 4 ‾1 0 ‾8                    -2 3⍴1 2 0 ‾3 ‾5 ‾8
‾3 ‾4 1 0 8                    ‾1 ‾2  0
      --2 ‾1 0 ‾1 ‾2            3  5  8
2 1 0 ‾1 ‾2
```

Don't confuse the negative sign (‾) with arithmetic negation (−). As pointed out on page 6, the negative sign should really be thought of as punctuation, not an operation to be performed; hence, the error message in the following:

```
    A←3 ¯1 0                         -A                              ¯A
                          ¯3  1  0                        SYNTAX_ERROR
                                                                ¯A
                                                                 ∧
```

Factorial

An expression like !X (for X an integer) means the product $1 \times 2 \times 3 \times \dots (X-1) \times X$. For example,

```
        !4                    !1 2 3 4                    !2 2ρ1 5 2 4
24                       1  2  6 24                      ¯1 120
                                                          2  24
```

If you got a *SYNTAX ERROR*, it was probably due to your failure to line up ' and . as discussed on **page 26**.

For those with a considerable background in mathematics, the factorial can be defined by the use of the gamma function, given by the following integral

$$\Gamma(n + 1) = \int_0^\infty x^n e^{-x} \, dx$$

which is equivalent to n! with n not restricted to integer values (negative integers are out of the domain, however).

```
        !2.5 0 ¯2.5
3.32335097 1 2.363271801
```

For those with minimal math background, forget it.

Magnitude

The *magnitude* (absolute value) function is defined as X if $X \geq 0$, or $-X$ if $X < 0$. In plain English, take the magnitude of the number and ignore any negative sign that may be present. Here are some examples:

```
        |3 5 ¯2 7 ¯3                     |2 3ρ3 ¯1 0 1 ¯5 ¯6
3  5  2  7  3                      3 1 0
                                   1 5 6
```

Reciprocal

In APL the division symbol, ÷, used monadically, is the multiplicative inverse, or reciprocal. Taking the reciprocal of a number is the same as dividing one by that number. As expected, ÷0 is a *DOMAIN ERROR*.

```
        ÷1 2 3 4 5                         1÷1 2 3 4 5
1 0.5 0.3333333333 0.25 0.2       1 0.5 0.3333333333 0.25 0.2

        ÷÷1 2 3 4 5                        ÷2 2ρ1 ¯2.5 4 5
1 2 3 4 5                         1              ¯0.4
                                  0.25            0.2
```

Exponential, natural logarithm and roots

The expression *X is equivalent to raising e, the base of the system of natural logarithms, which has the value 2.71828..., to the X power. This means that *X is the same as e*X. In this example, the second element of the argument results in the value of e itself:

```
        *2.5 1
12.18249396 2.718281828
```

Natural logarithms are obtained by the monadic ⊕. ⊕X yields the same result as the dyadic logarithm using e, 2.17828... as the left argument. Since the base e is frequently used in mathematics, conventional notation for it is 'ln' or 'log$_e$'. Logarithms were originally invented as an aid in doing calculations involving products, quotients, powers and roots. With the advent of modern calculators and computers they are rarely used for this purpose. What's more important, however, is that they do occur frequently in the solutions of equations representing many physical problems. This is generally the case where the changes involved in the phenomena to be analyzed are exponential in nature, such as unrestrained population growth or monetary calculations for compound interest.

Here is a sample:

```
      ⊛1 10 100 1000
0 2.302585093 4.605170186 6.907755279
```

Logarithms and exponentials are inverse functions, that is, each undoes the effect of the other as the example below shows:

```
      ⊛*1 2 3
1 2 3
```

Furthermore, the dyadic logarithm function $B⊛N$ (page 21) can be defined as $(⊛N)÷⊛B$.

No special symbol is provided for the square root (or any other root) in APL. To take the Nth root of X, use $X*÷N$. Recall that in algebra, roots are shown to be equivalent to fractional powers (see **page 20**).

Logical negation

Like the dyadic logical functions ∧ ∨ ⍲ ⍱, logical negation, also called *not* and using the symbol ~, can have only 0 or 1 as an argument. As you have probably guessed, ~1 is 0 and ~0 is 1.

```
      ~1 0 1 1           ~2 2ρ1 0 1 1              ~3
0 1 0 0                0 1            DOMAIN ERROR
      ~~1 0 1           0 0                   ~3
1 0 1                                         ∧
```

The last two examples show that ~ is its own inverse, and works only for 0's and 1's.

Ceiling and floor

There are a few more monadic functions in APL that don't have corresponding symbols in conventional notation, yet are important to know. The first of these is *ceiling*. It uses the symbol ⌈, and is defined as the smallest integer not smaller than the argument. Practically speaking, taking the ceiling of a number 'rounds up' the number.

```
      ⌈3.14 3.9 4 4.1
4 4 4 5
```

Its usefulness becomes apparent when you have to change a decimal fraction to the next higher integer. For example, the U. S. Postal Service charges 20 cents for the first ounce of first class mail and 17 cents for each additional ounce (at this writing). Any fractional ounces are counted as a full ounce. If X is the actual weight of a letter, then $.03+.17×⌈X$ is the cost in dollars.

Floor (⌊) is a mirror image of ceiling. It results in the largest integer not larger than the argument ('rounding down').

```
      ⌊3.14 3.9 4 4.1            ⌊2 3ρ2.999 3.542 7.931 6 1.08 4
3 3 4 4                        2 3 7
                              6 1 4
```

What about the ceiling and floor of a negative number? Let's try two examples:

```
      ⌈¯4.1              ⌊¯4.1
¯4                   ¯5
```

If this puzzles you, it can be cleared up by reference to the number line (**page 22**). Rounding ¯4.1 up gives the next larger integer, ¯4, while rounding down gives the next smaller integer, ¯5.

Finally, before going on to an illustrative problem, if we assign X as

> X←1.1 4.2 ¯3.9 0 3

then by executing

```
         ⌊X                         ⌈X
1 4  ¯4 0 3               2 5  ¯3 0 3
       ¯⌈-X                      ¯⌊-X
1 4  ¯4 0 3               2 5  ¯3 0 3
```

we can see that our APL system is richer by two identities, no simple equivalent of which exists in conventional notation. Other identities will be introduced from time to time in the text.

Now back to earth. Here is a practical problem which uses the floor and ceiling functions. It involves rounding off bills with fractional pennies (so-called half-cent adjustment). For purposes of illustration let's assign a vector X as

> X←3 3.1 3.49 3.5 3.51 3.9 4

To make the half-cent adjust work properly, we round up if the fractional part is 0.5 or more, and round down if it is less than 0.5. So for the above values we want the result to be 3 3 3 4 4 4 4.

Looking at the floor of X, we get

```
         ⌊X
3 3 3 3 3 3 4
```

This isn't exactly what we want. What about the ceiling?

```
         ⌈X
3 4 4 4 4 4 4
```

which isn't right either.

Suppose we add 0.5 to each element of X and then try the floor again:

```
         X+.5
3.5 3.6 3.99 4 4.01 4.4 4.5
         ⌊X+.5
3 3 3 4 4 4 4
```

Success! And the result suggests that a half-cent adjustment that rounds down (that is, makes 3.5 come out to 3 instead of 4) is done this way:

```
         ⌈X-.5
3 3 3 3 4 4 4
```

Roll

Let's try the monadic function *roll*, whose symbol is ? (upper shift Q):

```
         ?6 6                ?6 6                ?3 4⍴6
1 5                 3 4                  2 1 5 5
                                         6 3 4 5
                                         1 1 4 5
```

What kind of oddball function can this be that doesn't return the same result each time? We seem to be getting numbers at random from it. Indeed, if you play around with it some more, you will see that $?X$ returns a random integer chosen from the integers 1 to X inclusive.

This means that ? 6 6 simulates the roll of a pair of dice, while

```
         ?2
```
1

is a simulation of a coin toss, with 1 standing for heads, say, and 2 for tails.

Where you put the symbol makes an important difference:

```
      ?3 4ρ6                      3 4ρ?6
3  1  3  5                   6  6  6  6
4  6  6  4                   6  6  6  6
1  4  3  5                   6  6  6  6
```

The example on the right generates only one random value and then repeats that value twelve times, as contrasted to the left example, which first made a matrix of 6's and then randomized the values.

When we try to execute the roll function with a noninteger, or with zero or a negative number, a *DOMAIN ERROR* results. The domain of the roll function consists of positive integers only.

Each time you sign on the terminal you will get the same sequence of random numbers if the same arguments are used. When you check out algorithms (called *debugging*), it is often desirable for testing purposes to use the same set of numbers so that valid comparisons can be made of successive runs. In Chapter 28 we'll show how to change the starting value for the built-in APL algorithm that generates random numbers.

Direction

Occasionally you may need to know whether a value is positive, negative or zero. The function $\times X$, called *direction*, does this for us. It returns as results 1, ‾1, or 0. Don't confuse it with $\times / X$:

```
        ×2 2ρ‾1 4 0 ‾8                    ×1 ‾3 0                    ×/1 ‾3 0
 ‾1  1                              1  ‾1  0                              0
  0  ‾1
```

Pi times

The function $\circ X$ is equivalent to πX. It uses the large circle ○ (upper shift *O*):

```
       ○‾1 0 1 2 3
‾3.141592654 0 3.141592654 6.283185307 9.424777961
```

Note that ○1 is π itself.

A short lesson on probability

The discussion which follows exercises some of the monadic functions introduced in this chapter. It may be of interest to the mathematically inclined or to those who visit Las Vegas or Monte Carlo. If you are of neither persuasion, we won't be disappointed if you skip this section and the next (trigonometry and related functions) and go directly to the drill on page 52.

A fallen member of Gamblers Anonymous with a flair for numbers comes up with the following formula for the probability of having exactly one match in a random matching of two equivalent decks of 52 distinct cards:

$$P1 = \frac{1}{0!} - \frac{1}{1!} + \frac{1}{2!} - \frac{1}{3!} + \cdots - \cdots + \frac{1}{52!}$$

He notes that this can be readily modified for 2, 3, ...m matches.

APL notation makes easy work of this formula. First, we develop the vector of denominators, stopping after 10 terms:

```
     D←!0 1 2 3 4 5 6 7 8 9
```

The reciprocals can be obtained by assigning

```
      R←÷D
      R
1 1 0.5 0.1666666667 0.04166666667 0.008333333333 0.001388888889 0.0001984126984
      2.48015873E¯5 2.755731922E¯6
```

and the alternating sum is given by

```
      P1←-/R
      P1
0.3678791887
```

Putting all of this together we have

```
      ∇P1←MATCH N                    MATCH 0 1 2 3 4 5 6 7 8 9
[1]   P1←-/÷!N                       0.3678791887
[2]   ∇
```

The series converges rapidly because of the factorials in the denominators. And, as our backsliding gambler soon found out, the probability P_m of m matches is approximately $e^{-1}/m!$, or $PM←(*¯1)÷!M$.

Circular, hyperbolic and pythagorean functions

For those of you who have an interest, be it perverse or legitimate, in the circular, hyperbolic and pythagorean functions, they are available as primitive scalar dyadics. As with π, the function symbol is the large circle.

Strictly speaking, these functions, being dyadic, don't belong in this chapter. Most users of APL will never need them. However, for those of you with a scientific bent, they are mentioned here.

0○X	$(1-X*2)*.5$		
1○X	sine X	¯1○X	arcsin X
2○X	cosine X	¯2○X	arccos X
3○X	tangent X	¯3○X	arctan X
4○X	$(1+X*2)*.5$	¯4○X	$(¯1+X*2)*.5$
5○X	hyperbolic sine of X (sinh X)	¯5○X	arcsinh X
6○X	hyperbolic cosine of X (cosh X)	¯6○X	arccosh X
7○X	hyperbolic tangent of X (tanh X)	¯7○X	arctanh X

The rules for conformability of the arguments are the same as for the standard scalar dyadic functions; that is, the shapes of the arguments must match, or either can be a scalar. The left argument cannot be any values other than those shown above, and is used to select which of the functions is to be performed. For the trigonometric functions, the right argument is taken to be radians (multiply degrees by $0÷180$). The inverse (arc) functions return only the principal value of the angle.

Here is a simple example testing the oft-heard rumor that $\sin^2\theta + \cos^2\theta = 1$ (at least for an angle of 45 degrees):

```
      THETA←45×0÷180
      +/(1 2○THETA)*2
1
```

Finally, besides their direct use in problems, readers familiar with the calculus will appreciate the value of having a complete set of circular functions. See any handbook containing tables of derivatives and indefinite integrals.

A drill exercise

On most APL systems there is a drill exercise in the various functions that have been described so far (it's located in common library 1 of the system on which this text is based). This is a stored program, much like STATISTICS in the first chapter. The details of how such programs are written and stored will be covered in later chapters.

Follow this sequence carefully on your terminal. You should also check to see what other exercises, if any, are available on your system. The more practice you get at this early stage, the better you will understand how the individual functions of APL can be used in programming.

First execute the following command:

```
)LOAD 1 AIDRILL
SAVED  14.15.05 07/06/79
```

A message comes back stating when the workspace *AIDRILL* (a block of storage containing the drill programs) was last saved. The *)LOAD* command, about which more will be said later, puts an exact image of the workspace *AIDRILL* in a place where you can use it directly.

You are about to go through an exercise in which you and the APL system will exchange roles. It will ask you to do problems and you will be required to enter the answers. To start off, enter *EASYDRILL* and put a *Y* under each function for which you want practice, as shown in the copy below. Be sure to type *Y* for the exercises in vectors because vectors are so important in APL. Also reply *Y* to the question about reduction. None of the problems require answers which are not integers, and the problems are relatively easy computationally. We suggest, however, that the first time through, you select only the easier functions.

```
EASYDRILL
TYPE Y UNDER EACH FUNCTION FOR WHICH YOU WANT EXERCISE
SCALAR DYADIC FUNCTIONS
+-×÷*⌈⌊<≤=≥>≠!|∧∨⍲⍱
YY         YY     YY
SCALAR MONADIC FUNCTIONS
YY YY

TYPE Y IF EXERCISE IN VECTORS IS DESIRED, N OTHERWISE
Y

TYPE Y IF EXERCISE IN REDUCTION IS DESIRED, N OTHERWISE
Y
```

Here are some sample problems generated by the program. These will be different each time you use the program, and different for each user as well.

```
              ¯1 9 ¯9 5 > ¯8 ¯10 4 8
☐:    1 1 0 0
              -8 ¯6 ¯4 ¯3 0
☐:    ¯8 6 4 3 0
```

If the problem is correctly answered, you get another problem as your reward. Let's enter a wrong answer for the next one:

```
          ⍱/ 2 2
☐:    0 1
TRY AGAIN
☐:    1
```

You get three tries altogether, after which you are given the correct answer, and, to add insult to injury, you get another problem of the same general kind:

```
          ∨/ 0 0 1 1
☐:    1
          ⌊ ¯2.333333333 ¯2 1.666666667 ¯2.666666667 ¯3

☐:    3 4 5 6
TRY AGAIN

☐:    4 2 10 4
TRY AGAIN

☐:    3 1 9 7
ANSWER IS  ¯3 ¯2 1 ¯3 ¯3
          ⌊¯1
☐:    ¯1
          × ¯7 ¯4
☐:    ¯1 ¯1
```

Entering $PLEASE$ gives you the answer and another problem of the same kind, while $CHANGE$ gives you the answer and moves you on to another problem involving a different function. To get out of the drill, enter $STOP$, after which you will receive a record of your performance, only part of which is shown here. $STOPSHORT$ exits you from the program but doesn't display your record, in case you're too embarrassed to look at it.

```
              ⌊ 1.333333333 ¯0.6666666667
☐:    PLEASE
ANSWER IS   1  ¯1
              ⌊ 0.5 1.75

☐:    STOP
```

```
YOUR RECORD IS
FUNCTION        FIRST TRY    SECOND TRY    THIRD TRY    FAILED
    +
    _
    >                 1
    ≠
    ∨                 1
    ⊕                                          1
    ×                 1
    _
    ⌈                                                      1
    ⌊                 2
```

PROBLEMS

1. DRILL

```
⌊¯2.7|¯15               |3.1 0 ¯5.6 ¯8          ?10 10 10 10
*3 4.7 ¯1.5             !3 5 7 4               ⊕14.1 86 .108
⌈¯1.8 0 ¯21 5.6         ⌊5.5 6.8 ¯9.1 ¯.12     ×¯5.6 0 42
?3 4 5                  ?¯1.2 ¯6.7 .52 19.5    ~0 1 1 0
÷3.5 ¯10 ¯.287         4×⌈5.8×¯31.046          1○○1 2
○1÷180                 4○1 2 3                 ¯1 ¯2○1 10.5
```

2. Using the residue function, write one-line definitions in APL of $\lfloor X$ and $\lceil X$.

3. If $A \leftarrow 3$ and $B \leftarrow 3\ 2\ 1\ ¯6$, evaluate

```
*2+A1←(¯1+A*3)÷2
~(2≤A)∧∨/3=B
C≠⌊C←((A*2)+(A+1)*2)*.5
```

4. Write an algorithm to test an integer N for the following: if the final digit is deleted, the original number is divisible by the new one.

5. January 1 fell on Thursday (the fifth day of the week) in 1970. Determine the day of the week on which January 1 falls in any given year Y. For simplicity, assume any year divisible by 4 is a leap year.

6. Given a vector V which is made up of one-and two-digit integers. **A** Write an expression that will yield a logical vector whose 1's correspond in position to the one-digit members of V; **B** do the same for the two-digit members of V.

7. Let $M \leftarrow 84.6129999993$. Display M. Compare $1E5 \times M$ with $\lfloor 1E5 \times M$. (See *comparison tolerance* on page 295 for an explanation.)

8. Construct an APL expression that will determine whether or not the first N significant figures of two whole numbers X and Y are identical.

9. **A** You are given D dollars with which to make purchases of books at B dollars each. How many books can be purchased? **B** How many books can be bought if it is required that the D dollars be used up and supplemented, if necessary?

10. **A** Write a general expression to round any number N to D positions to the right of the decimal point. **B** How does your answer change if the rounding is to take place to the Dth position to the *left* of the decimal point?

11. Write an APL expression that rounds numbers down if the decimal part is less than .5, and up if greater than .5. For numbers ending in .5, your expression should round to the nearest *even* integer.

12. For $A \leftarrow 0\ 1\ 0\ 1$, $B \leftarrow 1\ 0\ 0\ 1$ and $C \leftarrow 1\ 1\ 0\ 0$ evaluate **A** $(\sim A) \vee \sim B$; **B** $A \vee C \wedge B$; **C** $(A \wedge \sim B) \wedge A \vee C$; **D** $(\sim B) \vee A \vee \sim C$

13. Show in APL that the following identity holds: $\cos 2x = \cos^2 x - \sin^2 x$

14. Use reduction to express the identity $\sin^2 x + \cos^2 x = 1$

15. Write an APL expression to construct a $4\ 4$ matrix made up of random integers in the range 1 to 100.

16. A certain number N may be either positive or negative. Write a one-line APL expression to compute its square root if it is positive or its square if it is negative.

17. Write APL expressions for each of the following. Use S for 'Sam's a ham', J for 'Joe is so-so' and T for 'Teddy is ready.' **A** Sam's a ham and Teddy is not ready; **B** Joe is not so-so or Teddy is ready; **C** Teddy is ready and Sam's a ham or Joe is so-so.

18. For the arbitrary vectors $V1 \leftarrow 0\ 1\ 1\ 1\ 0\ 1$ and $V2 \leftarrow 1\ 1\ 0\ 1\ 0\ 1$ show that $\sim(V1 \wedge V2)$ is equivalent to $(\sim V1) \vee \sim V2$ and $\sim(V1 \vee V2)$ is equivalent to $(\sim V1) \wedge \sim V2$.

19. A teacher gives the following grades in an exam: 40 55 75 92 98 60 71 74 59 67 ($GRADES$). On a retest the same pupils scored 67 79 81 90 95 62 68 75 54 80 ($NEWGRADES$). The teacher (a rare and generous soul!) decides to record only the new grades or 20% more than the old grades, whichever is greater. What grades (whole numbers, no grades higher than 100) are actually recorded?

20. An insurance company sells three types of homeowners' policies with optional deductible amounts of $100, $250 and $500 respectively. The total number of policies of each type sold by one of their agencies is 608, 1277 and 942. If the agency's experience is that in a given year 2%, 3.5% and 5% of the three types of policies suffered losses in excess of the deductible, how much money beyond the premiums was paid out by the owners themselves?

21. The Board of Directors of a company decides to split the stock by issuing one additional share for each four now held. Fractional shares are to be redeemed in cash at the rate of $16.50 a share. If stockholder holdings are stored in the vector $SHARES$, how many additional shares are to be issued to each stockholder? How much does each receive in cash for fractional shares?

22. Convert a vector $DATES$ written as YYMMDD to the format MMDDYY.

23. Write an expression to extract out of a vector of numbers the digits in a specified position. Assume the positions are specified as ...2 1 0 ‾1 ‾2... for ...hundreds, tens, units, tenths, hundredths,...

24. A school district buys pencils for its elementary school population of 3412 pupils and 175 teachers, administrators and others. Each individual is expected to use 11 pencils a year on the average. If pencils are sold only in boxes of one gross (144), and it is desired to have 20 extra boxes for stock, how many gross should be purchased?

25. The rounding algorithm $\lfloor X + .5$ on page 50 gives inconsistent results with negative numbers ending in .5. Rewrite it to take care of this exception.

Chapter 8: Function definition

In Chapter 3 we introduced the concept of a user defined function to supplement the primitive functions available on the keyboard. In this and the next few chapters we will review and considerably extend that concept, which allows you to develop (or borrow from other users with similar interests) and store functions of your choice on the APL system. This is equivalent to giving you the ability to tailor the generalized APL system to suit your own requirements. You can't use symbols like the hypothetical ⌷ in Chapter 3 (at least not in most commercially available APL systems), but, as you have already seen, you are able to use multiple character names with potential for mnemonic meanings, such as *HYP* for computing the length of the hypotenuse of a right triangle from the lengths of its legs. With this facility, solutions like (12 *HYP* 5)+4 *HYP* 3 become available.

The Defined Function HYP

The function *HYP* has already been developed and stored by the authors, and you may 'borrow' it by entering

```
     )COPY 1 CLASS HYP
SAVED   14.45.33 02/20/83
```

Don't worry at this point about the details of the above entry and response (unless you got a message like *WORKSPACE NOT FOUND* or *OBJECT NOT FOUND*, in which case check with your system librarian); we'll cover that later. The workspace 1 *CLASS*, incidentally, contains many illustrations and examples that will be of use throughout this book.

Experiment with *HYP* by entering

```
     3 HYP 4                    (12 HYP 5)-4 HYP 3                      1 3 12 HYP 1 4 5
5                            8                               1.414213562 5 13
```

The last example shows that *HYP* works with vector arguments as well as scalars. In fact, the defined function *HYP* has the same requirements on the shapes of its arguments as the primitive scalar dyadic functions + or × or ⌈.

So far, we've looked only at the external behavior of the function *HYP*. Before we can design our own functions we will have to be able to understand how *HYP* and similar functions are constructed.

Displaying a defined function

You have already seen the command which displays functions like *HYP* stored in the APL system. It is ∇*HYP*[⌷]∇, which you should carefully enter on your keyboard at this point. *Do not* press RETURN until your entry looks exactly like the one below. If you make a mistake, correct it before you press RETURN, not after, using the correction procedure introduced on page 7.

```
     ∇HYP[⌷]∇
```

The symbol ∇ is the upper shift *G* and the box ⌷ (called a *quad*) is the upper shift *L*. We won't explain the rationale behind the particular combination of symbols now, but you will see in Chapter 10 how this command relates to others that will be needed to define, display and edit functions.

Here is the system's response:

```
     ∇C←A HYP B
[1]     C←((A*2)+B*2)*0.5
     ∇
```

The first line, beginning with ∇, is called the *header* of the function. *HYP* is the name of the function; it has two arguments, *A* and *B*, with a *result* *C* (i.e., the answer). Notice that the arguments are separated from the function name by spaces. Can you imagine what would happen if the spaces were omitted?

Line 1 gives the familiar algorithm for calculating the hypotenuse. As has been pointed out, the ∇s send signals to the system that function definition is about to begin or end.

HYP can be used like a primitive scalar dyadic function, though an error results if we try to execute *HYP*/3 4, *HYP*\ι10 or *A*∘.*HYP* *B* in many APL implementations.

Interface diagrams

To help you understand the role of defined functions like *HYP*, here is a pictorial representation, called an *interface diagram*, of the entry and execution of *HYP*. Think of the outer box as holding the entire APL system:

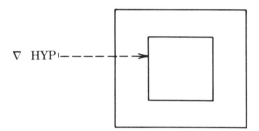

The first ∇ 'opens the door' to an appropriate place in storage (inner box) for the instructions comprising the function *HYP*. Entering the final ∇ in effect 'closes the door,' and the system reverts to execution mode.

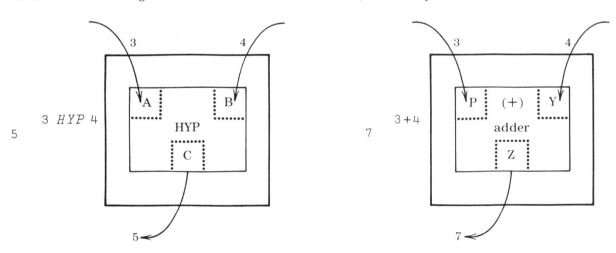

After opening, the paths leading to the dotted boxes *A* and *B* (left diagram), and the path leading from the dotted box *C* are set up automatically as part of the instructions incorporated in *HYP* to allow for receipt of data (*A* and *B*) and for temporary storage of the answer *C* before release to the outside. These latent paths are transformed into operational ones when the function is executed. Dotted boxes *A*, *B* and *C* have a similar ephemeral existence, coming into play only during function execution. In this example, the process shown is really not much different from that involved in a simple addition problem, summing 3 and 4 to give 7 (right diagram).

    3 *HYP* 4

5

In the diagram of the adder the temporary boxes have been given arbitrary names *P*, *Y* and *Z*. The two pictures are conceptually identical, except that in the second case the box representing the adder is a primitive part of APL, courtesy of the designers and implementors of the APL system. You may wonder what purpose the dotted storage boxes serve. More about this in Chapter 9.

Composing and entering functions

Now get some practice entering functions yourself. First enter,

)CLEAR
CLEAR WS

which is a system command that clears out your active workspace (where you are doing your APL work) and replaces it with a fresh blank workspace, just like the one you received when you signed on.

Suppose we try to execute *HYP* now:

        3 HYP 4
SYNTAX ERROR
        3 HYP 4
        ∧

Are you surprised that we got an error message? You shouldn't be. After all, our new workspace isn't supposed to have anything in it, and this leaves the way open for us to insert the function *HYP* ourselves. Start by entering

        ∇C←A HYP B
[1]   C←((A*2)+B*2)*.5
[2]   ∇

The initial ∇, as pointed out previously, tells the system you want to enter a function and 'opens the door' to a place in storage. More formally, after you enter the opening ∇, you are said to be in *function definition mode*, as opposed to *execution mode*. The rules for making up function names in APL, by the way, are the same as those for variable names (see page 12).

The rules for entering a function in APL2 are similar, but the system response is slightly different. After the header is entered it is returned as line zero ([0]), and subsequent lines are not numbered by the system until after the function is closed out.

This completes entry of the function *HYP*, and it can now be executed:

        3 HYP 4
5

If at this point you don't get 5 as your result, enter)CLEAR and repeat the previous steps.

We haven't squeezed all the juice out of *HYP* yet. Just as we can enter

        2+3×4
14

so we can ask the system for

        2+3 HYP 4
7

What makes this possible is the fact that the calculation involved in *HYP* produced a result which was stored away *temporarily* under the name *C* and hence was available for further calculations. Such a function is said to *return an explicit result*.

Using an interface diagram for this example, we can see that the existence of the temporary storage box C makes the result of 3 HYP 4 available to the adder, which adds it to 2, to yield the final result 7.

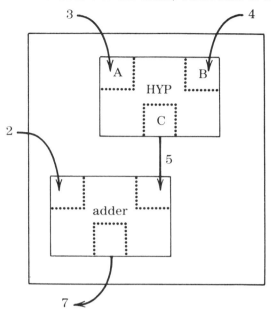

In the next chapter we'll explore the uses and consequences of writing headers *without* results, equivalent in our diagram above to leaving out the box C.

A defined monadic function

As a concession to those of you with backgrounds in other programming languages we'll now define a function to simulate $A*.5$, that is, a square root. It's unnecessary, but who cares? It makes an interesting simple illustration. If we had such a function, say $SQRT$, then line 1 of HYP could be [1] $C \leftarrow SQRT$ $(A*2)+B*2$ instead of [1] $C \leftarrow ((A*2)+B*2)*.5$.

Now define such a function by entering the header

        $\triangledown R \leftarrow SQRT$ X
[1]

Don't forget the space between $SQRT$ and X. Only the one argument X is needed here (the numbers we are calculating the square root of). It is placed to the *right* of the function name. The system responds, as before, with [1]. Incidentally, this suggests that a good way to tell whether you are in function definition or execution mode is to see if you get a number in brackets when RETURN is pressed. Just remember that if you do get it, anything you enter from that point on until the closing $\triangledown$ becomes part of the function you are defining.

If you were to press RETURN again, you would once more get [1], indicating that the system is still waiting for line 1.

Now enter the algorithm and close out the function. A couple of examples show that $SQRT$ seems to work acceptably.

```
[1]    R←X*.5            SQRT 1 2 4
[2]    ∇              1 1.414213562 2
```

Earlier we had suggested that $SQRT$ could be used to simplify the function HYP. Having just defined $SQRT$, let's now write another HYP function in which $SQRT$ can be embedded. Starting off as before, enter the function header and wait for the response:

```
      ∇R←A HYP B
DEFN ERROR
      ∇R←A HYP B
              ∧
```

But this time it appears that something is wrong. Apparently reentering the function with the same name and in the same workspace doesn't wipe out the old function. There is no analogy between the behavior of a function header and an assignment of values to a variable, the old values of which are lost when a new assignment is made.

You may argue that this replacement feature could be a very handy thing to have around for function headers, but if you think about it you will see that it can have some very grave consequences too. Suppose, for example, you had a big complicated function that was really valuable in your work, and you inadvertently used the same function name for something else. All your hard work, unless you kept a record of it somewhere else, would then be gone. So the APL system deliberately makes it hard for you to destroy defined functions.

This leaves you with two alternatives for redefining *HYP*. You can get rid of *HYP* by an appropriate system command (to be taken up later) or, better yet, use a different name for your new function, say, *HY*. Here is the function *HY*, which works just as well as *HYP* did:

```
      ∇C←A HY B
[1]   C←SQRT (A*2)+B*2
[2]   ∇
```

```
      3 HY 4
5
      1 3 HY 1 4
1.414213562 5
```

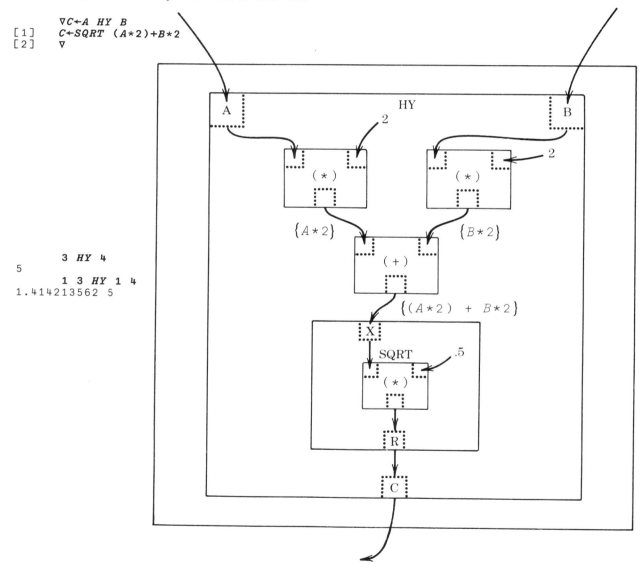

The interface diagram shows *SQRT* embedded within *HY*, along with the square and adder (not detailed). The arrow leading to the box *X* in *SQRT* carries the result of the operation on *A* and *B* of the square and adder functions.

Documenting functions

Most of the APL expressions and functions that we have seen so far are so simple that they are self-explanatory to an experienced user. However, suppose a function to calculate cosines was called C instead of $COSDEM$. How long might it take you to discover what it really does? You'd be wise to include comment statements in your functions to avoid the frustrating experience of not being able to figure out what you did a month or two later (and as a way of showing mercy to others who may be working with your functions).

With this in mind, here is a documented function that uses a MacLaurin series to calculate the cosine of an angle. You needn't know anything about cosines or MacLaurin series to appreciate the importance of some of the comments:

```
      ∇T←COSDEM X
[1]   ⍝ COSINE EXAMPLE.  ARGUMENT IS IN DEGREES.  DEMONSTRATES CONVERGENCE
[2]   ⍝ GILMAN AND ROSE, 1980
[3]   T←0 2 4 6 8 10 12 14 16
[4]   ⍝ T ABOVE IS USED AS A TEMPORARY VARIABLE.
[5]   T←-\((○X÷180)*T)÷!T
[6]   ⍝ FOR PRODUCTION WORK OR COMPARISON, USE 2○○X÷180
[7]   ∇
```

On older APL systems a separate line must be used for comments, but on most modern systems a comment can be put on the same line as instructions. The rule is that everything to the right of a ⍝ is taken as commentary.

Unfortunately, most casual APL users (as opposed to professionals) seem to develop all kinds of afflictions when it comes to documenting. They suddenly become blind, deaf and dumb. The typical arguments (no pun) given as to their failure to document include the following gems:

> Who needs it?
>
> It's obvious
>
> APL is self-documenting
>
> No one else will ever use my functions.

Hogwash! People with those attitudes act as though they're going to be around in the same job forever, which is absurd. They refuse to leave an understandable legacy to their successors. Moreover, if they haven't used some of their own (nontrivial) code for some time and then need to modify it, the odds are great that they'll have as much difficulty picking through their *own* undocumented functions as someone else's!

This whole topic deserves much more attention than we can give it here. Many information systems managers require formal documentation of functions, groups of related functions comprising major production applications, and workspaces. Whether you are a casual user or full-time programmer, some record of what you did and how it works is useful.

System commands to list and delete functions

Our workspace, which was originally empty, now has four functions. We can find out what functions are in our workspace with the system command $)FNS$, introduced in Chapter 3,

```
      )FNS
COSDEM   HY       HYP      SQRT
```

which works in exactly the same way as $)VARS$ did earlier; that is, it provides us with an alphabetized listing of the functions available in the active workspace. As was the case for the command $)VARS$, if the listing is long and we are interested only in whether a particular name, say, HYP is included, we can ask for

```
      )FNS HY
HY       HYP      SQRT
```

and we get that part of the listing from the letter sequence HY on. The display can be interrupted at any time by pressing ATTN or its equivalent on your terminal.

We can watch the behavior of the system as we add and delete functions. For example, let's include the following simple monadic function designed to give the square of a number:

```
      ∇R←SQ U
[1]   R←U×U∇
```

Two observations should be made at this point. First, the rule could have been stated in either of two ways: $U \times U$ or $U * 2$. Second, waiting until the next line number is returned by the system is really unnecessary. Since the function is finished at the end of line 1, it's perfectly proper to close it out there, as was done in this case.

SQ seems to be in working order,

```
      SQ 4
16
```

and in fact SQ and $SQRT$ are inverse functions, with one undoing the effects of the other:

```
      SQRT SQ 4
4
```

Displaying the list of functions now available, we see SQ has been added to the list:

```
      )FNS
COSDEM  HY      HYP     SQ      SQRT
```

To delete functions that are no longer needed in the workspace, use the system command $ERASE$ introduced earlier:

```
      )ERASE HYP
```

A new display of functions shows that HYP is gone:

```
      )FNS
HY      SQ      SQRT
```

The $ERASE$ command can be used to delete several functions and variables at the same time. Just separate the names you want deleted. If you try to erase nonexistent objects, APL will let you know which ones weren't there.

Of course, to get rid of all the functions and variables at once, use

```
      )CLEAR
CLEAR WS
```

Now the commands $)FNS$ and $)VARS$ will elicit 'empty' responses. The cursor just moves over six spaces.

Some observations on function definition

Now that you have been introduced to function definition, called 'programming' in other languages, some guidelines on the subject are in order. Let's look first at what is involved: formulating the problem, developing the algorithm, translating the algorithm into APL instructions, testing and debugging the resulting functions, and documenting.

The user's imagination and creativity are called on to a far greater extent in the first two of these activities than in the others, which are generally more mechanical. Half the battle is formulating the problem well. And victory can be almost guaranteed if, building on this foundation, intelligent algorithms can be developed. Many of the errors that must be identified and removed in debugging arise because the user rushed into an APL translation of a half-baked algorithm. While it is true that APL instructions can be changed easily in defined functions (see Chapter 9), and error messages are usually a clue as to what is wrong, nonetheless, in APL as in medicine, an ounce of prevention is worth a pound of cure. Our advice to you, therefore, is to spend more time thinking through the problem and how you plan to solve it. If you do this, you will spend considerably less time correcting mistakes after the fact.

Moreover, if the developed function will be used by you again in the future, or will be used by others, it should be documented. For simple applications comments within the function will suffice, but for extensive work, formal users' manuals and maintenance aids should be written.

Those of you who are following the discussion of direct definition are reminded to see page 298.

PROBLEMS

We haven't explained how to correct typographical errors in defined functions (Chapter 10), so for now you'll have to be very careful entering these exercises. If you do make mistakes, $)CLEAR$ and reenter. Most of the exercises don't depend on any other, so you can usually $)CLEAR$ before each exercise. On some systems you can't even $)CLEAR$ while in function definition, so you may have to enter a ∇ (to close function definition) before you can $)CLEAR$.

1. Define a function EQ which evaluates the expression $(X-2)\times X-3$ for various integer values of X and identifies the solutions to the equation $0=(X-2)\times X-3$.

2. Define a function BB which generates the batting averages of players by dividing the number of hits obtained by the number of times at bat for each player.

3. Define a function $HERO$ to calculate the area of a triangle by Hero's formula. (See problem 5, Chapter 5.)

4. The ABC Manufacturing Company reimburses its employees 100% of the first $200 spent per semester for college work in an approved program, and 50% of the next $300. No reimbursement is made for expenses above $500 per semester. Write a function called $REFUND$ that will calculate the refund due each employee in the program.

5. A well-known formula (Ohm's Law) in electrical work gives the combined resistance RT of several resistances R1, R2, etc., wired in parallel as follows (conventional notation):

$$\frac{1}{\text{RT}} = \frac{1}{\text{R}_1} + \frac{1}{\text{R}_2} + \cdots$$

Define a function PR that will calculate RT for a vector M of resistances in parallel.

6. To find the standard deviation of a set of numbers, the following steps are necessary: (1) compute the mean; (2) find the difference of each number from the mean; (3) square these differences; (4) take the square root of the average of step 3. Write a function SD to compute the standard deviation of some data X. Assume you already have a monadic function AVG (which computes averages) in storage.

7. In relativity theory the mass of a body depends on its velocity V relative to the observer. Specifically, in conventional notation $m = m_0 \div \sqrt{1 - v^2/c^2}$ where m_0 is the mass of the object at rest and c is the velocity of light (3E8 meters/sec.). Write a defined function REL to compute the mass of a body moving at speed V and with a rest mass MR.

8. Define functions called $PLUS$, $MINUS$, $TIMES$, $DIVIDEDBY$ to give mathematical meaning to these words, e.g., 3 $PLUS$ 4 returns 7, etc.

9. (For the more sophisticated) Rewrite HYP using one or more of the circular functions introduced in Chapter 7.

10. Write a function that does what $\div$ does, except that any number divided by zero results in a zero, rather than an error.

11. A well known rule of thumb in personal finance states that the number of years required to double money on deposit is roughly equal to 72 divided by the annual interest rate in percent. Write a function to estimate the doubling time for various rates of interest.

12. A company wants to maximize its profit (who doesn't?) on a new line of widgets. The cost accountants estimate that the overhead of the assembly line making the widgets is $50,000 regardless of the number sold. The first 5000 are calculated to cost $20 each, and all those in excess of 5000 cost $25 each. **A** Define a function $EXPENSE$ to calculate the total cost based on the number produced. **B** A survey shows the probable sales expected for a range of possible prices. Use the function $EXPENSES$ along with the revenue estimates from the survey to obtain the potential profit at each price.

Chapter 9: The syntax of functions

The last chapter showed how to enlarge the set of functions that is a primitive part of APL with functions of your own choosing or need. We observed that no matter how many primitive functions APL has, you are likely to need some that the implementors didn't anticipate. And even if there were many more primitive functions, the keyboard would have to be so large to incorporate them that it would be physically impractical. Actually, the ability to define functions (that is, to program) is what separates general purpose computer systems from fixed-application devices such as calculators, automated bank tellers and airline reservation systems.

Analogous to the primitive functions, we've seen two forms of defined functions: the dyadics HYP and HY, and the monadics $SQRT$ and SQ. There are four more variants to learn about, helpful illustrations of which are stored in the workspace 1 $CLASS$, which was accessed in the last chapter. Let's reload this workspace and find out what is in it by executing the following sequence of commands. The system responses are included after each command:

```
     )LOAD 1 CLASS
 SAVED   14.45.33 02/20/83

     )FNS
 ADD       AGAIN     AREA     AUTO     AVG     AVG1     AVG2     AVG3
 AVG4      AVG5      AVG6     CHANGE   CHARMAT CLR      CMP      CMPN
 CMPX      CMPY      COMPINT  COMPOSE  COS     CP       C2GT99   DEC
 DENUMCODE           DESCRIBE          DICE    DUPLICATES        ENT
 EVAL      F         FACT     FACTORIALS       FIND     FINDROW  FIX
 FUNEDIT   GAME      GEO2     GEO3     GETFN    GO       GRAPH    HEXA     HY
 HYP       INPUT     INT      INVOICERUN       LASTVISIT         MEAN
 NAMESONLY           NEWPATIENT        NEWVISIT         NUMCODE  OBSERVE ON
 PEREL     RECT      REP      REPF     REPL     REPLENISH        RETIE
 RIGHTJUST           ROWNAMES          RUN      SALES    SD      SELECT
 SELECT    SETUP     SHOWME   SIGN     SLAM     SORT     SPELL
 SPLINECALC          SPLINEEVAL        SPRED    SQ       SQRT     STAT    STATEMENT
 STATISTICS          SUB      SUBST    SUM      SUSPENDED         TOSS
 TOTVISITS           TRANSP   VIG      WSSHOW   DSLOPE   ESLOPE   XSLOPE
```

Your listing may not be identical to this one, since changes are made from time to time in the common library workspaces. Be that as it may, most of the functions in this list will be illustrated and explained as we go through the remaining chapters. The ones we will be interested in now are HYP, $SIGN$, $DICE$, $RECT$, $STAT$ and $GAME$.

Remember that to display the contents of a function, enter ∇name[□]∇, after which the system displays the function header followed by all the steps which comprise the function, including even the opening and closing dels. Here is our old friend HYP:

```
     ∇ HYP[□]∇
   ∇ C←A HYP B
[1]   C←((A*2)+B*2)*0.5
   ∇
```

This display command will be useful as we examine in the rest of this chapter some additional ways of constructing defined functions.

Function Headers

There are six types of APL function headers. Each has its own particular uses, as will be seen from the illustrative examples to be displayed. These six forms are summarized in the table below.

	Dyadic	Monadic	Niladic
Returns Explicit Result	∇E←A HYP B	∇R←SIGN X	∇R←DICE
No Explicit Result	∇L RECT H	∇STAT X	∇GAME

Don't worry for the moment about what all this means; all in good time.

The formal term for the number of explicit arguments that a function takes is *valence*. It also refers to the number of operands (the functions or arrays on which an operator acts to produce a derived function) associated with an operator. Some APL systems return a *VALENCE ERROR* instead of some other error message whenever you try to execute a monadic function (with no dyadic definition) with left and right arguments, or a primitive dyadic function (with no monadic definition) with a right argument only.

Functions with explicit results

To start off, display the function *SIGN*:

```
    ∇SIGN[□]∇
  ∇ R←SIGN X
[1]   R←(X>0)-X<0
  ∇
```

It takes a single argument which, if negative, returns ‾1, if positive, 1 and if zero, it returns 0. In fact, it duplicates the monadic direction function introduced earlier. Executing this for various arguments, we get

SIGN ‾5.2	SIGN 0	SIGN 3 ‾2 0
‾1	0	1 ‾1 0

You can see how *SIGN* works by tracing through it with a few examples. If X is negative, X < 0 would be 1 and X > 0 would be 0. So 0−1 gives ‾1. Similarly, for X positive, X < 0 is 1, with 1−0 resulting in 1. And for X = 0, X < 0 is 0 and X > 0 is also 0, so that 0−0 gives 0.

Here is an interface diagram for *SIGN*:

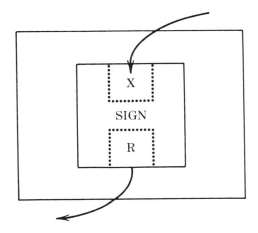

Now enter *DICE* a few times and then display it.

```
      DICE
9

      DICE
4

      DICE
4

      ∇DICE[☐]∇
    ∇  R←DICE
[1]    R←+/? 6 6
    ∇
```

DICE simulates the sum of a random roll of two dice. The header has no arguments. It is a *niladic* function, to coin a word. The function really doesn't need any arguments. It selects the numbers for the roll itself, using the random number generator. As shown by the interface diagram, there is no external input path because the data required comes from within the APL system itself (dotted arrow):

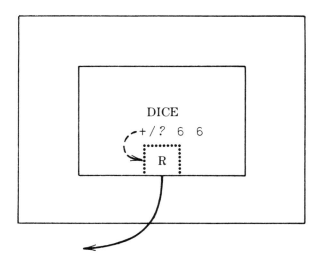

Functions without explicit results

We have just seen examples of function headers that take no arguments (*DICE*), one (*SIGN*), or two (*HYP*). They all returned *explicit results*, that is, a result that could be used for subsequent computation. Now let's look at one that doesn't give explicit results, but merely displays them, the function *RECT*:

```
      ∇RECT[☐]∇                    3 RECT 4
    ∇  L RECT H              14
[1]    2×L+H                 5
[2]    L HYP H               12
[3]    L×H
    ∇
```

The first thing that should hit your eye is that there is no arrow in the header. Line 1 gives the perimeter of a rectangle of length *L* and height *H*; line 2 is the length of the diagonal, using the previously defined *HYP*; line 3 is the area of the rectangle. Notice also that there is no assignment arrow on any line. This means that the results of each line aren't stored anywhere but will be displayed.

This function displays information, but that information can't be easily used for further work. Watch what happens when we try to use its 'result' for further computation:

```
      5+3 RECT 4
14
5
12
VALUE ERROR
      5+3 RECT 4
           ∧
```

Here the results of the three lines of the function again are displayed, but we can't add 5 to them because the numbers weren't stored anywhere, as contrasted to

    5+3 *HYP* **4**
10

A comparison of their interface diagrams highlights their differences:

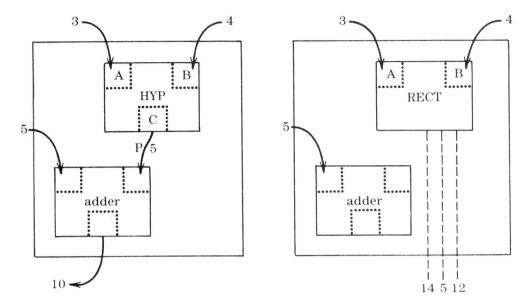

In the diagram for *RECT* one of the input paths has no values to feed into the adder, since the output from *RECT* was 'deposited' on the paper or display screen but not retained anywhere else. By contrast, the output from *HYP* was stored temporarily in *C* to permit its movement to the adder.

The two headers ∇*C*←*A* *HYP* *B* and ∇*A* *RECT* *B* differ in that an assignment (←) is made in *HYP* and not in *RECT*, and in the body of *RECT* there are no assignments of results to any variables. We'll have more to say about the significance of the variables used in the header and in the function itself later in this chapter.

Now consider the monadic function *STAT*:

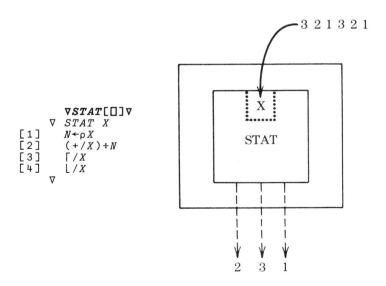

```
      ∇STAT[□]∇
    ∇ STAT X
[1]   N←ρX
[2]   (+/X)÷N
[3]   ⌈/X
[4]   ⌊/X
    ∇
```

Again the header has no explicit result, and the display will be three lines. The first two compute the average of the elements of X and could easily have been combined into one line. N is just a convenient handle for transferring the results of line 1 (which is the number of elements) to line 2. Line 2 displays the average, and lines 3 and 4 display the largest and smallest elements of X. Executing $STAT$ we get

```
      STAT 3 2 1 3 2 1
2
3
1
```

Since no explicit results are returned, it doesn't make any sense to try to work further with them. If we do try it, we get an error message as before:

```
      2×STAT 8 1 4 10
5.75
10
1
VALUE ERROR
      2×STAT 8 1 4 10
          ^
```

To complete the table on **page 65**, display the function $GAME$:

```
      ∇GAME[□]∇
    ∇ GAME
[1]   MINE←DICE
[2]   YOURS←DICE
[3]   ×MINE-YOURS
    ∇
```

After executing the function a few times,

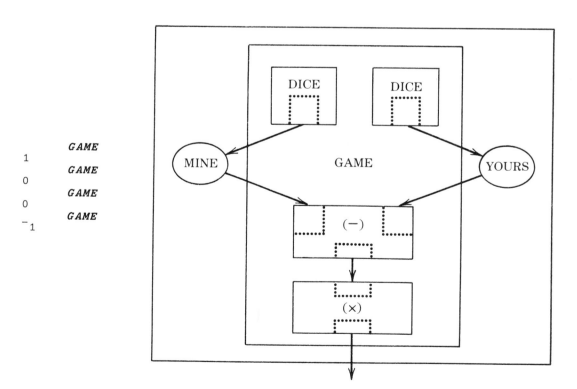

```
        GAME
1
        GAME
0
        GAME
0
        GAME
¯1
```

you should be able to see that this function simply generates one of the three random integers ¯1, 0, 1. It needs no arguments because the random numbers come from the niladic function $DICE$.

The interface diagram for *GAME* shows the results of *DICE* being ultimately deposited in permanent (as opposed to temporary) storage boxes in the APL system.

Another function like *GAME* that you have already encountered is *EASYDRILL* in the workspace 1 *AIDRILL*. This also required no arguments and returned no explicit results. It displayed the answers and accepted inputs, but you couldn't do any computations with them. Functions of this type are commonly called *main programs*.

Some of these programs can be quite large. In most systems the only limit is the space available, but VS APL has a limit of 2047 lines in a single function. Of course, common sense should tell you not to make your programs too long because they will be hard to read and maintain. A good rule of thumb to follow is to keep the length to a page or less.

Different types of variables

The variables that we have encountered so far all appeared to have similar behavior. Now we will see that this isn't quite true, and that APL has a feature that provides protection against variables being accidentally respecified as a result of function execution. Another aspect of this feature lets the same variable name be used repeatedly in different functions without the possibility of confusion.

In the workspace 1 *CLASS*, which you should now load,

```
)LOAD 1 CLASS
SAVED  14.45.33 02/20/83
```

there are five functions, *AVG*1, *AVG*2, *AVG*3, *AVG*4, *AVG*5, which are quite similar and which are all intended to calculate averages. We will use the small but significant differences among them to study the different kinds of variables that can exist in APL.

Dummy variables

Display *AVG*1. The header shows it to be a monadic function that returns an explicit result. The first line gives the number of elements in X and stores that value in N, while the second line divides the sum of the elements by N and stores it temporarily in R when the function is executed.

```
      ∇AVG1[☐]∇
    ∇ R←AVG1 X
[1]   N←ρX
[2]   R←(+/X)÷N
    ∇
```

Let's give X and N values and then execute *AVG*1 with an arbitrary argument. What will happen to X and N?

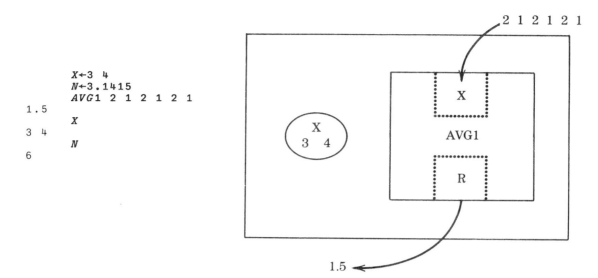

```
        X←3  4
        N←3.1415
        AVG1 2 1 2 1 2 1
1.5
        X
3  4
        N
6
```

Is something wrong here? We put in 3.1415 for *N* and got back 6. On the other hand, *X* was set at 3 4 and apparently wasn't affected, although we used the vector 2 1 2 1 2 1 for the argument *X* in the header of *AVG*1. According to what was presented in an earlier chapter, the latest value of *X* is supposed to supersede a previous value. So why didn't we get 2 1 2 1 2 1 when we called for *X*?

For a clue look at the function header. One of its arguments is named *X*. Apparently this isn't the same variable as the *X* we set before (3 4), even though the symbols are the same. When we executed this function for 2 1 2 1 2 1, *for the time being X* inside the function must have had the value 2 1 2 1 2 1. The *X* outside (3 4) wasn't affected, since we were able to retrieve it afterwards unaltered. Are there then really two *X*'s?

This can be clarified by reference to an interface diagram for *AVG*1. The *X* in the header is a *temporary* storage box for the argument (dotted box). It is filled in this case by the vector 2 1 2 1 2 1, while the variable *X* previously assigned the value 3 4 is sitting elsewhere in storage (oval). The *X* within *AVG*1 is a different *X* from the *X* in the oval.

If, however, we failed to specify another argument for *AVG*1, and instead executed *AVG*1 *X*, the data flow would look as in this interface diagram.

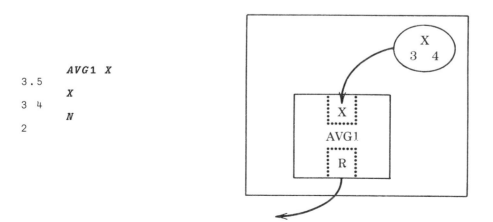

```
        AVG1 X
3.5
        X
3  4
        N
2
```

It's as though the system looked around for an *X* in storage to use as an argument and found 3 4. This situation is exactly the same as though we had called for *AVG*1 *A* for some *A* in storage. What may be confusing is the use of the same name at two different levels here.

The variables used as the argument and result of the header are in a very real sense 'dummy' variables. This means that they have values assigned to them only *inside* the function itself. We can find out what these values are only when we ourselves are 'inside' the function, that is, when execution is suspended part way through because we interrupted it or because of an error.

To illustrate the point further, define this function and then execute it with arguments 3 and 4:

```
      ∇Z←A FN G                    3 FN 4
[1]   Z←A+G∇                  7
```

If after execution we ask for A, G and Z, we get *VALUE ERROR*s instead, because A, G and Z simply don't exist once the function *FN* is completed.

```
        A                        G                      Z
VALUE ERROR              VALUE ERROR            VALUE ERROR
        A                        G                      Z
        ∧                        ∧                      ∧
```

Interface diagrams of the situations during and after execution show this graphically:

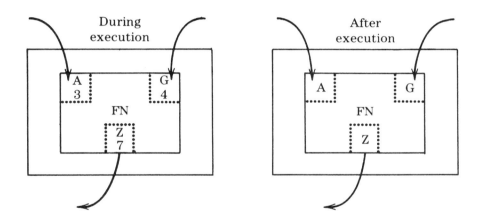

Since the A and G boxes are empty after execution, the *VALUE ERROR* messages received above should be understandable. However, now let's assign A and G and then display them after execution of *FN*:

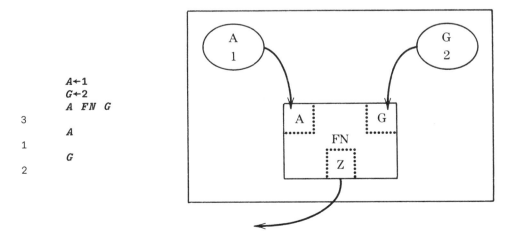

```
      A←1
      G←2
      A FN G
3
      A
1
      G
2
```

The values of A and G stored outside the function (ovals) weren't affected by the execution, even though copies of their constants were fed into the A and G dotted boxes.

It may be dawning on you by this time that it doesn't make any difference what names we use for the arguments of a function. They serve only to indicate that two arguments are called for and to indicate which is which. In a sense, they act like the zeros in the number .00032. All the zeros do is fill up space, but you need them to read the number correctly. This is why the arguments associated with the function name are sometimes called *dummy variables* and have values only within the function, acquired during execution and disappearing when execution is complete. They are special cases of a general class of variables called *local variables*. More about this later.

As the interface diagrams suggest, we can make similar points about results in the headers. They also are dummy variables, and may acquire values during execution. And in the case of the arguments, once execution is finished, the value is lost. That's why *Z* produced a *VALUE ERROR* in the previous example.

Global variables

There is still a little more juice to be squeezed out of the original function *AVG*1. We have answered the question of why calling for *X* returned the value 3   4. But what about *N*?

In contrast to *X*, *N* does not appear in the header, but only in the body of the function. Lacking any instructions from us to the contrary, it ought to behave the same way all of our variables had been behaving before we learned about function definition. That is to say, whenever the system encounters an instruction reassigning a variable whose value has been previously set, it changes that value accordingly. In our case, *N* was originally set at 3.1415, but during execution it was reset to 6 as a result of the instructions in line 1 of *AVG*1. Interface diagrams would show *N* as follows:

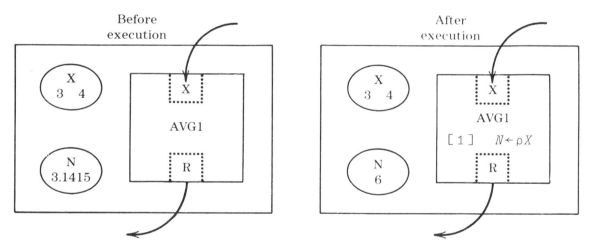

When the variable *N* is given a value during execution, that new value replaces any existing value of *N* outside *AVG*1; or if *N* didn't exist, *N* is created for the first time (again outside *AVG*1). The key word here is *outside*, with variables like *N*, appearing in the executable lines of a function (but not in the header), ending up outside the function once a value has been assigned to them. In this sense they behave exactly like the variables you worked with in Chapter 2, and are called *global variables*.

The next section will describe how these variables can be protected from surprise replacement by having the names appear in the header of the function.

Local variables

Let's look at another way in which variables can be used in function definition. For this, display $AVG2$:

```
      ∇AVG2[□]∇
   ∇  R←AVG2 X;N
[1]   N←ρX
[2]   R←(+/X)÷N
   ∇
```

Something new has been added to the header: a variable N, preceded by a semicolon. When a variable is used in the header in this fashion, it is a *local variable*, whose value can be set and used only within the function itself. It behaves like the dummy variables we discussed previously.

To restore the values of the variables to what they were before we first executed $AVG1$ for comparison purposes, reset N:

```
   N←3.1415
   X
3 4
```

Using the same argument as before, let's execute $AVG2$ and then display X and N:

```
   AVG2 2 1 2 1 2 1              X              N
1.5                           3 4            3.1415
```

As you expected, X hasn't changed. This time N still holds the original value set when we made it a global variable. The instructions for N on line 1 now refer to a *local* N within the function itself, it being only an accident of choice that we used the same name for both a local and a global variable.

In the following interface diagrams for $AVG2$ we see an example of how local variables such as N, in a very real sense *shield* or protect previously defined names.

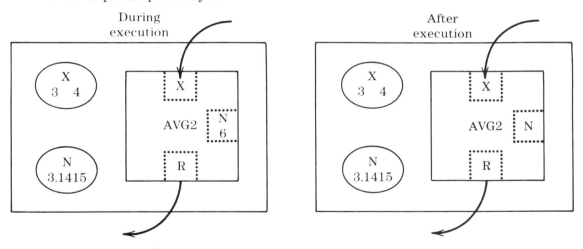

It should now be clear that the APL system keeps the record straight for variables used in these different ways. This is fortunate for us because we may have used the same variable name previously for something entirely different and probably want to preserve it. To prevent accidental reassigning of the variable, it is wise to make it local by putting it in the header preceded by a semicolon. If more than one variable is to be localized, they can be strung out, separated from each other and the rest of the header by semicolons.

$AVG3$ is another example of the use of a local variable. It has a local variable P and is a niladic function returning an explicit result:

```
      ∇AVG3[□]∇              AVG3
   ∇  R←AVG3;P            3.5
[1]   P←ρX                   X
[2]   R←(+/X)÷P            3 4
   ∇
```

You ought to be able to figure out for yourself why the result 3.5 was returned. (Hint: is X a local, global or dummy variable?) In any event, $AVG3$ is a poorly designed function because it depends on the existence of the global variable X for its successful execution. Such dependencies should be employed only when there are no reasonable alternatives, and they should always be documented.

Now reassign X and execute $AVG3$ again. Clearly, the X being averaged is from the most recent global assignment:

```
        X←2 1 2 1 2 1
        AVG3
1.5
```

Things get more complicated when you define functions that in turn execute other functions (subroutines). Local variables in the outermost function still shield globals of the same name from the inner functions as well. And if there is local name duplication in the subroutine, the value associated with it is that in the particular subroutine being executed at the moment.

The following example will either clarify the confusion above, or cause you to swear off duplication of names in subroutines altogether.

```
        ∇R←A OPN B;D          ∇Z←OPN1 A          D←5
[1]     D←A+B            [1]  A                  3 OPN 4
[2]     R←OPN1 D ∇       [2]  D             7
                         [3]  Z←A*2 ∇       7
                                            49
```

Global variables as counters

$AVG4$ adds a new twist:

```
        ∇AVG4[□]∇
     ∇  R←AVG4 X
[1]     R←(+/X)÷ρX
[2]     COUNT←COUNT+1
     ∇
```

This function is intended to illustrate a practical reason to change the value of a global variable inside a function. It is designed so that each time it is used a counter (called $COUNT$) increases by one. A record can thus be kept of the total number of times the function is executed.

Here is an attempted execution of $AVG4$:

```
        AVG4 2 1 2 1 2 1
VALUE ERROR
AVG4[2] COUNT←COUNT+1
        ∧
```

Why do we get an error message? If you think about it, you will see that we goofed by failing to assign an initial value for $COUNT$. So naturally the system didn't know where to start counting, and was unable to execute line 2. This is confirmed by asking for the value of $COUNT$:

```
        COUNT
VALUE ERROR
        COUNT
        ∧
```

Setting $COUNT$ to 0 and reexecuting $AVG4$ twice, we get

```
        COUNT←0
        AVG4 2 1 2 1 2 1                    AVG4 5 4 3 2 1
1.5                                3        
        COUNT                              COUNT
1                                  2
```

$COUNT$ now behaves as we had intended. It is a global variable because it doesn't appear in the header.

In *AVG*5 below, *COUNT* is a local variable:

```
     ∇AVG5[□]∇                          AVG5 2 3 2 3
   ∇ R←AVG5 X;COUNT                  VALUE ERROR
[1]  R←(+/X)÷ρX                      AVG5[2]  COUNT←COUNT+1
[2]  COUNT←COUNT+1                                 ∧
   ∇
```

What's wrong? *COUNT* was set earlier to 0, so why the error message? True, *COUNT* was set, but as a global variable. Its value can't be used in *AVG*5 because we said in the header that *COUNT* was local. There's no way this function can work, because the local *COUNT* shields the global *COUNT*.

Suppose we put a line before line 1 which sets *COUNT* to 0. Then each time we executed it, the local variable *COUNT* would be reset to 0. It would never get beyond 1. Furthermore, because it would be local, all trace of it would be lost once we exited the function.

Up to this point in the chapter we have managed to bungle the execution of two functions, *AVG*4 and *AVG*5. Such partial executions, called *suspensions*, stay with us until we sign off or remove them. They take up valuable space and may cause other unanticipated things to happen. For the time being, clear up each such suspension by typing →, followed by *RETURN*. More about this phenomenon in Chapter 16.

There is a limitation on the use of local variables. It isn't possible to use a subfunction by the same name as a local variable. For example, if *COUNT* were also a function, we couldn't ask for it to be executed in *AVG*5 and still retain *COUNT* as a local variable.

By this time you should be getting an appreciation of the usefulness of local variables, as well as an awareness (we hope) of some of their pitfalls. It is not only variables that can be localized; functions can be made local to functions. This advanced concept is treated in Chapter 24.

Before leaving the topic this is a good place to point out that most people have difficulty remembering more than a half dozen things at a time. This physiological limitation suggests that you would do well to restrict the number of different variables you use in your programs. They not only take up space in the workspace, but also make your programs harder to read and maintain. If you use the same names over again in another part of your program, make sure it is in a place where no confusion is likely to arise when the statements are reviewed later, and use comments liberally to document your techniques.

PROBLEMS

Define the functions as required in problems 1 to 6:

1. Dyadic, explicit result: to calculate the FICA (social security tax) at the rate of P percent on gross yearly income IN up to an annual maximum of MAX.

2. Dyadic, no explicit result: to store in the variable T the square of the difference of its two scalar arguments.

3. Monadic, explicit result: to generate a limited set of prime numbers, using Fermat's formula 2^{2^n} (conventional notation).

4. Niladic, no explicit result: to see if either of two previously defined variables A and B divides the other evenly. The answer should be 1 if they divide evenly, or 0 otherwise.

5. Monadic, no explicit result: accepts a vector argument V and makes these changes to global variables: **A** adds to NV the number of numbers in V; **B** adds to SV the sum of the elements in V; **C** adds to $SVSQ$ the sum of the squares of the elements in V. Don't $)CLEAR$ yet; problem 6 uses these variables.

6. Niladic, explicit result: uses NV, SV and $SVSQ$ of problem 5 to compute the sample standard deviation, using the formula $((SVSQ-(SV*2)\div NV)\div ^-1+NV)*.5$.

7. What is wrong with the following function headers (A and B are arguments)?
   A SQ A $\nabla Z \leftarrow B$ HYP ∇A $1FIB$ B ∇A HYP B C ∇A HYP $B;B;C$

8. Enter the function HYP (page 56) and use it to evaluate each of the following:
   $(3$ HYP $4)$ HYP 3 HYP 1 $4+3$ HYP $4-3$ $(4+3)$ HYP $4-3$

9. $)LOAD$ 1 $CLASS$ and then define a dyadic function D which returns an explicit result that is the larger of its two arguments. Explain the system's behavior.

10. Define a dyadic function $ROUND$ that returns an explicit result which is the right argument rounded off to the number of decimal places indicated in the left argument. Example:
    2 $ROUND$ 123.456 1.33333 3.5 gives 123.46 1.33 3.5

11. $)LOAD$ 1 $CLASS$. Enter $CLR \leftarrow 52$ 78 90 and account for the result.

12. $)LOAD$ 1 $CLASS$ and enter this function :

    ```
         ∇F
    [1]  Z←(A*2)+B*2
    [2]  Z←Z*.5∇
    ```

    After assigning arbitrary values for A and B, execute $T \leftarrow F+7$ and $T \leftarrow Z+7$. Explain your results.

13. $)CLEAR$ and define these three functions:

    ```
         ∇PERIM1              ∇R←B PERIM2 C              ∇R←PERIM3 C
    [1]  R←2×B+C∇       [1]  R←2×B+C∇             [1]  R←2×B+C∇
    ```

    Now make these assignments $R \leftarrow 3$ $B \leftarrow 2$ $C \leftarrow 5$ $M \leftarrow 7$ $S \leftarrow 1$.
    A Execute $PERIM1$. Observe the changes to the variables.
    B Reset the variables R, B, C, M and S to their original values and execute $S \leftarrow M$ $PERIM2$ R. Again observe the changes to the variables.
    C Reset the variables again and execute $S \leftarrow PERIM3$ R. Observe the changes to the variables. Can you explain every change?

14. Write a function $MARGIN$, which returns an explicit result, to solve the following problem. Experience shows that sales S of a toy depend on the price, P, as $40000-5000×P$. The total cost C of production is $C \leftarrow 35000+2×S$. For each price $1, $2, $3, $4, $5, $6 and $7, what is the profit margin?

15. Write a function $COST$ to figure the total cost of a shopping trip by adding the cost of nontaxable items to that of the taxable items (on which 5% sales tax must be calculated).

Chapter 10: Function editing

The two previous chapters explained how to enter and use different types of functions, but didn't show how to change a function which had an error in it. Since we can't do much without the capability for such change, this chapter will be concerned with ways of editing functions after they have been written and entered.

To speed things up, we'll use the prepared function $STAT$ in the workspace 1 $CLASS$:

```
      )LOAD 1 CLASS
SAVED  14.45.33 02/20/83

      ∇STAT[☐]∇
    ∇ STAT X
[1]    N←ρX
[2]    (+/X)÷N
[3]    ⌈/X
[4]    ⌊/X
    ∇
```

It isn't possible to enter it or redefine it because we already have a copy of it in our workspace. Suppose we didn't know that it was already in and tried to reenter it:

```
      ∇STAT X
DEFN ERROR
      ∇STAT X
             ∧
```

As was discussed earlier on **page 59** the error message shows that the system has built-in protection against accidental replacement of a function. However, we can make changes to functions that have already been defined, as we shall see. Given our all too-human propensity to make mistakes or to change our minds, this APL feature is an obvious necessity.

Adding a line

The four lines of the function $STAT$ as presently written give information on the average and largest and smallest elements of a vector argument X. Suppose we want to add a fifth line which will give the range (difference between the largest and smallest element).

How is this done? The first step is to open up the function by entering a single ∇ and the function name, followed by RETURN as usual:

```
      ∇STAT
[5]
```

Notice that the system replies with [5]. In general the next available line number will be returned. It's as though we had just entered the first four lines and are ready to continue our writing on the fifth line. (This is a way, if somewhat sneaky, to find out how many lines are in the function.) Now enter

```
[5]    (⌈/X)−⌊/X
[6]    ∇
```

and we see that the system replies with a [6], waiting for the next line of input. Since we don't want to add anything further, a closing ∇ has been entered as a signal that we want to get back into execution mode.

Execution with a vector 2 9 1 gives us four lines of output, the fourth line being range as we had intended, and a display of the function now shows that line 5 has indeed been added:

```
        STAT 2 9 1                        ∇STAT[□]∇
4                                      ∇  STAT X
9                               [1]       N←ρX
1                               [2]       (+/X)÷N
8                               [3]       ⌈/X
                                [4]       ⌊/X
                                [5]       (⌈/X)-⌊/X
                                       ∇
```

Replacing a line with another line

Also in the workspace 1 *CLASS* is a function called *AVG* which computes the average of the elements of an argument *X*. We are going to change line 2 of *STAT* to *AVG*, but first we'll check out *AVG* to see if it works:

```
    AVG 1 2 3
2
```

To replace line 2, we need to open up the function as before by entering

```
    ∇STAT
```

The system's response is [6], which we override with [2]:

```
[6]   [2]
```

After pressing RETURN, the system replies with a [2] and we can now enter *AVG X*:

```
[2]   AVG X
```

Having accepted the change to line 2, the system displays [3], anticipating that's the next line you want to change. Since we aren't going to make any more changes right now, ∇ is used to close out the function:

```
[3]   ∇
```

It should be emphasized that in making this change, only line 2 was changed. All the other lines of the function were *not* affected.

Here is an execution of *STAT* and a display of the revised function:

```
        STAT 2 9 1                        ∇STAT[□]∇
4                                      ∇  STAT X
9                               [1]       N←ρX
1                               [2]       AVG X
8                               [3]       ⌈/X
                                [4]       ⌊/X
                                [5]       (⌈/X)-⌊/X
                                       ∇
```

The change has been made and the rest of the function is unaltered.

Changing the header

You can change the header itself in exactly the same way as any other line by using [0] as the line number:

```
        ∇STAT                            ∇STAT[□]∇
[6]     [0]                          DEFN ERROR
[0]     NEWNAME X                        ∇STAT
[1]     ∇                                   ∧
```

Since *STAT* as been renamed *NEWNAME*, we get an error message when we attempt to display *STAT*, because it no longer exists. Naturally, any changes in the header must be consistent with what is in the body of the function itself, unless of course the corresponding changes are made in the body of the function also.

You can display *NEWNAME* now if you wish, but after you do, change the name of the function back to *STAT* because there are more function editing commands yet to learn, and it will be easier if we get back on track.

```
        ∇NEWNAME
[6]     [0]
[0]     STAT X
[1]     ∇
```

Inserting a line between two other lines

Suppose we want to insert between lines 1 and 2 a statement whose purpose is to display the original values of *X*. This is done by first opening the function as usual, and then entering some number in brackets that is between 1 and 2, say [1.1]:

```
        ∇STAT
[6]     [1.1]
```

Any number will do as long as it is between the numbers of the two lines bracketing the location of the insertion. The system returns [1.1] and we can then enter *X*, which when encountered during execution will cause the values of *X* to be displayed.

```
[1.1]   X
[1.2]
```

The next line number provided by the system is 'one greater' in its last significant digit to provide for still other entries between lines 1 and 2. Let's ask first for a display of what we have so far while we're still in function definition mode, and then close it out:

```
[1.2]   [□]∇
     ∇ STAT X
[1]     N←ρX
[1.1]   X
[2]     AVG X
[3]     ⌈/X
[4]     ⌊/X
[5]     (⌈/X)-⌊/X
     ∇
```

Your cursor should have moved over six spaces after this. If it did, you are in execution mode. However, if a number in [ ] was returned, then enter ∇, followed by RETURN.

Of course, a line numbered 1.1 is somewhat awkward, to say the least. Fortunately, after the function is closed out the lines are automatically renumbered, as seen in the following display:

```
        ∇STAT[□]
     ∇ STAT X
[1]     N←ρX
[2]     X
[3]     AVG X
[4]     ⌈/X
[5]     ⌊/X
[6]     (⌈/X)-⌊/X
     ∇
[7]
```

The lines of the function have been renumbered. But since [7] was returned, we are still in function definition mode. Pressing RETURN gives [7] again, and since there is to be no more entry at this time, we close out the function to get back to execution mode.

```
[7]     ∇
```

Doing several things at once

It is possible to put several of the editing instructions on a single line. For our example we'll take line 3, AVG X, change it back to what it was originally, and then return to execution mode. To do this, enter the following:

       $\nabla STAT[3](+/X)\div N\nabla$

The [3] moves control to line 3, what follows it becomes the new line 3, and the second ∇ closes it out after the change. We can now check this by displaying the function in the usual manner:

```
        ∇STAT[□]∇
    ∇ STAT X
[1]    N←ρX
[2]    X
[3]    (+/X)÷ρX
[4]    ⌈/X
[5]    ⌊/X
[6]    (⌈/X)-⌊/X
    ∇
```

But observe the following entry, which inserts a comment after line 5:

      $\nabla STAT[5.1]$ ⍝ *NEXT LINE DISPLAYS RANGE* ∇
[5.2]

Why is function definition still open? The reason is that even though a closing ∇ was entered, it came after a comment symbol ⍝, and hence was taken as part of the comment itself. Entering a ∇ on the *next* line now closes the function and renumbers the comment as line 6.

[5.2] ∇

Deleting a line

How do we remove a line completely? For example, suppose we want to get rid of line 4. As usual, we first open up the function and direct control to line 4:

      $\nabla STAT[4]$

The computer responds with [4], indicating it is ready to work on line 4. What you do next depends on the particular APL system you are using. On many older versions of APL, the only way you can delete a line is to press ATTN followed by RETURN. For most modern systems, [Δ4] deletes line 4, but on APL*PLUS Systems it is [~4].

[4]   [Δ4]

Next, [8] is displayed, it being the next available line at the end of the function. We now ask for a display of the function, but without closing it out:

```
[8]    [□]
    ∇ STAT X
[1]    N←ρX
[2]    X
[3]    (+/X)÷N
[5]    ⌊/X
[6]  ⍝ NEXT LINE DISPLAYS THE RANGE∇
[7]    (⌈/X)-⌊/X
    ∇
[8]
```

Notice that line 4 has been deleted and the display continues with [8]. Let's remove line 6 (incidentally, some systems let you remove many lines at once, e.g., [Δ4 6 7]) and close the function:

[8]   [Δ6]∇

Since the function is closed, the lines are now renumbered:

```
        ∇STAT[□]∇
      ∇ STAT X
[1]     N←ρX
[2]     X
[3]     (+/X)÷N
[4]     ⌊/X
[5]     (⌈/X)-⌊/X
      ∇
```

Just remember that if the number of ∇'s *you* (and not the system) have entered is even, you are in execution mode; if odd, you are in function definition mode. An exception is ∇'s following a comment; they are regarded as part of the comment itself.

Erasing the entire function

Occasionally, while making extensive changes, you might get so messed up that you want to start over. You can get rid of the entire function using the system command)ERASE followed by the name of the function you no longer want. Don't do it now, because we need *STAT* for some more examples. The response to a successful erasure is simply that the cursor moves over six spaces. As you would expect, attempts to display an erased function result in an error message.

Locking functions

You can lock a function by closing it with the ⍒ character (formed by overstriking ∇ and ~) instead of ∇. On some systems you can use ⍒ for either starting or ending functions to be locked. Once a function is locked, it can't be edited or displayed, although it can be executed and erased. Make sure you keep an unlocked reference version as a base for future work. Locking is useful for protecting proprietary algorithms or things like classroom exercises which a teacher might not want students to see, or to prevent others from tampering with the programs. APL2 has a more general way to lock functions using the dyadic system function □FX, described in Chapter 24.

Displaying only part of a function

Thus far we have asked for the entire function to be displayed. What if the function is a long one and we are interested only in a single line, say, 4? The display command for this is very similar to what we have used previously:

```
        ∇STAT[4□]∇
[4]     ⌊/X
```

If there had been no second ∇, line 4 would have been displayed and then the system would ask us what we wanted to do to it by returning [4] again,

```
        ∇STAT[4□]
[4]     ⌊/X
[4]
```

and now we can close out the function by entering ∇:

```
[4]     ∇
```

By now you should be getting the idea that the □ (quad) is used in APL to display things. Fancifully speaking, you can think of it here as a window to see what's going on inside the function. The rules are that [□] displays everything, [n□] displays the particular line, and [□m] displays all lines beginning with the one specified to the end of the function.

```
        ∇STAT[□3]
[3]     (+/X)÷N
[4]     ⌊/X
[5]     (⌈/X)-⌊/X
      ∇
[6]
```

After listing lines 3, 4 and 5, the system offers the next available line number, 6, to let us continue adding lines. What's a user to do if the function has, say, fifty lines and he wants to display only lines 3, 4 and 5? The way to display only these lines is to enter [□3] and let it run until you've seen what you need to see. Just press ATTN or BREAK to stop the display. However, unless the original display command was closed with a ∇, you will be in function definition mode after interrupting. Plan your next step accordingly.

Detailed editing of part of a line

Getting into more specific and limited changes, let's start over again with a fresh copy of 1 *CLASS*.

```
)LOAD 1 CLASS
SAVED  14.45.33 02/20/83
```

As we've already said, this wipes out what was in the active workspace and replaces it with an exact image of the workspace being loaded.

Now display *STAT*, but without the closing ∇:

```
      ∇STAT[□]
    ∇  STAT X
[1]    N←ρX
[2]    (+/X)÷N
[3]    ⌈/X
[4]    ⌊/X
    ∇
[5]
```

It is again in its original form, and the system is waiting for us to enter line 5.

Up to now we have replaced entire lines. But suppose a line is very long and complicated, and our change is to involve only a few characters. For example, say we'd like to change the variable N to $COUNT$ in lines 1 and 2 of *STAT*. Obviously, in this case we could type both lines over since they are quite short. However, it will be more instructive to use the detailed editing capabilities of APL to make the changes.

We're still in function definition mode, since pressing RETURN gets

```
[5]
```

To direct the cursor to the specific characters that need revising, what we enter has the following format:

[line number □ estimate of what display position the first change occurs at]

In this case we'll deliberately make the cursor space over twenty positions (from the left margin) and then backspace manually to the N just to show that our estimate doesn't have to be accurate:

```
[5]    [1□20]
```

The system will respond by displaying [1] and then positioning the cursor twenty spaces over on the next line:

```
[1]    N←ρX
               ⊠
```

We wish to strike out the letter N. For this, the slash (/, same symbol as reduction) is used. $COUNT$ has five characters for which space needs to be provided. To be sure we get enough space we enter 8 after the slash as shown, once we have manually backspaced the cursor to the N. This inserts eight spaces just prior to the character (here ←) above the number entered:

```
[1]    N←ρX
       /8
```

After pressing RETURN, the system responds as follows, with the cursor finally resting at the position where ⊠ is shown.

```
[1]    ⊠         ←ρX
```

We can now enter $COUNT$ in the space provided:

```
[1]    COUNT    ←ρX
```

Having made this change we are asked if we want to do anything with line 2. Before doing anything else, display line 1:

```
[2]    [1□]
[1]    COUNT←ρX
[1]
```

N is gone, $COUNT$ has been inserted, and the extra blanks have been deleted.

Now directing control to the eighth position on line 2, we use the same procedure to insert $COUNT$ at the end of the line. Eight positions are too few in this case, so we'll have to use the space bar to move the cursor over some more after it comes to rest in the eighth position:

```
[1]    [2□8]
[2]    (+/X)÷N
                /
[2]    (+/X)÷COUNT
[3]    ∇
```

Since the insertion is to be made at the end of the line, no provision for extra space is necessary. Displaying the entire revised function, we see that the changes have been made:

```
       ∇STAT[□]∇
[1]    COUNT←ρX
[2]    (+/X)÷COUNT
[3]    ⌈/X
[4]    ⌊/X
    ∇
```

Here are more things you can do with detailed editing. First, the command [n□0] displays line n and moves the cursor to the end of the line to allow for additions on the right as shown,

```
       ∇STAT[2□0]
[2]    (+/X)÷COUNT▨
```

and we can now extend the line:

```
[2]    (+/X)÷COUNTER∇
```

Local variables are conveniently added to the header of a function by using [0□0] to position the cursor at the right end of the header line.

Second, if more than nine spaces have to be inserted at any one place in a line, the letters of the alphabet may be used, each letter being assigned a numerical value equal to five times its index position in the alphabet. Here is an example:

```
       ∇STAT[1□12]
[1]    COUNT←ρX
          B
[1]    COUNT▨               ←ρX
```

The letter B causes 10 spaces to be inserted, and the cursor comes to rest at the position marked by the ▨ above. Now it's as though *you* had entered the line as shown above, and you can make whatever additions you choose. In the example below, the letters ER are entered in that space and followed by ∇ at the end of the line:

```
[1]    COUNTER               ←ρX∇
```

You can apply detailed editing to the line number itself. The effect is to generate a new line with the new number. The old line still remains. If you make other changes, those changes are carried to the new line, but the original line is unchanged.

The APL*PLUS and Sharp Systems make use of the comma, period and semicolon to give added flexibility to detailed line editing. When a comma is entered, all characters following it are placed directly in the line to be changed, and then the line is redisplayed. The cursor comes to rest at the first created blank position, or at the end of the line if there were no blank positions created. For example:

```
        ∇STAT[1□7]
[1]     COUNTER←ρX
        ///////,N
[1]     N←ρX▨
```

Pressing RETURN now directs control to the next line. Alternatively, if you have more than one change to make on the same line, use the semicolon instead of the comma. It works the same way, except that the line is again displayed, with the cursor coming to rest just after the last character you inserted. If you have only one change to make to the line, use the period instead of the comma or semicolon. In this case the change is inserted as usual, but control goes immediately to the next line.

```
[2]     [2□10]
[2]     (+/X)÷COUNTER
                ///////.N
[3]     ∇
```

Editing the last line entered in calculator mode

On the APL*PLUS and Sharp Systems, you can apply detailed editing to the last line you entered in calculator mode. You inform the system you wish to make changes to the last line entered by the system command)EDIT followed by the position number. That is,)EDIT 12 is similar to [n□12]. The line is redisplayed, and you can now use any of the characters / , ; . as well as digits and letters to delete, insert or position changes to the line. When the editing is complete, the line is again executed for you, or at least attempted, if you make a mistake like the one that follows here:

```
        X←2 3 7 4 2
        +/X
4.5
        )EDIT 7
        +/X
        /..5×(⌈
SYNTAX ERROR
        0.5×(⌈/X
               ∧
        )EDIT
        0.5×(⌈/X)+⌊/X
```

In the last example,)EDIT without a number following it is equivalent to [n□0]—the cursor moved to the end of the line to allow for additions to the right.

)EDIT works on the last executable line only. It ignores intervening system commands entirely. It also ignores all lines entered in function definition. However, there is one very interesting and useful quirk in its behavior. It can be used to capture the last executed line and include it in a function. This can be a real blessing when developing subsequent lines of a function by experimenting with each line in execution mode. Suppose you had just developed an algorithm for midrange, .5×(⌈/X)+⌊/X, in execution mode and now wanted to include it as the last line in STAT:

```
        ∇STAT
[5]     )EDIT
[5]     0.5×(⌈/X)+⌊/X∇
```

Because)EDIT is such a popular feature, it has been made even easier to use. The entry)20 is just as good as)EDIT 20, and) is equivalent to)EDIT or)EDIT 0.

Other ways to edit functions and lines

Besides the editing facilities that are provided as an inherent part of APL systems, many terminals provide features that can be employed to edit lines and functions. On the IBM 3278 display terminal, for instance, the cursor may be moved under any line previously displayed, even on a prior page, or belonging to some other function. After RETURN is pressed, the line, complete with its line number, appears in the input area of the screen. The INSERT and DELETE keys may then be used with the cursor to perform very detailed and sophisticated editing. However, no matter what value you give m in the command [n□m], the cursor comes to rest at the end of the line. In other words, it is always equivalent to [n□0].

There are additional variants on the standard APL editing commands which are available in APL2. These make life a little easier for the user who may have access to them.

commands	[Δ]	all lines (be careful!)
to delete	[ΔS]	all lines in vector S
	[ΔL1-L2]	all lines from L1 through L2
	[Δ-L2]	all lines from the beginning through L2
	[ΔL1-]	all lines from L1 to the end
commands	[□S]	all lines in S
to display	[□L1-L2]	all lines from L1 through L2
	[□-L2]	all lines from the beginning through L2
	[□L1-]	all lines from L1 to the end

Should you goof in deleting lines, the action can be rescinded with [→] or →, which restores the function.

Full screen editors

Many APL systems which support display terminals also offer more advanced editing capabilities than those included in the traditional APL editor described in this chapter. These full-screen editors differ from system to system in how they are invoked and in the specific commands and features available to the user.

But they all have these common characteristics: (1) changes can be made in place anywhere on the screen; (2) there are commands to do global finds of names, etc. within the function and change them; and (3) users always see the current version of the function displayed (although line renumbering still doesn't take place until after the function is closed and redisplayed). If you have a display terminal on a system which offers this capability, use it. The ease with which changes can be made will more than compensate for having to learn the commands specific to the editor.

Much later in the book we will discuss other powerful ways to modify functions, which provide an adjunct or alternative to the ones of this chapter. There are even ways to convert a function to a character variable, change the character variable under program control, and then reconvert it to a function.

Summary of editing features

The editing facilities covered in this chapter will 'soak in' as you write more involved functions. You should refer to this chapter frequently until editing becomes second nature for you. For that reason, we provide the following synopsis of the major features:

∇*FN*	open *FN*, ready for entry of first new line.
[3]	ready for entry or reentry of line 3.
[3.1]	ready for entry of a line to follow line 3.
[3□]	display line 3, ready for reentry of line 3.
[□]	display entire *FN*, ready for entry of first new line.
[□3]	display line 3 and all following ready for entry of first new line.
[Δ3]	(or [~3]) delete line 3, ready for entry of first new line.
[3□0]	display line 3, ready to add onto end of line 3.
[3□10]	display line 3, cursor at position 10 ready for insertions.
/	delete character above.
digit	insert specified number of spaces.
letter	insert 5 spaces for *A*, 10 for *B*, etc.
.	insert following text, ready for next line (Sharp and APL*PLUS Systems).
,	insert following text, ready at end of same line (Sharp and APL*PLUS Systems).
;	insert following text, cursor positioned at end of inserted text (Sharp and APL*PLUS Systems).
∇	close function definition.
⍫	close function definition and lock function.
)*ERASE FN*	erase function entirely.
)*EDIT* 10	display last line executed, ready to insert at position 10 (Sharp and APL*PLUS Systems).
)10	display last line executed, ready to insert at position 10 (Sharp and APL*PLUS Systems).
)*EDIT*	display last line executed, ready at end of line (Sharp and APL*PLUS Systems).
)	display last line executed, ready at end of line. (Sharp and APL*PLUS Systems).

PROBLEMS

)*LOAD* 1 *CLASS* and enter the following sample program to calculate the standard deviation of a set of numbers (see problem 6, Chapter 8):

```
       ∇ STD N
[1]    R←AVG N
[2]    R←R-N
[3]    R←AVG R*2
[4]    ANS←R*0.5 ∇
```

1. Display the function and direct control to line 5.

2. Use detailed editing to change *ANS* on line 4 to *R*.

3. Edit the header to return an explicit result *R*.

4. Eliminate line 2.

5. Display the function and remain in function definition mode.

6. Change line 3 to *R←AVG(R-N)*2*.

7. Display lines 3 and 4.

8. Close out the function.

9. Use a single entry to open up the function again and reinsert the original contents of line 2.

10. Change line 3 back to its original form with detailed editing.

11. Insert just prior to line 1 a command that will display the number of elements in *N*. Then close out the function.

12. Delete the function from the active workspace.

13. Without reloading the workspace or copying the function you just erased, try to display it now.

Chapter 11: Workspaces

In the previous chapters, all variables that you assigned and functions that you defined were lost whenever you signed off. The only recoverable work was in 1 *CLASS* and 1 *AIDRILL*. And the only reason you could still access them was that when you loaded one of these workspaces into your own active workspace, you were actually taking an exact *image* of the original, not the original itself. Although you lost the image whenever you signed off, you could always obtain another image later.

We need to know how to preserve what we do for posterity. In this chapter we'll go through a series of exercises designed to show how you can manipulate workspaces. To ensure continuity while learning the features covered in this chapter, you should repeat the entire sequence of commands exactly as they are given in this chapter. Diagrams of the workspace contents are included at appropriate points to help you.

Workspace contents

Start off by entering

```
)CLEAR
CLEAR WS
```

As we pointed out earlier, this is one of a family of system commands, like the sign-on and sign-off. It has the effect of wiping out all the work done in the active workspace and replacing it with a clean workspace, such as is normally obtained at the sign-on. Remember that the active workspace is the one that you have currently available to you, in which all your work is now being done.

In VS APL the *)CLEAR* command may be followed by a number, e.g., *)CLEAR 256000,* to set up a clear workspace whose size in *bytes* (a byte is a space needed for one character) is the number entered.

To show that this workspace is now empty as a result of the *)CLEAR* command, we can use the commands

```
)FNS
)VARS
```

ACTIVE WS

```
CLEAR WS
─ ─ ─ ─ ─ ─ ─

```

to see that there isn't anything in the active workspace.

Since the purpose of this chapter is to show you how to save functions and variables for future use, we'll need some example functions. For this, let's enter the function *HYP*:

```
      ∇R←A HYP B
[1]   R←((A*2)+B*2)*.5∇
```

ACTIVE WS

```
CLEAR WS
─ ─ ─ ─ ─ ─ ─

HYP
```

Let's now set a couple of variables and observe that they appear in the $)VARS$ listing:

```
PI←3.14159
V←1 2 3 4 5
```

and the command

```
      )VARS
PI       V
```

ACTIVE WS

```
┌──────────────┐
│ CLEAR  WS    │
│ ─ ─ ─ ─ ─ ─  │
│ HYP     PI   │
│         V    │
│              │
└──────────────┘
```

For a second function, enter

```
      ∇TOSS
[1]   ?2∇
```

and then obtain a new listing of functions to confirm that $TOSS$ has indeed been stored.

```
      )FNS
HYP      TOSS
```

ACTIVE WS

```
┌──────────────┐
│ CLEAR  WS    │
│ ─ ─ ─ ─ ─ ─  │
│ HYP     PI   │
│ TOSS    V    │
│              │
└──────────────┘
```

Saving and recovering a workspace

We could continue entering functions and variables, but for purposes of illustration let's pretend that we're through with our work at this point and want to preserve these functions and variables for use later.

The system command $)SAVE$ does this. It puts an image of the active workspace into a more permanent storage facility, called your *private library*. When a workspace is saved, you give it a name so that it can be retrieved later. Many systems limit the name to eight or fewer characters. There is no relation between this name and the names of variables and functions inside the workspace, although you should always try to select names with some mnemonic content.

We'll use the name $FIRST$ for the work previously entered:

```
      )SAVE FIRST
14.12.04 02/26/83
```

We get a message back giving the time and date. This means that $)SAVE$ was successful and an image of the workspace is now stored with the name $FIRST$ in your private library.

There is a command which lists the names of all the saved workspaces in your library. This command is $)LIB$ or $)WSLIB$, depending on the particular system.

```
      )LIB
FIRST
```

ACTIVE WS

```
┌──────────────┐
│ FIRST        │
│ ─ ─ ─ ─ ─ ─  │
│ HYP     PI   │
│ TOSS    V    │
│              │
└──────────────┘
```

PRIVATE LIBRARY

```
┌──────────────┐
│ FIRST        │
│ ─ ─ ─ ─ ─ ─  │
│ HYP     PI   │
│ TOSS    V    │
│              │
└──────────────┘
```

Only one workspace is listed because that's all we have saved so far.)*FNS* shows that *HYP* and *TOSS* are still around:

```
     )FNS
HYP    TOSS
```

Remember that we saved an *image* of the active workspace. Let's now get a fresh workspace:

```
     )CLEAR
CLEAR WS
```

ACTIVE WS	PRIVATE LIBRARY
CLEAR WS	*FIRST*
	HYP PI *TOSS V*

Imagine that it's now the following day and we are ready to do some work with *HYP* and *TOSS*. They were lost from the active workspace when we cleared, but there is an exact image stored in our library in the workspace named *FIRST*. To recover this image, execute the command

```
     )LOAD FIRST
SAVED  14.12.04 02/26/83
```

The response tells when it was last saved. In VS APL, the)*LOAD* command can be followed by a number specifying a desired size of the active workspace. For example,)*LOAD FIRST* 200000 changes the size of the active workspace to 200000 bytes. Or, if the size of the saved workspace forces a change of size for the active workspace, you'll get a *WS SIZE IS...* message.

Our functions and variables are available to us once again:

```
     )FNS
HYP    TOSS
     )VARS
PI    V
```

ACTIVE WS	PRIVATE LIBRARY
FIRST	*FIRST*
HYP PI *TOSS V*	*HYP PI* *TOSS V*

Let's check on *V* to see whether it's still what it's supposed to be:

```
     V
1 2 3 4 5
```

Most people have more than one project cooking at any one time, and usually save a separate workspace for each project. How is this done? To illustrate the procedure,

```
     )CLEAR
CLEAR WS
```

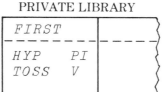

ACTIVE WS	PRIVATE LIBRARY
CLEAR WS	*FIRST*
	HYP PI *TOSS V*

and define the function *SQRT*:

```
      ∇R←SQRT X
[1]   R←X*.5∇
```

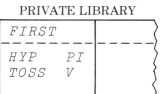

Now save an image of the active workspace (which contains only the function *SQRT*) with the name *SECOND*:

```
      )SAVE SECOND
14.12.21 02/26/83
```

Before going on, let's be sure we understand that all we have immediate access to at this point is the active workspace with only the function *SQRT* in it. An image of this workspace, with the name *SECOND*, is also in your private library.

```
      )FNS
SQRT
      )LIB
FIRST
SECOND
```

If we want to use any of the functions or variables in the workspace named *FIRST* now, we must load it. Then we see that *HYP* and *TOSS* are back in the active workspace:

```
      )LOAD FIRST
SAVED   14.12.04 02/26/83
      )FNS
HYP      TOSS
```

ACTIVE WS		PRIVATE LIBRARY		
FIRST		FIRST	SECOND	
HYP PI		HYP PI		
TOSS V		TOSS V	SQRT	

Now we'll load *SECOND* and look at its contents. We don't need to clear between loadings because the act of loading replaces the contents of the active workspace with the material in the workspace being loaded.

```
      )LOAD SECOND
SAVED   14.12.21 02/26/83
      )FNS
SQRT
```

ACTIVE WS		PRIVATE LIBRARY		
SECOND		FIRST	SECOND	
		HYP PI		
SQRT		TOSS V	SQRT	

The examples above show that we can access the contents of only one workspace at a time, specifically, the one whose image is in the active workspace.

Let's save yet another workspace with the name *THIRD*. This time, just to be different, load 1 *CLASS*, and get a list of the functions:

```
      )LOAD 1 CLASS
SAVED  14.45.33 02/20/83

      )FNS
ADD       AGAIN    AREA      AUTO     AVG      AVG1     AVG2     AVG3     AVG4     AVG5
AVG6      CHANGE   CHARMAT   CLR      CMP      CMPN     CMPX     CMPY     COMPINT  COMPOSE
COS       CP       C2GT99    DEC      DENUMCODE         DESCRIBE          DICE
DUPLICATES         ENT       EVAL     F        FACT       (list interrupted.)
```

ACTIVE WS   PRIVATE LIBRARY

```
┌─────────────┐     ┌─────────────┬─────────────┬────────┐
│   1 CLASS   │     │ FIRST       │ SECOND      │        │
│─────────────│     │─────────────│─────────────│        │
│ ADD    AUTO │     │ HYP     PI  │             │        │
│ AGAIN  AVG  │     │ TOSS    V   │ SQRT        │        │
│ AREA   ...  │     │             │             │        │
└─────────────┘     └─────────────┴─────────────┴────────┘
```

The contents (or more precisely, an *image* of the contents) of 1 *CLASS* will now be saved as *THIRD*:

```
      )SAVE THIRD
14.12.35 02/26/83
```

Our listing of saved workspaces has grown:

```
      )LIB
FIRST
SECOND
THIRD
```

ACTIVE WS   PRIVATE LIBRARY

```
┌─────────────┐     ┌─────────────┬─────────────┬─────────────┐
│   1 CLASS   │     │ FIRST       │ SECOND      │ THIRD       │
│─────────────│     │─────────────│─────────────│─────────────│
│ ADD    AUTO │     │ HYP     PI  │             │ ADD    AUTO │
│ AGAIN  AVG  │     │ TOSS    V   │ SQRT        │ AGAIN  AVG  │
│ AREA   ...  │     │             │             │ AREA   ...  │
└─────────────┘     └─────────────┴─────────────┴─────────────┘
```

The *LIB* command produces an alphabetized list. Furthermore, just as with *FNS* and *VARS*, a partial listing can be obtained:

```
      )LIB SE
SECOND
THIRD
```

APL2 allows a variant of this command: *)LIB PE ST* lists all workspaces whose names begin with *PE* through *ST*.

Let's clear again, define a couple of variables, and save them in *FOURTH*:

```
      )CLEAR
CLEAR WS
      X←4 6 8 10
      Y←2 5 8

      )SAVE FOURTH
NOT SAVED, USER STORAGE FULL
```

We are told, in effect, that we have only three workspaces allotted to us and they are used up, so we're out of luck.

Some versions of APL have a *)QUOTA* command. In APLSV, the first number in the reply is the number of workspaces allowed and the fourth number is the number of workspaces actually used. (The other parts of the reply will be explained later.) In VS APL, the amount of library space is based on the number of bytes actually stored rather than the number of workspaces. The first line of the reply tells the total number of bytes permitted in your private library and the number of bytes already used.

Dropping a saved workspace

If X and Y were really some big functions or tables of data and we wanted desperately to save them, then our question is: which of the three workspaces in our library can we afford to sacrifice? Again, look at the list:

```
    )LIB
FIRST
SECOND
THIRD
```

Assuming we don't need $THIRD$, let's try to save X and Y, which are still in the active workspace, in $THIRD$:

```
    )SAVE THIRD
NOT SAVED, THIS WS IS CLEAR WS
```

We are prevented from saving it in $THIRD$ because we already stored a workspace named $THIRD$. Again APL keeps you from inadvertently destroying a saved workspace by replacing it with another workspace with the same name.

As we'll soon see, there is a way to include X and Y in $THIRD$ without destroying what is already there. But for now, suppose we really wanted to get rid of $THIRD$. The command

```
    )DROP THIRD
14.12.47 02/26/83
```

does this, the response giving the time and day when the workspace was dropped. $THIRD$ is now gone, as shown by

```
    )LIB
FIRST
SECOND
```

ACTIVE WS
CLEAR WS
X
Y

PRIVATE LIBRARY		
FIRST	SECOND	
HYP PI		
TOSS V	SQRT	

We have no functions in the active workspace, but it still contains the two variables X and Y:

```
    )FNS
    )VARS
X       Y
```

This isn't a surprise, since we haven't done anything to the active workspace yet. Now that there is room available, let's save these variables in a workspace called $XYDATA$.

```
    )SAVE XYDATA
14.12.48 02/26/83
    )LIB
FIRST
SECOND
XYDATA
```

ACTIVE WS
XYDATA
X
Y

PRIVATE LIBRARY		
FIRST	SECOND	XYDATA
HYP PI		X
TOSS V	SQRT	Y

Altering a saved workspace

What if we wanted to merge the variables X and Y into $FIRST$? Here is what happens when we try this:

```
    )SAVE FIRST
NOT SAVED, THIS WS IS XYDATA
```

What this means is that the contents of our active workspace have already been saved with the name $XYDATA$ and therefore can't be saved also with the name $FIRST$. To save the material in the active workspace into $FIRST$, we would have to drop $FIRST$ and then save the active workspace with the name $FIRST$. Later we'll see how the $COPY$ command can be used to merge two workspaces.

Another way to change the status of a saved workspace is illustrated by the following sequence:

```
      )LOAD FIRST
SAVED  14.12.04 02/26/83
```

ACTIVE WS			PRIVATE LIBRARY		
FIRST			FIRST	SECOND	XYDATA
HYP	PI		HYP	PI		X
TOSS	V		TOSS	V	SQRT	Y

Let's now define the function $SIGN$:

```
      ∇R←SIGN X
[1]   R←(X>0)-X<0∇
      )FNS
HYP      SIGN      TOSS
```

ACTIVE WS			PRIVATE LIBRARY		
FIRST			FIRST	SECOND	XYDATA
HYP	PI		HYP	PI		X
SIGN	V		TOSS	V	SQRT	Y
TOSS						

Here is what happens when we try to save this active workspace into $SECOND$:

```
      )SAVE SECOND
NOT SAVED, THIS WS IS FIRST
```

We are again prevented from doing so because the active workspace contains an image of $FIRST$, not $SECOND$. However, we can save into $FIRST$. Since the active workspace has the name $FIRST$ already associated with it, when we now save, it isn't necessary to repeat the name $FIRST$ (though it wouldn't hurt matters any to use it):

```
      )SAVE
14.13.00 02/26/83 FIRST
```

ACTIVE WS			PRIVATE LIBRARY		
FIRST			FIRST	SECOND	XYDATA
HYP	PI		HYP	PI		X
SIGN	V		SIGN	V	SQRT	Y
TOSS			TOSS			

The response is the time of the saving and the name of the saved workspace.

$FIRST$ is now updated. This can be shown by clearing and reloading. Notice that the time and day reported by the $LOAD$ are those associated with the most recent $SAVE$.

```
      )CLEAR
CLEAR WS
      )FNS
      )LOAD FIRST
SAVED  14.13.00 02/26/83
      )FNS
HYP      SIGN      TOSS
```

The CONTINUE workspace

On time sharing systems each user has provision for a special workspace named *CONTINUE*. Should you lose your telephone connection with the APL system before signing off, everything in your active workspace would be available automatically to you when you sign back on. This is because the system places an image of your active workspace into a workspace named *CONTINUE*, and reloads it at the next sign-on, as indicated by the response *SAVED...* following the system identification message.

CONTINUE is really an extra workspace that isn't part of the regular user allotment, and it can be used for emergencies if the other workspaces aren't available. However, you have to be very careful with it. Usually, whenever there is a failure in the system or the telephone lines, the contents of *CONTINUE* are replaced by whatever is in the active workspace. So if you must, you can save work into *CONTINUE*, since it is always available to you. But it isn't a wise move for long-term storage because of the danger posed by the possible involuntary replacement of its contents.

Following our example, let's define a vector *X* in the active workspace:

X←2 3 7 4 2

ACTIVE WS		PRIVATE LIBRARY			
FIRST		*FIRST*		*SECOND*	*XYDATA*
HYP	*PI*	*HYP*	*PI*		*X*
SIGN	*V*	*SIGN*	*V*	*SQRT*	*Y*
TOSS	*X*	*TOSS*			

If you were to lose your connection with the computer at this point, an image of your active workspace would be automatically placed in *CONTINUE*. And of course your active workspace doesn't exist when you're not signed on. The next time you sign on, rather than starting with a clear workspace, the *CONTINUE* workspace is automatically loaded for you.

ACTIVE WS		PRIVATE LIBRARY						
CONTINUE		*FIRST*		*SECOND*	*XYDATA*		*CONTINUE*	
HYP	*PI*	*HYP*	*PI*		*X*		*HYP*	*PI*
SIGN	*V*	*SIGN*	*V*	*SQRT*	*Y*		*SIGN*	*V*
TOSS	*X*	*TOSS*					*TOSS*	*X*

You can simulate losing your telephone connection with the *)CONTINUE* command. It places an image of your active workspace in *CONTINUE*, then signs you off the system and severs the phone connection as does *)OFF*. *)CONTINUE HOLD* and *)OFF HOLD* are similar except that they keep the phone line active briefly so someone else can sign on without having to redial.

Locked workspaces

Workspaces which contain material of a sensitive or private nature can be protected with passwords in a manner similar to the user sign-on. A password, whose use is strictly optional, may be included, changed or dropped when saving the workspace. Once included, it must be be used to load it:

```
      )LOAD FIRST
SAVED  14.13.00 02/26/83
        )SAVE FIRST:GW33
   14.13.10 02/26/83
        )LOAD FIRST
WS LOCKED
        )LOAD FIRST:GW33
SAVED  14.13.10 02/26/83
```

A password is removed by resaving the workspace using the colon only, as follows:

```
)SAVE FIRST:
14.13.11 02/26/83
```

In VS APL the password is ignored for your own workspaces.

Using other people's libraries

You know how to use the *LIB* command to get a listing of the saved workspaces in your private library. Someone else may have saved workspaces in his private library with the same names as yours, but there is never any confusion, since each user's workspaces are associated with his own user identification (same as sign-on).

In APLSV, Sharp and APL*PLUS Systems you can load an image of someone else's workspaces into your active workspace like this:

```
)LOAD 78974 INTERACT
SAVED 12.30.59 05/09/80
```

ACTIVE WS		PRIVATE LIBRARY 78974

```
ACTIVE WS                          PRIVATE LIBRARY 78974
┌──────────────────┐           ┌──────────────────────────┐
│ 78974 INTERACT   │       >   │ 78974 INTERACT   │        >
│ ---------------- │  - - - -  │ ---------------- │ - - - -
│    (FNS)         │       <   │    (FNS)         │        <
│    (VARS)        │           │    (VARS)        │
└──────────────────┘           └──────────────────────────┘
```

Here we are loading the workspace named *INTERACT* that is stored in user 78974's private library. Since for reasons of privacy you can't execute)*LIB* on anyone else's library, user 78974 would have had to tell you which workspace names he is using for you to load them.

Such easy promiscuity isn't possible in VS APL. Instead, VS APL has a feature called a *project library* for groups of users who need to freely share workspaces. For authorized users, loading and copying material from their project library takes place in the same way as common libraries (see below).

VS APL workspaces can be moved between people who are not in the same project, but it is a cumbersome procedure. You should consult your system administrator for assistance should you need to do this.

Common libraries

The libraries with numbers between 1 and 999 are intended to hold workspaces of general or common interest, and are called *common libraries*. The contents of any of these can be displayed using the *LIB* command followed by the library number. As discussed on page 91, a partial listing beginning, say, at *AI* can be obtained by:

```
)LIB 1 AI
AIDRILL
CLASS
FILEAID
FILEPRINT
FILES
FORMAT
NEWS
TYPEDRILL
WSFNS
```

```
    ACTIVE WS              COMMON LIBRARY 1
┌──────────────────┐  ┌────────────────────────────┐   ┌──────────────────────────┐
│ 78974 INTERACT   │  │ APLCOURSE │ CLASS      │    │ > │ NEWS      │ TYPEDRILL │  │
│ ---------------- │  │ --------- │ ---------- │    │ < │ --------- │ --------- │  │
│    (FNS)         │  │ DESCRIBE  │ ADD   AUTO │    │   │  (FNS)    │  (FNS)    │  │
│    (VARS)        │  │ EASYDRILL │ AGAIN AVG  │    │   │  (VARS)   │  (VARS)   │  │
│                  │  │ TEACH     │ AREA  ...  │    │   │           │           │  │
└──────────────────┘  └────────────────────────────┘   └──────────────────────────┘
```

The list you get will probably differ from what is shown here because common libraries aren't static; they are different on each APL system, and they change from time to time. Notice that *CLASS* and *AIDRILL*, which have been used before, are in the list. Ordinarily, individual APL users cannot save material into a common library or drop any workspaces from it. If you were to try to save an image of your active workspace into someone else's private library or into a common library such as 1 *CLASS*, you would not be permitted to because yours wasn't the user number that saved it the first time:

```
        )SAVE 1 CLASS                              )SAVE 78974 LITTER
NOT SAVED, THIS WS IS 78974 INTERACT        IMPROPER LIBRARY REFERENCE
```

In some systems certain libraries have been designated as 'load only' for security reasons. Attempts to save, rename or copy workspaces in such a library won't be successful.

Library 1 is a general interest library on most APL systems. Other common libraries may or may not be present on a given system. The library listings may seem meaningless to you, but there are practical ways to find out what is in a strange workspace. As an example, enter

```
     )LOAD 1 CLASS
SAVED  14.45.33 02/20/83
```

The load commands are slightly different for one's own workspaces as compared to those in the common libraries or other private libraries: you must include the library number. Its use is optional for your own library.

Having loaded the workspace 1 *CLASS*, the first thing to do is to get a list of the functions and variables:

```
        )FNS
ADD        AGAIN     AREA      AUTO      AVG       AVG1      AVG2      AVG3      AVG4      AVG5
AVG6       CHANGE    CHARMAT   CLR       CMP       CMPN      CMPX      CMPY      COMPINT   COMPOSE
COS        CP        C2GT99    DEC       DENUMCODE           DESCRIBE            DICE
DUPLICATES           ENT       EVAL      F         FACT      FACTORIALS          FIND      FINDROW
FIX        FUNEDIT   GAME      GEO2      GEO3      GETFN     GO        GRAPH     HEXA      HY
HYP        INPUT     INT       INVOICERUN          LASTVISIT           MEAN      NAMESONLY
NEWPATIENT           NEWVISIT            NUMCODE   OBSERVE   ON        PEREL     RECT      REP
REPF       REPL      REPLENISH           RETIE     RIGHTJUST           ROWNAMES            RUN
SALES      SD        SELECT    SELECT̲    SETUP     SHOWME    SIGN      SLAM      SORT      SPELL
SPLINECALC           SPLINEEVAL          SPRED     SQ        SQRT      STAT      STATEMENT
STATISTICS           SUB       SUBST     SUM       SUSPENDED           TOSS      TOTVISITS
TRANSP     VIG       WSSHOW    D̲SLOPE    E̲SLOPE    X̲SLOPE

        )VARS
A          ADBASE    B         CARDS     CIRCUIT   D         FURN      M         MILEAGE   NUMDATA
P          PREVIOUSTIME        PRODREV   QUOTE     SPL       TAB0      TAB1      TAB2      TAB3
VECT       X         Y         WSID̲      ΔCH
```

Look for names that are suggestive of instructions, like *HOW* or *DESCRIBE*. Executing a few of them will usually give you the information you need, since most professional APL system librarians and managers use these conventions.

```
        DESCRIBE
THE FUNCTIONS IN THIS WORKSPACE ARE USED AS EXAMPLES IN THE TEXT,
APL - AN INTERACTIVE APPROACH (THIRD EDITION),
BY LEONARD GILMAN AND ALLEN J. ROSE (WILEY, 1983).

CONTENTS OF THIS WORKSPACE ARE COPYRIGHT 1983 BY GILMAN AND ROSE.
```

Even if there is no description of the contents of a workspace, you can often gain some information by displaying functions with interesting names. In particular, looking at the header will tell you how many arguments a function has and whether it returns an explicit result.

Some workspaces require so much description that complete documentation in the workspace would take up too much space and take a lot of time to display. For many of these, separate instruction manuals may be available or the documentation may be stored in another workspace.

Workspace descriptions are very important. You'll realize just how important the first time you have to use someone's workspace which is not adequately described. Furthermore, you should always prepare descriptions for your own workspaces. It makes it much less painful to use the functions after they and you have lain fallow for a while.

The workspace identification command

After an hours-long session at the keyboard, with your fingers worn down to the bone, you can't be blamed for having forgotten the name of the workspace you started with. The command)*WSID* (for *workspace identification*) command will tell you:

```
    )WSID
IS 1 CLASS
```

ACTIVE WS
1 *CLASS*
ADD   AUTO
AGAIN AVG
AREA . . .

PRIVATE LIBRARY

FIRST	*SECOND*	*XYDATA*
HYP PI		*X*
SIGN V	*SQRT*	*Y*
TOSS		

CONTINUE
HYP   PI
SIGN V
TOSS X

It gives the name (and library number, if not your own) of the last workspace you loaded or saved. In other words, when you save an image of the active workspace, the workspace identification of the active workspace becomes the name of the saved workspace. Of course, if you just signed on and haven't yet loaded or saved a workspace,)*WSID* replies with *CLEAR WS*.

The)*WSID* command can also be used to change the workspace identification of the active workspace:

```
    )WSID XYDATA
WAS 1 CLASS
```

ACTIVE WS
XYDATA
ADD   AUTO
AGAIN AVG
AREA . . .

PRIVATE LIBRARY

FIRST	*SECOND*	*XYDATA*
HYP PI		*X*
SIGN V	*SQRT*	*Y*
TOSS		

CONTINUE
HYP   PI
SIGN   V
TOSS   X

At this point, you have tricked the active workspace into thinking it came from *XYDATA*. If you now issue a *SAVE*, it will put an image into saved workspace *XYDATA*:

```
    )SAVE
14.13.36 02/26/83 XYDATA
```

ACTIVE WS
XYDATA
ADD   AUTO
AGAIN AVG
AREA . . .

PRIVATE LIBRARY

FIRST	*SECOND*	*XYDATA*
HYP PI		*ADD AUTO*
SIGN V	*SQRT*	*AGAIN AVG*
TOSS		*AREA . . .*

CONTINUE
HYP   PI
SIGN   V
TOSS   X

Without)*WSID*, the shortest way you could have moved the contents of the active workspace to workspace *XYDATA* would have been)*DROP XYDATA* followed by)*SAVE XYDATA*.

Copying a workspace

The command)*COPY* provides the very important ability to gather selected functions and variables from saved workspaces into the active workspace without having to reenter them at the keyboard. Unlike the)*LOAD* command,)*COPY* doesn't replace the contents of the active workspace. It merges the copied variables and functions with those already there.

The following sequence puts the function $SIGN$ (from workspace $FIRST$) in workspace $SECOND$:

```
)LOAD SECOND
SAVED  14.12.21 02/26/83
```

ACTIVE WS   PRIVATE LIBRARY

SECOND
SQRT

FIRST		SECOND	XYDATA		CONTINUE	
HYP	PI	SQRT	ADD	AUTO	HYP	PI
SIGN	V		AGAIN	AVG	SIGN	V
TOSS			AREA	...	TOSS	X

```
)COPY FIRST SIGN
SAVED  14.13.11 02/26/83
```

ACTIVE WS   PRIVATE LIBRARY

SECOND
SIGN
SQRT

FIRST		SECOND	XYDATA		CONTINUE	
HYP	PI	SQRT	ADD	AUTO	HYP	PI
SIGN	V		AGAIN	AVG	SIGN	V
TOSS			AREA	...	TOSS	X

While the active workspace now contains the function $SIGN$, the saved workspace $SECOND$ doesn't until it is saved again:

```
)SAVE
14.13.46 02/26/83 SECOND
```

ACTIVE WS   PRIVATE LIBRARY

SECOND
SIGN
SQRT

FIRST		SECOND	XYDATA		CONTINUE	
HYP	PI	SIGN	ADD	AUTO	HYP	PI
SIGN	V	SQRT	AGAIN	AVG	SIGN	V
TOSS			AREA	...	TOSS	X

Here are some variants of the $)COPY$ command, shown by examples:

```
)COPY 1 CLASS AVG1              )COPY 78974 INTERACT FREQ
SAVED  14.45.33 02/20/83   SAVED  17.20.57 08/28/82
```

For security reasons, you can't copy from a $CONTINUE$ workspace belonging to someone else. When copying from someone else's workspace or a common library workspace, the number (and password, if present) must be included. Several functions and variables may be copied at once. Just separate them with spaces. A $)COPY$ command without a list of objects copies *all* functions and variables in. It is useful when you want to merge the contents of two workspaces, but shouldn't be used as an alternative to loading a workspace. A $COPY$ uses much more computer resources than a $LOAD$ does (like emptying a bag of sugar one spoonful at a time, instead of dumping it all at once).

Protected copying

If you copy a function or variable from some saved workspace, and there already is an object with the same name in the active workspace, then the new object replaces the old one in the active workspace *without warning*. If that's what you intended to do, fine. But with the ability to copy all objects without giving a specific list of which ones to copy, it's almost too easy to clobber something you wanted to keep.

To avoid this problem, use the $)PCOPY$ command. It works exactly like $)COPY$, except that if there is an ambiguity (same name in the active workspace and the copied workspace), the object is $NOT\ COPIED$, preserving the original object in the active workspace.

Groups

Users who often have to copy a collection of objects from a heavily used workspace, their own or in a common library, will be pleased to hear that APL provides a facility to make such copying less burdensome.

This feature lets the owner of the workspace *group* a collection of global objects. Users of that workspace can then copy (or erase from their own version of the workspace) the entire group as though it were a single object.

For example, let's group in workspace *SECOND* the various functions (copied from 1 *CLASS*) that attempt to calculate averages:

```
        )COPY 1 CLASS AVG1 AVG2 AVG3 AVG4 AVG5 AVG6
SAVED   14.45.33 02/20/83
        )GROUP AVGFNS AVG1 AVG2 AVG3 AVG4 AVG5 AVG6
        )SAVE SECOND
   14.14.06 02/26/83
        )CLEAR
CLEAR WS
        )COPY SECOND AVGFNS
SAVED   14.14.06 02/26/83
        )FNS
AVG1    AVG2     AVG3     AVG4     AVG5     AVG6
```

The assigned name of the group immediately follows the group command. It obeys the same rules for naming functions and variables, but cannot be the same as that of any other global object in the workspace. In other words, you use the same rules for naming variables, functions and groups, but any chosen name can be used only for one object at a time.

To display the groups in a workspace use the command)*GRPS*, or)*GRPS MA* to get a partial listing starting at, say, *MA*. The command)*GRP AVGFNS* displays the members of the group *AVGFNS*.

The group *AVGFNS* can be enlarged to incorporate new variables and functions:

```
        DATA←ι0
        )GROUP AVGFNS AVGFNS DATA
        )GRP AVGFNS
AVG1    AVG2     AVG3     AVG4     AVG5     AVG6     DATA
```

It may be *dispersed* (i.e., broken up, but with its members not erased) by entering

```
        )GROUP AVGFNS
        )GRPS
        )FNS
AVG1    AVG2     AVG3     AVG4     AVG5     AVG6
```

All the objects in a group may be erased at one time by executing)*ERASE* on the group name, which is handy when you want to make room in the workspace, or frustrating if you had intended only to disperse the group.

Finally, groups can be made up of other groups. However, in copying, the constituent objects of the copied group aren't copied over—just the group name is.

Groups are convenient for a lot of activities, but they are not as well thought out as most other parts of APL systems, and their behavior may differ widely on different APL systems. For these reason, we suggest you not make heavy use of groups, but rather use the storage management techniques covered later in this book.

As if in recognition of this fact, APL2 doesn't support the group commands. Instead, it provides two facilities called *indirect copy* and *indirect erase*, which use the conventional *COPY* and *ERASE* commands with character matrices each of whose rows contains the name of an object to be copied or erased. The matrix must be enclosed in parentheses in the name list following the command.

```
        )CLEAR
CLEAR WS
        )COPY SECOND AVG1 AVG2 AVG3 AVG4 AVG5 AVG6
SAVED   14.14.06 02/26/83 (GMT-5)
```

```
      ANAMES←7 6ρ'AVG1   AVG2   AVG3   AVG4   AVG5   AVG6   ANAMES'
      )SAVE APL2DEMO
 14.20.55  2/28/83 (GMT-5)
      )ERASE (ANAMES)
      )FNS
      )COPY APL2DEMO (ANAMES)
·SAVED  14.20.55 02/28/83 (GMT-5)
      )FNS
AVG1     AVG2     AVG3     AVG4     AVG5     AVG6
      )VARS
ANAMES
      )ERASE (ANAMES)
      )FNS
      )VARS
```

The name of the matrix itself can be included as one of its own rows, so that it can be erased at the same time.

System functions that match system commands

On most APL systems, system commands cannot be included inside a function, but in many cases *system functions* are provided which achieve the desired effect. For example, to copy the variable $TAB3$ from 1 *CLASS* on the APL*PLUS System, use $\Box COPY$ '1 *CLASS* $TAB3$' and to erase $TAB3$ from the active workspace use $\Box EX$ '$TAB3$'. Most of the system functions return explicit results (sometimes coded) that are equivalent to the corresponding replies or error messages from the system commands. Those that most directly match the system commands treated in this chapter are in the table below. We'll deal with system functions in depth later; for now just be aware that they exist.

A summary of the effects of system commands on workspaces

To avoid unpleasant surprises such as having used)*DROP* where you meant)*ERASE*, learn how each system command affects your stored and active workspaces. The equivalent system functions listed below aren't all available in every APL system.

| SYSTEM COMMAND | CHANGES | | | INFORMATION ONLY | EQUIVALENT SYSTEM FUNCTION |
	ACTIVE WS NAME	ACTIVE WS CONTENTS	LIBRARY CONTENTS		
CLEAR	X	X			
CONTINUE	X		X		
COPY		X			$\Box COPY$ 'WS OBJ'
DROP			X		
ERASE		X			$\Box EX$ 'OBJ'
FNS				X	$\Box NL$ 3
GROUP		X			
GRP				X	
GRPS				X	
LIB				X	$\Box LIB$
LOAD	X	X			$\Box LOAD$
OFF	X	X			
OFF HOLD	X	X			
PCOPY		X			$\Box PCOPY$ 'WS OBJ'
SAVE			X		
SAVE NAME	X		X		
VARS				X	$\Box NL$ 2
WSID				X	$\Box WSID$
WSID NAME	X				
WSLIB				X	$\Box WSLIB$

Some thoughts about workspace storage

We can't end this chapter without a few words about the limitations imposed on the APL user who insists on storing information only in workspaces. It should be apparent by this time that workspaces are somewhat constrained in what they can hold (although less so in VS APL than in other versions). As you become more knowledgeable you will learn other ways to 'stretch' the workspace by using space-saving algorithms, the APL equivalent of cars that get more miles to a tank of gasoline. But all they can accomplish for you is to let you go a bit farther with what you have.

This doesn't help you when you have a database which may be, say, ten times as large as the workspace you want to put it in. Something more is needed. This something is the notion of *files*, which are collections of information stored in a place other than the workspace. To manipulate such data in APL it has to be brought into the active workspace in appropriate sized chunks, although some systems have facilities for doing certain tasks in a non-APL environment like CMS. More about files later in the book.

PROBLEMS

1. Carry out the following instructions and APL system commands in the order given.

    Define a few arbitrary functions and variables. Then enter

)SAVE WORK1
)CLEAR
    and repeat these instructions several times until your workspace quota is used up. Use workspaces named *WORK*2, *WORK*3, etc.

)LIB

    How many workspaces can you save in your APL system?

)DROP WORK1
)LIB
)LOAD WORK3
)FNS
)VARS

    Define additional functions and variables.

)SAVE WORK2

    Why wasn't the material saved?

)WSID WORK2
)SAVE
)CLEAR
)LOAD WORK2
)FNS
)VARS

    Has *WORK*2 been superseded?

    Delete several functions and variables from *WORK*2.

)ERASE FN1 FN2 V1 V2 ...
)SAVE
)LIB
)FNS
)VARS

2. Follow the instructions given and carry out the indicated system commands:

```
)LIB 1
)LOAD 1 ADVANCEDEX
```

(If your system does not have workspace 1 *ADVANCEDEX*, load any other workspace from common library 1.)

```
)FNS
)VARS
```

If there is a function or variable named *DESCRIBE* or *HOW*, execute it.

```
)WSID
```

Define a function *RECT* which gives only the area of a rectangle of length L by W. Display it after executing.

```
)COPY 1 CLASS RECT
```

Was your own defined function *RECT* unchanged?

```
)ERASE RECT
```

Redefine *RECT* as above to give only the area of a rectangle.

```
)PCOPY 1 CLASS RECT
```

Does this command behave the same as)*COPY*?

```
)SAVE JONES
```

If the workspace was not saved, drop one of those in your library and then save it. Then change the name of your active workspace to *SMITH*.

```
)WSID SMITH
)SAVE
)CLEAR
)LOAD 1 ADVANCEDEX (or whichever LIB 1 workspace you used before)
)SAVE 1 ADVANCEDEX
```

Why couldn't *ADVANCEDEX* be saved?

```
)CONTINUE HOLD
```

Now sign on again.

```
)LIB
)FNS
)VARS
```

3. You have saved your work in a workspace called *GOOD* and have just developed a function *OK* in your active workspace. Write out a sequence of commands which will get *OK* into *GOOD* without carrying with it any unwanted 'trash' which may be in the active workspace.

4. Compose a group $\underline{A}$ consisting of the variables *TAB*0, *TAB*1, *TAB*2, *TAB*3 and a group $\underline{B}$ consisting of functions *AVG*1, *AVG*2, *AVG*3, *AVG*4, *AVG*5 of workspace 1 *CLASS*. Enlarge group $\underline{A}$ by including the variable *PI*. List the groups, list the members of group $\underline{A}$, and then disperse group $\underline{A}$.

Chapter 12: Mixed functions

Thus far we have worked mainly with primitive scalar dyadic and monadic functions. One of their characteristics is that the shape of the result is the same as the shape of the argument. For example, if the arguments are vectors, so is the result. If the arguments are scalars, then the result is a scalar. In this and subsequent chapters, functions will be introduced for which the result has the *data type* (i.e., character or numeric) of the right argument, but the contents and shape depend on the arguments in some way. These are appropriately called *mixed* functions. Both dyadic and monadic ρ, introduced in Chapter 2, are examples of mixed functions.

Interval

Regular sequences of numbers like 1980 1981 1982 1983 or .05 .06 .07 .08 .09 .10 are frequently used in business. You may already have discovered that you could generate the sequence 1 2 3 4 5 by expressions like +\5ρ1 and probably wondered why it takes so much effort to get such a simple result.

Rest assured that the developers of APL knew you would often need this type of result, and they provided a monadic mixed function to do it for you. It is called the *interval function* or *interval generator* or *count*, and it employs the ι symbol (shift *I*, also referred to as *iota*).

We can see what it does by entering a few examples,

```
      ι5                ι6                  ι10                           ι2
1 2 3 4 5        1 2 3 4 5 6       1 2 3 4 5 6 7 8 9 10            1 2
```

but suppose we want the sequence 1980 1981 1982 1983. It's pretty easy. Just cook up the sequence 1 2 3 4 and add 1979 to it:

```
      1979+ι4
1980 1981 1982 1983
```

Similarly, to get the sequence .05 .06 .07 .08 .09 .10 enter

```
      .04+.01×ι6
0.05 0.06 0.07 0.08 0.09 0.1
```

Not quite so intuitive, but it surely works. Very often a need for a sequence will be expressed in terms of 'I want numbers starting at .05 up to .1 in steps of .01'. The function *STEP* does this for us:

```
       ∇Z←L STEP R;POINTS;RANGE
[1]    ⍝L IS START,END; R IS INCREMENT
[2]    ⍝NO ERROR CHECKING   AJ ROSE SEPT 1982
[3]    RANGE←--/L ⍝ HIGH-LOW
[4]    POINTS←⌊RANGE÷R ⍝ INCLUDE BOTH ENDS
[5]    Z←0,(×POINTS)×ι|POINTS ⍝ INCLUDE BOTH END POINTS
[6]    Z←R×Z ⍝ SCALE RESULT
[7]    Z←(1ρL)+Z ⍝ DISPLACEMENT
[8]    ⍝ ON ONE LINE: Z←(1ρL)+R×0,ι⌊(--/L)÷R
[9]    ∇

       .05 .1 STEP .01
0.05 0.06 0.07 0.08 0.09 0.1

       1980 1983 STEP 1
1980 1981 1982 1983
```

The ability to deal with sequences makes it easier to explore functions with operation tables—you don't have to do the counting.

```
        (ι5)∘.≤ι5          (1.075 1.15 STEP .025)∘.*10 12 STEP 1
1 1 1 1 1              2.061031562    2.215608929    2.381779599
0 1 1 1 1              2.59374246     2.853116706    3.138428377
0 0 1 1 1              3.247321025    3.653236154    4.109890673
0 0 0 1 1              4.045557736    4.652391396    5.350250105
0 0 0 0 1
```

You may recognize the second result above as compound interest at 7.5%, 10%, 12.5% and 15% over 10, 11 and 12 periods.

The remainder of this section is for those readers who are of a mathematical bent. We'll meet the rest of you at the next section.

Remember the card matching algorithm (page 51),

$$P1 = \frac{1}{0!} - \frac{1}{1!} + \frac{1}{2!} - \frac{1}{3!} + \cdots - \cdots + \frac{1}{52!}$$

With interval we can simplify our execution of the function *MATCH*:

```
        ∇P1←MATCH N              MATCH 5              MATCH 20
[1]     P1←-/÷!ιN ∇           0.6333333333         0.6321205588
                                 MATCH 10             MATCH 52
                              0.6321205357         0.6321205588
```

Its evaluation for a varying number of terms indicates that this probability estimate converges very rapidly as the number of terms increases.

Index set

This APL2 function is a close cousin of the interval function. Its symbol is the *squad* (skinny quad), *R*▯, formed by overstriking the left and right brackets. Applied monadically to a scalar or vector of nonnegative integers, it produces all permutations of the intervals of the argument:

```
        R▯4                  R▯2 3
1 2 3 4                  1 1
                         1 2
                         1 3
        R▯1 2
1 1                      2 1
1 2                      2 2
                         2 3
```

Empty vectors and vectors of length one

These concepts, which are not intuitively apparent to most of us, are important to master. We have previously covered certain topics which we suggested most students might want to skip; however, *everyone* needs to understand empty vectors and vectors of length one.

Look at the following examples:

```
        ι3              ι2              ι1              ι0
1 2 3            1 2             1
```

ιN obviously generates a *vector* of N elements, starting with 1. That doesn't bother you as long as N is 2 or greater, but what about ι1? Is it a vector with one element, or is it the same as the scalar 1?

```
        1
1
```

They look the same, but they are not the same. The expression 1 (or 1−0, or ×72, etc.) results in a scalar. The result of ι1 is a vector, even though it is only a single element. In mathematics there is a term which is associated with the distinction—*rank*, which we introduced earlier and about which we will have more to say shortly.

We have seen the results of ι5, ι4, ι3, ι2 and ι1. Now we're ready to examine ι0. This is a vector of *no* elements. The system in its response is trying to display a vector of length 0, but there just aren't any elements to display! The important thing to remember is that ι*N* always returns a vector, and the length of that vector is *N*.

Of what use is a vector of length 0? A good question. One might ask, 'What use is an empty warehouse?' The empty warehouse is a place in which goods can be stored. An empty vector (you should pardon the comparison) is somewhat analogous. Think about this: if you needed to generate vectors of varying length and you were looking for a starting place to store elements as they were accumulated, what better place to start with than a vector of no elements, an empty 'warehouse,' the vector ι0? Although you won't really appreciate its many uses until you begin to get more deeply involved in function definition in APL, some examples of empty vectors will be introduced in this and subsequent chapters to help motivate you.

Shape

In Chapter 5 the shape function ρ was introduced and used to give information about the sizes of vectors, matrices and other arrays. It was stated that ρ could be applied to *any* array. Let's explore this by using some samples that are in 1 *CLASS*. Bring copies of these arrays, called *TAB*0, *TAB*1, *TAB*2 and *TAB*3 into your active workspace with the *COPY* command:

```
    )COPY 1 CLASS TAB0 TAB1 TAB2 TAB3
SAVED  14.45.33 02/20/83
```

Display *TAB*0:

```
    TAB0                ρTAB0
4.1
```

It's just the scalar number 4.1 and has *no* dimensions. Hence, ρ*TAB*0 results in a vector with *no* elements. Unlike vectors and matrices, scalars don't 'extend out' in any direction. In this sense scalars are like idealized geometric points, which are also considered to be dimensionless.

Let's now investigate *TAB*1:

```
    TAB1                                      ρTAB1
1.414213562 1.732050808 2 2.236067977        4
```

*TAB*1 is obviously a vector of four elements. ρ*TAB*1 confirms that *TAB*1 has only one dimension, with four elements along that dimension.

Now display *TAB*2:

```
    TAB2            ρTAB2
3   1   7        4 3
7  10   4
6   9   1
1   6   7
```

Here we have a two-dimensional array (matrix), with four elements along one dimension (number of rows) and three elements along the other (number of columns).

Finally, display $TAB3$:

```
        TAB3                  ρTAB3
111 112 113          2  4  3
121 122 123
131 132 133
141 142 143

211 212 213
221 222 223
231 232 233
241 242 243
```

This may look peculiar, but remember that we are restricted to two-dimensional paper to depict a three-dimensional array. The result of $\rho TAB3$ indicates that we do indeed have a three-dimensional array, two elements deep (number of planes), four elements down (number of rows), and three elements across (number of columns).

If you are wondering how $TAB3$ was constructed, here's how it was done. Try both the following algorithms which use the outer product twice:

```
    100 200∘.+10 20 30 40 ∘.+ι3          (100×ι2)∘.+(10×ι4)∘.+ι3
111 112 113                          111 112 113
121 122 123                          121 122 123
131 132 133                          131 132 133
141 142 143                          141 142 143

211 212 213                          211 212 213
221 222 223                          221 222 223
231 232 233                          231 232 233
241 242 243                          241 242 243
```

Rank

Rank was mentioned as a way to talk about the number of dimensions of an array. Let's see how this is handled in APL. First consider

```
    ρρTAB0
0
```

An unexpected response? Not really, when you think about it. Let's see if we can construct a plausible explanation. First, we'll line up the responses from $\rho TAB0$, $\rho TAB1$, $\rho TAB2$ and $\rho TAB3$:

```
        ρTAB3                ρρTAB3
2  4  3                  3

        ρTAB2                ρρTAB2
4  3                    2

        ρTAB1                ρρTAB1
4                      1

        ρTAB0                ρρTAB0
                       0
```

What do you see? The shape of an array of N dimensions is itself a vector of N elements. So $\rho TAB0$ must really be a vector with no elements (same as $\iota 0$), and $\rho\rho TAB0$ is equivalent to $\rho\iota 0$.

Thus, $\rho\rho$ of any array gives the number of dimensions of the array. We have already attached the name *rank* to this concept. A scalar has rank 0; a vector, rank 1; and a matrix, rank 2. Arrays of rank 3 and higher don't have generally accepted names.

At last we are ready to tell the difference between 1 and $\iota 1$. This distinction was left unanswered when it was introduced on page 104. They have different shapes and different ranks:

```
      1              ρ1              ρρ1
1                               0
     ι1              ρι1             ρρι1
1               1               1
```

In spite of the identical appearance of the results of 1 and ι 1 on the screen or paper, 1 and ι 1 are viewed as different in the APL system. Your failure to observe the difference can lead to the downfall and subsequent painful debugging of otherwise well-constructed programs.

Catenate

You have probably sensed a need to have a way to stuff more elements into a vector. This would certainly be desirable if the vector represented, say, the individual charges run up over a period of time by a customer in a department store. Our only recourse thus far has been to reassign the vector by reentering it with both old and new values—an unsatisfactory method.

APL does have a function which allows us to enlarge an array. To illustrate how it can be done, let's design a simplistic calculator capable of summing a list of numbers. Here is its description:

key	purpose or action
CLR	clears accumulator
ENT	allows entry of values and prints number of values accumulated since last entry
SUM	prints sum of accumulated numbers

A simulation of this calculator is provided in 1 *CLASS*. Let's use it first and then see how it's constructed.

```
)LOAD 1 CLASS
SAVED  14.45.33 02/20/83
```

First, we clear the 'memory':

```
CLR
```

Next, enter *ENT* followed by some data as shown:

```
ENT 5 3 1
3
```

The system responds with a 3, indicating that three values have been entered. Make another entry:

```
ENT 5 6
5
```

Entering *SUM* gives the sum of the values accumulated:

```
SUM
20
```

We can continue to enter values and get the sum:

```
ENT 2
6
SUM
22
```

Now clear the memory again and make a new entry:

```
CLR
SUM
0
ENT 1 2 3
3
SUM
6
```

What do the functions look like that comprise this simple calculator?

```
      ∇CLR[□]∇              ∇ENT[□]∇                ∇SUM[□]∇
    ∇ CLR              ∇ ENT X                  ∇ SUM
[1]   VECT←ι0      [1]   ρVECT←VECT,X       [1]   +/VECT
    ∇                  ∇                      ∇
```

CLR is niladic and doesn't return an explicit result. Reasonable enough, since its purpose is only to set the accumulator $VECT$ to $\iota 0$ each time it is executed. $VECT$ is a global variable. It is initialized as an empty vector, a good place to start.

ENT takes the elements in its argument X and joins them onto the end of $VECT$. This result is stored in $VECT$ and the number of elements resulting is displayed. In effect, we update $VECT$ and display information about its elements at the same time. A new dyadic function is introduced in ENT. It is called *catenate*, the symbol for which is the comma. Its job is to join or chain together its two arguments.

All the third function SUM does is calculate and display the sum of the values that have been accumulated in $VECT$.

The catenate function has some noteworthy characteristics. For example, if we make the assignments

        $J \leftarrow \iota 3$ $K \leftarrow 9\ 8\ 7\ 6$

and catenate J and K, putting the result in Y, then there are seven elements in Y:

        $Y \leftarrow J,K$ Y ρY
                        1 2 3 9 8 7 6   7

Two vectors can be catenated. What about a scalar? Can it be catenated to a vector? Consider

        $J,6$
1 2 3 6

For the purpose of catenation, scalars are regarded as vectors of length 1. Therefore, catenation of two scalars makes a vector:

        $X \leftarrow 3,5$ X ρX
                        3 5   2

Catenating $\iota 0$ to a vector gives the same vector, as we would expect:

        $J,\iota 0$ $(\iota 0),J$
1 2 3   1 2 3

What about catenating a vector of length 0 to a scalar?

        $R \leftarrow 6$ $T \leftarrow R,\iota 0$
        R T
6   6
        ρR ρT
                        1   1
        $\rho \rho R$ $\rho \rho T$
0   1

T is a vector of one element, while R is a scalar. Anytime you catenate vectors or scalars in any combination, the result is always a vector.

When applied to matrices, catenation allows us to increase the number of rows or columns. This extension of the function is often needed to merge data from several sources, or to tack on a row or column of totals to some table. It will be discussed in Chapter 19.

Ravel

If we're not careful, the distinction between vectors and scalars can cause difficulties. Sometimes it's advantageous to have a vector of length one instead of a scalar. As an example consider AVG in $1\ CLASS$, which you should still have in your active workspace. When used on a vector argument, it works as expected, but see what it does with a scalar argument:

        $AVG\ 2\ 3\ 4$ $AVG\ 4$
3

Something must be wrong. Check to see what ρ*AVG* 4 is:

```
      ρAVG 4
0
```

This means that *AVG* 4 must result in a vector of length 0. Why should this be? Let's display the function:

```
      ∇AVG[□]∇
    ∇ R←AVG X
[1]   R←(+/X)÷ρX
    ∇
```

Working from right to left on line 1, if *X* is a scalar, then ρ*X* is an empty vector. But the algorithm calls for dividing +/*X* (a scalar) by ρ*X* (in this case a vector of length 0). Dividing a scalar by a vector gives a result which has the same shape as the vector argument. Need we say more?

Interesting though all this may be, it doesn't solve our problem. Our function, to be consistent, should return a result of 4 in this case. We have to make the argument *X* a vector if it isn't one already. The monadic function *ravel* is used for this. It uses the same symbol, the comma, as the dyadic function catenate. Let's insert a comma between ρ and *X* in *AVG*:

```
      ∇AVG[1□16]
[1]   R←(+/X)÷ρX
            1
[1]   R←(+/X)÷ρ,X∇
```

Now executing *AVG* 4, we get the desired result:

```
      AVG 4

    4
4
```

Ravel has some interesting uses. *TAB*2 is a good example. Notice that the last dimension is raveled first, and that there are as many elements in the result as in the original array:

```
      TAB2              ρTAB2              ,TAB2
  3   1   7          4 3          3 1 7 7 10 4 6 9 1 1 6 7
  7  10   4
  6   9   1              ×/ρTAB2            ρ,TAB2
  1   6   7          12                 12
```

Raveling proceeds similarly on a three-dimensional array like *TAB*3. The last dimension is again raveled first. No matter what the rank of the array with which we start, ravel converts the array to a vector.

```
      TAB3
  111 112 113
  121 122 123
  131 132 133
  141 142 143

  211 212 213
  221 222 223
  231 232 233
  241 242 243
      ,TAB3
111 112 113 121 122 123 131 132 133 141 142 143 211 212 213 221 222 223 231 232
    233 241 242 243
```

In APL2 ravel has been extended to allow raveling along an existing axis, or the creation of a new one:

```
      R←2 3ρι6               ,[1 2]R
      R                  1 2 3 4 5 6
  1 2 3                      ,[2 3]2 3 4ρι24
  4 5 6                   1  2  3  4  5  6  7  8  9 10 11 12
      ,[1]R                13 14 15 16 17 18 19 20 21 22 23 24
  1 4                          ,[ι0]5 6
  2 5                       5
  3 6                       6
```

```
        ,[1.5]1 2                    ,[2.2]2 2ρι4
1                               1
2                               2
        ,[.2]1 2
1 2                             3
                                4
```

The result, for A a scalar or vector of integer axes (only continuous and increasing order allowed) combines those axes and has rank $1+(\rho\rho R)-\rho$, A where R is the argument and A the axis specifiers. For fractional axis specifiers the result has in the appropriate position in its shape a new axis and has rank $1+\rho\rho R$. (See page 183 for a discussion of axis specifiers.)

Similar extensions to catenate are found in other APL systems, and are described in Chapter 19.

Reshape

This function was introduced in Chapter 2. By way of review, assign

```
    U←4  3 5 7 8 9
```

Suppose we want to build a two-dimensional table with the first row 4 3 5 and the second row 7 8 9. The reshape function rearranges the elements in the right argument to have the shape of the left argument:

```
        2 3ρU
4  3  5
7  8  9
```

Here is an example where the left argument contains a single element:

```
        3ρU
4  3  5
```

The number of elements in the left argument gives the rank of the resulting array. Here are some more examples:

```
        5ρ3                 5ρ0 1                1 5ρ0 1              5 1ρ0 1
3  3  3  3  3        0  1  0  1  0        0  1  0  1  0          0
                                                                1
                                                                0
                                                                1
                                                                0
```

So far our right arguments have been vectors or scalars. What happens when the right argument of ρ is a matrix?

```
    A←2 3ρ2 3 4 5 6 7              5ρA                  3 4ρA
    A                    2  3  4  5  6          2  3  4  5
2  3  4                                         6  7  2  3
5  6  7                                         4  5  6  7
```

From this we can conclude that whatever the shape of the right argument for ρ, for reshaping purposes it is in effect , A. This is perfectly reasonable, since raveling an array of rank 2 or more before reshaping is just what most people would do if they had to do it by hand.

Finally, what if the right argument contains no elements, i.e., is an empty vector?

```
        3ρι0
LENGTH ERROR
        3ρι0
        ^
```

There are no elements on the right with which to carry out the desired reshaping, so the instruction can't be executed. But now try these two examples:

```
    0ρι0                        (ι0)ρι0
                       LENGTH  ERROR
                            (ι0)ρι0
                            ^
```

Can you explain the results?

PROBLEMS

1. DRILL Assign $A \leftarrow 0 \ 8 \ {}^-3 \ 4 \ 6 \ 10$, $M \leftarrow 2 \ 4 \rho \iota 8$ and $V \leftarrow 3 \ 3 \rho \iota 9$ and execute

ρA	ρM	${}^-7 \times \iota 1$	$\div \iota 5$
$\rho \rho A$	$({}^-2) \ 1 \ 2$	$\iota \lceil /A$	$\iota 28 \div 3 + 1$
$\rho \rho \rho A$	$\iota 10$	${}^-2, \ 1 \ 2$	$\rho \rho V$
$A \lceil 0.8 \times \iota 6$	$(\iota 5) + 3$	$+/\iota 15$	V, M

2. What is the difference in meaning of the two expressions $\rho A = 6$ and $6 = \rho A$?

3. Load 1 *CLASS* and execute each of the following:

   $\times / \rho TAB0$ $\qquad$ $\times / \rho TAB1$ $\qquad$ $\times / \rho TAB2$ $\qquad$ $\times / \rho TAB3$

   What information is gained from these instructions?

4. For the vector A (problem 1) execute $\iota \rho A$ and $\rho \iota \rho A$. What meaning can be assigned to each of these expressions?

5. Write one-line monadic functions returning an explicit result to give: **A** the sum of the square roots of the first N positive integers; **B** the square root of the sum of the first N positive integers; **C** the geometric mean of the first N positive integers (the Nth root of the product of the N numbers)

6. Construct each of the following sequences using ι:

$1 \ 3 \ 5 \ 7 \ 9 \ 11 \ 13 \ 15$	${}^-250 \ {}^-150 \ {}^-50 \ 50 \ 150 \ 250$
${}^-7 \ {}^-2 \ 3 \ 8 \ 13$	$5 \ 4 \ 3 \ 2 \ 1$
$0 \ 0.3 \ 0.6 \ 0.9 \ 1.2 \ 1.5$	$1 \ 0 \ 1 \ 0 \ 1 \ 0$

7. Enter $\iota 3 \ast \iota 3$. Account for the error message.

8. Fill in the blanks in the following expressions to generate 50 1's:

   _____50 $\qquad$ 50_____ $\qquad$ _____50_____50

9. Rewrite each of the following statements without parentheses:

   ${}^-1 + (-/(\iota 5)) \times 2$ $\qquad$ $+/(\iota 5) - 1$ $\qquad$ $+/((\iota 5) + 1) = 5$ $\qquad$ $+/0 = (\iota 5) = 6$

10. Write functions that would approximate each of the following series to N terms:

    A $\qquad$ $1 - \dfrac{1}{2} + \dfrac{1}{3} - \dfrac{1}{4} + \cdots$

    B $\qquad$ $\dfrac{1}{0!} + \dfrac{x^1}{1!} + \dfrac{x^2}{2!} + \cdots$

11. Write an APL expression that yields 1 if the array A is a scalar, 0 otherwise.

12. What is the difference between $\rho A, \rho B$ and $(\rho A), \rho B$ for two vectors A and B?

13. Assume you have defined a dyadic function E. How could you tell the difference between it and, say, $6E8$ in scaled notation?

14. Make the scalar S a vector without using the ravel function.

15. Construct a table of sines of angles from 0 to $O \div 2$ radians in steps of $O \div 20$ radians.

16. Show how to find the sum of the alternate elements in ιN, beginning with the second.

17. How do you set up an 'empty' matrix with 5 columns?

18. Express each of the following numbers in APL and determine which is the smallest:

$$\frac{321,400}{\sqrt{27.8}} - \frac{17}{.00065} \qquad \log_5 \frac{1}{\sqrt[4]{.0000068}} \qquad \sqrt[9]{(32,200)^2}$$

19. Find the sum of the first 30 terms in the series $\quad 1 - \frac{1}{2} + \frac{1}{4} - \frac{1}{6} + \frac{1}{8} - \cdots + \cdots$

20. Create an $N \times N$ matrix with an arbitrary vector of elements V along the major diagonal and 0's elsewhere.

21. Use the outer product to form the 4 4 matrix

```
1 1 1 1
2 2 2 2
3 3 3 3
4 4 4 4
```

22. You owe a kind-hearted loan shark $10,000 and are required to pay as interest 1/2 of this sum the first year. Because of the lender's generosity, the second year you pay only 1/2 of the first year's repayment, and during the third year, only 1/2 of the second year's payment, etc. in perpetuity. There being no discount for prepayment, how much would you have to repay to wipe out the debt?

23. Write expressions to generate logical vectors of length L and **A** R leading ones **B** R trailing ones.

Chapter 13: Character data

All of the functions, problems and solutions you've learned so far have been fundamentally quantitative or numerical in nature. However, computers are used as much for nonnumerical work as for numerical work. Just consider all the applications of word processing, information retrieval, electronic mail, language translation and 'talkative' computer games that abound. And don't forget that most quantitative applications (such as business reports) combine text and data to provide meaningful headings and descriptions for those who receive the reports.

Simple titles for results

In workspace 1 *CLASS* the function *RECT* calculates and displays the length of the perimeter, the length of the diagonal and the area of a rectangle. Load 1 *CLASS*, try *RECT* for a rectangle with sides 3 and 4, and then display the function:

```
      )LOAD 1 CLASS                    ∇RECT[☐]∇
SAVED  14.45.33 02/20/83           ∇  L RECT H
      3 RECT 4                  [1]    2×L+H
14                              [2]    L HYP H
5                               [3]    L×H
12                                 ∇
```

The three lines of output are the perimeter, diagonal and area (in that order) of the rectangle whose sides are 3 and 4. But we had to look inside the function to see what each of the answers represented. Even if you had used comments, they wouldn't help identify the results when you execute the function.

Now try the function *GEO2*, which is similar to *RECT*:2

```
      3 GEO2 4                         ∇GEO2[☐]∇
PERIMETER IS:                     ∇  L GEO2 H;X
14                              [1]    X←' IS:'
AREA IS:                        [2]    'PERIMETER',X
12                              [3]    2×L+H
DIAGONAL IS:                    [4]    'AREA',X
5                               [5]    L×H
                                [6]    'DIAGONAL',X
                                [7]    L HYP H
                                   ∇
```

Line 1 looks like nothing we've done so far. It introduces a new use for the quote symbol, to enclose characters. As a matter of fact, not only are there obvious alphabetic characters *I* and *S* but also a colon used as a punctuation mark, and even a blank space at the beginning.

APL interprets each of these, including the blanks, as a separate character. But it does more than that. Since in line 2 catenation is used between the set of characters on the left and those on the right (stored in *X*), there is a strong suggestion that such characters are elements of an array, in this case of rank 1. It's a fancy way of calling what is between the quotes a vector. However, since we could conceivably have a table (or matrix) of characters, the rank will depend, as with numerical information, on the shape. *X* here is a vector of length 4.

Continuing down the function, lines 4 and 5 respectively catenate the words '*AREA*' and '*DIAGONAL*' to *X*, which consists of the characters '*IS:*'.

You don't have to be in function definition mode to use characters literally. For instance:

```
      A←'HELLO '
```

Again, notice the space after the `'O'`. Counting the space, it's a vector of length 6:

```
      ρA
6
```

We can do some pretty cute things with character data. If we assign

```
      B←'HOW ARE YOU'
```

then catenation forms the message

```
      A,B
HELLO HOW ARE YOU
```

Now back to more serious business. Suppose we had a family of rectangles we wanted information about:

```
      1 3 5 GEO2 1 4 12
PERIMETER IS:
4 14 34
AREA IS:
1 12 60
DIAGONAL IS:
1.414213562 5 13
```

Our answers are OK, but the grammar is a little peculiar. It would be nice to have identification that matches the output grammatically. Specifically, the labels should be followed by `'ARE'` or `'IS'`, depending on the number of elements in the arguments. Let's now explore the function `GEO3`:

```
      ∇GEO3[□]∇
    ∇ L GEO3 H;X;FLAG
[1]   FLAG←((ρ,L)>1)∨(ρ,H)>1
[2]   X←((4×~FLAG)ρ' IS:'),(6×FLAG)ρ'S ARE:'
[3]   'PERIMETER',X
[4]   2×L+H
[5]   'AREA',X
[6]   L×H
[7]   'DIAGONAL',X
[8]   L HYP H
    ∇
```

```
      1 3 5 GEO3 1 4 12
PERIMETERS ARE:
4 14 34
AREAS ARE:
1 12 60
DIAGONALS ARE:
1.414213562 5 13
      3 GEO3 4
PERIMETER IS:
14
AREA IS:
12
DIAGONAL IS:
5
```

`GEO3` does exactly what we want it to, and changes the alphabetic information to fit the conditions of the problem. The first thing to note is the presence of the two local variables X and $FLAG$. On line 1, if there is more than one element in either L or H, then the variable $FLAG$ is set to 1; otherwise it is 0. If the result of line 1 is 1 (i.e., we ask for information about more than one rectangle), $6×FLAG$ is 6 and $6ρ'S ARE:'$ is simply the characters `'S ARE:'`. At the same time $\sim FLAG$ would be 0 and $4×0$ is 0, so $0ρ' IS:'$ results in an empty vector. Thus, no characters are displayed. When catenated, the effect is just `'S ARE:'`. You should be able to figure out for yourself what happens in this line if $FLAG$ is 0. Line 2 tells the system to pick up `'IS:'` or `'S ARE:'`, depending on the length of the arguments. The rest of the function is like `GEO2`. Finally, some food for thought before leaving this function: why must the arguments L and H in line 1 be raveled?

Mixed output

You may have wondered why in both `GEO2` and `GEO3` the numeric and alphabetic information was placed on separate lines when a more natural format would call for them to be on the same line, as, for example, `'PERIMETERS ARE: 4 14'`.

Unless you are using an APL system that allows mixed arrays (page 257), attempts to catenate characters and numeric values run into trouble:

```
      M1←'GIVE '          M2←' DOLLARS'          COST←15
      M1,COST,M2
DOMAIN ERROR
      M1,COST,M2
      ∧
```

While character data and numeric data can't be catenated directly, numeric data can be converted to character data using the monadic *format* function ⍕, formed by overstriking ⊤ and ∘ (upshift *N* and *J*). What you get is a character vector or character scalar that when displayed looks exactly like the original numeric value.

      ⍕COST   **ρ⍕COST**
15   2

Using ⍕ we can now make more natural looking displays:

      M1,(⍕COST),M2
GIVE 15 *DOLLARS*

Practice makes perfect, so you should now go back and modify *GEO*2 and *GEO*3 to give more attractive displays.

The format function has many other uses than the simple conversion to characters shown here. Chapter 17 will discuss these in more detail.

Assigning character variables

Character data must begin and end with quotes. It's important that when character data is entered, *both* quotes are present. Otherwise you have an open quote, the results of which are system dependent, as described on page 26.

Occasionally you may need to use a word with an apostrophe in it. Since this is the same character as the quote, how can it be handled? For example, look at the following attempted assignment:

      'ISN'T'
SYNTAX ERROR
      'ISN'T'
           ∧

That didn't help at all. Use double quotes to get the apostrophe in:

      W←'ISN''T'
      W
ISN'T

A handy rule to remember when using quotes is that there must be an even number on any line (but comments don't count). Some early APL systems won't give an error message for unmatched quotes, but rather appear to gobble up whatever you enter like some voracious video game monster. The only way to stop it is to enter a matching quote.

Character variables can contain any of the printable characters, including the overstruck ones, that can be entered at the keyboard. Besides these, you can also use certain special effects characters such as *new line*, *linefeed* and *backspace*. They are described on page 238.

Functions that work with characters

What about all the functions we've studied so far? Do they work with characters? Let's try some and see:

      A←'X'   **A+B**   **A<B**
      B←'Y'   *DOMAIN ERROR*   *DOMAIN ERROR*
                             A+B   **A<B**
                              ∧   ∧

These functions make no sense operating on characters because characters aren't orderable. That is, 5.3 is greater than 2.45, but who can say whether the character '*F*' is greater or lesser than the character '***'? Indeed, most of the primitive functions behave similarly. But consider

      A=B   **A≠B**
0   1

Here we are asking the system to compare each element of the left argument A with the corresponding element of B. There is only one element on each side, and they don't match, so we get the responses shown.

A more sophisticated application of = is shown in the following example, which asks how many occurrences of the letter `'E'` there are in a vector:

```
    D←'ENGINEER'              'E'=D                    +/'E'=D
                        1 0 0 0 0 1 1 0           3
```

Another function which works with a character argument is the dyadic ρ, which isn't surprising since all it does is reshape the argument:

```
    ALF←'ABCDEFGHIJKLMNOPQRSTUVWXYZ'
    4 6ρALF
ABCDEF
GHIJKL
MNOPQR
STUVWX
```

We can create all kinds of interesting character arrays this way. Here is another example in which words that will comprise the rows are of varying lengths:

```
    FURN←4 6ρ'DESKS CHAIRSTABLESFILES '
    FURN
DESKS
CHAIRS
TABLES
FILES
```

In such cases you should be extra careful to 'pad' each prospective row with the right number of blanks to ensure a proper display. Otherwise the consequences can be ludicrous:

```
    4 6ρ'DESKSCHAIRSTABLESFILES'
DESKSC
HAIRST
ABLESF
ILESDE
```

You will find the function *ROWNAMES* in workspace 1 *CLASS* convenient for making character matrices without having to count the number of characters between words. *ROWNAMES* makes use of a few APL features to be described later. But because it is so handy for building matrices of names or titles, we are introducing it here. However, don't bother to try to understand why it works. Just use it.

```
    )COPY 1 CLASS ROWNAMES
SAVED  14.45.33 02/20/83

    ∇ROWNAMES[□]∇
    ∇ Z←S ROWNAMES T;A;B;R
[1]    T←,T ◇ B←T=1↑T
[2]    A←(+/B)↑▼B ◇ A←(1↓A,□IO+ρT)-1+A ◇ R←⌈/A
[3]    Z←((ρA),R)ρ(,A∘.≥(~□IO)+ιR)\(~B)/T ◇ R←ρZ
[4]    S←2↑(2× 3 2 ⊥(ρ,S),0=¯1↑S)↓((¯2↑0,S),R,-R)[2 3 2 3 2 1 2 5 0 1 0 5 +□IO]
[5]    →BY×R∨.≠S
[6]    BY:Z←(S× 1 ¯1 ⌈×S)↑Z ◇ →OUT×0>¯1↑S
[7]    OUT:Z←(1-(Z=' ')⊥1)⌽Z
    ∇
```

```
    FURNV←'/DESKS/CHAIRS/TABLES/FILES'              FURN2
    FURN2←(ι0)ROWNAMES FURNV              DESKS
    ρFURN2                               CHAIRS
4 6                                      TABLES
                                         FILES
```

The right argument of *ROWNAMES* is a character vector. Its first character is arbitrary (we used the `'/'`) and serves as a *delimiter* (separator). The resulting matrix has as many rows as there are delimiters. The left argument can be a variety of things. If it is an empty vector, as above, the result contains as many columns as the longest character sequence between delimiters. If it is a scalar positive integer, then the number of columns is chopped (or extended with blanks). If the left argument is a scalar zero, each column is as long as the longest character sequence between delimiter characters, but each row is *right-justified*:

```
        4 ROWNAMES FURNV                    0 ROWNAMES FURNV
DESK                                 DESKS
CHAI                                 CHAIRS
TABL                                 TABLES
FILE                                 FILES
```

If the left argument is a negative number, then that sets the number of columns, with each row again right-justified. Finally, if the left argument is a two-element vector, the first element sets the number of rows (positive from the top or negative from the bottom), while the second element controls the configuration of the columns, as in the scalar left arguments described above:

```
      ‾9 ROWNAMES FURNV                    ‾3 5 ROWNAMES FURNV
    DESKS                             CHAIR
   CHAIRS                             TABLE
   TABLES                             FILES
    FILES
```

Characters that look like numbers

Up to this point we have used only letters, punctuation marks and space as characters. Any keyboard character, including overstruck ones, can be employed in this manner. This can lead to some mystifying situations with numbers:

```
        T←'10'            (or T←⍕10)

        T
10
```

But *T* doesn't have the value of 10:

```
        T=10
0  0
```

Neither element of *T* matches the `'10'` on the right! If this is puzzling to you, remember that *T* is a *vector* of two elements, `'1'` and `'0'`, neither of which is equal to the numeric value 10.

On page 115 we saw how the format function ⍕ was used to convert a numeric value to its character representation. That function can be used to test whether a variable contains character information or numeric information. The trick is based on the fact that ⍕ applied to numeric values converts it to characters.

The following commented function is the test. It covers all cases except where the argument is empty; that's treated on page 131.

```
        ∇R←TYPE VAR
[1]     VAR←1⍴VAR ⍝ DEALS ONLY WITH FIRST ELEMENT--FAILS IF VAR IS EMPTY
[2]     R←(9×∧/VAR=⍕VAR)⍴'CHARACTER' ⍝ IF CHARACTER, OTHERWISE R IS EMPTY.
[3]     R←R,(7×∨/VAR≠⍕VAR)⍴'NUMERIC' ⍝ IF NUMERIC--HENCE R IS EITHER
[4]     ⍝THE VECTOR 'CHARACTER' OR THE VECTOR 'NUMERIC'
[5]     ∇
```

Just as ⍕ is used to convert numeric data to its character representation, ⍎ (upshift *B* with upshift *J*), called *execute*, can be used to convert character vectors to their numeric representation.

```
        V←'10 72.4 93'          VN←⍎V                VNV←⍕VN
        V                       VN                   VNV
10 72.4 93              10 72.4 93            10  72.4 93
        ⍴V                      ⍴VN                  ⍴VNV
10                      3                     10
        TYPE V                  TYPE VN              TYPE VNV
CHARACTER              NUMERIC               CHARACTER
```

For users of APL*PLUS and APL2 there is a primitive function *type*, monadic ∊, that gives the same information as the defined function *TYPE*. It returns a zero for numeric values and a blank for character values:

```
      εV                                εVN
                          0 0 0
      ρεV                               ε2 4ρι8
10                        0 0 0 0
      +/' '=εV            0 0 0 0
10
```

Executing character strings

The execute function does much more than just converting character representations into numbers. Execute treats its character vector argument as though you had entered it in calculator mode. For example, A←'B←2+3'◇⍕A is equivalent to your having entered B←2+3 at the keyboard. This means you can assign character variables which will subsequently be executed.

Both execute and direct definition (see page 298) give you a vast increase in programming flexibility and power because you can reassign the character variables on which they are based, under program control. This leads to application systems that can appear intelligent (in the sense of programs that write or edit other programs), a topic we address in Chapter 24.

Ranking

Earlier in this chapter we said that character data is unorderable. Yet there are many times when it is necessary to impose an artificial ordering on character data. Dictionaries and telephone books would be impossible if words or names weren't listed in some order.

To see how this can be done, let's first assign a vector consisting of the letters of the alphabet in their normal sequence:

```
      X←'ABCDEFGHIJKLMNOPQRSTUVWXYZ'
```

Now try

```
      Xι'CAFE'
3 1 6 5
```

The dyadic use of ι (called *ranking* or *index of*) can be used to convert a character vector such as '$CAFE$' above to a numeric vector holding the index position of each character in the left argument. In other words, 'C' is the *third* element of X, 'A' is the *first*, 'F' is the *sixth* and 'E' the *fifth*.

The following function uses *index of* to convert a character vector or scalar to a single number, which can then be ordered:

```
      ∇S←ORDER CONVERT CHVEC;WEIGHTS;INDEX         X CONVERT 'CAFE'
[1]   CHVEC←, CHVEC                             3010605
[2]   WEIGHTS←100*(ρCHVEC)-ιρCHVEC                  X CONVERT 'CHAD'
[3]   INDEX←ORDERιCHVEC                         3080104
[4]   S←+/INDEX×WEIGHTS∇                            X CONVERT 'CASH'
                                                3011908
```

This method has some flaws, however. It won't work reliably for vectors of more than 8 characters because the computer can store only about 16 decimal digits in a scalar (that value will vary from system to system). To see the failure, compare X $CONVERT$ '$ABCDEFGHIJKLMN$' with X $CONVERT$ '$ABCDEFGHIJKLMZ$'.

A second flaw is apparent in the following examples:

```
      X CONVERT 'DAME'              X CONVERT 'DAY'
4011305                      40125
```

We would expect 'DAY' to appear in the dictionary after '$DAME$'; this method doesn't work unless the compared words are the same length. This can be dealt with by making all words the same length inside the function, and by augmenting to include a blank as its first element (since 'DAM' should come before '$DAME$'). A new function to do this has a built-in ranking vector, and makes all arguments eight characters long:

```
      ∇S←CONV2 CHVEC;WEIGHTS;INDEX
[1]   CHVEC←8ρCHVEC,'        '
[2]   WEIGHTS←100*8-ι8
[3]   INDEX←' ABCDEFGHIJKLMNOPQRSTUVWXYZ'ιCHVEC
[4]   S←+/INDEX×WEIGHTS ∇
```

```
      CONV2 'DAME'                    CONV2 'DAY'
5.02140601E14              5.02260101E14
```

Here are a few more details to know about dyadic ι. Its left argument must be a vector, but its right argument can be arrays of any shape whatever. The shape of the result is always the same as that of the right argument.

```
      M←2 3ρ'CATDOG'            XιM              ρXιM
                            3  1 20         2 3
                            4 15  7
```

What happens if the right argument contains a character which isn't present in the left argument, or if the same character appears more than once in the right argument?

```
      Xι'BABBAGE, CHAS.'
2 1 2 2 1 7 5 27 27 3 8 1 19 27
```

The example shows you that all characters that aren't found (such as the comma, space and period) result in a value that is one larger than the length of the left argument. Generally, the left argument should contain all characters you expect to encounter in the right argument. Any repeated characters in the right argument return the same value: that of the *first match* in the left argument. This is true even if the left argument has duplicate occurrences.

```
      'BABBAGE, CHAS.'ι'BABBAGE, CHAS.'
1 2 1 1 2 6 7 8 9 10 11 2 13 14
```

Note that the repeated letters aren't used up. This feature can be used to test whether a vector has duplicate characters or not:

```
      TD←'BABBAGE'              TU←'COMPUTER'
      TDιTD                     TUιTU
1 2 1 1 2 6 7             1 2 3 4 5 6 7 8
      (TDιTD)=ιρTD             (TUιTU)=ιρTU
1 1 0 0 0 1 1             1 1 1 1 1 1 1 1
      ∧/(TDιTD)=ιρTD          ∧/(TUιTU)=ιρTU
0                         1
```

Ranking works with numeric arrays in exactly the same way that it does with characters.

Membership

Suppose you want to know which characters in some vector are also present in some other vector 'CHSET'. One way to do it is this:

```
      CHSET←' ABCDEFGHIJKLMNOPQRSTUVWXYZ0123456789'
      (1+ρCHSET)≠CHSETι'ALL FOUND'
1 1 1 1 1 1 1 1 1
      (1+ρCHSET)≠CHSETι'SOME NOT FOUND'
1 1 1 1 0 0 0 1 1 1 1 1 1
```

A more direct way to check for membership is to use the *membership* function, ∈, found on the E key:

```
      'ALL FOUND'∈CHSET           ∧/'ALL FOUND'∈CHSET
1 1 1 1 1 1 1 1 1                              1
      'SOME NOT FOUND'∈CHSET      ∧/'SOME NOT FOUND'∈CHSET
1 1 1 1 1 0 0 0 1 1 1 1 1                      0
```

For membership, the shape of the result is always the same as that of the left argument. Both arguments may be arrays of any rank whatever:

```
        (3 4ρι12)ε2 2ρ4 15 2 ‾3                    (2 2ρ4 15 2 ‾3)ε3 4ρι12
 0  1  0  1                                   1  0
 0  0  0  0                                   1  0
 0  0  0  0
```

A few more points about character data

Look at this sequence of entries:

```
        ρ'ABC'                  ρ'AB'                   ρ'A'                    ρ''
3                           2                       0
```

A single character in quotes in APL is a scalar, while any other number of characters in quotes is a vector. Of course, to make a single character a vector, just ravel it.

```
        ρ,'A'
1
```

Don't make the common mistake of putting the comma inside the quotes. Why?

And finally, ' ' is an empty vector, just as ι0 is an empty vector. There is actually a difference between ' ' and ι0, but don't worry about that now.

PROBLEMS

1. DRILL: Assign X←'MISSISSIPPI' and Y←'RIVER'

```
'ABCDE'='BBXDO'              1 2<'MP'                 ρρAL←3 3ρ'ABCDEFGHI'
ρV←'3172'                    YεX                      X='S'
(ρV)ρV                       +/X='S'                  +/'P'=X
3172=V                       +/X≠'S'                  +/(X,' ',Y)≠'S'
X,Y                          X,' ',Y                  ∨/X='R'
```

2. Determine what D is from the following record of executions:

```
        D
        ρD
15
        5×D
DOMAIN ERROR
        5×D
         ∧
        ' '=D
 1 1 1 1 1 1 1 1 1 1 1 1 1 1 1
```

3. Define a function F which takes a single argument A and displays its shape, rank and number of elements with appropriate descriptive messages. Assume rank $A≥1$.

4. Show how to display 1-and 2-digit positive integers I so that 1-digit integers are indented one space and the 2-digit integers begin at the left margin.

5. Copy the functions HYP and $GEO3$ in 1 $CLASS$. Open up the function and direct control to line [0.5]. Use the comment symbol ⍝ on this line and the next to write a message describing what the function does. Then close out the function, display it and execute it. Do comments introduced in this manner affect execution?

6. The matrix $GR3$ contains the grade records (A, B, C, D and F) of 25 students in a class, with the first row listing the number of A's received by each student, the second row the number of B's, etc. Each course represented in the matrix is three credits. A similar matrix $GR2$ records grades for two-credit courses, and $GR1$ for one-credit courses. Write a program to calculate the grade point average for each student and for the class. (The grade point average is computed by multiplying 4 times the number of A credits, 3 times the number of B credits, etc., adding them up and dividing by the total number of credits earned.)

7. How many consonants are in the vector $CHAR$←'WHY AM I DOING THIS PROBLEM?'?

Chapter 14: Selecting data from an array

Most of the time we find ourselves in possession of far more data (from business records, surveys, experiments, observations of natural phenomena, government statistics, etc.) than we need for the job to be done. So the problem of how to pull out the 'good stuff' from the mass of extraneous information is an important one for most APL users. In fact, data selection is one of the most common activities in APL, and for that matter, in any computer language. This chapter will describe five mixed functions that will assist you in the data selection process.

Indexing

Of all the selection functions *bracket indexing* is the most general. Let's define a character vector X:

        X←'ABCDEFGHIJK'

We can select from X the characters forming the word CAFE by

        X[3 1 6 5]
    CAFE

The expression in square brackets (not parentheses) is usually read as 'X sub 3 1 6 5' (for *subscripting*).

Any valid APL expression that results in integers can be used for indexing. For instance, execute

        X[2 5ρ3 1 8 9 4 2 10 6 7 5]   X[4ρ3]
    CAHID   CCCC
    BJFGE

The result has the shape of the expression in the brackets. But the following produces a new kind of error:

        X[12]
    INDEX ERROR
        X[12]
        ∧

To avoid an error message the expression in brackets must refer only to left argument indices that exist. In the last example, because X has just 11 characters there is no way to get the twelfth one.

Not only does bracket indexing have a different form from the other functions, it is also unique in being the only function that can appear on the left side of the assignment arrow (except in APL2; see Chapter 25). For example, suppose we want to change the character 'D' in X above to the character '$?$':

        X   X[4]←'?'   X
    ABCDEFGHIJK   ABC?EFGHIJK

The replacement has taken place.

More generally, elements can be rearranged by indexing:

        X   X[5 6]←X[6 5]   X
    ABC?EFGHIJK   ABC?FEGHIJK

If no indices are entered, every element of the vector is changed to the specified value:

        X   X[]←'T'   X
    ABC?FEGHIJK   TTTTTTTTTTT

You can index numeric as well as character arrays. Say we are given the heights (in inches) of five students:

```
L←51 63 60 62 59 62
```

If the third student's height had been entered incorrectly, and should have been 61 instead of 60 inches, the change can be made easily by

```
L[3]←61
L
51 63 61 62 59 62
```

Indexing matrices

To illustrate bracket indexing on a two-dimensional array, let's define a matrix which contains a company's revenue (in thousands of dollars) over a four-month period for three products:

```
                 |    M  O  N  T  H
                 |    1     2     3     4
         --------+-----------------------------
PRODUCTS    A    |   11    23    80   100
            B    |   18    19    99   122
            C    |   16    14   128   112
```

The sales data is stored in a matrix called *PRODREV* in 1 *CLASS*.

```
    )COPY 1 CLASS PRODREV              PRODREV
SAVED  14.45.33 02/20/83          11   23   80  100
                                  18   19   99  122
                                  16   14  128  112
```

To specify any element of this array requires two numbers, one to tell the row and the other the column in which the element is located. Suppose we want the element in the second row and fourth column. The expression

```
    PRODREV[2 4]
RANK ERROR
    PRODREV[2 4]
    ∧
```

doesn't work because the two elements of the expression in the brackets refer to two different dimensions of the array *PRODREV*. We get a *RANK ERROR* message because we have failed to take into account that *PRODREV* is of rank 2, not rank 1. What is needed here is a separator for the row number and column number. The semicolon is used for this purpose.

```
    PRODREV[2;4]
122
```

More than one element can be specified at a time, like the sales of products A and C in the second month or that of product C in months 1 and 2:

```
    PRODREV[1 3;2]              PRODREV[3;1 2]
23 14                      16  14
```

There is a shorthand way of specifying *all* the elements along a particular dimension. Curiously enough, it's done by not entering *any* indices of the dimension in question. This is an extension to two dimensions of a previous example, *X[ ]←'T'*. If we wanted to see the sales for product C for all the months stored, we could enter either of the following:

```
    PRODREV[3;1 2 3 4]              PRODREV[3;]
16 14 128 112                  16  14 128 112
```

Similarly, we can get the revenue for all products for the fourth month with

```
    PRODREV[;4]
100 122 112
```

This implies that to get all of *PRODREV* we could use

```
      PRODREV[;]
11   23   80 100
18   19   99 122
16   14  128 112
```

which is perhaps a bit silly, but at least consistent.

As with vectors, you can change values in a matrix by using bracket indexing to the left of the assignment arrow. For example, to change the sales figures for month 1, products C and D, enter

```
      PRODREV[1;3 4]←90 105            PRODREV
                                  11   23   90 105
                                  18   19   99 122
                                  16   14  128 112
```

Unless the right argument is a single element, its shape must match the shape of the part of the array being indexed on the left.

Now for some miscellaneous but useful observations about bracket indexing. When indexing a matrix, there must be one semicolon to separate the row and column indices. But since vectors are one-dimensional, no semicolon is needed. Scalars are dimensionless and cannot be indexed at all.

The shape of the result in bracket indexing is the same as the shape you would get by taking outer products among the indices. This may not seem significant to you, but it does explain the following:

```
      X←2 3ρι6
      X[1 2;3]
3 6

      ρX[1 2;3]              ρ1 2∘.+3
2                         2

      X[1 2;,3]
  3
  6

      ρX[1 2;,3]            ρ1 2∘.+,3
2 1                     2 1
```

Previously you saw that APL permitted multiple assignments. If you are using this feature extensively, you should observe and remember this example, whose result varies on different APL systems:

```
      X←5ρ0          Z←X[2 3 4]←1            X                    Z
                                        0  1  1  1  0              1
```

We close this section on indexing by posing a question. Given the array *FURN* (page 116), how do you select the scattered elements `'F'`, `'I'`, `'R'` and `'E'`? If you have been thinking about how bracket indexing works, you will already be aware that it is the nature of the beast to couple in all possible combinations the indices specified for each dimension. You can't use this form of indexing directly to index scattered points in an array unless they all lie along a single row or column. Here is how you would pick out the vector `'FIRE SALE'` from the matrix *FURN*. We readily agree that it's a lot of work. If you have access to APL2, Chapter 25 describes functions that select scattered elements from arrays of any rank.

```
      FURN
DESKS
CHAIRS
TABLES
FILES
      FURN[4;1 2],FURN[2 3;5],FURN[1;6],FURN[1 2;3],FURN[3;4 5]
FIRE SALE
```

Replication and Compression

Replicate is a function whose left argument elements specify how many copies of corresponding right argument elements are to be selected. It uses the same symbol, /, as does reduction, but there's no confusion because reduction always has a function (such as + or ×) to its left while replicate has a vector of nonnegative integers. For vector right arguments the shape of the result of replicate is the sum of the left argument.

```
      2 3 0 1 3/10 20 30 40 50
10 10 20 20 20 40 50 50 50
```

Replicate is a relatively new function in the world of APL. Some older systems don't have it, and for them we provide the following simulation:

```
      )COPY 1 CLASS REP REPF REPL
SAVED  14.45.33 02/20/83
```

```
      ∇REPF[□]∇                                    ∇REPL[□]∇
   ∇ Z←L REPF R;AXIS                           ∇ Z←L REPL R;AXIS
[1]   ⍝ SIMULATION OF L/[1]R                [1]   ⍝ SIMULATION OF L/[ρρR]R
[2]   ⍝ JILL WADE   SEPT. 82                [2]   ⍝ JILL WADE   SEPT. 82
[3]   ⍝ AXIS IS GLOBAL TO REP               [3]   ⍝ AXIS IS GLOBAL TO REP
[4]   AXIS←1 ◇ Z←L REP R                    [4]   AXIS←1⌈ρρR ◇ Z←L REP R
   ∇                                           ∇
```

The function *REP* which is used by *REPF* and *REPL* does contain some features not yet covered in the text—don't worry, we'll get to them soon.

```
      ∇REP[□]∇
   ∇ Z←L REP R;IX;RHO;RT;TRANS
[1]   ⍝ SIMULATES Z←L/[AXIS] R  USED BY REPF AND REPL (JILL WADE SEPT 82)
[2]   ⍝ CREATE A MATRIX WHOSE LAST DIMENSION CONTAINS THE REQUIRED
[3]   ⍝ DATA, INDEX WHAT'S NEEDED, THEN REARRANGE SHAPE OF RESULT
[4]   R←1/R ◇ L←((ρR)[AXIS]ρ1)/L ⍝ DEAL WITH SCALAR ARGUMENTS
[5]   IX←(,L∘.≥⍳⌈/L)/,(⍳ρL)∘.×(⌈/L)ρ1 ⍝  INDICES IN REQUIRED DIMENSION
[6]   TRANS←((AXIS≠⍳ρρR)/⍳ρρR),AXIS ◇ RT←(⍋TRANS)⍉R
[7]   RHO←ρRT ◇ RT←((×/¯1↓RHO),¯1↑RHO)ρRT ⍝  RESHAPE TRANSPOSED ARRAY
[8]   Z←TRANS⍉((¯1↓RHO),ρIX)ρRT[;IX⌊¯1↑ρRT] ⍝ ADJUST FOR SCALAR RIGHT ARGUMENT
   ∇
```

When the left argument of replicate consists of only 0's and 1's, it is usually called *compression*. Compression is on virtually all APL systems, and it is a very popular function because it has so many uses.

In Chapter 4 we examined a group of relational functions which resulted in logical arrays (1's and 0's only) when applied to data. These logical arrays can be used as 'sieves' with holes where the 1's are, and barriers for the 0's to strain out unwanted data.

The vector *L* represents the heights of a group of students. We could find the heights of the second and third students by indexing, but we could as well use compression:

```
      L
51 63 61 62 59 62
      L[2 3]
63 61
      0 1 1 0 0 0/L
63 61
```

This can be read as 'the 0 1 1 0 0 0 compression of *L*.' Where there is a 0 in the left argument, the corresponding element on the right isn't picked up. The only elements returned are in those positions where there is a 1 to match it on the left. This means that for vector arguments the lengths must be the same.

To illustrate a practical use of compression, here is a bank account problem. For *A*, a vector of accounts with the negative values representing overdrawn accounts, the instruction *A*<0 produces a vector with 1's in the positions of the offenders and 0's elsewhere. This is made to order for compression,

```
      A←3 ¯4 5 0 ¯6              A<0              (A<0)/A
                             0 1 0 0 1        ¯4 ¯6
```

and we have extracted from *A* only the overdrawn accounts.

We can go a little further with compression. For instance, the instruction

```
      (A<0)/⍳ρA
```

tells us that accounts 2 and 5 are the guilty parties and should be flagellated, dunned or whatever, depending on the circumstances.

Both arguments normally must have the same length, unless the left argument is a scalar. If all or none of the elements are desired, use a single 1 or 0:

```
     A←'ABCDEF'              1/A              0/A                   2/A
                           ABCDEF                            AABBCCDDEEFF
```

Otherwise, if the lengths don't agree, an error message results:

```
        1 0 1 0/A
LENGTH ERROR
        1 0 1 0 /A
               ∧
```

In `1 CLASS` the function `CMP` uses compression to compare two scalar arguments for size and returns a character vector stating whether the left argument is less than, equal to or greater than the right argument. Use the `COPY` command to get it into your active workspace, try it out on a few examples and display it.

```
      )COPY 1 CLASS CMP            ·
SAVED  14.45.33 02/20/83
      3 CMP 5                 5 CMP 3                 5 CMP 5
LESS                    GREATER                 EQUAL


      ∇CMP[□]∇
    ∇ A CMP B
[1]   ((A>B)/'GREATER'),((A=B)/'EQUAL'),((A<B)/'LESS'
    ∇
```

It doesn't return an explicit result, since we wouldn't be apt to have any further use for the result. Notice the practical use for catenation with characters, not unlike line 2 of the function `GEO3` on page 114. Starting from the right, we pick up either all of the character vector `'LESS'` or none of it, depending on whether `A` is less than `B`. The vectors `'EQUAL'` and `'GREATER'` are treated similarly and catenated. Since only one of the three conditions can possibly hold at any one time, we are actually catenating two empty vectors and one nonempty character vector to get the right display. The fact that the left argument of compression is a logical vector makes it an ideal candidate for selecting on the basis of a true-false condition, as `CMP` shows.

There are several other ways of doing what `CMP` does, but most of them require features that we haven't introduced yet. They'll be discussed in Chapter 22. One method that we can explore now, however, employs indexing rather than compression:

```
      (3 7ρ'LESS   EQUAL  GREATER')[2+×A-B;]
```

It is further evidence that the old adage 'There's more than one way to skin a cat' holds for most problems in APL, and reflects the richness of the language.

Replication and compression on two-dimensional arrays

When using replication or compression with two-dimensional arrays, you have to keep one additional piece of information in mind: the left argument must have as many elements as the number of elements in the dimension across which replication or compression occurs. The symbol / works along the second dimension of a matrix, and ≠ along the first dimension. Here are examples in which the third month (column 3) in `PRODREV` is elided, and `'CHAIRS'` is repeated three times but `'DESKS'` and `'FILES'` are elided in `FURN`:

```
      )COPY 1 CLASS PRODREV FURN
SAVED  14.45.33 02/20/83

      PRODREV                     1 1 0 1/PRODREV
  11  23  80 100            11  23 100
  18  19  99 122            18  19 122
  16  14 128 112            16  14 112
```

```
          FURN                          0 3 2 0≠FURN
DESKS                          CHAIRS
CHAIRS                         CHAIRS
TABLES                         CHAIRS
FILES                          TABLES
                               TABLES
```

Formally, the conditions for replication or compression of matrices are as follows:

If $Z \leftarrow L/R$, then
1. L must be a vector or a scalar consisting of nonnegative integers
2. ρL must be $(\rho R)[1]$ for $\neq$, or $(\rho R)[2]$ for $/$
3. $\rho \rho Z$ is $\rho \rho R$

Unlike indexing, replication and compression can't reorder data. Although their selection capability is limited to a single dimension, they can pick out elements, rows, columns or planes that aren't adjacent, but only in the order in which they occur. So to select products A and C for months 2 and 3 in $PRODREV$ (represented by $PRODREV$ [1 3;2 3]) we would have to compress twice:

```
       1 0 1≠0 1 1 0/PRODREV
23   80
14  128
```

The replicate function on APL2 also permits the use of negative integers in the left argument. Wherever they occur, as many copies of the fill element (zero for numeric arrays, blank for characters) as the magnitude of the (negative) integer are inserted into the result. This allow you to compress, replicate and expand in one step:

```
       0 1 2 ‾2 1 1 0 ‾2/0 5 10 15 20 25
5 10 10 0 0 15 20 0 0
```

Selecting data with membership

Membership, because it produces a logical array based on the presence or absence of elements, is frequently used as the left argument for compression. Like the relational and logical functions, it acts like a sieve to separate wanted from unwanted elements in an array. The following example removes vowels from a sentence:

```
       PHRASE←'THE QUICK BROWN FOX JUMPED OVER THE LAZY PROGRAMMER'
       (~PHRASEϵ'AEIOU')/PHRASE
TH QCK BRWN FX JMPD VR TH LZY PRGRMMR
```

Most systems don't have a primitive function that says 'not a member of.' To get results like 'those elements of L that aren't members of R,' use membership with logical negation.

```
       L←1 5 50 17 13
       R←13 45 17 5 50 19
```

```
       (LϵR)/L                       (~LϵR)/L
5 50 17 13                  1
```

However, APL2 does have a dyadic function *without*, $\sim$, whose action is equivalent to the expression $(\sim L \epsilon R)/L$. Its syntax is $L \sim R$. R may be any array, while L is a scalar or vector. The result is the vector of elements in L which aren't in R.

```
       'HELP'~'L'              3 1 5 6 7~1 3 7          3 1 5 6 7~2 3ρι6
HEP                    5 6                     2 4
```

The idiom $L \sim L \sim R$ gives the *intersection* (i.e., the common items) of L and R:

```
       3 1 5 6 7~3 1 5 6 7~1 3 7
3 1 7
```

Expansion

Just as compression gives us a way to get a subset of an array, so there is also in APL a function called *expansion*, which allows us to insert additional elements. The symbol for expansion is \, the backward pointing slash, on the same key as the compression symbol.

```
      1 0 1 0 0 1 1 1 1 1\'ABCDEFG'
A B  CDEFG
```

```
      1 0 0 1 0 1\3 2 3
3 0 0 2 0 3
```

These examples show that where 0 appears in the left argument, a blank (for characters) or 0 (for numeric array) is inserted in the result, which otherwise is identical to the right argument. Notice also that the number of 1's in the left argument must be the same as the dimension of the right argument, i.e., we have to pick up *all* of the right argument.

The following example shows that when a scalar right argument is used, it is repeated to match the number of 1's in the left argument, with the shape of the result the same as the shape of the left argument:

```
      1 0 0 1 0 1\323
323 0 0 323 0 323
```

With two-dimensional arrays the treatment is similar to that for compression.

```
      PRODREV
 11  23  80 100
 18  19  99 122
 16  14 128 112
```

```
      1 1 1 0 1 0\PRODREV
 11  23  80   0 100   0
 18  19  99   0 122   0
 16  14 128   0 112   0
```

We made room for two new columns by inserting zeros in the positions shown. To place 'LAMPS' between 'DESKS ' and 'TABLES' in 'FURN', use this sequence:

```
      FURN
DESKS
CHAIRS
TABLES
FILES
```

```
      MOREFURN←1 0 1 1 1⍀FURN

      MOREFURN
DESKS

CHAIRS
TABLES
FILES
```

```
      MOREFURN[2;]←'LAMPS '

      MOREFURN
DESKS
LAMPS
CHAIRS
TABLES
FILES
```

Here is a summary of the conditions governing the use of the expansion function on matrices:

If Z←L\R, then
1. L must be a vector consisting of all 1's and 0's.
2. (+/L) must be (⍴R)[1] for ⍀ or (⍴R)[2] for \.
3. (⍴Z) is (⍴L),(⍴R)[2] for ⍀ and (⍴R)[1],⍴L for \.

Although it may seem a bit far-fetched, in a way, expansion is a selection function since it allows us to 'select' everything and make room for extra elements needed in the array.

Take and drop

Besides compression and indexing, there are two other versatile function which select portions of an array. Their behavior and syntax are best explained with a few well-chosen examples. First, let's examine the *take* function ↑, (upper shift *Y*), with vector and scalar right arguments:

```
      V←8 5 3 9 ¯1 ¯4
      1↑V
8
      2↑V
8 5
      8↑V
8 5 3 9 ¯1 ¯4 0 0

      2 3↑5
 5 0 0
 0 0 0
```

```
      ¯1↑V
¯4
      ¯2↑V
¯1 ¯4
      ¯8↑V
0 0 8 5 3 9 ¯1 ¯4

      ¯2 ¯3↑'X'

     X
```

If L is the left argument and is positive, ↑ selects the first L elements from the right argument. If L is negative, the last $|L$ elements are taken. When L is greater than ρR the result is R with sufficient 0's (or blanks for character data) on the right or left to make a vector of length L. L must be an integer or a vector of integers. With a vector left argument and a scalar right argument, ↑ returns an array whose shape is the left argument and whose elements consist of zeros (or blank characters), except for the element in the upper left corner.

Here is how ↑ can be applied to *PRODREV*. In each case the elements of the left argument refer to what is to be taken across each dimension:

```
      PRODREV                  2 3↑PRODREV               2 ¯3↑PRODREV
 11   23   80  100       11 23 80                   23   80  100
 18   19   99  122       18 19 99                   19   99  122
 16   14  128  112              ¯2 3↑PRODREV              ¯2 ¯3↑PRODREV
                         18   19   99               19   99  122
                         16   14  128               14  128  112
```

Drop, ↓, (upper shift U) behaves in much the same way, except that if A is the left argument, A elements are dropped instead of taken. As with ↑, A must be a scalar integer or a vector of integers.

```
      0↓V                    2↓V              8↓V             ¯2↓V
 8 5 3 9 ¯1 ¯4          3 9 ¯1 ¯4                         8  5  3  9
```

Again, here are some illustrations with *PRODREV*.

```
      2 1↓PRODREV             ¯1 2↓PRODREV            2 ¯1↓PRODREV
 14  128  112             80 100               16   14  128
                          99 122                      ¯2 3↓PRODREV
                                               100
```

Generally speaking, for $Z \leftarrow L \downarrow R$, ρZ is $(\rho R) - |L$. This means that the result always has the same rank as the right argument. In the example $\,^{-}2\ 3 \downarrow PRODREV\,$ above, the result is a matrix (one row and column), *not* a scalar. Similarly, the result of $\,^{-}2\ 1 \downarrow PRODREV\,$ is also a matrix (one row, three columns) even though it looks like a vector.

Take and drop allow only solid blocks of data to be selected, with no capability to reorder or replicate. Where large blocks of data are needed, ↑ and ↓ are much faster than bracket indexing on most APL systems.

As you saw above in the examples using *PRODREV*, ↑ and ↓ are handy for picking out corners of an array, and appropriate combinations of them can be used to select a solid block located away from a corner. For example, here are some ways to 'take the edges' off a matrix:

```
      MAT←4 6ρι24
      MAT                     ¯1 ¯1↓1 1↓MAT             2 4↑1 1↓MAT
  1  2  3  4  5  6        8  9 10 11                8  9 10 11
  7  8  9 10 11 12       14 15 16 17               14 15 16 17
 13 14 15 16 17 18
 19 20 21 22 23 24
```

In APL2 take and drop have been extended to allow for selection along specified axes. The extended form and its equivalent in other APL systems are shown side-by-side:

```
      1↑[1]MAT                1 6↑MAT
 1 2 3 4 5 6            1 2 3 4 5 6

      2↑[2]MAT                4 2↑MAT
  1  2                   1  2
  7  8                   7  8
 13 14                  13 14
 19 20                  19 20

      2↓[1]MAT                2 0↓MAT
 13 14 15 16 17 18      13 14 15 16 17 18
 19 20 21 22 23 24      19 20 21 22 23 24
```

Reshape

This function was introduced in Chapter 2 and has been used right along in the text. Reshape isn't commonly thought of as a selection function. However, when you're interested in the front of an array, it's a handy way of picking out elements. For example,

```
      6ρPRODREV
11  23  80  100  18  19
```

picks out the first 6 elements, while

```
      3 3ρPRODREV
 11   23   80
100   18   19
 99  122   16
```

selects the first 9 and reshapes them—not too useful in this example but handy in building *identity matrices* used in matrix algebra. These are simply square matrices with 1's on the major diagonal and 0's elsewhere:

```
      4 4ρ1, 4ρ0
1  0  0  0
0  1  0  0
0  0  1  0
0  0  0  1
```

You may wonder what happens when the left argument of ρ is an empty vector. Let's explore this with the matrix *PRODREV*:

```
      (ι0)ρPRODREV               ''ρPRODREV
11                          11
```

The shape of the result is a scalar, the first element of the right argument. You should be able to figure out for yourself why it has to be a scalar.

We can enlarge any array with reshape as well as shrink it, provided we don't mind replicating data from the front end:

```
      4 7ρPRODREV
 11   23   80  100   18   19   99
122   16   14  128  112   11   23
 80  100   18   19   99  122   16
 14  128  112   11   23   80  100
```

In a way reshape is like APL food. Too much and you have a 'fat' array; too little and your array may end up looking like a dieter's delight.

More APL2 functions

Many APL'ers have wished for a primitive function that locates where in an array another array is. Although you would have to define a function for it in most APL systems, APL2 provides a *find* function, $\underline{\epsilon}$ (ε overstruck with underbar) that does just that.

It's as easy to use as membership—no restrictions on the sizes, shapes and ranks of the arguments. The result is a logical array of the same shape as that of the left argument L (the array being searched), with a 1 in every position of L where the pattern (the right argument R) begins. Find may be used with an axis specifier to indicate a direction other than the normal last axis.

```
      L←'ABRACADABRA'          L∈'AB'            L∈[1]'AB'
      L∈'AB'                 1 0 0 0 0         0 0 0 1 0
1 0 0 0 0 0 0 1 0 0 0       0 0 1 0 0         0 0 1 0 0
      1 2 3 4 1 2 3 4∈1 2   0 1 0 0 0         0 0 0 0 1
1 0 0 0 1 0 0 0             0 0 0 1 0         0 0 0 1 0
      L←5 5ρL               0 0 1 0 0         0 0 0 0 0
```

	L			$L\in 2\ 2\rho\text{'}ABAD\text{'}$					$L\in 2\ 1\rho\text{'}AB\text{'}$				
$ABRAC$		1	0	0	0	0		0	0	0	1	0
$ADABR$		0	0	0	0	0		0	0	1	0	0
$AABRA$		0	1	0	0	0		0	0	0	0	1
$CADAB$		0	0	0	0	0		0	0	0	1	0
$RAABR$		0	0	0	0	0		0	0	0	0	0

A companion function is *find index*, $\underline{\iota}$. Its result is a matrix of integers containing the indices of the starting positions of the pattern. Again the arguments, like find, have no restrictions on them:

	$L\underline{\iota}\text{'}AB\text{'}$			$L\underline{\iota}2\ 1\rho\text{'}AB\text{'}$			$L\underline{\iota}[1]\text{'}AB\text{'}$			$L\underline{\iota}2\ 2\rho\text{'}ABAD\text{'}$
1	1		1	4		1	4		1	1
2	3		2	3		2	3		3	2
3	2		3	5		3	5			
4	4		4	4		4	4			
5	3									

Another selection function available in APL2 is *unique*, $\cap$. As its name suggests, when applied to any array R the result is a logical array of the same shape, with 1's marking the first occurrence of the items of R in row major order:

```
      ∩R←3 2 3 4 2 1 0 1                    ∩2 4ρ1 2 1 3 2 4 3 6
1 1 0 1 0 1 1 0                       1 1 0 1
      (∩R)/R                          0 1 0 1
3 2 4 1 0
```

One or more axes may be specified in testing for uniqueness:

```
      R←5 5ρ'HE   SELLSWHAT HE   SELLS'
      R                                  ∩[1]R
HE                                   1 1 1 0 0
SELLS
WHAT
HE
SELLS
```

Putting the functions to work

Our parting gifts to you before leaving this chapter are two useful defined functions for working with character data. It is well worth your time to understand how these functions work, and why.

The first, $SQUEEZE$, is a monadic functions that removes contiguous blank characters in a vector of text. It works by comparing each element to its immediate neighbor. If both are blank, then the second of the pair is compressed out. Notice also the treatment of leading and trailing blank elements.

```
      ∇Z←SQUEEZE X
[1]   ⍝REDUCES CONSEC. BLANKS
[2]   Z←((X≠' ')∨(1↓X≠' '),1)/X∇

      SQUEEZE '  HOW      NOW BROWN     COW     '
HOW NOW BROWN COW

      SQUEEZE 'BEES    KNEES'
BEES KNEES
```

Does it work on *all* vectors? Will it work on empty vectors?

The next function converts a vector of text into a matrix with no more than one word per row. It is a simpler version of *ROWNAMES* (page 116).

```
      )COPY 1 CLASS CHARMAT
SAVED  14.45.33 02/20/83

      CHARMAT ' HOW    NOW BROWN COW'
HOW


NOW
BROWN
COW

      CHARMAT SQUEEZE ' HOW    NOW BROWN COW'
HOW
NOW
BROWN
COW

      ∇CHARMAT[□]∇
    ∇ Z←CHARMAT V;A
[1]   V←V,' ' ◊ A←V∈' ,' ◊ V←(~A)/V ⍝ V HAS COMMA, SPACES REMOVED
[2]   A←A/⍳ρA ⍝ A IS LOCATIONS OF COMMAS, SPACES
[3]   A←A-1+0,¯1↓A ◊ A←(A≠0)/A ⍝ A IS LENGTHS OF RESULTANT ROWS.
[4]   A←A∘.≥⍳⌈/0,A ⍝ A IS LOGICAL MATRIX FOR EXPANSION.
[5]   Z←(ρA)ρ(,A)\V ⍝ RAVEL A TO EXPAND, THEN RESHAPE RESULT.
    ∇
```

Our last function is a classical idiom for determining whether a variable is character or numeric. It depends on the fact that ↑ (and \) fills in with blanks for character data and 0's for numeric data. Note that even when an APL array is empty, its type (character or numeric) is still preserved.

```
      ∇Z←DATATYPE R
[1]   Z←' '=1↑0ρR ⍝ 1 FOR CHARACTER, 0 FOR NUMERIC
[2]   ∇
```

Summary

Before leaving the subject of data selection, let's summarize the selection capabilities of traditional APL:

function	syntax	description
indexing	$A[B]$	picks out isolated elements, rows, columns, etc. in known positions
replication, compression	B/A	selects repeated items (or none at all) along some dimension
expansion	$B\backslash A$	inserts zeros or blanks along some dimension
take, drop	$B{\uparrow}A$ and $B{\downarrow}A$	selects a chunk of an array by specifying its boundaries
reshape	$B\rho A$	selects data from the front of an array, recycling if needed
membership	$B\in A$	tests for presence of elements in an array.

There is still one more selection function, the transpose, $A\mathbin{\lozenge}B$, which can be used to select elements lying on a diagonal plane. This advanced function will be discussed in Chapter 19.

PROBLEMS

1. DRILL. Assign

```
A←0 ¯5 ¯8 6.2 15 ¯2 25
B←1 0 0 1 0 1 1
C←'ABCDEFGHIJKLMNOPQRSTUVWXYZ ?'
M←3 4ρι12
```

`(2<ι5)/ι5`	`M[2;3 1]`	`1 0 1≠M`
`B/A`	`1 1 0 1\'TWO'`	`A[1]+A[2 3 4]×A[7]`
`A[ρA],B[¯2+ρB]`	`A[8]`	`1 0 0 1 1 1\M`
`A[3 6]←2E5 4E¯4`	`Aι⌈/A`	`B\2 3 4 5`
`'ABD'∊C`	`2 10 15∊M`	`0 2↓M`
`4↑A`	`¯3↓C`	`1 3↑M`
`2 3ρM`	`3 3ρ1,3ρ0`	`10ρ100`

2. Assign $D←$ ¯2.1 4 1.9 0 ¯1 ¯4 ¯1.4 .7 2.5 2. Select those elements which are **A** less than .5 **B** positive **C** equal in magnitude to 4 **D** negative and greater than ¯1 **E** equal to 2 **F** less than 1 and greater than or equal to ¯2.

3. Define a monadic function to insert the character ∘ between each pair of adjacent elements in vector V.

4. For any arbitrary vector V write a function $INCR$ to compute increments between adjacent elements.

5. For mathematicians only: obtain the approximate area under the curve $Y = 3X^2$ between X_1 and X_2 by breaking it up into rectangles of width I in that interval. Hint: first define F to compute $3 \times X * 2$.

6. Write a program $WITHIN$ to select from a vector W those elements which lie within an interval R on either side of the average of W.

7. Write an APL expression to select those elements in a vector which are integers.

8. Define a function IN to tell what percent of the elements in a vector A lie within the interval B $\pm$ C.

9. Construct an expression that selects the largest element in a three-element vector V and displays a 1 if it exceeds the sum of the remaining two elements, 0 otherwise.

10. Show how to select the elements with even indices in a vector Y.

11. You are given a vector X whose elements are all different and arranged in ascending order. Write a program to insert a given scalar S into the appropriate place in the sequence so that the result is still in ascending order. Be sure that your function is able to handle the case where S is identical to some element in X.

12. Define functions to remove from a vector V all duplicate elements.

13. Write a program $SELECT$ which takes two arguments and prints that element in the left argument X whose position corresponds to the position of the largest element in the right argument Y.

14. Why is $V[^-1 + \iota \rho V]$ not executable?

15. Write an APL expression which returns the index of the largest element in a vector W.

16. V is a vector of bank account balances. Write expressions to get: **A** negative balances; **B** total of all the negative balances; **C** account number(s) (consecutive, beginning with 1) of the positive balances; **D** account number(s) with the largest balance; **E** sum of the balances in accounts 1, 5 and 6. Ditto for 2, 4 and 8.

17. Write an APL expression to calculate the sum of the first eight elements of a vector Q (or all of them if the number of elements is less than eight).

18. You are given a matrix M whose shape is 4 5. Use drop to pick out the section of M represented by $M[2 3; 2 3 4]$

19. Construct APL expressions to insert for $V \leftarrow \iota N$ a zero **A** between each two adjacent elements of V; **B** before each even element of V; **C** after each odd element of V.

20. Write a function whose explicit result is all the factors of a given integer N (i.e., the integers which divide evenly into N).

21. Define a monadic function which takes a character argument and selects the longest word in it. Hint: look for the longest set of consecutive nonblank characters.

22. Define a function $COMFACT$ to display a list of common factors, if any, of two integers A and B.

23. Write an expression to eliminate from a vector V elements with specified indices I.

24. What is the difference between $M[1;2]$ and $M[,1;,2]$?

25. Write an APL expression to delete the letter A from a character vector W.

26. Show how to pick out the elements of a vector X which are **A** divisible by 2 and/or 3, and **B** divisible by neither 2 nor 3.

27. A vector A contains the ages of all the employees of the Zee Manufacturing Company. Define an APL function that will yield the two ages which are closest to one another.

28. For an arbitrary matrix, $M \leftarrow 5\ 5\rho\iota 25$, show how to obtain **A** the first three rows of M; **B** the four elements in the upper left corner; **C** the last two columns of M; **D** the four corner elements.

29. Redo problem 23, Chapter 6, assuming that all the data is stored in a 3 5 matrix $INFO$. The fifth column is the average cost per gallon of gas.

30. The auditors of a progressive company find that the total cost of sampling information for accounting purposes can be described by the expression $(.08\times N)+10.24\div N\star.5$ where N is the number of items to be sampled, \$.08 the unit cost of sampling an item and \$10.24 the cost of a unit error in estimation. How many items should be sampled to minimize the total cost? Assume $N\leq 50$.

31. Write a function $CENTER$ to center the title T above the body of a report R.

32. Use expansion to double-space a character matrix M.

33. A vector V is broken up into fields marked by a delimiter character W. Write a function $FWIDTH$ to return the widths of these fields.

34. A survey is conducted in which interviewers are asked 10 questions to which they must respond 'yes' or 'no.' Find the percentages of positive responses to each question if the answers are stored in a logical matrix ANS, with one row for each person interviewed.

35. You are given a vector of stored messages $V \leftarrow {}'GOOD\ DAYHI\ YOURSELFHELLO\ AND\ WELCOMEGO$ $AWAY\ I''M\ BUSY'$. Define a function HI to return a random message from V.

36. **A** Construct a matrix whose shape is always random and not greater than 8, made up of elements which are random positive integers not greater than 150. **B** Modify your result to make the upper bound for the elements itself a random number less than 300.

37. Use the membership function to identify and select the one-digit integer elements of a vector V.

38. Write an APL expression to determine if two sets of numbers, $S1$ and $S2$, have identical elements, except possibly for order.

39. You are given a vector of characters $S \leftarrow {}'WE\ ARE\ ALL\ GOOD\ MEN'$. Write an APL expression to determine how many occurrences of the letters ${}'ABCDEFGHIJKL'$ are in S.

40. Let C be a vector of characters. Construct an expression which replaces every ${}'X'$ in C with a ${}'Y'$.

41. For a vector of eight elements, construct two expressions for selecting the last three elements. Use the compression function in one and the take function in the other.

42. Write an APL expression to select N random elements from a matrix M.

43. Show how to add a scalar N to each element in the even columns of a matrix M.

44. You are given five vectors $V1$ through $V5$ of invoices from fifteen customers. The first represents bills under 30 days old, the second 30 through 59 days old, the third 60 through 89 days, etc. All entries with a given index are associated with the same customer. Write a program that will **A** construct a matrix of these invoices with each vector $V1$ through $V5$ occupying a single row; **B** print the total amount of receivables in each category and separately for each customer, with an appropriate message; **C** print the grand total of all receivables with an identifying message; and **D** identify which customers are deadbeats (have invoices outstanding more than 59 days).

45. Using *only* the take ($\uparrow$) function, select from the character vector $V \leftarrow 'INDUBITABLY'$ the characters $'DUB'$. Ditto for drop($\downarrow$).

46. As production and sales manager for one of your company's products, you must decide how much to produce and what to charge for it. Your compensation is a salary plus 2% of the total receipts from the sale of the product. The company will not sell the product for less than $7.00. At the same time, if the price goes above $7.50 then the company's facilities are liable to be picketed by local consumer groups. The demand function for this product is $Q = 600 - 3.7P^2$, where Q is the quantity sold and P the price charged. What price should you charge and how much should you produce to maximize your personal income? Assume you produced only enough to cover sales, and can vary the price only in increments of one cent.

47. Write an APL expression to compare two sets of 50 random integers each (generated without duplication from $\iota 100$) and select those integers common to both.

48. Given $V1 \leftarrow 2\ 3\ 4\ 5\ 6\ 9\ 15$ and $V2 \leftarrow 4\ 9\ 15\ 6\ 20\ 25\ 40$, write APL expressions to find **A** those elements in both $V1$ and $V2$; **B** those elements in either $V1$ or $V2$; **C** those elements of $V1$ not in $V2$.

49. Write an expression to delete a specified row R from a matrix M, storing the result in $M1$.

50. Write an expression to take from a vector V all the elements after the first occurrence of a specified element, S. That is, if $V \leftarrow 3\ 1\ 2\ 7\ 2\ 1\ 1\ 2\ 6$ and $S \leftarrow 2$, the result should be $7\ 2\ 1\ 1\ 2\ 6$.

51. Why does $MAT[I;]\iota VECTOR$ give a $RANK\ ERROR$ for some row I?

52. The $4\ 3$ matrices $PRICES$ and $ORDERS$ contain information about four sizes (S,M,L,XL) and three styles (A,B,C) of shirts from a manufacturer. When the prices on style B are decreased by 10% to meet competition, the orders received increase by 15% for all sizes in that style. How does total revenue from all styles now compare with the original?

53. Again with $PRICES$ and $ORDERS$, **A** identify those sizes and styles that sold less than 10,000 and were also high priced (more than $20); **B** how many combinations fall in this category?; **C** how much revenue is attributable to them?

Chapter 15: Transformations and rearrangements

One of the earliest commercial uses of computers was rearranging data, particularly alphabetic information (commonly referred to as *sorting*). Those of you who are jigsaw puzzle buffs or who have had to produce an index for a book such as this will appreciate the desirability of having a systematic way to go about the job.

And who is there among us who hasn't at one time or another wondered why the grated cheese in certain supermarkets is to be found over the frozen foods, rather than being nestled among the boxes of pasta and tomato sauce, where you might expect it? Then there's the frustration we have all felt when a house number in an unfamiliar neighborhood isn't where it's 'supposed to be.' The need for order when searching clearly permeates most everyday activities.

This chapter is concerned with rearranging data in arrays. The topic isn't really new because some of the functions covered already, like bracket indexing and reshape, can be used to rearrange data as well as to select data.

Two very common rearrangements are reversing or rotating the elements in an array. For example, if you wished to reverse the elements of a vector V you could use the expression $V[1+(\rho V)-\iota \rho V]$. And the expression $V[1+(\rho V)|{}^{-}1+\iota \rho V]$ will rotate the elements N positions to the left. Reversal and rotation requirements occur frequently enough that APL provides functions specifically designed for the jobs.

Reverse

To *reverse* the elements in a vector, use the symbol ϕ (O overstruck with |). As with all selection and rearrangement functions, reverse can be applied to character data as well as numeric data:.

```
   φ10 10 20 12          φι3        φ'ABCDEF'        φ'POTS'
12 20 10 10             3 2 1       FEDCBA           STOP
```

When applied to matrices, ϕ reverses the order of the columns (last dimension). To reverse the order of the rows (first dimension), use $\ominus$ (O and −) instead. The example matrix $DATA$ here was chosen so that you can easily see how the elements are moved:

```
   DATA←(10×ι5)∘.+ι4
```

```
     DATA              φDATA              ⊖DATA
11 12 13 14        14 13 12 11        51 52 53 54
21 22 23 24        24 23 22 21        41 42 43 44
31 32 33 34        34 33 32 31        31 32 33 34
41 42 43 44        44 43 42 41        21 22 23 24
51 52 53 54        54 53 52 51        11 12 13 14
```

To reverse both columns and rows, use either of

```
   φ⊖DATA             ⊖φDATA
54 53 52 51        54 53 52 51
44 43 42 41        44 43 42 41
34 33 32 31        34 33 32 31
24 23 22 21        24 23 22 21
14 13 12 11        14 13 12 11
```

Reverse is a very easy function to remember. The shape of the result is always the same as the shape of the argument, as for the primitive scalar monadic functions. The elements themselves are unchanged, but they appear in element reverse order for vectors or reverse row ($\ominus$) or column (ϕ) order for matrices.

Rotate

The same symbols φ and ⊖, when used dyadically, mean *rotation*. For vectors, the left argument is the number of positions to rotate, while the right argument is the array to be rotated:

```
      2φ10 10 20 12                2φι3              1φ'ABCDEF'
20 12 10 10               3 1 2                BCDEFA
      0φ10 10 20 12               ¯1φι3             ¯5φ'ABCDEF'
10 10 20 12               3 1 2                BCDEFA
```

There are always as many elements in the result as in the right argument. The shape of the result is the same as the right argument. The elements are just pushed left for positive left arguments or right for negative left arguments.

What happens if you rotate more positions than there were in the vector originally?

```
      103φ'ABCDEFGHIJ'              ¯30φ1 2 3
DEFGHIJABC                    1 2 3
```

This little function, which can be regarded as a *formal description*, tells what really happens:

```
     ∇ R← N ROTATE V
[1]    ⍝FORMAL DESCRIPTION OF ROTATION.  NOTE USE OF RESIDUE
[2]    N←(ρV)|N ◇ R←NφV ∇
```

Matrices can be rotated as well. If the left argument is a single number, then all rows or columns are rotated the same amount:

```
     DATA              1φDATA            ¯2⊖DATA
11 12 13 14       12 13 14 11       41 42 43 44
21 22 23 24       22 23 24 21       51 52 53 54
31 32 33 34       32 33 34 31       11 12 13 14
41 42 43 44       42 43 44 41       21 22 23 24
51 52 53 54       52 53 54 51       31 32 33 34
```

Each row or column can be rotated an independent amount. For those cases, the left argument must be a vector containing one element for each row or column of the right argument. That is, for φ, ρLEFT must be ¯1↑ρRIGHT and for ⊖, ρLEFT must be 1↑ρRIGHT:

```
     1 2 0 ¯1 5φDATA            3 2 1 0⊖DATA
12 13 14 11               41 32 23 14
23 24 21 22               51 42 33 24
31 32 33 34               11 52 43 34
44 41 42 43               21 12 53 44
52 53 54 51               31 22 13 54
```

Applications of rotation

Here are some applications of rotation drawn from text processing, finance and mathematics. If you're not interested in any of these topics, you can skip to the next section.

Given a matrix of words, we want to *right justify* each row; that is, slide each word to the right so that the right margin lines up.

```
     )COPY 1 CLASS FURN RIGHTJUST
SAVED  14.45.33 02/20/83

     ∇RIGHTJUST[□]∇
     ∇ R←RIGHTJUST M;BLANKS;TRAILBLANKS
[1]    ⍝RIGHT JUSTIFY CHARACTER MATRIX.  AJR/LG AUG 1980.
[2]    BLANKS←M=' ' ◇ TRAILBLANKS←∧\φBLANKS ◇ R←(-+/TRAILBLANKS)φM
     ∇

     FURN              RIGHTJUST FURN
DESKS                  DESKS
CHAIRS                 CHAIRS
TABLES                 TABLES
FILES                   FILES
```

For our second application let's multiply two polynomials. The longhand method is shown here:

$$\begin{array}{r} x^3 + 3x^2 + 5x - 6 \\ 2x^2 - 4x + 7 \\ \hline 2x^5 + 6x^4 + 10x^3 - 12x^2 \\ - 4x^4 - 12x^3 - 20x^2 + 24x \\ + 7x^3 + 21x^2 + 35x - 42 \\ \hline 2x^5 + 2x^4 + 5x^3 - 11x^2 + 59x - 42 \end{array}$$

In APL it can be worked this way:

```
      P1←1 3 5 ¯6
      P2←2 ¯4 7
      PROD←P1∘.×P2
      AUGMENT←((ρP1),¯1+(ρP1)+ρP2)↑PROD
      SHIFTED←(1-ιρP1)⌽AUGMENT
```

```
        PROD                      AUGMENT                         SHIFTED
    2   ¯4    7           2   ¯4    7    0    0    0          2   ¯4    7    0    0    0
    6  ¯12   21           6  ¯12   21    0    0    0          0    6  ¯12  ¯21   0    0
  ¯10  ¯20   35         ¯10  ¯20   35    0    0    0          0    0  ¯10  ¯20   35   ¯0
  ¯12   24  ¯42         ¯12   24  ¯42    0    0    0          0    0    0  ¯12   24  ¯42
        +/SHIFTED
  2 2 5 ¯11 59 ¯42
```

The interesting part of the method is augmenting the outer product result matrix with enough columns of zeros to permit lining up each row of coefficients properly.

An important financial planning use of rotation is in calculating leading or lagging cash flows. For example, a planner knows that 50% of his customers pay in the month they are billed, 30% pay in the first following month, 10% pay in the second following month, and 5% pay in the third following month. The rest of the customers are deadbeats who never pay. If the expected monthly billings are as shown in the vector $BILLINGS$, what is the cash stream?

```
      BILLINGS←1000 1020 1350 1200 900 950 990 1030 1000 800 800 900
      LAGPAY←.5 .3 .1 .05

      ∇CASHSTREAM←B FLOW L;T
[1]    T←B∘.×L
[2]    T←(+\ρT)↑T  ⍝ ENLARGE TO PREVENT WRAP-AROUND
[3]    T←(1-ι1↑ρT)⌽T  ⍝ LAG EACH ROW ONE MORE MONTH
[4]    CASHSTREAM←¯1↓+/T∇

      BILLINGS FLOW LAGPAY
500 810 1081 1157 996 932.5 930 952 955.5 852.5 791.5 820 390 130 45
```

Transpose

Transposition is the interchanging of elements along two or more dimensions. The *transpose* function ⍉ has both monadic and dyadic forms. This chapter will consider only monadic transpose, leaving dyadic transpose (powerful, but difficult for many people to master) for a later chapter.

Monadic transpose applied to a matrix simply turns the matrix on its side:

```
        DATA                    ⍉DATA
   11 12 13 14          11 21 31 41 51
   21 22 23 24          12 22 32 42 52
   31 32 33 34          13 23 33 43 53
   41 42 43 44          14 24 34 44 54
   51 52 53 54               ρ⍉DATA
        ρDATA           4 5
   5 4
```

In other words, any element that could be reached by $DATA[I;J]$ can be reached as $(\lozenge DATA)[J;I]$ and $\rho DATA$ is the same as $\phi\rho\lozenge DATA$. It doesn't make any sense to transpose vectors or scalars; in both cases the results are the same as the arguments.

Transposition is almost indispensable for some tasks. Suppose you wanted to produce a compound interest table for 5%, 7.5% and 10% interest for 1, 2, 3 and 4 years, but with the interest rates running across the page and the periods running down:

```
      ⍉(1+0.05 0.075 0.1)∘.*⍳4
1.05                1.075              1.1
1.1025              1.155625           1.21
1.157625            1.242296875        1.331
1.21550625          1.335469141        1.4641
```

You would be hard pressed to think of any way to get this result *without* transpose. You certainly can't do it with $(\iota 4)\circ.*1+0.05\ 0.075\ 0.1$ because $*$ isn't commutative.

A transformation mnemonic

By this time you have probably noticed that the appearance of the symbols ϕ, $\ominus$ and $\lozenge$ is related to the kind of transformation which results when they are applied to certain arrays.

```
     DATA            φDATA             ⊖DATA             ⍉DATA
11 12 13 14      14 13│12 11       51 52 53 54      11 21 31 41 51
21 22 23 24      24 23│22 21       41 42 43 44      12 22 32 42 52
31 32 33 34      34 33│32 31       31 32 33 34      13 23 33 43 53
41 42 43 44      44 43│42 41       21 22 23 24      14 24 34 44 54
51 52 53 54      54 53│52 51       11 12 13 14
```

In each case the slant of the line in ϕ $\lozenge$ and $\ominus$ represents the axis (shown as a dotted line) about which the transformation occurred.

Arranging data in ascending and descending order

A director of a musical comedy has the following dancers available for the chorus line:

```
      )COPY 1 CLASS ROWNAMES
SAVED  14.45.33 02/20/83

      NAMES←(⍳0) ROWNAMES '/JUDY/MINDY/JEFF/JILL/DAVID/ANNETTE/LISA'
      EMPNO←⍳7

      HEIGHT←63 65 69 62 69 64 64

      RECORDS←(⍕⍉2 7⍴EMPNO,HEIGHT),' ',NAMES

      RECORDS
1 63 JUDY
2 65 MINDY
3 69 JEFF
4 62 JILL
5 69 DAVID
6 64 ANNETTE
7 64 LISA
```

He wants to line them up so that the shortest dancer is at the left and the tallest is at the right. If he were to do this manually, he might designate an area as the place to line up, and then ask the shortest person in the set of dancers to report there. He would repeat the procedure until no dancers were left in the original place.

With APL he can move them all at once:

```
      ORDER←⍋HEIGHT
      ORDER
4 1 6 7 2 3 5
```

```
        NAMES[ORDER;]                     RECORDS[ORDER;]
JILL                              4 62 JILL
JUDY                              1 63 JUDY
ANNETTE                           6 64 ANNETTE
LISA                              7 64 LISA
MINDY                             2 65 MINDY
JEFF                              3 69 JEFF
DAVID                             5 69 DAVID
```

The new symbol above, ⍋, *grade up*, formed by overstriking the △ and the |, is the key to this type of ordered rearrangement. When applied to a vector of numbers it gives the indices of the lowest, next lowest, and so on to the highest value in the original vector. Thus, the result always has the same shape as the argument.

The result is frequently used to index some related array to reorder it, as we did with *NAMES* above. We could have applied it to *HEIGHT* as well, producing them in ascending order:

```
        HEIGHT[⍋HEIGHT]
62 63 64 64 65 69 69
```

If there are two or more identical values in the original vector, the first from the left is taken as the lowest. Look at the last two elements of *ORDER*. The first 69 encountered was the third element of *HEIGHT*, and the next 69 was in the fifth element. And if all the elements of the vector were identical, then ⍋*VECTOR* would be the same as ι⍴*VECTOR*.

Sometimes you need to arrange data in descending order. An obvious approach is to reverse the results of ⍋:

```
        HEIGHT
63 65 69 62 69 64 64
```

```
        ⍋HEIGHT                           ⌽⍋HEIGHT
4  1 6 7 2 3 5                     5 3 2 7 6 1 4
```

```
        HEIGHT[⌽⍋HEIGHT]                  ⌽HEIGHT[⍋HEIGHT]
69 69 65 64 64 63 62              69 69 65 64 64 63 62
```

```
        NAMES                 NAMES[⌽⍋HEIGHT;]              ⊖NAMES[⍋HEIGHT;]
JUDY                     DAVID                        DAVID
MINDY                    JEFF                         JEFF
JEFF                     MINDY                        MINDY
JILL                     LISA                         LISA
DAVID                    ANNETTE                      ANNETTE
ANNETTE                  JUDY                         JUDY
LISA                     JILL                         JILL
```

But a specific function, ⍒, *grade down*, does it directly:

```
        ⍒HEIGHT               HEIGHT[⍒HEIGHT]              NAMES[⍒HEIGHT;]
3 5 2 6 7 1 4            69 69 65 64 64 63 62         JEFF
                                                     DAVID
                                                     MINDY
                                                     ANNETTE
                                                     LISA
                                                     JUDY
                                                     JILL
```

Observe that while this gives an equally good arrangement for the chorus line, it is not identical to ⊖*NAMES*[⍋*HEIGHT*;] or *NAMES*[⌽⍋*HEIGHT*;]. This is because both ⍋ and ⍒ start their search for smallest or largest from the left end of the vector:

```
        ⍋HEIGHT                  ⍒HEIGHT
4  1 6 7 2 3 5           3 5 2 6 7 1 4
        ⌽⍒HEIGHT                 ⌽⍋HEIGHT
4  1 7 6 2 5 3           5 3 2 7 6 1 4
```

You can sometime take advantage of this subtle difference. For instance, a test for unique elements is ∧/(⍋*VECTOR*)=⌽⍒*VECTOR*, although ∧/(*VECTOR*ι*VECTOR*)=ι⍴*VECTOR* may be easier to understand.

Grading matrices up and down

In most APL systems, grade up and grade down work only on vectors. If that's the case on your system, read the rest of this section and the next on alphabetic sorting. If you are using APL2, skip to page 142, advanced grade features. While the result of ⍋ or ⍒ can be used to rearrange a matrix, as we did with *NAMES*, sometimes a matrix has to be rearranged taking into account more than one column.

For example, each row of the following table represents the date of hiring of a group of employees:

month	day	year
5	12	1970
6	3	1969
5	12	1965
3	30	1965
6	3	1969
1	12	1970

There are several ways to do the reordering, but they all depend on one principle: rearrange on the least significant column first (days), and do the most significant column last (years).

The first approach simply converts each three-part date into a single number:

```
     H←6 3⍴5 12 70 6 3 69 5 12 65 3 30 65 6 3 69 1 12 70
     H[;3]←H[;3]+1900
     H
5    12 1970
6     3 1969
5    12 1965
3    30 1965
6     3 1969
1    12 1970
```

Each row of the data matrix *H* is now converted to a single element in a new vector in which years have the greatest weight, months have an intermediate weight, and days have the least weight:

```
     SQUASHED←+/H×(⍴H)⍴100 1 10000
     SQUASHED
19700512 19690603 19650512 19650330 19690603 19700112

     ⍋SQUASHED
4 3 2 5 6 1

     H[⍋SQUASHED;]
3    30 1965
5    12 1965
6     3 1969
6     3 1969
1    12 1970
5    12 1970
```

Well, it worked. We took advantage of the fact that no value in the 'days' column would exceed 99 and that the months also would not exceed 99. All in all, we took up around 8 decimal digits for each value in *SQUASHED*. But if we had had many data columns to include in the 'squashed' ordering, this method wouldn't work because most APL systems can't handle more than around 16 decimal digits in one element.

A more general approach is to reorder the array once for each column that contributes to the ordering:

```
     HD←H[⍋H[;2];]             HMD←HD[⍋HD[;1];]            HYMD←HMD[⍋HMD[;3];]
     HD                        HMD                         HYMD
6     3 1969              1    12 1970               3    30 1965
6     3 1969              3    30 1965               5    12 1965
5    12 1970              5    12 1970               6     3 1969
5    12 1965              5    12 1965               6     3 1969
1    12 1970              6     3 1969               1    12 1970
3    30 1965              6     3 1969               5    12 1970
```

This approach also worked, and it was not limited by the number of columns involved in the ordering. But we moved a *lot* of data around to get it done. All the elements of what was *H* were moved three times. A better method is to move only the elements of the grade vector for each column, and rearrange the original matrix only after all the grading is complete, as in the following sequence:

```
GD←⍋H[;2]                          H[GYMD;]
GMD←GD[⍋H[GD;1]]              3    30  1965
GYMD←GMD[⍋H[GMD;3]]          5    12  1965
                             6     3  1969
                             6     3  1969
                             1    12  1970
                             5    12  1970
```

With only three columns to arrange, a hard-coded solution in a defined function doesn't appear unreasonable here:3

```
      ∇R←GRADE3 M
[1]   ⍝REARRANGES 3-COLUMN NUMERIC MATRIX.   GILMAN, OCT 1980
[2]   R←⍋M[;2]
[3]   R←R[⍋M[R;1]]
[4]   R←R[⍋M[R;3]]  ∇
```

We feel compelled to cite an instance where an APL one-line solution for this problem achieved conciseness, but destroyed readability. Here is the controversial one-liner:

```
      ∇R←ONELINEGRADE M
[1]   R←R[⍋M[R←R[⍋M[R←R[⍋M[;3]];2]];]]∇
```

Alas, it works, but not in all APL implementations

Alphabetic sorting

Rearranging the rows of character matrices in alphabetic order is not different from working with numeric matrices, once you get past the first step: changing the characters to their index positions in some character set, called a *collating sequence*.

```
      NAMES                   ' ABCDEFGHIJKLMNOPQRSTUVWXYZ,.'⍳NAMES
JUDY                     11 22   5 26   1   1   1
MINDY                    14 10  15   5  26   1   1
JEFF                     11  6   7   7   1   1   1
JILL                     11 10  13  13   1   1   1
DAVID                     5  2  23  10   5   1   1
ANNETTE                   2 15  15   6  21  21   6
LISA                     13 10  20   2   1   1   1
```

Again the rearranging begins in the least significant column. But because there are many columns to do, it's wise to write a little function to make entry easier.

```
      ∇R←C UP V
[1]   ⍝USES GLOBAL MATRIX ND.  V IS LESS SIGNIFICANT GRADE VECTOR.
[2]   ⍝C IS COLUMN OF ND TO BE GRADED.   R IS NEW GRADE VECTOR.
[3]   R←V[⍋ND[V;C]]∇
      ND←' ABCDEFGHIJKLMNOPQRSTUVWXYZ,.'⍳NAMES

      NAMES[1 UP 2 UP 3 UP 4 UP 5 UP 6 UP 7 UP ⍳1↑⍴NAMES;]
ANNETTE
DAVID
JEFF
JILL
JUDY
LISA
MINDY
```

Why the ⍳1↑⍴NAMES? That's the original grade vector, meaning that NAMES[⍳1↑⍴NAMES;] is identical to NAMES itself. Also, see how we have taken advantage of APL's right-to-left execution sequence.

You must be thinking that there's got to be a better way to alphabetize than using 1 UP 2 UP 3 UP... etc., and there is, but it comes in a later chapter.

Advanced grade features

In APL2, ⍋ and ⍒ have been enhanced to accept arrays of rank greater than one:

```
     TAB2                     ⍋TAB2
3   1   7            4  1  3  2
7  10   4
6   9   1
1   6   7
```

The shape of the result is the same as the first dimension of the argument and places the subarrays of the argument (defined along the first dimension) in ascending order.

The most interesting part of the extension is with character arrays,

```
    NAMES                 ⍋NAMES              NAMES[⍋NAMES;]
JUDY              6 5 3 4 1 7 2            ANNETTE
MINDY                                      DAVID
JEFF                                       JEFF
JILL                                       JILL
DAVID                                      JUDY
ANNETTE                                    LISA
LISA                                       MINDY
```

using the default sort sequence ' A_AaB_Bb ... 0123456789'. If, as frequently happens, we have a list which is a combination of alphabetic and numeric characters (for example, a parts list), then ⍋ will neatly sort the alphabetic prefixes and numeric suffixes:

```
     INV←6 4ρ'CX20AC10AM2 AB8 AB3 CD14'

     INV                 INV[⍋INV;]
CX20                AB3
AC10                AB8
AM2                 AC10
AB8                 AM2
AB3                 CD14
CD14                CX20
```

Any desired sort sequence can be used with a dyadic version of grade. For instance, let $S←$'□*LXO' and $M←5$ 3ρ'***XXXZZZ⌊⌊⌊□□□':

```
     S⍋M                 M[S⍋M;]
5 1 4 2 3           □□□
                    ***
                    ⌊⌊⌊
                    XXX
                    ZZZ
```

As with dyadic ι, characters not present in the sort sequence are relegated to the end of the list.

Exotic uses of grade

Grade up and grade down are easy enough to work with for their obvious applications in rearranging vectors or matrices for display. However, don't think that's all they are good for. They are profoundly versatile, and professional APL'ers continue to discover interesting uses for them. This section mentions a few of the more surprising ones. Some of the points are admittedly of academic or recreational interest only. You can skip this entire topic if you wish, without loss of continuity.

⍋ and ⍒ can be used instead of monadic ι:

```
    ι5                   ⍋5ρ0                 ⍒5ρ0
1 2 3 4 5            1 2 3 4 5            1 2 3 4 5
```

The more curious among you may wonder whether ⍋⍋VECTOR has any special meaning. Let's explore it with

```
     Z←40 80 50 10 40              ⍋Z                  ⍋⍋Z
                              4 1 5 3 2            2 5 4 1 3
```

What you get is the cardinal ordering of each of the elements of the original vector. ▲▲Z tells you that Z's first element is the second largest, its second element is the largest, its third element is the fourth largest, and so on.

▲▲ can be used to *merge* or *collate* two or more arrays much as you would collate pages of paper from several stacks into one. For example, the two matrices ITEMS and SUMMARIES can be merged in whatever pattern is required:

```
       ITEMS                    SUMMARIES                        LINES
REVENUES                 *GROSS MARGINS             REVENUES
COST OF GOODS            *TOTAL EXPENSES            COST OF GOODS
SELLING EXPENSE          *NET BEFORE TAX            *GROSS MARGINS
GEN AND ADMIN            *NET AFTER TAX             SELLING EXPENSE
TAXES                                               GEN AND ADMIN
                                                    *TOTAL EXPENSES
      TEMP←((ρITEMS)+1 0×ρSUMMARIES)ρ(,ITEMS),,SUMMARIES   *NET BEFORE TAX
      LINES←TEMP[▲▲1 1 2 1 1 2 2 1 2;]                      TAXES
                                                    *NET AFTER TAX
```

Observe that the result of ▲VECTOR is always some permutation of the numbers ιρVECTOR. *Permutation vectors* have interesting mathematical properties when used with functions ▲, ▼, monadic φ, dyadic ι and indexing. We'll state a few of the identities here as brain teasers. All of these examples assume that P is a vector consisting of the numbers ιN, but scrambled in an arbitrary manner.

```
     ▼P       φ▲P                    P      ▲▲P      ▼▼▼▼P

     ▼▲P      φP              ▲P      ▲▲▲P     ▲▼▲P

   P[P]     (▲P)ιP        P[▲P]    (▲P)[P]    ιρP    PιP
```

Another practical use of ▲ and ▲▲ is in the following linear interpolation algorithm. Given a set of actuarial data like the following,

```
     PRESENT AGE               1   5  10  20  30  50  65  70
     ADDITONAL LIFE EXPECTANCY 75 74 66 54 40 23  9  7
```

calculate the expectancies for a group of people aged 5, 20, 24, 61 and 12. The first two are easy and can use dyadic ι directly,

```
      AGE←1 5 10 20 30 50 65 70          EXP[AGEι24 61 12]
      EXP←75 74 66 54 40 23 9 7     INDEX ERROR
      EXP[AGEι5 20]                      EXP[AGEι 24 61 12]
74 54                                            ∧
```

but those that don't match exactly will require us to estimate between values. One of the simpler methods for doing this is linear interpolation. For example, age 24 is four-tenths the distance between 20 and 30, and the corresponding life expectancies are 54 and 40:

```
      54+((24-20)÷30-20)×40-54
48.4
```

The question is, how to find that 24 is between the 20 and the 30; and the answer is a clever use of grade up:

```
      ▲▲AGE,24
1 2 3 4 6 7 8 9 5
```

The last element represents the relative ranking of 24 among the elements of the vector AGE. From here it's all downhill (pun intended):

```
      POS←¯1↑▲▲AGE,24
      EXP[POS-1]+((24-AGE[POS-1])÷-/EXP[POS-1 0])×-/EXP[POS-1]
69.42857143
```

This will interpolate only one value at a time. But one of the major beauties of APL is its ability to work with arrays of data. The following function interpolates entire arrays, and even extrapolates if the values are outside the range of numbers.

```
      )COPY 1 CLASS INT
SAVED   14.45.33 02/20/83
```

```
      (⍉ 2 8⍴AGE,EXP) INT 5 20 61 24 12
74 54 12.73333333 48.4 63.6

      ∇INT[⎕]∇
    ∇ R←X INT D;DI;Y;RQ;P
[1]   ⍝LEFT ARG IS 2 COL MATRIX. COL 1 IS INDEPENDENT VARIABLE
[2]   ⍝COL 2 IS RESULT VARIABLE.
[3]   ⍝RIGHT ARG IS VALUES [SCALED TO COL 1] TO BE INTERPOLATED
[4]   ⍝    OR EXTRAPOLATED INTO COL2.   AJROSE 26 AUG 79.
[5]   RQ←⍴D ◇ DI←⍋D←,D ◇ D←D[DI] ◇ Y←X[;2] ◇ X←X[;1]
[6]   P←¯1+2⌈(((⍴X)+⍋⍋X,D)-¯1+⍳⍴D)⌊⍴X
[7]   R←(Y[P]+((D-X[P])÷-/X[P∘.+ 1 0])×-/Y[P∘.+ 1 0])[RQ⍴⍋DI]
    ∇
```

Match

Occasionally there is a need to determine whether two arrays are identical, that is, their contents, shape and rank are the same. APL2 and APL*PLUS both provide a dyadic function *match*, ≡ (= overstruck with _) to do the checking. It returns a scalar 1 if the arguments are identical, 0 otherwise. Note its behavior on these look-alikes:

```
      '' ≡ ⍳0
0

      1 ≡ ,1
0

      (2 3⍴⍳6) ≡ 2 3⍴⍳6
1

      '23' ≡ 23
0
```

Deranged data

All of this chapter has focused on transforming or rearranging data into some orderly pattern. Now we're going to introduce a function that deliberately scrambles data.

Suppose, for example, that the dancers' union protests having the chorus line in ascending order, and demands that each person be given an even chance of being in any position. A way to do it fairly would be to write each dancer's identification number on a slip of paper, put it in an urn, and have an honest person, blindfolded, sequentially draw slips from the urn and announce the lineup. The function *deal*, ?, does exactly that.

Ordering for the dancers could be any of these:

```
      7?7                    7?7
4 2 5 3 7 6 1          3 1 2 7 4 6 5

      ARB←7?7                ARB
                        3 1 6 2 7 5 4
      NAMES                 NAMES[ARB;]
JUDY                   JEFF
MINDY                  JUDY
JEFF                   ANNETTE
JILL                   MINDY
DAVID                  LISA
ANNETTE                DAVID
LISA                   JILL
```

We've already used the symbol ? in a monadic sense to mean *roll*. Roll, you may recall, selects each value with possible replacement. Thus, ?7⍴7 may or may not have values repeated in it, while 7?7 is guaranteed not to have any repeats.

Suppose you needed only 5 dancers. Then

```
     5?7                    5?7                    5?7
3  2  1  7  4          1  2  6  5  3          3  1  4  7  6
```

is a way to select 5 items from a population of 7, again without repeats. Both arguments must be single integers, and the left argument must not be larger than the right. The result is a vector whose length is the same as the value of the left argument.

To help you keep deal and roll straight, associate their names with games of chance. Deal implies random selection of a subset (or complete set) of unique objects like a deck of cards (4 13ρ52?52 is a perfect way to simulate a bridge round). Roll implies random selection with the possibility of repeated values, as in a roll of dice (?2ρ6), the readout of a one-armed bandit (?3ρ10), or even a coin toss (?2). Of course, 1?N and ?N both select one number from ιN, although their ranks may differ.

Both roll and deal are random selections from an underlying uniform frequency distribution, each value of which has an equal chance of being selected. Suppose you wanted to build a game of chance, such as Russian roulette (a six-position revolver with only one live bullet). Here the probability of living is 5/6 and the probability of dying is 1/6 on any given spin and trigger pull.

This function would do it:

```
      ∇RISKY
[1]      [1]  ((2 4ρ'LIVEDEAD')[1 1 1 1 2;])[1?6]∇
```

The program *TEACH* in the next section employs a similar technique, assuring that all exercises have a chance of being selected, but weighting the probability of choice toward those on which the student has done poorly.

Another drill

In Chapter 7 the tutorial exercise *EASYDRILL* was introduced to give you practice in the functions discussed up to that point. You're ready now for some tougher problems. In workspace 1 *AIDRILL* there is a drill called *TEACH*. Load the workspace and type *TEACH*. Indicate which functions you want practice in. Be brave and try exercises with vectors of length 1 and 0. Here is a short sample session with *TEACH*:

```
      )LOAD 1 AIDRILL
SAVED  14.15.05 07/06/79

      TEACH
ARE YOU ALREADY FAMILIAR WITH THE INSTRUCTIONS? (TYPE
Y FOR YES AND N FOR NO.
NO

THIS IS AN EXERCISE IN SIMPLE APL EXPRESSIONS.  YOU WILL FIRST
HAVE THE OPPORTUNITY TO SELECT THE FEATURES YOU WISH TO BE
DRILLED IN.  THE EXERCISE THEN BEGINS.  FOR EACH PROBLEM YOU MUST
ENTER THE PROPER RESULT.  ANSWERS WILL CONSIST OF SCALAR INTEGERS
IF EXERCISES WITH VECTORS ARE NOT DESIRED; OTHERWISE ANSWERS WILL
CONSIST OF SCALARS OR VECTORS.  A VECTOR OF LENGTH ZERO REQUIRES
THE RESPONSE ι0, A VECTOR OF LENGTH ONE REQUIRES THE RESPONSE ,X
WHERE X IS THE VALUE OF THE ELEMENT.  YOU HAVE THREE TRIES FOR
EACH PROBLEM.  TYPE STOP AT ANY TIME TO TERMINATE THE EXERCISE
AND PRODUCE A RECORDING OF YOUR PERFORMANCE.  TYPING STOPSHORT
WILL TERMINATE THE EXERCISE BUT WILL NOT PRODUCE A RECORD OF
PERFORMANCE.  TYPING PLEASE FOR ANY PROBLEM WILL LET YOU PEEK AT
THE ANSWERS.  TYPE Y UNDER EACH FUNCTION FOR WHICH YOU WANT
EXERCISE:

SCALAR DYADIC FUNCTIONS
+-×÷*⌈⌊<≤=≥>≠!|∧∨⊛*↑↓
     YY        YY

SCALAR MONADIC FUNCTIONS
+-×÷⌈⌊!|~
   Y  Y

TYPE Y IF EXERCISES ARE TO USE VECTORS, N OTHERWISE
Y
```

```
TYPE Y IF REDUCTION EXERCISES ARE DESIRED, N OTHERWISE
Y

TYPE Y IF VECTORS OF LENGTH ZERO OR ONE ARE DESIRED,
N OTHERWISE
Y

MIXED DYADIC FUNCTIONS
ρι,∈⊥⊤/↑↓\φ
YYY

MIXED MONADIC FUNCTIONS
ιρ,φ
YY

                        !,0
□:
        1
TRY AGAIN
□:
        ,1

                        !ι0
□:
        ι0

                        ρ0
□:
        ι0

                        ÷ 1 ‾1 0.1111111111
□:
        1 ‾1 9

                        ⌈/ ‾8 ‾10 4
□:
        4

                        ι5
□:
        STOPSHORT
```

PROBLEMS

1. DRILL.   Assign $A \leftarrow 3\ 2\ 0\ ^-1\ 5\ ^-8$, $N \leftarrow 4\ 3\rho 9\ 7\ 1\ 2\ 3\ 5\ 6\ 9\ 15\ 22\ 1$ and $M \leftarrow 3\ 4\rho\iota 12$.

$3\phi A$	$\phi 0, \iota 3$	$A[\Psi 0\ 1\ 0\ 1\ 0\ 1]$
$2\phi A[\iota 4]$	$2\phi\phi\iota 7$	$2\phi 1\Theta M$
$\Delta\Psi A$	$\phi\Theta N$	$(\phi\iota 6)\iota M$
$2\uparrow ^-3\phi A$	$A[\Delta\Delta A]$	$(\iota 6)=\Delta A[\Delta A]$
$^-2\ 1\ 3\phi M$	$M[\Delta M[1;];]$	$\Diamond N$

2. Use APL to rearrange the character vector $S \leftarrow$ '*THE QUICK BROWN FOX JUMPS OVER THE LAZY DOG*' so that the letters (including duplicates and blanks) are in alphabetical order.

3. Construct this matrix using the monadic transpose:

    ```
    0 3 2 1
    1 0 3 2
    2 1 0 3
    ```

4. For an arbitrary numerical vector V which has been sorted in ascending order, show how to insert another vector $V1$ so as to preserve the ordering.

5. For a given numeric vector V of length N, write an APL expression that tests whether V is some permutation of the vector ιN (i.e., every element of V is in ιN and vice versa).

6. Write a program to find the median of a set of numbers. The median is defined as the scalar in the middle of the list after it has been sorted. When the number of elements is even, average the two middle elements.

7. Define a function to delete all leading, trailing and redundant occurrences of some element S in a vector V.

8. If the lengths of the sides of a box are stored in the 3-element vector $LENGTHS$, write expressions to compute **A** the volume of the box, and **B** its surface area (assuming it is closed on all sides).

9. Define a function $STRAIGHTLINE$ to compute a straight line depreciation schedule. The function should take a 3-element vector as its argument indicating the initial value of the asset, its life in years and its salvage value, in that order. It should return a vector showing the depreciated value of the asset at the end of each year. For example, $STRAIGHTLINE$ 1000 4 200 should result in 1000 800 600 400 200.

10. Write an expression to move all elements greater than 10 in a vector V to the front of the vector.

11. (A toughie!) A magic square of order n is one made up of the integers 1 through n. The sums over each row, column and diagonal are the same. One way to construct the squares of odd order is to start with a matrix of the right size, made up of the successive integers ordered rowwise. Then set up a vector of n successive integers with 0 in the middle to rotate the matrix successively over the last and first dimensions. Define a monadic function MS to do this.

12. You are given a 13-card bridge hand whose face values are the top row of a character matrix $HAND$ and the corresponding suit the bottom row (T=10):

    ```
         HAND
    JA9T36QTQ48K7
    DHCHSCHSCHDHD
    ```

    Write instructions to sort the hand **A** by suit, **B** by value and **C** by value within suit.

13. Write a function to separately sort each row of a numeric matrix M.

14. Construct a function LOC that locates all occurrences of a word or phrase W in a character vector V.

15. The vector G contains the grade point averages of all the seniors in a certain college. Find the two highest grades.

16. Show how to use ∧\ and ⌽ to **A** left-justify a matrix M, and **B** right-justify it.

17. Use the results of problem 16 to rotate a function that centers each line in a matrix whose lines before padding are of different lengths.

18. The vector S lists the amounts of individual holdings of shares of stock in the Squeaky Wheel Company. Show how to find the smallest number of individuals who together control 50% of the shares.

19. You are given a vector V of scholastic grades. Write an expression to drop off the lowest four and find the average of the rest.

20. Using *only* four characters, construct an expression that returns 1 if the first element in a given vector V is the largest, and 0 otherwise.

21. Write an APL expression that returns the index of the rightmost nonzero element in a vector V, that is, we get 5 for $V \leftarrow 3$ 2 0 0 8 0 0.

22. $NAMES$ is a character matrix containing the names of golf players in a tournament. The numeric vector $SCORES$ contains their scores in the same order as $NAMES$. Print $NAMES$ and $SCORES$ together and rank them high to low score.

23. Generate the indices of the last occurrences of elements $V1$ in vector $V2$.

24. Use ranking to delete the **A** leading and **B** trailing occurrences of some scalar S from a vector V.

25. Define a function $TRIANGLE$ to construct an n-row triangle out of the character ' ∘ '.

26. Construct a function $SUBST$ that makes a simple letter substitution for a message M which uses only the 26 letters of the alphabet (no blanks).

27. (For cryptography buffs). Design a function VIG to simulate the Vigenère code, which adds a 'key' to the indices resulting from $ALF \iota MESSAGE$.

28. Write a program to decode the message resulting from execution of the function $SUBST$ (problem 26).

29. Execute the following instructions and explain what they do:

$$B \leftarrow \phi A \leftarrow \iota 25 \qquad \qquad \diamond 3 \ 25 \rho A, B, A \times B$$

Chapter 16: Branching

One of the more prominent features of most programming languages is the concept of program flow and control, commonly referred to as *branching*. If you are familiar with other languages, you may be wondering why this notion, which involves selection of only some of the steps of a function or causes repeated execution under specified conditions, hasn't yet been presented in this text. The reason is that APL solves many problems in a more straightforward way, without branching.

The branch instruction

A branch instruction is usually called for whenever an algorithm requires a choice to be made as to what the next step should be, based in the results of some previous step. It is nothing more than an instruction to alter the regular sequence of steps.

We can demonstrate how this can be done by using a function called *SORT* in 1 *CLASS*. The problem that *SORT* is designed to handle is a very simple one: rearrange the elements of a vector in ascending order. Actually, there isn't any need to write a function to do this, since grade up can be used with indexing to accomplish the same thing very concisely (see page 140). The function, however, is a classic example of controlling the sequencing of the steps in a program.

Let's talk ourselves through the algorithm needed to solve the problem. The first and most obvious step is to start with a clean sheet of paper. Don't laugh. Try doing a large sorting problem by hand without it (or its equivalent). And as we'll see when we 'translate' the steps required into their APL equivalents, this part of the algorithm really does have an APL analogue.

The sensible next step is to pick out the smallest value in the vector. Right? Yes, but... suppose this value occurred many times (say, 100) in the vector. Then we would be inefficiently searching the vector 100 times for the same value. Wouldn't it make more sense to pick up all occurrences of that value in a single pass? Having done that, we write the smallest value 100 times on our paper and cross them off the original vector, go back and pick out the smallest value from what's left and repeat the process until all the numbers are used up.

It isn't any great challenge to devise a function to go through the repetitive steps, but it would need a safeguard built into it. We know when to stop, but a function would have to be explicitly instructed; otherwise it would continue to cycle through the sequence of steps indefinitely. This means that our algorithm needs a step which says in effect: 'look each time through to see if any numbers are left in the vector. If there are any, go on; if not, stop.'

Now we are ready to explore the function *SORT*.

```
      )LOAD 1 CLASS                    ∇SORT[]∇
SAVED  14.45.33 02/20/83        ∇ R←SORT X
      SORT 2 3 7 4 4 2          [1]    ⍝BRANCHING EXAMPLE NO. 1.
2 2 3 4 4 7                      [2]    R←⍳0
                                [3]    TEST:→(DONE,MORE)[1+×⍴X]
                                [4]    MORE:R←R,(X=⌊/X)/X
                                [5]    X←(X≠⌊/X)/X
                                [6]    →TEST
                                [7]    DONE:⍝SORT IS COMPLETED.
                                 ∇
```

It is a monadic function and expects a numeric vector argument X. The result is to be the numbers in X arranged in ascending order (same as $X[⍋X]$). Line 2 defines R as an empty vector (remember the clean sheet of paper?).

Line 3 is the branch instruction. If X were empty (i.e., nothing to sort), then $\times\rho X$ is 0 and $(DONE,MORE)[1+\times\rho X]$ would select $DONE$, whose value is 7. The arrow $\rightarrow$, *branch*, then directs the computer to move immediately to line 7, bypassing all the others. In other words, a sorted empty list is still an empty list.

On the other hand, if X were not empty, then $\times\rho X$ is 1 and $(DONE,MORE)[1+\times\rho X]$ is $MORE$, whose value is 4. The arrow then directs the computer to line 4, where all copies of the smallest value in X are catenated to R, the equivalent of writing them on the clean sheet of paper. On line 5, all copies of the smallest value in X are compressed out of X.

Line 6 gives the computer no choice whatsoever. It is an instruction to go directly to the line on which $TEST$: appears. The above sequence of instructions is repeated until there are no numbers left to sort.

Labels

In the $SORT$ function above, $TEST$, $MORE$ and $DONE$ are *labels*. Labels follow the same naming rules as variables, functions and groups. A label is set off from the rest of the line by a colon. Although they are local to the function, they don't appear in the header. Labels can be used like scalar variables or constants, except that you can't assign new values to them; their values are the line numbers on which they appear. If the line number changes (by editing the function), so does the value of the label.

Infinite loops

It takes no great talent to write functions that will run forever. For example, if line 5 of $SORT$ had been omitted, X would never become empty. The result R would grow wildly until the inevitable WS $FULL$ stopped execution. What do you think would happen if line 3, which is a checkpoint, were left out?

Errors in the calculation of which line to branch to next are also common. And it can be hard to ferret out these errors, particularly in functions with many branches.

For these reasons, we make an obvious recommendation: don't use branches unless you have to. If you don't have iterative branching (also called *looping*), you can't have an infinitely running program. But there are still many algorithms that either can't be executed without branching, or which are easier to develop using branches; so you're not going to be able to avoid branching forever. Fortunately, APL provides features which help you to figure out what's happening inside functions with branches. The next two sections treat the most fundamental of these.

Tracing the sequence of execution

Suppose you just wrote your first function using branches, and it doesn't work. What do you do? Let's assume you don't have an APL expert handy, so you have to find the problem and fix it yourself. First, get a new listing of the function and review it for obvious errors. Ask yourself if the APL expressions on each line do what they are supposed to do, especially in the branch instructions themselves.

But it is likely that you won't catch many subtle errors this way. You really need a way to watch each line as it is executed, and see if it is delivering what you expected at that point.

APL comes to the rescue! The *trace* system function does exactly that. To trace each execution of every line in $SORT$, enter

```
      (ι7) ⎕TRACE 'SORT'
      SORT 30 70 40 40
SORT[1]
SORT[2]
SORT[3]→4
SORT[4]30
SORT[5]70 40 40
SORT[6]→3
SORT[3]→4
SORT[4]30 40 40
```

```
SORT[5]70
SORT[6]→3
SORT[3]→4
SORT[4]30  40  40  70
SORT[5]
SORT[6]→3
SORT[3]→7
SORT[7]30  40  40  70
```

(On older systems, use $T\Delta SORT\leftarrow\iota 7$ instead.) As you can see, the result of each line and branch is shown. If you have avoided using long, complicated expressions it will be easier to trace because more intermediate results will be displayed.

Rather than tracing all the lines of a function, you can select only those lines that are central to the analysis. This avoids voluminous displays that don't add to the understanding.

```
      3  4  □TRACE 'SORT'
      SORT 30  70  40  40
SORT[3]→4
SORT[4]30
SORT[3]→4
SORT[4]30  40  40
SORT[3]→4
SORT[4]30  40  40  70
SORT[3]→7
30  40  40  70
```

The trace stays set until you change it or remove it. You can view the current trace setting by the monadic use of □TRACE, and you can remove all tracing by using an empty left argument:

```
      □TRACE                              (ιO) □TRACE 'SORT'
3  4                                      SORT 30  70  40  40

                                    30  40  40  70
```

Stopping the sequence of execution

Sometimes tracing isn't enough; and you'd like to halt execution dead in its tracks so you can poke around. It is very unlikely that you can stop a running function at the right place using BREAK—APL moves too swiftly for that. One simplistic approach is to deliberately cause an error where you want to stop. For example, if line 6 of *SORT* were →*TEST*÷0 instead of →*TEST*, you'd have a *DOMAIN ERROR* every time you got to line 6.

But there is a cleaner way to do it. You can set *stops* before whichever lines you wish in a manner similar to the trace:

```
      6 □STOP 'SORT' ⍝FOR OLDER SYSTEMS, USE S∆SORT←6
      SORT 2 3 7 4 4 2
SORT[6]
```

Now you can view any of the variables that have acquired values prior to (but not including) line 6. At this point you are free to change the variables or enter other commands as though they were already lines of the function. And most important, you can resume execution by issuing a branch instruction:

```
      →6
SORT[6]
```

The function stopped again before line 6. Let's look at *R* and *X*:

```
      R                    X                        →3
2  2  3                7  7  4                  SORT[6]
```

When we resumed execution (→3), we bypassed line 6. No harm was caused in this particular function, but in general it's not a wise procedure.

This time, after viewing *R* and *X* and having concluded that the function is running properly, we remove the stop. The function runs uninterrupted to completion.

```
      R                          (ιO) □STOP 'SORT'
2  2  3  4  4                     →6
      X                    2  2  3  4  4  7
7
```

Suspended functions

When a function is interrupted by encountering a stop (or by an error, or by your having pressed BREAK), it is called *suspended*. As you saw in the last section, you can explore, or even do unrelated calculations while suspended.

It is easy to forget that your function is suspended, because most of APL's features are still available to you. Most novices will stubbornly start another execution of the function while suspended. This is a bad practice. Without going into detail now, two of the horrors that result are that some of your global variables may be shielded, and your workspace becomes littered with a stack of partly executed functions and their associated variables. This littering reduces the space available to you for other work, and increases your storage charges on commercial systems.

Hence, always remove a suspension as soon as you have fixed whatever caused it. The usual fix is a branch to the proper line to continue running, but there are other alternatives, to be discussed soon.

You can produce a list of the suspensions with the system command $)SI$ (for *state indicator*). Let's now define a trivial function $FAILURE$ to generate suspensions:

```
      ∇FAILURE
[1]    5÷0
[2]    5 □STOP 'SORT'
[3]    SORT 2 3 7 4 2
[4]    (2+3 ∇
```

There are three potential suspensions above: line 1 will cause a $DOMAIN$ $ERROR$; line 2 will cause $SORT$ to suspend at its line 5; and line 4 is an obvious $SYNTAX$ $ERROR$.

Here goes $FAILURE$:

```
      FAILURE                              )SI
DOMAIN ERROR                         FAILURE[1]*
FAILURE[1]  5÷0
          ∧
```

It is hung as expected on line 1. Now push on to line 2:

```
      →2                                   )SI
SORT[5]                              SORT[5]*
                                     FAILURE[3]
```

Note that the stack of litter has grown. Not only is $SORT$ suspended, but $FAILURE$, which initiated $SORT$ on line 3, is also on the stack. Manually execute $FAILURE$ again:

```
      FAILURE                              )SI
DOMAIN ERROR                         FAILURE[1]*
FAILURE[1]  5÷0                      SORT[5]*
          ∧                          FAILURE[3]
```

What a mess! But look carefully at the $)SI$ report. The most recent suspension appears at the top, the oldest at the bottom. Did you observe the *'s following the top two entries? They indicate that these are true suspensions; on the other hand, $FAILURE[3]$ (without a *) indicates that it is *pendent*, not having been suspended itself, but rather waiting for $SORT$, which it invoked, to finish.

As promised, there are several ways to reduce the $)SI$ stack. Saving the workspace, clearing, and copying the entire workspace will remove all the stack. Copying removes all stops and traces as well.

```
      )SAVE CONTINUE                       )COPY CONTINUE FAILURE SORT
21.29.25 12/09/82                    SAVED  21.29.25  12/09/82
      )CLEAR                               )SI
CLEAR WS
```

Many APL systems support the system command) *RESET*, which removes all the clutter:

```
     )LOAD CONTINUE                            )RESET
SAVED  21.29.25 12/09/82                       )SI
     )SI
FAILURE[1]*
SORT[5]*
FAILURE[3]
```

Occasionally, when an error halts execution in a lengthy run, you may want to 'back out' part way to preserve some of the work. A branch to zero (→0) will remove the immediate suspension:

```
     )LOAD CONTINUE                               )SI
SAVED  21.29.25 12/09/82                      SORT[5]*
     )SI                                      FAILURE[3]
FAILURE[1]*                                        →0
SORT[5]*
FAILURE[3]                                    2  2
     →0                                       SYNTAX ERROR
                                              FAILURE[4]  (2+3
                                                          ^
                                                   )SI
                                              FAILURE[4]*
```

It hung again, but this time because of the missing parenthesis on line 4 of *FAILURE*. When backing out, it is wise to set stops in the pendent function which invoked the suspended one. This gives you a chance to look around and maybe patch up some errors, so you may resume your execution.

The arrow used by itself is called a *naked branch*. It removes the current suspension and any pendencies that invoked it. After using it, the stack still has earlier suspensions in it. In other words, each time you use → alone, you 'peel' one layer from the suspension stack.

```
     →
     )SI
```

In our case, since there was only one suspension in the stack, entry of → restored the stack to its normal, empty state.

Two variants of the) *SI* system command are available in some APL systems. They give more detail about the suspensions.) *SINL* (or) *SIV* on older systems) reports suspensions like) *SI* and lists the local variables for each suspended or pendent function.) *SIS* (in APL2) lists the statements being executed at the time of suspension, with an indication (as in the typical error message) of the point where the suspension happened and the statements being executed at the time.

Some APL systems treat locked functions as though they were primitives. Unlike old soldiers, locked functions do die when execution is interrupted. To avoid compromising security they are never suspended or pendent. Three kinds of error message are possible: *DOMAIN ERROR* if there was an actual error, *WS FULL* (or something similar) if a system limitation halted execution, or *INTERRUPT*. See page 300 if you need more detail.

The line counter system function

Some of the same information reported by) *SI* is available in a feature called the *line counter system function*, □*LC*. It results in a vector whose first element is the most current line number that is suspended or being executed, whose second element is the most immediate previous line, etc. Compare the following displays:

```
     )LOAD CONTINUE                  )SI                  □LC
SAVED  21.29.25 12/09/82        FAILURE[1]*          1  5  3
                               SORT[5]*
                               FAILURE[3]
```

Its most important use is to resume execution at the point of interruption by the instruction →□*LC*. In the case above, this would result in the function *FAILURE* restarting at line 1.

$\Box LC$ is also used to direct control to some line that is a fixed number of lines distant from the present one. For example, here's a stupid way to sum a vector, somewhat reminiscent of more primitive programming languages:

```
[N]     S←0
[N+1]   I←0
[N+2]   I←I+1
[N+3]   →(2×I>ρVECTOR)+1+□LC[1]
[N+4]   S←S+VECTOR[I]
[N+5]   →□LC[1]-2
[N+6]   ...
```

No matter where these statements are in a program (so long as they are adjacent), line [N+5] causes a branch back two lines. And line [N+3] causes a branch ahead one line, provided that all the elements in *VECTOR* haven't been added yet, or ahead 3 lines, if they have all been added. Caution: if you use this method instead of the using labels, you must be sure to make appropriate adjustments if you insert or delete lines.

Another simple use of the line counter is using ρ□LC to test how deep you are in the suspension stack. It's shorter, albeit less informative, than)SI.

Absolute branches

It is technically possible to branch to an absolute line number instead of to a label or relative to $\Box LC$. For example, *SORT* could have been written as

```
        ∇R←BADSTYLESORT X
[1]     ⍝USES ABSOLUTE BRANCHES; SHOWN ONLY AS COUNTEREXAMPLE
[2]     R←⍳0
[3]     →(7 4)[1+ρX]
[4]     R←R,(X=⌊/X)/X
[5]     X←(X≠⌊/X)/X
[6]     →3
[7]     ⍝SORT IS COMPLETED
[8]     ∇
```

However, this style is not recommended because it requires too much maintenance for even simple changes. For example, in *BADSTYLESORT*, if a new line were inserted between lines 1 and 2, all the line numbers would have to be changed. About the only absolute branch in lieu of a label that is condoned is →0, which means 'leave the program immediately.' And even here it is recommended that the function have only one exit point, preferably the last line.

Conditional branching

A branch expression consists of right arrow followed by an APL expression (naked branch is a special case). The expression must result in scalar or vector integer values. Decimals, characters and arrays of rank greater than 1 cause an error. If it is a vector, only the first element is used for the branch. If the value (including labels) matches a line in the function, then that line is executed next. If the value doesn't match (for example, →100 in a function with 20 lines, or →0 in any function), then execution is ended and control returns to the pendent function which used it, or to calculator mode if the stack is empty.

An important, special case is a branch to an empty vector (→⍳0). Then *no branch* happens, since there is no first element in the vector. Control flows to the next statement as though the branch expression wasn't there at all.

This gives rise to the most popular use of branching—one which causes a branch if some logical condition is met. For example, here is a more efficient version of *SORT*:

```
        ∇R←SORT X
[1]     ⍝BRANCHING EXAMPLE NO. 3
[2]     R←⍳0
[3]     LOOP:→(0=ρX)/DONE
[4]     R←R,(X=⌊/X)/X
[5]     X←(X≠⌊/X)/X
[6]     →LOOP
[7]     DONE:⍝SORT IS COMPLETED.
[8]     ∇
```

An even shorter version would omit line 7 entirely, and change line 3 to LOOP:→(0=ρX)/0.

Examples of branch expressions

There are many ways to compute the branch target in APL—any expression that returns an integer scalar or vector with integer first element would do. In the list of popular forms that follows, $L1$, $L2$, $L3$ are labels, X and Y are numeric scalars to be compared, I is an iteration counter, and N is the relative distance between the line being executed and the target line.

1) Branch unconditionally to a fixed point in the function:
>   →5
>   →LABEL

2) Branch unconditionally out of the function:
>   →0 (or any nonexistent line number)

3) Branch to one of the two possible lines:
>   →(L1,L2)[1+X≥Y]
>   →((X≥Y),~X≥Y)/L1,L2
>   →(1 0≠X≥Y)/L1,L2

4) Branch to one of several lines:
>   →(L1,L2,L3)[2+×X−Y]
>   →((X>Y),(X<Y),X=Y)/L1,L2,L3
>   →IϕL1,L2,L3,...
>   →I+□LC

5) Branch to a given line or drop through to the next line:
>   →(X≥Y)/L1
>   →(X≥Y)ρL1
>   →(×X−Y)↑L1,L2
>   →L1⌈ιX≥Y
>   →(L2,L3,L1)[I]×ιX≥Y
>   →((X>Y),(X<Y)/L1,L2

6) Branch to a line a fixed distance from the current line:
>   →N+□LC

7) Branch out of the program or to a specific line:
>   →((X≥Y),X<Y)/L1,0
>   →L1×X≥Y

8) Branch to a given line or the line following it:
>   →L1+X≥Y

Rules for branching

As you can see below, the rules for branching in defined functions are very simple, yet using these rules most popular forms of structured programming can be emulated.

>   → (any APL expression)
>   is

INVALID	if the expression results in other than an integer or a vector whose first element (the only one which can cause a branch) is an integer or a valid label.
VALID	if the expression results in
(a)	an empty vector, which causes a branch to the next statement (→ι0 for example).
(b)	an integer outside the range of statement numbers of the function, which causes an exit from the function (such as →0, but don't confuse with →ι0).
(c)	an integer inside the range of statement numbers of the function, which causes a branch to that line number.
(d)	a label, which causes a branch to that line of the function on which the label is to be found.

Structured branching and control

In the 1970's much was written about *structured programming*. Some of its advocates have charged APL with being devoid of structure. No doubt the allegation comes from the fact that APL has only one form of program control, the branch expression. Virtually anything goes in that expression, as we saw in the last section. There are situations where too much variety can blemish the appearances of functions. The careful user should consider limiting his choice of branching techniques to the following forms.

Normal program flow should be downward, rather than jumping around. Error or warning messages should appear immediately after the test. For APL*PLUS and Sharp Systems, the message can even appear on the same line as the test, by using diamonds.

```
→(VALUE>0)/L3
'NEGATIVE VALUE ENCOUNTERED FOR SQUARE ROOT'
'CHANGING TO POSITIVE AND PROCEEDING'
VALUE←|VALUE
L3:R←VALUE*.5
```

The notion of branching if some logical condition exists is so prevalent that it's wise to employ a function whose name is descriptive:

```
       ∇R←BRANCH IF CONDITION                →L3 IF VALUE ≥0
[1]    R←CONDITION/BRANCH ∇                   L3:R←VALUE*.5
```

Iteration, particularly when based on some arithmetic progression, such as 'do some sequence of lines for *J* having values of 10, 12, 14, 16, 18 and 20,' should follow a pattern like this:

```
J←10
LOOPJ:→(J>20)/PASTJ
(whatever is to be done based on J)
J←J+2
→LOOPJ
PASTJ:
(whatever should follow)
```

Many users prefer to increment on the same line as the test. While it does use embedded assignment, it's worthwhile in this case.

```
J←8 ⍝ NOTE STARTING VALUE
LOOPJ:→(20<J←J+2)/PASTJ
(whatever is to be done based on J)
→LOOPJ
PASTJ:
(whatever is to follow the loop)
```

Because this type of iteration is so common, we have a gift for you: a set of functions that will let you write the above sequence as

```
J←DO 8 20 2
(whatever is to be based on J)
→NEXT J
```

We now present the functions *DO*, *NEXT*, *SETDO* and *OUT*. Although they use no new primitives, the techniques employed are tricky, to say the least. Understanding how they work is not a prerequisite for using them.

```
       ∇R←DO X;N
[1]    ⍝X IS 3 ELEMENT VECTOR: START, END, INCREMENT
[2]    ⍝DC IS A GLOBAL VARIABLE THAT CONTROLS IT ALL.
[3]    ⍝LAST TWO ELEMENTS ARE BOOLEAN INDICATORS.
[4]    →(∧/ 0 1 =¯2↑DC)/POST ⍝ OTHERWISE THIS IS A NEW DO STMT.
[5]    N←⌊(X[2]-X[1])÷X[3]+X[3]=0 ⍝N IS NUMBER OF ITERATIONS TO DO.
[6]    →((N>0)∧X[3]≠0)/OK
[7]    'LINE ',(⍕⎕LC[2]),' INFINITE LOOP: ',⍕X
[8]    DC← 1 1 ⍝RESET DC IN HOPELESS SITUATION.
[9]    → ⍝ AND BLAST OUT OF )SI STACK.
[10]   OK:DC←0,(N+1),X[1 3],⎕LC[2],DC ⍝ SET UP FOR THIS LEVEL.
[11]   POST:R←DC[3]+DC[1]×DC[4] ⍝RETURN VALUE FOR THIS ITERATION.
[12]   DC[1]←1+DC[1] ⍝COUNT THIS ITERATION.
[13]   DC[⍴DC]←0 ⍝ 0 MEANS JUST EXECUTED DO.  SEE NEXT[4].
[14]   ∇
```

```
          ∇ R←NEXT X
[1]       ⍝X IS IGNORED, BUT RECOMMENDED. USE NAME OF ITEⱠATION VARIABLE.
[2]       R←(DC[1]≠DC[2])/DC[5] ⍝BRANCH TO DO OR BEYOND.
[3]       DC[ ̄1+⍴DC]←DC[1]=DC[2] ⍝1 MEANS COMPLETED ITERATION.
[4]       DC[⍴DC]←1 ⍝1 MEANS JUST EXECUTED NEXT.  SEE DO[13].
[5]       →PEEL×DC[1]=DC[2]
[6]       PEEL:DC←5↓DC ∇


          ∇ R←TD OUT CONDITION
[1]       ⍝SPECIAL FUNCTION FOR PREMATURE ESCAPE FROM LOOP.
[2]       ⍝TD[1] IS TARGET LINE, TD[2] IS NUMBER OF LEVELS OUT.
[3]       R←CONDITION/TD[1]
[4]       →REALLYOUT×CONDITION
[5]       REALLYOUT:DC←(5×TD[2])↓DC ⍝CHOP 5 ELEMENTS OFF FOR EACH LEVEL.
[6]       ∇


          ∇ SETDO
[1]       ⍝EXECUTE THIS TO INITIALIZE AND AFTER ANY ABORTED RUN.
[2]       DC← 1 1 ⍝ INITIAL SETTING FOR DO CONTROL.
[3]       ∇
```

Here is an example of the use of looping functions to perform a matrix multiplication (the hard way—APL has a built-in function we'll see later):

```
          ∇ C←A MATMULT B;I;J;K;T                  A←2 3⍴⍳6
[1]       SETDO                                    A
[2]       →(( ̄1↑⍴A)=1↑⍴B)/OK                       1 2 3
[3]       'ERROR - DIMENSIONS DO NOT MATCH'        4 5 6
[4]       S∆MATMULT←⎕LC+1
[5]       OK:C←((1↑⍴A), ̄1↑⍴B)⍴0                    B←100×3 4⍴⍳12
[6]       I←DO 1,(1↑⍴A),1                          B
[7]       J←DO 1,( ̄1↑⍴B),1                         100   200   300   400
[8]       T←0                                      500   600   700   800
[9]       K←DO 1,( ̄1↑⍴A),1                         900  1000  1100  1200
[10]      T←T+A[I;K]×B[K;J]
[11]      →NEXT K                                  A MATMULT B
[12]      C[I;J]←T                                 3800   4400   5000   5600
[13]      →NEXT J                                  8300   9800  11300  12800
[14]      →NEXT I ∇
```

Some thoughts on branching

Branching in APL is a powerful programming tool about which much sense (and nonsense) has been written. There is one school of thought that says 'avoid branching wherever possible.' Two reasons are usually given by adherents of this school: (1) each time around there is a costly translation of source code into internal code, and (2) branching complicates the normal flow of a program, and therefore makes it harder to debug and maintain.

A second school proclaims the virtues of 'intelligent' loops which can run rings around (sorry about that) complicated one-liners.

As usual, neither side has a monopoly on wisdom. The truth lies somewhere in between. While it's true that some loop programs are virtually indecipherable, that is probably the fault of the coder, not APL. You will find many occasions where branching just can't be avoided or where the nonbranch solution, while ingenious, is unnatural. So branch if you must, but do so with style.

If the previous section on structured programming touched a responsive chord, you are well prepared. If not, here are a few simple guidelines with illustrations to help you avoid pitfalls in branching.

1. Avoid branching around a branch. Instead of

```
     →(A=B)/L1
     →L2
```

use

```
     →(A≠B)/L2
   L1:
```

2. Put the test for a condition at the beginning of a loop (*leading decision*) rather than at the end (*trailing decision*). This tends to eliminate unnecessary looping. The function *SORT* at the beginning of this chapter employs a leading decision. It branches immediately to the end if the argument *X* has no elements.

3. Replace branches with array operations. The function below uses looping to summarize by quarter the sales for each item (row) in a matrix, each of whose 12 columns contains the sales for a particular month:

```
        ∇R←SUMQ M;I
[1]     R←((1↑ρM),4)ρ0
[2]     I←1
[3]     →(5=I)/0
[4]     L:R[I;]←+/M[;(3×I-1)+ι3]
[5]     I←I+1
[6]     →L ∇
```

This problem is one of those that can be solved without branching:

```
        ∇R←BETTERSUMQ M                              ∇R←BESTSUMQ M
[1]     R←(+\M)[;3×ι4]                      [1]      R←+/((1↑ρM),4 3)ρM ∇
[2]     R[;2 3 4]←R[;2 3 4]-R[;1 2 3] ∇
```

BESTSUMQ reshapes the sales matrix to a three-dimensional array (see Chapter 19) each of whose planes represents a single item. Within any plane each row contains a quarter's sales data. The reduction is carried out over the rows. The lesson learned here is that thinking the problem through again may lead to a different solution which takes advantage of APL's lesser used, but no less powerful features, or suggests the use of a higher dimensional array than was initially contemplated.

4. Always branch to a label, not a line number. We've said it before (page 154), but it bears repeating here.

5. Do as much as possible a) before you enter a loop, and b) with each iteration, testing and incrementing counters no more than is absolutely necessary. This last guideline is proposed to get you 'thinking lean,' to reduce the overhead involved in looping.

6. Avoid 'gluing.' Even the best APL'ers do it, but that doesn't make it right:

```
    →LABEL,0ρ[]←'THIS IS A MESSAGE TO THE USER'
```

Here two completely unrelated concepts, the message and the branch, are placed in a single executable line. Just as in writing there should be but one idea in a sentence, so having one concept (or at least only closely related concepts) makes an APL line more readable. Besides, in some cases gluing another instruction might change the rank of an array and lead to an error. These problems can be avoided by using separate lines for the unrelated pieces, or the diamond as a separator if your system supports it.

Even when the ideas are closely related, problems can arise when execution is interrupted. For instance, in the last section an example was given which incremented a counter on the same line as the test:

```
    LOOPJ:→(20<J←J+2)/PASTJ
```

If the function is interrupted past the point where *J* is incremented but *before the line is completed*, when execution is resumed the entire line will be reexecuted with an incorrect value for *J*. Hence branch lines, like all the others, should be written to be *restartable* in case of interruption.

There is another technique that avoids branching altogether by the use of *execute*. This concept will be discussed in Chapter 24.

The foregoing discussion has touched on only one aspect of style in writing APL programs, although an important one. Programming style is a whole subject in itself, and one about which reasonable people can differ. Indeed, whole books have been written just on the related subject of structured programming.

Our intent is to be expository, and not dogmatic, since no one can dictate by fiat what 'good' style is. Whatever it is, it certainly changes with time, like fashions in clothes, and depends on the features available on the system being used.

'Good' can probably be best translated as 'readable,' which isn't necessarily synonymous with efficiency of execution and effective use of storage. Those of you who have to modify or maintain someone else's code will appreciate our emphasis on readability. But don't be too quick to point a finger at others. We assure you that your own code is just as likely to be unreadable after you haven't looked at it for six months.

Recursion

This section is entirely optional. Recursion is rarely used in practical business programming. But it is an intriguing topic for most neophyte computer scientists, so we include it for your entertainment.

The classic example of recursion is that of the factorial. An alternate way to describe how to calculate the factorial of N is to multiply N by the factorial of $N-1$. But that would require being able to calculate the factorial of $N-2$ and so on. That is a recursive definition. To make sense out of it, there must be some special ending value or else the dependencies go on forever. In the case of factorials, the special ending value is the factorial of zero, defined to be 1. Once you have that, you can work your way out and ultimately produce the factorial of N. Now, here is what we just said, but written in APL:

```
      )COPY 1 CLASS FACT COMB
SAVED  14.45.33 02/20/83

      ∇FACT[☐]∇
    ∇ R←FACT N;NM1
[1]   →(N≠|⌊N)/0
[2]   →(N=0)/L6
[3]   NM1←N-1
[4]   R←N×FACT NM1
[5]   →0
[6]   L6:R←1
    ∇
```

As you can see, the function *FACT* calls upon itself. And as you can also see, if it didn't have (or can't get to) an ending value of 0, you would be in deep trouble. You might want to set ☐*TRACE* or ☐*STOP* on this function and explore it with *small* positive integer arguments.

Recursive techniques are used in sophisticated computer programs for artificial intelligence research, compilers and interpreters. An example is wading through sets of nested parentheses in APL statements to get to the innermost level, and then working the way out with the solution.

One of the more useful examples of recursion is the following function *COMB* that enumerates all combinations of N things taken from a population of P. This function is particularly interesting because it calls upon itself twice (line 2) at each level of the recursion.

```
      ∇COMB[☐]∇                                              3 COMB 4
    ∇ R←M COMB N                                         1 2 3
[1]   →(M=1,N)/L,R  ⍝RECURSIVE    AJROSE 1976            1 2 4
[2]   R←1+(0,(M-1) COMB N-1),[1] M COMB N-1              1 3 4
[3]   →0                                                2 3 4
[4]   L:R←(⍳N)∘.×⍳1
[5]   →0                                                  5 COMB 5
[6]   R:R←(⍳1)∘.×⍳N                                     1 2 3 4 5
    ∇
```

PROBLEMS

1. Tell what each of the following does:

   A $\rightarrow((5<W),5>W)/\ 3\ \ 2$
   B $\rightarrow3\times\iota A=8$
   C $\rightarrow END\times Y>,R\leftarrow\ 1\ \ 1\ \rho1$
   D $\rightarrow(\vee/,B\epsilon C)/7$
   E $\rightarrow\ 5\ \ 0[1+A>C]$

   F $\rightarrow^-1\uparrow\phi\ \ 3\ \ 4\ \ 7\ \ 9$
   G $\rightarrow8\times\iota 0\neq J\leftarrow J-1$
   H $\rightarrow4\times(\mid X\mid)\geq I\leftarrow I+1$
   I $\rightarrow AGAIN\lceil\iota N=2\times1\rho R\leftarrow\ 2\ \ 4\ \rho\ \ 5\ \ 7\ \ 1\ \ 8$

2. Let T be a vector of 'trash' characters, some of which may occur in the character vector V. Define an APL function that will eliminate the trash from V.

3. Write a version of the function CMP (page 125) that uses branching.

4. Use branching to find the median of a set of numbers. (see problem 6, Chapter 15 for more information about the median.)

5. Define a dyadic function $DUPL$ that will locate all occurrences of some scalar N in a vector V and print an appropriate message if the desired scalar is not present.

6. Design an APL function so that it ignores all nonscalar input and takes the square root of any scalar argument. Assume all input is positive.

7. Take the opening two sentences of this chapter, eliminating all punctuation, underlining and blanks, and define a function to arrange the characters in alphabetic order.

8. Write an APL program to find the *mode* (most frequently occurring number) of a set of data.

9. The Fibonacci series is of the form $1\ \ 1\ \ 2\ \ 3\ \ 5\ \ 8\ \ 13\ \ \ldots$, where each term after the first two is the sum of the preceding two terms. Define a function which prints N terms of the series.

10. Define a function which will produce a histogram of a vector A of nonnegative integers, i.e., the height of the histogram for $A[1]$ is $A[1]$, the height for $A[5]$ is $A[5]$, etc. Show how the histogram can be 'cleaned up' by replacing the 0's with blanks and the 1's with $\star$'s.

11. Use branching to construct a function which prints an annual compound interest table. Design your function to produce three columns, the first to be the year, the second the value of the principal at the beginning of the year, and the third the interest accumulated during the year. Include appropriate column headings and round off each figure to the nearest cent.

12. Estimate the odds that 3 or more cards of any one suit will appear in a 5-card poker hand from a well-shuffled deck.

13. ACK is a function constructed for the purpose of proving that nonprimitive recursive functions do exist, and is named after its creator (see Communications of the ACM, page 114, Vol. 8, No.2, February 1965.) Use *small* integers for I and J. Follow the execution of ACK with the trace and stop controls:

```
        ∇R←I ACK J
[1]     →(0=I,J)/4 3
[2]     R←(I-1) ACK I ACK J-1 ◇ →0
[3]     R←(I-1) ACK 1 ◇ →0
[4]     R←J+1∇
```

14. Write a program $EQUAL$ that compares any two APL arrays and returns a 1 if they are identical, 0 otherwise.

15. Define a dyadic function $PRINT$ to print a message (argument) if a given condition (other argument) is met.

16. Define a program $DELE$ to delete a given name from a matrix of names or print an appropriate message if the name isn't in the matrix.

17. Use branching to solve the matrix grade problem cited on **page 140** in the last chapter.

18. Define a function $FINDROW$ that locates those lines in a literal matrix that match a given name.

19. Write a function $CARDSORT$ that uses the cardsort technique (from the days of mechanical punched card sorters) to sort one column of a literal matrix at a time, working backwards from right to left.

20. Redo problem 9 and define a dyadic recursive function $FIB1$ whose right argument A specifies the first two terms of·the series, with the left argument N the number of terms desired.

Chapter 17: Report formatting

This chapter covers what you need to know to produce a neat report for someone else. You have probably observed by now that you haven't been able to exercise much control over the way APL prints numeric results on the terminal. If this limit on your options for producing attractive reports doesn't bother you, skim over this chapter lightly. If on the other hand you have developed some concern (or consternation) over this, then you will find the features described here very helpful.

Thus far it would appear that APL decides how displayed numbers will be formed, how they will be spaced, and how many significant digits will be shown. However, while you can always get the answers out in a readable form, they may not necessarily be in the proper shape to hand to your boss, who may have a preference for reports with such features as column and row headings, and data with a fixed number of decimal positions, each neatly lined up. Be tolerant. The boss needs good formatting because as he gets older his eyes start to go. More seriously, if the data that you submit to him is easy for him to read, the quicker he can make his business decisions. And besides, you owe it to yourself to finish up any important programming assignment by producing the final results in an attractive format.

The treatment in this chapter is intended to be only an introduction, covering some elementary ideas to get you started. Many APL systems include prepared formatting packages to make life easier for you. The more elaborate format packages generally have user guides to assist both the novices and the pros. Consult your computer center management for further information.

The monadic format function

In Chapter 13 we introduced ⍕ as a device to convert numeric values to their character representation. While we used it only for scalars there, it can take any array as its argument, and the result is a character array whose appearance when displayed is identical to the original argument. In this example we have a table of compound interest (on one dollar) for interest ranges of 4, 8 and 12 percent, for years 1 through 4:

```
      TABLE←((1+.04×⍳3)∘.*⍳4)-1
      TABLE
0.04        0.0816      0.124864    0.16985856
0.08        0.1664      0.259712    0.36048896
0.12        0.2544      0.404928    0.57351936
```

Now suppose we didn't want to see all those digits, three digits being sufficiently accurate for our purpose. If we use a rounding algorithm such as

```
      .001×⌊.5+TABLE×1000
0.04        0.082       0.125       0.17
0.08        0.166       0.26        0.36
0.12        0.254       0.405       0.574
```

the numbers are still spread out more than is desired. Some of the blank columns could be eliminated by storing a character representation of *TABLE* as *CTABLE* and then compressing out some of the blank columns:

```
      CTABLE←⍕TABLE
      ⍴CTABLE
3 64
      CTABLE
0.04        0.0816      0.124864    0.16985856
0.08        0.1664      0.259712    0.36048896
0.12        0.2544      0.404928    0.57351936
```

While *TABLE* had only four columns of numbers, *CTABLE* has 64 columns of characters. In general, monadic ⍕ preserves all the dimensions of the array argument except for the last dimension.

```
      (64ρ16↑7ρ1)/CTABLE
 0.04    0.081   0.124   0.169
 0.08    0.166   0.259   0.360
 0.12    0.254   0.404   0.573
```

Printing precision

In the above example, we did eliminate the trailing digits, but the numbers are truncated (chopped off) rather than rounded. We could combine the rounding algorithm with compression to fix it, but it seems a lot of work for something that can be stated as simply as 'I want three digits of printing precision.' APL to the rescue! The *printing precision* system variable, $\Box PP$, is a special feature (actually, there are many system variables and system functions in APL, but we'll hold back on a general discussion so we don't clutter up the presentation of the present topic) that lets you control the maximum number of digits that are displayed for a numeric array, or the number of significant digits that are provided in the result of ▼ for each column of its argument.

The default value of $\Box PP$ on most APL systems is 10. That's why we never showed a result with more than 10 significant digits. But you can change it on most systems to any integer value between 1 and 16:

```
      □PP
10                           □PP←1                 □PP←16
      ÷7                      ÷7                     ÷7
0.1428571429           0.1      0.1428571428571428
                                                  □PP←10
```

Monadic ▼ uses the present $\Box PP$ setting in determining the width of the result. The rules for spacing with monadic ▼ (and APL raw output as well) differ from system to system, and are subject to change. And while the above formatting was a little easier to do, it's still not an ideal result. No more than three significant digits are shown, and the result is properly rounded in the last digit, but the display still looks ragged. For these reasons feel free to use monadic ▼ and $\Box PP$ for casual displays, but avoid them in applications where the result must be aligned with other displays, such as headings and titles. Read on, the next section contains one answer.

The dyadic formatting function

The dyadic use of ▼ extends the control you have over printed results. Its right argument is the data to be formatted, and its left argument holds the format instructions, which are the total number of characters in the result and the number of decimal positions to be shown. The following example forms each column of *TABLE* into a *field* six characters wide, with three decimal places:

```
      6 3▼TABLE
 .040   .082   .125   .170
 .080   .166   .260   .360
 .120   .254   .405   .574
```

The left argument 6 3 was (conceptually) repeated for each column of *TABLE*. On the other hand, if you enter

```
      (8ρ8 3 7 4)▼TABLE                    ρ(8ρ8 3 7 4)▼TABLE
 .040    .0816    .125    .1699        3 30
 .080    .1664    .260    .3605
 .120    .2544    .405    .5735
```

you get a pattern of alternating field specifications. ▼ applies each *pair* of numbers in the left argument to a column of the right argument. The format function returns an explicit result which is a character representation (in this case a matrix) of the right argument.

The shape of the result is the same as the shape of the right argument, except that the last dimension of the result is the sum of the field widths. Thus, if the right argument is a (numeric) vector, the result is a (character) vector. Of course, if the right argument is a scalar, you'll still get a vector as a result. If you want a complete table with numeric row and column headings, the following program will do it:

```
      ∇RATES COMPINT TIMES
[1]    (4ρ' '),6 0⍕TIMES
[2]    (4 2,(2×ρTIMES)ρ6 3)⍕RATES,((1+RATES)∘.*TIMES)-1 ∇
      (.04×⍳3) COMPINT ⍳5
              1      2      3      4      5
      .04   .040   .082   .125   .170   .217
      .08   .080   .166   .260   .360   .469
      .12   .120   .254   .405   .574   .762
```

If the number of decimal positions is given as zero, as in line one of *COMPINT*, then the decimal point itself is suppressed. The result is rounded, not truncated.

If the second number of the pair is negative, then the corresponding field will be printed in scaled notation. Most commercial reports don't employ scaled notation, so unless you are making reports involving very large or very small numbers, skip the rest of this paragraph. If in spite of this warning you're still here, the first number in the pair still dictates the field width, but the second number controls the minimum number of significant digits of *mantissa* (the number before the *E*) that will be produced. The magnitude of this number must be at least six smaller than the field width to allow for a negative sign and the characters of the exponent itself, as for example

```
      10 ¯4 20 ¯3 10 ¯4⍕12345 .000001234567 ¯1
1.23450E4              1.235E¯6 1.00000E0
```

To recap, we have seen that the shape of the left argument must be a vector with either two elements (implied replication) or with one pair of elements for each column in the right argument. The first element of the pair gives the field width, and the second gives the number of digits after the decimal point (or the number of significant digits for scaled notation). If the second element of the pair is zero, the result appears as an integer, with no decimal point at all.

Special cases of dyadic format

If the first element of the pair is zero, the width is then taken to be whatever is required to represent the value, allowing for one blank space in front. Fractional values (i.e., have no integer parts) are formed without a zero before their decimal points. Look at this example:

```
      0 5 0 0 4 0 4⍕101.49   101.49 .1234 ¯.1234
101.49000 101 .1234 ¯.1234
```

If you format a matrix using zero (automatic) width specification, the resulting width is whatever is needed to cause each column of the result to line up properly and yet not run together, as shown by

```
      X←2 2ρ¯79.68 ¯.91 .5 1234567
      0 3 0 0⍕X
¯79.680          ¯1
  .500 1234567
```

When using implied replication and automatic widths (that is, formatting several columns of the right argument using a left argument pair of elements the first of which is zero), the width is based on the number of characters required to represent the largest value in the right argument, rather than dealing with it column by column. Observe the difference in these two examples:

```
      0 2 0 2⍕X
¯79.68          ¯.91
  .50 1234567.00

      0 2⍕X
¯79.68          ¯.91
  .50 1234567.00
```

As a special case, the left argument can be a single element. If it is a positive value, the result has automatic width, with the number of decimal positions taken from the left argument:

```
      Y←20 .012345 ¯7.2
      5⍕Y
20.00000   .01235 ¯7.20000
```

If the left argument is a single zero, the result will be formed with automatic width and no decimal positions. When the left argument is a negative integer, the result is formed in scaled notation:

```
        0⍕Y                    ¯3⍕Y
20  0 ¯7            2.0000E1  1.235E¯2  ¯7.2000E0
```

Lest you have any doubts, a character array as an argument is a *DOMAIN ERROR*, and left arguments that aren't scalars or vectors give *RANK ERRORs*. A vector left argument must be the proper length (2 or $2 \times ^-1 \uparrow \rho ARRAY$) to avoid a *LENGTH ERROR*. And, not unexpectedly, if the field width specified is too small to accommodate the display without overlap, a *DOMAIN ERROR* results.

A method for producing complete reports

Most commercial reports consist of at least some title lines, column headings and line names, as well as the data in the body of the report. As we pointed out earlier, this pattern is so common that most commercial APL systems provide report writing programs to make it easy for the user (who may not even know how to program in APL!) to produce decent-looking reports. We can't assume you have access to such facilities on your system, but we'll provide you with a method which will help you produce the reports you need.

The fundamental idea here is to use a character matrix whose dimensions are large enough to hold all the information that must be in the report—in other words, think of a page of paper if you are using a printing terminal, or one full screen if you are using a display terminal, many of which are 24 vertical lines by 80 characters across.

The illustration which follows produces an expense report for a traveling salesperson addicted to three-martini lunches and living high on the hog. As you study it, make sure you understand how each of the parts of the report goes into the character matrix *PAGE*. A display of the completed report is at the end of this section.

```
        ∇DATA PLACE INDS;ROWIND;COLIND
[1]     ⍝PLACES CHAR MATRIX DATA IN GLOBAL CHAR MATRIX PAGE
[2]     ⍝   STARTING AT POSITIONS GIVEN BY INDS.    A.J.ROSE  DEC 18 1980
[3]     DATA←(¯2↑ 1 1 ,⍴DATA)⍴DATA ⍝MAKE VECTORS, SCALARS INTO 1-ROW MATRIX
[4]     ROWIND←INDS[1]+¯1+⍳(⍴DATA)[1]
[5]     →(∧/ROWIND≤(⍴PAGE)[1])/L1 ◊ 'ROW INDEX TOO LARGE' ◊ →0
[6]     L1:COLIND←INDS[2]+¯1+⍳(⍴DATA)[2]
[7]     →(∧/COLIND≤(⍴PAGE)[2])/L2 ◊ 'COLUMN INDEX TOO LARGE' ◊ →0
[8]     L2:PAGE[ROWIND;COLIND]←DATA∇

        )COPY 1 CLASS ROWNAMES
SAVED  14.45.33 02/20/83

        PAGE← 24 80 ⍴' '
        LODGING← 45.7 60.42 55.2 0 50.19
        TRAVEL← 94.65 0 42.8 23.34 76
        FOOD← 40.25 51.4 66.5 42.34 35.9
        MISC← 37.9 32.2 28.75 0 35.45
        EXPENSES←⍉ 4 5 ⍴LODGING,TRAVEL,FOOD,MISC
        'GAIL PATTERSON' PLACE 1 1
        'EXPENSE REPORT FOR WEEK OF 12/3/82' PLACE 2 1
        (,¯8 ROWNAMES ' LODGING TRAVEL FOOD MISC. TOTAL') PLACE 4 11
        (40⍴' ───────') PLACE 5 11
        (10 ROWNAMES ' MONDAY TUESDAY WEDNESDAY THURSDAY FRIDAY  TOTAL') PLACE 6 1
        (8 2 ⍕EXPENSES) PLACE 6 11
        (8 2 ⍕ 5 1 ⍴+/EXPENSES) PLACE 6 43
        (40⍴' ───────')PLACE 11 11
        (8 2 ⍕(+⌿EXPENSES),+/+⌿EXPENSES) PLACE 12 11
```

```
            PAGE
GAIL PATTERSON
EXPENSE REPORT FOR WEEK OF 12/3/82

            LODGING  TRAVEL   FOOD    MISC.   TOTAL
            ───────  ───────  ───────  ───────  ───────
MONDAY       45.70    94.65    40.25    37.90    218.50
TUESDAY      60.42      .00    51.40    32.20    144.02
WEDNESDAY    55.20    42.80    66.50    28.75    193.25
THURSDAY       .00    23.34    42.34      .00     65.68
FRIDAY       50.19    76.00    35.90    35.45    197.54
            ───────  ───────  ───────  ───────  ───────
TOTAL       211.51   236.79   236.39   134.30    818.99
```

Dressing up displayed values

Most business people like to see their numbers decorated more than just aligning decimal points. Three of the most common requests are currency symbols such as ' $ ' in front of the values, commas in every third position of the integer parts, and negative values placed in parentheses instead of using the APL '⁻' symbol. Virtually all commercial APL systems provide this sort of thing (see the next chapter); but for those of you who don't have such access, we provide the following functions. Besides, understanding how these functions work will help improve your own APL skills.

The function *FLOAT* takes a single character as its left argument and a character matrix or vector (the result of a ⍕) and places the symbol just before each leading nonblank character. It's the user's responsibility to make sure the matrix has enough blank spaces to get the result looking right.

```
      ∇R←SYMBOL FLOAT MATRIX;SHAPE
[1]   SHAPE←ρMATRIX
[2]   R←,MATRIX
[3]   R[((R=' ')∧1⌽R≠' ')/⍳ρR]←SYMBOL
[4]   R←SHAPEρR∇
```

```
      DATA←4 2ρ1 2.75 .5 12345.678 ⁻12 ⁻.03 0 999
```

```
      10 2⍕DATA                    '$' FLOAT 10 2⍕DATA
         1.00        2.75            $1.00       $2.75
          .50    12345.68            $.50    $12345.68
       ⁻12.00        ⁻.03          $⁻12.00       $⁻.03
          .00      999.00            $.00      $999.00
```

Placing a comma between every third digit in the integer parts is a tougher job. The function *COMMAS* is one way to do it. If you're looking for a challenge, rewrite *COMMAS* so that it can handle more than one field across, with varying field widths. You may want to employ loops to do it.

```
      ∇R←DEC COMMAS N;B;D;S;T;U
[1]   N←(⁻2↑1 1,ρN)ρN ⍝ SHAPE INTO MATRIX
[2]   R←DEC ⍕((×/ρN),1)ρN ⍝ FORMAT
[3]   T←ρR
[4]   D←R[1;]⍳'.' ⍝ FIND DECIMAL PT (IF ANY)
[5]   B←⌽(⌊4×(D−1)÷3)ρ1 1 1 0 ⍝ SET UP EXPANSION
[6]   B←B,(1+(1↓ρR)−D)ρ1 ⍝ REST OF EXPANSION
[7]   R←B\R ⍝ EXPAND RESULT AND
[8]   R[;(~B)/⍳1↓ρR]←',' ⍝ PUT COMMAS IN
[9]   U←ρR
[10]  R←,R
[11]  B←R∈','
[12]  S←B/⍳ρB ⍝ REMOVE COMMAS AS IN ,123 OR ,⁻12
[13]  S←((R[(ρR)⌊1+S]∈' ')∨R[1⌈⁻1+S]∈'⁻ ')/S
[14]  R[S]←' '
[15]  R←(1 ⁻1×T)↑UρR
[16]  R←((1↑ρN),T[2]×1↓ρN)ρR∇
```

```
      15 2 COMMAS 6 1 ρ0 1 123 1234 123456 1234567.89
              .00
             1.00
           123.00
         1,234.00
       123,456.00
     1,234,567.89
```

Our final task for this section is to develop a function to place parentheses around negative numbers. Placing the left parenthesis in front of the negative values is easy enough—simply replace the ⁻ by a (. However, to line up the positive values with the negative values, it is necessary to shift every character left one position, and then insert the) only in those fields that start with (, as shown in the following function:

```
        ∇Z←DEC PARENS N;L;R;S;T
[1]     T←ρN
[2]     N←1⌽DEC⍕((×/ρN),1)ρN ⍝ RESHAPE AND FORMAT
[3]     S←' '=N ⍝ IDENTIFY POSN OF LEFT PAREN
[4]     S[;¯1↑ρS]←2×+/S ⍝ IDENTIFY POSN OF RIGHT PAREN
[5]     S←,S
[6]     L←(S=1)/⍳ρS ⍝ LOCATIONS OF LEFT PARENS
[7]     R←(S=2)/⍳ρS ⍝ LOCATIONS OF RIGHT PARENS
[8]     N←,N
[9]     N[L]←'('
[10]    N[R]←')'
[11]    Z←((1↑T),(ρN)÷1↑T)ρN⍨
```

```
        12 2 PARENS ¯5  0 ¯.00003 ¯55559.98 123.4
        (5.00)
            .00
            .00
     (55559.98)
        123.40
```

Picture format

Some versions of APL, including IBM's APL2, offer an enhanced format feature called *picture format*, and a *format control* system variable, $\Box FC$, used with ⍕.

$\Box FC$ is a 6-element character vector whose default value is `'.,*0_J'`, with the following definitions:

$\Box FC$ element	default	use in picture format
1	.	decimal point
2	,	comma
3	*	fill to replace blank
4	0	fill to indicate overflow
5	_	fill to display blank
6	J	complex number formatting (to be discussed in Chapter 28)

The picture format is a character vector used as the left argument of ⍕. As its name suggests, it specifies the pattern to be applied to the right argument. Digits are control characters. Their positions show where digits will appear in the result. All other characters (called *decorators*) are displayed in the result. The dot and comma are used as a decimal point and comma in the usual sense.

Each control character has a specific meaning:

```
0 pad result with zeros up to this position
1 float decorator if negative
2 float decorator if nonnegative
3 float decorator
4 do not float nearest decorator
5 display digit
6 end field at right of noncontrol character
7 exponential E at right of noncontrol character
8 fill with ⎕FC[3] when blank
9 if nonzero, pad result with zeros to this position
. decimal point
, comma
```

Here are some examples:

```
      ' 5555.5'⍕6 0 45.26 350            ⍝ WHEN ONLY 5'S ARE USED, LEADING AND
     6           45.3  350                   TRAILING ZEROS ARE SUPPRESSED

      ' 5.5 55.5 5555.55'⍕7.5 62.78 100.452
  7.5 62.8  100.45

      ' 005 5.550'⍕32.56 4.1             ⍝ 0 PADS A FIELD WITH ZEROS
  033 4.100

      '05/05/05'⍕20382                   ⍝ USE OF EMBEDDED DECORATORS
  02/03/82

      ' ⁻51.550'⍕⁻6 0 6 ⁻12.24           ⍝ 1 FLOATS DECORATOR AGAINST NEGATIVE NUMBERS
   ⁻6.000    .000   6.000 ⁻12.240

      '(51.550)'⍕⁻6 0 6 ⁻12.24
  (6.000)    .000   6.000 (12.240)

      ' +52.552'⍕⁻6 0 6 ⁻12.24           ⍝ 2 FLOATS DECORATOR AGAINST POSITIVE NUMBERS
     6           +6       12.24

      ' $53.552'⍕⁻6 0 6 12.24            ⍝ 3 FLOATS DECORATOR AGAINST ALL NUMBERS
    $6           $6      $12.24

      ' $51.45*'⍕⁻6 0 6 ⁻12.24           ⍝ 4 BLOCKS EFFECT OF 1,2 OR 3
    $6       *      *   6    * $12.24*

      '06/06/06'⍕2 3 82                  ⍝ 6 ENDS A FIELD
  02/03/82

      '1.700E0'⍕342.789                  ⍝ 7 INDICATES EXPONENTIAL E
  3.428E2

      '1.700*00'⍕342.789                 ⍝ * REPLACES E
  3.428*02

      ⎕FC[3]←'?'
      ' 8855.5'⍕6 0 6 12.24              ⍝ 8 REPLACES BLANK POSITIONS WITH ⎕FC[3]
  ???6    ????    ???6   ??12.2

      ' 55.59'⍕6 0 6 12.24               ⍝ 9 PADS ONLY NONZERO FIELDS WITH ZEROS
   6.00          6.00 12.24

      ' 55,555'⍕32879                    ⍝ USE OF COMMA IN PICTURE FORMAT
  32,879

      ⎕FC[4]←'*'                         ⍝ ⎕FC[4] FILLS IN FOR OVERFLOWING FIELD
      2 0 4 1 4 2⍕2 3⍴4 7 32 2 1 .4
  4 7.0****
  2 1.0 .40
      ' 555'⍕36824
  ***

      ⎕FC[4]←'0'
      ' 555'⍕36824                       ⍝ ⎕FC[4] DEFAULT VALUE (0) CAUSES ERROR
  DOMAIN ERROR
      ' 555'⍕36824
            ∧
      ⎕FC[5]←'A'
      ' $AA35555.5'⍕43287                ⍝ ⎕FC[5] IN PICTURE FORMAT PRODUCES BLANKS
    $  43287
```

Is the report still useful?

We can't resist one last tip, based on our own extensive and sometimes unhappy experience with business reports generated by others. It is that periodic reports, once begun, seem to take on a life of their own, and continue to be produced even when no one needs them. Circumstances do change. The initial recipients die or move on. Their successors wonder why they keep getting those weighty and impressive reports, but are reluctant to take their names off the distribution list or to question their value.

If you are the producer of such a long-lived 'standard' report, you might after a while unilaterally and without fanfare terminate it, and wait for a reaction. The odds are high that few of the recipients will even notice the loss. And you will have done your employer a service by reducing his overhead.

PROBLEMS

1. Format the array $TABLE$ (page 161) according to each of the following specifications: **A** field width 10, 4 decimal places; **B** field width 10, E-notation, 3 mantissa places; **C** automatic width, 3 decimal places; **D** columns 1 and 3 having 3 decimal places and field width 8, columns 2,4,5 having 5 decimal places and width 10.

2. Use ⍕ to display a logical matrix more compactly.

3. Define a dyadic function SAL to print a table of salaries showing the amount earned per week, month and year for a specified range and given increments of weekly salaries.

4. Design a report for a bank to identify currently overdrawn accounts, those with more than $100, and the weekly high and low balances for all accounts for the month. Assume you have two tables, $NAMES$ for customer names and $ACTIVITY$ for the weekly activity during the month (deposits −withdrawals). Each column in $ACTIVITY$ represents the net activity by customer for a particular week. Negative values mean withdrawals exceeded deposits. The first week's activity includes the opening balance.

5. Write a function which uses ⍕ to distinguish between literal and numeric arguments.

6. DAT is a numeric table whose columns contain respectively part numbers, quantity in inventory, quantity on order (by customer), unit cost and standard reorder quantity. Produce a report with appropriate column headings and a set of stars to flag those items for which the number in stock is less than the standard reorder quantity.

7. Insurance coverage in a dental plan pays 60% of all costs over $15 for each visit. Write a function to display the bill, amount paid by insurance and net cost to the policy holder for a given visit.

8. Format a date which is in numeric form, e.g., 121582 becomes 12/15/82.

9. Write a function $FORM$ to replace with blanks all zero elements in a matrix M.

10. Define a function $COLHEAD$ to spread the rows of a matrix of column headings across the top of a report. The left argument should have two elements, the first being the number of positions from the left margin at which printing begins, the second the column width.

Chapter 18: Comprehensive report formatting

Given dyadic ⍕ and a lot of enthusiasm, the accomplished APL programmer can produce formatted number displays with infinite variety and utility. However, it is time-consuming to develop functions like *FLOAT*, *COMMAS* and *PARENS* (Chapter 17). Besides, functions like those seem to use up more computer resources than you may feel appropriate; after all, they do apparently obvious, simple things to the display. Even worse is that unless you invest a vast amount of time in design and analysis, they won't work well together. Suppose you needed floating currency symbols, commas and negative numbers in parentheses all in the same formatted value?

Most commercial APL systems offer powerful solutions to this dilemma. In this and the following sections we'll discuss the dyadic system function □*FMT*. The version we will discuss is that of Sharp APL and the APL*PLUS System, but variants are found on other systems as well.

The left argument is always a character vector with its own set of rules about how the data, which is the right argument, will be formatted and decorated. Regardless of the shape of the right argument, the result is always a character matrix. The left argument is called the *format string* and the right argument the *data list*. Going over the examples used in Chapter 17, we first format the variable *TABLE* so that each field is six characters wide, with three digits after the decimal point:

```
      TABLE←((1+.04×⍳3)∘.*⍳4)-1
      'F6.3' □FMT (TABLE)
0.040 0.082 0.125 0.170
0.080 0.166 0.260 0.360
0.120 0.254 0.405 0.574
```

Parentheses aren't really needed around the right argument. However, since you'll need the parentheses later to format two or more data items at the same time, you might as well form the habit now. One difference from ⍕ is that for all numbers between ‾1 and 1, leading zeros are produced in the result.

Let's now examine the format string. The character *F* indicates that the result is to be produced in *fixed point*; in other words, a decimal point will be present. The 6 indicates the fields are to be six characters wide, and the 3 calls for three positions after the decimal point.

In the above example, it is implied that the *format phrase F*6.3 is repeated once for every column in the data list. To produce fields of varying width, use format strings composed of several format phrases, with each phrase set off by a comma:

```
      'F8.3,F7.4,F8.3,F7.4,F8.3' □FMT (TABLE)
0.040 0.0816   0.125 0.1699
0.080 0.1664   0.260 0.3605
0.120 0.2544   0.405 0.5735
```

For that matter, since □*FMT* will cycle through a list of format phrases and start again at the front (much like the dyadic ρ) 'F8.3,F7.4' could have been used above as well.

Integer formatting is done using the letter *I* instead of *F*, followed by the desired field width. If the value to be formatted by an *I*-code is not an integer, it is rounded to the nearest integer. Look carefully at the next example, because we're sneaking in yet another new feature:

```
      'I4,2F10.5,I4' □FMT ((⍳4)∘.*1 .5,(÷3),2 3)
1    1.00000    1.00000    1    1
2    1.41421    1.25992    4    8
3    1.73205    1.44225    9   27
4    2.00000    1.58740   16   64
```

The above table of numbers, square roots, cube roots, squares and cubes has two main formats. The *I*4 produced fields one, four and five, and the *F*10.5 produced fields two and three. The new feature we introduced was the explicit *replication factor*, namely, the 2 that comes before the $F10.5$. Its meaning is straightforward: you could just as well replace the phrase $2F10.5$ by the two phrases $F10.5,F10.5$.

Replication factors can apply to several format phrases by using parentheses. For example, $2(I4,2F10.3)$ is the same as $I4$, $F10.3$, $F10.3$, $I4$, $F10.3$, $F10.3$ and $I4$, $2(F6.2,2(I3,I2),I5),F10.6$ is the same as $I4$, $F6.2$, $I3$, $I2$, $I3$, $I2$, $I5$, $F6.2$, $I3$, $I2$, $I3$, $I2$, $I5$, $F10.6$.

You can express results in scaled notation by using a format phrase of the form $E14.8$. The 14 stands for the field width, and the 8 stands for the number of significant digits in the mantissa that will be represented. The number of significant digits requested must always be at least six less than the width to allow for the letter E, the decimal point, possible negative signs in the mantissa and exponent, and the two-digit exponent itself. To give you the flavor of the E-format code, try some variants of this example:

```
      'I4,E10.3,E20.12' ⎕FMT (2 ¯5 10 ∘.* 1 ¯4 15)
   2   6.25E¯2     3.27680000000E4
  ¯5   1.60E¯3    ¯3.05175781250E10
  10   1.00E¯4     1.00000000000E15
```

So far every illustration we have used as the right argument to $⎕FMT$ has been a matrix. When the data list contains a vector, it is treated as though it were a one-column matrix, as in

```
      'I1' ⎕FMT (!ι4)
 1
 2
 6
 *
```

which produces a character matrix with four rows and one column. This is particularly handy because a very common use of $⎕FMT$ is to list several data items side-by-side. Note that stars are produced whenever the value is too big for the field width.

Here is an example which displays the first five integers, their factorials, reciprocals, exponentials and natural logarithms:

```
      '2I4,F15.7,2E14.6' ⎕FMT (ι5;!ι5;÷ι5;*ι5;⍟ι5)
   1   1      1.0000000     2.71828E0      0.00000E0
   2   2      0.5000000     7.38906E0      6.93147E¯1
   3   6      0.3333333     2.00855E1      1.09861E0
   4  24      0.2500000     5.45982E1      1.38629E0
   5 120      0.2000000     1.48413E2      1.60944E0
```

Since semicolons are used to separate items in the data list, parentheses aren't needed for any of the expressions.

Suppose you really wanted the example $'I4'$ $⎕FMT$ $(!ι6)$ to produce a one-line result. You could do it either by making the data items into a one-row matrix or by raveling the result:

```
      'I4' ⎕FMT (1 6ρ!ι6)              ,'I4' ⎕FMT (!ι6)
 1    2    6   24  120  720      1    2    6   24  120  720
```

The shape of the first result is a matrix with one row and 24 columns, and the shape of the second result is a character vector with 24 elements. Can you explain the difference?

Working with alphabetic data

Most business reporting has character information (such as names of items or people) shown next to whatever numbers apply to them. For example, with this data

```
      NAMES←4 6ρ'NUTS  SCREWSBOLTS NAILS '
      COSTS←.05 .03 .20 .01
      QUANT←150 200 4 1000
```

a quite readable report (or invoice) can be obtained:

```
    '6A1,F10.2,I8,F10.2' □FMT (NAMES;COSTS;QUANT;(COSTS×QUANT),+/COSTS×QUANT)
NUTS        0.05        150        7.50
SCREWS      0.03        200        6.00
BOLTS       0.20          4        0.80
NAILS       0.01       1000       10.00
                                  24.30
```

The main point here is the format phrase 6*A*1. The *A*-code is used to format character data items. Its width specification is usually 1, and its repetition factor is usually the number of columns in the character matrix you are formatting. But width factors other than 1 can be useful, as shown here:

```
    '6A2' □FMT (NAMES)
N  U  T  S
S  C  R  E  W  S
B  O  L  T  S
N  A  I  L  S
```

Each character position in the variable *NAMES* produced two positions in the result. In a sense, this is a very limited way to perform an expansion on the second dimension of a character matrix. However, it is introduced here because reports can sometimes be made more attractive by spreading out the text a bit.

It is easy to get messed up when using the *A*-code if you forget that each column of a character array is a separate entity. We will emphasize that point by this example:

Dotted lines have been drawn to emphasize the result produced by each part of the format string.

The picture code

The picture code helps you produce specialized decorative effects. Embellishments such as placing slashes between the day, month and year in a date, separating the parts of a Social Security number, or 'dressing up' a telephone number are easily accomplished. To use it, the letter *G* is followed by a *picture pattern*. The pattern starts with the character ⊂ and ends with ⊃, and the result field width is the number of characters between ⊂ and ⊃. The characters between determine how the result appears: a character 9 says 'put a digit here,' and the character Z says 'if this position would have been a leading or trailing zero, put a blank here, otherwise use the appropriate digit character.' Any other character that appears in the picture pattern is literally placed in the result in that position.

```
      X←72.71 0 ‾12 .026

      'G⊂ZZZ9⊃' □FMT (X)              'G⊂ZZZZ⊃' □FMT (X)
  73                              73
   0
 ‾12                            ‾12
   0

      'G⊂9999⊃' □FMT (X)              'G⊂$Z9.99⊃' □FMT (X)
0073                            $ 0.73
0000                            $ 0.00
****                            $‾0.12
0000                            $ 0.00
```

Only the integer part of the values are taken, as for an *I*-code. In the top right example, those values that would have printed as all zeros have disappeared (replaced by blanks). You may be surprised by the stars in the lower left example. The reason they appear is that the *G*-code demanded that every position be a digit, and there wasn't room for the negative sign here.

Even though a period was used in the bottom right example, it didn't scale the data. The period has no special meaning in a picture code. You have two options for properly placing the decimal point: you can multiply the data by the appropriate power of 10 before □*FMT* works on it; or you can use the scaling code, *K*:

```
      'G⊂$ZZ9.99⊃' □FMT (100×X)              'K2G⊂$ZZ9.99⊃' □FMT (X)
$  72.71                               $  72.71
$   0.00                               $   0.00
$⁻12.00                                $⁻12.00
$   0.03                               $   0.03
```

The *K*-code is preferred, because it uses fewer computer resources. The number following *K* is the power of 10 (either positive or negative) by which the data is to be multiplied. You may find it easier to think of it as the number of positions that the decimal point is being shifted over. The *K*-code can be used with *F*, *I* and *E* as well, although its use there is rather infrequent.

Here are some examples of typical uses of the *G*-code. Pay special attention to the first example; it shows a common error. Characters taken from the picture pattern are placed in the result field only if they would be surrounded by digits in the result field. This may be frustrating when dealing with decimal points, but quite handy when placing commas. See how the value .87 is treated in the next examples:

```
      'K2G⊂$ZZZ,ZZZ.99 REFUND⊃' □FMT (1063.24 .87 150)
$    1,063.24 REFUND
$          87 REFUND
$      150.00 REFUND

      'K2G⊂$ZZZ,ZZ9.99 REFUND⊃' □FMT (1063.24 .87 150)
$    1,063.24 REFUND
$        0.87 REFUND
$      150.00 REFUND

      'G⊂PHONE (999) 999-9999⊃' □FMT (9143475565 5198373216)
PHONE (914) 347-5565
PHONE (519) 837-3216
```

Qualifiers

If you are warming up to the idea that APL can do commercial formatting, you will be convinced after learning about *qualifiers* and *decorations*, which are much like the control characters used in APL2 (Chapter 17). They are used with format codes *F*, *I* and *G* to tailor the report further to specific needs. All qualifiers and decorations come after the repetition factor, if there is one, and before the format codes. Here is an example using two qualifiers:

```
      'BCF13.2' □FMT (10 ⁻4 0 1234567.9 ⁻.004 ⁻1000)
       10.00
       ⁻4.00

 1,234,567.90

    ⁻1,000.00
```

The *B*-qualifier says 'if the number would have been represented as a zero, make the field all blanks.' Notice that since we're showing only two decimal positions, the result is rounded to the nearest whole number, and hence the value ⁻.004 is rounded to zero and subsequently blanked. The *C*-qualifier simply inserts commas separating the digits of the integer parts in groups of three.

The *Z*-qualifier is used to insert leading zeros (instead of leading blanks) in a field. It would ordinarily be used when preparing output destined for punched card transfer to another (non-APL) computer as shown:

```
      'ZI9,▨/▨' □FMT (3 4⍴⍳12)
000000001/000000002/000000003/000000004/
000000005/000000006/000000007/000000008/
000000009/000000010/000000011/000000012/
```

In the following illustration, the *L*-qualifier is used to *left-justify* the represented values within the field:

```
      ∇FACTORIALS
[1]   28⍴14↑' N  !N'
[2]   'I2,X2,LI10,I2,X2,LI19' □FMT (⍳10;!⍳10;10+⍳10;!10+⍳10) ∇
```

```
        FACTORIALS
   N   !N          N    !N
   1   1           11   39916800
   2   2           12   479001600
   3   6           13   6227020800
   4   24          14   87178291200
   5   120         15   1307674368000
   6   720         16   20922789888000
   7   5040        17   355687428096000
   8   40320       18   6402373705728000
   9   362880      19   1216451004088320__
  10   3628800     20   2432902008176640___
```

Note the dashes at the lower right of the display. They appear because the internal value stored in APL is accurate only to approximately 16 decimal places, and the positions shown as dashes indicate that there is no accuracy in those positions.

We've already seen the K-qualifier applied to the G-code, so we'll just remind you that it can also be used with F-, I-and E-codes.

Decorations

The codes $MNOPQR$, each followed by a string of text enclosed between ⊂ and ⊃, are used to inject that text into the field according to these rules:

M⊂text⊃   places text to left of negative result
N⊂text⊃   places text to right of negative result
O⊂text⊃   substitutes this text in place of zero result
P⊂text⊃   places text to left of nonnegative result
Q⊂text⊃   places text to right of nonnegative result
R⊂text⊃   fills in 'unclaimed' spaces with text.

Since some people still aren't accustomed to the way negative numbers are shown in APL, you can use the M-decoration to replace the APL overbar by the dash:

```
     'M⊂−⊃P⊂$$⊃F10.2' □FMT (¯79.32 10000 0 ¯123.45)
    -79.32
$$10000.00
    $$0.00
  -123.45
```

Besides using the M-decoration to get the minus sign in the above example, P was used to place two dollar signs before each nonnegative value. This is called a 'floating currency symbol' because it is placed adjacent to the first visible digit.

It is often desirable to substitute some indication like $NONE$ or N/A for those fields that would print only zeros, such as the third row in the above example. Use the O-decorator for that:

```
     'O⊂NONE⊃P⊂$$⊃F10.2' □FMT (¯79.32 10000 0 ¯123.45)
    ¯79.32
$$10000.00
      NONE
  ¯123.45
```

If the O-decorator is not present, zero fields are decorated with P-text and Q-text. If the O-code is used, however, it takes precedence over P and Q.

Business reports often indicate losses or decreases by placing any negative values in parentheses, rather than prefixing them with a negative sign. This can be done with the following combination of codes:

```
     'M⊂(⊃N⊂)⊃Q⊂ ⊃CI10' □FMT (¯79 1000 0 ¯123.45)
    (79)
  1,000
      0
    (123)
```

Do you know why the Q⊂ ⊃ decoration is used in this example?

The next illustration shows a typical 'check protection' application in which the field is protected against someone tampering with the printed value. The R-text fills in all 'unclaimed' positions, except that if an O-code is also present, it dominates:

```
      'O⊂NIL⊃P⊂$⊃CR⊂*⊛⊃F14.2'  □FMT  (7932.56 .002 312.5)
*⊛*⊛*$7,932.56
*⊛*⊛*⊛*⊛*⊛*NIL
*⊛*⊛*⊛*$312.50
```

Stars in the result

Decorations and qualifiers consume additional character positions, and the field width must be sufficient to hold them all. If you try to put more characters in a field than will fit, the field will be entirely filled with the $\star$ character, but no other indication of error is given. This is so that in an involved commercial format, you can see which field caused the problem and revise your format string.

The most frequent cause of $\star$'s appearing is the attempt to format character data with an F-, I-, E-or G-code, or trying to format numeric data with the A-code. This often happens when you haven't counted the number of columns carefully in a character matrix, so that there is a mismatch between the format phrases and the columns of the data items in the right argument. For example, if you used the format

```
        '5A1,F10.2,I5,F10.2'  □FMT  (NAMES;COSTS;QUANT;COSTS×QUANT)
NUTS *********        0      150.00*
SCREW*********        0      200.00*
BOLTS*********        0        4.00*
NAILS*********        0     1000.00*
```

you get the stars in the second field because the matrix $NAMES$ has six columns instead of five. The remaining data items are displaced one field to the right, with the consequences shown.

Filler and positioning codes

So far we've covered the F-, I-, E-and G-codes for formatting numeric values, and the A-code for formatting character values. The remaining formatting codes don't associate with any data in the right argument, but rather are used to supply filler spaces or text between fields. The X-code supplies blanks:

```
    'I4,X3,6A1'  □FMT  (ι4;NAMES)
1     NUTS
2     SCREWS
3     BOLTS
4     NAILS
```

Can you think of an alternate way to produce this display without using the X-code?

Fields of constant character information can be sandwiched between data fields in the result by placing the text between ⊂ and ⊃:

```
      '⊂PRODUCT⊃,I2,⊂ IS ⊃,6A1'  □FMT  (ι4;NAMES)
PRODUCT 1 IS NUTS
PRODUCT 2 IS SCREWS
PRODUCT 3 IS BOLTS
PRODUCT 4 IS NAILS
```

The last of the codes is the T-code (for horizontal tabbing). It is used to specify in which visible column of the result the next characters will be placed. For example,

```
    'I3,T20,I1'  □FMT  (ι3;2×ι3)
1                    2
2                    4
3                    6
```

starts the second field in column 20 of the result. T and X are quite similar. The major difference is that X-positioning is relative to the present position, while T-positioning is relative to the left margin. Both T-and X-

codes may be used to position to the left (backwards). For instance, assume you are presently at display position 50. The phrase $T40$ will cause the characters that were in position 40 and beyond to be replaced by any following formatted characters. X^-10 moves backward 10 positions from wherever it presently is.

The T-code, when used without a number following it, repositions the cursor to the right to the first 'unused' position. You'd use it in a very complicated formatting job in which backspacing is needed.

Substitution of standard symbols

The previous discussion introduced some characters with special meanings in $\Box FMT$ left arguments and results. Here is a summary of them:

character	code	meaning
9	*G*	digit selector
Z	*G*	zero-suppress digit selector
⋆	*F G I*	overflow indicator
.	*F*	decimal point
,	*C*	comma insert
_	*F G I*	nonsignificant digit marker
$\overline{0}$	*Z*	fill character
(blank)	*G*	lead zero fill character

For special effects, any of the above can be replaced by a different character through use of the *S*-qualifier. The first character in each pair is the standard symbol, and the second is the substitute. In this expression commas are replaced by dashes and the star by a question mark:

```
      'SC,-*?⊃CI10'  ⎕FMT  (1234567 123456789)
1-234-567
?????????
```

The characters Z and 9 are reserved in their use in the picture code. If you ever had to use them literally (for example, to include the word '*FRAZZLE*' or '*MODEL Z9*' in a picture), you'd be in trouble without the *S*-qualifier. It works this way: if you put $SC9\circledast Z\underline{Z}\supset$ in front of the G, then for that picture, $\circledast$ now means 'put a digit here' and $\underline{Z}$ has the meaning that Z used to have, so that 9 and Z are released from their regular duties, as shown below:

```
      'SC9⊛ZZ⊃GCZZZ⊛ UNITS OF PRODUCT Z9⊃'  ⎕FMT  (73)
73 UNITS OF PRODUCT Z9
```

The characters used to enclose text, ⊂ and ⊃, can also be substituted by other characters if you need to use ⊂ and ⊃ within the text itself. Other pairs that are valid are <text>, ⍈text⍈ and ⎕text⎕. Thus, $G\Box999Z\Box$ is the same as $GC999Z\supset$.

Symbol substitution is a convenient way to match the European number formatting convention, in which commas and periods are interchanged from the North American style:

```
      'SC.,,.⊃CF14.2'  ⎕FMT  (123479.32 10000000 123.456)
    123.479,32
 10.000.000,00
        123,46
```

Ragged data

$\Box FMT$ really doesn't care whether all of the data items have the same number of rows; it simply fills in any 'ragged edges' with blank fields. Note how we can produce the whole report, including a total line at the bottom:

```
      QC←COSTS×QUANT  ◊  NAMT←5 6ρ(,NAMES),'TOTAL '
      '6A1,F10.2,I5,F10.2'  ⎕FMT  (NAMT;COSTS;QUANT;QC,+/QC)
NUTS       0.05   150      7.50
SCREWS     0.03   200      6.00
BOLTS      0.20     4      0.80
NAILS      0.01  1000     10.00
TOTAL                     24.30
```

This implies that $\Box FMT$ can be used to join character matrices together, even if they aren't the same size.

Chapter 19: More on higher dimensional arrays

Most APL users feel quite comfortable with scalars, vectors and matrices. Which is why, except for a few illustrations earlier in the text, that's all we have used so far. But when it comes to three-(and higher-) dimensional arrays, the story is quite different. The comfort vanishes, to be replaced by queasiness and a lingering suspicion that there's something fishy about how APL manipulates such arrays.

Perhaps this is due to our inability to visualize them satisfactorily on a two-dimensional screen or paper. Or maybe our brains can't operate readily on more than two dimensions at a time. Be that as it may, this chapter will attempt to give you a warm feeling for three-dimensional arrays and how they can be used more effectively than a collection of matrices containing the same data.

As for arrays of rank greater than three (some APL implementations can deal with up to 63 dimensions), we concede that a certain measure of dedication and ingenuity is required, though the rewards are often commensurate with the effort. Also to be described in this chapter will be an extension of catenate and a new function, *laminate*, which allows us to construct arrays of rank greater than those of the arguments.

There are many examples of potential three-dimensional arrays which suggest themselves, more often than not as a set of separate two-dimensional arrays. For instance, an accounting system may be set up with 4 expense categories for each of 7 departments to keep track of expenditures by month. We could store each month's data in a separate 4 by 7 matrix. But it then becomes awkward to generate reports on selected departments and categories over a span of many months. However, if we structure the data as a single three-dimensional array, each of whose planes (or pages, if you prefer) contains all the data for a single month, we can slice up the data in many ways to answer any request the auditors may make.

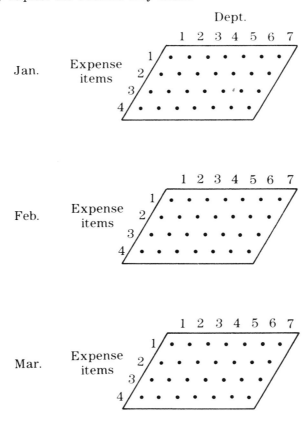

Three-dimensional arrays

We'll use as our primary example a couple of three-dimensional databases which will consist of 2 planes, one for each of two months. Each plane has 4 rows (for different sizes) and 3 columns (for different styles). The data elements are orders and wholesale prices:

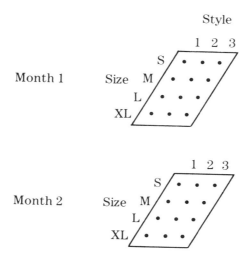

```
ORD←2 4 3ρ50 88 32 34 62 20 10 21 5 3 4 2 15 30 10 20 50 20 5 12 2 1 2
PRICE←20 22 19 20 22 9 20 22 19 22 24 21
PRICE←2 4 3ρPRICE,36 40 34 36 40 34 36 40 34 38 42 36
```

```
        ORD                     PRICE
50 88 32                  20 22 19
34 62 20                  20 22  9
10 21  5                  20 22 19
 3  4  2                  22 24 21

15 30 10                  36 40 34
20 50 20                  36 40 34
 5 12  2                  36 40 34
 1  2  1                  38 42 36
```

Observe how *ORD* and *PRICE* were built by reshaping a vector of data. The left argument of dyadic ρ dictates that the result is of shape 2 by 4 by 3, just as in the expression *T*←5 8ρι40 the result will be a matrix of shape 5 by 8.

All of the standard scalar functions work on three-dimensional arrays in the same way they work on arrays of lesser rank. For example, to get the total revenue for each month-size-style (with prices increasing uniformly by 15%), enter

```
    ORD×1.15×PRICE
 1150          2226.4        699.2
  782          1568.6        207
  230           531.3        109.25
   75.9         110.4         48.3

  621          1380          391
  828          2300          782
  207           552           78.2
   43.7          96.6          41.4
```

The new revenues can be rounded to the nearest hundred with

```
      100×⌊.5+(ORD×1.15×PRICE)÷100
1200 2200  700
 800 1600  200
 200  500  100
 100  100    0

 600 1400  400
 800 2300  800
 200  600  100
   0  100    0
```

The rules for primitive scalar dyadic and monadic functions stated earlier can be boiled down to

any-dimensional array ← any-dimensional array f any-dimensional array

any-dimensional array ← g any-dimensional array

with f standing for any primitive scalar dyadic function and g standing for any primitive scalar monadic function. The arrays must have identical dimension and rank (or one can be a single element).

Indexing multidimensional arrays

To index an item or items of a multidimensional array, you must provide an index for each of the dimensions of the array. A quick check is whether you have used exactly one fewer semicolon than the rank of the array. Thus, to get the scalar value corresponding to the second month, fourth size, third style of ORD, use

```
      ORD[2;4;3]
1
```

or to get the matrix that is all of the second month's data,

```
      ORD[2;;]
15 30 10
20 50 20
 5 12  2
 1  2  1
```

Operations along a single dimension

In Chapter 5 we saw how reduction could be used along the rows or columns of a matrix with / and ⌿ respectively. But what symbols do we use when there are more than two dimensions? APL has a feature called the *axis* operator. It has the syntax $[I]$, where I is a scalar or one-element vector representing the index of the axis or dimension along which the associated function is to be applied. What this means is that +/[1]M is the same as +⌿M and +/[⍴⍴M]M is the same as +/M (that is, reduce over the last dimension). The need for the brackets when dealing with three-dimensional objects should be obvious: there should be a way to reduce over any dimension. For instance, in the example used previously, here are some ways to get summaries:

```
      +/[1]ORD      ⍝ BY SIZE AND STYLE FOR ALL MONTHS (COULD BE +⌿ORD)
 65 118  42
 54 112  40
 15  33   7
  4   6   3
      +/[3]ORD      ⍝ BY SIZE FOR ALL STYLES FOR EACH MONTH (COULD BE +/ORD)
170 116  36   9
 55  90  19   4
      +/[2]ORD      ⍝ BY STYLE FOR ALL SIZES FOR EACH MONTH (ONLY WAY
 97 175  59            TO DO THIS ONE)
 41  94  33
```

As you can see from the three examples above, $f/[K]ARRAY$ results in an array whose shape is the same as $\rho ARRAY$, except that the K-th dimension or axis disappears. Hence the term *reduction*—the result is reduced in rank. More formally, $\rho f/[K]ARRAY$ is $(K \neq \rho ARRAY)/\rho ARRAY$.

The dyadic function *MEAN* takes a given dimension of an array and divides the sum across that dimension by the number of elements comprising that sum. Its left argument is the dimension of the array across which we are averaging:

```
      )COPY 1 CLASS MEAN                     ∇MEAN[□]∇
SAVED  17.28.02 06/12/81                ∇ R←K MEAN X
                                   [1]    R←(+/[K] X)÷(ρX)[K]
                                        ∇
```

Let's try it on *ORD*:

```
      1 MEAN ORD        ⍝AVERAGE ORDERS FOR ALL MONTHS BY SIZE AND STYLE
32.5              59              21
27                56              20
 7.5              16.5             3.5
 2                 3               1.5

      2 MEAN ORD        ⍝AVERAGE ORDERS FOR EACH STYLE FOR EACH MONTH
24.25             43.75           14.75
10.25             23.5             8.25

      3 MEAN ORD        ⍝AVERAGE ORDERS FOR EACH SIZE FOR EACH MONTH
56.66666667       38.66666667     12           3
18.33333333       30               6.333333333  1.333333333
```

The overall average is

```
      1 MEAN 2 MEAN 3 MEAN ORD       ⍝AVERAGE ORDER FOR ANY MONTH, SIZE AND STYLE
20.79166667
```

Can you think of why 3 *MEAN* 2 *MEAN* 1 *MEAN ORD* won't work?

The same dimension selection scheme outlined above for reduction applies to other operators and functions as well. Here are a few representative examples using *TAB3*:

```
      )COPY 1 CLASS TAB3
SAVED  14.45.33 02/20/83

      TAB3                      +\[3]TAB3
111 112 113               111 223 336
121 122 123               121 243 366
131 132 133               131 263 396
141 142 143               141 283 426

211 212 213               211 423 636
221 222 223               221 443 666
231 232 233               231 463 696
241 242 243               241 483 726

      +\[1]TAB3                 1⌽[3]TAB3  ⍝OR  1⌽TAB3
111 112 113               112 113 111
121 122 123               122 123 121
131 132 133               132 133 131
141 142 143               142 143 141

322 324 326               212 213 211
342 344 346               222 223 221
362 364 366               232 233 231
382 384 386               242 243 241

      +\[2]TAB3                 (2 3ρ1 2 3 2 0 1)⌽[2]TAB3
111 112 113               121 132 143
232 234 236               131 142 113
363 366 369               141 112 123
504 508 512               111 122 133

211 212 213               231 212 223
432 434 436               241 222 233
663 666 669               211 232 243
904 908 912               221 242 213
```

The last illustration needs careful examination to see what is happening. Note that the left argument is itself a matrix:

```
      2 3ρ1 2 3 2 0 1
1 2 3
2 0 1
```

To see what is happening, look at the value in row 2, column 3. It is 1 and therefore rotates $TAB3[2;;3]$ one position. Can you describe the result of $(4\ 3\rho\iota12)\ominus TAB3$?

Here are some more examples:

```
      1 0/[1]TAB3 ∧OR 1 0/TAB3              1 1 1 0 1\[2]TAB3
111 112 113                            111 112 113
121 122 123                            121 122 123
131 132 133                            131 132 133
141 142 143                              0   0   0
      1 2 ‾2↑TAB3                       141 142 143
112 113
122 123                                211 212 213
      R←2 4ρTAB3                        221 222 223
      R∈TAB3                            231 232 233
1 1 1 1                                   0   0   0
1 1 1 1                                 241 242 243

      TAB3∈R                               1 ‾1 2↓TAB3
1 1 1                                   213
1 1 1                                   223
1 1 0                                   233
0 0 0

0 0 0
0 0 0
0 0 0
0 0 0
```

Note that $+\backslash[2]TAB3[;4;]$ is the same as $+/[2]TAB3$. Can you generalize this?

Catenation

Our earlier discussion of catenation (Chapter 12) was limited to combinations of vectors and scalars, with the result always a vector. Now that we have the axis operator $[n]$ as an APL 'signpost' to mark the dimension over which we want to use a function, we can extend catenation to arrays of all shapes.

This is easier to see than to talk about in the abstract. The character arrays P, Q, R, S and T will be used here for illustration. But first, a couple of brief rules. Two arrays whose shapes are *conformable* (i.e., the 'right size') can be joined along an existing dimension. If no dimension is specified, the catenation is along the last dimension:

```
      P←2 2 7ρ'P'              Q←4 7ρ'Q'              R←2 7ρ'R'
      P                        Q                      R
PPPPPPP                  QQQQQQQ                  RRRRRRR
PPPPPPP                  QQQQQQQ                  RRRRRRR
                         QQQQQQQ                        S←7ρ'S'
PPPPPPP                  QQQQQQQ                        S
PPPPPPP                                           SSSSSSS
                                                       T←4ρ'T'
                                                       T
                                                 TTTT

      Q,[1]R                   Q,[1]S                   Q,T ∧OR Q,[2]T
QQQQQQQ                  QQQQQQQ                  QQQQQQQT
QQQQQQQ                  QQQQQQQ                  QQQQQQQT
QQQQQQQ                  QQQQQQQ                  QQQQQQQT
QQQQQQQ                  QQQQQQQ                  QQQQQQQT
RRRRRRR                  SSSSSSS                        ρQ,T
RRRRRRR                        ρQ,[1]S            4 8
      ρQ,[1]R            5 7
6 7
```

A scalar argument is extended for purposes of catenation:

```
      W←'W'
      Q,W  AOR  Q,[2]W                    Q,[1]W                          W,[2]P
QQQQQQQW                            QQQQQQQ                        WWWWWW
QQQQQQQW                            QQQQQQQ                        PPPPPPP
QQQQQQQW                            QQQQQQQ                        PPPPPPP
QQQQQQQW                            QQQQQQQ
     ρQ,W                           WWWWWWW                        WWWWWW
 4  8                                   ρQ,[1]W                    PPPPPPP
                                     5  7                          PPPPPPP
                                                                        ρW,[2]P
                                                                    2  3  7
```

Remember the function *PLACE* in Chapter 17? We used it to create a report with row and column headings by placing the pieces in the desired row and column positions in a predefined character matrix or page. Here is an alternative approach, which emphasizes catenation. First, let the expenses be stored in the matrix *EXP*:

```
      EXP←45.7 94.65 40.25 37.90 60.42 0 51.40 32.2 55.2 42.8 66.5 28.75
      EXP←5 4ρEXP, 0 23.34 42.34 0 50.19 76 35.9 35.45
```

Now we append the row totals:

```
      EXP1←EXP,+/EXP ◇ EXP1
 45.7              94.65             40.25            37.9            218.5
 60.42              0                51.4             32.2            144.02
 55.2              42.8              66.5             28.75           193.25
  0                23.34             42.34             0               65.68
 50.19             76                35.9             35.45           197.54
```

To include the column totals and the grand total, enter

```
      EXP2←EXP1,[1]+/EXP1 ◇ EXP2
 45.7              94.65             40.25            37.9            218.5
 60.42              0                51.4             32.2            144.02
 55.2              42.8              66.5             28.75           193.25
  0                23.34             42.34             0               65.68
 50.19             76                35.9             35.45           197.54
211.51            236.79            236.39           134.3           818.99
```

The numeric matrix is then converted to characters by

```
      EXP3←11 2▼EXP2 ◇ EXP3
  45.70             94.65            40.25            37.90           218.50
  60.42               .00            51.40            32.20           144.02
  55.20             42.80            66.50            28.75           193.25
    .00             23.34            42.34              .00            65.68
  50.19             76.00            35.90            35.45           197.54
 211.51            236.79           236.39           134.30          818.99
```

The row headings are formatted next. We could assign them as

```
      ROWS←7 9ρ'          MONDAY    TUESDAY   WEDNESDAYTHURSDAY  FRIDAY    TOTAL    '
```

(why the spaces before *MONDAY*?), but if you are doing a lot of this it would be handy to have a utility like the following:

```
      )COPY 1 CLASS ON
SAVED  14.45.33 02/20/83

      ∇ON[□]∇
    ∇ Z←A_ON B;PAD
[1]     A←(¯2↑ 1 1 ,ρA)ρA A FORCE A TO BE A MATRIX
[2]     B←(¯2↑ 1 1 ,ρB)ρB A FORCE B TO BE A MATRIX
[3]     PAD←(¯1↑ρA)⌈¯1↑ρB A PICK LARGER DIMENSION FOR PAD
[4]     Z←(((1↑ρA),PAD)↑A),[1]((1↑ρB),PAD)↑B
    ∇

      ROWS←'' ON 'MONDAY' ON 'TUESDAY' ON 'WEDNESDAY'
      ROWS←ROWS ON 'THURSDAY' ON 'FRIDAY' ON 'TOTAL'
```

Next we form a vector of the column headings, keeping in mind that *ROWS* is 9 positions wide and each of the columns in *EXP*3 was formatted as a field of width 11:

```
HDGS←5 11↑'LODGING' ON 'TRAVEL' ON 'FOOD' ON 'MISC' ON 'TOTAL'
HDGS←,(-+/∧\⌽HDGS=' ')⌽HDGS ⍝ RIGHT ADJUSTS
```

To complete the body of the report the pieces are catenated:

```
RPT←ROWS, HDGS,[1]EXP3 ⍝ OR ROWS, HDGS ON EXP3
RPT
            LODGING      TRAVEL        FOOD        MISC       TOTAL
MONDAY       45.70       94.65        40.25       37.90      218.50
TUESDAY      60.42         .00        51.40       32.20      144.02
WEDNESDAY    55.20       42.80        66.50       28.75      193.25
THURSDAY       .00       23.34        42.34         .00       65.68
FRIDAY       50.19       76.00        35.90       35.45      197.54
TOTAL       211.51      236.79       236.39      134.30      818.99
```

Suppose we belatedly discover that the amount for food on Tuesday is incorrect. It should be $54.50 instead of $51.40. *EXP*3 is a character array on which we can't do calculations. So unless we want to go to the bother of figuring out the exact positions in *EXP*3 to change, it's back to the original numeric array *EXP* or intermediate steps *EXP*1 or *EXP*2. Do you now see the wisdom in saving it separate from the augmented and formatted version?

The final step is to put the title on. First, let's add some space on top of *RPT*,

```
RPT←' ' ON RPT
```

and then execute the utility function *CENTER*, since titles on reports are generally centered:

```
      ∇Z←T CENTER R
[1]    Z←(‾1↑⍴R)-⍴T
[2]    Z←((⌈.5×Z)⍴' '),T
[3]    Z←Z ON ' ' ON R∇
```

```
'JILLIAN AUSTEN' CENTER 'EXPENSE REPORT FOR WEEK OF 12/3/80' CENTER RPT
                      JILLIAN AUSTEN

            EXPENSE REPORT FOR WEEK OF 12/3/80

            LODGING      TRAVEL        FOOD        MISC       TOTAL
MONDAY       45.70       94.65        40.25       37.90      218.50
TUESDAY      60.42         .00        51.40       32.20      144.02
WEDNESDAY    55.20       42.80        66.50       28.75      193.25
THURSDAY       .00       23.34        42.34         .00       65.68
FRIDAY       50.19       76.00        35.90       35.45      197.54
TOTAL       211.51      236.79       236.39      134.30      818.99
```

If you had guessed wrong on the spacing in *HDGS*, it's no big deal to go back and reassign it, particularly if you are working on a display terminal with good editing capabilities. It would be much nicer if we had still another utility that would take a matrix of column headings and spread it over the columns of data, no matter how they might be spaced. This capability, as well as other cosmetic features needed for professional formatting, is generally included in the formatting packages found in most APL systems.

Lamination

By now you have probably tried on at least one occasion to make a matrix out of two vectors of the same length, using catenate:

```
      V←⍳5                    V,[1]V                      V,[2]V
      V,V              1 2 3 4 5 1 2 3 4 5          INDEX ERROR
1 2 3 4 5 1 2 3 4 5                                    V,[2] V
                                                          ∧
```

Catenate can be used only to produce a result of the same *rank*, but enlarged *shape*. (The sole exception is when both arguments are scalars; in this case they are treated as vectors of length one.)

What we were trying unsuccessfully to do with *V* above was to make a matrix (rank 2) out of two vectors (rank 1). This means joining the vectors along a new, not yet existing dimension. If you think about the vectors as layers of data, the technique of forming a matrix out of them is akin to the building up of a sheet of plywood, that is, the data is *laminated*.

The *laminate* function, which shares the use of the comma with catenation, does this. Don't be intimidated by the fractional axis specifiers in the following examples; they're not as haphazardly chosen as they seem to be (ρ*Q* is 4 7, ρ*R* is 2 7 and *W* is a scalar):

```
        Q,[.5]W                    Q,[1.4]W              R,[2.9]W
QQQQQQQ                     QQQQQQQ              RW
QQQQQQQ                     WWWWWWW              RW
QQQQQQQ                                          RW
QQQQQQQ                     QQQQQQQ              RW
                            WWWWWWW              RW
WWWWWWW                                          RW
WWWWWWW                     QQQQQQQ              RW
WWWWWWW                     WWWWWWW
WWWWWWW                                          RW
      ρQ,[.5]W              QQQQQQQ              RW
2  4  7                     WWWWWWW              RW
                                  ρQ,[1.4]W      RW
                            4  2  7              RW
                                                 RW
                                                 RW
                                                 RW
                                                       ρR,[2.9]W
                                                 2  7  2
```

```
      L←3  4ρ'ABCDEFGHIJKL'          L,[1.1]R        L,[2.75]R  L,[.5]R
      R←3  4ρ'1234567890KR'    ABCD              A1                ABCD
                               1234              B2                EFGH
                                                 C3                IJKL
                               EFGH              D4
                               5678              E5                1234
                                                 F6                5678
                               IJKL              G7                90KR
                               90KR              H8

                                                 I9
                                                 J0
                                                 KK
                                                 LR
```

Here is a way to think about laminating arrays. Suppose you wish to laminate two matrices of shape 3 by 4. The result will have *three* dimensions, and the shape will be 3 4 2, 3 2 4 or 2 3 4. The only question is where the 2 will go. Much like inserting a line in a function, to squeeze the 2 between the existing dimensions, use a value between 1 and 2; in the first position use a number between 0 and 1. As in catenation, scalars are extended to match the array being laminated. The catenation of two scalars to form a two-element vector is really an example of lamination.

Laminate is commonly used to build up a three-dimensional array from already existing matrices. As an example, let's use the two separate planes of *ORD* (here we obtain them by indexing):

```
      )COPY 1 CLASS TAB3
SAVED  14.45.33 02/20/83

      TB1←TAB3[1;;]              TB2←TAB3[2;;]
      TB1                        TB2
111 112 113                211 212 213
121 122 123                221 222 223
131 132 133                231 232 233
141 142 143                241 242 243
```

These two arrays can be combined in several ways:

```
        TB1,[.4]TB2                    TB1,[1.3]TB2                   TB1,[2.5]TB2
  111 112 113                    111 112 113                    111 211
  121 122 123                    211 212 213                    112 212
  131 132 133                                                   113 213
  141 142 143                    121 122 123
                                 221 222 223                    121 221
  211 212 213                                                   122 222
  221 222 223                    131 132 133                    123 223
  231 232 233                    231 232 233
  241 242 243                                                   131 231
        ρTB1,[4]TB2              141 142 143                    132 232
  2 4 3                          241 242 243                    133 233
                                       ρTB1,[1.3]TB2
                                  4 2 3                         141 241
                                                               142 242
                                                               143 243
                                                                     ρTB1,[2.5]TB2
                                                                4 3 2
```

These laminations produced three-dimensional arrays, while the following catenations give us only larger matrices, as we pointed out earlier:

```
        TB1,[1]TB2                     TB1,[2]TB2
  111 112 113                    111 112 113 211 212 213
  121 122 123                    121 122 123 221 222 223
  131 132 133                    131 132 133 231 232 233
  141 142 143                    141 142 143 241 242 243
  211 212 213
  221 222 223
  231 232 233
  241 242 243
```

Dyadic transpose

ORD, you will recall, is a three-dimensional array with two planes (one for each of two months), four rows (sizes) and three columns (styles). In the last section, we used laminate to reconstitute the display with differing points of view, as it were. A more general method of interchanging among planes, rows and columns employs the dyadic transpose function, ⍉. First, let's rearrange the data so that the planes are style and the columns are months. In other words, if the original data was in month, size, style order, we now want style, size, month.

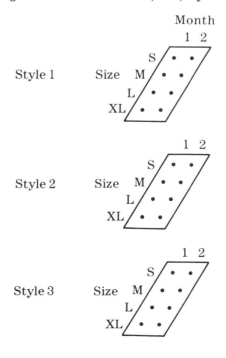

What was the third dimension becomes the first, the second remains as the second, and the new third dimension is what was the first. The result is identical to that obtained from the monadic transpose, $\lozenge ORD$:

```
        3 2 1◊ORD              ◊ORD                  ρORD
50  15                  50  15              2 4 3
34  20                  34  20                     ρ◊ORD
10   5                  10   5              3 4 2
 3   1                   3   1                     ρ3 2 1◊ORD
                                            3 4 2
88  30                  88  30
62  50                  62  50
21  12                  21  12
 4   2                   4   2

32  10                  32  10
20  20                  20  20
 5   2                   5   2
 2   1                   2   1
```

Another transpose makes the styles the rows and the sizes the columns, leaving the planes as months:

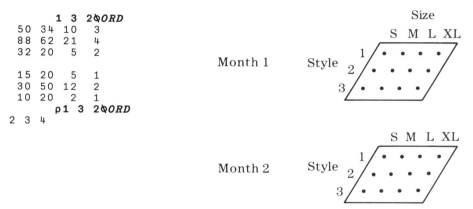

```
        1  3  2◊ORD
50  34  10   3
88  62  21   4
32  20   5   2

15  20   5   1
30  50  12   2
10  20   2   1
          ρ1 3 2◊ORD
2 3 4
```

Size

S M L XL

Month 1   Style

In this case the first dimension is unchanged, but what was the third dimension becomes the second, and what was the second becomes the third.

Note how dyadic transpose allows alteration of the axes in the last two and next four examples:

```
        2  1  3◊ORD           2  3  1◊ORD             3  1  2◊ORD           1  2  3◊ORD
50  88  32             50  34  10   3         50  15               50  88  32
15  30  10             15  20   5   1         88  30               34  62  20
                                              32  10               10  21   5
34  62  20             88  62  21   4                               3   4   2
20  50  20             30  50  12   2         34  20
                                              62  50               15  30  10
10  21   5             32  20   5   2         20  20               20  50  20
 5  12   2             10  20   2   1                               5  12   2
                               ρ2 3 1◊ORD    10   5                1   2   1
 3   4   2             3 2 4                  21  12                      ρ1 2 3◊ORD
 1   2   1                                     5   2               2 4 3
        ρ2 1 3◊ORD
4 2 3                                          3   1
                                               4   2
                                               2   1
                                                    ρ3 1 2◊ORD
                                              4 3 2
```

You should now be able to determine for yourself how different left arguments rearrange the month, style and size data. By the way, the 1 2 3◊ isn't very useful since the result is the same as the right argument, but we included it for completeness. There are 6 (!3) different transpositions of three-dimensional objects into three-dimensional objects.

For transposition, the left argument meets the requirement that each element of the normal axis order (1,2,3,...) is replaced by the axis number it is to end up as in the result. In the example 3 1 2⍉ORD, month (axis 1 originally) is now the third axis, while size (axis 2) is now planes (first axis), and style (original third axis) is now rows (second axis).

Confused? We're not through yet. The following section looks at ways to take diagonal slices of an array with the dyadic transpose. In the authors' experience, this is one of the most difficult features of APL. For that reason the section is optional and left to those readers who are looking for a challenge.

Using dyadic transpose to get a diagonal slice

The sales analyst for the company whose database is the array ORD, a true APL buff, decides to examine the data in still other ways. Comparison of each line with the other lines of the plane from which it was taken shows that in the second month, the best seller was actually a size larger than the best selling size in the first month! The analyst concludes that the advertising campaign was aimed at the fashion setters, who tend to be smaller, and awareness of the product only gradually filtered through to those for whom the blouses the company makes would be less flattering.

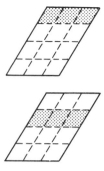

All the relevant data can be extracted with

```
      1 1 2⍉ORD
50 88 32
20 50 20
```

Here the desired plane and row indices are the same.

The transposition

```
      2 2 1⍉ORD
50 20
88 50
32 20
```

gives the same information, but the result is the (monadic) transpose of the previous result, as can be seen if we remove duplicate elements from the left argument.

A second slice is the 2 1 1 (or 1 2 2) transpose, which consists of all elements whose row and column indices are the same:

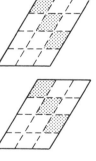

```
      2 1 1⍉ORD              1 2 2⍉ORD
50 15                   50 62  5
62 50                   15 50  2
 5  2
```

This extracts for each month the sales for style A small size, style B medium size and style C large size.

The final slices are

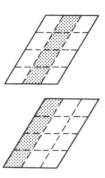

```
      1 2 1⍉ORD              2 1 2⍉ORD
50 34 10  3             50 30
30 50 12  2             34 50
                        10 12
                         3  2
```

which gets those elements whose first and third indices are identical. The result is the sales for style A the first month and style B the second month.

What about left arguments like

```
      1 3 3⍉ORD
DOMAIN ERROR
      1 3 3 ⍉ORD
              ∧
```

All positive integers up to the largest one present in the left argument must be included to avoid the error message. In the example, 2 was missing.

The most commonly used diagonal slice is that of a matrix (usually a square one), and fortunately it's an easy one to remember—the 1 1⍉.

```
   M←3 3⍴⍳9              M              1 1 ⍉M
                     1 2 3           1 5 9
                     4 5 6
                     7 8 9
```

As in the above matrix example, in a three-dimensional array the 1 1 1 ⍉ selects those elements all of whose indices are the same.

Although the dyadic transpose is one of the most powerful APL functions, its action on arrays of rank greater than 2 isn't always easy to see. For that reason, the function is not among the more popular with many APL users. And that's a pity, because it is so useful. You can do quite well experimenting at the terminal to find the proper transpose. If you do experiment, avoid arrays with the same dimension—it's much clearer to deal with an array of shape 2 by 4 by 3 than one of shape 3 by 3 by 3.

Using the relationships below will help you become a dyadic transpose expert, if that's your goal in life. The rules apply only when the elements of the left argument are all different; in other words, the rules don't apply for diagonal slices.

ρ right argument is (ρ result)[left argument]
left argument is (ρ ,result) ⍳ρ right argument
ρ result is (ρ right argument)[left argument ⍳ ⍳ρ left argument]

An application of dyadic transpose

Here is an application which uses dyadic transpose to reformat a character matrix (each row representing a word) into several columns of words, so that the order is preserved by reading down the first column, then the second, etc. The function is *SPRED* and the sample matrix is *SPL*:

```
        )COPY 1 CLASS SPRED SPL                      SPL
SAVED  14.45.33 02/20/83                             ZERO
        ∇SPRED[□]∇                                   ONE
      ∇ R←F SPRED X                                  TWO
[1]     R←⌈(ρX)[1]÷F ⍝CALCULATE AND PAD EXTRA        THREE
[2]     X←((R×F),1↓ρX)↑X ⍝BLANKS IF F IS NOT A       FOUR
[3]     X← 2 1 3 ⍉(F,R,1↑ρX)ρX ⍝FACTOR OF 1↑ρX       FIVE
[4]     R←(×/ 2 2 ρ1,ρX)ρX ⍝GILMAN AND ROSE, 1976    SIX
      ∇                                              SEVEN
        ρSPL                                         EIGHT
10 5                                                 NINE
```

To produce a two-field spread and a three-field spread, try

```
        2 SPRED SPL,' '                   3 SPRED SPL,' '
ZERO    FIVE                       ZERO   FOUR    EIGHT
ONE     SIX                        ONE    FIVE    NINE
TWO     SEVEN                      TWO    SIX
THREE   EIGHT                      THREE  SEVEN
FOUR    NINE                              ρ3 SPRED SPL,' '
        ρ2 SPRED SPL,' '          4 18
5 12
```

Do you know why a column of blanks was catenated to *SPL* in these examples?

Indexing scattered points

As we pointed out in Chapter 14, it isn't possible to pick out scattered elements of arrays of rank greater than one with primitive bracket indexing without getting more than we need. However, the previous sections showed how dyadic transpose can select various slices of an array. You may have a sneaking suspicion that if indexing is used to select parts of an array that include the desired points, maybe the dyadic transpose can then pull out the right slice.

Let's put this to the test on the array *CARDS* in 1 *CLASS*:

```
        )COPY 1 CLASS CARDS
SAVED  14.45.33 02/20/83

        CARDS
SPADE
CLUB
HEART
DIAMOND
```

The following set of separate indices will produce the characters *SUITS*,

```
        CARDS[1;1],CARDS[2;3],CARDS[4;2],CARDS[3;5],CARDS[1;1]
SUITS
```

but if the indices are merged, the result looks like some long-dead ancestor of the English language:

```
        AA←CARDS[1 2 4 3 1;1 3 2 5 1]
        AA
SAPES
CUL C
DAIOD
HAETH
SAPES
```

Each index is coupled with *all* the other indices along the remaining dimension.

If you're looking for *SUITS* in this mess, you probably noticed that the correct combinations of indices are those along the major diagonal of *AA*. But we already know how to get these points:

```
      1 1⍉AA
SUITS
```

It isn't too difficult a generalization to extend this to three dimensions. Say the elements 112 142 143 221 are wanted from *TAB*3:

```
    TAB3                     1 1 1⍉TAB3[1 1 1 2;1 4 4 2;2 2 3 1]
111 112 113              112 142 143 221
121 122 123
131 132 133
141 142 143

211 212 213
221 222 223
231 232 233
241 242 243
```

By taking other slices of a three-dimensional array, you can index scattered rows or columns.

The use of dyadic transpose for scatter-indexing may be summarized as follows, where *P,R,C* are the vectors of plane, row and column indices:

select scattered	from a matrix	from a rank-3 array
points	1 1⍉M[R;C]	1 1 1⍉T[P;R;C]
columns	M[;C]	2 1 2⍉T[P;;C]
rows	M[R;]	1 1 2⍉T[P;R;]
planes	M	T[P;;]

Those users who have access to APL2 or APL*PLUS will find that scatter-indexing can be done more easily with the index or choose functions (page 264).

PROBLEMS

1. Drill. Assign *U*←2 3 4ρι24, *C*←2 4 3ρ'ABCDEFGHI'

   ```
   ⌈/⌈/⌈/U            +≠U[;2;3]          ⍉C                ⊖C
   ⌈/,U               ¯1 1 2↓C           1 0 1 0/[2]C      3 1 2⊖C
   ×≠U                (2 4ρι3) ⌽C        0 2 2↓U           1 2 2⊖U
   +/[2]U             +/U[;1;3]
   ```

2. Make the first row first plane of *U* equal to the third row second plane of *U*.

3. Starting with a matrix *M*←3 4ρι4, produce another matrix *R* whose shape is 3 3 4 and made up of the columns of *M*. Use only indexing.

4. Write a one-line function to produce a table of three columns listing the integers 1 through *N*, their factorials and their reciprocals.

5. The XYZ advertising agency currently has 10 accounts. Each of these accounts represents an amount of money which is budgeted to be spent over a 12-month period in the following categories: 1) radio, 2) TV, 3) newspapers, 4) magazines, 5) direct mail. Assume the financial data is stored in an array *BUDGET* whose first dimension is time (in months), whose second dimension consists of the cost categories above, and whose third dimension is the accounts themselves. Write APL expressions to answer each of the following:
   A Find the total yearly cost for accounts 4 and 10.
   B How much was spent for the year for newspaper advertising in account 6?
   C What is the total yearly cost by account?
   D Which account spent the least money on TV during any month? In which month did this occur?
   E How much was spent each month in accounts 1 and 3 for magazine and direct mail advertising?
   F Construct a matrix of total monthly costs/account. Include appropriate row and column headings.
   G Enlarge the array *BUDGET* to include extra planes after the 6th and 12th months that will contain cumulative semiannual or annual costs/account/budget category.

6. You are given a long character vector V. Use laminate to follow each character with a semicolon.

7. A magazine subscription service sells 25 different magazines in 16 cities. The 12 by 25 by 16 array $MAGSALES$ contains a record of the number of subscriptions sold by month, magazine and city. Construct a function that will print in matrix form the name of the leading magazine each month. Assume the names of the magazines are stored in a matrix $MAGNAMES$, with the names of the months in the matrix CAL. Ignore the possibility of a tie for total sales per month to simplify the algorithm.

8. Write a program to underline nonblanks in a character vector V.

9. The 5 4 4 array SP contains selling price information on a company's primary product. Each plane represents data for one year (1978-82) for each of four models A, B, C, D (rows) in each of four sizes S, M, L, XL (columns). A similar array $SALES$ has the number of units sold each year for each model and size. Find the
   A gross volume for 1979
   B sales by size for 1980 and 1981
   C increase in sales volume by model from 1978 to 1982
   D revenue for models A and C (medium size) in 1978 and 1979
   E total revenue for 1982.
   F create a new table for 1983 prices (20% higher than 1982) and append it to SP.

10. Using the same three-dimensional database as in problem 9,
    A By what percent did sales in 1980 for mediums (all models) exceed those for extra large?
    B How many units (by model) were sold during 1981 and 1982 of those models whose sales exceeded 50,000 for all sizes sold?

11. During the year a hardware store bought each quarter a certain amount of nails, tacks and screws. The pounds of each bought per quarter are stored in the 3 by 4 table HWR. Print a report with an appropriate title and row and column headings and totals showing the year's purchases.

12. Write a function to number a given list of names.

13. Define a function $TABLE$ which formats a numeric table M as a character table with no decimal places if all the elements are integers, otherwise 2. The table should be bordered by '_' and '⁻', and the columns separated and bordered by '|'.

14. Write functions $WITH$ and $ABOVE$ to do the following: $WITH$ is to append and pad out row headings (stored in $SIDE$); $ABOVE$ is used to append column headings (stored in TOP). The expression $SIDE \; WITH \; TOP \; ABOVE \; DATA$ should then return a report which includes row and column headings.

15. Define a function $BESIDE$ to join two matrices of different shapes horizontally.

16. Decorate (i.e. outline) a literal matrix M with a character A.

17. For a 5 by 5 matrix $SALES$, use ⍉ to construct a new matrix $SALES1$ with column headings 10 through 14 and row headings $STORE1$ through $STORE5$.

18. Use the dyadic transpose to add a vector V to each row of a vector M.

19. Write an expression to obtain the diagonal that runs from the upper right to the lower left of a matrix.

Chapter 20: Generalized inner product and matrix inverse

In Chapter 2 the concept of an operator was introduced as something which can be applied to a function to obtain a different function; i.e., like the action of an adverb on a verb in grammar, operators modify a function. The operators common to most versions of APL are the outer product $\circ.f$, reduction $f/$, scan $f\backslash$, the axis operator $f[n]$, and the *inner product* $f.g$. It is this last very useful operator which will be introduced in this chapter.

We illustrate the inner product with a common problem. A company employs three sales persons who are engaged in selling four products A,B,C,D. Their sales volumes are shown in the matrix $VOLS$. $COSTS$ contains the price for each product and the shipping charges per unit.

Costs

Product	Unit price	Unit ship cost
A	4	0.05
B	2	0.06
C	1	.03
D	1	.02

		A	B	C	D
Salesperson	1	2	3	0	1
	2	0	2	1	4
	3	1	1	2	1

Volumes

```
VOLS←3 4ρ2 3 0 1 0 2 1 4 1 1 2 1
COSTS←4 2ρ4 .05 2 .06 1 .03 1 .02
```

The total revenue generated by salesperson 1 can be calculated as either of

```
      +/2 3 0 1 × 4 2 1 1                        +/VOLS[1;]×COSTS[;1]
15                                        15
```

and in the same way we can generate the total shipping costs for salesperson 3:

```
      +/1 1 2 1 × .05 .06 .03 .02               +/VOLS[3;]×COSTS[;2]
0.19                                      0.19
```

191

In fact, *all* the revenue and shipping costs associated with the three salespersons can be obtained by executing

```
      +/VOLS[1;]×COSTS[;1]              +/VOLS[1;]×COSTS[;2]
15                               0.3
      +/VOLS[2;]×COSTS[;1]              +/VOLS[2;]×COSTS[;2]
9                                0.23
      +/VOLS[3;]×COSTS[;1]              +/VOLS[3;]×COSTS[;2]
9                                0.19
```

or, more compactly, with

```
      +/[2]1 2 2 3 ⍉VOLS∘.×COSTS
   15                0.3
    9                0.23
    9                0.19
```

Inner product

The inner product concisely states and executes this complete set of instructions:

```
      VOLS+.×COSTS
   15                0.3
    9                0.23
    9                0.19
```

This particular operator, +.×, corresponds to *matrix multiplication* in mathematics. With matrix arguments it separately multiplies each row of the left argument by each column of the right argument and then carries out plus-reduction on the results. The inner dimensions must agree. That is, the number of columns in the left argument must match the number of rows in the right argument. Hence, the name *inner product*.

We're not through with this problem yet. Let's try

```
      VOLS⌈.×COSTS
   8                 0.18
   4                 0.12
   4                 0.06
```

By the same reasoning as before this represents the greatest revenue and shipping charge per item produced by each salesperson.

In present implementations of APL there are 441 distinct inner products possible, although most users tend to stay with +.×, ∧.=, ∨.≠, ∧.≠, ⌊.+ and ⌈.+. There appears to be plenty of room for those of you who are adventurous enough to explore new uses for the remaining 435. Who knows? You may become famous!

The inner product is *not* the same as $A∘.+B$ or $A∘.×B$ and it can't even be compared with $A×B$ since the latter operation works only when the two arrays are the same size, and the multiplication is carried out between corresponding elements only. The inner product, $Af.gB$, operates on any pair of arrays, provided that the last dimension of the left argument is the same as the first dimension of the right argument. Except for scalar arguments, the dimensions of the result in each case are $(^-1↓\rho A),1↓\rho B$. Here are more examples involving scalars, vectors and multidimensional arrays:

```
      10+.×3 2 8                      (2 3 4⍴⍳24)+.-4 2⍴⍳8
130                              ⁻6  ⁻10
      1 2 3 4+.*0 1 2 3          10   6
76                              26   22
      2 1 6+.×3 2⍴⍳6
35 44                           42   38
      (3 4⍴⍳12)+.=⍳4             58   54
4 0 0                           74   70
```

Numerical applications of the inner product

One interesting application involves a pipeline network between cities on a map. The diagram below shows not only the intercity pipeline lengths in miles between A, B, C and D, but also the directions in which they are measured:

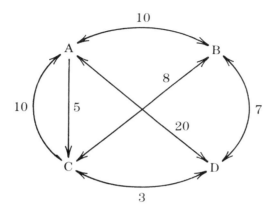

```
FM↓ TO→| CITY A   CITY B   CITY C   CITY D
-------|---------------------------------
CITY A |    -       10       5       20
CITY B |   10       -        8        7
CITY C |   10       8        -        3
CITY D |   20       7        3        -
```

Notice that the distances are not necessarily the same in both directions between any two cities. This is to allow for the most general case where there may be competing pipelines between two cities along different rights of way. The same information is provided in 1 *CLASS* as the variable *MILEAGE*. Believe it or not, a table of the longest pipeline distances from any city to any other city passing through some intermediate city is given by *MILEAGE⌈.+MILEAGE*:

```
      )LOAD 1 CLASS
SAVED  14.45.33 02/20/83
```

```
       MILEAGE              MILEAGE⌈.+MILEAGE
  0  10   5  20          40  27  23  20
 10   0   8   7          27  20  15  30
 10   8   0   3          23  20  16  30
 20   7   3   0          20  30  25  40
```

The longest distance from A to B is 27 miles (A→D→B), from B to C 15 miles (B→A→C), etc.

Why does this work? Let's arrange the matrices for the inner product in the same form used for the the last section:

0	10	5	20
10	0	8	7
10	8	0	3
20	7	3	0

$\lceil . +$

0	10	5	20
10	0	8	7
10	8	0	3
20	7	3	0

[1;1]	[1;2]	[1;3]	[1;4]
[2;1]	[2;2]	[2;3]	[2;4]
[3;1]	[3;2]	[3;3]	[3;4]
[4;1]	[4;2]	[4;3]	[4;4]

The longest distance from B to C is represented by the contents of box [2 ; 3]. This is formed by operating on the second row of the left argument and the third column of the right argument. It requires adding 10 and 5, and taking the greater of that sum and the sum of 0 and 8, which is 15, then taking the greater of 15 and the sum of 8 and 0, which is still 15, and finally taking the greater of 15 and the sum of 7 and 3.

There are many other interesting and useful variants of the inner product, only a few of which will be considered here. For instance, the shortest two-leg pipeline distance is *MILEAGE*⌊.+*MILEAGE*. The shortest distance from A to C is 5 miles, which is A→A→C or A→C→C. We are allowed this possibility because the distance from each city to itself is zero (the entries on the major diagonal of *MILEAGE*):

```
        MILEAGE                    MILEAGEL.+MILEAGE
    0 10   5 20                  0 10   5   8
   10  0   8  7                 10  0   8   7
   10  8   0  3                 10  8   0   3
   20  7   3  0                 13  7   3   0
```

One way to prevent such a sneaky result is to put arbitrarily large numbers along the major diagonal of a new array Q (to avoid destroying or rewriting *MILEAGE*). Then $Q\lfloor .+Q$ is the matrix of shortest two-leg distances, given that the intermediate city is different from the start or end. The shortest such distance from A to C is 18 miles (A→B→C). Application of this operation a second time ($Q\lfloor .+Q\lfloor .+Q$) gives the shortest three-leg distances:

```
        Q+MILEAGE+1000×(ı4)∘.=ı4
        Q                          QL.+Q                    QL.+QL.+Q
 1000    10     5    20      15  13  18   8          23  15  11  20
   10  1000     8     7      18  14  10  11          20  18  14  13
   10     8  1000     3      18  10   6  15          16  14  18   9
   20     7     3  1000      13  11  15   6          21  13   9  18
```

We can continue this process ad nauseam, but there is a prepared function *AGAIN* in 1 *CLASS* that will do it for us. It is niladic and simply reassigns a global T as $T\lfloor .+Q$. If we set T equal to Q initially, the first time we execute *AGAIN* we will get the shortest two-leg distances, the next time the shortest three-leg distances, and so on:

```
        ∇AGAIN[□]∇              T+Q ◇ AGAIN              AGAIN                  AGAIN
     ∇ AGAIN             15  13  18   8          23  15  11  20        21  19  23  14
 [1]   T+TL.+Q           18  14  10  11          20  18  14  13        24  20  16  17
 [2]   T                 18  10   6  15          16  14  18   9        24  16  12  21
     ∇                   13  11  15   6          21  13   9  18        19  17  21  12
```

Circuit analysis applications

Imagine a circuit with six functional units connected as follows:

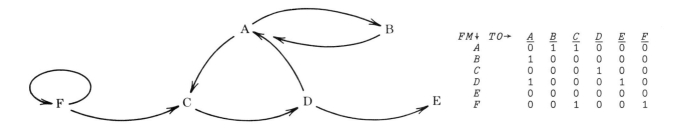

$FM\downarrow$ $TO\rightarrow$	$\underline{A}$	$\underline{B}$	$\underline{C}$	$\underline{D}$	$\underline{E}$	$\underline{F}$
A	0	1	1	0	0	0
B	1	0	0	0	0	0
C	0	0	0	1	0	0
D	1	0	0	0	1	0
E	0	0	0	0	0	0
F	0	0	1	0	0	1

A, B, C, D, E and F are some kind of functional units which can be either energized or not. The circuit works this way: if C is energized, after a certain increment of time D is energized, and after another increment of time E and A are energized; if A is energized, after an increment of time C and B are energized, etc. F is the oddball unit here. Once it is energized it stays on permanently, but unless we start with F on there is no way to turn it on. E is a terminus. It doesn't turn anything on. All this information is summarized in the matrix $CIRCUIT$, with 1 standing for the existence of a connection from the unit named on the left to the one whose name is on the top:

```
     CIRCUIT
0  1  1  0  0  0
1  0  0  0  0  0
0  0  0  1  0  0
1  0  0  0  1  0
0  0  0  0  0  0
0  0  1  0  0  1
```

We can assign a vector ST with six elements (one for each unit in the circuit) in which a 1 signifies that that unit is energized initially. For example, if only A is on, we assign ST as

```
      ST←1 0 0 0 0 0
```

What units are on after one increment of time? From the matrix $CIRCUIT$ it appears that B and C will be turned on and all the others, including A, will be off. The result should be 0 1 1 0 0, which can be achieved by

```
      STv.∧CIRCUIT
0  1  1  0  0  0
```

(Why is ∨.∧ used?) and after another increment of time,

```
      0 1 1 0 0 0v.∧CIRCUIT
1  0  0  1  0  0
```

A is energized during alternate cycles because of the loop between A and B.

To step this through several increments of time use the function RUN in 1 $CLASS$:

```
      ∇RUN[□]∇
    ∇ NETWORK RUN STATUS;COUNT
[1]   COUNT←0
[2] LOOP:COUNT
[3]   STATUS
[4]   STATUS←STATUSv.∧NETWORK
[5]   COUNT←COUNT+1
[6]   →LOOP
    ∇
```

The left argument is $NETWORK$, the matrix which describes the circuit connections. The right argument $STATUS$ represents the initial conditions. $COUNT$ is a local variable which is set to 0 on line 1 and displayed on line 2. Line 3 prints the current status of the circuit elements. $STATUS$ is updated on the next line and the counter upped on line 5. The final line causes a branch to line 2.

Does this program look a bit peculiar to you? It should. There is no safeguard in it to turn it off once it starts, and it will run forever! The proper thing to do would be to put a line in it that will cause execution to cease once *COUNT* reaches a certain value. Since there is no such check, we'll let it go and manually interrupt execution when we've seen enough.

Start by turning on only A:

```
        ST←1 0 0 0 0

        CIRCUIT RUN ST
0
1 0 0 0 0

1
0 1 1 0 0 0

2
1 0 0 1 0 0

3
1 1 1 0 1 0

4
1 1 1 1 0 0

5
1 1 1 1 1 0

6
1 1 1 1 1 0

7
1 1 1 1 1 0
RUN[3]
        )SI
RUN[3]   *
        COUNT
10
```

Execution has been manually interrupted, as discussed above, and we are suspended on line 3. F will never turn on no matter how many runs we make, while *COUNT* is up to 10, the display having lagged behind execution. Ordinarily we can't get a value for *COUNT* because it is a local variable. But remember that we are still in the function as a result of the suspension. Don't forget to remove the suspension by → or)*RESET*.

Character applications

One of the most frequent applications of inner product is finding which row of a character matrix matches a given character vector, commonly called *table lookup*. For example, if *DATA* is a matrix with each row holding the name of a product,

```
        DATA←'TACO' ON 'BURRITO' ON 'ENCHALADA' ON 'TOSTADA' ON 'TUMS'
```

then a function like this

```
        ∇HITS←MATRIX FIND VECTOR
[1]     HITS←MATRIX∧.=(1↓ρMATRIX)↑VECTOR∇
```

returns a bit vector with a 1 corresponding to which rows of the matrix match the vector.

```
        DATA FIND 'TOSTADA'
0 0 0 1 0
```

By this time some of you may be thinking how nice it would be if the example above could be modified to handle a matrix right argument, i.e., to simulate ranking. Let's see how a function can be built to do this.

Remember that ranking locates the first match of right argument elements in the left argument:

```
      A←3 4 ρ1 4 3 28 10 50 60 15 4 9 13              B←3 10 15 3 8
      A                                               B ι A
 1   4   3 28                                    6  6  1  6
10  50  60 15                                    2  6  6  3
 4   9  13  1                                    6  6  6  6
```

The 6's represent those elements in *A* not found in *B*. The right argument can be of any shape, but the left argument must be a vector.

A useful extension of this idea is locating the indices of rows in the left argument which are the first occurrences of matches to rows of the right argument. If we had such a function, *MDI*, for the arrays

```
      FURN1←5 6ρ'DESKS CHAIRSTABLESFILES CHAIRS'
      LOOKUP←4 6ρ'CHAIRSLAMPS PHONESTABLES'
```

```
      FURN1                    LOOKUP
DESKS                    CHAIRS
CHAIRS                   LAMPS
TABLES                   PHONES
FILES                    TABLES
CHAIRS                        ρLOOKUP
      ρFURN1             4  6
5  6
```

then *FURN*1 *MDI LOOKUP* should return 2 6 6 3.

How do we go about building *MDI*? Two ideas suggest themselves here. The inner product ∧ . = will be useful for getting matches of the rows. Locating the *first* match is trickier. In Problem 8, Chapter 5, we showed that ∧ \ on a logical vector returns 1's until the first 0 is encountered, with all 0's thereafter. These two techniques are the basis for *MDI*.

We can't execute *FURN*1∧ . =*LOOKUP* (why not?), but the expression *A*1←*FURN*1∧ . =⍉*LOOKUP* works quite nicely. The 'highest' 1 in each column marks the spot. To turn that into a recognizable index, we'll first define *A*2←∧⍀~*A*1 and then add 1 to *A*2's column sums:

```
      A1←FURN1∧.=⍉LOOKUP          A2←∧⍀~A1              A3←1++⌿A2
      A1                         A2                    A3
 0  0  0  0                  1  1  1  1            2  6  6  3
 1  0  0  0                  0  1  1  1
 0  0  0  1                  0  1  1  0
 0  0  0  0                  0  1  1  0
 1  0  0  0                  0  1  1  0
```

The function *MDI*, assembled from these steps, is shown below, along with another version, *MDI*1, which works no matter what the rank of *LOOKUP*.

```
      ∇Z←MATRIX MDI LOOKUP                  ∇Z←MATRIX MDI1 LOOKUP
[1]   Z←1++⌿∧⍀MATRIX∧.=⍉LOOKUP∇      [1]    Z←1++/∧\LOOKUP∨.≠⍉MATRIX∇
```

The inner product ∨ . ≠ returns a result which is the logical complement of that from ∧ . =. In all cases, of course, the shapes of the two arrays must be acceptable for use with the inner product.

The rest of this chapter is optional. It covers, at least superficially, many uses of APL in matrix algebra, curve-fitting and splines. If you are a member of that class of users for whom the above topics are esoterica, skip to the next chapter. But if your curiosity has gotten the better of you, or you have a genuine need to know, read on.

Linear equations

There are many uses for APL in the branch of mathematics known as *matrix algebra*. Since this text is a teaching introduction to the language, only a few of these will be considered, the first being the solution of a set of exactly determined simultaneous linear equations.

For those who have forgotten their high school algebra, simultaneous linear equations are of this form in conventional notation,

$$aX + bY + cZ = r$$
$$dX + eY + fZ = s$$
$$gX + hY + iZ = t$$

the problem being to find values of the variables X, Y, Z that satisfy all the equations. a, b, c,..., i and r, s, t are numerical constants.

Suppose that in three successive weeks we bought quantities of items A, B and C, spending the amounts listed:

```
       | TOTAL |  A  |  B  |  C
-------+-------+-----+-----+---
WEEK 1 | $1.10 |  4  |  6  |  0
WEEK 2 | $0.59 |  3  |  2  |  2
WEEK 3 | $0.78 |  1  |  3  |  4
```

What are the unit costs of the various items? The answer happens to be $.05 for A, $.15 for B and $.07 for C. Let's work back from the answer to see how we can solve similar problems. From our previous work with the inner product, we ought to be able to get the vector of total costs from the number-of-items matrix and the unit-costs vector (try this for yourself). We'll call the total-costs vector D, the matrix of the number of each item purchased X, and the unit-costs vector B. Our trouble is that in a real problem we would know X and D but not B.

Before proceeding, here is a quick review of some elementary rules about matrices. M, N, P and R are matrices of the appropriate size and $+.\times$ is ordinary matrix multiplication. You can demonstrate all of these rules on any APL system:

(1) If M equals N, then $R+.\times M$ equals $R+.\times N$
(2) $(M+.\times(N+.\times P))$ equals $(M+.\times N)+.\times P$
(3) If M has an inverse, MI, then $MI+.\times M$ equals I, where I is the identity matrix
(4) $(M+.\times I)$ equals $(I+.\times M)$ equals M

The third fact introduces two new concepts, the *identity matrix* and the *matrix inverse*. The identity matrix is simply a square matrix with ones on the major diagonal and zeros elsewhere. An identity matrix of size N can be formed by $(\iota N)\circ.=\iota N$ or $(N,N)\rho 1,N\rho 0$. It is called the identity matrix because when any matrix is multiplied (in the $+.\times$ sense) by it, the result is unchanged.

The matrix inverse concept is similar to other types of inverses we have encountered. For example, adding the additive inverse to a number results in 0, the identity element for addition, while multiplying a number by its multiplicative inverse results in 1:

```
      R←ι5
    0=R+-R                      1=R×÷R
1  1  1  1  1                 1  1  1  1  1
```

$-R$ here is the additive inverse and $\div R$ the multiplicative inverse. So the inverse of a matrix M is a matrix which, when it multiplies M (matrix multiplication, not element-by-element), yields the identity matrix.

If $M+.\times MIR$ results in I, then MIR is said to be a *right inverse*. If $MIL+.\times M$ results in I, MIL is a *left inverse*. If the same matrix is both a left and a right inverse of M, then M must be square (why?), and we refer to *the inverse* of M. From this point on, MI will stand for *the inverse* of M.

Now getting back to our problem, with the dimensions underneath as shown, we had

$$\begin{array}{cccc} D & \leftarrow & X & +.\times & B \\ (3) & & (3\ 3) & & (3) \end{array}$$

and we want to find B. The following sequence of algebraic substitutions does it for us. The rules are the ones stated above.

$$\begin{array}{lll} XI+.\times D & \text{is } XI+.\times(X+.\times B) & \text{rule 1} \\ & \text{or } (XI+.\times X)+.\times B & \text{rule 2} \\ & \text{or } I+.\times B & \text{rule 3} \\ & \text{or } B & \text{rule 4} \end{array}$$

The last line is our conclusion, that $B\leftarrow XI+.\times D$.

To find the inverse of a matrix, APL provides a primitive monadic function ⌹, formed by overstriking the quad and divide symbols, and usually called *quad-divide, domino* or *matrix divide*. Let's use it to solve the unit costs problem at the beginning of this section.

```
       X                        ⌹X
 4  6  0          ‾0.03846153846    0.4615384615   ‾0.2307692308
 3  2  2           0.1923076923   ‾0.3076923077    0.1538461538
 1  3  4          ‾0.1346153846    0.1153846154    0.1923076923
       D                        (⌹X)+.×D
1.1  0.59  0.78          0.05  0.15  0.07
```

If the right argument X is a scalar, then ⌹X is equivalent to ÷X, while for X a vector, ⌹X returns a vector result which is a multiple of X.

Use of the inner product in the solution of simultaneous equations can be eliminated by the dyadic matrix divide, $R \leftarrow D⌹X$, instead of $(⌹X)+.×D$. The right argument is the matrix of coefficients, and the left argument the vector of constants:

```
      D⌹X
0.05  0.15  0.07
```

More generally, for ⌹M to yield a result, the matrix must be invertible, i.e., have at least as many rows as columns. Its determinant must not be zero, otherwise a *DOMAIN ERROR* results. If M is nonsquare, the result is a left inverse,

```
      M←4 2ρ2 1 1 3 4 5 6 7
      ⌹M
‾0.3377926421   ‾0.3913043478    0.003344481605   0.1170568562
‾0.2575250836    0.347826087     0.05685618729   ‾0.01003344482
```

while if the matrix is square, the result is the inverse of the matrix:

```
      P←3 3ρ3 4 5 6 7 8 9 10 2
      ⌹P
‾2.444444444     1.555555556   ‾0.1111111111
 2.222222222    ‾1.444444444    0.2222222222
‾0.1111111111    0.2222222222  ‾0.1111111111
```

In the first case, ρ ⌹M equals ρ ⍉M. The use of the dyadic ⌹ as in $R \leftarrow B⌹A$, requires that ρ ρ A be 2, with ρ ρ B either 1 or 2. The first dimension of A must be equal to or greater than the second dimension of A, and must equal the first dimension of B. A right argument which is nonsquare (first dimension greater than second dimension) indicates a system of equations with more equations than unknowns, and the solution is a *least-squares* solution (next section). It is also possible for both A and B to be vectors. In this case the result is a scalar. Similarly, if A and B are both scalars, $A⌹B$ is equivalent to $A÷B$.

APL2 offers more advanced matrix algebra features. ⎕IR (implicit $r$esult) holds the rank (matrix algebra definition, largest submatrix with an inverse) of the right argument of the last execution of ⌹. ⊟, polynomial zeros, is a monadic function whose argument is the coefficients of the powers (decreasing to the right) of the polynomial. The result is a vector containing the roots of the polynomial. ⊞ (eigen) is a monadic function whose argument must be a square matrix of real numbers and whose result is a matrix with one more row than the argument. The first row is the *eigenvalues* of the argument, and the remaining rows are the right *eigenvectors*.

Least square fits, trend lines and curve fitting

If you wish to fit a straight line of the form $Y = a + bX$ through two points, such as (1.5,2) and (3.5,3), you can use the dyadic ⌹ as shown:

```
      2 3⌹2 2ρ1 1.5 1 3.5
1.25  0.5
```

1.25 is the value of the Y-intercept, and 0.5 is the value for b, the slope. Any predicted Y-value along the line can be found by the defined function *EVAL*:

```
        ∇EVAL[☐]∇
      ∇ Y←EVAL X
[1]     Y←(X∘.* 0 1)+.× 1.25 0.5
      ∇

        EVAL 0 .5 1 1.5 2 2.5 3
1.25 1.5 1.75 2 2.25 2.5 2.75
```

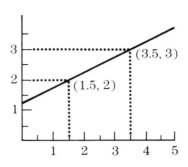

Now suppose a business analyst has spent effort, time and funds obtaining the following data, and wishes to find the linear (straight line) relation between X and Y:

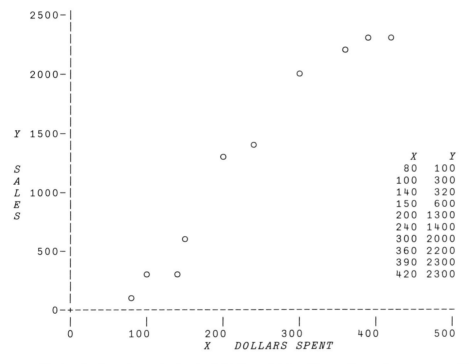

Obviously there is no single straight line which will pass through every one of the points. We are left with the problem of choosing the one particular straight line which is 'best' in some sense.

One approach in wide use is to fit a line such that the sum of the squared vertical distances from the line to each point is the smallest possible value—the *least squares* fit. The problem, therefore, is to find the coefficients a and b such that $+/(((b,a)+.×X∘.*0 1)-Y)*2$ is the smallest possible value. The expression $Y⌹X∘.*0 1$ does it, and is called a *linear least squares* solution. There is no other set of coefficients you can pick which will get a smaller sum-of-squares of differences, given that you decide a straight line is the correct *model*.

The following figures use a typical graphics workspace as found on commercial time sharing systems or available for purchase. It is one of a family of graphics workspaces for specific models of printing terminals, in this case an Anderson-Jacobsen Model 832 or 833 terminal).

```
      X←80 100 140 150 200 240 300 360 390 420
      Y←100 300 320 600 1300 1400 2000 2200 2300 2300
      PX←(⌊/X)+0,(⍳100)×.01×(⌈/X)-⌊/X
      OT←PX,[1.5](PX∘.*0 1)+.×Y⌹X∘.*0 1
```

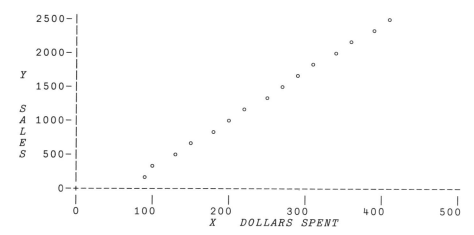

Alternatively, you might want to fit a simple curved line through the points. There are an infinite number of curved lines you could pick, but a typical first choice is to fit a quadratic of the form $Y = a + bX + cX^2$. a, b and c are the three elements of the result of

```
      R←Y⊞X∘.*0 1 2
      R
‾996.8729766 13.2153557 ‾0.01230306278
```

There is no other set of three values which will give a smaller result to the expression $+/((R+.\times X\circ.*0\ 1\ 2)-Y)*2$.

```
      OT←PX,[1.5](PX∘.*0 1 2)+.×Y⊞X∘.*0 1 2
```

Statisticians concern themselves with selecting the proper model (should it be $A + B \times X$, or $A + (B \times X) + C \times X*2$, or something else?) and then making formal tests of statistical significance. Usually these tests involve comparison of the size of the coefficients to the sum of the squares of the differences. You should *not*, however, conclude that the models used above exhaust the ingenuity of statisticians and mathematicians.

Splines

Since the computer has made their calculation manageable, a great deal of research effort has gone into models called *splines*. A spline is a mathematical analogue of a draftsman's curve-fitting instrument. Splines have a solid mathematical basis, and they also have the desirable property of fitting curves to a set of points in an esthetic fashion. Their greatest application is for graphing data for which the underlying model is unknown (or even nonexistent !).

It is far beyond the scope of this book to treat splines in any detail. We will present working programs for evaluating natural cubic splines, with no comment on the programming style or algorithms.

```
∇SPLINECALC[□]∇
    ∇ C←X SPLINECALC Y;N
[1]    N←4×¯2+ρY←0,Y
[2]    C← 1 0 0 0 0 0 1 1 1 1 0 0 0 0 1 2 3 0 ¯1 0 0 0 2 6 0 0 ¯2
[3]    C←(N- 2 0)ρ(4+4×N)ρ(5,N)↑ 4 7 ρC
[4]    C←(C,[1] N↑ 0 0 2),[1](-N)↑ 2 6
[5]    C←X,((ρX),4)ρY[,1⌈(1↓ιρX)∘.+ 0 1 ,2ρ-N]⌹C
    ∇


∇SPLINEEVAL[□]∇
    ∇ R←X SPLINEEVAL C;J
[1]    J←1⌈+/X∘.>R←C[;1]
[2]    R←+/C[J;1+ι4]×((X-R[J])÷((1↓R)-¯1↓R)[J])∘.*¯1+ι4
    ∇

    OT←PX,[1.5] PX SPLINEEVAL X SPLINECALC Y
```

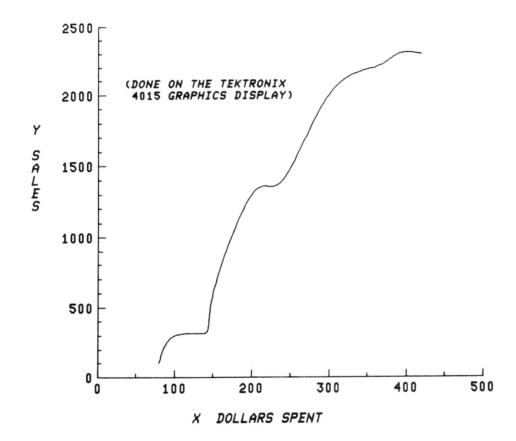

Notice that the spline technique ingeniously fits the curve through each of the points, without any jagged edges.

The few examples shown barely begin to cover the wide range of possible applications of the inner product. Many of the problems appearing in the previous chapters can be redone more compactly with the inner product. Exercises for the reader are deferred to the end of Chapter 21, which covers the outer product.

Chapter 21: Generalized outer product

This chapter is somewhat anticlimactic in that there are no surprises or new APL features in it. The outer product, you will recall, was introduced way back in Chapter 3 as a shortcut to generate operation tables for the primitive scalar dyadic functions, and has been used in most of the succeeding chapters. Here we will review the syntax of the outer product and emphasize it with suitable examples other than just the vectors and scalars used heretofore.

The arguments of the outer product can be arrays of any rank. And the *rank* of the result in all cases is the *sum of the ranks* of the arguments, while the *shape* of the result is the *catenation of the shapes* of the arguments. Below are some examples:

```
      3 6 ∘.⌈ 5 8 7 ¯1 ⍝ALL POSSIBLE COMBINATIONS OF ELEMENTS OF THE TWO VECTORS
5 8 7 3
6 8 7 6

      'HELLO'∘.='GOODBYE' ⍝OCCURRENCES OF LEFT ARG ELEMENTS IN RIGHT ARG
0 0 0 0 0 0 0
0 0 0 0 0 0 1
0 0 0 0 0 0 0
0 0 0 0 0 0 0
0 1 1 0 0 0 0
      SOLD←2 3⍴3 8 5 10 6 20 ⍝ SALES OF PRODUCT OVER 2 WEEKS BY 3 SALESPEOPLE
      COST←2 2⍴11 15 30 20 ⍝ POSSIBLE TEST PRICES FOR THE PRODUCT
      COST∘.×SOLD ⍝ RESULT HAS 4 DIMENSIONS
 33  88  55
110  66 220

 45 120  75
150  90 300


 90 240 150
300 180 600

 60 160 100
200 120 400
```

Some of the patterns in the result are interesting. Here again is the identity matrix (see page 198) of order 4 and its logical complement:

```
      (⍳4)∘.=⍳4            (⍳4)∘.≠⍳4
1 0 0 0                0 1 1 1
0 1 0 0                1 0 1 1
0 0 1 0                1 1 0 1
0 0 0 1                1 1 1 0
```

The other relational functions also yield interesting patterns of 1's and 0's, which when 'overlaid' by multiplication on a matrix of the same size, will sieve out unwanted elements by replacing them with 0 while leaving alone the others:

```
      (⍳5)∘.≤⍳5        M←5 5⍴⍳25           M×(⍳5)∘.≤⍳5
1 1 1 1 1                            1  2  3  4  5
0 1 1 1 1                            0  7  8  9 10
0 0 1 1 1                            0  0 13 14 15
0 0 0 1 1                            0  0  0 19 20
0 0 0 0 1                            0  0  0  0 25
```

Some uses for the outer product have already been explored in the text and exercises. Others will be found in the problems at the end of this chapter. Until then, for those of you in whom the gambling instinct runs strong and unrestrained, consider the following 'practical' problem: you wish to use the facilities of APL to simulate 20 rolls of a single die. Identify those successive rolls which between them result in a 7.

We must first generate the 20 rolls by

```
      R←?20ρ6
      R
1 5 3 4 2 1 5 5 6 3 4 5 1 1 4 5 1 3 1 3
```

The corresponding vector of the 'neighbors' of these rolls is easily obtained by $1\phi R$ and the sums by $^-1\downarrow R+1\phi R$. Why is $^-1$ used?

```
      1φR
5 3 4 2 1 5 5 6 3 4 5 1 1 4 5 1 3 1 3 1
      ¯1↓R+1φR
6 8 7 6 3 6 10 11 9 7 9 6 2 5 9 6 4 4 4
```

Those successive rolls adding up to 7 can be identified by

```
      HIT←(7=¯1↓R+1φR)/ι¯1+ρR
      HIT
3 10
```

while the rolls represented by HIT are $HIT\circ.+0\ 1$ and the actual values of R selected can be displayed with $R[HIT\circ.+0\ 1]$:

```
      HIT∘.+0 1            R[HIT∘.+0 1]
   3   4                3 4
  10  11                3 4
```

As a corollary to the last problem, consider the following question: how many 4's are there in R? Clearly this is $+/R=4$. But suppose we modify the question slightly and ask how many times each of the integers 1 through 6 occurs in R. We could repeat the above expression for each integer. But the outer product lets us do it all at once:

```
      +/R∘.=ι6
6 1 4 3 5 1
```

If you are still in a gambling mood you might try your luck by defining a function to simulate the action of a slot machine, the so-called 'one-armed bandit,' to see how many times you get, say, three 'lemons' or three 'cherries.' You may find the outer product useful here, or, as is frequently the case given the richness of the APL language, come up with a completely new and innovative approach.

String searching

Our next example is a function $STRINGSEARCH$ designed to locate all occurrences of a given phrase W in some character vector T of text, sometimes called a *string*. There are several ways in which the problem can be approached. The one to be shown here makes use of the fact that an outer product with vector arguments results in a matrix, each of whose rows corresponds to the execution of the given function between each element of the left argument and the entire right argument. (Compare with $R\circ.=ι6$ in the last example.)

With the function =, this will result in a logical matrix, each row of which checks for the presence of one character of the phrase W in the text T. To illustrate, assign

```
      W←'IN'              T←'IT DOES NOT RAIN IN SPAIN'         AA←W∘.=T
      AA
1 0 0 0 0 0 0 0 0 0 0 0 0 0 1 0 0 1 0 0 0 0 0 1 0
0 0 0 0 0 0 0 0 1 0 0 0 0 0 1 0 0 1 0 0 0 0 0 1
```

The interesting thing about this array is the location of the 1's in the rows, corresponding to the occurrences of I and N in T. Note the shift of the 1 corresponding to the location of N in the second row, compared with the location of I in the first row (except the letter N in the word NOT).

One way to distinguish between occurrences of IN and those of isolated I's and N's is to shift the second row one element to the left, which produces columns of all 1's, corresponding to the locations of IN:

```
      BB←(¯1+ιρW)φAA
      BB
1 0 0 0 0 0 0 0 0 0 0 0 0 0 1 0 0 1 0 0 0 0 0 1 0
0 0 0 0 0 0 0 1 0 0 0 0 0 0 1 0 0 1 0 0 0 0 0 1 0
```

Next, to identify these columns, ∧-reduce across the first dimension:

```
      CC←∧⌿BB
      CC
0 0 0 0 0 0 0 0 0 0 0 0 0 0 1 0 0 1 0 0 0 0 0 1 0
```

This result can now be used to pinpoint in T the indices representing the locations of the first elements of occurrences of IN in W:

```
      CC/ιρT
15 18 24
```

Finally, the complete defined function looks like this:

```
      ∇R←T STRINGSEARCH W
[1]   R←(∧⌿(¯1+ιρW)φW∘.=T)/ιρT ∇
```

What would change if we wanted to locate all occurrences of the *word* IN instead of just the successive *characters* I and N?

$STRINGSEARCH$ isn't very efficient in its use of space or time if T is very large. If we really wanted to produce, say, a concordance of a text, first, the text itself isn't likely to fit into the available workspace and would therefore have to be stored on a file (Chapter 27), to be brought in one piece at a time. Second, the individual words would be pre-indexed, and the search would then be confined to identifying words with the same indices as the ones desired.

Text processing is such an important application that some systems provide special system functions for doing it efficiently. On many systems T $\square SS$ W is equivalent to $∧⌿(¯1+ιρW)φW∘.=T$, but runs much faster.

Our next illustration also has to do with text searches. The problem is to replace all occurrences of a single character in a character vector with a specified string. This is a simpler version of the customary replacement of a given string by another string, wherever it occurs in the text.

We first define a character vector:

```
      VEC←'HOT POT'
```

The character $'T'$ is to be replaced by the string $'CUS'$.

Let's build a function $REPSTRING$ to do this. First, we catenate the string to each element of VEC:

```
      AA←,VEC,((ρVEC),ρ'CUS')ρ'CUS'
      AA
HCUSOCUSTCUS CUSPCUSOCUSTCUS
↑     ↑     ↑↑↑↑    ↑      ↑     ↑↑↑
```

The arrows show the characters to be selected. Next, we use the outer product to define a sieve of 1's and 0's to do the selection and then compress to get the desired result:

```
      BB←,(VEC='T')∘.=0,(ρ'CUS')ρ1           BB/AA
                                           HOCUS POCUS
```

The function $REPSTRING$ which incorporates this algorithm is show below:

```
      ∇R←V REPSTRING C;STR;TEMP1;TEMP2          VEC REPSTRING 'T','CUS'
[1]   STR←1↓C                                  HOCUS POCUS
[2]   TEMP1←,V,((ρV),ρSTR)ρSTR
[3]   TEMP2←,(V=1↑C)∘.=0,STR=STR
[4]   R←TEMP2/TEMP1 ∇
```

This sneaky solution is an ingenious but slower alternative to looping, a more natural approach for most people:

```
        ∇R←V REPSTRING1 C;STR;TEMP1;TEMP2
[1]     R←'' ⍝ TO HOLD RESULT
[2]     STR←1↓C  ⍝ REPLACEMENT STRING
[3]     C←1↑C ⍝ CHARACTER TO BE REPLACED
[4]     TEMP1←(C=V)/⍳⍴V ⍝ ALL OCCURRENCES OF C IN V
[5]     TEMP1←¯1+TEMP1-0,¯1↓TEMP1 ⍝ CHARACTERS BETWEEN ADJACENT C'S
[6]     L:→END IF 0≥⍴TEMP1 ⍝ EXIT IF NO MORE REPLACEMENTS
[7]     TEMP2←1↑TEMP1 ⍝ CHARACTERS TO NEXT C
[8]     R←R,(TEMP2↑V),STR ⍝ MAKE THIS REPLACEMENT IN R
[9]     TEMP1←1↓TEMP1 ⍝ REMOVE THIS OCCURRENCE
[10]    V←(1+TEMP2)↓V  ⍝ STRIP THE CHARACTERS OFF V
[11]    →L⍝ TO REPEAT PROCESS
[12]    END:R←R,V ⍝ IF NO CHARACTERS REMAIN IN V
[13]    ∇
```

Removing duplicate rows from a matrix

Frequently it happens that we have a table which contains duplicate rows, for example, a mailing list, to be cleaned up. The key to the problem is to find a way to identify the duplicate rows.

We'll use the matrix *NAMS* to illustrate the technique:

```
    NAMS←5 3⍴'ANNJOEJOEMAYANN'            AA←NAMS∧.=⍉NAMS
    NAMS                                   AA
ANN                                  1 0 0 0 1
JOE                                  0 1 1 0 0
JOE                                  0 1 1 0 0
MAY                                  0 0 0 1 0
ANN                                  1 0 0 0 1
```

AA indicates that rows 1 and 5 of *NAMS* are duplicates, as are rows 2 and 3. What we need is a vector whose elements are 1 1 0 1 0. This can be gotten by $BB←(⍳1↑⍴NAMS)∘.>⍳1↑⍴NAMS$ which produces a lower triangle of 1's, and combining it with the array *AA*:

```
    BB←(⍳1↑⍴NAMS)∘.>⍳1↑⍴NAMS           CC←AA∧BB
    BB                                    CC
0 0 0 0 0                            0 0 0 0 0
1 0 0 0 0                            0 0 0 0 0
1 1 0 0 0                            0 1 0 0 0
1 1 1 0 0                            0 0 0 0 0
1 1 1 1 0                            1 0 0 0 0
```

Notice that there are now 1's only in the duplicate rows. The rest is easy:

```
    (~∨/CC)⌿NAMS
ANN
JOE
MAY
```

Here is the complete algorithm:

```
    ∇R←DUPELIM X;T                        DUPELIM NAMS
[1]    T←X∧.=⍉X                        ANN
[2]    R←(~∨/((⍳1↑⍴T)∘.>⍳1↑⍴T)∧T)⌿X    JOE
[3]    ⍝ OR  R←(∧/T≁(⍳1↑⍴T)∘.>⍳1↑⍴T)⌿X ∇  MAY
```

Graphing

This topic has to do with the use of the outer product to build up a simple-minded but instructive graphing function. To begin with, define

```
      X← ̄5+⍳9                        Y←⌽X
      X                              Y⍝
 ̄4  ̄3  ̄2  ̄1 0 1 2 3 4        4 3 2 1 0  ̄1  ̄2  ̄3  ̄4
```

Because the middle elements in both X and Y are 0's, their outer product will produce 0's along the 'axes' of the matrix:

```
      M←Y∘.×X
```

The next step is to replace the 0's with some character, say, +, and everything else with blanks. One way to do this is to use the matrix M to index a suitable character vector:

```
      ' +'[1+0=M]
       +
       +
       +
       +
+++++++++
       +
       +
       +
       +
```

Since the horizontal axis looks somewhat out of scale (one horizontal character space isn't as wide as one vertical character space), we adjust our 'graph' as follows:

```
      (18⍴1 0)\' +'[1+0=M]
       +
       +
       +
       +
+ + + + + + + + +
       +
       +
       +
       +
```

Suppose now we wish to plot on this set of axes a number of points (X,Y), where $Y←X+1$. Our axes are made up of characters, so that the points themselves would have to be represented as characters to include them. It is more interesting, however, to go back to our original outer product, which is numeric, and superimpose the desired set of points FP on it before converting to characters:

```
      FP←Y∘.=X+1
      FP
0 0 0 0 0 0 0 1 0
0 0 0 0 0 0 1 0 0
0 0 0 0 0 1 0 0 0
0 0 0 0 1 0 0 0 0
0 0 0 1 0 0 0 0 0
0 0 1 0 0 0 0 0 0
0 1 0 0 0 0 0 0 0
1 0 0 0 0 0 0 0 0
0 0 0 0 0 0 0 0 0
```

FP produces a matrix of 1's where the points are. We next add the matrices FP and $1+2×0=M$. You should be able to see why multiplication by 2 is necessary if you execute the next step but with and without the multiplication by 2:

```
        FP+1+2×0=M                      FP+1+0=M
  1  1  1  1  3  1  1  2  1       1  1  1  1  2  1  1  2  1
  1  1  1  1  3  1  2  1  1       1  1  1  1  2  1  2  1  1
  1  1  1  1  3  2  1  1  1       1  1  1  1  2  2  1  1  1
  1  1  1  1  4  1  1  1  1       1  1  1  1  3  1  1  1  1
  3  3  3  4  3  3  3  3  3       2  2  2  3  2  2  2  2  2
  1  1  2  1  3  1  1  1  1       1  1  2  1  2  1  1  1  1
  1  2  1  1  3  1  1  1  1       1  2  1  1  2  1  1  1  1
  2  1  1  1  3  1  1  1  1       2  1  1  1  2  1  1  1  1
  1  1  1  1  3  1  1  1  1       1  1  1  1  2  1  1  1  1
```

Finally, our expanded plot is

```
        (18ρ1 0)\' o+o'[FP+1+2×0=M]
            +           o
            +         o
            +       o
            o
  +   +   +   o   +   +   +   +   +
        o       +
      o         +
  o             +
                +
```

Now that we have built up the algorithm for the plot routine, we can incorporate it into a defined function, *GRAPH*, and try it out after setting *FP* and *X*:

```
        ∇Z←GRAPH
[1]     Z←((2×ρX)ρ1 0)\' o+o'[FP+1+2×0=(φX)∘.×X] ∇
        X← ̄5+ι9
        FP←(φX)∘.=X+1

        GRAPH
            +           o
            +         o
            +       o
            o
  +   +   +   o   +   +   +   +   +
        o       +
      o         +
  o             +
                +
```

Plotting functions can get quite complicated when it is necessary to include such amenities as labeling of the axes, provision for changing the scale of the plot, and rounding off the computed values for the coordinates, since the terminal can't type characters between lines and spaces. Most APL systems provide prepared plotting routines in the common libraries. Some of these, however, may be specific packages designed to work only on graphics terminals like those manufactured by Tektronix or Hewlett-Packard Corporations. The plotting facilities available may differ somewhat from system to system, so carefully read the instructions in *DESCRIBE* or *HOWPLOT* or whatever your system provides. Problem 11 will give you some practice in simple plotting, using a widely distributed APL workspace.

Operators

This section is optional. Its purpose is twofold: to discuss in more detail the nature of the class of APL features called 'operators,' and second, to describe APL2 enhancements in this area.

One reason for this emphasis on operators is that, as the present and preceding chapters show, a single operator, because it can act on many different functions, becomes a powerful tool in the hands of a knowledgeable user. Just inner products alone added 441 possible derived functions to your APL vocabulary.

Quantity, of course, doesn't automatically make for quality. But the operator concept has been generalized to enrich the APL dictionary in the same way that the ability to convert old words or coin new ones has greatly broadened the scope and versatility of the English language.

Let's now look at the operator itself. As we mentioned earlier in the text, an operator takes a function (sometimes with another function or an array) and converts it into something different, called a *derived function*.

Those functions or arrays that the operator acts upon are formally called *operands*. They are analogous to the arguments of functions.

The left operand of an operator must be a function, while the right operand may be either a function or an array. Reduce is an example of a monadic operator, while inner and outer products are dyadic. For, say, +/, + is the left operand of the reduce operator /, while for ∘.× and +.×, ∘ and + are left operands, with × the right operand.

We mentioned in Chapter 6 that there is a sort of hierarchy in APL after all. It's limited to operators taking precedence over functions. Operators are said to have 'long scope' on the left, which means that the left operand is the longest function expression on the left. If the operator is dyadic, it has 'short scope' on the right, that is, its right operand is the single function or array on the right. Functions, by way of contrast, have long scope on the right.

You'll appreciate what all this means by following this APL2 example:

```
      A←2 3ρ⍳6                 B←3 4ρ⍳12              A+.×.⌈B
      A                        B                  45 120 122 384
1 2 3                     1   2   3   4          180 240 308 384
4 5 6                     5   6   7   8
                          9  10  11  12
```

It isn't as weird as it looks. The rows of A combine, using ⌈, with the columns of B in the usual manner of the inner product to give

```
1   2   3   4
5   6   7   8
9  10  11  12

4   4   4   4
5   6   7   8
9  10  11  12
```

and then +.×/ is carried out on each column of this intermediate result. But what kind of oddball expression is +.×/ ?

Three comments are in order here. First, the reason that the expression +.×.⌈ was grouped as (+.×).⌈ is that operators have long left scope and short right scope. Second, the sensible (and correct) way to look at +.×/ is to put × between every pair of elements in each column and perform +/ on the result. The first column in the first plane, for example, becomes +/1×5×9, or 45. And last, the plus reduction bought us nothing since it was carried out on a scalar. The original extended inner product would have made more sense on higher-dimensional arguments.

Reduce and scan have been extended in APL2 to allow the use of any dyadic function, including defined functions, that produces a result. This can lead to some interesting possibilities. In what follows, the new expression on the left side is equivalent to the traditional expression on the right:

```
      ρ/2 3                        2ρ3
3 3                         3 3


      ρ/2 2ρ2 1 3 2                2 3ρ1 2
1 2 1                       1 2 1
2 1 2                       2 1 2
```

If this last example seems incomprehensible to you, look at it this way:

$$\begin{pmatrix} 2 \\ 3 \end{pmatrix} \rho \begin{pmatrix} 1 \\ 2 \end{pmatrix}$$

ρ is applied to the subarrays along the last dimension, giving 2 3ρ1 2.

```
      ,/2 3ρ2 1 3 2 4 5              2 2,1 4,3 5
2 2 1 4 3 5                 2 2 1 4 3 5
```

```
        HYP/12 3 4                        12 HYP 3 HYP 4
13                                  13
        +.,≠2 3ρι6                         +/ι6
21                                  21
        ∘.+≠2 3ρι6                         1 2 3 ∘.+4 5 6
5 6 7                               5 6 7
6 7 8                               6 7 8
7 8 9                               7 8 9
```

You can get partial reductions across an array in APL2. This *n-wise reduction* has the syntax $Z \leftarrow L\ F/R$, where F is any dyadic function producing a result and L is any integer. It works like this:

```
        5+/1 2 3 4 5                       0+/1 2 3 4 5
15                                  0 0 0 0 0
        4+/1 2 3 4 5                       2+≠3 3ρι9
10 14                              5    7    9
        3+/1 2 3 4 5               11   13   15
6 9 12                                    3,/5 6 7 8 9
        2+/1 2 3 4 5               5 6 7 6 7 8 7 8 9
3 5 7 9                                   ¯2-/1 5 8 14 50
        1+/1 2 3 4 5               4 3 6 36
1 2 3 4 5
```

A negative value for L reverses the subarrays before applying the function.

If your system supports this extension, don't confuse these two similar appearing expressions:

```
        2+/1 2 3 4 5                       2++/1 2 3 4 5
3 5 7 9                             17
```

Inner and outer products have also been generalized to allow any primitive or defined function that produces a result:

```
        A←2 3ρ1 0 1 1 1 0               A,./C                    2 4 6⌊.ιB
        B←3 3ρ1 2 2 4 5 6 7 8 9     1   9                  2 1 1
        C←3 4ρι12                   2  10
        A                          3  11                       2 3∘.HYP 3 4
1 0 1                              4  12                  3.605551275 4.472135955
1 1 0                                                     4.242640687 5
        B                          1   5
1 2 2                             2   6                       2 3+.HYP 3 4
4 5 6                             3   7                  8.605551275
7 8 9                             4   8
        C
1  2  3  4                             ρA,./C
5  6  7  8                        2 4 2
9 10 11 12
```

You might be surprised at the shape of the result of outer product, and we suggest you draw a table like the one on the right to see that it works out the same as any other outer product:

```
        ρ1 2 3 ∘., 10 20 30 40
3 4 2
        1 2 3 ∘., 10 20 30 40
   1 10
   1 20
   1 30
   1 40

   2 10
   2 20                          ,  |   10       20       30       40
   2 30                          ---+----------------------------------
   2 40                          1  | (1,10)   (1,20)   (1,30)   (1,40)
                                 2  | (2,10)   (2,20)   (2,30)   (2,40)
   3 10                          3  | (3,10)   (3,20)   (3,30)   (3,40)
   3 20
   3 30
   3 40
```

We didn't tell you the whole story earlier when we said that the shape of the result was the catenation of the shapes of the two arguments. APL2 uses a definition common to all IBM versions of APL, in which for $Z \leftarrow L \circ .fR, \rho Z$ is $(\rho L), (\rho R), \rho S1fS2$, where $S1$ and $S2$ are scalars. Since $\rho S1fS2$ is empty for scalar functions, the difference never showed up before.

There are two more primitive operators available in APL2. *Each* (¨) applies a function to each element in an array. Since its usefulness is more apparent with nested arrays, discussion is deferred to Chapter 25. Another operator is *bracket axis*. It specifies the subarrays to which a function is to be applied *and* the axes along which to assemble the result.

Here we have to digress to describe a somewhat similar operator which is available in most APL systems, but which is restricted to a few functions that transform an array or select from it. We refer here to *axis specification*, which you have already seen with reduction, scan and the mixed functions replicate, expand, rotate, catenate and laminate. APL2 permits it to be used also with ravel, take and drop, unique, find and find index. These extensions have been described where the functions are introduced in the text. Those specific to nested arrays are described in Chapter 25.

That's only part of the story. APL2 extends axis specification to all primitive scalar monadic and dyadic functions. Now you can do what you wanted to do at the beginning of the text: add a vector to a matrix.

```
      1 2 3 +[2]2 3ρι6              (2 3ρι6) +[1 2] 2 3ρ5+ι6
2 4 6                          7  9 11
5 7 9                         13 15 17

      5 6+[1]2 3ρι6                 (2 3ρι6) +[2 1] 2 3ρ5+ι6
 6  7  8                       7  9 11
10 11 12                      13 15 17
```

Let's get back to *bracket axis*. Two forms are recognized:

```
Z←  F[AZ;AR] R
Z←L F[AZ;AL;AR] R
```

The names in the brackets refer to axes associated with the right and left arguments (*AR* and *AL*) and the result (*AZ*). If no values are specified for *AR* or *AL*, all axes are taken. If there is no value given to *AZ*, the last axes of *Z* are taken.

Although there appear to be similarities between this operator and axis specification (which has no semicolons), the way in which the latter works is function dependent, while bracket axis, like other operators, acts on functions in a consistent way, independent of the specific functions. It can be used with any function that produces a result.

Bracket axis works with defined functions as well as primitive functions. If *AR* or *AL* is empty (ι0), the monadic *F* is applied to each subarray (i.e., is like *F* ¨).

```
      A←2 3ρι6              ,[;1]A              ,[1;]A
      A                  1 4              1 2 3 4 5 6
1 2 3                   2 5                 ,[1;ι0]A
4 5 6                   3 6              1 2 3
      ,[;ι0]A               ,[;2]A           4 5 6
1                       1 2 3                 ,[1;1]A
2                       4 5 6              1 2 3
3                         ,[;1 2]A         4 5 6
                       1 2 3 4 5 6           ,[1;2]A
4                                          1 4
5                                          2 5
6                                          3 6

      A1←2 3ρ1 0 2 ¯7 ¯8 0
      ×[;1]A1
1 ¯1
0 ¯1
1 0

      A2←3 4ρ5 2 0 4 ¯5 6 15 1 8 3 11 ¯5
      A2                                        ⍋[;1]A2
¯5  2  0  4                              2 1 3
¯5  6 15 ¯1                             1 3 2
 8  3 11 ¯5                             1 3 2
                                       3 2 1
```

So far we haven't shown you anything which couldn't be obtained in other ways without too much fuss. But here's a perhaps unanticipated goody which falls out of all this: you can convert a character matrix directly into a number matrix (in other APL systems ⍎ works only on scalars and vectors).

```
      CHAR←⍕A
      CHAR
1 2 3
4 5 6
      ⍴CHAR
2 5
```

```
      NUM←⍎[;2]CHAR
      NUM
1 2 3
4 5 6
      ⍴NUM
2 3
```

With dyadic functions, if *AR* or *AL* is empty, the other subarrays will be replicated like a scalar:

```
      10 20 30 40,[;⍳0;⍳0]⍳4
10 1
20 2
30 3
40 4

      10 20 30 40,[;1;⍳0]⍳4
10 20 30 40  1
10 20 30 40  2
10 20 30 40  3
10 20 30 40  4

      10 20 30 40,[;⍳0;1]⍳4
10  1  2  3  4
20  1  2  3  4
30  1  2  3  4
40  1  2  3  4

      10 20 30 40 [;1;1]⍳4
10 20 30 40  1  2  3  4
      10 20 30 40 [1;⍳0;⍳0]⍳4
10 20 30 40
 1  2  3  4

      10 20 30 40[1;⍳0;1]⍳4
10 20 30 40
 1  1  1  1
 2  2  2  2
 3  3  3  3
 4  4  4  4

      10 20 30 40[1;1;⍳0]⍳0
10 10 10 10
20 20 20 20
30 30 30 30
40 40 40 40
 1  2  3  4
```

Defined operators

Just as the concept of a defined function allowed us to assemble various combinations of primitive functions and operators for repeated use with different arguments, so the idea of a *defined operator*, available in APL2, lets you invent your own operators, to be used with different operands. Defined operators are handy when you need to apply several different functions in the same way to data in a manner not already covered by the existing operators.

There are eight allowable header forms, depending on the number of arguments and operands and whether an explicit result is to be returned:

	return result	no result
2 arguments, 2 operands	*Z←L (F OP G)R*	*L (F OP G) R*
2 arguments, 1 operand	*Z←L (F OP) R*	*L (F OP) R*
1 argument, 2 operands	*Z←(F OP G) R*	*(F OP G) R*
1 argument, 1 operand	*Z←(F OP) R*	*(F OP) R*

F and *G* are operands, *L* and *R* are arguments, and *OP* is the name of the defined operator.

Operators are defined in the same way as functions, subject, of course, to the header format restrictions above. Here is a universal operator that tries to be all things to all users:

```
      ∇Z←L (F ALLPURP) R
[1]   Z←R F L
[2]   ∇

      R←5 12
      L←.5
      L *ALLPURP +/R*2      ⍝ FINDS HYPOTENUSE OF RT TRIANGLE WITH LEGS R
13

      R←'ABCDEFGHIJKLMNOP'
      L←'HELP'
      L ⍳ALLPURP R    ⍝ SIMULATES RANKING
8 5 12 16
```

Another problem: suppose you had to do different outer products on square matrices of the same size and wanted to limit the arithmetic to the elements on or above the main diagonal. The following defined operator will do it:

```
        ∇Z←L (F OUTP) R;K;M
[1]     K←ι1↑ρL
[2]     M←K∘.≤K
[3]     Z←(M×L)∘.F M×R
[4]     ∇
```

Thus, the outer products could be easily executed on L and R by expressions of the form $L +OUTP R$, $L ×OUTP R$, $L \lceil OUTP R$, etc.

To complete the picture and help you keep track of defined operators in your workspace, a system command $)OPS$ is provided that works like $)FNS$ and $)VARS$.

PROBLEMS

1. DRILL. Assign $A←ι4$, $B←2$ $3ρ'ABCDEF'$, $C←'ABD'$, $D←3$ $1ρι3$, $E←3$ 4 5, $F←4$ $3ρι10$, $G←3$ $4ρφι7$

$C∘.=B$	$A∘.+3×D$	$~(A∘.=A)∘.∧1$ 0 0 1
$D∘.×A$	$D∘.÷A$	$ФD∘.*A$
1 3 $9∘.>D$	$B∘.≠C$	$A∘.\lceil ^-1$ 3 2 4
$E+.=E$	$E∧.>G$	$F×.=E$
$F×.-G$	$E∨.≠F$	$G\|.-F$
$F∨.<G$	$3+.×F$	$(ФG)\lceil.+E$

2. What is the shape of the result when the outer product is used to add the elements of a vector of length 4 to the elements of a 2 2 matrix?

3. Define a function $DIST$ that computes the rounded off (nearest integer) distances between any two cities whose X and Y coordinates are given in a matrix L. Assume $ρL$ is N, 2 and the cities are all located north and east of the origin of the coordinate system.

4. Write an APL expression to find the number of occurrences of each of the letters $ABCDEFG$ in the word $CABBAGE$.

5. Construct expressions which will give the sum and carry digits for addition of two numbers in any number system B (for B less than 10). Write a function to generate an additional table of a set of integers INT in the base B.

6. For mathematicians only: write a program to multiply two polynomials together. Assume their coefficient vectors $C1$ and $C2$ are arranged in descending order of powers of X.

7. Use the function $GRAPH$ (page 208) for each of the following:
   A $Y←|X←^-5+ι9$
   B $Y←^-5+X*2$
   C $Y≤X+1$
   D $(Y≤X+1)∧Y≥3-|X$
   E $Y≤3|X$

8. Execute the following instructions in order and explain the resulting display.

   ```
   X←^-13+ι20
   Y←φX
   R←(0=(^-3×Y)∘.+(2×X)-2)∨0=(2×Y)∘.+X-8
   R
   ```

9. Modify $GRAPH$ (page 208) to scale down all the data X by a factor S.

10. Write an expression to show the growth of various amounts of principal accumulating interest compounded at different rates and for different numbers of years.

11. After loading the workspace with plotting routines in your APL system, execute each of the following. (As pointed out at the end of the chapter, the syntax, name of the function, and auxiliary features may be different, so be sure to call for *DESCRIBE* or *HOWPLOT* or *HOWFORMAT*, or whatever instructions are available in your system.)

A
```
X←ι20
Y←X*2
Z←2×X*2
20 60 PLOT X VS Y
20 60 PLOT (Y AND Z) VS X
```

B
```
X←1,50×ι7
Y←÷X
20 60 PLOT Y VS X
20 30 PLOT Y[1+ι7] VS X[1+ι7]
```

12. To evaluate the strength of a bridge hand (13 cards dealt from a standard deck), a point count is used. This assigns 4 points for each Ace, 3 for each King, 2 for each Queen and 1 for each Jack. Out of a possible 40 points in the deck, a particular hand can have up to 37 high card points (HCP), with the average being 10. Define a function to simulate the dealing of a large number of bridge hands and use a histogram (problem 10, Chapter 16, or in the *PLOT* workspaces if available) to determine the shape of the HCP distribution.

13. Modify the function *STRINGSEARCH* (page 205) so that it uses ↑ to point to occurrences of W in T.

14. **A** For two vectors A and B of the same length, and the matrices M and U ($U←(\iota N)\circ.\leq\iota N$) give a meaning to each of the following:

   A $A\wedge.=B$ $M\wedge.=B$ $A+.\neq B$ $(M=0)\wedge.\geq U$ $A\times.*B$
   B For a logical square matrix N, what is the significance of $R←N\vee.\wedge N$?
   C For the matrices C and D, what is the meaning of $C+.=D$ and $C\lceil.\lfloor D$?

15. (Again for the math buffs.) Write a program to evaluate at various points X a polynomial with coefficients C. Assume the terms of the polynomial are arranged in ascending order of powers of X. Use the inner product.

16. The Parochial Computing Systems Corporation reimburses its employees for travel on company business at the rate of 20 cents per mile for the first 100 miles, 15 cents per mile for the next 50 miles and 10 cents per mile for all mileage in excess of 150. Define a monadic function which uses the inner product to compute mileage allowances for employees.

17. Redo using the inner product
   A problem 6, Chapter 6
   B problem 4, Chapter 8
   C problem 5, Chapter 16

18. The Shallow Water Pump Company manufactures four different sump pumps. Each model requires different numbers of five basic parts:

part type		1	2	3	4	5
	1	1	2	0	5	2
pump	2	0	3	0	1	5
model	3	1	1	4	2	2
	4	1	2	4	5	5

The Company anticipates orders for 300 of model 1, 500 of model 2, 200 of model 3 and 1000 of model 4. Assuming no margin for bad parts, how many of each part should be ordered from the vendors? These parts cost respectively $32.00, $9.75, $3.20, $.78, $7.20. What is the cost of all the parts needed? What is the cost of each pump model?

19. The Shocking Appliance Company has a distribution system which consists of 2 warehouses, 8 distribution centers and 100 stores. Highway distances between the warehouses and distribution centers are stored in the 2 by 8 matrix WD, while the distances between the centers and stores are in the 8 by 100 matrix DS. Find the shortest distance between each warehouse and store, given that merchandise must pass through a distribution center on its way to the store.

20. A solution in search of a problem: for a given vector A what does $A<.\geq1\phi A$ do?

21. The table below shows how many kilograms of each fruit were purchased at what cost in four trips made to the supermarket.

item	kilograms/trip	cost/kilogram
apples	5 2 6 8	$.89
oranges	2 4 3 1	.50
pears	5 6 2 5	.95
grapes	2 2 4 3	1.70
bananas	5 6 2 7	.55

Assume that the item names are stored in the matrix *FRUIT*, the purchased amounts in *QUANT* and the cost per kilogram in the vector *VCOST*. Find the

A cost of each trip
B total weight purchased each trip
C total weight of each fruit purchased
D total cost of each fruit
E total cost of the four trips
F largest amount paid for a single fruit in each trip
G average cost/kilogram of all fruit purchased.
H amount spent on grapes ('grapes' may not necessarily be the fourth rows of *FRUIT* and *QUANT*)

22. Another puzzler: what is the significance of the inner product $(M,0)<.-\lozenge M,0$ for *M* an integer matrix?

23. Use the inner product to locate the index of the first occurrence of a vector in a table.

24. Find the inverse of the identity matrix.

25. Use ⊞ to solve the following set of equations:

$$2x + y + 3z = 10$$
$$4x + 3y - z = 13 \quad \text{(conventional notation)}$$
$$2x + y - 4z = 3$$

26. In algebra it is shown that for the system of equations

$$ax + by = c \quad \text{(conventional notation)}$$
$$dx + ey = f$$

the application of Cramer's rule gives as solutions

$$x = (ce - bf) \div (ae - bd) \quad \text{(conventional notation)}$$
$$y = (af - cd) \div (ae - bd)$$

Write an APL program to solve by Cramer's rule a given set of two linear equations and print the message *NO UNIQUE SOLUTION* if ae - bd = 0. Then define a function *SOLVE* which uses ⊞ to solve the equations.

27. Nearly every calculus book ever printed has a problem similar to the following: A farmer has 300 feet of fencing material which he wants to use to enclose as large a rectangular area as possible. One side of the property to be enclosed is a relatively straight stretch of river, and needs no fencing. How should the fence be put in? (To solve this problem, set up an expression for the area, apply the *SLOPE* function to it, and see where the slope is 0. This corresponds to a maximum point on the graph of area vs the variable representing the length of one side.)

28. Sales forecasters for the Sticky Wicket Company predict the following sales for the next 7 years (in millions of dollars):

year	sales
1985	38
1986	52
1987	64
1988	82
1989	98
1990	128
1991	156

Assuming a linear model, find the equation which best fits this data.

29. (For matrix algebra buffs). A factory makes three finished products, P1, P2, P3. Four subassemblies A1, A2, A3, A4 are involved, along with two detail parts D1, D2. The table below shows how many of each (row) part are used directly in each (column) part:

	P1	P2	P3	A1	A2	A3	A4	D1	D2
P1	0	0	0	0	0	0	0	0	0
P2	0	0	0	0	0	0	0	0	0
P3	0	0	0	0	0	0	0	0	0
A1	1	2	0	0	0	0	0	0	0
A2	0	1	1	0	0	0	0	0	0
A3	0	0	2	1	1	0	0	0	0
A4	0	0	0	1	2	2	0	0	0
D1	3	2	0	0	0	0	1	0	0
D2	0	0	0	0	0	1	3	0	0

What are the total parts required? Hint: if the above matrix is designated as U and the requirements matrix as R, then the following matrix equation (conventional notation) is true: $R = UR + I$ (I is the identity matrix).

30. Tests conducted by the U.S. Environmental Protection Agency yielded the following data on fuel economy of light duty vehicles:

weight class	fuel consumption, gal/100 mi.
2000	4.14
2200	4.67
2500	5.35
2750	5.61
3000	6.77
3500	7.39
4000	9.29
4500	10.45
5000	10.95
5500	12.16

Find the linear least-squares fit of fuel consumption to weight.

Chapter 22: The representation and storage of data

It is impossible to think of a number in the abstract without associating it with some concrete representation. Take the number 3, for instance. Can you think of the concept of 'threeness' without imagining three objects or visualizing the character 3 in some system of notation, be it Roman numerals, scaled notation, base-2 notation or whatever?

No matter how many different ways of depicting the number 3 we may come up with, they all stand for the same thing—the abstract notion of *threeness*. Yet most of the time we have no difficulty recognizing the number if it is embedded in a context which conditions our thinking along the right lines:

0.03E2

003

3.0000

EXACTLY***$3*DOLLARS*AND*00*CENTS

III

00011

The last line above might be eleven in decimal notation, but because of the other more familiar ways of expressing three that preceded it, we would quite likely accept it as being the value 3 in its binary representation.

What it all boils down to is this: just as a rose by any other name is still a rose and smells just as sweet, so there are many ways to express the same number; and their value to us depends on what we are most used to, and what form is most useful to us.

Thus far in all our APL work we have been using ordinary decimal notation. But many other systems are in common use. Mixed systems like clock time and number systems to the bases 2, 8 and 16 are examples. In this chapter we will examine how APL makes it possible for us to switch conveniently from one number system to another. For this, two powerful functions, *decode* and *encode*, will be introduced.

Decode

Suppose we are in a room whose length is 3 yards, 0 feet and 1 inch. This is an example of the English system of measurement at its worst! How can we express the length in a single unit of measure, say inches? If we were to do it by hand, we would probably set up something like the following:

$$\begin{array}{ccccccc}
3\,yds & & 0\,ft & & 1\,in & & \\
\underline{\times (12 \times 3)} & & \underline{\times 12} & & \underline{\times 1} & & \\
108 & + & 0 & + & 1 & = & 109\,in
\end{array}$$

APL has a dyadic function that makes this conversion for us. It is called the *base* or *decode* function, and its symbol is the upper shift B, $\perp$. The right argument is the array to be converted, while the left argument is a vector whose elements are the increments needed to make the conversion from one unit to the next, like from yards to feet. Since each of the elements on the left can be thought of as acting somewhat like the base of a number system (sometimes called a *radix*), the left argument is usually referred to as the *radix vector*.

In a *mixed number system* like the one involving our length measurements of the room, the syntax of $\perp$ requires that the number of elements in both arguments be the same. There is one exception to this, namely, that either argument may be a scalar or vector of length 1, a case which will be considered shortly. For our particular problem, we'll use 1760 (the number of yards per mile) as the multiplying factor for the next increment even though it won't be used specifically in the conversion:

      1760 3 12⊥3 0 1
109

As a matter of fact, any number will do in that position, as long as there is something there:

      0 3 12⊥3 0 1   **3 1⊥3 0 1**
109   *LENGTH ERROR*
                                      3 1 ⊥ 3 0 1
                                          ^

Here is another example, the conversion to seconds of 2 minutes and 10 seconds:

      60 60⊥2 10   **0 60⊥2 10**
130   130

We can formally express the action of the radix vector on the right argument by letting $W[J]$ be the weighting factor that tells us what the increments should be from one unit to the next in our reduction. In our example of the room size, if A is the radix vector and B is the right argument, then $W[3]$ is 1, $W[2]$ is $A[3] \times W[3]$ or 12, $W[1]$ is $A[2] \times W[2]$ or 3×12. This is equivalent to $+/36\ 12\ 1 \times 3\ 0\ 1$, or $+/W \times B$.

Clock time and English length measurements are examples of mixed number systems. The decode function works equally well for decimal or other uniform base number systems. For instance, suppose the following is a picture of the odometer reading (in miles) of a car:

This can be regarded as a scalar 3521 or a vector 3 5 2 1. If it is a vector, we can convert it to the scalar number 3521 by executing

      10 10 10 10⊥3 5 2 1   **0 10 10 10⊥3 5 2 1**
3521   3521

The decode function can be applied to number systems other than decimal. Here is a binary counter:

1	0	1	1	0

This can be converted to a decimal number by

      2 2 2 2 2⊥1 0 0 1 1
19

But if the counter were to be interpreted as readings on an odometer, our result will be different:

      10 10 10 10 10⊥1 0 0 1 1
10011

Obviously, we need to know what the representation is to tell what a particular number stands for.

As we have already seen with many primitive functions, APL extends a scalar argument to match the length of the other argument:

      10⊥3 5 2 1   **2⊥1 0 0 1 1**   **10 10 10 10⊥5**
3521   19   5555

To help you understand how the decode function works, we diagram the last three problems side-by-side:

	room length	odometer	binary counter
radix vector R	1760 3 12	10 10 10 10	2 2 2 2 2
weighting vector $W \leftarrow \phi 1 , \times \backslash 1 \downarrow R$	36 12 1	1000 100 10 1	16 8 4 2 1
vector to be decoded B	3 0 1	3 5 2 1	1 0 1 1 0
result $+ / W \times B$	109	3521	22

The weighting matrices are obtained by cumulative multiplication, so that the Kth element is the product of the elements 1 to K-1 of the radix vector beyond the first K. For mixed radix systems such as English length measure, you have to use that much detail to describe it, but for uniform radix systems such as the odometer or binary counter examples, the weighting vectors are simply the radix raised to the powers ...3 2 1 0.

Decoding matrices

Although decode acts on any multidimensional array, we'll introduce here only a few simple examples with matrices. The array $SAMPLE$ will be used for illustration:

        SAMPLE←4 4ρ10 15 8 14 13 1 18 25 10 15 1 14 2 15 2 27

Let's assume we want to get the 100 decode of the rows. Since decode acts along the first dimension, we'll have to transpose the sample:

        DCD←100⊥⍉SAMPLE
        DCD
    10150814 13011825 10150114 2150227

We must confess that the matrix $SAMPLE$ isn't completely arbitrary, but was derived from

        ASAMPLE←4 4 ρ'JOHNMARYJOANBOB '

so that $SAMPLE$ is equivalent to ' $ABCDEFGHIJKLMNOPQRSTUVWXYZ$'$\iota ASAMPLE$. Although it may not be obvious, $\text{⍋}DCD$ applied to the rows of $SAMPLE$ yields the same results as the defined function $GRADE3$ (page 141), which was used to sort the columns in a numeric matrix beginning at the right, and $ASAMPLE[\text{⍋}DCD;]$ is really an alphabetic sort!

        ⍋DCD   ASAMPLE[⍋DCD;]
    4 3 1 2 BOB
                   JOAN
                   JOHN
                   MARY

All of this is incorporated in a program $ALFSORT1$ (B is the radix for decoding):

        ∇Z←B ALFSORT1 M;ALF
    [1]   ALF←' ABCDEFGHIJKLMNOPQRSTUVWXYZ0123456789'
    [2]   Z←M[⍋,B⊥⍉ALF⍳M;]∇

This method avoids a looping solution which might seem more natural to those of you who were brought up on card sorters and the like. But we must warn you that it has several disadvantages. First, with large tables there are apt to be $WSFULL$ problems. Second, there is a limitation to the ability of the function to discriminate among long, nearly identical rows because the large numbers which result can't be represented in APL as distinct numbers. For example, if $B\leftarrow 38$, then rows whose first 10 or more columns are the same won't be differentiated. And third, if there are too many columns you may get a $DOMAIN\ ERROR$ because of the very large values resulting from the decoding. An algorithm to determine how many columns can be handled by one decimal number is $\lfloor 56 \div 2 \circledast \rho ALF$, 56 being the number of usable bits in a decimal (floating point) number. B should also be at least 1 greater than ρALF.

$ALFSORT2$ completes the picture, when one field is required to be in sequence within another:

```
        ∇Z←BFLDS ALFSORT2 M;ALF;B
[1]     ALF←' ABCDEFGHIJKLMNOPQRSTUVWXYZ0123456789'
[2]     B←1↑BFLDS
[3]     BFLDS←1↓BFLDS
[4]     Z←M[⍋B⊥⍉ALF⍳M[;BFLDS];]∇
```

In this function, *BFLDS* contains the radix as its first element. The remaining elements in *BFLDS* are the selected column indices used to key the sort (leftmost values are the most major fields).

*ALFSORT*1 and *ALFSORT*2 will handle most ordinary sorting problems. However, if the sort sequence is very long and you run into the limitations mentioned earlier, you might try sorting in two passes, first the minor, then the major fields. There are many variations employed in sorting, particularly where upper and lower case alphabets are involved. Programs to handle these and other cases are found in utility workspaces in nearly every APL system. If you are using an APL system that has enhanced primitive grade capability (Chapter 15), then the use of sorting routines like the above is unnecessary.

Like the dyadic transpose (Chapter 19), decode can be employed to select or identify scattered elements in a matrix. Let's get a sample matrix to work on:

```
        )COPY 1 CLASS TAB2                       TAB2
SAVED   14.45.33 02/20/83                  3   1   7
                                           7  10   4
                                           6   9   1
                                           1   6   7
```

Suppose you wanted to select from *TAB*2 a vector consisting of *TAB*2[1;3], *TAB*2[4;2], *TAB*2[3;2], *TAB*2[1;1]. If you place all the desired indices in a matrix and apply ⊥ to that array,

```
        PICK←4 2⍴1 3 4 2 3 2 1 1          1+(⍴TAB2)⊥⍉PICK-1
        PICK                                3 11 8 1
   1 3
   4 2
   3 2
   1 1
```

what you get are the positions you want if *TAB*2 were raveled (check it!). This gives rise to a general method for selecting arbitrary elements from an array:

```
        ∇R←DATA SELCT INDICES
[1]     ⍝INDICES IS A MATRIX WITH AS MANY ROWS AS DATA HAS RANK.
[2]     R←(,DATA)[1+(⍴DATA)⊥⍉INDICES-1] ∇
        TAB2 SELCT PICK
7 6 9 3
```

The diagram below clarifies how the raveled positions (*RP*) are related to the original positions (*OP*). In each case, *RP*←1+(⍴*DATA*)⊥¯1+*OP*.

value	OP	RP	value	OP	RP	value	OP	RP
3	1 1	1	1	1 2	2	7	1 3	3
7	2 1	4	10	2 2	5	4	2 3	6
6	3 1	7	9	3 2	8	1	3 3	9
1	4 1	10	6	4 2	11	7	4 3	12

Here's an offbeat but useful application of ⊥. Suppose you have an 'irregular' matrix of characters *M* (the irregularity is really illusory since the apparently ragged edges are padded with blanks that don't show):

```
        M←5 6ρ' ANN     EVA JILL         JANICE'
        M
ANN
   EVA
JILL

JANICE
```

The problem is to right-justify the matrix (see also the defined function *ROWNAMES*, page 116). We first identify the location of the blanks with $M=$' '. This logical matrix, used as the left argument of the decode function with 1 as the right argument, results in a vector whose elements are related to the number of blanks to the right of the first nonblank character in each line of M (why?):

```
    Q←(M=' ')⊥1              Q
                        3 2 3 6 1
```

Subtracting Q from 1 should tell us how much to shift each line to the right (any value will do for the fourth row):

```
    QS←1-Q          QS                  QS⌽M
                ¯2 ¯1 ¯2 ¯5 0            ANN
                                        EVA
                                        JILL

                                      JANICE
```

Putting all this in one expression, the completed algorithm is $(1-(M=$' '$)⊥1)⌽M$. Another way to do the same thing, not using ⊥, is $(-+/\wedge\backslash\phi M=$' '$)\phi M$ (page 136).

Encode

Like so many of the other functions we've encountered in APL, there is a function that 'undoes' the work of the decode function, that is, converts from a value to some predetermined representation. Appropriately, it is called *representation* or *encode*, and its symbol is ⊤ (upper shift N). Thus, if we execute

```
    2 2 2 2⊥0 1 0 1
5
```

then the function ⊤ brings back our initial argument:

```
    2 2 2 2⊤5
0 1 0 1
```

Here are our room length and odometer problems in reverse:

```
    1760 3 12⊤109                10 10 10 10⊤3521
3 0 1                         3 5 2 1
```

The latter example describes how 3521 would appear on a 4-digit odometer. How would 43521 appear on the same odometer?

```
    10 10 10 10⊤43521
3 5 2 1
```

We can draw an analogy here. It's like an odometer which reads only up to 9999 and then starts over from 0 again. In fact, in this case the right argument has been reduced by $10*4$:

```
    (10*4)|43521
3521
```

What happens when we're not sure how many elements are needed in the radix vector, yet we don't want to lose anything, as was unfortunately the case in the example above? Using zero as the first element of the left argument puts everything remaining in the first element of the result, as shown below:

```
    0 10 10 10⊤43521              0 60⊤130
43 5 2 1                      2 10
```

The encode function also operates on matrices. This feature doesn't have many uses, and will not be reviewed here. Both encode and decode yield some rather interesting results when used with negative numbers and nonintegers. Explore these on your own, because we're hard put to think of practical examples for them.

Hexadecimal to decimal conversion

An obvious application is the conversion of decimally represented information to another numbering system. Since the bases 2, 8 and 16 have been used extensively for computers, our first illustration builds an algorithm to convert from the decimal to the *hexadecimal* (base-16) system.

In our ordinary decimal (base-10) system, we require ten distinct symbols 0123456789, and in the base-16 system, 16 symbols are needed. Values larger than 9 in the base-10 system are represented by adding positions on the left (provided, of course, we are talking about whole numbers and not fractions). For example, 10 is a two-position number, 9 being the largest number that can be represented by a single symbol.

In the hexadecimal system the symbols are 0123456789ABCDEF. If you were to ask why the letters ABCDEF, the most appropriate response would be, why not? We need symbols for each of the values 10 through 15. New symbols could be invented or old ones used differently (like upside down or with a bar across them), but it really doesn't matter as long as they are distinct from one another and are used consistently.

A decimal system number such as 6325 can be represented in so-called expanded notation as $6 \times 10^3 + 3 \times 10^2 + 2 \times 10^1 + 5 \times 10^0$. We can represent a hexadecimal number in exactly the same way, except that powers of 16 instead of powers of 10 are involved. Here is the expansion of the hexadecimal number 1AF2, which is equivalent to 6898 in decimal form: $1 \times 16^3 + 10 \times 16^2 + 15 \times 16^1 + 2 \times 16^0$.

In 1 *CLASS* there is a dyadic function *HEXA* which makes the conversion for us. The left argument is the number of positions we want to see represented; the right argument is the value to be converted:

```
      )COPY 1 CLASS HEXA                          3 HEXA 254
SAVED  14.45.33 02/20/83              0FE
      ∇HEXA[□]∇                                   2 HEXA 254
    ∇ R←N HEXA X                      FE
[1]     R←'0123456789ABCDEF'[1+(Nρ16)⊤X]          1 HEXA 254
    ∇                                 E
```

$N \rho 16$ generates a vector of N elements, each of which is 16. If, for example, N is 3 and X is 254, $(N \rho 16) \top X$ is $(3 \rho 16) \top 254$ or 0 15 14. In expanded notation this is the same as $0 \times 16^2 + 15 \times 16^1 + 14 \times 16^0$.

Looking through the vector of characters 0123456789ABCDEF, we see that the 0 is in the first position, 1 in the second position, etc. It is necessary to add 1 to $(3 \rho 16) \top 254$ to pick up the subscripts for the proper characters:

```
      1+(3ρ16)⊤254
1 16 15
```

Now let's execute *HEXA* for, say, the number 257, for which at least three hexadecimal positions are needed: $1 \times 16^2 + 0 \times 16^1 + 1 \times 16^0$.

```
      4 HEXA 257                    2 HEXA 257
0101                            01
```

We get a false result if we don't specify sufficient positions. Incidentally, 0101 is a vector of characters. Do you see why?

```
      ρ4 HEXA 257
4
```

What about the reverse operation, converting from hexadecimal to decimal representation? The function *DEC* in 1 *CLASS* does this. It is monadic and requires a character argument:

```
      )COPY 1 CLASS DEC                           DEC '0FE'
SAVED  14.45.33 02/20/83              254
      ∇DEC[□]∇                                    DEC 'FE'
    ∇ R←DEC H                         254
[1]     R←16⊥¯1+'0123456789ABCDEF'⍳H              DEC 'E'
    ∇                                 E
```

H represents the vector of characters in hexadecimal notation. The ranking picks up the positions of the corresponding characters in the left argument. Trying this out with 0*FE*, we get

        '0123456789*ABCDEF*'ɩ'0*FE*'
1 16 15

which is one position too high to use as the right argument of ⊥. Hence ¯1 is added before the decode function is applied:

        16⊥0 15 14
254

DEC doesn't need a left argument because the decode function automatically extends the scalar 16 to match the shape of the right argument.

If we were to try *DEC* with undefined characters, say, *WER*, we still get a result,

        DEC 'WER'
4336

but it is meaningless. To find out why, remember what ranking does for an element in the right argument not found on the left. It will produce here the vector 17 15 17; and after adding ¯1 to each element we have

        16⊥16 14 16
4336

Now try

        DEC 5 HEXA 321   *DEC 2 HEXA 321*
321   65

and we see that *DEC* and *HEXA* are inverse functions, provided that sufficient positions have been allowed.

Numeric encrypting

In some of the problems at the end of Chapter 15 we experimented with cryptographic techniques by converting readable messages into 'scrambled' characters. Using ⊤ and ⊥ we can now code several characters into a single number. The function *NUMCODE* (from 1 *CLASS*) breaks up a character vector *M* into groups of four characters each, and codes each group into a single numerical value. *B* is a scalar which must be at least one greater than ρ*ALF*. The key to this function is line 4, which takes the four-row character matrix into which *M* has been transformed (lines 2 and 3), converts it into indices (*ALF* ɩ *M*) and then changes each column into a unique number in base *B*. As you will learn in the next section, there is an upper limit on the value of *B* which depends on the way in which numbers are represented in the computer. Decrypting can be done using *DENUMCODE*, provided that one knows the base *B*:

```
      ∇NUMCODE[□]∇                        ∇DENUMCODE[□]∇
   ∇ Z←B NUMCODE M                     ∇ Z←B DENUMCODE MESSAGE
[1]   M←(4×⌈0.25×ρM)↑M              [1]   MESSAGE←(4ρB)⊤MESSAGE
[2]   M←(4,0.25×ρM)ρM               [2]   Z←,ALF[MESSAGE]
[3]   Z←B⊥ALFɩM                        ∇
   ∇
```

      ALF←' ABCDEFGHIJKLMNOPQRSTUVWXYZ'

      M←'REBELS ADVANCING ON ALL FRONTS'

      MESSAGE←30 NUMCODE M

      MESSAGE
517537 183199 83266 175545 354681 549410 40891 61231

      30 DENUMCODE MESSAGE
REBELS ADVANCING ON ALL FRONTS

How data is stored in APL

In the IBM based versions of APL (VS APL, STSC, Sharp, APL2) discussed in this book, a number can have 16 decimal digits without loss of precision. More specifically, the mantissa is represented as 56 binary elements, and $10 \circledast 2 \star 56$ is $16.8+$, which suggests that each 16-bit machine 'word' can pack eight 2-digit numbers. Before showing how decode can be used to do the packing, let's examine the way in which APL stores information.

Ultimately, every numeric or character element that you use in APL is represented inside the computer as a sequence of binary (0 or 1) values or *bits*. Each character is represented internally as 8 bits, called a *byte*. This implies that APL has a maximum of 256 ($2 \star 8$) different characters. Your terminal can represent about 150 of them. These are the display characters, including the overstruck ones such as $\lozenge$ $\ominus$ $\square$ $\neq$ $\underline{A}$ $\underline{Z}$ $\cap$.

Integers in the range ¯2147483648 to 2147483647 are usually stored in 32 adjacent bits, called a *word*. Here is what the number 5 looks like internally:

$$00000000000000000000000000000101$$

Negative numbers are denoted with a 1 in the leftmost position, and the number itself is stored as $(32\rho 2)\top VALUE$, called 2's *complement* form. Some examples follow:

```
¯2147483648    10000000000000000000000000000000
¯2147483647    10000000000000000000000000000001
¯2147483646    10000000000000000000000000000010
         ¯2    11111111111111111111111111111110
         ¯1    11111111111111111111111111111111
          0    00000000000000000000000000000000
          1    00000000000000000000000000000001
          2    00000000000000000000000000000010
 2147483646    01111111111111111111111111111110
 2147483647    01111111111111111111111111111111
```

Nonintegers, as well as integers smaller than ¯2147483648 or larger than 2147483647, take 64 bits for internal storage, called *double-word floating point*. But the value isn't represented in a straightforward manner like 2's complement. Rather, it is stored as follows:

bit 1	Sign of mantissa (1 if negative, 0 if positive or 0)
bits 2 to 8	Value of exponent, in hexadecimal. Decode as $16 \star (2 \bot STORAGE[1+\iota 7])-64$
bits 9 to 64	Value of mantissa, as a binary fraction. Decode as $(2 \bot STORAGE[8+\iota 56]) \div 2 \star 56$ or $.5 \bot 0, STORAGE[65-\iota 56]$

The value is assembled by the computer with this algorithm:

$$(1-2 \times STORAGE[1]) \times (.5 \bot 0, STORAGE[65-\iota 56]) \times (16 \star ^-64+2 \bot STORAGE[1+\iota 7])$$
$$\text{(sign)} \qquad\qquad \text{(mantissa)} \qquad\qquad \text{(exponent)}$$

Positive and negative values within the approximate range $10 \star ^-75$ and $10 \star 75$ can be accommodated.

When the values you use in APL are only 0 or 1, each is stored as a single *bit*. This is an extremely compact way to store information, and in part explains why APL is so well suited for analysis of binary choice data— market research studies, for example. You can pack 32 times as much of this kind of information into a workspace as you could if you were using integers, or 64 times as much as when using floating point.

Conversion from one storage type to another

An important factor to consider is that if one element of an array requires integer (32 bits) or floating point (64 bits) internal representation, then *every* element in the array is stored in the same manner. Thus, we have:

```
0  1  1  0  1  1  0  0  takes 8 bits, or 1 byte
0  1  1  0  2  1  0  0  takes 256 bits, or 32 bytes
.5                      takes 512 bits, or 64 bytes
'01101106'              takes 64 bits, or 8 bytes.
```

Although on most older APL systems characters and numeric values can't be mixed in the same array, APL2, Sharp and APL*PLUS Systems have relaxed the restriction (see **page 257**).

APL tries to pick the most compact internal representation for your data, but in the interests of practicality, certain types of checking are not done by the computer. For example, when you multiply two integers, the result is integer (32 bits) if it fits; otherwise the result is made floating (64 bits). However, if you multiply .2 by 10, the result is stored as floating, even though it would be expressible as an integer. Likewise, $5-4$ results in integer (32 bits) storage, rather than taking only one bit.

You can usually force APL to store data the way you wish by using $X \leftarrow \lfloor X$ or $X \leftarrow \lceil X$ to convert from floating to integer. The only time it won't work is when the integer part is too large to fit into a 32-bit word. Use $X \leftarrow 2 \times .5 \times X$ to convert bits or integers to floating point representation. To convert integer or floating to bit storage, use $X \leftarrow \sim \sim X$ or $X \leftarrow X = 1$. $\sim \sim X$ gives *DOMAIN ERROR* if any of the values to be converted are neither 0 nor 1, while $X = 1$ will produce 0 for any value not equal to 1.

These conversions may differ from system to system. If these matters are important to you, you'll have to ask someone who knows the particulars of your system, or do lots of experimentation.

Finally, here is a function which will internally represent any numeric array in the most compact manner:

```
      ∇R←INTREP N;S;NULL
[1]   S←ρN
[2]   NULL←(×/S)ρ0
[3]   NULL[]←N
[4]   R←SρNULL∇
```

All of the above discussion was specific to APL on IBM 370-based hardware. Things may be entirely different on other computers. For example, on STSC's TRS80 model III and IBM PC versions, integers are 16 bits long and there is no bit type storage at all! Binary data is stored as integer instead, taking 16 bits for storing each bit. On those systems, floating point data still uses 64 bits per number, but the mantissa and exponent arrangement differs. You can get a hint of that by trying $\lfloor / \iota 0$.

Measuring the amount of storage

The amount of storage available in your active workspace can be measured by the $\Box WA$ (for *working area*) system variable. Its result is a scalar holding the number of bytes available to you. When you define a variable, you will find that $\Box WA$ decreases roughly by the number of bytes actually taken by the data. It isn't usually exact because of storage taken by the name and the dimension information, as well as other scraps of internal information that the APL system stores or erases, almost as though it has a mind of its own.

```
      □WA                 Q←10000ρ'CLUTTER '              □WA
149544                                                  139524
```

If you explore $\Box WA$, make sure your tests use enough data to get accurate readings. Also, in some systems vectors of the form $D+M \times \iota N$ aren't stored as N-element vectors, but rather as only three elements holding D, M and N. Some systems are clever enough to save only one copy of data from a sequence like $B \leftarrow 99 \quad 6\rho'BOTTLE'$ followed by $C \leftarrow B$.

$\Box WA$ can be employed in programs which use an alternative algorithm (usually involving looping) to solve a problem when there isn't enough space to do the job directly. The value of $\Box WA$ in a clear workspace varies from system to system, usually between 24000 and 256000, as decided by the system management.

Data compaction

To illustrate how decode can be used to pack data in a form requiring less internal storage, we first define

```
      NUMBERS←100-ι8
      NUMBERS
99 98 97 96 95 94 93 92

      □WA
139468

      PACKED←100⊥NUMBERS

      PACKED
9.998979696E15
```

```
      □PP←16

      PACKED
9998979695949392

      )ERASE NUMBERS
      □WA
139480
```

As you might expect, to unpack the numbers use T:

```
      (8ρ100)TPACKED
99 98 97 96 95 94 93 92
```

We can easily demonstrate the inability to pack accurately more than eight 2-digit numbers:

```
      NUMBERS←100-ι9                        PACKED←100⊥NUMBERS
      NUMBERS                               (9ρ100)TPACKED
99 98 97 96 95 94 93 92 91      99 98 97 96 95 94 93 92 80
```

Generally speaking, packing like this isn't recommended because it tends to obscure what's going on. Moreover, how much you can pack is very implementation dependent. You will very likely have to redo all compaction work if you change systems. Because APL does a pretty good job conserving storage, it isn't necessary for you to resort to techniques like this unless there's a desperate need to conserve space.

In-place storage

During execution APL usually needs space for both the argument and the result at the same time. This is why you may encounter WS FULL when trying to catenate a row to a very large array in a workspace whose □WA indicates lots of space available.

Most APL implementations are sophisticated enough to sense when the result will fit into the space occupied by an argument and use the same space for it. For example, in the instruction $R←+\ι1000$ the result is in-place storage, with R replacing the temporary values $ι1000$. However, for $R←+\R$, the scan argument isn't temporary, and there is no in-place storage.

Some other functions for which there is in-place storage are rotate, reshape, bracket indexing and addition. The first two will make copies if room exists, and use in-place storage only to avoid WS FULL's.

Some instructions produce a result that is the same as the argument. These cause no data movement in the workspace and take up no extra storage (e.g., $A[ ]$). And finally, there are a few instructions which appear to defy logic by requiring much less space to execute than you might expect. One such example is the common expression $V/ιρV$, which needs space only for the result. Another is $→□LC$, which takes only 40 bytes no matter how big □LC itself is.

These space-saving features are highly implementation dependent and may even change from release to release.

Hints for saving storage

As applications grow and become more sophisticated, storage requirements tend to grow also. Sooner or later you reach a point where something has to go to make room for currently needed functions and data, unless your computer center upgrades its machines to provide bigger workspaces. With VS APL you may be able to stave off the inevitable for a while because of the large workspace size, but even here there are steps you can take to save space. Some are obvious and have already been discussed; others will be taken up in later chapters.

Localize variables. If you must use global variables don't enter them into a function as arguments, to avoid doubling the space required.

Expunge unneeded information.

Load or copy only what you need.

Store large amounts of data and functions on files.

Segregate data by data type where practicable, e.g., don't mix one column of floating point with 10 columns of integers.

Pack data if feasible into characters or use ⊥ to store more than one value in a single element. Scale decimal data by a power of 10 to convert it to integers.

Avoid APL operations that require an array argument to coexist temporarily with the result.

Store large character matrices with many trailing blanks in raveled form with the blanks removed. Use a table of pointers to record start and stop positions for each item in the vector.

Eliminate unnecessary suspensions.

Production programming

Having said all this, we now make some observations about the *production* environment (tested and debugged programs to be used generally by others), contrasted with that of the do-it-yourselfer. In the latter case no one really cares if your specifications are nonexistent, the code is inefficient and is giving the computer a headache, or the program itself is likely to fail if it encounters an unusual situation (sometimes called an edge condition) such as empty vectors or negative inputs.

But when programming for production, this laissez-faire attitude leads to disaster. Programs whose code is obscure, whose design is illogical and whose resistance to modification would make a diamond seem soft by comparison, are the bane of support groups who try to maintain them. There are two choices: change either APL or the programmers' work habits and style. Since the former occurs only slowly, and then with much disagreement on how to change it, the only reasonable alternative is to change the way programmers write APL.

This is where standards come in. Reasonable people can (and do) differ about them. In a way it's like asking how much government regulation is necessary to protect people from themselves and others without stifling individual initiative. It is not the authors' intent to prescribe a set of guidelines, which probably wouldn't help those of you whose anarchical bent is beyond redemption, but to sensitize you to the fact that the production environment is, and must be, more restrictive than the personal environment.

Application to computer design

This optional section is intended for those of you who are curious about the design of computers. APL has been widely used to design and simulate digital devices. Here is an example of how the addition operation of a typical 16-bit microcomputer can be simulated. The addition operation adds the 16 bits of its argument $WORD$ to the accumulator $\underline{A}$, itself a 16-bit register, and sets the carry flag $\underline{C}$ (a 1-bit register) to 1 if the result would have 'overflowed' into a seventeenth binary position.

```
      ∇ADD16 WORD;TEMP
[1]    TEMP←(17ρ2)⊤(2⊥A)+2⊥WORD
[2]    A←1↓TEMP
[3]    C←1↑TEMP∇
```

This use of APL as a *formal definition* of a digital system or subsystem is a viable alternative to the lengthy (and often ambiguous or incomplete) written specifications that are normally used for this purpose. With APL, the formal definition is a program that can be tested, validated and run.

Check protection

Our last illustration is the function CP, which fills in the space before a number with stars up to a preset position. Its use for check protection should be evident. CP, which is in 1 $CLASS$, is dyadic. The left argument is the number of characters in the result (field width), and the right argument is the amount of the check. The function is superfluous for those APL systems with picture format, $\square FMT$, or their equivalent (Chapters 17 and 18).

```
        )COPY 1 CLASS CP                          5 CP 301
SAVED   14.45.33 02/20/83                      **301
        ∇CP[□]∇                                    5 CP 12345
    ∇ R←N CP X;P                                12345
[1]     R←'0123456789'[1+(Nρ10)⊤X]               5 CP 0031
[2]     P←¯1+(R≠'0')ι1                          **301
[3]     R←(Pρ'*'),P↓R ∇
```

Line 1 makes a vector of characters out of X, the argument, and adds enough 0's in front to make ρR equal to N. Line 2 sets P as one less than the index of the first nonzero character, while line 3 puts into R, P copies of $*$ followed by all but the first P elements of R.

PROBLEMS

1. DRILL

```
(3ρ40)⊥8 7 2          2ι5 1 9 6            1 4 7ι3 5ρι15
1 ¯4.1 .8⊥1 2 3       7 8 9ι7 8 9          3⊤5217
3 3⊤5217              3 3 3⊤5217           (5ρ3)⊤5217
(4ρ8)⊥¯14             1 4 6⊤345            2 4 5⊤78
```

2. Write APL expressions to **A** convert 2 gallons, 8 quarts and 1 pint to pints; **B** find the number of ounces in 3 tons, 568 pounds and 13 ounces.

3. Find the

    A base-8 value of 2 1 7 7
    B base-2 value of 1 0 1 1 0 1
    C base-3 representation of 8933
    D base-5 representation of 4791

4. Write expressions that will show that ⊥ and ⊤ are inverses of each other (not, however, for all arguments).

5. Define a function to remove commas from a character vector consisting of digits and commas, and convert the result to a numerical vector.

6. Write an APL expression which determines whether or not, for a given three-digit number N, N is equal to the sum of the cubes of its digits.

7. For $M←$'1234583', what are the differences between each of the following expressions?

    A $M←¯1+$'0123456789'ιM
    B $M←10⊥¯1+$'0123456789'ιM
    C $M←10⊥0$ 1 2 3 4 5 6 7 8 9['0123456789'ιM]

8. It is a fact that a number N is divisible by 11 if the alternating sum of its digits is divisible by 11. Construct an expression that uses the encode function with this condition to test for divisibility by 11.

9. Write an APL function to illustrate the following well-known arithmetic 'trick': given any 3-digit number N whose first and last digits are different, reverse the digits and subtract the smaller number from the larger. Reverse the digits in the answer and add this value to the original difference. The sum will always be 1089.

Problems 10-14 are designed to show you a little of the often unappreciated power of the decode and encode functions.

10. Describe the action of each of the following (N a scalar and V a vector): **A** $1⊥V$ **B** $0⊥V$ **C** $-1⊥\phi V$ **D** 0 $1⊤N$

11. Use ⊥ to write a dyadic function $EVAL$ to evaluate at the point X a polynomial with coefficients C (descending powers of X). Compare with page 43.

12. Define a function $ENCODE$ to simulate ⊤ and provide the necessary number of positions in the left argument.

13. How can you use decode on the room measurement example (page 217) to get the answer in feet or yards?

14. Show how to delete **A** leading and **B** trailing occurrences of some element S from a vector V.

15. Array C contains the costs for various items of clothes purchased by Abigail Adams for Polly Jefferson and her maid in 1787. (First column is pounds, second column shillings and the third is pence.) The total submitted to Thomas Jefferson was 10 pounds, 15 shillings, 8 pence. Jefferson changed this to 11 pounds, 16 shillings and 2 pence. Which sum is correct? (Pound=20 shillings; shilling=12 pence.)

```
C←0 5 6 3 10 0 0 15 0 1 10 0 0 6 6 0 5 0 0 7 6 0 13 0
C←C,0 2 4 0 5 10 0 13 6 0 3 0 0 5 6 0 1 6 1 5 6 0 7 4
C←20 3ρC,0 6 0 0 2 0 0 4 6 0 6 8
```

16. Define a function $DIAG$ that takes as its right argument a matrix M whose elements are positive integers, and forms a decimal number out of the diagonal elements.

17. A challenge for those of you who are so in love with APL they can't fall asleep at night without saying to themselves 'Let me count the ways ...' Find at least 9 different ways to compute the average of a vector of numbers.

18. Execute `1000 100 10 1 +.×3 5 2 1` (the odometer problem). What does the result tell you about the relationship between inner product and decode?

Chapter 23: Input and output

Observe the following dialogue with a computer, using a program which simulates a psychiatrist (derived from the program *Eliza*, J.Weisenbaum, *Communications of the ACM*, Volume 9, Number 1, January 1966).

```
WOULD YOU PREFER TO TALK TO A DOCTOR (CLIENT-CENTERED PSYCHOTHERAPIST),
OR A FREAK (LONG-HAIRED STUDENT TYPE)?
TYPE 'DOCTOR' FOR THE DOCTOR, OR 'FREAK' FOR THE STUDENT.
□:   DOCTOR

YOU MAY END THE CONVERSATION ANYTIME BY TYPING THE SINGLE WORD 'BYE'

HOW DO YOU DO.  PLEASE STATE YOUR PROBLEM
□:   I AM TRYING TO LEARN ABOUT INPUT AND OUTPUT.
DO YOU BELIEVE IT IS NORMAL TO BE TRYING TO LEARN ABOUT INPUT AND OUTPUT
□:   IN THE CONTEXT OF AN APL COURSE IT IS NORMAL.
WHAT DOES THAT SUGGEST TO YOU
□:   THAT I MAY HAVE TO LEARN EVEN MORE
YOU SAY THAT YOU MAY HAVE TO LEARN EVEN MORE
□:   YES, I NEED TO GAIN AN UNDERSTANDING OF IT.
I SEE
□:   WHAT DO YOU SEE?
WHAT ANSWER WOULD PLEASE YOU MOST
□:   I DON'T KNOW.  YOU ARE NOT VERY HELPFUL.
DO YOU WISH TO BE ABLE TO KNOW
□:   WHAT SORT OF QUESTION IS THAT?
THAT'S A FREAKY QUESTION
□:   THIS CONVERSATION IS GETTING SILLY.
I'M NOT SURE I UNDERSTAND YOU FULLY
□:   I SAID, I DON'T THINK YOU KNOW WHAT YOU'RE DOING.
DO YOU SAY YOU SAID FOR SOME SPECIAL REASON
□:   WHAT?
ARE SUCH QUESTIONS MUCH ON YOUR MIND
□:   NOT UNTIL I STARTED TALKING TO YOU.
YOU SEEM TO NEED TO STARTED TALKING TO ME
□:   THAT'S SILLY.
PLEASE GO ON
□:   I DON'T WANT TO GO ON; I WANT TO STUDY MORE.
WHY DO YOU WANT TO GO ON
□:    I DON'T WANT TO GO ON.
WHAT DOES WANTING TO GO ON HAVE TO DO WITH THIS DISCUSSION
□:   THAT'S WHAT I'D LIKE TO KNOW.
HAVE YOU ASKED SUCH QUESTIONS BEFORE
□:   GOOD HEAVENS.
WHAT DOES THAT SUGGEST TO YOU
□:   HELP!

PLEASE GO ON
□:   HOW DO I GET OUT OF HERE?
HAVE YOU ASKED SUCH QUESTIONS BEFORE
□:   BYE

I EXPECT TO TALK TO YOU AGAIN SOON
```

The function appears to converse or interact with the user. While running, it prompts the user for an entry on the keyboard, comes up with an appropriate answer (well, most of the time) and decides what the next prompt is. This is different from all of the programs and functions you have written so far; all your functions communicated with the user only through arguments or global variables, and as a consequence the user had to know *something* about APL to use them. With the facility to 'converse' with the computer, users need to know only how to type an appropriate response. Depending on the level of sophistication that the program employs to deal with a user's entry, it can appear almost human in its reply. In particular, if the program lets the user know what his choices are, treats him gently when he errs, and can deal with minor typing errors, the program can rightly be termed *user friendly*.

Accepting character data

The most important APL feature to accept input from the user is the *quote-quad*, ⍞. When it is encountered in an APL statement, the computer accepts whatever characters the user types at the keyboard, until he enters RETURN. The characters that have been entered are then available for assignment to a variable as a character vector or for other purposes.

Here is an APL function that you might employ to deal with yes-or-no choices in a user-friendly application. Its argument is used as a prompt. The explicit result is a 1 for a *YES* reply or 0 for *NO*.

```
      ∇Z←YESORNO PROMPT;TRIES;ANS
[1]   ⍝ RETURNS 1 FOR YES, 0 FOR NO.
[2]   ⍝ AFTER 3 UNSUCCESSFUL TRIES, WARNS USER AND EXITS.
[3]   ⍝ A.J. ROSE SEPT 1982
[4]   TRIES←0
[5]   AGAIN2:PROMPT
[6]   AGAIN1:ANS←,⍞
[7]   Z←((2 3ρ'YESNO ')∧.=3↑ANS)/1 0
[8]   →(1=ρZ)/0
[9]   TRIES←TRIES+1 ◊ 'PLEASE ANSWER YES OR NO'
[10]  →(AGAIN1,AGAIN2,DEFAULT)[TRIES]
[11]  DEFAULT:'WARNING - BECAUSE I CANNOT UNDERSTAND YOUR REPLY,'
[12]  'YOUR INTENTIONS WILL BE INTERPRETED AS ''NO'''∇

      YESORNO 'DO YOU UNDERSTAND WHAT THIS FUNCTION DOES?'
MAYBE
PLEASE ANSWER YES OR NO
???
PLEASE ANSWER YES OR NO
DO YOU UNDERSTAND WHAT THIS FUNCTION DOES?
PERHAPS
PLEASE ANSWER YES OR NO
WARNING - BECAUSE I CANNOT UNDERSTAND YOUR REPLY,
YOUR INTENTIONS WILL BE INTERPRETED AS 'NO'
0
```

The input is accepted on line 6. The effect of ⍞ is to halt execution at that point until you press the RETURN key. Whatever characters you typed on the line prior to RETURN will be in the variable *ANS* as a character vector. (Some older APL systems treat a single character of ⍞ input as a scalar. For them, you should ravel so that you are always dealing with a vector.)

You can use your APL system as a word processor or electronic typewriter to help you edit text. The following program both accepts text and lets you edit what you've entered.

```
      )COPY 1 CLASS CHANGE COMPOSE
SAVED  14.45.33 02/20/83

      ∇CHANGE[□]∇
   ∇  Z←CHANGE TEXT;CMD;W;C
[1]   Z←W←0 ◊ →(1=ρρTEXT)/L2 ◊ 'NOT A VECTOR' ◊ →0 ⍝ DEMO TEXT
EDITOR. AJR 10/1/82
[2]   L2:CMD←'' ◊ →(0=ρTEXT)/INS ◊ →(' '=1↑0ρTEXT)/EDIT ◊ 'NOT CHARACTER' ◊ →0
[3]   EDIT:(50↑W↓TEXT), 7 0 ⍕W+1 ◊ CMD←,⍞ ◊ →(0=ρCMD)/HELP
[4]   Z←+/∧\' '=CMD ◊ C←1↑Z↓CMD ◊ CMD←(1+Z)↓CMD
[5]   →(C='H0123456789FBL/\EI')/HELP,(10ρDIG),FWD,BACK,LOC,SL,SL,END,INS
[6]   'UNKNOWN COMMAND' ◊ →EDIT
[7]   HELP:'NNN          MOVE WINDOW TO NNN'
[8]   'FNNN  BNNN    MOVE FORWARD OR BACK NNN CHARACTERS'
[9]   'F     B       MOVE FORWARD OR BACK 50 CHARACTERS'
[10]  'LPHRASE       MOVE TO NEXT PHRASE'
[11]  '//NEW \\NEW   REPLACE WHAT''S OVER // OR \\ BY NEW'
[12]  'E            END THE PROGRAM'
```

```
[13]    'H              HELP MESSAGES'
[14]    'INEW            INSERT NEW AT THIS POINT, SWITCH TO ENTRY MODE'
[15]    'SPACES          SWITCHES FROM ENTRY MODE TO EDIT MODE'
[16]    →EDIT
[17]    DIG:W←0⌈(⁻50+ρTEXT)⌊≢C,(∧\CMD∈'0123456789')/CMD ◇ →EDIT
[18]    FWD:W←0⌈(⁻50+ρTEXT)⌊W+Z+⁻1↑≢'50 ',(∧\CMD∈'0123456789')/CMD ◇ →EDIT
[19]    BACK:W←0⌈(⁻50+ρTEXT)⌊W+Z-⁻1↑≢'50 ',(∧\CMD∈'0123456789')/CMD ◇ →EDIT
[20]    LOC:W←W+Z ◇ CMD←∧≠(⁻1+ιρCMD)⌽CMD∘.=W↓TEXT ◇ →(∨/CMD)/HIT
        ◇ 'NOT FOUND' ◇ →EDIT
[21]    HIT:W←⁻1+W+CMDι1 ◇ →EDIT
[22]    SL:W←W+Z ◇ Z←+/∧\C=CMD ◇ TEXT←(W↑TEXT),(Z↓CMD),(W+Z+1)↓TEXT ◇ →EDIT
[23]    INS:W←W+Z ◇ Z←(W↑TEXT),CMD,(' '≠⁻1↑CMD)/' ' ◇ TEXT←W↓TEXT
[24]    INMORE:CMD←,⎕ ◇ →(' 'v.≠CMD)/INM2 ◇ TEXT←Z,TEXT ◇ →EDIT
[25]    INM2:Z←Z,CMD,(' '≠⁻1↑CMD)/' ' ◇ →INMORE
[26]    END:Z←TEXT
      ∇
```

The argument is a character vector, *TEXT*. If *TEXT* is not empty, *CHANGE* assumes you want to edit *TEXT*; line 3 then assigns to *CMD* those characters which you enter on the keyboard. In particular, if you enter only RETURN, then *CMD* is an empty vector and execution moves to line 7 where user instructions are displayed. Entry of valid commands (see lines 7 to 15) causes the appropriate action to be performed, after which execution moves to line 3 again.

CHANGE starts out in entry mode if the argument was empty. In this mode, new characters are repeatedly accepted in line 24 and catenated to *Z*. If the entered line doesn't end with a space character, one is supplied so that words don't run together. Entry of a totally blank line causes a switch to edit mode as in the previous paragraph. You can switch from edit mode to entry mode with the *I* command. Whatever follows *I* becomes part of the newly entered text.

```
      NT←CHANGE ''
BECAUSE THE ARGUMENT WAS EMPTY, WE START IN
ENTRY MODE AND STAY THERE UNTIL AN ENTIR
ELY BLANK LINE IS INPUT.

BECAUSE THE ARGUMENT WAS EMPTY, WE START IN ENTRY         1
LENTIRELY
NOT FOUND
BECAUSE THE ARGUMENT WAS EMPTY, WE START IN ENTRY         1
LENTIR
ENTIR ELY BLANK LINE IS INPUT.                          80
/////////COMPLETELY
COMPLETELY BLANK LINE IS INPUT.                         80
B20
STAY THERE UNTIL AN COMPLETELY BLANK LINE IS INPUT       60
              /
  COMPLETELY BLANK LINE IS INPUT.                       78
                              IHERE WE SWITCH
BACK TO ENTRY MODE.

HERE WE SWITCH BACK TO ENTRY MODE.                      111
                              /AND BACK AGAIN TO EDIT MODE.
AND BACK AGAIN TO EDIT MODE.                            144
B10
CH BACK TO ENTRY MODEAND BACK AGAIN TO EDIT MODE.       123
              / A
  AND BACK AGAIN TO EDIT MODE.                          144
0
BECAUSE THE ARGUMENT WAS EMPTY, WE START IN ENTRY         1
F
MODE AND STAY THERE UNTIL A COMPLETELY BLANK LINE        51
STOP
UNKNOWN COMMAND
MODE AND STAY THERE UNTIL A COMPLETELY BLANK LINE        51
END
      20↑NT
BECAUSE THE ARGUMENT
```

Although it doesn't contribute to our discussion of ⎕, *CHANGE* needs a companion function, *COMPOSE*, to produce final copy. The right argument is a vector of *CHANGE*d text, and the left argument is whatever maximum line width you want.

```
      ∇COMPOSE[□]∇                              40 COMPOSE NT
      ∇ N COMPOSE TEXT;P                     BECAUSE THE ARGUMENT WAS EMPTY, WE START
[1]   LOOP:→(N≤ρTEXT)/MORE ◊ TEXT ◊ →0       IN ENTRY MODE AND STAY THERE UNTIL A
[2]   MORE:P←(TEXT=' ')/ιρTEXT               COMPLETELY BLANK LINE IS INPUT. HERE WE
[3]   P←¯1↑N,(P≤N+1)/P                       SWITCH BACK TO ENTRY MODE AND BACK AGAIN
[4]   P↑TEXT ◊ TEXT←P↓TEXT ◊ →LOOP           TO EDIT MODE.
      ∇
```

Escaping from quote-quad

The following program has a fatal flaw. It swallows up whatever you enter at the keyboard like an APL equivalent of the video game PacMan:

```
      ∇TEXT←GOTCHA
[1]   TEXT←''
[2]   MORE:'GIMME SOME WORDS'
[3]   TEXT←TEXT,▯
[4]   →MORE∇
```

No matter what you type (including character errors) the program continues to gobble up your input (until you ultimately reach *WS FULL*). You can't even sign off because *')OFF'* would just be catenated to *TEXT*! But there is an emergency escape from situations like this—entering the sequence *O* backspace *U* backspace *T* RETURN will rescue you, as will use of the CLEAR or PA2 keys or their equivalent on terminals that don't have a backspace. The exact form of rescue may differ, though on most systems you will be suspended. Check *)SI* to be safe.

Needless to say, programs that don't include a graceful way to escape a ▯ loop shouldn't be written. Plan for some sequence of characters which when entered will provide an escape from the loop. Typical escapes are entry of a blank line, or only the RETURN key, or some word like *END*, *STOP*, *QUIT* or *HELP*. It's very important for the program to tell the user what his choices are and how to escape. Programs that don't are user-hostile, and they are largely responsible for the feeling of alienation that many people have for computers and computer programmers.

Prompts and replies on the same line

Most of the techniques described here differ significantly in their details from one system to another. You will need to try these ideas and experiment on your own to discover the idiosyncrasies of your system.

Just as in the expression *REPLY←,* ▯ you move characters from the keyboard into the variable *REPLY*, in the expression ▯*←PROMPT* characters are being moved from the variable *PROMPT* to the terminal's printer or screen. Using this form of display, no new line signal is sent to the printer or screen. That means that if you follow ▯*←PROMPT* with an expression like *REPLY←,* ▯, then the prompt and reply are on the same line. In a very real sense ▯ is a window between APL and the outside, sharing information between the two environments.

The following example shows how this feature, called *bare output* works in APLSV and VS APL:

```
      ∇ Z←BAREOUTPUT R                    REPLY←BAREOUTPUT 'ENTER YOUR NAME: '
[1]   ▯←R                          ENTER YOUR NAME: FLOYD
[2]   Z←,▯ ∇                              REPLY
                                                      FLOYD
                                          ρREPLY
                              22
```

REPLY has 22 elements because in these versions of APL the input is prefixed with as many space characters as there are characters in the prompt.

Removal of the blanks is easy. We'll change line 2 and reexecute to show that the result now has only the characters that were entered:

```
        ∇BAREOUTPUT[2]Z←(ρR)↓,⍞ ∇
        ρBAREOUTPUT 'ENTER YOUR NAME: '
ENTER YOUR NAME: FLOYD
5
```

On some other systems, the reply holds an image of the prompt instead of the blanks above. On still other systems only the characters that were typed in are retained. But APL2 lets you decide for yourself how to treat replies on the same line as the ⍞ prompt. Whatever value you set in the *prompt replacement* system variable is what goes into the reply. Its default value is □*PR*←' ', which matches the behavior of APLSV and VS APL by supplying leading blanks. Here are some other values:

```
        □PR←'∘'                           □PR←''
        BAREOUTPUT 'TEST'                     BAREOUTPUT 'TEST'
TESTENTRY                          TESTENTRY
∘∘∘∘ENTRY                          ENTRY
```

Setting □*PR* to an empty character vector, ' ', eliminates the leading blanks.

Evaluated input

One application of ⍞ input occurs so frequently that it has been given a separate symbol, the □ (quad). When control in a line of APL reaches a □, the prompt □: is displayed. Whatever you enter on the keyboard is accepted as though you were in calculation mode, rather than accepting the characters literally as with ⍞. Informally, this is what □ does in terms of ⍞:

```
        ∇R←QUADINPUT
[1]     ⍝ INFORMAL SIMULATION OF □ FOR INPUT. DOES NOT HANDLE
[2]     ⍝ EDGE CONDITIONS SUCH AS ∇ FN DEF, )SYS COMMANDS, BLANK LINES
[3]     ⍞←'□:',□TCNL,6ρ' ' ◇ R←⍎⍞ ∇
```

The symbol ⍎ on line 3 was mentioned on page 117 and is called *execute*; it treats character vectors as though they were entered in calculation mode. (In other words, Z←⍎'2+3' or ⍎'Z←2+3' is equivalent to Z←2+3. More in Chapter 24). □*TCNL* (page 238) makes the next display start on a new line.

Any valid APL expression can be entered through □. Recall that the drill *TEACH* in workspace 1 *AIDRILL* accepts the student's replies through □. Here is a much simpler computer drill—one to exercise a child's skills in elementary subtraction:

```
        SUB                           ∇ SUB;HELP;STOP;P1;P2
ENTER STOP TO STOP            [1]     HELP←∘∘1 ◇ STOP←∘∘∘1
14-10                         [2]     'ENTER STOP TO STOP, HELP FOR HELP'
□:                           [3]     L3:P1←?20
        4                     [4]     P2←¯1+?P1+1
THATS RIGHT                   [5]     (⍕P1),'-',⍕P2
19-7                          [6]     L6:→((1↑,□)=(P1-P2),HELP,STOP)/OK,HELP,0
□:                           [7]     (⍕P2),' + ___ = ',(⍕P1),□TCNL,'TRY AGAIN'
        11                    [8]     →L6
7 + ___ = 19                  [9]     OK:'THATS RIGHT'
TRY AGAIN                     [10]    →L3
□:                           [11]    HELP:(P1ρ'∘'),' TAKE AWAY',□TCNL,P2ρ'∘'
        HELP                  [12]    →L6 ∇
∘∘∘∘∘∘∘∘∘∘∘∘∘∘∘∘∘∘∘ TAKE AWAY
∘∘∘∘∘∘∘∘
□:
        12
THATS RIGHT
11-9
□:
        STOP
```

Line 1 assigns values to *HELP* and *STOP* that are unlikely to be matched by a student's entry at the keyboard. On line 3 a random integer from 1 to 20 is stored in *P*1. *P*2 is then assigned a random integer from 0 to *P*. This guarantees that *P*2 will never be greater than *P*1, so that no problems requiring negative answers will be generated. Line 5 displays the problem. Line 6 accepts input, tests the correctness of the answer and branches. If *HELP* was entered, the branch is to line 11, where a hint is offered to the student. Entering *STOP* causes execution to cease.

If an incorrect answer is entered, line 7 rephrases the problem. If the problem is answered correctly this time we go to line 9 and then to line 3 for a new problem to solve.

In this exercise, *HELP* and *STOP* are local variables with unlikely (but arbitrary) values. This technique is a simple way to give programs a touch of user-friendliness, although for serious applications ⍞ should be used instead. Even in *SUB*, a student could cheat on the answer by replying with $P1-P2$; he would be right every time!

As with ⍞, it is possible to write loops including □ which don't have planned escapes. Emergency escape from □ input differs from one system to another. Try → or)*RESET* or BREAK or *O* backspace *U* backspace *T*. One or more of these will likely work.

Other uses and limitations of the quad

Don't get the impression from the previous section that □ must be used only within defined functions. When entering voluminous data, □ is very handy for coping with entries that would overrun the right margin. Suppose within some function there are lines like

```
[9]    'ENTER DATA'
[10]   'SUM IS ',⍕+/□
```

If the number of values being added is large, □ can be used in the manner shown below:

```
ENTER DATA
□:
      5 9 14 6 3 12 15,□
□:
      6 2 3,(10ρ21),8,7,□
□:
      3 2 1
SUM IS 306
```

It works because □ admits any APL expression, including □ itself. A line of numeric input that ends with ,□ has the meaning 'to be continued.'

Here are some limitations of □ input. You can't use it for function definition; it is intended only for APL statements which return an explicit result. System commands entered as □ input are executed, but the response to the command isn't considered as input. If you reply to □ with just a RETURN or spaces and RETURN, it acts as though you haven't entered anything and comes back with another □: prompt. If your reply to □ is a line with multiple statements, the rightmost statement must return an explicit result, or a *VALUE ERROR* is produced. *GAME* in this example does not have an explicit result:

```
        Z←□                              STMT1              ∇GAME[□]∇
□:                               5                       ∇ GAME
        STMT1←2+3 ◊ GAME                 Z               [1]    MINE←DICE
1                                VALUE ERROR             [2]    YOURS←DICE
VALUE ERROR                              Z               [3]    ×MINE-YOURS
        Z←□                              ∧                    ∇
        ∧
```

□ can also be used on the left side of the assignment arrow. A statement like □←2 3ρ⍳6 has the same effect as simply 2 3ρ6; but to both display and store the values *STORE*←□←2 3ρ⍳6 or □←*STORE*←2 3ρ⍳6 replaces the two statements *STORE*←2 3ρ⍳6 ◊ *STORE*. Some APL experts always use □← instead of implicit output because they feel the explicit reference makes the programs more readable.

If you are lost in some horribly complicated APL line trying to figure out what went wrong, it may be helpful to temporarily embed □← at critical points to detail the sequence of events, as we demonstrate on our old friend *HYP*. □← used in this way serves as a trace within the line.

```
        ∇HYP[□]∇                            ∇HYP[1□10]
      ∇ C←A HYP B                    [1]    C←((A*2)+B*2)*0.5
[1]     C←((A*2)+B*2)*0.5                    22  2
      ∇                             [1]
                                    [2]    C←(□←(□←A*2)+□←B*2)*0.5
      3 HYP 4                              ∇
5                                  →1
      3 5 HYP 4 12 100             16 144 10000
LENGTH ERROR                       9 25
HYP[1] C←((A*2)+B*2)*0.5           LENGTH ERROR
         ∧                         HYP[1] C←(□←(□←A*2)+□←B*2)*0.5
                                          ∧
```

Conversions of character input to numeric values

Many large commercial applications have need to accept voluminous numeric data from the terminal. Often the people assigned to entering the data are not experienced in the use of computers. To err is human; to forgive is user-friendly. So it is important that your programs handle input errors gently. For that reason, most applications use 🛡 input instead of □, with the input being checked in the program for errors before being converted to numeric values.

The usual means of doing the conversion is with the execute function, ♣ (see Chapter 24). However, input validation must be done first or else the program may suspend with errors from invalid data. In both Sharp and APL*PLUS Systems, monadic system functions $\Box FI$ and $\Box VI$ are provided to do this efficiently. $\Box FI$ takes as its argument a character vector (or scalar) and converts it to a vector of numbers, using a subset of the rules for □ input. If there is anything in the argument that can't be converted, a zero is placed in that position of the result.

```
      □FI '10    25.4 9'              □FI '10 23SKIDOO 9 ¯.25'
10 25.4 9                       10  0  9  ¯0.25
```

To distinguish between true zeros and those arising from bad data, the system function $\Box VI$ may be used. It accepts the same arguments as $\Box FI$, but returns a vector with 1's in the positions where the result is valid, and 0's where it isn't.

```
      □VI '10    25.4 9'              □VI '10 23SKIDOO 9 ¯.25'
1 1 1                           1  0  1  1
```

$\Box FI$ and $\Box VI$ are both usually employed in a sequence like this:

```
      INPUT←,🛡
      →(0∈□VI INPUT)/ERRORANALYSIS
      DATA←□FI INPUT
```

Friendly design

The last section described facilities for checking and cleaning up entries and thereby protecting naive users from the consequences of their limited experience. It is a fact that input and output considerations consume a vast amount of the time and energy of computer people. Perhaps more than any other single factor, properly designed input and output is what lets non-computer people use computers. Imagine the chaos that would result if an automatic bank teller machine didn't have built-in error checking to exclude unacceptable input!

When someone begins using an application, he benefits by explicit prompts and unabbreviated replies, all of which tend to reinforce learning the application. As he gains experience, the prompts can become more terse, and abbreviated replies are sufficient. This holds true for most applications. $YESORNO$ at the beginning of this chapter is a trite example of generic prompting functions.

Most commercial APL systems feature libraries of prompting and input functions that can be embedded in your applications. If you have access to such functions, you should use them rather than write your own, because they save development time and tend to make for more consistent use of prompts and input conventions across diverse applications.

We've only hinted at some of the ways to deal with naive users so far. Those of you who will be designing applications for others to run should always take the user's viewpoint, skill and experience level to heart. Test your work on people who are representative of the ultimate audience. Don't rely on your own judgment; the fact that you've arrived here in this book says you are no longer a novice, and prompts that suit you may be too cryptic for a truly naive user.

Direct communication with the operator and other users

Most time-shared APL systems provide ways to send messages to other users via shared files or shared variables. The messages are kept in a common file until the intended recipient decides to read his 'mail.' However, there is occasional need to contact another user immediately, and system commands are provided for this purpose. The system command $)PORTS$ gives a listing of *port numbers* (remember your first sign-on in Chapter 1?) and the three-letter codes for the users presently signed on. This command, as well as the message commands described below, is usually not supported on personal computer systems when used as a stand-alone, since there is no one else to send messages to.

```
     )PORTS
OPR OPE      036 LGI       226 ADF
003 AJR      064 JIL
035 LMB      079 KEI
```

In the interests of privacy, the $)PORTS$ command is usually restricted on commercial APL systems. But if you know the three-letter code, say, JIL, for the person you want to reach, you can enter

```
     )PORT JIL
064 JIL
```

You can communicate with that person by the $)MSG$ or $)MSGN$ commands. The command consists of $)MSG$ or $)MSGN$ followed by the port number and your one-line message.

```
     )MSG 64 THIS IS AL. DID YOU FIX THE PLANNING PROGRAM?
```

The message will not be sent while the other user is typing, and your keyboard is locked during that time. As soon as he enters a RETURN, the message will appear on his terminal,

```
003:R THIS IS AL. DID YOU FIX THE PLANNING PROGRAM?
```

and you will get the message $SENT$ on your terminal. If you used $)MSGN$ instead of $)MSG$ (i.e., no reply expected, as evidenced by the absence of $\underline{R}$ in the message received), your terminal unlocks as soon as the message $SENT$ appears on your terminal. In either case, a lock can be broken at any time by BREAK, but $MESSAGE\ LOST$ appears on your terminal if you do so prematurely.

A message can be sent to the computer operator with the command $)OPR$ or $)OPRN$, followed by your message. With $)OPR$, your terminal remains locked, while it becomes available for use immediately after the $SENT$ message is you used $)OPRN$.

```
     )OPR A.J. ROSE HERE; MAY I PLEASE HAVE 2 MORE WORKSPACES?
SENT
OPR: DONE ... /BETSY
     )OPRN THANKS
SENT
```

Good manners are even more important in the use of APL's message commands than in voice telephone communication. Do not send messages capriciously, as you may disturb some important report being prepared by the other user. Remember also that a one-line printed message cannot carry your voice inflections, so be very explicit when you request something or when you reply to a request for information.

To avoid the intrusion of a message while you are working at the terminal, use $\square MSGR\ 'OFF'$. Then no one (except the operator to advise you of an emergency) can send you a message. The would-be sender is informed (by seeing $INCOMMUNICADO$) that you're not willing to take messages. When you're ready to receive them again, use $\square MSGR\ 'ON'$.

You can use $\square KEYB\ 'LOCK'$ to place your terminal in a permanently locked state, so that messages can be received even if you've stepped away from the terminal. To use the terminal, just press BREAK before each line of input. To restore the keyboard to its normal state use $\square KEYB\ 'OPEN'$.

$\square KEYB$ and $\square MSGR$, along with $\square HT$ and $\square PW$ (to be introduced later in this chapter), are session-related system variables. That means that their values don't get reset when you $)LOAD$ a new workspace, but rather they stay until sign-off or until you deliberately reset them.

Special characters

Most terminals have features such as backspace, linefeed, new line, and bells (or even whistles) that you may wish to exercise. Inside APL, these features are represented as characters; for example, if you had a character vector containing '$OVERBAR$', three backspace characters, and three overbars (' ‾ '), then on most terminals it would display as $OVER\overline{BAR}$.

The rub is there's no direct way to enter the backspace character from the keyboard. But there are ways to get it. The system variable □AV (atomic vector) contains the entire character set, including overstruck characters like ⍒, ⍟ and ≠, as well as terminal control characters such as the backspace.

The definition of □AV is completely dependent on the particular implementation of APL being used. Hence, you should avoid expressions with □AV within functions which may be transferred to a different version of APL.

All is not lost, however, since some systems provide the more useful special characters in an alternate form:

| | | □AV position | | | special terminal character | |
Character	Sharp, SV	VS	APL2	APL*PLUS	APL2	APL*PLUS
linefeed	160	170	38	202	□TC[3]	□$TCLF$
backspace	165	38	23	201	□TC[1]	□$TCBS$
new line	157	74	22	203	□TC[2]	□$TCNL$
idle	1	1	1	205		□$TCNUL$
audible tone				204		□$TCBEL$

For other characters consult your local information center, system manager or system manual.

Some of the 256 elements of □AV may produce weird results on your terminal; some are associated with characters not reproducible with your particular display or keyboard printer; and some may vary from country to country. There are even combinations of characters which have a particular significance on specific terminals. For instance, a user of the Tektronix 4015 graphics terminal on APLSV may blank the screen by entering □AV[47 92 47 91] or trigger the Tektronix 2631 hard copy unit with □AV[47 92 47 87]. On other terminals these instructions would simply appear as $\omega F\omega E$ and $\omega F\omega A$ respectively, or as pure gibberish.

Sophisticated APL programmers occasionally employ □AV to save space when storing data which is known to have 256 or fewer different possible values. For example, imagine dealing with survey data in which multiple choice replies were 1 2 3 4 5 6. Storing each value as an integer would consume 32 bits (on IBM 370 or equivalent systems; varies on other systems). If you were to convert each value to character, as in $CODED$←□AV[$INTEGERS$], there would be a four-fold saving in space because each character consumes only 8 bits (see page 224). You can reconstitute the original values by □AVι$CODED$ whenever you need them. Caution: if you use this technique, do not attempt to display the coded values on your terminal. It may produce unpredictable results and might even cause physical damage!

Getting the most out of your terminal

APL can be run on a wide variety of terminals. For much of what you do with APL you don't have to worry about the type of terminal you are using; however, you can take advantage of the special features of your terminal if you want to.

If your terminal is equipped with horizontal tabs, you can speed up significantly the printing of reports with a lot of 'white space' between the columns of information. Some screen display terminals come with built-in tab stops, usually 6 apart. To use them simply inform the APL system you are using tabs with □HT←6×ι20 for a terminal with 120 characters per line, or □HT←6×ι13 for one with 80 characters.

Printing terminals usually require that you set their physical or electronic tab stops. Page 240 gives an example of setting tabs. Once they are set, use the □HT system variable to inform the APL system where you have set the tabs. Some systems require that tabs be evenly spaced (i.e. some multiple of ιN) but IBM APL systems are more permissive, allowing any integer values up to the width of the printer. You then proceed without any further consideration of tabs. Whenever it takes less time for APL to tab over to the next printed position (rather than spacing over), it will do so automatically. □HT by itself gives you the present tab settings.

For input, entry of the TAB key is treated exactly like the equivalent number of spaces. A novel application of this involves using ⍞ input to build the rows of a character matrix. If the tabs are set to the column dimension of the result matrix, then tabbing to the next typed word ensures that the result matrix will have text left-justified on each row.

Here is an example with tabs set at 10, 20, 30 etc. The symbol ⍈ denotes where the TAB key was pressed:

```
      ⎕HT←6×⍳20                                        ⍴T
      ∇R←INPUT                                  3  10
[1]   R←,⍞  ◇  R←(⌈(⍴R)÷10),10)⍴R  ∇                   T
      T←INPUT                                  PICKLES
PICKLES⍈ONIONS⍈KETCHUP⍈                        ONIONS
                                               KETCHUP
```

Not all terminals can print the same number of characters on a line. For example, many desktop printing terminals provide 130 or more characters per line, but screen display devices often provide only 40, 64 or 80. Professional business reports should be designed to fit on the narrowest terminal likely to be used for the application, to ensure that nothing is lost by trying to display lines too long to fit. Most APL systems assume a display width of 60 to 130 characters. Longer displays are continued on following lines. You can usually tell when a display has been continued because all lines after the first are indented six spaces.

If your application requires it, and if your terminal has the physical capability, you can vary the print or display width from 30 to about 250 characters. The way to do it is with the ⎕PW (print *width*) system variable.

```
      ⎕PW
130
      ⎕PW←60
      90⍴'1234567890'
123456789012345678901234567890123456789012345678901234567890
      123456789012345678901234567890

      ÷⍳10
1 0.5 0.3333333333 0.25 0.2 0.1666666667 0.1428571429
      0.125 0.1111111111 0.1

      ⎕PW←50
      90⍴'1234567890'
12345678901234567890123456789012345678901234567890
      123456789012345678901234567890123456789012345678901234567890
```

As you can see, character displays are broken at exactly the specified width, but numeric displays are broken earlier to avoid splitting a value in the middle. The ⎕PW system variable is handy when you have to make emergency use of a terminal that is narrower than your usual one, or when your application requires wide lines and you have access to a terminal with suitable width.

The print width setting is ignored for entry of data from the terminal. Even if the print width is set to 50, you are free to enter characters up to the right margin. Similarly, direct messages from the operator or other users ignore the print width.

Many screens don't need the built-in delays and idles required by electromechanical typewriter-style terminals, and on some systems the ⎕TERM system function can be used. ⎕TERM 'NOIDLES' removes all delays; ⎕TERM 'IDLES' restores them.

To permit the use of new overstruck symbols on display terminals such as the IBM 3278, which doesn't have a backspace character, APL2 includes the system command)PBS followed by a nonblank character of your choice. If, for example, you entered)PBS ←, then to simulate the equal underbar =, you enter =←_ or _←=. Only legitimate new overstruck characters can be represented in APL2 (at this writing) in this way (⍫ ⍳ ∊ = ⍉ ⍫ ⍠).

For applications that might be run at a variety of terminals, such as electronic mail applications for traveling executives, the program can even determine the terminal type (⎕TT, but interpretation varies from system to system) and set ⎕PW, ⎕HT and ⎕TERM to suit.

If a given application will be run so frequently as to dominate the use of the terminal, you should consider acquiring the right terminal for that job. This means shopping carefully and evaluating the features. You can get a good start by reading 'A Consumers' Guide to Choosing an APL Terminal', by Carl M. Cheney and Scott N. McAuley, pages 356-367 of *APL In Practice* (Wiley, 1980).

Arbitrary output and input

The rest of this chapter discusses features and details useful for tailored input and output applications, including intersystem communication and making the terminal do tricks. You may safely skip it without loss of continuity.

APL*PLUS and Sharp APL Systems provide the system functions, $\Box ARBOUT$ and $\Box ARBIN$ which, while a little trickier to use than $\Box AV$, give you total control and flexibility in moving information between the computer, the terminal and the outside world.

$\Box ARBOUT$ is a monadic system function which does not have an explicit result. Rather, it sends unadorned byte sequences to the terminal without any delays, idles, linefeeds or other padding that is normally transmitted when producing character results on the terminal. It is inadvisable to rely on the $\Box HT$ settings when using $\Box ARBOUT$ because the terminal needs certain delays and padding to physically move the printing mechanism to the right position. Ironically, the tab stops themselves are usually set by a $\Box ARBOUT$ sequence. For instance, to set tabs on a NEC Spinwriter to correspond to $\Box HT \leftarrow 10 \times \iota 10$, use the sequence $\Box ARBOUT$ 27 55, 120ρ(10ρ32),27 49.

To switch the display of a Human Design Systems Concept 400 terminal from white-on-black to black-on-white (i.e., reverse video image), the terminal must first be placed in 'programmer mode' by $\Box ARBOUT$ 27 85, and then $\Box ARBOUT$ 27 68 will produce the reverse image (found by reading the HDS manual):

```
      ☐ARBOUT 27 85 27 68
      'THIS IS BLACK ON WHITE'
```

Now all following displays show as black on white. You can switch back to white-on-black by $\Box ARBOUT$ 27 100, and disable programmer mode with $\Box ARBOUT$ 27 117.

But suppose you want to switch to and from reverse image in the middle of a line. To do that, use $\Box ARBOUT$ for the entire line, including the characters that you would normally print directly. The phrase $WATCH\ IT$ $SWITCH$ is coded into the argument here:

```
      ☐ARBOUT 119 97 116 99 104 32 27 100 105 116,☐
☐:
      27 68 32 115 119 105 116 99 104 13
WATCH IT SWITCH
```

The numbers in $\Box ARBOUT$'s argument correspond to ASCII (American Standard Code for Information Interchange) codes and can be found in their published tables. Because APL overstruck characters like ⍒ aren't in the table, they are formed with sequences such as 79 8 63 or 63 8 79.

Just as you can send any arbitrary byte pattern from the computer to the terminal, you can also send arbitrary patterns from the terminal or other input device to the computer. $\Box ARBIN$ is a function (monadic or dyadic depending on the system) that accepts signals from an outside source (typically the keyboard but could be an analog sensor, voice input, bar code reader, or whatever) and translates those signals to $\Box ARBOUT$-compatible values. $\Box ARBIN$'s right argument is a prompt, and it works much like $\Box ARBOUT$. To suppress the prompt just use ι0.

On the APL*PLUS VM System, $\Box ARBIN$ is monadic, as shown by the following:

```
      ARB←☐ARBIN 101 110 116 101 114 62 ⍝  ☐ARBIN VALUES FOR 'ENTER:'
ENTER:THIS IS O̅V̅E̅R̅
      ARB
244 232 233 243 160 233 243 160 239 246 229 242 136 136 136 13
6 192 192 192 192 141
      ☐ARBOUT ARB
THIS IS O̅V̅E̅R̅
```

Every keystroke is taken verbatim, which means that there are three elements for APL overstruck characters such as ⍕. $\Box ARBIN$'s result may differ from the expected value in the ASCII table by 128, depending on how the parity switch on the terminal was set. It's always safe to resolve that by $ARB \leftarrow 128 | ARB$.

Intersystem communication and distributed computing

On STSC's APL*PLUS systems for small computers, $\Box ARBIN$ is a dyadic function. The right argument, which may be character, is the prompt, and the left argument is an integer vector specifying how, where and when the signals will be sent.

element no.	possible values	meaning
1 outbound	0	No outport used
	1	Send to first serial (ASCII) port
	2	Send to second serial port
	3	Send to parallel port (usually a printer)
	4 - 15	Other ports or peripheral devices
2 inbound	0	No response is expected
	1	Response comes from first serial port
	2 - 15	Response comes from designated port
3 translation	‾1	Untranslated numeric codes are transmitted and received
	0 - 2	Various ASCII translations (0 is normal for APL)
	3	IBM and Epson parallel printer graphics mode
4 protocol	0 - 3	3 is normal for many time sharing computers
5 wait	positive integer	If no response in this number of seconds, continue execution of program (called a dead-man timer)
	0	No response expected; no wait (similar to use of $\Box ARBOUT$)
	negative integer	Infinite wait
6 char limit	positive integer	Maximum number of characters accepted in response
	0	Default value (check for your computer)
7 terminators	list of values, 0 to 255	$\Box ARBIN$ stops accepting data when any transmission code in the list is encountered (the list can be empty)

What this all means is that $\Box ARBIN$ will send information to, and accept information from, the ports designated in elements 1 and 2. It will stop accepting signals when the time limit has been reached, or the maximum number of characters has been received, or a terminating code was entered or the BREAK key was pressed.

$\Box INKEY$ is a special niladic system function for working with the display screen to do full-screen management. It accepts a single keystroke, which may occur anywhere on the screen. As soon as you have entered one keystroke, the program resumes (without waiting for you to press RETURN). In this manner you can manage the screen on a character by character basis.

If you use a line like $REP \leftarrow 1\ 1\ 0\ 1\ 20\ 250\ 7\ 10\ 13\ \Box ARBIN\ 'PROMPT'$, it means you are sending $PROMPT$ to serial port 1, and you expect a reply to come from there as well. Input continues to be accepted until 20 seconds have elapsed since the last character was entered, or 250 characters have been received, or a RETURN, LINEFEED or BACKSPACE has been entered. The result will be characters.

You can tell which one of the termination rules stopped the transmission by looking at the last element of the result (caution, system dependent):

last value in result	what caused termination	relevant elements
One of the termination codes	Termination code encountered	7 and beyond
129 or $\Box AV[129+\Box IO]$	Time limit exceeded	5
130 or $\Box AV[130+\Box IO]$	Character count exceeded	6
131 or $\Box AV[131+\Box IO]$	BREAK was pressed	not applicable

The most important thing about $\Box ARBIN$ is that with it you can use a low-cost personal computer such as the TRS80 Model III or the IBM Personal Computer as an intelligent node of a distributed computing network. A typical configuration might consist of several IBM PCs attached via modems to a time-sharing APL system running in a VM environment on an IBM 3081 or other large-scale computer.

The function *ET* (for executed transmission) lets the remote user phone his home base and transfer data between the time-sharing computer and the personal computer. *ET* is a rather primitive function, but it does demonstrate distributed computing capabilities. Assume the time-sharing computer's active workspace is 1 *CLASS*. The dialogue below is on the remote personal computer:

```
      )CLEAR
CLEAR WS


      ∇Z←ET R
[1]   ⍝ EXECUTES R ON TIME+SHARING COMPUTER
[2]   ⍝ RESULT TRANSMITTED TO REMOTE PERSONAL COMPUTER
[3]   Z←1 1 0 1 ¯1 32000 7 ⎕ARBIN R,⎕TCNL ⍝ STOP ON ⎕TCBEL
[4]   ⍝ TO TIME+SHARING COMPUTER, APPEARS AS KEYBOARD USER
[5]   Z←2↓¯9↑Z ⍝ CHOP OFF TRANSMISSION EMBELLISHMENTS – MAY VARY ON OTHER SYSTEMS
[6]   Z←(Z≠⎕TCLF)/Z ⍝ MAY VARY ON OTHER SYSTEMS
[7]   ∇
      ET ')LOAD 1 CLASS'
SAVED   21.53.11 02/19/83


      LV←ET ')WSID'

      LV
IS 1 CLASS

      ⎕←X←ET 'TAB1'
1.414213562 1.732050808 2 2.236067977

      ρX ⍝ X IS CHARACTERS
37
      X←⍎X ⍝ CONVERT TO NUMERIC
```

The transactions above moved an image of *TAB*1 on the time-sharing computer into *X* on the personal computer. Data and programs can also be moved from the personal computer to the time-sharing computer:

```
      X←X+3
      ET 'NEWX←',⍕X
      ET 'NEWX'
4.414213562 4.732050808 5 5.236067977

      NEWX
VALUE ERROR
      NEWX
      ∧
```

We generated that last *VALUE ERROR* on purpose to demonstrate that *NEWX* is in the time-sharing computer, not the personal computer.

Elaborations of this general idea of intercommunicating computers make possible such sophisticated activities as a small personal computer programmed to dial a larger one to access a database, or to hand off some computing task that's too intensive for a small machine.

PROBLEMS

1. Define a function that will give multiplication drill with integers *?N* for some argument *N* in the header. Have your function print a message *TRY AGAIN* for wrong answers. Use *STOP* as a variable for escape from the function.

2. Modify your answer to the above problem so that three tries are allowed, after which the correct answer is printed and another problem is posed.

3. Add a further refinement to the multiplication drill so that when *HELP* is typed, the answer to the problem is given as *X*[1] rows of *X*[2] stars each, with an appropriate message and a repetition of the problem. *X* is the vector of random integers generated in the problem.

4. Still another refinement: keep track of the number of right answers and display the percent right when finished.

5. Since quote-quad input doesn't prompt with ▯, show how to force literal input and display ▯ at the same time.

6. Replace the message *TRY AGAIN* on line 6 of *SPELL* (in 1 *CLASS*) with a statement that reveals the answer.

7. Define a function *ENTER* that will take the literal spelling of numbers, like those in *SPL* (in 1 *CLASS*), and put them in successive rows of a 20-column matrix. Exit from the function will be effected by entering an empty vector.

8. Define a dyadic function *LIST* that lets you input and list a specified number of names of specified length.

9. Write a monadic function *LOOKUP* whose right argument is a list *L* of names in matrix form, and which asks you to input a name to be looked up by the function, identifies its row location(s), or prints an appropriate message.

10. Define a function *BALANCE* to prompt for an opening balance and a vector of transactions (positive for deposits and negative for withdrawals) and produce a report showing the opening and closing balances, total deposits and total withdrawals.

11. Write a function whose syntax is *Z←MAT INS N* to prompt for a vector to be inserted after row *N* in a literal array *MAT*.

12. Define a function *MONTHLYINPUT* to ask for 12 months of data and a control total. If the control total equals the sum of the first 12 numbers, the program should return these 12 numbers as a result. Any error should cause an appropriate error message to be printed and prompt for the numbers again.

Chapter 24: Advanced programming features and techniques for controlling exceptions

With the rapid spread of microcomputers and the phenomenal growth of end-user application packages designed for them, there has developed great interest in the concept of user friendly programs. This chapter will concentrate on those features of APL that will, when properly used, dissuade users from heading for the nearest bar to drown their frustrations.

Consider the following compound interest program, which was written to be used by a friend who doesn't like computers:

```
        ∇SAVINGS;PIN;P;I;R;CF
[1]     TOP:'ENTER PRINCIPAL, INTEREST RATE AND NUMBER OF PERIODS'
[2]     PIN←□
[3]     P←PIN[1] ◊ I←PIN[2] ◊ N←PIN[3]
[4]     CF←P×(1+I)*ιN
[5]     'BALANCE EACH PERIOD ',8 2⍕CF ∇
        SAVINGS
ENTER PRINCIPAL, INTEREST RATE AND NUMBER OF PERIODS

□:
        1000 .08 4.5
DOMAIN ERROR
SAVINGS[4] CF←P×(I-1)*ιN
                ∧
```

A person who started out with a dislike for computers would not be won over by the display above. While professionals understand the meaning and intent of the diagnostic message *DOMAIN ERROR*, its tone is unfriendly to the naive user.

We would like to insulate unwitting users from such messages. There are two traditional means of keeping the user out of trouble: the first is to admonish the user to follow the instructions precisely (e.g., put in a positive integer only, or else suffer embarrassment or frustration). The second is for the application developer to anticipate every possible thing that can go wrong (ha!) and include steps to deal with these potential errors, or events, or exceptions. The first approach is inhumane to the user; the second is inhumane to the developer. If one had to choose between the two, the recommended choice would be to put the burden on the developer to do it right.

Error trapping

Some modern APL systems provide a third option, to 'trap' the unfriendly message just before it is displayed, replace it by something less offensive, and even fix or bypass the problem and keep running. The underlying philosophy is that an error is an exception to the normal running of the program. The default behavior of APL when an exception happens is to display the cause of the exception and halt execution.

On APL*PLUS Systems, □*ELX* (for exception latent expression) is used to change what the system does when an exception (i.e, an error like *DOMAIN ERROR*) happens. You assign □*ELX* as a character vector holding whatever APL statement you would like executed should an error occur.

For example, if you wanted the *SAVINGS* program to print *'I CANNOT UNDERSTAND YOUR REQUEST, PLEASE TRY AGAIN'* and branch to line 1, set

```
    □ELX←'MESSAGE◊→TOP'
    MESSAGE←'I CANNOT UNDERSTAND YOUR REQUEST, PLEASE TRY AGAIN'
```

```
        SAVINGS
ENTER PRINCIPAL, INTEREST RATE AND NUMBER OF PERIODS
□:
        1000 .08 4.5
I CANNOT UNDERSTAND YOUR REQUEST, PLEASE TRY AGAIN

ENTER PRINCIPAL, INTEREST RATE AND NUMBER OF PERIODS
□:
        1000 .08 5
BALANCE EACH PERIOD   1080.00 1166.40 1259.71 1360.49 1469.33
```

Now, when an error happens, regardless of what error it is, whatever is in $\Box ELX$ gets executed rather than the normal system behavior of displaying the diagnostic message and halting. You can even take different actions depending on the type of error, since $\Box DM$ (next section) holds the text of the *diagnostic message*. $\Box ELX$'s default value is '$\Box DM$'; that is, display the error message (and halt execution).

A similar facility is found on APL2. There the dyadic system function $\Box EA$ (for execute *alternate*) is used. Its right argument is the APL expression you wish to compute; and its left argument is what to do if there is an exception in the right argument.

```
        ∇SAVINGS[4] '→ERCODE' □EA 'CF←P×(1+I)*⍳N'
[5]     →0 ⍝ NORMAL EXIT
[6]     ERCODE:'I CANNOT UNDERSTAND YOUR REQUEST, PLEASE TRY AGAIN'
[7]     →TOP ∇
```

Analyzing the diagnostic message

For both versions above, the same treatment was given without regard to the type of the exception or where it happened. Most professional applications benefit by more detailed analysis of the nature of the exception; depending on what happened it might be possible to make changes and move on. For example, you might decide that a noninteger N could be rounded up, but other exceptions, such as character data, should result in a halt.

Both APL*PLUS and APL2 capture the most recent diagnostic message, albeit somewhat differently. On the APL*PLUS System, the system variable $\Box DM$ is a character vector holding the last *diagnostic message* encountered ($\Box DM$ is an empty vector if no exceptions have happened). On APL2, the same information is in the system variable $\Box EM$ (for event *message*), but as a character matrix. $\Box EM$ starts out as 3 0⍴' '.

```
    ρ□DM ⍝ APL*PLUS SYSTEMS          ρ□EM ⍝ APL2 SYSTEM
63                              3 25
    □DM                             □EM
DOMAIN ERROR                    DOMAIN ERROR
SAVINGS[4]  CF←P×(1+I)*⍳N        SAVINGS[4]   CF←P×(1+I)*⍳N
              ∧                              ∧
```

The first row of $\Box EM$ contains the error message, the second the offending statement, and in the third carets point to where the error occurred and the extent of the execution prior to the error. There may be further information in following rows.

```
    ⍎'1 2+3 4 5'
LENGTH ERROR
    1 2+3 4 5
    ∧   ∧
    ⍎'1 2+3 4 5'
    ρ□EM
5 18
```

APL2 provides additional information about the most recent event or exception with $\Box ET$, for event type. Its value starts as 0 0, and is reset by each error. At this writing, there are 32 codes:

0 0	No error		3 1	*VALUE*, name with no value
0 1	Unclassified (monadic *□ES*)		3 2	*VALUE*, no result for function
1 1	*INTERRUPT* (attn)			
1 2	*SYSTEM ERROR*		4 1	Implicit *□PP ERROR*
1 3	*WS FULL*		4 2	Implicit *□IO ERROR*
1 4	*SYSTEM LIMIT*, symbol table		4 3	Implicit *□CT ERROR*
1 5	*SYSTEM LIMIT*, shares		4 4	Implicit *□FC ERROR*
1 6	*SYSTEM LIMIT*, interface quota		4 5	Implicit *□RL ERROR*
1 7	*SYSTEM LIMIT*, interface capacity		4 6	Implicit *□MD ERROR*
1 8	*SYSTEM LIMIT*, array rank		4 7	Implicit *□PR ERROR*
1 9	*SYSTEM LIMIT*, array size			
1 10	*SYSTEM LIMIT*, array depth		5 1	*VALENCE ERROR*
1 11	*SYSTEM LIMIT*, prompt length		5 2	*RANK ERROR*
			5 3	*LENGTH ERROR*
2 1	*SYNTAX*, no array (3÷)		5 4	*DOMAIN ERROR*
2 2	*SYNTAX*, ill-formed line [( ]		5 5	*INDEX ERROR*
2 3	*SYNTAX*, name class 13←*A*		5 6	*AXIS ERROR*
2 4	*SYNTAX*, context (*X←Y*)←0			

Controlling interruptions

APL*PLUS Systems treat differently those exceptions caused by errors and those caused by the user pressing BREAK or ATTN. *□ALX*, for *attention latent expression*, works like *□ELX*, but traps only BREAKs. You would use it to prevent a program from halting in a critical section, such as an update of a database. For instance, place the statements *GLOBSW←0* ◊ *□ELX←'→RESUME'* prior to the critical section, with this program to handle the interruption:

```
       ∇Z←RESUME;□ALX
[1]    □ALX←'→□LC' ◊ GLOBSW←1 ⍝ LOCAL □ALX TO PREVENT SECOND INTERRUPTION HERE
[2]    'I AM WORKING ON A CRITICAL PART OF YOUR JOB'
[3]    'AND WILL HALT WHEN I GET TO A SAFE PLACE'
[4]    Z←1↓(0≠□LC)/□LC ∇
```

At the end of the critical section, reset *□ALX* to turn off its current action (if it was not localized), and test *GLOBSW* to see if an interrupt had been deferred.

Interruptions in APL2 are handled with *□EA* and the detection of the code 1 1 in *□ET*. There is also a dyadic *□FX* (*fix*) that can make a function uninterruptable. The left argument is a four-element vector consisting of ones and zeros signifying whether certain properties are active or not:

element	effect
1	function cannot be displayed or edited
2	function cannot be suspended
3	weak interrupts (attn or break) are ignored
4	most errors are changed to *DOMAIN ERROR*

A left argument value of 0 0 0 0 is equivalent to a normal unlocked function, and a value of 1 1 1 1 is equivalent to using ⍫ to lock the function. In particular, setting element three to 1 prevents interruptions in the function.

□FX's right argument requirements will be covered later in this chapter, but for now you can impose the effects you want using sequences like 0 1 1 0 *□FX □CR 'FNNAME'*, where *FNNAME* is the name of the unlocked function that you want to make uninterruptable.

Simulating events

Sometimes when testing a new application system, you may need to simulate an error or event even though one hasn't happened. Or you may want the application to signal an exception to the function which called the currently executing function. The unmodified hypotenuse program below will display a diagnostic message and halt if its arguments disagree in shape or rank, or if either is character:

```
      )LOAD 1 CLASS
SAVED  14.45.33 02/20/83

      1 2 3 HYP 'ABC'
DOMAIN ERROR
HYP[1]  C←((A*2)+B*2)*0.5
                  ∧
      )RESET
```

Suppose we don't want to leave the function suspended, but prefer instead to compose a friendlier message and pass it to the calling environment. □ERROR is an APL*PLUS monadic system function whose character argument is the message to be carried back to the calling environment; it will be displayed as though it were the diagnostic message.

```
      ∇HYP[0] C←A HYP B;□ELX
[1]   [.1]□ELX←'□ERROR ''PLEASE REENTER WITH A DIFFERENT '',(∧\□DM≠'' '')/□DM'∇
      3 5 HYP 4 12
5 13
      1 2 3 HYP 4 12
PLEASE REENTER WITH A DIFFERENT LENGTH
      1 2 3 HYP 4 12
             ∧
      □DM
PLEASE REENTER WITH A DIFFERENT LENGTH
      1 2 3 HYP 4 12
             ∧
```

In the above example, □ERROR doesn't actually get invoked unless an exception occurs which wakes up □ELX. If □ERROR's argument is empty, then □ERROR does not become effective. This feature can be used to conveniently control conditional use of the facility.

In APL2, the event simulation system function is □ES. In its dyadic form, the left argument is the character vector message to be carried back to the calling environment. The right argument is usually a two-element integer vector which sets □ET.

Here is HYP in APL2 form:

```
      ∇C←A HYP2 B
[1]   'ALT' □EA 'C←((A*2)+B*2)*.5'∇
      ∇ALT;ERTEXT
[1]   ERTEXT←(∧\(□EM[1;]≠' ')/□EM[1;] ⍝ UP TO FIRST SPACE
[2]   ('PLEASE REENTER WITH A DIFFERENT ',ERTEXT) □ES □ET ∇
```

As with □ERROR, if □ES's right argument is an empty vector, then □ES does not become effective, permitting conditional control.

□ES also has a monadic form whose argument may be a character vector or scalar or a zero or two-element integer vector. Non-empty character vectors are displayed and an error condition generated in the statement executing the function containing □ES. □ET is set to 0 1 (unclassified). If the argument of □ES is a two-element integer vector, it goes into □ET and an event simulation generated in the statement executing the function containing □ES, along with an error message if the argument is a legitimate error code for □ET. Finally, if the argument is 0 0, the workspace is cleared unless the error is trapped with □EA.

Controlling the environment

Normally, when a user signs onto an APL system, the terminal keyboard becomes 'open' to the user's taking control of the session. There are circumstances, however, where it is undesirable for the user to have such power. An automated banking application, for instance, would be chaotic if a customer were to gain control: he might break the bank!

We have already seen some control mechanisms in □EA, □ELX and □ALX. Once a program starts running, control can be maintained with these. Still to be considered are ways to start a session under complete control, and how to keep control when a function completes.

The latent expression and variants of workspace loading

The system variable $\square LX$ causes a workspace to 'come out running' in the sense that when it is loaded, a designated APL expression begins executing immediately:

```
      )CLEAR
CLEAR WS
      )COPY 1 CLASS SPELL SPL GO
SAVED  14.45.33 02/20/83

      ∇GO[□]∇
   ∇ GO
[1]   'TIME FOR YOUR SPELLING EXERCISE!'
[2]   □RL←⌈1000×□TS[6]
[3]   SPELL
   ∇

      □LX←'GO'
      )SAVE SPELIT
  14.43.44 02/26/83
```

The *latent* expression can be any APL expression held in a character vector. It is executed when the workspace is loaded, as seen from the following display:

```
      )LOAD SPELIT
SAVED  14.43.44 02/26/83

TIME FOR YOUR SPELLING EXERCISE!
5
FIVE
THATS RIGHT

8
EIGHT
THATS RIGHT
2
STOP
```

Besides making the use of application and tutorial workspaces convenient for non-APLers, the latent expression provides a valuable assist to restarting critical applications after a communications line failure. Since $\square LX$ can be reassigned any number of times, you can store anticipatory resumption instructions in it. Particularly in shared file or shared variable applications (Chapters 27 and 28), you will probably need different resumption actions depending on whether a sequence of file updating statements was completed or not.

When a user signs on again after a line failure, his $CONTINUE$ workspace is loaded for him, and the latent expression executes. It may reactivate relevant files, and it should branch into the interrupted program at whatever line is appropriate (within noncritical sequences), or it should force a complete restart if there is no way to resume at the interruption.

On the APL*PLUS System, $\square LX$ can be used in conjunction with $\square LOAD$, $\square QLOAD$ and $\square XLOAD$ to develop application systems that encompass many workspaces, loading the next one automatically. Each initiates loading of a designated workspace. The argument is the name (and number and lock, if necessary) of the workspace to be loaded. An example is $\square LOAD$ '1 $CLASS$'. $\square LOAD$ and $\square QLOAD$ operate identically, except that $\square LOAD$ prints the $SAVED$ message while $\square QLOAD$ does not.

Usually, the succeeding workspaces are saved with a latent expression set by the author of the application system. Just prior to executing $\square LOAD$, all pertinent intermediate data is placed on a file. Then $\square LOAD$ brings in the next workspace, and the latent expression brings in the data that was placed on the file and executes the main function of that workspace. Using these techniques, very large applications are tackled conveniently and economically.

$\square XLOAD$ and its companion system command $)XLOAD$ cause the workspace to be loaded without the latent expression being activated. This is so that the application developer has a way to maintain the programs in an unencumbered manner. Only the owner of a workspace can load it with $\square XLOAD$ or $)XLOAD$; other users are prohibited for security considerations.

Keeping control when the program stops

When a function stops running because of an untrapped exception or interruption, or a simulated event, or a $\Box STOP$, or even a normal finish, control is usually turned over to the user. But in some applications (or for some users) this may not be desirable; you may want the user to be prohibited from free-form use of the system, constraining him to the use of specific applications only. A global declaration of $\Box EA$ or $\Box ELX$ or $\Box ALX$ (perhaps in $\Box LX$ itself) will trap the exceptions. What remains to be discussed is what to do with the session if it can't be resumed or if the application has completed normally.

On APL2 you can force a $CLEAR\ WS$ by using an expression like ($'CLEARING\ THE\ WORKSPACE'$ $\Box ES$ 0 0) as the left argument to $\Box EA$. That is, a $\Box ES$ right argument of 0 0 is a special signal to clear the active workspace. This prevents users from poking around in the functions.

APL*PLUS systems clear the active workspace with the expression $\Box SA$ $'CLEAR'$. $\Box SA$ (for stop action) operates in a latent manner; that is, you can set it early in the program but it doesn't become effective until the function is about to halt. Of course, if you had set $\Box ELX$ or $\Box ALX$ they would dominate. $\Box SA$ is the ultimate tool to use where $\Box ELX$ or $\Box ALX$ haven't been set, or where they themselves fail, or when the function completes normally.

Besides $\Box SA$ $'CLEAR'$ you can use $\Box SA$ $'EXIT'$ to have the same effect as $\rightarrow$ (i.e., clearing the $\Box SI$ to the most recent suspension), or $\Box SA$ $'OFF'$ to sign off the system, or $\Box SA$ $''$ to reset its original, default condition of no stop action.

Automatic program generation and modification

Since the earliest days of the stored program computer there has been speculation (mostly in jest, but some serious) about when computers would become self-perpetuating. We will not join this discussion here, except to note that one technological requirement for that to happen would be the ability of a computer to write computer programs by itself.

No, your APL system can't write or modify programs without your active participation. But it can reduce the amount of work you do by taking over virtually all aspects of the job except thinking. As such, your APL computer is considerably more than the mindless assistant we described in the opening pages of this book.

The rest of this chapter considers programs that help write programs and modify programs. The need for this ability is apparent: suppose you had written a 30-line function making frequent use of a local variable P and you now wish to change every occurrence of it to T. Or you may want to include in a function you are developing large chunks of other, existing functions. Making those changes manually is tedious work.

To modify a program, we will first convert it to a character variable because it is easy to make changes to character variables in APL. For example, to change all occurrences of the letter P in the vector VEC to T, use $VEC[(VEC='P')/\iota\rho VEC]\leftarrow'T'$. Then after the desired changes are made, the character variable is reconverted to a defined function.

The system function $\Box CR$ (for canonical representation) produces a character matrix in which each row is a line of the function.

```
)LOAD 1 CLASS                          XSUB←□CR 'SUB'
SAVED  14.45.33 02/20/83               ρXSUB
                                       11 30
      ∇SUB[□]∇                         XSUB
    ∇ SUB;HELP;STOP;P1;P2;BR           SUB;HELP;STOP;P1;P2;BR
[1]   HELP←001 ◊ STOP←0001             HELP←001 ◊ STOP←0001
[2]   L2:P1←?20 ◊ P2←¯1+?P1+1          L2:P1←?20 ◊ P2←¯1+?P1+1
[3]   (⍕P1),'-',⍕P2                    (⍕P1),'-',⍕P2
[4]   L4:BR←(1↑,□)=(P1-P2),HELP,STOP    L4:BR←(1↑,□)=(P1-P2),HELP,STOP
[5]   →BR/OK,HELP,0                    →BR/OK,HELP,0
[6]   (⍕P2),' +___  = ',(⍕P1)          (⍕P2),' +___  = ',(⍕P1)
[7]   'TRY AGAIN' ◊ →L4                'TRY AGAIN' ◊ →L4
[8]   OK:'THATS RIGHT' ◊ →L2           OK:'THATS RIGHT' ◊ →L2
[9]   HELP:(P1ρ'○'),' TAKE AWAY'       HELP:(P1ρ'○'),' TAKE AWAY'
[10]  P2ρ'○' ◊ →L4                     P2ρ'○' ◊ →L4
    ∇
```

The name of the function to be worked on must be supplied as a character vector argument. There doesn't have to be any relation between the name of the function being converted and the name of the result, but you may find it convenient to choose related names.

The function header line becomes the first row of the result. Line numbers themselves, as well as the starting and closing ∇s, are stripped off. Each line of the function is left-justified, and the column dimension is determined by the number of characters in the longest line.

When you have a canonical representation of a function, you can apply all the character-manipulating tricks of APL to do function editing and searching for patterns. You could, for example, find the row and column positions of each occurrence of the letter *P* with this sequence:

```
    1+(ρXSUB)⊤¯1+('P'=,XSUB)/ιρ,XSUB
 1  1  1  1  2  2  3  3  3  4  4  5  5  5  5  6  7  7 10 10 11
 8 13 15 18  4 15  4 13 20  3 12 15 18 25 30 11  3 21  4  7  1
```

Let's change the message *TAKE AWAY* to *SUBTRACT* (note that line 9 of the function is row 10 of its character representation):

```
    XSUB[10;]←(1↓ρXSUB)↑'HELP:(P1ρ''∘''),'' SUBTRACT'''
```

We haven't changed the function *SUB* yet. All we've done is change the variable *XSUB*. A canonical representation is converted to a function by the monadic system function □*FX*, for *fix*:

```
    □FX XSUB
SUB
```

If the canonical representation is proper, □*FX* returns a character vector consisting of the name of the function. That the function has been replaced becomes obvious by displaying part of it in the normal manner:

```
    ∇SUB[□8]∇
[8]   OK:'THATS RIGHT' ◊ →L2
[9]   HELP:(P1ρ'∘'),' SUBTRACT'
[10]  ¯P2ρ'∘' ◊ →L4
    ∇
```

The canonical representation being converted to a function must be properly formed. If the argument is numeric, you get *DOMAIN ERROR*. If it isn't a matrix, you get *RANK ERROR*. You can fix suspended or pendent functions, but no change takes place in the definition until execution is completed. It's best to clear the state indicator before making changes to functions.

Other errors, such as improperly formed headers, blank rows, unmatched quotes and characters which cannot be entered in normal function definition mode (like backspace) get you an explicit numeric result indicating the first row of the function that is causing the problem. To help catch these kinds of errors, people frequently use tools like this one to 'cover' □*FX*:

```
    ∇FIX[□]∇
    ∇ FIX X;Z
[1]   →(' '=1↑0ρZ←□FX X)/0
[2]   'CANNOT CONVERT ';X;' ERROR AT ';Z
    ∇
```

Besides □*CR*, APL*PLUS Systems offer □*VR*, for *vector representation*. Like □*CR*, it is monadic, and its argument is a character vector holding the name of a function. The result of □*VR* is a character vector, which when displayed looks exactly as though you had displayed the function in the normal manner. Both the starting and trailing ∇'s are in the vector. Also present are the line numbers in brackets, and a new line character at the end of each line. □*VR*'s result usually requires less space than that of □*CR* because there is no 'padding' to fill out short lines. Which one to use in a given application depends on space considerations and whether what you want to do is easier with the function in vector form or matrix form. Generally speaking, use □*CR* if you are displaying or changing entire lines; use □*VR* if the changes tend to be less structured. Doing things like changing all occurrences of *P*1 to *FIRSTNUM* is much easier with □*VR* than with □*CR*.

Here is a very useful function employing □*VR* to search and modify functions. It employs *CHANGE* (page 231) to do the actual modification of the character vector *TEXT*:

```
    □VR 'FUNEDIT'
    ∇ R←FUNEDIT X;TEXT;REPLY
[1]   ⍝PROTOTYPE MODEL OF APL*PLUS WS 11 FNED FNED
[2]   ⍝ORIGINAL BY J. M. SPENCER AND C. E. YATES
```

```
[3]    START:TEXT←⎕VR X ◇ →(' '=1↑0ρTEXT)/REWORK ◇ 'CANNOT EDIT ',X ◇ →0
[4]    REWORK:TEXT[(TEXT=⎕TCNL)/⍳ρTEXT]←'⊞' ◇ 'USE ⊞ TO STAND FOR CARRIER RETURN'
[5]    TEXT←CHANGE TEXT ⍝ LET USER EDIT AS HE WISHES.
[6]    TEXT[(TEXT='⊞')/⍳ρTEXT]←⎕TCNL ⍝REPLACE CARRIER RETURNS
[7]    R←⎕DEF TEXT ⍝ ATTEMPT TO RECONSTITUTE FUNCTION
[8]    →(' '=1↑0ρR)/0 ⍝ IF CHARACTER RESULT IT WAS SUCCESSFUL.
[9]    →(E1,E2,E3,E4,E5,E6,E7)[1↑R] ⍝EXPLAIN ERRORS
[10]   E1:'WS FULL: NOT ENOUGH ROOM FOR THE FUNCTION DEFINITION.' ◇ →EX
[11]   E2:'DEFN ERROR: MALFORMED HEADER; FN NAME IN USE; MISSING OR EXTRA ∇ OR ⍢;'
[12]      'MISSING A LINE NUMBER [N]; OR NONCONSECUTIVE LINE NUMBERS' ◇ →EX
[13]   E3:'CHAR ERROR: CONTAINS CHARACTER SUCH AS ⎕TCNL OR ⎕TCBS' ◇ →EX
[14]   E4:'SYMBOL TABLE FULL: CREATING THE FUNCTION WOULD REQUIRE MORE'
[15]      'SYMBOL TABLE ENTRIES THAN ARE AVAILABLE' ◇ →EX
[16]   E5:'UNMATCHED QUOTES: THERE IS AN ODD NUMBER OF QUOTES' ◇ →EX
[17]   E6:'*** UNUSED ⎕VR ERROR CODE.  ERROR IN CHANGE PROGRAM'
[18]      'ABANDONING EFFORT.  CONTACT A. J. ROSE.' ◇ →0
[19]   E7:'EMPTY LINE: NO TEXT BETWEEN TWO CARRIAGE RETURNS' ◇ →EX
[20]   EX:'ERROR OCCURRED AROUND POSITION ',⍕R[2]
[21]   PROMPT:⍞←'REWORK, START OVER, QUIT? ' ◇ REPLY←1↑⍞
[22]     →(REWORK,START,0,PROMPT)['RSQ'⍳REPLY]
       ∇
```

Rather than using ⎕FX, line 7 of FUNEDIT uses ⎕DEF (define), a somewhat more powerful cousin of ⎕FX on the APL*PLUS System. It can accept matrices and properly formed character vectors as its argument. A vector must be similar to the result of ⎕VR. New line characters not contained within quotes are used to mark the lines of the function. The characters up to the first new line character make up the function header. Headers must begin with a ∇ or ⍢ (if ⍢, then the function is created as a locked function). As in the result of ⎕VR, the lines of the argument must be numbered consecutively beginning with 1, and must be contained within brackets. A trailing ∇ or ⍢ is required, and it may appear on or after the last numbered line.

If ⎕DEF can't convert its argument to a function, its result is a two-element numeric vector. The first element is the error code (see lines 10-19 of FUNEDIT). The second element is the location of the error—the character position for a vector argument, or the row number for a matrix argument.

Local functions

The example here creates, executes and discards a local function:

```
     ∇XSLOPE[⎕]∇
     ∇ Z←X∆X XSLOPE F;X;∆X;F;SINK
[1]    ⍝ CALCULATES SLOPE OF CURVE F AT POINT X.
[2]    X←1↓X∆X ◇ ∆X←X∆X[1]
[3]    SINK←⎕FX F
[4]    Z←((F X)-F X-∆X)÷∆X
     ∇
     (.0001,⍳5) XSLOPE 2 13ρ'Y←F X          Y←(3×X*2)+5×X'
10.9997 16.9997 22.9997 28.9997 34.9997
```

Line 3 of the function is the important one here. The character matrix right argument of XSLOPE, F, was made into the function F. The explicit result of ⎕FX is stored in SINK simply to avoid its being implicitly displayed. Another way to suppress it is 0 0ρ⎕FX F.

Then line 3 was executed, and we got the expected result. However, were we to display)FNS after the execution, we find that the function F isn't there. That's because it was declared to be a local function by the presence of F in the header. And like any local variable, when the function XSLOPE finishes executing, F disappears and the space it had taken is freed up.

The slope example we used here is a trivial one, because ⍢ does it more directly. But remember that ⍢ can handle only one line at a time, and it is clumsy with branching, while ⎕FX has no such restrictions.

An important use of local functions is storing functions in their character array representation as components of an APL file, and bringing into the workspace only those needed for the particular job at the time they are needed.

Local functions follow the same conventions as local variables. You can have a global and a local function with the same name. The display of a function using ⎕CR or ⎕VR displays the local version.

Erasing objects under program control

Functions, variables and group can be erased with the $)ERASE$ system command, but like all system commands this requires manual intervention. The monadic system function $\Box EX$ (for *expunge*) is provided to erase functions and variables under program control.

To erase a function named $STAT$ from the workspace, use $\Box EX$ '$STAT$'. You can erase several things at once by making the argument a character matrix with each row an object to be erased. On APL*PLUS Systems the argument can also be a character vector in which spaces separate names to be erased.

$\Box EX$ always returns a vector of 1's and 0's whose length matches the number of names in the argument. 1 means that the object either didn't exist in the first place or that it was successfully erased. 0 means that the object either could not be erased ($\Box EX$ won't let you erase a label or group, or (except in APL2) a function that is currently in the state indicator). And it won't work if the name you supplied was an impossible one, such as $23SKIDOO$. $\Box EX$ operates on the most local version of the object, while $)ERASE$ operates only on global objects.

Locking functions

$\Box DEF$ produces a locked function if the argument is in vector form and $\nabla\!\!\!\!\sim$ is used instead of the starting or ending ∇. However, there is no way to contain locking instructions in the matrix form. For this reason the $\Box LOCK$ system function is provided on the APL*PLUS System. Its argument is a character vector or matrix holding the names of the functions to be locked. The result is an empty matrix (its shape is $0\ \ 0$) if all the names were in fact functions; otherwise it is a character matrix holding the names that could not be locked. APL2 provides dyadic $\Box FX$ for locking functions. The right argument is the canonical representation of the function to be locked, and the left argument is a four element binary vector (see **page 300**). If the first element is a 1, the function will be locked.

Name list and name classification

We have just seen how functions can be created, modified and erased using $\Box CR$, $\Box FX$, $\Box VR$, $\Box DEF$, $\Box LOCK$ and $\Box EX$. They wield substantial power over their weaker brothers, the system commands and ∇ editing of Chapter 10, particularly because they can be executed under program control. To complement these facilities, some inquiry functions are also provided. The first is $\Box NL$, for *name list*. The argument of $\Box NL$ is the class of the object you are inquiring about. Its result is a character matrix holding names of objects satisfying the inquiry.

$\Box NL$ can be either monadic or dyadic. If monadic, the right argument is a scalar or vector of coded values (1 for labels, 2 for variables and 3 for functions) of the classes of objects you are trying to list. For example, to find all function and variable names in the workspace, use $R\leftarrow\Box NL\ 2\ 3$. The most local definition of the object is used.

When $\Box NL$ is used in dyadic form, the left argument is a character vector or scalar. Only objects whose names start with a character in the left argument are returned. Thus, to get a list of all labels starting with P or Q or R, use $LIST\leftarrow'PQR\ '\Box NL\ 1$.

The monadic system function $\Box NC$ is closely related to $\Box NL$. The argument is a character matrix of names (APL*PLUS Systems also allow a character vector), and the result is a numeric vector telling how each of the names is used. The most local use of the names is given.

result	interpretation
0	The name is not in use at this level of the state indicator, and hence can be used to define a function, label, variable or group.
1	The name is in use as a label.
2	The name is in use as a variable.
3	The name is in use as a function.
4	The name is not available for use (i.e., it is a group, and the state indicator is empty and the name is not shielded, or the name is not properly formed).

In APL2, $\Box NL$ and $\Box NC$ have been extended. $\Box NL$ accepts 4 as an argument to list defined operators (page 212), and $\Box NC$ returns $^-1$ for an invalid name. The return code of 4 for $\Box NC$ means the name is in use as a defined operator. There is also a related system command $)NMS$. An example of its use is $)NMS\ PE\ ST$, which lists the names of all global variables, defined functions and defined operators from PE through ST (optional), along with an integer designating the name class.

Functions on files

Here is the key part of a system for using functions stored on files (see Chapters 26 and 27) as a means of conserving workspace. The general idea is to pull in functions only when they are needed, and to erase functions when required to make room for new ones. Component one of the file is a directory holding the names of the functions that are on file.

```
      ∇GETFN[□]∇
    ∇ Z←NAME GETFN FILENO;IF;ROWMATCH;DIR;SINK;STK;CANERASE;HOWMANY;LOCVEC;SIZES
[1]   ⍝BRINGS FN NAME IN FROM FILE FILENO [IF IT CAN]   AJROSE NOV 82
[2]   ⍝FIRST COMPONENT OF FILE IS DIRECTORY MATRIX;
[3]   ⍝   FIRST ROW IS '***DIRECTORY'
[4]   ⍝   OTHER ROWS HOLD FN NAMES; ROW INDEX IS COMPONENT NO.
[5]   ⍝RESULT CODES:   1 IF SUCCESSFUL, NAME ASSEMBLED
[6]   ⍝   2 NAME ALREADY IN WS      3 ERROR, NAME NOT ON FILE
[7]   ⍝   4 ERROR, NOT ENOUGH WS    5 ERROR IN FILED FUNCTION
[8]   SINK←□DEF 2 8 ρ'Z←B IF C   Z←C/B ' ⍝ IF IS A LOCAL FN
[9]   SINK←'∇Z←L ROWMATCH R',□TCNL ⍝ROWMATCH IS A LOCAL FN
[10]  SINK←□DEF SINK,'[1]Z←1+(¯1↑ρL)⌈¯1↑ρR◊Z←(((¯1↑ρL),Z)↑L)∧.
=(Z,1↓⍉ρR)↑⍉R∇',□TCNL
[11]  NAME←(NAME≠' ')/NAME ◊ Z←2 ◊ →0 IF∨/(□NL 3) ROWMATCH NAME ⍝IF ALREADY IN WS
[12]  DIR←□FREAD FILENO,1 ◊ LOCVEC←DIR ROWMATCH NAME
[13]  →(∨/LOCVEC)/L1 ◊ Z←3 ◊ →0 ⍝ IF NAME NOT IN FILE
[14]  L1:STK←□SI ⍝BUT MUST REMOVE ALL BUT THE FN NAMES FROM IT
[15]  STK←(ρSTK)ρ(,∧\STK≠'[')\(,∧\STK≠'[')/,STK
[16]  →L3 IF □WA>5000
[17]  ⍝THIS IS THE TRICKY PART.  TRY TO ERASE FNS TO MAKE SOME ROOM.
[18]  ⍝ERASE LARGEST FNS THAT ARE IN WS, ON FILE, BUT NOT IN STK.
[19]  CANERASE←(∨/(□NL 3) ROWMATCH DIR)≠□NL 3
[20]  CANERASE←(~∨/CANERASE ROWMATCH STK)≠CANERASE
[21]  SIZES←□SIZE CANERASE
[22]  HOWMANY←1++/(+\SIZES[⍒SIZES])<5000-□WA ⍝ERASE AT LEAST 5000 BYTES
[23]  →L2 IF HOWMANY≤ρSIZES ◊ Z←4 ◊ →0
[24]  L2:SINK←□EX CANERASE[HOWMANY↑⍒SIZES;]
[25]  L3:SINK←□DEF □FREAD FILENO,(DIR ROWMATCH NAME)⍳1
[26]  Z← 1 5[1+0=1↑0ρSINK] ⍝ IF NUMERIC RESULT, IT WAS UNSUCCESSFUL
    ∇
```

Here is a narrative of what happens. If the function is already in the workspace, exit (line 11). Otherwise, check if the function is in the file: if it isn't, exit (lines 12 and 13). If there was no exit, clean up the execution stack (lines 14 and 15) for later use. If there aren't 5000 bytes of storage available (line 16), try to make space by erasing the largest functions which are reconstitutable and not in the execution stack (lines 19 through 22). If there is not enough space after that attempt, exit (line 23). Finally, erase the old function (line 24) and bring the new function from the file (line 25), and exit with result code (line 26).

This function was written to be an expository prototype rather than a comprehensive production program. In particular, *GETFN* can't deal with functions whose names conflict with local variables. This problem is usually circumvented in production systems by using very unlikely (and unmnemonic) names for the locals such as Δ1, Δ2, Δ3, etc.

Two local functions are embedded in *GETFN. IF* (line 8) is kept in □CR form, while *ROWMATCH* (lines 9 and 10) is kept in □VR form. There was no particular reason for the choice of forms in this example except to demonstrate both forms to the reader.

GETFN employs □SIZE on line 21 to help determine which functions should be erased, the idea being to erase a few large ones rather than a lot of little ones. □SIZE finds the amount of space used by objects in the workspace. The right argument is either a character vector with the names separated by blanks, or a character matrix with one name per row. The result is a numeric vector, one element per name holding the number of bytes used. Unused names result in a zero, while for groups the value is the sum of the space taken up by the individual objects, plus some overhead for the group name itself.

Execute

This monadic function, whose symbol is ⍎, is a partial alternative to $\Box FX$ or $\Box DEF$ in that it allows the direct evaluation of character vectors. Indeed, its argument is a character vector (or scalar), and the result (explicit or not) is what would have happened if you had entered the characters in calculator mode. Compare these examples:

```
      A←ι5            ⍎'A←ι5'           A←⍎'ι5'
      R←A+2           ⍎'R←A+2'          R←⍎'A+2'
      R               R                 ⍎'R'
3 4 5 6 7       3 4 5 6 7         3 4 5 6 7
```

When used within a function, statements like `[5] X←⍎'3+Y'` or `[8] →⍎'LOOP'` are equivalent to `[5] X←3+Y` or `[8] →LOOP`.

You can overcome APL's limit of two arguments per function by passing a character matrix holding the names, all in one argument. Here, for example, is a function that displays whatever information (such as shape, datatype, size, etc.) is requested about named objects in the workspace:

```
      ∇SHOWME[□]∇
    ∇ LIST SHOWME ACTION;OBJ
[1]   ⍎(2≠⍴⍴LIST)/'LIST←(ι0) ROWNAMES LIST' ⍝CONDITIONAL EXECUTION.
[2]   LOOP:→(0=1↑⍴LIST)/0 ◇ OBJ←LIST[1;] ◇ LIST← 1 0 ↓LIST
[3]   OBJ ◇ OBJ←⍎OBJ ◇ ⍎ACTION ◇ →LOOP
    ∇
```

```
      ' TAB0 TAB1 TAB2 TAB3' SHOWME '''RANK='',(⍕⍴⍴OBJ),''  SHAPE='',⍕⍴OBJ'
TAB0
RANK=0    SHAPE=
TAB1
RANK=1    SHAPE=4
TAB2
RANK=2    SHAPE=4 3
TAB3
RANK=3    SHAPE=2 4 3
```

Execute is frequently used as an alternative to simple conditional branching as it was on line 1 of $SHOWME$. Now for another example, in which if the variable DC doesn't exist, it is created as the vector 1 1, but if DC already exists, nothing is done: `⍎(0=□NC 'DC')/'DC←1 1'`. Can you see how inclusion of this expression in the function DO (**page 156**) eliminates the need for $SETDO$ for initialization?

Execute is useful for numerical approximations to the functions of calculus because the *form* of an expression (rather than the *value*) can be used as an argument. The mathematical representation of the slope of a function f(X),

$$\frac{F(x + \Delta x) - F(x)}{\Delta x}$$

can be evaluated with the following function. Note that the left argument of $ESLOPE$ passes the formula to the function, avoiding having to hard-code the formula in $ESLOPE$.

```
      ∇ESLOPE[□]∇
    ∇ Z←FX ESLOPE XΔX;FX;FXΔX;ΔX
[1]   ⍝RIGHT ARG IS 2-ELE VECTOR X AND ΔX    AJROSE NOV 82
[2]   ⍝LEFT ARG IS FORMULA IN TERMS OF X.
[3]   X←XΔX[1] ◇ ΔX←XΔX[2]
[4]   FX←⍎FX ⍝EVALUATE AT X
[5]   X←X-ΔX
[6]   FXΔX←⍎FX ⍝EVALUATE AT X-ΔX
[7]   Z←(FX-FXΔX)÷ΔX
    ∇
```

```
      '(3×X*2)+5×X' ESLOPE 4 .001
28.997
      '(3×X*2)+5×X' ESLOPE 4 .00001
28.99997
```

This function can be adapted to handle more than one X and ΔX with this change,

```
∇ESLOPE[3] X←XΔX[1;;] ◊ ΔX←XΔX[2;;]∇
```

which expects the right argument to be a three-dimensional array whose first plane is X values and whose second plane is ΔX values.

The function $SLAM$ can be used to format sets of X's and ΔX's together:

```
∇SLAM[□]∇
∇ XΔX←X SLAM ΔX
[1]    ⍝USED IN CONJUNCTION WITH SLOPE FUNCTIONS.  AJR NOV 82
[2]    X←,X ◊ ΔX←,ΔX ⍝ MAKE ARGUMENTS VECTORS.
[3]    XΔX←(⍉((ρΔX),ρX)ρX),[0.5]((ρX),ρΔX)ρΔX
∇
```

```
      4 5 6 SLAM .01 .001 .0001 .00001
4.000000000E0     4.000000000E0     4.000000000E0     4.000000000E0
5.000000000E0     5.000000000E0     5.000000000E0     5.000000000E0
6.000000000E0     6.000000000E0     6.000000000E0     6.000000000E0

1.000000000E‾2    1.000000000E‾3    1.000000000E‾4    1.000000000E‾5
1.000000000E‾2    1.000000000E‾3    1.000000000E‾4    1.000000000E‾5
1.000000000E‾2    1.000000000E‾3    1.000000000E‾4    1.000000000E‾5

      '(3×X*2)+5×X' ESLOPE 4 5 6 SLAM .01 .001 .0001 .00001
    28.97             28.997            28.9997           28.99997
    34.97             34.997            34.9997           34.99997
    40.97             40.997            40.9997           40.99997
```

Which method of automatic program generation to use (canonical or vector representation, or execute, or direct definition) depends on three factors: what is supported on your system, your personal taste, and which technique most closely fits the job at hand. If you are anticipating moving an application from one system to another, $□CR$ and ⍎ tend to be consistent on most systems. $□VR$ differs from system to system in its fussiness (presence of new lines, starting and ending ∇'s, etc.).

PROBLEMS

1. Write a function $ARITH$ with argument $DATA$ to branch (using execute) to ADD, SUB or BAL if the first element of a vector $DATA$ is 15, 25 or 35 respectively. Otherwise, the branch is to ERR.

2. Show how execute can be used to **A** generate a new name for some data DAT, and **B** change a standard variable name NAM to $NAM1$, $NAM2$ etc. for various data D.

3. Write a function $DECOM$ to decomment any function, using $\Box CR$.

4. Rewrite the recursive function $FACT$ (page 159) using $\pounds$.

5. Generalize problem 2B to select the Ith column of an array M of unknown rank (but either 2 or 3).

6. If you have the diamond $\Diamond$ available on your system, show how to recursively execute (although inefficiently) an instruction *outside* function definition mode.

7. Write a function that will erase all functions in the workspace except those in the argument M.

8. What does $A \leftarrow \pounds (\Phi A), ' ', \Box$ do if executed within a function?

9. Define functions to edit a matrix as though it were a function.

10. Write a calling function $REPORT$ which prompts a user for the name of a report and then executes a program of the same name as the report he has chosen.

11. Define a function $OMIT$ to prompt for a matrix name and the rows to be omitted from it.

12. After loading 1 $CLASS$, define a function $DRILL$ which allows the user to choose between the exercises SUB, ADD and $SPELL$, and automatically initiates execution once a choice has been made.

13. Use execute to define a function with header $A \quad CHECK \quad B$ that prints $TRUE$ or $FALSE$ for $A > B$.

14. Edit the canonical representation of CMP in 1 $CLASS$ to change $GREATER$ to $MORE$.

15. Make HYP local to the function $RECT$ in 1 $CLASS$.

16. Construct a function $DISP$ to display automatically the canonical representations of functions beginning with specified letters.

17. Write APL instructions that force an absolute branch ($\rightarrow$) whenever there are more than six entries in the state indicator.

18. Define a function $LIST$ to display all the functions in a given workspace. (Hint: use $\Box NL$ to get the names, and convert them to character representation.)

19. Construct a dyadic function $OPROD$ to produce operation tables, given that the left argument is an APL operator and the right argument R is a two-element vector of positive integers such that the table is made up of combinations of $\iota 1 \uparrow R$ and $\iota 1 \downarrow R$.

Chapter 25: Nested arrays

Some APL systems now allow you to build *nested arrays* made up of other arrays of different shape, rank and type (i.e., mixed character and numeric). This added power doesn't come for free, however. You will have to learn new concepts about data, and quite a few new functions as well.

But it will be well worth it. For example, defined functions will now accept multiple explicit arguments and yield multiple explicit results. Numeric and character data may now be directly combined in a single variable for convenient formatting and storage. Mixed data in files is easier to read and write. The need for looping is significantly reduced. In building arrays there is no need to count characters to insure proper padding, and because padding isn't needed, storage is conserved. These are just a few of the many uses of nested arrays that illustrate, more than anything you have seen so far, the power of APL.

Mixed arrays

You learned in Chapter 13 that character and numeric data could not normally be mixed in an array. On several occasions we have discussed methods for converting from numeric to character or vice versa to compensate for the inability to handle mixed data types. You still can't mix types in most APL systems, but some newer versions have removed the restriction. For example, in APL2 and newer APL*PLUS Systems the following works:

```
      V←'T',4 12,'PEOPLE'              M←2 7ρι14
      V                               M[1;1+ι6]←'2BV~2B'
T 4 12 PEOPLE                         M
      ρV                        1 2  B  V  ~  2  B
9                               8 9 10 11 12 13 14
      V∈ι20                           M∈□AV
0 1 1 0 0 0 0 0 0          0 0 1 1 1 1 1
      V∈□AV                     0 0 0 0 0 0 0
1 0 0 1 1 1 1 1 1
```

As you can see, each position in an array can now be either character or numeric, and both types can be in the same array.

The *type* function, ∈, a new member of the family of primitive scalar monadic functions, indicates which items are numeric (returns a 0) or character (returns a blank):

```
      ∈V                              ∈M
  0 0                          0
      ρ∈V                      0 0 0 0 0 0 0
9                                   0≠∈M
      0≠∈V                     0 1 1 1 1 1 1
1 0 0 1 1 1 1 1 1             0 0 0 0 0 0 0
      ' '=∈V
1 0 0 1 1 1 1 1 1
```

You may recall that for uniform arrays (all character or all numeric), the fill element for expand and take was zero for numbers and blank for characters. For mixed arrays, the fill element is determined by the type of the first item. If the first item is numeric, the fill element is zero, while for a character first item the fill element is the blank. The fill element of an empty array is determined by the type of the most recent first item:

```
      V                        M                     ¯3 8 ↑M
T 4 12 PEOPLE             1 2  B  V  ~  2  B    0 0  0  0  0  0  0 0
      (18ρ 0 1)\V         8 9 10 11 12 13 14    1 2  B  V  ~  2  B 0
 T  4   12  P E O P L E                         8 9 10 11 12 13 14 0
```

257

All APL functions work on mixed arrays. In particular, those for selecting or rearranging require no change in thinking at all. You still can't do arithmetic on the character items, but it's very easy to compress them out. For example, you can sum all the numeric items in a vector V by $+/(0=\epsilon V)/V$.

Vector notation and nested arrays

In traditional APL, numeric vectors are implied whenever two numeric values are separated only by spaces. Thus, $V2\leftarrow4\ 12$ is a two-element uniform numeric vector. Similarly, character vectors are implied when two or more characters are surrounded by single quotes. For example, $V3\leftarrow'PEOPLE'$ is a six-element uniform character vector, while $S1\leftarrow'T'$ is a character scalar.

Nested array systems extend the concept of vector notation by allowing *variables* separated only by spaces to be regarded as the *items* of a vector. The expression $V2\ V3$ is a two-element nested vector (sometimes called a *strand*), while $V2,V3$ is an eight-element simple mixed vector.

One benefit of this extension is easier expression of commonly used idioms. Just as you would write $5\ 3\rho\iota15$ rather than $(5,3)\rho\iota15$ in traditional APL, you can now write $A\ B\ \rho\iota15$ instead of $(A,B)\rho\iota15$ (assuming A is 5 and B is 3). Seasoned APL'ers reading this section may cry heresy; however, the evidence is strong that new APL users, unbiased by habit, readily take to this notational freedom.

To encourage you to read on, see if you can figure out these examples:

```
      ρ'T', 4 12 ,'PEOPLE'
9

      ρ'T' 4 12 'PEOPLE'
4

      S1←'T' ◊ V2← 4 12 ◊ V3←'PEOPLE'
      ρS1,V2,V3
9

      ρS1 V2 V3
3
```

The expression $S1\ V2\ V3$ above—three variables with no functions between them—yielded a three-item vector. Let's capture the result to examine it more closely:

```
      NA←S1 V2 V3              NA                    ΦNA
      ρNA                   T  4 12  PEOPLE     PEOPLE  4 12  T
3
      NA[1]                    NA[2]                 NA[3]
T                          4 12                  PEOPLE
      ρρNA[1]                  ρρNA[2]               ρρNA[3]
0                          0                     0
```

The display of the result gives some clue about what's going on. Notice the extra spaces in some of the results. They indicate that the items between extra spaces are enclosed by an incredible shrinking process so that it is stored in a single array position as though it were a scalar. To make the point even more dramatic, in the APL*PLUS System NA would have been displayed as $T\ (4\ 12)\ (PEOPLE)$, the parentheses showing exactly where the nesting has occurred. From all appearances, it seems that the number vector $4\ 12$ and the character vector $'PEOPLE'$ have been enclosed so that each vector is now stored in a single array position as though it were a scalar.

The enclose function

That's exactly what happened. Each item of the result has become a nested scalar. The enclosures in our example happened as an implicit effect of vector notation, but there are also explicit ways to enclose arrays to make them nested scalars. The *enclose* function is the monadic use of the symbol $\subset$:

```
        S3←⊂'PEOPLE'  ⍝  OR  S3←NA[3]
        ρS3

        ρρS3
0
        S3
  PEOPLE
```

Because *S*3 is a scalar, its contents can be stored in a single position of any array:

```
        M                              M[2;3]
1 2    B    ∨    ∼    2    B       10
8 9  10  11  12  13  14                M[2;4]
        M[2;4]←S3                PEOPLE
        M                              M[2; 3 4]
  1 2    B   ∨          ∼    2    B    10   PEOPLE
   8 9  10    PEOPLE   12  13  14
        ρM
2 7
```

Simple scalars (contrasted to nested scalars) cannot be enclosed; for them the application of ⊂ is ignored. All other arrays can be enclosed. The result of ⊂ is always a scalar, either simple (the do-nothing case) or nested. See how the vector , '*V*' can be nested while the scalar '*S*' cannot:

```
      'S'                          ,'V'
S                          V
      ⊂'S'                         ⊂,'V'
S                          V
      ⊂⊂⊂'S'                       ⊂⊂⊂,'V'
S                              V
```

Actually, there are two major schools of thought about nested arrays, and the difference centers on whether a simple scalar can be enclosed or not. The systems described in this book are termed *floating*, and do not enclose simple scalars. Those systems that do allow scalars to be enclosed are called *grounded*. For elementary uses such as described in this book either system will do, and the differences won't be dramatic. However, for advanced use and commercial applications the distinction becomes important.

The depth function

The *depth* function, monadic ≡ (= overstruck with _), indicates the maximum nesting of an array. It always returns a scalar result. When applied to a simple scalar the result is 0, and for other simple arrays the depth function returns 1.

```
        ≡5                       ≡⍳10                   ≡ 2 3 4 9 ρ'FOO'
0                        1                      1
```

Nested arrays are another story. For them the result is the maximum nesting expressed as a positive scalar integer one more than the number of nest levels:

```
        U←2ρ⊂⊂⊂4 1ρ'NEST'         U[2]←⊂U[2]             U[2]←25
        U                        U                      U
    N        N                N        N            N   25
    E        E                E        E            E
    S        S                S        S            S
    T        T                T        T            T
        ≡U                       ≡U                     ≡U
4                        5                      4
```

APL*PLUS Systems determine depth somewhat differently. There, ≡*A* is always 0 for any simple array; for nested arrays the result is positive if the nesting is uniform, and negative otherwise. The results for the examples in this section would be 0, 0, 0, 3, ¯4, 3.

Simple scalars, such as the most recent *U*[2], don't figure into the determination of nesting depth or uniformity, just as scalars don't affect the shape of the result of primitive scalar dyadic functions like + − × and ÷ (remember them?).

Enclose with axis

APL2 features an interesting extension to enclose which can change simple arrays to nested arrays or increase the nesting depth. It works like this:

```
      ⊂[1]3 2ρι6                        ⊂[2]3 2ρι6
 1 3 5    2 4 6                    1 2    3 4    5 6
      ρ⊂[1]3 2ρι6                       ρ⊂[2]3 2ρι6
2                                 3
```

```
      ARG←2 3 5ρ'HOW   NOW   BROWNCOW  SO    QUIET'
HOW
NOW
BROWN                        ⊂[1 3]ARG                        ⊂[2 3]ARG
                     HOW      NOW     BROWN          HOW        COW
COW                  COW      SO      QUIET          NOW        SO
SO                                                   BROWN      QUIET
QUIET                        ρ⊂[1 3]ARG                       ρ⊂[2 3]ARG
                 3                                2
```

If $Z←⊂[K]ARG$, except when K is empty and ARG is simple, $ρρZ$ is $(ρρARG)-ρ,K$, and each item in the result has rank $ρ,K$. The shape of the result is $(∼(ιρρARG)∈K)/ρARG$. Alert readers will note some similarities between this use of enclose and the function $SPRED$ (Chapter 19), which used dyadic transpose to restructure arrays for display.

APL*PLUS provides a function similar to enclose with axis, *split*, the monadic ↓. If no axis is specified, it encloses along the last axis; otherwise it encloses on the axis given.

```
      ↓ARG                        ↓[1]↓[3]ARG                     ↓[2]↓[3]ARG
HOW    NOW    BROWN         HOW    NOW    BROWN          HOW      LOW
COW    SO     QUIET         COW    SO     QUIET          NOW      SO
                                                         BROWN    QUIET
      ρ↓ARG                       ρ↓[1]↓[3]ARG                    ρ↓[2]↓[3]ARG
 2 3                        3                           2
```

The first function

You have already seen that when a nested item is selected from a nested array, it is obtained as a nested scalar. In other words, it still 'wears' its enclosure implicitly:

```
      NA
 T  4 12    PEOPLE
      X←NA[3]
      X
PEOPLE
      ρρX
0
```

The *first* function (also called *disclose*), monadic ⊃, removes one level of enclosure from an item:

```
      ⊃X                         ρ⊃X                    ρρX
PEOPLE                      6                      1
```

When first is applied to an array with more than one item, the result is the first item and all the others are ignored:

```
      NA
 T  4 12    PEOPLE
      ⊃NA                        ⊃⊃NA                       ⊃⊃⊃NA
T                          T                          T
      ⊃φNA                       ⊃⊃φNA                      ⊃⊃⊃φNA
PEOPLE                     P                          P
      ⊃NA[2]                     ⊃⊃NA[2]                    ⊃⊃⊃NA[2]
 4 12                      4                          4
```

If the item is not nested (in other words, it is already a simple scalar), then first just delivers that scalar as its result.

Disclose with axis

This function has the syntax $Z \supset [K] ARG$, where all the nonscalar items in ARG must have rank ρ , K. K itself is a simple scalar or integer vector (except that if ARG consists of scalar items only, K must be empty). The depth of the result Z is less than that of ARG (except when ARG is simple and K is empty). For the case where the items of ARG have different shapes, they are padded on the right with their fill elements to conform to the shape of the biggest item. One other point: unlike its use in other axis sensitive functions, $[K]$ refers to the axes of the result rather than the axes of the argument.

```
      Z←⊃[1](3 2 4)(10 8 16)         Z←(3 2ρ'ABCDEF')(3 2ρ'UVWXYZ')

      Z                                Z
3 10                             AB   UV
2  8                             CD   WX
4 16                             EF   YZ

      ρZ                               Z←⊃[2 3]Z
3 2                                  Z
      Z←⊃[2](3 2 4)(10 8 16)     AB
      Z                          CD
   3  2  4                       EF
  10  8 16
      ρZ                         UV
2 3                              WX
      Z←⊃[1]'ABC' 'DEFG'         YZ
      Z                                ρZ
 AD                              2 3 2
 BE                                    Z←⊃[2](2 3)(4 5 6)
 CF                                    Z
  G                              2 3 0
                                 4 5 6
```

The APL*PLUS System uses the function *mix*, monadic ↑, to replace a level of nesting by a new axis. It uses the same fractional index notation as laminate; however, while in laminate the new axis has only two levels, mix produces as many levels as there were nested objects in the argument. If there is no index specified for mix, the new axis becomes the last axis of the result:

```
      ↑[0.5]'ABCD' 'EFGH' 'IJKL'
AEI
BFJ
CGK
DHL
```

```
      ↑[1.5]'ABCD' 'EFGH' 'IJKL'              ↑'ABCD' 'EFGH' 'IJKL'
ABCD                                    ABCD
EFGH                                    EFGH
IJKL                                    IJKL
```

The items being disclosed by mix must be of identical shape; otherwise $RANK$ or $LENGTH$ $ERROR$s result:

```
      ↑(1 2 3)(4 5)(6 7 8)
LENGTH ERROR
      ↑(1 2 3)(4 5)(6 7 8)
      ∧
```

Split and mix (or enclose and disclose with axis) can rearrange arrays to achieve transpose-like effects. For $X←3$ $4\rho\iota 12$, all the following expressions get the same result. Can you think of any others?

```
      ↑[0.5]↓X          ↑↓[1]X          ⊃[1]⊂[2]X          ⊃[2]⊂[1]X
```

Pick

The dyadic form of disclose is called *pick*. When applied to a nested vector right argument, it selects the item named on the left, with a layer of enclosure removed. Each item of the left argument picks through a progressively deeper layer of the nest. Picking a nonexisting item causes an error:

```
            NA
     T   4  12    PEOPLE
            1⊃NA                           2  1  ⊃NA                      3  1  ⊃NA
     T                              4      2  2  ⊃NA               P      3  2  ⊃NA
            2⊃NA                           2  2  ⊃NA                      3  2  ⊃NA
     4  12                          12     2  3  ⊃NA               E      3  3  ⊃NA
            3⊃NA

     PEOPLE                       INDEX ERROR                      O
                                        2  3  ⊃NA                         3  1  1  ⊃NA
                                           ∧                      LENGTH ERROR
                                                                         3  1  1  ⊃NA
                                                                            ∧
```

The results of using pick on vectors are simpler than the arguments, as the above examples show. Successive applications of pick show this clearly:

```
       V←'APL' 2 (5ρ'ABC' 'XYZ')
       V
 APL 2   ABC XYZ ABC XYZ ABC
       ρV
 3
       3 4 2⊃V
 Y
```

```
       A←3⊃V                      B←4⊃A                 C←2⊃B
       A                          B                     C
 ABC XYZ ABC XYZ ABC       XYZ                  Y

       ρA                         ρB                    ρC
 5                        3                     
       ρρA                        ρρB                   ρρC
 1                        1                     0
```

When the right argument is more complicated than a vector, the items of the left argument must be nested vectors, indicating the axes of the right argument to be picked:

```
           M                              (⊂ 1 1)⊃M               (⊂ 2 4)⊃M
  1 2   B  ∨           ~   2   B     1                       PEOPLE
  8 9 10   PEOPLE  12 13 14               (⊂ 1 3)⊃M               5⊃(⊂2 4)⊃M
                                    B                       L
```

Pick can do many of the same things that traditional bracket indexing can. In general, the disclosed item in the *I;J*th position of a matrix can be selected by ⊃*ARRAY*[*I*;*J*] or (⊂*I J*)⊃*ARRAY*. But there are differences between pick and indexing: pick is restricted to getting single items, while indexing can get various slices or planes of items. That is, pick has no direct analogue for *ARRAY*[*I*;]. Another obvious difference is that while indexing selects *elements*, pick selects *items*.

Pick is very powerful in its ability to reach into an array of any shape whatsoever and draw out desired data. However, like some other powerful functions, it requires a lot of learning to use it for complicated cases.

By the way, did you notice anything odd about the statement *V←'APL' 2 (5ρ'ABC' 'XYZ')*? It ends with a right parenthesis, and that is indeed never required—for traditional APL. But the convenience of strand notation costs you here. The *DOMAIN ERROR* below comes from trying to use the strand *'APL' 2 5* as the left argument to reshape.

```
       'APL' 2 5ρ'ABC' 'XYZ'
 DOMAIN ERROR
       'APL' 2 5ρ'ABC' 'XYZ'
        ∧          ∧
```

Assigning to vectors of variables

A bonus feature of the nested arrays facility is the ability to disperse the items of a vector into a group of variables. For example, the three items of the nested vector *NA* can be stored in three variables with a statement like this:

```
       ITA ITB ITC←NA
       ITA                         ITB                    ITC
T                              4 12                    PEOPLE
```

The item to the right of the assignment must be a scalar or vector (higher dimensional arrays won't work and will result in *RANK ERROR*), and there must be exactly as many variable names on the left as there are items on the right (*LENGTH ERROR* otherwise). As with pick and disclose, one layer of enclosure is removed by vector notation assignment. A handy consequence of all this is that you can now exchange the contents of two variables. Try doing *ITA ITB←ITB ITA* in one step in traditional APL!

Vector notation can be used to remove the limitation of two arguments in defined functions. Here is a function to replace a substring in text. Focus your attention on the argument and line 2. The rest of the function is a mundane looping solution.

```
          ∇Z←REPLACE R;TEXT;OLD;NEW;LOC
[1]       ⍝ R IS A 3-ELEMENT NESTED VECTOR
[2]       TEXT OLD NEW←R
[3]       Z←''
[4]       LLP:LOC←(∧/(⁻1+⍳⍴OLD)⊖TEXT∘.=OLD)⍳1
[5]       ⍝ABOVE FINDS LOCATION OF FIRST OCCURRENCE OF OLD IN TEXT.
[6]       →(LOC=1+⍴TEXT)/DONE
[7]       Z←Z,((LOC-1)↑TEXT),NEW
[8]       TEXT←(⁻1+LOC+⍴OLD)↓TEXT
[9]       →LP
[10]      DONE:Z←Z,TEXT ∇

          REPLACE 'VECTOR ← VECTOR + VECTOR' 'VECTOR' 'MATRIX'
MATRIX ← MATRIX + MATRIX
```

Selective assignment

In traditional APL you could assign an entire variable (*Z←* ...) or parts of a variable using bracket indexing (*Z[* ... *]←* ...). In APL2 this idea of assigning parts has been broadened. Most of the selection and ordering functions now work on the left of the assignment arrow. For example, (1 1⍉*MATRIX*)←0 sets the diagonal of a matrix to zero. To change the last element of a vector to twice what it was, execute (⁻1↑*VECTOR*)←2×⁻1↑*VECTOR*.

Selective assignment considers the expression on the left as an array of locations, or positions that can be indexed, for the variable being assigned. It works with those functions that select or rearrange elements without changing their values.

Unite

In APL2 there is a handy function, *unite*, monadic ∪, which does just what it says. On simple arrays it is equivalent to , *ARG*:

```
          ARG←∪(3 5 6) (2 3⍴⍳6) (⍳0)
          ARG
3 5 6 1 2 3 4 5 6
          ⍴ARG
9
```

One consequence of this is that we can easily partition a vector. Try doing the following example in traditional APL:

```
          V←'NORTH/SOUTH/EAST/WEST'
          V[(V='/')/⍳⍴V]←⊂''' '''
          V
NORTH ' ' SOUTH ' ' EAST ' ' WEST
```

```
      NV←'''',(∪V),''''
      NV
'NORTH' 'SOUTH' 'EAST' 'WEST'

      NV←⍕NV
      NV
NORTH SOUTH EAST WEST
      ρNV
4
```

Scatter-indexing

Besides its traditional uses to obtain single items or vectors or planes of items, indexing has been extended in some APL*PLUS Systems to allow working with scattered items. This form of indexing is called *choose*:

```
      X← 2 3 ρ'BAFDEC'
      X
BAF
DEC

      X[1;2],X[1;1],X[2;3]
ABC
      X[(1 2)(1 1)(2 3)]
ABC
```

The rule is that each item of the (nested) array in the brackets must call for a valid position of the left argument. The same idea can be used to assign into indexed positions. To swap $X[1;2]$ with $X[2;3]$ you can use $X[(1\ 2)(2\ 3)]←X[(2\ 3)(1\ 2)]$. You can use either traditional bracket indexing with semicolons or the new choose form, but you can't use them together in the same selection.

Index

APL2 extends indexing through the dyadic function *index*, ⌷. Its left argument L is a simple integer array whose values are in the range 1 to the axis length to be indexed in the right argument R. Each column of L is associated with an axis of R, and each element in L determines the element to be selected along the associated axis of R. This means, for example, that $2\ 1\ 3\ ⌷\ R$ is the same as $R[2;1;3]$. The real benefit comes when L itself is multidimensional, with each row of L then indexing R independently. The function then scatter indexes.

```
      3⌷10×⍳4                           (10×⍳4)[3]
30                              30

      R←3 5ρ'DRINKWATEROFTEN'
      2 3⌷R                             R[2;3]

T                              T
      (3 2ρ⍳4)⌷R                        R[1;2],R[3;4],R[1;2]
RER                            RER
```

Conformability requires that $ρρR$ be the same as $^-1↑1,ρL$.

An extension of index is *index with axis*. It works the same way as index except that the left argument contains indices only for the axes selected. For the other axes all the indices are used, like bracket indexing when axes are omitted. Unselected axes are placed last in the result.

```
      2⌷[1]R                            R[2;]
WATER                          WATER
      3⌷[2]R                            R[;3]

ITT                            ITT
      (2 1ρ2 3)⌷[1]R                    R[2 3;]
WATER                          WATER
OFTEN                          OFTEN
      (2 1ρ2 3)⌷[2]R                    R[;2 3]
RAF                            RAF
ITT                            ITT
```

Match

To check that two arrays are exactly identical, use dyadic *match* (= overstruck with _). This function returns a scalar 1 if the two arguments are identical in shape, rank, nesting and contents, and returns scalar 0 if there are any differences at all.

```
      (×/ι0)≡5-4                  (,1)≡⊂1                       (ι0)≡''
1                          0                          0
      1≡,1                        (,1)≡⊂,1                      (⊂ι0)≡⊂''
0                          0                          0
      1≡⊂1                        (⊂1)≡⊂,1                      (ι0)≡0↑ι5
1                          0                          1
      1≡⊂,1                       (⊂,1)≡⊂,,1                    ''≡0ρ'ABC'
0                          1                          1
```

The each operator

This powerful operator, *each*, ¨, greatly reduces the need to use looping or complicated loopless APL idioms. The formal definition is deceptively simple: the each operator applies a function to its arguments item by item. The best way to understand each's potential is to write some examples to show how they would be done both with and without each:

```
      'ABC',¨'EFG'                        ('A','E')('B','F')('C','G')
AE  BF  CG                           AE  BF  CG

      1 2 3 ρ¨10                           (1ρ10)(2ρ10)(3ρ10)
10    10 10    10 10 10               10    10 10    10 10 10

      ×/¨ι¨ι3
1 2 6

      ×/¨(1)(1 2)(1 2 3)                  (×/1)(×/ 1 2)(×/ 1 2 3)
1 2 6                                1 2 6
```

The arguments of each follow the rules for scalar dyadic functions; that is, both arguments must have the same shape, unless one of them is a single element.

How traditional APL operators work on nested arrays

When working with the operators outer product, reduction, scan and inner product in the next few pages, think about the rules for defining the shape of the result. Even though the arguments can now be nested arrays, in each case the rules for determining the shape of the result haven't changed:

```
      Z←L ∘.f R      (ρZ) is (ρL),ρR  (catenation of all the axes)
      Z←f/[K]R       (ρZ) is (K=ιρρR)/ιρR  (all axes except the one reduced over)
      Z←f\[K]R       (ρZ) is ρR  (all axes preserved)
      Z←L f.g R      (ρZ) is (¯1↓ρL),1↓ρR  (catenation of all axes except the inner two)
```

The rules above look simple enough; however, it may take some examples to convince you they really work on nested arrays. First, we explore outer product:

```
      A←(1 2 3)(4 5)
      B← 10 20 30
      A∘.+B
11 12 13    21 22 23    31 32 33
14 15       24 25       34 35
```

To see what's happening, set up an operation table and start filling it in.

```
        +    |    10          20          30
    --------+---------------------------------
      1 2 3 |  11 12 13    21 22 23    31 32 33
        4 5 |   14 15        24 25        34 35
```

You may be surprised to find that $A\circ.+A$ won't work. That's because it would require a table like

```
    +    |    1 2 3                4 5
---------+--------------------------------
  1 2 3  |    2 4 6              LENGTH ERROR
    4 5  | LENGTH ERROR            8 10
```

In other words, even though the shapes of the arrays are conformable for outer product, the individual items must be conformable for addition, and 1 2 3 + 4 5 won't work.

When you apply the each operator to outer product, you get entirely different results; an outer product is performed on each pair of items:

```
      A∘.+¨A
 2  3  4      8  9
 3  4  5      9 10
 4  5  6
```

Think of this as (1 2 3 ∘.+ 1 2 3) (4 5 ∘.+ 4 5) and you'll see how the result is developed. However, $A\circ.+\ddot{}B$ won't work because A's first item, (1 2 3), would be added with B's first item, 1 0, and A's second item, (4 5), would be added with B's second item, 2 0; but there would be no match for the third item of B.

You know that reduction over simple arrays is equivalent to writing the function between adjacent items; that is, $+/1$ 2 3 is the same as $1+2+3$. The same holds true with nested arrays, as you can see by writing out the steps:

```
      +/(10 20 30) 4 (5 6 7)
 19 30 41
      (⊂ 10 20 30)+4+⊂5 6 7
 19 30 41

      ρρ+/(10 20 30) 4 (5 6 7)  ⍝NOTE THE RESULT IS A NESTED SCALAR
 0
      ⊂(10+4+5)(20+4+6)(30+4+7)
 19 30 41
```

Moreover, the shape of the result still follows the familiar rules for reduction of simple arrays: all axes are preserved except the one being reduced.

```
      ρTAB3
 2 4 3
      T3X←⊂[3] TAB3
      T3X
 111 112 113   121 122 123   131 132 133   141 142 143
 211 212 213   221 222 223   231 232 233   241 242 243

      ρT3X
 2 4

      ⌈/[1] T3X
 211 212 213   221 222 223   231 232 233   241 242 243
      ρ⌈/[1] T3X
 4
```

Suppose you want to obtain a result consisting of the sum of the elements of each item? That's literally how you do it:

```
      +/¨(1 2 3) 4 (5 6 7)  ⍝ READ AS SUM OVER EACH
 6 4 18
      (+/ 1 2 3)(+/4)(+/ 5 6 7)
 6 4 18
```

Since scan is the repeated application of reduction, it follows that it will work where reduction works:

```
      +\(10 20 30) 4 (5 6 7)
 10 20 30   14 24 34   19 30 41
      +\¨(10 20 30) 4 (5 6 7)
 10 30 60   4   5 11 18
```

Incidentally, because of mixed arrays, some *DOMAIN ERROR*s associated with scan no longer appear; `=\'AAAA'` produces the mixed vector `A 1 0 0` rather than *DOMAIN ERROR*.

Inner products calculated with nested arrays are also possible, but in practice are rarely used. Since inner product includes repeated application of reduction, all the conformability rules for reduction apply here as well. Inner product will result in a *LENGTH ERROR* unless each of the items of both arguments are the same shape or are scalars.

You must be ready now to leap on your terminal to try out all this new power that nested arrays brings to you. But hold on—one of the bigger surprises is just about to be disclosed (no pun) to you. Here it is: all of the traditional operators, reduction, scan, inner and outer products, now work with dyadic mixed functions as well as the dyadic scalar functions. We already saw in Chapter 21 that catenation could be used with the outer product. It wasn't mentioned at that time, but the result of `1 2 3°.,10 20 30 40` is nested.

Practical applications? You bet. For example, here's how to read the first three records of a file (next chapter) tied to 20 on an APL*PLUS System:

```
      DATA←[]FREAD¨20°.,ι3          or          DATA←[]FREAD 20,¨ι3
      ρDATA
3
      DATA
 100 103  200 201 202  300 301 302 303 304 305
```

How traditional APL functions work on nested arrays

Many of the APL functions take on additional capabilities in the world of nested arrays. We have already encountered the shape function, monadic ρ, in this chapter. It gives the shape of the array at the outermost level:

```
      A←(2 3 ρ'HOWNOW') 'BROWN' 'COW'
      A
HOW   BROWN   COW
NOW
      ρA
3
```

To see the shapes of items at the next level of nesting, use the each operator with shape (think of 'the *shape* of *each* item'). To get the ranks at the next level, apply the 'shape of each' twice:

```
      ρ¨A
2 3   5  3
      ρ¨ρ¨A
2  1  1
```

To see how these work, look at the process in detail:

```
      ρ¨ρ¨A
2  1  1

      ρ¨ρ¨(2 3 ρ'HOWNOW') 'BROWN' 'COW'
2  1  1

      ρ¨(ρ 2 3 ρ'HOWNOW')(ρ'BROWN')(ρ'COW')
2  1  1

      ρ¨(2 3)(,5)(,3)
2  1  1

      (ρ 2 3)(ρ,5)(ρ,3)
2  1  1

      (,2)(,1)(,1)
2  1  1
```

The items of the result are enclosed because they are one-item vectors. To remove the enclosure, use `⊃¨ρ¨ρ¨A` or `,↑ρ¨ρ¨A`.

Here is how you would calculate the averages of the nested vector $DATA$ gathered in the last section:

```
     (+/¨DATA)÷ρ¨DATA
101.5   201   302.5
```

Those mixed functions that select or rearrange generally work on the items of nested arrays as they do on simple arrays. This includes reverse, rotate, compress (replicate), expand, index, transpose, take, drop, reshape, ravel, catenate and laminate, as well as the new ones, enclose, disclose, split and mix. For all the dyadic ones except catenate and laminate, the left argument must be simple (that is, not nested).

All the functions above work at the outer level only. For instance, reverse changes the order of the three items in A, but not the order of the characters enclosed in those items:

```
      φA                             φ¨φA
COW      BROWN    HOW        WOC    NWORB    WOH
                  NOW                        WON


      φ¨A                            φφ¨A
WOH    NWORB    WOC          WOC    NWORB    WOH
WON                                          WON


      φ¨φ¨A                          φ····A
HOW    BROWN    COW          HOW    BROWN    COW
NOW                          NOW
```

···· reaches into the second level of the nest, which consists of scalars. That's why the last example above has no effect.

Here are some more examples for you to ponder:

```
      2↑A                          ,¨A
HOW      BROWN           HOWNOW  ..  BROWN      COW
NOW                           2↑¨,¨A
      2↑¨A               HO    BR     CO ..
LENGTH ERROR                 (ι3)↑¨,¨A
      2↑¨A               H     BR    COW
      ^
```

Index of (dyadic ι) and membership also work on the outer level of nested arrays. Their results are simple and the shape of the result is still the same as the shape of the right argument for ranking or the left argument for membership. Technically, the implied = comparison is replaced by ≡.

```
      AιA                 'NOW' 'COW' ιA              Aε 'NOW' 'COW'
1 2 3                        3 3 2                      0 0 1
```

The rest of the mixed functions, monadic ⊞ ⍋ ⍒ ⍉ and dyadic ⊞ ⊤ ⊥ ⍉ \ ⍋ ⍒ work only on non-nested arrays. Thus, ⍋(20 10 5 10) (20 30 10) won't work, but you can grade each of the items:

```
      ⍋¨(20 10 5 10)(20 30 10)
3 2 4 1   3 1 2
```

Rearranging the contents of the items according to their grades (the equivalent of $X[⍋X]$ for a non-nested vector) is somewhat harder to do. Bracket indexing can't be used with each, so pick has to be used. Note that the items have to be enclosed one more level (by ⊂¨X) to make it work.

```
      X←(20 10 5 10) (20 30 10)
      (⍋¨X)⊃····⊂¨X
(5 10 10 20) (10 20 30)
```

All the primitive scalar functions, dyadic + − × ÷ * ⍟ ⌈ ⌊ | ! ○ < ≤ = ≥ > ≠ ∨ ∧ ⍱ ⍲ and monadic + − × ÷ * ⍟ ⌈ ⌊ | ! ○ ~ ? ε work on the data at the bottom of the nest, as opposed to the mixed functions, which work on the items at the outermost level of the nested array:

```
      A                      'O'=A                       ('O'=A)+2×'W'=A
HOW    BROWN    COW      0 1 0  0 0 1 0 0  0 1 0      0 1 2  0 0 1 2 0  0 1 2
NOW                      0 1 0                        0 1 2
```

As with simple arrays, scalars and one-element arrays are conformable for the dyadic functions. Remember that the functions associate with each pair of items and you'll understand why these work: `(1 2 3) 4 + (,5)(20 30)` is the same as `(1 2 3+,5) (4+20 30)`. It's as though the each operator were applied an arbitrary number of times.

Since the primitive scalar functions already work on the data at the bottom of the nest (the formal term is *pervasive*), each does not have any effect on them. For that reason, `(1 2 3) 4+¨(,5)(20 30)` is the same as `(1 2 3) 4 + (,5)(20 30)`.

When and where to use nested arrays

Some people feel that the concept of nested arrays and the associated extensions to traditional APL is as significant an advance as APL was over other programming languages. In terms of the new power and freedom of expression that is no doubt true, but there is a dark side to the story also.

Others feel that APL has been made more confusing by all these new features—for example, no longer can arrays be regarded as just plain rectangular. Moreover, at this writing there are differences among the various commercial implementations which can affect the portability of applications.

We suggest that you do explore nested arrays, but that you adopt a limited approach to its use. Begin by avoiding the use of nesting for data that has permanence (i.e., is filed or stored in the workspace between sessions). On the other hand, do employ nested arrays and the new functions in local algorithms if they make programming easier for you. As with the rest of APL, shorter is probably clearer, but make sure you use comments liberally. And be prepared to revise your work if you must change APL systems. When you gain experience and confidence in nested arrays it is then appropriate to use them for saved data. Ultimately, nested arrays gives you the power to represent data realistically and naturally, without artifices like padding.

Our own experience in adapting to nested arrays was that it was harder for us than for our students. This we attribute to our own habits formed by sixteen years of traditional APL use. Newcomers to the APL scene accept nested arrays as useful, powerful, and not particularly difficult to learn.

If you are beginning to see how nested arrays can be put to practical use, you'll appreciate the applications illustrated in some of the problems. We especially recommend that you work through problems 9 (report formatting), 13 (branching), 14 (side-by-side display), 15 (text processing) and 16 (vectors of different lengths).

PROBLEMS

1. On each expression indicate if the array produced is simple or nested.

```
3 4 5                3 (4 'A')            'ABC' 'XYZ'
(,3)(,4)(,5)         ((3)(4)(5))          'ABC','XYZ'
(3)(4)(5)            (,3),(,4),(,5)       'A' 'B' 'C'
3 4 'A'              3 4 'AB'             'A' ('B' 'C')
```

2. Given the variables `A←2 3⍴⍳6   B←99   C←'APL'`, show the depth, shape, rank and display of the array produced by each expression.

```
⊃A                   (⊂A),(⊂B),(⊂C)       2 3⍴C C
⊂A                   ⊃⊃A                  2 3⍴⊂C
⊂⊂A                  3 4⍴A B C            B B B
⊂⊃A                  2 3⍴C                ⊂A B C
```

3. Using the variables defined above and $D \leftarrow A$ B C , show the depth, shape and display of the array produced
    by each expression.

D	$(\supset D[1]),D[2]$	$\supset \ddot{\ } D$
$D[1]$	B	$,\ddot{\ } D$
$\supset D[1]$	$\subset B$	$\rho \ddot{\ } D$
$\supset \supset D[1]$	$\subset \subset B$	$\rho \ddot{\ } \rho \ddot{\ } D$
$D[2]$	$\supset B$	$\supset \rho \ddot{\ } \rho \ddot{\ } D$
$\supset D[2]$	$\supset \supset B$	$+/ \ddot{\ } ^-1 \downarrow D$
$D[1],D[2]$	$C,\ddot{\ } B$	$(\subset A),\ddot{\ } C$
$D[1 \ 2]$	$A,\ddot{\ } B$	

4. Describe what these expressions do: $1 \geq \underline{=} A$ and $\Box CR \ddot{\ } \subset [2] \Box NL \ 3$

5. Write an expression to change a vector of character vectors that contains no blanks into a simple vector with
    one blank between each of the original vectors. For example, $'APL'$ $'IS'$ $'FUN'$ would be changed
    to $'APL \ IS \ FUN'$.

6. Write an expression to change a simple vector that may contain blanks into a vector of vectors that are split
    at the blanks. Do not include the blanks in the result. For example, $'APL \ IS \ FUN'$ would be changed
    to $'APL'$ $'IS'$ $'FUN'$.

7. Write an expression that will enclose an array only if the array is simple.

8. Write an expression to attach row numbers onto the left edge of any matrix.

9. Given the variables

    ```
    COLS←'JANUARY' 'FEBRUARY' 'MARCH'
    ROWS←'SHOES' 'TIES' 'WORK BOOTS' 'SHIRTS'
    DATA←2 3ρ100 523 0 95 0 192 3 12 18 38 0 0
    ```
    Write an expression to produce the following display:

    ```
                JANUARY   FEBRUARY   MARCH
    SHOES           100        523       0
    TIES             95          0     192
    WORK BOOTS        3         12      18
    SHIRTS           38          0       0
    ```

    The expression should work regardless of the number of items or their length as long as $\rho ROWS$ is
     $1\uparrow\rho DATA$ and $\rho COLS$ is $^-1\uparrow\rho DATA$.

10. Write a monadic function named $SHAPES$ that takes as its argument any array and returns a nested vector
    of the shapes of all the simple arrays that it contains. For example, $SHAPES \ 'APL' \ (45 \ ((3 \ 4$
     $\rho \iota 6) \ (\iota 0)))$ results in $(,3) \ (\iota 0) \ (3 \ 4) \ (,0)$

11. The following function is very similar to monadic format. How does it differ and why?

    ```
         ∇ Z←FORMAT A
    [1]    Z←0 1↓0 ¯1↓∓⊂((-2⌈ρρA)↑1 1,ρA)ρA ∇
    ```

12. If $X \leftarrow P1 \supset V$, $Y \leftarrow P2 \supset V$ and $Z \leftarrow P3 \supset V$, express $P1 \ P2 \ P3 \supset \ddot{\ } \subset V$ in terms of X , Y and Z .

13. Use pick with execute to branch to $L1$ if $X > Y$, $L2$ otherwise.

14. For $A \leftarrow 3 \ 4\rho\iota 12$ and $B \leftarrow 4 \ 2\rho 10 \times \iota 8$, display A , B and $A+. \times B$ side by side.

15. Show how to **A** get a count of the number of occurrences of each word in a text
    string $TEXT \leftarrow 'THIS \ IS \ AN \ EXAMPLE \ OF \ WORD \ PROCESSING \ IN \ THIS \ CHAPTER'$; **B**
    check for the presence of the phrase $'AN \ EXAMPLE'$; **C** produce a listing of those words in $TEXT$ not in
    the word list $REFERENCE$.

16. You are a businessman with only three accounts, each of which consists of debits for goods purchased and
    credits for returned goods. The data is stored in a nested vector $ACCOUNTS$, with two vectors (debits,
    credits) for each account: $ACCOUNTS \leftarrow ((100 \ 350) \ (10)) \ ((5000 \ 290 \ 450 \ 600)$
     $(\iota 0)) \ ((150) \ (\iota 0))$. **A** Find the total credits and debits by account; **B** Find the net sales for each
    account.

Chapter 26: Introduction to Data Files

Almost all commercial data processing applications and a good many scientific applications involve more data than can be jammed into a workspace. Even though sophisticated coding and packing techniques may be employed, sooner or later the workspace will fill up. Also, there is a class of applications, such as airline reservation systems, in which several users must be able to read or update values almost simultaneously. For example, imagine that your terminal is one of many serving as a reservation station, and you and the other reservation agents are all trying to sell whatever seats are still unclaimed. There would have to be a variable to serve as an inventory record to keep count of how many seats remain. It would be decreased whenever any agent reserves a seat or increased when a seat is cancelled.

Both of these classes of applications can be handled through careful and tedious use of the system commands $)COPY$ and $)SAVE$, but at best they would be prone to error. Furthermore, in the case of a reservation system, you would have the problem of deciding whose saved workspace holds the most recent updating of the inventory. There are good odds that you would never resolve the situation of two agents attempting to decrement the inventory at the same time.

Large database applications and shared database applications are both properly handled using a *file system*. There are many different file systems, but the two major types are those based on IBM's *shared variables* concept (next chapter) and those based on the *component file* concept (here). The examples used in this chapter are based on STSC's APL, but Sharp's is almost identical, the major difference being the names used. For example, STSC uses $\Box FCREATE$ and $\Box FREAD$ to create a file and to read from it, while Sharp uses $\Box CREATE$ and $\Box READ$.

A *file* is a place to put data so that it is available to the programs in your active workspace, but doesn't take any space away from the active workspace. You don't have to be concerned with where the data is actually put; it is enough to say that it is stored in the same type of equipment that holds the workspaces of your library.

Like workspaces, files have names, and data can be stored in them. In fact, the data items stored in a file can have the same variety of structures that variables have. However, unlike workspaces, instead of referring to a data item by name, you refer to it by a number, that number being the position of that data item in the file. Each data item in a file is called a *component* (instead of a variable) and the file itself consists of a sequence of these components. You could have a file with, say, three thousand components, and each component could be a character matrix of shape 100 by 90. This would amount to nearly three million bytes if you had to stuff it into a workspace all at once, which would be impossible in most APL systems and grossly inefficient in the rest. When using files you have to contend with only one component at a time in your workspace.

File creation

Now that we have the generalities out of the way, let's approach learning file use by considering an example of a simplistic customer information system containing both identifying and geographic data.

Imagine that you are responsible for keeping business related data on some 5000 customers. When a new customer is added to the list, 25 items of information, including size, address, type of business, etc., are recorded. Some customers may have multiple locations, which may change from time to time as, say, branch offices, warehouses or factories are opened or closed. We will assume that no company in our customer set has more than 100 locations.

A reasonable structure for holding this data (if it could fit in the workspace) would be a three-dimensional array of customers by location and by associated data category (25 items). There would be lots of wasted space because the second dimension, locations, would either have to be as long as the number of locations associated with the most dispersed customer or limited to some fixed amount, say, 100, as suggested above.

In the file we're going to create, the component numbering will correspond to the first dimension of this hypothetical three-dimensional array, and each component will consist of a given customer's data. Each component will be a matrix whose row dimension is the number of locations recorded, with 25 columns for the 25 pieces of associated data.

Let's name the file we will create *'CUSTOMERS'*:

> *'CUSTOMERS' □FCREATE 98*

The dyadic function *□FCREATE* is used to create the file. Its left argument is the name of the file. The naming rules are similar to those of workspaces: names must consist of letters and numbers, and can be up to eleven characters in length. Note that the name is in quotes, which is different from the way workspaces are referenced in system commands.

The right argument is called the *file tie number*. It is a unique number for referencing the file when it is in active use. A number is used rather than the file name so that if you have two or more files active (tied) at the same time, you can 'index' from file to file much as you index an array in the workspace. The number you choose doesn't really matter much except that it must be a positive integer, and there must be a different number for each file in active use at any one time. You can find out which files are tied at any time by the niladic function *□FNAMES*:

> *□FNAMES*
> 78975 *CUSTOMERS*

The result is a 22-column character matrix. Columns 1 through 10 hold the user numbers of the owners of the files, column 11 is blank and columns 12 through 22 hold the names of the files. Our particular matrix has only one row, but if you had six files active, the matrix would have six rows. The order of the file names in the matrix corresponds to the chronological order in which they were tied.

A listing of file tie numbers in use can be obtained by the niladic function *□FNUMS*:

> *□FNUMS*
> 98

The result is a vector holding the file tie numbers in the same sequence as the names in *□FNAMES*. Thus, if you already have some files tied, to find a unique file number for activation of another file, execute

> *1+⌈/0,□FNUMS*
> 99

In the expression above, the 0 is necessary to cover the case where no files are currently activated. Without it, the result would be *⌈/⍳0*, which is *¯7.237005577E75*. Of course, 1 added to that is not a positive number.

Whenever you sign off or lose your telephone connection, your files are automatically deactivated or *untied*. They are *not* automatically reactivated when you sign back on, even if *CONTINUE* is reloaded. You have to reactivate them with the *□FTIE* function:

> *'CUSTOMERS' □FTIE 76*

The syntax is similar to *□FCREATE*, except that this function is used to tie files that had been created previously. Actually, *□FCREATE* both *creates* and *ties* a file, while *□FTIE* only *activates* a file. Note that in this session, we tied *'CUSTOMERS'* to the number 76 instead of the number 98. There is no permanent connection between a file name and a file tie number. A file can be tied to whatever number you choose in any session.

To untie a file in midsession, use the monadic function *□FUNTIE*. Its argument is the vector of tie numbers of the files that you want to deactivate. *□FUNTIE □FNUMS[ρ□FNUMS]* would untie the file that was tied most recently in this session.

□FSIZE is a 'shape of' operation applied to a file. It is monadic, and takes an active file tie number as its argument. The result is a four-element vector holding (1) the lowest numbered component in the file, (2) the number of the next available component in the file, (3) the amount of space that you are presently using in the file and (4) the total space available in the file.

> *□FSIZE 79*   *□FSIZE 76*
> *FILE TIE ERROR*   1 1 128 100000
>   *□FSIZE 79*
>   ∧

We got an error because there is no file tied with 79. But 76 is an active tie number for the *'CUSTOMERS'* file.

The lowest component in our file is 1, but the next available component is also 1. This tells you that the file is empty, which is certainly what we'd expect for a file that we had never put anything into. The third element is the amount of storage currently used by the file. Depending on which system you are using, it may be zero for a new file, or it may be a small amount of overhead storage that even an empty file needs. The last element is 100000, the nominal amount of space available for storage in this file. Both the third and fourth elements are expressed in bytes and their values may differ from system to system.

Our file certainly doesn't have the capacity to hold all the data we intend for it. There are two ways to provide this space. If we had created the file as `'CUSTOMERS 52000000' ⎕FCREATE 98`, then it would have had the required capacity (computed from 4 bytes per integer to be stored, times 5000 customers, times 100 rows, times 25 columns), plus 4 percent overhead. Alternatively, we could have used the dyadic function `⎕FRESIZE`, whose right argument is the file tie number, and whose left argument is the amount of space to be reserved for the file:

```
      52000000 ⎕FRESIZE 76              ⎕FSIZE 76
                                  1  1  128  52000000
```

Updating a file

Let's now store some data in the file. We'll use the following variables as data for two customers:

```
      C1←2 25ρι50
      C2←(ι4)∘.×⌽ι25
```

We are simulating customer 1 with two locations and customer 2 with four locations. In particular, `C1[1;1]` is 1 and `C2[1;1]` is 25. Let's put customer 1 on the file, using the dyadic function `⎕FAPPEND`:

```
      C1 ⎕FAPPEND 76
      ⎕FSIZE 76
1  2  384  52000000
```

`⎕FAPPEND` puts the value of its left argument as a new component at the end of the file designated in the right argument. The lowest component is still number 1, but the next available component is now number 2. (Incidentally, some file systems would return the component number being appended as an explicit result.) Continuing, we add customer 2:

```
      C2 ⎕FAPPEND 76
      ⎕FSIZE 76
1  3  840  52000000
```

The amount of space used (third element of the result of `⎕FSIZE`) increases as you store more data. Although it may appear to increase erratically, it is that the file system reclaims space where possible, and occasionally uses extra chunks of space to manage its internal directories.

Now we're going to do what looks like a foolhardy act:

```
      )CLEAR
CLEAR WS
```

Before you began using files, doing that operation would have meant permanent loss of the data (unless, of course, you had)SAVEd an image of the workspace). However, our customer data is stored safely in a file and isn't affected by clearing the workspace.

We now have to learn how to read information from files, using `⎕FREAD`:

```
      C1←⎕FREAD 76 1                      C2←⎕FREAD 76 2
      ρC1                                 ρC2
2 25                             4 25

      C1[1;1]                            C2[1;1]
1                                25
      ρC2
VALUE ERROR
      ρC2
      ∧
```

The $\Box FREAD$ function brings into the active workspace an image of what's in the file component that you ask for. Note that, as in Chapter 11, we used the term *image*. The file is no more changed by reading it than a variable in the workspace is changed by using it as part of an expression. Also, while we frequently read the values back into the same variables that they came from, it is not a requirement. For example, we could have entered $C2\leftarrow\Box FREAD$ 76 1 and $C1\leftarrow\Box FREAD$ 76 2, which would interchange the data for customers 1 and 2 in the workspace (but *not* in the file).

You may have observed that the file tie numbers are preserved even if the workspace is cleared. File tie numbers are changed only by the functions $\Box FCREATE$, $\Box FTIE$, $\Box FUNTIE$, $\Box FSTIE$ or $\Box FERASE$ (the last two will be explained subsequently), or by signing off.

Here is a simple function to find the total number of locations of all customers (that is, the total number of rows in the file):

```
      ∇R←TOTCUST N;I
[1]   ⍝N IS THE FILE NUMBER
[2]   R←0 ◇ I←(¯1+⎕FSIZE N)[1]
[3]   LOOP:I←I+1 ◇ →(I=(⎕FSIZE N)[2])/0 ◇ R←R+1↑ρ⎕FREAD N,I ◇ →LOOP ∇
      TOTCUST 76
6
```

By this time you should be catching on to the use of files. More file operations will be introduced later in the chapter, along with example functions to utilize our customer database. There are two operations that are obvious necessities: (1) establishing a new customer in the file by methods a bit more friendly than what was done above; and (2) adding a new location to any individual customer's data already in the file. The first is handled by the defined function $NEWCUST$:

```
      ∇NEWCUST N
[1]   ⍝N IS THE FILE NUMBER
[2]   ⍝ APPENDS AN EMPTY MATRIX FOR NEW CUSTOMER
[3]   ⍝ AND PRINTS THE CUSTOMER NUMBER ASSIGNED.
[4]   (0 25ρ0) ⎕FAPPEND N
[5]   'THIS IS CUSTOMER ', ⍕(⎕FSIZE N)[2]-1 ∇
```

$CUSTDATA$ records the data gathered on a customer:

```
      ∇C CUSTDATA N;DATA
[1]   ⍝C IS CUSTOMER NUMBER, N IS TIE NUMBER
[2]   →((C≥(⎕FSIZE N)[1])∧C<(⎕FSIZE N)[2])/OK
[3]   'NO SUCH CUSTOMER NUMBER' ◇ →0
[4]   OK:'ENTER 25 VALUES' ◇ →(25=ρDATA←,⎕)/UPDATE
[5]   'INVALID INPUT' ◇ →0
[6]   UPDATE:DATA←(⎕FREAD N,C),[1]DATA ◇ DATA ⎕FREPLACE N,C ∇
```

You probably spotted the new file function $\Box FREPLACE$ on line 6. It replaces the C-th file component with new data from the workspace. In our case it's the catenation of the existing component with another row, $DATA$, on the bottom. There doesn't need to be any relation between what is being replaced and what you're replacing it with, although in the above case there happened to be. The requirement that only the first 100 locations are to be kept in the file can be satisfied simply by changing the second statement on line 6 to read $(100\ 25\uparrow DATA)\ \Box FREPLACE\ N,P$.

Getting data from a file

Having written functions to enter a new customer and his associated data, we now turn to programs for getting selected data from the file. *Information retrieval* is the computer industry's term for this procedure. Much effort is spent by computer professionals to develop and improve both file design (how the data is laid out in the files) and functions to access the database. In general, it requires more time to take one value from each of several components than it does to take several values out of one component. And if your database includes vast amounts of data, you really need to study how the information is to be used before you choose the layout of your file. As you have already seen, the nature of APL is such that even if you first happen to choose the wrong layout for your file, it's no big deal to revise it. However, the limited scope of this text doesn't permit our going into all the fine points of file design.

Complete data on each customer can be obtained by reading his component. Here is a function for obtaining a matrix of data from one or more customers' latest locations added to the database:

```
      ∇R←V LASTLOC N
[1]   ⍝V IS CUSTOMER NUMBER; N IS TIE NUMBER
[2]   R←0 25ρ0
[3]   LOOP:→(0=ρV)/0 ◊ R←R,[1]¯1 25↑⎕FREAD N,1↑V ◊ V←1↓V ◊ →LOOP ∇
```

The following function returns a vector of customer numbers with at least one location having more than 99 employees (item number 2, i.e., the second column):

```
      ∇R←C2GT99 N
[1]   R←⍳0 ◊ I←(⎕FSIZE N)[1]
[2]   LOOP:→(I=(⎕FSIZE N)[2])/0
[3]   R←R,(∨/(⎕FREAD N,I)[;2]>99)/I
[4]   I←I+1 ◊ →LOOP ∇
```

The approach in *C2GT99* can be generalized to produce a function which returns customer numbers all of which satisfy some relation on some column; for example, all customers who have ordered product 100 (the 25th column), or all customers whose state code is less than 7 (the New England states) in column 12:

```
      ∇R←REL SELECT NCV;N;C;V;COMP;T
[1]   ⍝NCV IS 3-ELE VECTOR - TIE NUMBER, COLUMN, VALUE
[2]   ⍝ REL IS RELATION SYMBOL (<≤=≥> OR ≠) AS A CHARACTER SCALAR
[3]   N←NCV[1] ◊ C←NCV[2] ◊ V←NCV[3]
[4]   R←⍳0 ◊ I←(⎕FSIZE N)[1]
[5]   REL←(LT,LE,EQ,GE,GT,NE)['<≤=≥>≠'⍳REL]
[6]   LOOP:→(I=(⎕FSIZE N)[2])/0 ◊ COMP←(⎕FREAD N,I)[;C] ◊ →REL
[7]   LT:T←∨/V<COMP ◊ →XX
[8]   LE:T←∨/V≤COMP ◊ →XX
[9]   EQ:T←∨/V=COMP ◊ →XX
[10]  GE:T←∨/V≥COMP ◊ →XX
[11]  GT:T←∨/V>COMP ◊ →XX
[12]  NE:T←∨/V≠COMP ◊ →XX
[13]  XX:R←R,T/I ◊ I←I+1 ◊ →LOOP ∇
```

```
      '=' SELECT 76 25 100
2

      '<' SELECT 76 12 7
1 2
```

More file functions

Some additional useful file functions will now be discussed briefly. First, the ⎕FLIB function is used to list the file names in a *library* of files. ⎕FLIB, with your user number as an argument, produces an explicit result: a character matrix with 22 columns and as many rows as you have different file names. Columns 1 through 10 hold your user number; column 11 is blank; and columns 12 through 22 hold the file name.

To illustrate the next function, ⎕FDROP, consider a file application involving order entry and invoicing. As each order is received, the pertinent information is appended as a new component on a file. Each order shipped causes an invoice to be produced, and the order information for that order is no longer needed. Most of the time, but not always, orders will be shipped in the order of receipt. It makes sense to let the component number be the order/invoice number, since there will be a different component for each one.

The only fly in the ointment is how to dispose of all the components holding order information that has already been invoiced. For that, we use ⎕FDROP. It is monadic, and its argument is the file number and the number of sequential components you want to drop from the front end (positive number) or back end (negative number) of the file.

For example, if some file tied to the number 20 presently has 153 components (that is, ⎕FSIZE 20 results in 1 154 40028 100000), then dropping 15 components from the front end (⎕FDROP 20 15) leaves 139 components. Then ⎕FSIZE 20 would now yield 16 154 35630 100000. Note that component numbering now starts with 16. If you now drop the last nine components, (⎕FDROP 20 ¯9), the result of ⎕FSIZE 20 would be 16 145 34918 100000.

An application in which components are appended to the file and other components are later dropped from the front end, is called FIFO (first-in, first-out), while an application which appends and drops from the back end is called LIFO (last-in, first-out).

Our order/invoice application is a member of the FIFO category. Here is a possible program to process an invoice, the argument N being the invoice number (component number) to be processed:

```
       ∇INVOICERUN N;ORD;FN
[1]    'ORDERS' □FTIE FN←1+⌈/0,□FNUMS
[2]    →(1=+/N<2↑□FSIZE FN)/OK1
[3]    'THIS NUMBER NOT IN FILE' ◊ □FUNTIE FN ◊ →0
[4]    OK1:ORD←□FREAD FN,N ◊ →(0≠ρORD)/OK2
[5]    'THIS NUMBER ALREADY PROCESSED' ◊ □FUNTIE FN ◊ →0
[6]    OK2: PRINTINVOICE ⍝ INVOICE PRINTING PROGRAM NOT SHOWN HERE
[7]    (⍳0) □FREPLACE FN,N ⍝ REPLACE WITH EMPTY AFTER PROCESSING
[8]    DROPLOOP:→(=/2↑□FSIZE FN)/DONE ⍝ DONE IF FILE IS EMPTY
[9]    →(0≠ρ □FREAD FN,1↑□FSIZE FN)/DONE
[10]   ⍝ STOP WHEN FIRST COMPONENT NOT EMPTY
[11]   □FDROP FN,1 ◊ →DROPLOOP
[12]   DONE:□FUNTIE FN ∇
```

We have departed from a pure FIFO scheme in using an empty vector to signal that an invoice has been processed. After processing, any empty components on the front end of the file are dropped.

When a file is no longer needed, it can be removed by the $□FERASE$ function. Once $□FERASE$ has been applied to a file, that file name no longer exists and any storage used by the file is available for reuse. The file to be erased must be tied. $□FERASE$ is a dyadic function whose left argument is the file name and whose right argument is the file tie number. It may seem redundant that both the name and tie number are required, but this is done to protect you from erasing the wrong file by accident.

```
       'CUSTOMERS' □FERASE 76
```

File access

Our discussion so far has assumed that you are the only person to access and update your files. This is satisfactory for many applications, but what do you do if the file in question contains, say, airline flight reservations which may be updated by any of thousands of ticket or travel agents across the country? We need a mechanism that permits sharing data among multiple users. To make a file shareable, its owner must overtly arrange for others to share it. For reasons of data security, when a file is first created, it is personal (i.e., not available to anyone other than the owner).

When a file owner decides to share his file, he must determine the type of *access permission* he wants to give others. For example, a bank systems manager may own (and hence control) a file of customer transactions. He might also want to allow the bank tellers to append new transactions on the file, but prevent their reading any of the already filed material. He might also want the bank president to be able to read any transaction, but (because the president has clumsy fingers) might not be willing to let him replace or append any components. And the people in the accounting department may have read, replace and append access, but are not allowed to drop or erase any transactions.

In the APL*PLUS and Sharp file systems, all these access rules are determined and recorded in an *access matrix*. Each file has associated with it an access matrix with three columns: the first contains the user numbers of those who have been given access permission of some sort; the second is the sum of *access codes* granted to each individual; and the third is an *access passnumber*, which provides a level of security to be discussed later in this chapter. For the time being the third column will be kept at zero, which means no access passnumber is required.

Here are the codes used to grant accesses to a file:

1 allows $□FREAD$	128 allows $□FRENAME$
2 allows $□FTIE$	512 allows $□FRDCI$
4 allows $□FERASE$	1024 allows $□FRESIZE$
8 allows $□FAPPEND$	2048 allows $□FHOLD$
16 allows $□FREPLACE$	4096 allows $□FRDAC$
32 allows $□FDROP$	8192 allows $□FSTAC$

A file's access matrix is brought into the workspace by an expression of the form $AM←□FRDAC\ FN$, where FN is the file number. As mentioned earlier, AM will always have 3 columns. For a file which has no accesses set, $ρAM$ is $0\ \ 3$.

Say you wanted user 78975 to be permitted to read components on a file which you own, and user 1729 to be able to append and replace components on your file. You would construct a matrix like this:

```
      AM←2 3ρ78975 1 0 1729 24 0
      AM
78975        1       0
 1729       24       0
      AM ⎕FSTAC 20
```

The ⎕FSTAC function is used to change the accesses for a file. Its left argument will be the access matrix of file 20 in this example. User 78975 has read access to the file because of the 1 in column two, and user 1729 has append and replace access because of the 24 (i.e., 8 for append plus 16 for replace) in AM[2;2].

Given that someone has granted you access to his file, how do you actually do it? You can list the file names to which another user (say 4176382) has given you some kind of access by using ⎕FLIB:

```
      ⎕FLIB 4176382
4176382 BONDS
4176382 STOCKS
```

Now that you know what files you have access to, you can tie them with ⎕FSTIE:

```
      '4176382 STOCKS' ⎕FSTIE 909
```

The left argument is the owner's user number and file name. ⎕FSTIE works much like the function ⎕FTIE introduced earlier. Once ⎕FSTIE has been executed, you can perform any of the file functions for which access permission has been granted.

Any number of users may tie the same file at the same time using ⎕FSTIE (called a *shared tie*), but only one person may tie a file using ⎕FTIE (*exclusive tie*). Normally, when using someone else's files, you 'share-tie' them. In fact, most shared applications don't permit ⎕FTIE (as controlled by the access matrix) except for emergency maintenance. ⎕FSTIE permission comes along with giving permission to do any of ⎕FREAD, ⎕FSIZE, ⎕FAPPEND, ⎕FREPLACE, ⎕FDROP, ⎕FHOLD, ⎕FRDAC, ⎕FSTAC, ⎕FRDCI, ⎕FRENAME and ⎕FRESIZE, while the function ⎕FERASE requires that the file be exclusively tied.

Here is another example of the use of shared files. Imagine that there is a class of students in a course in computer technology and that the instructor tells them to 'mail' their semester project reports as character vectors appended to a file he created, called PROJECT. The students' user numbers are 1001, 1002, 1003, ... ,1020. Since the instructor doesn't want them to read each other's work, the access permissions are set at 8, i.e., append only:

```
      'PROJECT' ⎕FCREATE 90
      ((1000+ι20),20 2ρ8 0) ⎕FSTAC 90
      ⎕FUNTIE 90
```

Each student can either share-tie and append his result, or he can append more than one component. Now there's always one wise-guy in a class of students who figures he can write whatever sort of graffiti he chooses into his instructor's file. But he won't go undetected. The function ⎕FRDCI (for *read component information*) is designed to let you know who did what to your file. Its syntax is like ⎕FREAD. The argument is a two-element vector consisting of the file number and component number.

The result is always a three-element vector. The first element is the number of bytes the component would use up if it were read into the workspace. This gives you the opportunity to bypass reading a large component in a crowded workspace. The second element is the user number of the person who last appended or replaced this particular component. A user who appends or replaces a component cannot suppress this information. The third element is the *timestamp*: when the component was appended or last replaced. This can be very useful when trying to analyze past actions performed on a file. The time is computed in milliseconds since midnight, January 1, 1900.

In workspace 0 or 1 FILEAID on APL*PLUS systems, you will find the monadic function TIMEN. Use the third element of ⎕FRDCI's result as its right argument. It will convert the argument into a more readable form, a six-element vector consisting of the year, month, day, hour, minute and seconds.

Real-time systems

The $\square FHOLD$ function is employed in sophisticated real-time systems where it is important that changes to the database be synchronized among several sharers. For example, suppose you had a shared file in which one component is a character matrix of names and another component is a vector of associated numbers (one number per row of the character matrix), and you did the following update:

```
NAMES←□FREAD 1 1 ◇ VEC←□FREAD 1 2
NAMES[K;]←20↑⍟ ◇ VEC[K]←□
NAMES □FREPLACE 1 1 ◇ VEC □FREPLACE 1 2
```

There is a risk that some other user might execute

```
NAMES←□FREAD 1 1 ◇ VEC←□FREAD 1 2
```

and get the data that existed on the file for the time between when you entered $NAMES$ $\square FREPLACE$ 1 1 and VEC $\square FREPLACE$ 1 2. If that were to happen, he'd have the new name but the old value.

To prevent this, the $\square FHOLD$ function is used. It is monadic, its argument consisting of the tie numbers of those shared files for which you want *temporary exclusive access*. The general idea is to bar you and the other sharers from doing anything with the file, if any of the sharers has already begun a critical updating sequence.

Thus, your update section should look like

```
NEWNAME←,⍟ ◇ NEWVALUE←□
□FHOLD 1 ◇ NAMES←□FREAD 1 1 ◇ VEC←□FREAD 1 2
NAMES[K;]←20↑NEWNAME ◇ VEC[K]←NEWVALUE
NAMES □FREPLACE 1 1 ◇ VEC □FREPLACE 1 2
□FHOLD ι0
```

and the other user's retrieval section should be

```
□FHOLD 1 ◇ NAMES←□FREAD 1 1 ◇ VEC←□FREAD 1 2 ◇ □FHOLD ι0
```

What actually happens when you execute $\square FHOLD$ is that a request for temporary exclusive use of the files is entered. If no one presently has the files in temporary exclusive use, you get them. If someone has an active $\square FHOLD$, execution of your function is suspended until his $\square FHOLD$ is broken (and all users who had executed $\square FHOLD$ prior to your request have been satisfied). Then it's your turn. To avoid hard feelings among disgruntled users, extensive updating should be done at times when the use of the file by others is likely to be minimal.

You might think that an uncooperative sharer could hog the file by executing a $\square FHOLD$ and not breaking it; however, $\square FHOLD$ is broken by any of these actions:

1. An interruption at the keyboard
2. Executing another $\square FHOLD$
3. Any return to execution mode
4. Untying the file
5. Signing off or being bounced

$\square FHOLD$ $ι0$ in the above example relinquishes your hold so that others don't have to wait unnecessarily to use the file. The conversational input $NEWNAME←,⍟$ $◇$ $NEWVALUE←□$ was moved outside the domain of $\square FHOLD$ for a similar reason. Other users might waste a lot of time waiting for you to input at the keyboard while hogging the file, although in some applications this might be a perfectly valid technique.

Transferring ownership and renaming files

The $\square FRENAME$ function, as its name suggests, lets you rename a file. The left argument is the new name, and the right argument is the tie number. If rename a file belonging to someone else (he would have to have given you access permission to do so), you now own it. Of course, $\square FRENAME$ can also be used to change the name of one of your own files.

Access passnumbers and secure applications

Even though you can control what types of file accesses a person can make through the access codes in the second column of a file access matrix, this is usually not enough. For example, you might have a file in which a certain user is permitted to read only the fifth component of a file, or one in which you won't permit him to append a component with more than, say, 500 elements.

Access passnumbers, the third column of the access matrix, are used to gain this level of security control. It works this way: if the access passnumber for a user is *not* 0, then to use the file, that person must supply the identical value in his file functions. Suppose user 666666 has been granted access to the file '78974 STREAK' by this row in the access matrix: 666666 25 6948520. This means that user 666666 has permission to share-tie, read, append and replace, but he must use expressions like this:

```
'78974 STREAK' □FSTIE 1 6948520
X←□FREAD 1 10 6948520
```

The access passnumber, when required, is the last element of the right argument of the file functions. The only exception is for □FHOLD. For it, use a 2-row matrix. The first row is the tie numbers of the files to be held, and the second row is the corresponding access passnumbers:

```
□FHOLD 2 1ρ1 6948520
```

It doesn't make such sense to go through all the bother of setting up a passnumber and then telling the user what that number is, so locked functions are employed. In secure applications, the designer or owner of the file usually supplies his correspondents with locked functions to do the file accessing. For instance, the following simple program allows other users to access only the even-numbered components of the file:

```
    ∇ Z←READ N
[1]   Z←□FREAD N[1],(N[2]×0=2|N[2]),6948520 ▽
```

Since the function is locked, there is no way the user can disclose the passnumber. Any attempts to read odd-numbered components will result in a *FILE INDEX ERROR*.

Summary of file functions

Here is a table showing all the file functions. *Z←* means that there is an explicit result. *tn*, *cn* and *pn* mean respectively file tie number, component number and access passnumber. The passnumber is required only if there is a nonzero value in column three of the access matrix. The access codes (column 2 of the access matrix) are shown for your convenience.

	function		code
arg	□FAPPEND	tn,pn	8
arg	□FCREATE	tn	none
	□FDROP	tn,arg,pn	32
arg	□FERASE	tn,pn	4
	□FHOLD	tn,tn,...	2048
Z ←	□FLIB	arg	none
Z ←	□FNAMES		none
Z ←	□FNUMS		none
Z ←	□FRDAC	tn,pn	4096
Z ←	□FRDCI	tn,cn,pn	512
Z ←	□FREAD	tn,cn,pn	1
arg	□FRENAME	tn,pn	128
arg	□FREPLACE	tn,cn,pn	16
arg	□FRESIZE	tn,pn	1024
Z ←	□FSIZE	tn,pn	any
arg	□FSTAC	tn,pn	8192
arg	□FSTIE	tn,pn	any
arg	□FTIE	tn,pn	2
	□FUNTIE	tn,tn,...	none

Chapter 27: Shared variables and communicating with other systems

IBM's shared variables concept is a general means of communication between your own APL programs and those of others, both APL and non-APL. The latter may even include the operating system under which APL and other (non-APL) services are running. A shared variable is, therefore, a window between your program and other environments to which your computer allows access.

What shared variables is all about

Chapter 23 introduced a feature that permits sharing a variable (though without specifically labelling the process as such)—the □ used for APL input and output. There, the □ is shared between you at your terminal and APL. We will now define a set of system functions that will generalize this simple sharing concept to include many other environments.

Just as you and your active workspace comprise a team to share the work of solving a problem, teams can be formed among two APL users and their active workspaces. Teams can also consist of an APL active workspace and the parent system that lives in the inner depths of the computer, and which controls all APL activities. They can further come into being between the parent APL system and alien languages or systems running on the same computer, such as FORTRAN, COBOL, Assembler language and their associated storage mechanisms.

For example, on most APL systems you can print voluminous reports on the high-speed printer attached to the computer, instead of at your terminal. This involves you, your terminal, your active workspace, the parent APL system, the system that runs the printer, the printer itself and the person at the computer center who puts the proper paper on the printer and delivers the printed results to you.

In practice, most APL users overlook most of these distinctions as unnecessary philosophy. But the ability to model shared processes is a characteristic of APL that is worth knowing. In this chapter we'll consider the formal sharing between a variety of commonly encountered environments.

Any APL variable in your active workspace, global or local, can be shared with any other consenting user. Both you and he can give the variable a new value. Then, when one of you uses the variable, it will have the most recent value that was given by either. A variable can be shared with the dyadic $\Box SVO$ (shared variable offer) system function. For example, the expression $78974 \ \Box SVO \ 'X'$ is an offer to share your variable X with user 78974.

User 78974 must make a similar offer to share his variable X with you. If your user number is 3677758, then he executes $3677758 \ \Box SVO \ 'X'$. $\Box SVO$ returns an explicit result, called the *degree of coupling*. The result is 1 when the first user has made an offer, and 2 when the second user makes a matching offer. A result of 2 indicates that the sharing arrangement has been consummated. A result of 0 means no offer has been made.

It isn't necessary that the two consenting users use the same name to refer to the shared variable. For example, users 78974 and 3677758 might agree that 3677758's variable $MZ3$ and 78974's variable SX are to be the same thing. Then, after 3677758 executes $MZ3 \leftarrow 'HELLO'$, 78974 would find that his SX is the character vector $'HELLO'$. Any of the following three independent sequences would have the same effect:

```
        USER 3677758                      USER 78974

   --------------------------------------------------------------
          78974 □SVO 'MZ3'                  3677758 □SVO 'SX MZ3'
     1                              2
   --------------------------------------------------------------
          78974 □SVO 'MZ3 SX'              3677758 □SVO 'SX'
     1                              2
   --------------------------------------------------------------
          78974 □SVO 'MZ3 COMM'           3677758 □SVO 'SX COMM'
     1                              2
   --------------------------------------------------------------
```

The second name mentioned in the right argument is called a *surrogate name*. It serves as a common link to establish the sharing. This is most evident in the third sequence, where both users offer the new name *COMM* as the surrogate. Surrogate names may not be more than 15 characters long.

You can make several offers to share at the same time. The right argument is then a matrix of names (one row per name, and if there is to be a surrogate it must be separated from the name by a blank). The left argument is a vector of coupling users, one for each variable of the right argument that is to be shared polygamously. The combination of a scalar left argument and matrix right argument offers to share all the variables with that user. For example,

```
     78974 □SVO 3 3ρ'MZ3MZ4MZ5'
 1 2 2
```

offers to share variables *MZ3*, *MZ4* and *MZ5*, but user *78974* has already offered variables *MZ4* and *MZ5*.

You can find out what variables are presently being offered for sharing with the □*SVQ* (shared variable query) monadic system function. It has two modes of operation. If the argument is an empty vector, the result is a vector holding the user numbers of all people offering to share something with you. And if the argument is one of those numbers, the result is a character matrix holding the names of the variables that user is offering to you. This matrix holds only the names that are *offered* for sharing, and not those which are presently being shared.

To determine whether a variable has been offered for sharing, is shared or hasn't been offered, use the monadic □*SVO* system function. Its argument is a character vector (or matrix) holding the names of the variables you are inquiring about. The result is a scalar (or vector) holding the degree of coupling: 0 if the variable has not been offered, 1 if it has been offered, and 2 if it is presently being shared with someone. For those cases where the degree of coupling is 1 or 2 the dyadic □*SVO* may also be used for inquiry, since a repeated offer under those conditions does not change the status of the original offer.

There are several possible error conditions that may occur. Attempts to exceed the quota of shared variables assigned by the system management result in *INTERFACE QUOTA EXHAUSTED* messages. Unavailability of the shared variable facility itself causes the report *NO SHARES*.

A variable need not have been assigned to share it. Or it is possible that both users have assigned a value to it prior to sharing. Here is how potential conflicts are resolved: if neither sharer has assigned a value, an attempt to use the variable results in the normal *VALUE ERROR*. If only one user has assigned it, that value is taken. If both have assigned values prior to sharing, then the value taken is the one set by the first person to make the offer to share.

For the lonely hearts among our readers, an offer to share a variable with user number 0 means you're willing to share it with any user who happens to be signed on at that time. Such unbounded generosity, however, can be reciprocated only with a counter-offer that specifically identifies the user making the original general offer.

After a variable is shared, it can be used much like any other variable. For example, you can set the (shared) variable *MZ3* by *MZ3*←56. You or anyone else among the sharers can now 'read' it in the usual way:

```
     MZ3
 56
```

Since any sharer can read or reassign it at any time independently of other sharers, the process is completely unconstrained. If *MZ3* represented a sharer's bank balance, such anarchy would lead to chaos if there were no rules governing who is allowed to do what under various conditions.

This *access protocol* is defined by the dyadic system function $\Box SVC$ (shared *variable* control). Its right argument is a vector (or matrix) of the names of the variables whose access protocol is to be changed. The left argument is a four-element vector (or matrix with four columns) whose values can be only 0 or 1 as specified below:

If the first element is 1	Your sharer must read or assign a value to the shared variable before you can reassign it.
If the second element is 1	Your sharer cannot reassign the shared variable until you either read or assign a value to it.
If the third element is 1	You cannot read the shared variable a second time unless your sharer has reassigned it.
If the fourth element is 1	Your sharer cannot read the shared variable a second time unless you have reassigned it.

It would appear that you can control your sharer's every move. That's not exactly the case, however, since he can make similar restrictions apply to your use of the shared variable. In fact, the resulting access protocol is determined by the logical OR ($\vee$) of both your access requests. Hence, the effect is always to become more restrictive. In one sense this is good, because there is no way that an uncooperative user can negate restrictions you have set. As a byproduct, dyadic $\Box SVC$ returns an explicit result which is the new setting of the access protocol combining your specifications with those of the sharer. It is the same shape as the left argument.

Monadic $\Box SVC$, whose argument is a character vector (or matrix) holding names of shared variables, returns the present access protocol as seen by the user, but doesn't change any of the control settings.

In actual operation, when one of the sharers is inhibited from proceeding and awaits some interlocking action on the part of the other sharer, his execution is held up until the action is performed. As soon as the conditions are satisfied, his execution continues. Interrupting may disturb the sharing aspects of a particular system.

An existing sharing arrangement can be retracted by the monadic system function $\Box SVR$ (shared *variable* retraction). The argument is a character vector (or matrix) holding the names of the variables you wish to stop sharing. The explicit result is the degree of coupling that the variables had prior to being withdrawn. Thus, you can annul an offer to share even before a prospective sharer has consummated the sharing arrangement.

A variable also ceases to be shared if you sign off, are disconnected because of a telephone failure, load or clear a workspace, or if the shared variable was local to some function which has completed execution, or if you erase the variable.

Once a variable has been offered for sharing, its access protocol does not have to be respecified. That is to say, after a nullification and subsequent offer to share again, the access protocol is whatever it was the last time it was set with $\Box SVC$. However, it's a good idea to verify the degree of coupling from time to time if the other sharer is believed to be unstable.

A variable can be shared with only one other person at any time. Polygamous sharing of information can be done by having one of the people serve as a steward, or 'communication center.' By sharing at least one variable with each of the other people, the communication center can mediate and route information among any of the people with whom he shares a variable.

System dependence

The shared variable commands described so far are fairly consistent across most APL systems offering them. Once we begin to use them to communicate with non-APL environments all sorts of system dependencies arise, which makes for problems in transporting APL data or programs from one system to another. Common sense suggests that to minimize the difficulty of making the required changes under these circumstances, the communication instructions should be isolated and well documented in a small number of subroutines. This has the obvious benefit of making the instructions to be changed not only more accessible but also more understandable.

Those non-APL programs that use the shared variable concept to interface with APL are called *auxiliary processors* (AP's). They provide access to many different non-APL environments. The rest of this chapter discusses some AP's found in various IBM systems, in particular *Time Shared Input/Output AP* (TSIO), which lets you use the data management facilities of the OS/VS and MVS operating systems and AP 100, 110, 111 and 123, found in CMS, a system operating in the virtual machine environment VM/370. They allow you to read and write files, execute VM and CMS commands, and access various peripheral devices. These AP's are also associated with other systems, such as TSO and CICS. (The authors regret having to deal with the computerese acronyms that pepper this section. We debated omitting the material entirely, but deferred because the facility provides the only way in many cases to use APL for important information handling tasks.)

TSIO file processing

This section will describe the access functions in the IBM supplied workspaces *APLFILES* and *TSIO* as part of APLSV. These workspaces let you use both TSIO and shared variables to set up, store and access files outside your workspaces.

```
)LOAD 1 APLFILES
SAVED   8.27.13 02/20/83
```

A file is created by using the dyadic function *CREATE*. The right argument, a character vector, is the name to be associated with the file. The left argument is a three-element vector. Element one contains the maximum number of components (APL arrays) that you can store in the file. Element two is the size (in characters) of the chunks[1]. A component may use several chunks, but a chunk cannot be used by two components. Therefore, use of many small chunks for a component results in a greater amount of retrieval time, while large chunks mean a lot of wasted storage in your file. The third element consists of the total number of chunks allowed.

For casual use of *CREATE*, you need not worry about all these details. If the third element is not given, 1.1 times the value of element one is supplied automatically. If the second element is not given, a chunk size of 550 is assumed. And if the first element is not supplied (that is, the left argument is ι0), then a file with a capacity for 100 components is created:

```
(ι0) CREATE 'SMALLFILE'
```

Here a file named *SMALLFILE* has been created with 100 components and a total of 110 chunks of 550 characters each.

Once a file has been created, it can be activated with the *USE* function:

```
USE 'SMALLFILE'
```

If you are using someone else's files, his user number must precede the file name and be separated by a blank, for example, *USE '1234 DATA'*. Use of that file by someone else doesn't preclude your reading it. *Caution:* the *USE* function sets three global variables, the first of which begins with the letters *CTL* and is followed by your file name. The second begins with the letters *DAT* and the last begins with *FD*. Avoid using these variables directly, as they are a critical part of the operation of the file processor.

Data is put on the file by using the function *SET*, aided by the function *AT*, in an expression of the form *(FILENAME AT COMPONENTNO) SET DATA*. As an example, let's put the character vector '3000 WESTCHESTER AVENUE' into the fifth component of the file *SMALLFILE*:

```
('SMALLFILE' AT 5) SET '3000 WESTCHESTER AVENUE'
```

The fifth component can be set without having set components one through four. However, you can't set any components beyond 100 with this particular file since only 100 were implied when the file was created.

Data is read from the file with the *GET* and *AT* functions. If you attempt to *GET* a component which has not been set, a *FILE INDEX ERROR* results.

```
R←GET 'SMALLFILE' AT 5
R
3000 WESTCHESTER AVENUE
```

The function *EXIST* can be used before *GET* to determine which components already have values. The result is ¯1 for components out of range, 0 for those components in the range but having no value, and 1 for those that do have values:

```
EXIST 'SMALLFILE' AT 3 4 5 6 100 101 102
0 0 1 0 0 ¯1 ¯1
```

---

[1] *Chunk* is the authors' term to refer to any physical or logical borders in storage such as tracks, sectors, extents, granules, etc., which impose some restriction on the smooth and contiguous storage of data in space set aside for you.

For files shared among users, you can tell who last set a particular component and its timestamp with the *GETL* function. *GETL FILENAME AT COMPONENTNO* returns the number of the user who has set the component, and when it was set.

A component can be removed with the *ERASE* command, which frees up the storage:

```
ERASE 'SMALLFILE' AT 5
EXIST 'SMALLFILE' AT 5
```
0

When there is only one file for an application, or when you reference the same file again, you can omit the *AT* and its right argument with *SET*, *GET*, *ERASE* and *EXIST*. These functions all use the global variable *FILEID*, which holds the name of the file last used as an argument to *USE* or *AT*.

Finally, when access to a file is no longer required, use the *RELEASE* function. *RELEASE* returns an explicit result 1 if the file was in use at the time of release, or 0 if it wasn't. *RELEASE* doesn't destroy the file, but simply retires it from active use. *USE* must be executed to regain access to a file after it has been released:

```
RELEASE 'SMALLFILE'
```
1

DELETE is used when a file is to be destroyed. It makes the file permanently unavailable, removes the file name and frees the previously occupied storage space for reuse:

```
DELETE 'SMALLFILE'
```

Other TSIO functions

Besides the TSIO functions in *APLFILES*, there are cover functions distributed with *APLSV* that provide an interface to the TSIO processor and incorporate the commands needed to share variables. There are two which are particularly useful, *TRY* and *CHK*.

TRY offers a share to the TSIO processor, uses surrogate names, checks for acceptable completion codes and sets up an interlock and file access. Here is an example:[1]

```
'A' TRY 'SW DSN=DS1'
```

CHK enables you to check the return codes (it is used by *TRY*):

```
B CHK C
```

B is a vector of return codes for which a message will *not* print. *C* is the shared variable. *CHK*'s result is a vector of length *B* with a 1 corresponding to the return code found and 0 elsewhere. If *B* is an empty vector, all error messages will be printed.

There are three global variables used in *TRY* and *CHK*. They are set by the application:

O	error conditions (1-31)
OLE	error messages corresponding to *O*
PID	processor ID (most often 370)

If TSIO returns a code not in *O*, the error message will be printed.

Although many of the error messages are self-explanatory (e.g., 12 *DATA SET NOT FOUND*), you may have to refer for help to the table of TSIO messages in the IBM publication SH 20-9087, APL Shared Variable Users Guide.

The rest of the discussion of TSIO will be concerned with the *direct* use of TSIO, as opposed to the cover functions like *USE*, *GET*, *ERASE* etc., that we have just described.

---

[1]With apologies to our readers, the standard terminology used in this and many subsequent commands in the rest of this chapter now begins to stray a little from 'looking like APL.' SW, to be explained later, stands for 'sequential write,' and DSN for 'dataset name.' A is the surrogate name of the control variable.

You may already have heard other programmers use words like *blocks* and *records* and wondered what they meant. To help you, we include a brief glossary of commonly used terms relating to how files are organized in many systems.

Terminology

dataset	The name given to a file in the operating system
block	A chunk of a dataset moved between the internal memory of the computer and the external device (tape, disk, etc.,) on which the dataset is stored.
record	A subunit of a block which contains the information you would normally access when you read or write to a dataset. It is sometimes called a *logical record*.
blocked (unblocked) data	Datasets whose blocks contain more than one data record are said to be blocked; otherwise they are unblocked.
fixed (variable) length	Applies to both blocks and records.
self-describing records	Begins with an indication of how long it is.
record format (RECFM)	A description of how blocks and records of a dataset are organized.
sequential access	Reading (SR) or writing (SW) records in a dataset in sequential order.
indexed access	Reading (IR) or writing (IW) records in a dataset by selecting the desired indices (records are indexed sequentially beginning with 0).

Our discussion of files hinted that the internal architecture of a block may differ significantly from one file to another, not just in the length of the records or the number of records in the block, but also in the kind of information in the record and in how it is encoded. The record format describes the organization of the block.

There are six different record formats provided in TSIO:

RECFM	Fixed length blocks
F	One fixed length record
FBS	The same number (>1) of fixed length records, each sent as a matrix
U	One variable length record
FB	Some number of fixed length records, each sent as a vector
V	One self-describing variable length record
VB	Some number of self-describing variable length records

The information itself may be stored in many different ways: in floating point, integer, character, APL or APL-EBCDIC representation. As you might expect, only the APL representation carries with it the shape and type of data. The others use only vectors.

Communicating with TSIO

In the description of the cover function *USE* (page 283), we pointed out that the file processor used several global variables. These variables are key to letting TSIO know that you want to work with a file.

The first of these is a *control variable* whose name must start with $\underline{CTL}$, followed by a dataset name. It serves two masters, letting you give commands to TSIO and letting TSIO in turn tell you how you made out with your commands. Where there may be multiple simultaneous accesses, TSIO uses this variable to keep things straight.

The second is a *data variable* whose name must start with $\underline{DAT}$, followed by a dataset name. For each data variable there is an associated control variable, the association being denoted by the use of the same dataset name (or surrogate name) with both variables. For example, if the dataset is DS1, the variables would be $\underline{CTLDS}1$ and $\underline{DATDS}1$. Of course, more than one control variable (or associated control/data variables) may be shared simultaneously for concurrent access to the dataset.

We haven't yet said how you identify the TSIO processor when you make your offer to share. On many (but not all) systems it is labeled '370'. Your sharing instruction would therefore be

```
370 ⎕SVO 'CTL'
```

1

Creating a dataset

A dataset may be built up only by writing records to it sequentially. If it has been sequentially written with RECFM=F, it may be indexed read or rewritten later.

To create a new dataset CTL must be set with several commands, SW for sequential writing, DSN=[name of dataset], DISP(for disposition)=NEW, RECFM=F (for indexed access, otherwise the default is RECFM=V), and BLKSIZE=[number of records per block]. Here is an example:

```
CTL←'SW DSN=DS1,DISP=NEW,RECFM=F,BLKSIZE=750'
CTL
0        (indicates successful execution)
```

Missing from the above is the space to be allocated and the data representation (default is CODE=A, for APL).

Now you are ready to write records to the data set. Once again the control variable is the key:

```
CTL←'RECORD1'
CTL←2 3ρφι6
CTL←10 20 30
CTL←'MARY HAD A LITTLE LAMB'
CTL←ι0
CTL
0
```

The data set is closed by assigning an empty vector to CTL.

Finally, to reopen an existing dataset, say, DS1, for sequential writing, set

```
CTL←'SW DSN=DS1'
```

Since DISP=OLD is the default value and the block size and record format are already known to TSIO, the dataset is ready for you to sequentially write records.

Now you have a problem. The above command erases the existing records and starts writing again with the first record. Most of the time, however, you merely want to write additional records to an existing dataset. For this use the command

```
CTL←'SW DSN=DS1, DISP=MOD'
```

To change the name of a dataset use the $RENAME$ command

```
CTL←'RENAME DSN=FRANKS, NEWNAME=HOTDOGS'
```

and to get rid of a dataset use $DELETE$:

```
CTL←'DELETE DSN=HOTDOGS'
```

Reading a dataset

As you might expect, you can sequentially read DS1 by the following commands:

```
CTL←'SR DSN=DS1'        (opens DS1)

      CTL
0
      CTL
RECORD1
      CTL
3 2 1
6 5 4
      ρ□←CTL
10 20 30

3
      CTL
MARY HAD A LITTLE LAMB
```

```
      ρZ←CTL          (end of dataset)
0
      CTL
0
```

If the empty vector had actually been entered as data, the response code to *CTL* would have been 1 4.

Indexed reading and writing

Thus far we have described how to sequentially read or write to a dataset starting at the first record. Many applications require access only to particular records in a dataset. TSIO provides this capability by associating sequential indices with the records. The numbering begins with 0, not 1. To index read or write a record two variables are needed—*CTL* to indicate whether we want to read or write, and *DAT* to send the data. As with *CTL*, *DAT* first has to be offered for sharing:

```
      370 □SVO 'DAT'
1
```

The following sequence of commands allows you to read the dataset:

```
      CTL←'IR DSN=DS1'      (open DS1 for indexed read)

      CTL
0
      CTL←0 2               (read [0 indicates read] third record)

      CTL
0
      DAT                   (third record)

      CTL←0 0               (read first record)

      DAT
RECORD1                     (first record)

      CTL←''                (close DS1)

      CTL
0
```

To read and write the commands are modified slightly:

```
      CTL←'IRW DSN=DS1'     (open DS1 for indexed read/write)

      CTL←0 2              (read third record)

      DAT                  (third record)
10 20 30
      DAT←'WHITE PLAINS, N.Y.'
      CTL←1 2              (write [1 indicates write] over third record with DAT)

      CTL←0 2              (read third record)

      DAT
WHITE PLAINS, N.Y.         (third record)
```

Sharing TSIO datasets

An owner may designate his dataset for sharing by DISP=SHR. Others may obtain access to it by also indicating DISP=SHR. Now the fun begins. If two users want to read the dataset at the same time, there is no problem since the contents of the dataset are static. But if writing is involved, there may be synchronization problems as to who does what when.

Much depends on what is being written. If the two users write independent records, they are home free. Even if they write the same record there is no difficulty, provided that what they write doesn't depend on what was previously in the record. TSIO acts as a scheduler, allowing one user to write and then the other.

The troublesome case arises where one user reads, say, record 20 and then decides, on the basis of what is in record 20, to add 5 to it. In the interval between his reading and writing of record 20, a second user reads record 20 and decides to add 10 to it. By the time he gets around to writing it, the first user has already rewritten record 20, so the change that the second user wants to make is based on an old reading of the record.

TSIO again comes to the rescue, with provisions for exclusive as well as shared holds on records, parts of datasets, functions on the datasets, or even things not connected with datasets at all, such as printers. All the things that a hold can be associated with are collectively designated as *facilities*, each of which is represented by a number.

A hold is exercised by setting

$$CTL \leftarrow C, F$$

F is the integer associated with the facility in question. C designates the type of hold desired. It has values 2,3,4 or 5 with the following meanings:

C	*request for*
2	Exclusive hold. Allow only if there is no current hold on F. The response code indicates whether the hold was successful. Continue execution.
3	Exclusive hold, but delay execution until all existing requests for holds on F have been fulfilled and the holds released.
4	Shared hold. Allow only if there are no existing requests for exclusive holds.
5	Shared hold, but delay execution as in C=3.

A second hold request on a facility releases an existing hold, as will retraction of the shared variable or its disappearance. Setting F=0 will also release a hold without requesting another. More than one hold can be requested by using multiple control variables.

Protection of datasets

TSIO automatically identifies every dataset you create by your account number. Explicitly adding your account number at the time of creation is allowable, but superfluous, much like loading or copying from one of your own workspaces:

$$CTL \leftarrow 'SW\ DSN=123456\ DS1,\ DISP=NEW,\ BLKSIZE=700'$$

But when you execute with a *negative* account number,

$$CTL \leftarrow 'SW\ DSN=^-123456\ DS1,\ DISP=NEW,\ BLKSIZE=700'$$

DS1 becomes a *reserved* dataset. Only you can access it, unless another APL user sets CTL with an *indirect command*, IC:

$$CTL \leftarrow 'IC\ DSN=^-123456\ CDS(10)'$$

$^-123456\ CDS$ is called a *command dataset*. Put simply, it is a 'laundry list' of commands each of which has associated with it a list of the users authorized to use that command. The example above refers to the 10th command stored in the dataset $^-123456\ CDS$:

$$SW\ DSN=DS1,\ DISP=NEW,\ BLKSIZE=700$$

If you are not on the list, access is denied. The dataset owner, of course, is free to access his reserved datasets at any time. To make it easy for administrators of collections of datasets designed to be accessed by large numbers of authorized users, many APL systems have utility functions which create and update command datasets.

There are other ways to control the setting up of files and use of specific devices. System administrators can allow users to allocate a certain amount of space on a storage device on their own to create new datasets, for example, 100 tracks on a disk. A dataset requiring more than 100 tracks would have to be specifically authorized by the system administrator. A user may be permitted to read other users' nonreserved datasets provided he knows their names. And some users (for example, systems programmers) may have special authorization for additional commands and reserved dataset access.

APL/TSIO datasets are really OS/VS datasets. They may be read directly, bypassing APL security, unless the system administrator has taken steps to prevent or control this access.

Finally, users authorized to allocate specific devices may perform physical I/O through TSIO. They can, for example, read a tape by including in the SR command the appropriate parameters like DENSITY, LABEL, UNIT, VOLUME.

VS APL file processing

In the VM environment programs run on *virtual machines*. This means each user has the perception that all the computer's resources are at his disposal, and are for him only. Since all the users are therefore virtual machine users, direct sharing of variables with others isn't possible. However, auxiliary processors enable users or APL functions to share variables in this environment.

Although there are many AP's in VS APL, our discussion in this chapter will address only those which are useful in working with files and in display screen management. At this time (1983) not all AP's are available or work in the same way in all host environments.

Cover functions

Just as a set of cover functions was provided in the workspace *APLFILES* to assist the TSIO user, so a series of environment dependent and file AP workspaces have been made available in VS APL. Those of you who have read the section on TSIO files will find the names of many of the cover functions similar to their TSIO counterparts. It is expected that more cover functions will be available in time to help the APL user. Readers wishing to explore the literature of the AP's in more detail should consult the references at the end of the chapter. Before reviewing these cover functions, here is an example using AP 110.

AP 110

Let's look at how a CMS file can be read or written using AP 110. Suppose, for example, we want to access the CMS file CUSTOMERS with fixed length records and character translation to the VS APL character set. The command

    DATA←'CUSTOMERS (FIX 192'

initializes the variable *DATA* with the name of the file to be accessed and the options to be used.

The next step is to offer the variable *DATA* for sharing with the AP:

    110 □SVO 'DATA'
2

AP110 then checks the initial value of the variable and assigns a return code. Each subsequent reference to the variable returns a record from the file:

    DATA
SMITH PUBLISHING COMPANY, NEW YORK, NY
    DATA
JONES AND KILPATRICK, INC., MOLINE, ILLINOIS

A new record is added to the file with

    DATA←40↑▯
MURPHY AND GREENBERG CO., ST. LOUIS, MO

and the file is closed by expunging the variable:

$\square EX$ '*DATA*'

Here is a set of utility functions to do this. We must warn you that these utilities may not exist on all VS APL systems; or if they do exist, they may have different names, syntax, restrictions or defaults from those listed here.

action	syntax	comment
file open	*FILEN OPEN R*	Opens the file *FILEN*, which may be new. *FILEN* is a character vector. *R* contains all the (optional) information needed to open the file: file type, mode, fixed length records, access control and conversion options. If missing there are default options.
file write	*Z←DAT PUT FILEN* or *DAT PUTFILE FILEN*	Puts the data in *DAT* sequentially into the file. *DAT* is a character vector in *PUT* and a character matrix in *PUTFILE*.
file read	*Z←GET FILEN* or *Z←GETFILE FILEN*	Gets the next sequential record in the file. The argument of *GETFILE* may contain, besides the file name, file type, mode and conversion option.
file close	*Z←CLOSE FILEN* *Z←CLOSEALL*	Closes the file and expunges the associated shared variables. *CLOSEALL* expunges all outstanding shared variables.

For the TSO environment there are similar functions available, along with a function *Z←FILEN RECID RECNO* which is used with *GET* and *PUT* to directly access a particular record, e.g., *GET CUSTOMER RECID* 30 will read record number 30 in the file *CUSTOMER*.

The CICS environment uses AP 132 to access what are called *transient data files* , which allow data to be exchanged with other CICS transactions. The files can be thought of as first in, first out queues where reading destroys a record at one end while writing appends it at the other.

file activated	*USE FILEN*	
file write	*QWRITE DAT*	A character scalar or vector is written at the back end of the current queue.
file read	*Z←QREAD*	Reads record at front end of queue and removes it from queue.
file close	*CLOSE*	Closes file and expunges shared variables.

Reading and writing APL variables

AP 121 reads and writes APL variables in their internal form. Objects are stored as they appear in the workspace. Here are the key functions:

file create	*L ACREATE FILEN*	Creates an APL file. *L* is a character vector beginning with '*S*' for a sequential file, otherwise a direct file is assumed. A numeric ending for *L* is the file size in bytes (default size if absent).
file activated	*USE FILEN*	Makes the referenced file available for reading or writing.
file write	*AWRITE DAT*	Writes *DAT* to the file. An empty vector closes it.
file read	*Z←AREAD*	Reads the next record (sequential) sequentially.
file read	*Z←AGET RECNO*	Reads the specified (direct) record number.
file update	*RECNO ASET DAT*	Replaces record *RECNO* with *DAT*.
file close	*CLOSE*	Closes currently open file and expunges associated shared variables.
file delete	*DROP FILEN*	Deletes the file.

Two monadic functions are provided to store large variables. *STORE VAR* (*VAR* is a character vector or scalar holding the name of the variable) creates an APL sequential file with the same name as in *VAR*, writes the variable as a single record, then expunges *VAR* from the workspace. *RETRIEVE VAR* opens the file and recreates *VAR* in the workspace.

For those users who have to access VSAM files, a similar set of utilities is provided. These are described in detail in the IBM manual 'A Guide to the VS APL Workspace Library,' Document Number GG22-9263.

Designing and using full-screen panels

Most computer systems these days provide facilities for full-screen panel design to take advantage of the capabilities available on newer display terminals. The miracles of modern electronics make it possible to access and use the entire screen, so that users aren't limited by the unidirectional start-stop movements of the keyboard printers that were popular when APL was in its infancy. VS APL provides AP 126 to assist in both designing and using the panels in APL programs.

In common with the other AP's, a set of cover functions has been developed to assist users in designing their own panels. Although the details may differ from system to system, the tasks which any good full-screen manager has to perform are the same. They include:

1. starting and stopping the use of AP 126
2. managing the pages themselves (creating, deleting, accessing, storing)
3. formatting text fields (defining new fields, reformatting existing fields, defining field attributes (e.g., color, highlighting, symbol sets, use of light pen, etc.)
4. managing screen I/O, including getting the output from 3 above to the screen so that it can be used
5. writing and reading text and attributes
6. getting screens to a printer
7. error handling
8. translating characters

A comprehensive set of cover functions that manage these tasks is in the distributed workspace *FSM*, which uses the IBM GDDM Program Product. To make things easier there is a companion workspace *FSDESIGN* which is a step-by-step do-it-yourself program, called *DESIGN*, that allows the user to query the process at each stage for a complete description of what is happening. The PF keys of the IBM 3278 terminal are employed in *DESIGN* not only to get help, stop execution or go back to the master design-control panel, but also to manipulate the viewing area of the screen as the panel is being laid out. Users will find the last two references particularly helpful here.

References (IBM Documents)

APLSV Shared Variables User's Guide, SH20-9087

VS APL for CMS, Terminal User's Guide, SH20-9067

VS APL for TSO, Terminal User's Guide, SH20-9180

VS APL for CICS, Terminal User's Guide, SH20-9167

Presentation Graphics Feature User's Guide, SC33-0102

Graphical Data Display Manager User's Guide, SC33-0101

A Guide to the VS APL Workspace Library, GG22-9263.

Chapter 28: Et cetera

This chapter consists of topics that didn't fit conveniently elsewhere. Some of it is very implementation specific. Nonetheless, these topics are important for advanced APL usage.

Working with time

Most APL systems have a clock that is accessed for a wide range of uses. In the case of a personal computer the user sets the clock when he turns on the computer; on larger systems the clock is set by the operations staff. The accuracy of the clock is no better than the accuracy of its initial setting, and it is possible that the clock may run slightly slow, particularly on small computers, if the system is heavily used.

The first manifestation of the clock that a user sees is typically in his sign-on banner, which will report the time and date.

When a workspace is saved a *timestamp* is supplied by the system; that timestamp is displayed when the workspace is loaded or copied. It can be invaluable to a developer trying to figure out which workspace is the most recent version.

On APL*PLUS Systems, the system variable $\Box WSTS$ is a scalar containing the time the active workspace was last saved. It is stored in millionths of a second from midnight January 1, 1900. In workspace 1 $FILEAID$ the monadic functions $TIMEN$ (for a result compatible with $\Box TS$, below) and $TIME$ (for a character vector result) are often used to convert this representation to year, month, day, hour, minute and second.

Similarly, when a file component is stored (via $\Box FAPPEND$ or $\Box FREPLACE$), a timestamp is stored with it. That timestamp can be retrieved by accessing the third element of $\Box FRDCI$'s result. It is in the same format as $\Box WSTS$.

The principal means of obtaining the current time on most APL systems is via the niladic system variable $\Box TS$, for time stamp. Its result is a vector whose elements are year, month, day, hour, minute, seconds and milliseconds. For example,

```
      ⎕TS
1983 3 10 21 54 7 867
```

means that the date and time is March 10, 1983, at 21:54 (9:54 p.m.) and 7.867 seconds.

On APL2 you can find the time when a function was last fixed by `2 ⎕AT R` where R is a character vector holding the name of the function. The result is in the same format as $\Box TS$. The full use of $\Box AT$ is covered on page 300.

The system clock on most time-sharing APL systems is set according to the time zone in which the system is located. On APL2 systems, however, the time stamp is Greenwich Mean Time (GMT) but you can change it to your local time by setting the system variable $\Box TZ$, for time zone. You would use $\Box TZ \leftarrow {}^{-}8$ for Pacific Standard Time, or $\Box TZ \leftarrow 1$ for European Standard Time. The permissible values are integers between ${}^{-}11$ and 13 inclusive.

Most systems make *account* information available to the user with the $\Box AI$ system variable. $\Box AI$ is quite system dependent, but a representative one produces a 4-element integer vector consisting of your user number, the amount of computer time used in the session, the amount of connect time since you signed on, and the typing time (that part of the elapsed time when it was your turn to type, as opposed to the time APL was typing or when the keyboard was locked). The last three elements are in milliseconds. To convert them to more comprehensible numbers (like hours, minutes, seconds and milliseconds) use a sequence such as

```
      X←□AI
      X
78975 1517 3809817 3113100
      ⍊0 60 60 1000⊤1↓X
1517 3809817 3113100
      0    0    1  517    1.517 seconds of CPU time
      1    3   29  817    1 hour, 3 minutes and 29.817 seconds of connect time
      0   51   53  100    51 minutes and 53.1 seconds of open keyboard time.
```

□AI in some systems may measure other usage, such as the number of characters transmitted, or the number of disk accesses or file resource units. Check your system reference manual for details.

Timing algorithms and applications

You can get an overall measure of how much time an application takes by the difference in □TS before and after running the application. On time-sharing systems the elapsed time an application takes depends also on how much resources the other users are taking, and elapsed times can vary widely. To smooth out these irregularities you should measure the application at different times and days, and average the results. You should run small applications in a loop several times so that your numbers are large enough to go beyond the granularity of the system clock. Also, do the same tests (including the loop, but with a placebo application instead) to account for the overhead of the test method itself. Besides measuring □TS, which is an approximation of elapsed time, consider some of the other resources reported in □AI.

The following program is a reasonably complete and precise tool for measuring the resources consumed. Its right argument is the character string representation of the statement to be timed, and the left argument is the number of repeated executions you want. The resources consumed are returned in the same format as □AI.

```
      ∇ ΔAI←N TIMER EXPR;FN;HEADER;WIDTH;TIMER
[1]     ⍝ TAKES TIMINGS FOR N ITERATIONS OF EXPR   BRIAN BECKER 3/83
[2]     ⍝ ASSUME EXPR RETURNS AN EXPLICIT RESULT; DISCARD IT IN SINK.
[3]     EXPR←'SINK←',EXPR ⍝ BEGIN TO BUILD LOCAL FUNCTION.
[4]     EXPR←(N,ρEXPR)ρEXPR ⍝ REPEATS THE EXPRESSION N TIMES
[5]     HEADER←'TIMER;SINK' ◇ WIDTH← ⌈/(ρHEADER),ρEXPR
[6]     FN←□FX (WIDTH↑HEADER),[1](N,WIDTH)↑EXPR ⍝ CREATE THE FUNCTION
[7]     ΔAI←□AI ◇ TIMER ◇ ΔAI←□AI-ΔAI ⍝ PRETIME, RUN, TAKE DIFFERENCE
      ∇
```

Delaying execution

□DL causes a *delay* for a fixed period of time. Its argument is the number of seconds of delay that is desired. The result is the number of seconds that actually transpired, because you may be delayed slightly longer than called for if the system is used heavily, or less if you interrupted by BREAK. When □DL is executed, your terminal keyboard stays locked, as when computing, but no computer time is used.

Asynchronous devices

Time is an important consideration when dealing with independent processors or devices. If your APL system communicates with devices such as microcomputers, printers, voice simulators or remote sensors, they must be synchronized, or chaos results. Often the application requires delaying the APL processing until a signal is received from the device. Much of this signalling happens automatically, as with buffered printers. For other devices or other applications you may have to specify the communication protocol.

One of the important considerations is what to do if the device doesn't respond when it should, similar to your own behavior when the system simply doesn't respond to your entries. □ARBIN (page 240), with its timeout feature, can be a lifesaver for this situation.

Imagine a time-shared computer that is programmed to routinely call several remote microcomputers and transfer the previous day's business transactions. The process needs to take alternate action if the telephone line was busy (try later), or if there was no answer (message the communications manager). During a successful connection there is the possibility of garbled transmission, indeterminate delays or unrecoverable communications failure. Detection and recovery, or at least alternate actions, are possible for all of these, and need to be developed if the application is to run without human intervention.

Detached and deferred tasks

The exact details of these facilities differ significantly from system to system. We will give only an introduction here. If you need these features for your application, consult your system reference manual.

Some time-sharing systems have facilities for initiating sessions without having a terminal attached. The *detached task* can communicate with regular users (here called *attached tasks*) via shared files or shared variables. Applications of this technology parallel supervisory or stewardship activities among humans. A major use of detached tasks is to serve as a 'security officer' to a shared database. The detached task intercepts the user's interactive request for data, and limits the flow to only that information to which the user is authorized.

A simple but useful application of detached tasks is to eliminate the use of a connected terminal for those jobs that aren't inherently interactive. You sign on the system from a regular terminal and create a detached task through the $\square SIGNON$ (for APL*PLUS) or $\square RUN$ (for Sharp APL) system function. Its argument consists of items like the name of the workspace to load (which usually has a latent expression set), the files that are to be used for input and output (in lieu of terminal keyboard and display), usage limits (to prevent runaways such as infinite loops), and what to do if there are untrappable errors.

When a detached task is running, the owner (that is, the user who initiated the task) can monitor it with the $\square TASKS$ or $\square RUNS$ system variable. The result is a matrix of task numbers and usage figures for all tasks currently running, including the current attached task. The result of $\square TASKS$ is roughly equivalent to $\square AI$, but for all tasks. A detached task can be terminated by the attached task or an initiating detached task using the $\square BOUNCE$ system function.

There is also a way to cause a detached task to 'wake up' much as you would set an alarm clock to wake you in the morning. The activation instructions can be very specific, and contingent on other tasks having completed, or a certain time having arrived, or certain data being available, or on a regular schedule such as every Friday night at 10 p.m. The specification is usually done by prompted programs supplied with the system. Detached tasks initiated in this manner are called *deferred tasks*. They are the ultimate mechanism for automating applications because once they are set up, no human need attend to them. This eliminates both the unnecessary human effort and errors. Where the deferred tasks are done at times other than normal working hours, they help to even out system workloads and thus make better use of the computing facilities.

Changing the index origin

APL normally operates in index origin 1. This means that the first element of a vector is obtained by $VECTOR[1]$. But there are branches of mathematics where by convention the first element of a vector is called the zero-th. To make APL more closely represent this convention, you can change the index origin to 0 by $\square IO \leftarrow 0$. Then the first element of a vector is obtained by $VECTOR[0]$. Affected are the monadic and dyadic forms of ι, $?$, $\spadesuit$ and Ψ, all forms of indexing and axis designation, and the left argument of ϕ.

```
      □IO←0                    X←2 6ρ'CHAIRSTABLES'         0 0 ⌽X
      ι5                       X[0;0 1 5]             CA
0 1 2 3 4                 CHS                               X,[0] 'DESKS '
      'ABCD'ι'CAXB'            +/[0]X='E'           CHAIRS
2 0 4 1                   0 0 0 0 1 0              TABLES
      ?1                       +/[1]X='E'           DESKS
0                         0 1                               'CAT',[¯.5]'DOG'
      3?3                                           CAT
0 1 2                                               DOG
```

These are the only things affected. In particular, the lines of functions still start at [1], file component numbers are always referenced in origin 1, and the shape of objects (ρ) is unchanged. The current origin can be determined by $\square IO$ and it can be reset with $\square IO \leftarrow 1$:

```
      □IO                     □IO←1               □IO
0                                            1
```

$\Box IO$ can be localized in defined functions, but you must give it a value before it is used by any of the affected primitive functions, or an *IMPLICIT ERROR* will result. Only 0 and 1 are acceptable values for $\Box IO$.

You may well ask what advantages there may be to work in either origin. To most do-it-yourselfers, 1 seems more 'natural.' But there are applications which seem made for 0-origin. For instance, algorithms like *HEXA* and *DEC* (Chapter 22) no longer need to add or subtract to adjust the indices. Boolean numbers are directly usable as indices, as in the branch instruction $\rightarrow(L1,L2)[X\geq Y]$.

In most APL systems, storage is saved by working in origin 0 if the results are in bit rather than integer form:

```
M←0  2  5  6  10  16  20  15  8  9  7  2
□IO←0                           □IO←1
SPACE←□WA                       SPACE←□WA
DATA0←M∘.≥1+ι⌈/M                DATA1←1+M∘.≥ι⌈/M
SPACE-□WA                       SPACE-□WA
116                        1008

    ' □'[DATA0]                    ' □'[DATA1]
```

```
□□                              □□
□□□□□                           □□□□□
□□□□□□                          □□□□□□
□□□□□□□□□                       □□□□□□□□□
□□□□□□□□□□□□□□□                 □□□□□□□□□□□□□□□
□□□□□□□□□□□□□□□□□□□□            □□□□□□□□□□□□□□□□□□□□□□□□
□□□□□□□□□□□□□□□                 □□□□□□□□□□□□□□□
□□□□□□□□                        □□□□□□□□
□□□□□□□□□                       □□□□□□□□□
□□□□□□□                         □□□□□□□
□□                              □□
```

Many programmers localize $\Box IO$ in every main function, setting it at the start and thereby passing it on to each function called by it (unless it is localized again). But the best solution is to write origin-independent APL instructions whenever possible, as for example:

```
V[ι4]            instead of     V[1 2 3 4]
→(X>Y)↑LABEL                    →LABEL ×ιX>Y
M,[□IO]V                        M,[1]V
V[1 7-~□IO]                     V[1 7]
```

Random link

When *roll* and *deal* were explained, we commented that you get the same sequence of random numbers each time you sign on. More accurately, there is a *random link*, $\Box RL$, associated with each workspace. Each time you use ?, a random number is generated based on the present value of $\Box RL$, and $\Box RL$ itself changes, ready for the next execution of ?. Actually, the numbers provided aren't really random; they cycle (on the IBM 370-based APLs) every 2147483646 numbers, but that's more than sufficient for practical purposes.

The value of $\Box RL$ in a clear workspace is 16807 ($7\star5$). It can be manually reset by assigning $\Box RL$ any value from 1 to 2147483646. The current random link can be captured by $X\leftarrow\Box RL$. $\Box RL$ can be localized, and must be assigned before any use of roll or deal.

There are two main reasons for changing the random link. You might want to reset it to some known previous value if you were rerunning some *simulation* or game to check its computations, or you might want to set it to an arbitrary random starting point, as happens in the exercise programs *EASYDRILL* (page 53) and *TEACH* (page 145). This is usually done by basing $\Box RL$ on $\Box TS$ or $\Box AI$. One of the more novel expressions is $\Box RL\leftarrow+/\Box AI$.

Comparison tolerance

On page 224 we mentioned that only about 16 decimal positions are kept in floating point internal representation. Thus, a rational number like $1\,1/3$ is accurate to approximately 1.333333333333333, which is slightly different from an exact value of $1\,1/3$. If you ponder this for a while, you'll accept the fact that it would take an infinite number of bits (as opposed to the 56 used for representation of the mantissa in floating point) to represent that number exactly.

If you must deal with rational numbers with exact precision, consider representing each value as a numerator and denominator pair of integer elements in an array, and developing a set of APL functions to perform rational arithmetic.

If 1 $^1/_3$ is represented in floating point storage as 1.333333333333333 then $3 \times 1 + \div 3$ should be 3.999999999999999. Why is it, then, that $4 = 3 \times 1 + \div 3$? They aren't *exactly* equal! The reason is that APL uses a little 'common sense' when comparing two numeric values. If values differ by no more than one part in 10000000000000, APL considers them equal. This feature is called the comparison *tolerance* (or *fuzz*, if you prefer), and is used by APL in the functions $<$ $\leq$ $=$ $\geq$ $>$ $\neq$ ι $\in$ $\lceil$ $\lfloor$ $\cap$ $\top$ $\underline{\epsilon}$ $\mathtt{I}$ and $|$.

You can change the comparison tolerance with the system variable $\Box CT$. It can take any value between 0 and just under 1:

```
      X←□CT                    □CT←0
      X                        4=3×1+÷3
1.419697693E¯14          0
      4=3×1+÷3                 □CT←X
1
```

$\Box CT$ can be localized in defined functions, but it must be assigned before any of the primitives that use it are executed, or an *IMPLICIT ERROR* results.

In APL2 there is a similar, but unrelated system variable $\Box MD$, for *matrix divide* tolerance, which may be set to any scalar nonnegative number. It acts for matrix divide and matrix inverse in the same way that $\Box CT$ does for functions which do comparisons. For singular right arguments, or those with more columns with rows, $\Box MD$ is a fuzz on the algebraic determination of the rank of R.

Horizontal tabs

For those APL users who work at typewriter terminals and some nonintelligent displays, the *horizontal tabs* system variable, $\Box HT$, is a scalar or vector containing tab settings. The cursor will move over to these tab settings on execution for faster output. Physical tab settings on the terminal must agree with those in $\Box HT$. $\Box HT$ is reset to $\iota 0$ when the current session is ended.

Terminal type

For those users who wish to create special effects that may be available only on certain terminals, there is a system variable $\Box TT$, for *terminal type*, which may be incorporated in a defined function to identify the terminal being used. There are five possible return codes (on VS APL—yours may differ): 0 for indeterminate; 1 for correspondence; 2 for PTTC-BCD; 3 for 1050; 4 for 3270 with APL; 5 for 3270 without APL.

User load

This system variable, $\Box UL$, returns the number of users on the system. In the early days of APL usage this was the main indicator of how saturated the system was. For versions of APL running on virtual machines or personal computers $\Box UL$ returns 1, which isn't particularly useful.

The symbol table

On most APL systems, there is a limit to how many different symbols (variables, functions, labels and groups) you can have in a workspace. That limit is quite liberal for most purposes. But as you might expect, sooner or later you may exceed the limit and get a *SYMBOL TABLE FULL* message (*SYSTEM LIMIT* on APL2).

You can view the current symbol table status by the system command $)SYMBOLS$:

```
       )LOAD 1 CLASS                        )CLEAR
SAVED  23.54.04 12/10/82          CLEAR WS
       )SYMBOLS                            )SYMBOLS
IS 512; 201 IN USE               IS 512; 0 IN USE
```

A symbol is used whenever you mention a new variable, function, label or group. However, if a name is used over again (such as *L*1 used as a label in one function, as a local variable in another, and as a group in the workspace) it doesn't increase the symbol count.

On the other hand, erasing variables or functions doesn't decrease the symbol count. Indeed, the symbol count is increased even by innocently mistyping a variable name:

```
       XY                                  )SYMBOLS
VALUE ERROR                      IS 512; 1 IN USE
       XY
       ∧
```

and it can increase substantially by forgetting to use quotes, as in this entry:

```
       XY←THIS IS AN ERROR                 )SYMBOLS
VALUE ERROR                      IS 512; 5 IN USE
       XY←THIS IS AN ERROR
                    ∧
```

If you use a workspace for extensive development and maintenance, eventually you will name more symbols than are allowed, as we have done maliciously here:

```
      ∇SYMBFULL                            SYMBFULL
[1]   I←1                          SYMBOL TABLE FULL
[2]   LP:♠'A',(♥I),'←99'           SYMBFULL[2]  LP:♠'A',(♥I),'←99'
[3]   I←I+1                                       ∧
[4]   →LP ∇                                 )SYMBOLS
                                  IS 512; 512 IN USE
```

When this happens, you should erase whatever variables, groups and functions you don't need and use the following sequence (assuming the original workspace was named *OLDWS*):

```
      )SAVE CONTINUE
      )CLEAR
      )COPY CONTINUE
      )WSID OLDWS
      )SAVE
```

This 'purifies' the workspace so that expired symbols are not retained. It is advisable to do this to a developing workspace every few weeks. On some systems,)*RESET* performs a similar cleanup of the symbol table.

Lest you feel that our example *SYMBFULL* is contrived, recall that any application using automatic program generation (□*FX*, □*DEF*, ♠, direct definition and latent expressions) can create new symbols. Similarly, applications that let the user roam in an executable environment (as opposed to keeping him tethered with □) are vulnerable to *SYMBOL TABLE FULL*s.

You can change the number of symbols, if you genuinely need more than the default, by an entry like)*SYMBOLS* 1000. This works only in a clear workspace, so you would still use the sequence above, resetting)*SYMBOLS* just before the)*COPY*. Increasing the symbol capacity decreases the available workspace (as measured by □*WA*) by as much as eight bytes per symbol, so plan accordingly. You can also specify fewer symbols, which gives you more □*WA*.

Some systems also offer a system variable, □*SYMB*. You can't use it to change the number of symbols, but you can use it in applications to see if the symbol table is getting full. Its result is a two-element vector holding the capacity and the number in use.

Direct definition

Direct definition is a form of expressing executable algorithms that most closely parallels the formal use of functions in mathematics. For this reason it is a popular APL feature in academic circles. For example, a mathematical definition of the conversion from Fahrenheit to Celsius is C(F)=(F-32)×(5÷9). Here is the same formula expressed and evaluated in defined function form and direct definition form on the Sharp APL System:

```
       )LOAD 1 DIRECTDEF
SAVED  10.59.31 09/25/80

       ∇C←FROMFAHREN F                    DEFINE
[1]    C←(F-32)×5÷9 ∇             DDFROMFAHREN:(ω-32)×5÷9

       FROMFAHREN 0 32 98.6 212           DDFROMFAHREN 0 32 98.6 212
¯17.77777778 0 37 100              ¯17.77777778 0 37 100
```

At this writing, direct definition has not stabilized in the APL language. APL2 doesn't have it at all. It is generally available on the Sharp APL System, but only as a simulation (workspace 1 *DIRECTDEF*) rather than as part of the APL system itself. On STSC's APL it has been implemented only on the 'experimental' system presently (August, 1983). Moreover, the syntax of direct definition used on each system is different.

But in spite of these drawbacks, direct definition has its advocates and its place in APL, particularly in expository work involving straightforward mathematics. It might be just right for you. However, if you came here from Chapter 3, you probably should go back there now, as the following paragraphs use features covered after Chapter 3.

On both systems the general idea is to provide a facility which lets you express your algorithms in an unencumbered way. For monadic functions on Sharp APL that idea carries well (the argument is always represented by ω):

```
DEFINE                             DEFINE
SQRT:ω*.5                          SQ:ω×ω
       SQRT 1 2 4                          SQ 4
1 1.414213562 2                    16
       SQ SQRT 1   4
1 2 4
```

On the STSC system, algorithms are stored as character vectors, and the operator ∇ is used to execute them:

```
       SQRT←'ω*.5'                        SQ←'ω×ω'
       (∘∇ SQRT) 1 2 4                    (∘∇ SQ) 4
1 1.414213562 2                    16
       (∘∇ SQ)(∘∇ SQRT) 1 2 4
1 2 4
```

The ∘ is used as a place holder to tell whether the function is being used as though it were monadic (∘∇ *NAME*) or dyadic (*NAME* ∇∘). Both Sharp and STSC use α to represent the left argument. The following examples compare the systems:

	traditional	*Sharp*	STSC
	∇Z←SUM W	*DEFINE*	
[1]	Z←+/W ∇	SUM:+/ω	SUM←'+/ω'
	∇Z←AVG W	*DEFINE*	
[1]	Z←(SUM W)÷ρW ∇	AVG:(SUM ω)÷ρω	AVG←'((∘∇SUM)ω÷ρω'
	AVG 2 3 7 4 2	AVG 2 3 7 4 2	(∘∇ AVG) 2 3 7 4 2
3.6		3.6	3.6
	∇Z←CEN W	*DEFINE*	
[1]	Z←W-AVG W ∇	CEN:ω-AVG ω	CEN←'ω-(∘∇ AVG)ω'

```
      ∇Z←SSQ W                    DEFINE                      SSQ←'(∘∇ SUM)
[1]   Z←SUM (CEN W)*2 ∇        SSQ:SUM (CEN ω)*2                  ((∘∇ CEN)ω)*2'


      ∇Z←VAR W                    DEFINE                      VAR←'((∘∇ SSQ)ω)
[1]   Z←(SSQ W)÷ρW ∇           VAR:(SSQ ω)÷ρω                     ÷ρω'


      ∇Z←SD W                     DEFINE                      SD←'((∘∇ VAR)ω)*.5'
[1]   Z←(VAR W)*.5 ∇           SD:(VAR ω)÷ρω                   (∘∇ SD) 2 3 7 4 2
      SD 2 3 7 4 2                SD 2 3 7 4 2                 1.854723699
1.854723699                 1.854723699
```

The final two examples are dyadic. In traditional APL they appear as

```
      ∇Z←A SXY W
[1]   Z←SUM (CEN A)×CEN W ∇

      ∇Z←A COR W
[1]   Z←(A SXY W)÷((SSQ A)×SSQ W)*.5 ∇▮

      2 3 7 4 2 COR 2 4 7 3 2
0.9418604651
```

and they follow closely in Sharp APL:

```
      DEFINE
SXY:SUM (CEN α)×CEN ω

      DEFINE
COR:(α SXY ω)÷((SSQ α)×SSQ ω)*.5

      2 3 7 4 2 COR 2 4 7 3 2
0.9418604651
```

But the form is quite different in APL*PLUS:

```
      SXY←'(∘∇ SUM)((∘∇ CEN)α)×(∘∇ CEN)ω'
      COR←'(α(SXY ∇∘)ω)÷(((∘∇ SSQ)α)×(∘∇ SSQ)ω)*.5
      2 3 7 4 2 COR 2 4 7 3 2
0.9418604651
```

As you can see, direct definition starts out simple, but tends toward long one-liners as the work gets more complicated. Although we won't cover it here, both systems allow more than one line, and they even have ways to branch or conditionally execute. The authors' feelings are that while direct definition is useful for very simple functions, the majority of users will continue to prefer and use regular function definition for most of their work.

More APL2 system functions and variables

The rest of this chapter explains still more advanced features of APL2. If you are new to APL, you can ignore them for now. Indeed, although these features are very powerful, you may not need them for years—the original APL was implemented in 1966, and none of these features existed until around 1982. That tells you that a lot of people somehow got by without them!

Attributes

This is a handy dyadic system function, represented by $\square AT$, which tells you in detail about the attributes of various objects in the workspace. The right argument is a character matrix of names, as for $\square NC$, while the left argument is 1, 2 or 3. Here is a table of results for each left argument value:

description	value	result position	meaning
valences	1	1	returns explicit result (0,1)
		2	function valence (0,1,2)
		3	defined operator valence (0,1,2)
fix time	2	1 through 7	$\square TS$ at fix time
execution properties	3	1	nondisplayable (0,1)
		2	nonsuspendable (0,1)
		3	weak interrupts ignored (0,1)
		4	nonresource errors converted to $DOMAIN\ ERRORs$ (0,1)

For variables, fix times and execution properties are all meaningless and zeros are returned. The execution properties may be independently set by use of the dyadic $\square FX$. The result is a numeric matrix with one row for each object whose attributes are being inquired after, and 3, 7 or 4 columns, depending on the value of the left argument.

```
      )LOAD 1 CLASS
SAVED  14.45.33 02/20/83

      □FX 'Z←(F REDUCE) R',[1]14↑'Z←F/R'
REDUCE


      1 □AT 3 7ρNAMES←'RECT    REDUCE MILEAGE'
0 2 0
1 1 1
1 0 0

      2 □AT NAMES
1982 10 7 9 22 35 685
1983 1 6 11 44 51 220
   0 0 0  0  0   0

      0 1 1 1 □FX 'L FN R',[1]6↑'L×R'
FN

      3 □AT 'FN'
0 1 1 1
```

Transfer forms

The dyadic system function $\square TF$ transforms an array or function into a character vector consisting of a data type code (F, N or C for a function, simple numeric array or simple character array), followed by the name of the object and a blank, the rank and shape of the array and a blank, and a raveled version of the array. Defined functions are represented in their raveled canonical form.

```
      ARRAY←3 3ρ⍳9
      Z←1 □TF 'ARRAY'
      Z
NARRAY 2 3 3 1 2 3 4 5 6 7 8 9
      Z←1 □TF 'HYP'
FHYP 2 2 16 C←A HYP B          C←((A*2)+B*2)*.5
```

There is an extended transfer form which has 2 as its left argument instead of 1 and displays the name and value of a variable or a (displayable) defined function or operator:

```
      2 □TF 'ARRAY'
ARRAY←3 3ρι9
      2 □TF 'HYP'
□FX 'C←A HYP B' 'C←((A*2)+B*2)*.5'
```

The result for a defined function or operator is a vector of vectors of the canonical form, beginning with □FX, if no execution properties have been set. Otherwise, the same display is prefixed by the execution properties:

```
      2 □TF 'FN'
0 1 1 1 □FX 'L FN R' 'L×R'
```

This transfer form is equivalent to the monadic □TF R.

The value of the transfer form is that it puts objects in a workspace in a standard form which allows for easy movement to another system which may be running a different version of APL. Once transferred, the character vectors containing the transfer forms can be executed to reconstitute the objects.

To assist users in the transfer, APL2 has two helpful system commands.)OUT filename creates a transfer file containing the transfer forms of objects in the active workspace. It may be followed by an optional list of specific objects (including system variables) to be transferred. At the receiving end)IN filename reads the file and defines the objects in the active workspace.

Left argument and right argument

These variables, □L and □R, are shared with the system. They are the array values of the referenced arguments of a function which has been interrupted by an error (except *SYNTAX ERROR* and *VALUE ERROR*). After the suspension is removed, they disappear.

```
      3 5 HYP 4 12 20                        □R
LENGTH ERROR                        16 144 400
HYP[1]    C←((A*2)+B*2)*.5                    □L
            ^       ^                9 25
```

Execution can proceed if we reassign □L or □R:

```
      □R←16 144
      →ι0
5 13
```

National language translation

A simple character vector is used as an argument to □NLT. It determines the language to be used for reporting errors and what language (besides English) will be accepted for system commands. The only recognized values at this time are

'DANSK'	Danish	'FRANCAIS'	French
'DEUTSCH'	German	'NORSK'	Norwegian
'ENGLISH'	English	'SUOMI'	Finnish
'ESPANOL'	Spanish	'SVENSKA'	Swedish

Anything other than the above sets □NLT to English. This variable can be set only for a session, but is not affected by clearing and loading.

System labels

APL2 provides two *system labels*, $\Box FL$ (fill) and $\Box ID$ (identity), which are used in defined functions and defined operators. The fill label $\Box FL$ is activated when the each, bracket axis, outer product and inner product operators are applied to certain empty arrays. It produces an empty result and avoids the *DOMAIN ERRORs* which would otherwise be produced. There is an elaborate set of conditions governing the use of this label and $\Box ID$ which interested users can reference in the IBM APL2 Language Manual SB21-3015.

Here is an example of how $\Box FL$ is used in a defined function with outer product:

```
      ∇Z←L POWER R                        ρ1 2 ∘.POWER 0ρ0
[1]   Z←L*R                            0 0
[2]   →0                                  1 2 ∘.POWER 3 4
[3]   □FL:Z←L*R+2 ∇                     1  1
                                        8 16
```

The identity label $\Box ID$ works similarly. It is activated when a dyadic defined function is applied to an empty array through the reduce operator or inner product whose intermediate result is empty along the last axis. In the following example the identity element is 3:

```
      ∇Z←L ADD R                         ADD/1ρ2
[1]   Z←L+R                        2
[2]   →0                                 ADD/0ρ2
[3]   □ID:Z←((L≠ιρρR)/ρR)ρ3 ∇B     3
                                         ADD/2 0ρ2
      ADD/2 5                      3 3
7
```

Complex arithmetic

APL2 treats all numbers as members of the complex number field. All arithmetic operations are defined on complex numbers, so that the real numbers with which we have been working thus far are only a subset of what is possible.

Here is how complex numbers may be represented:

```
APL2                 conventional notation
2J3                  2+3i
0J1                  i
3.4E2J¯2E¯3          340−.002i
2R.5                 2(cos.5 + i sin .5) in radians
2D50                 2(cos 50 + i sin 50) in degrees
```

Our assumption is that if you are reading these words now, you don't need Gilman and Rose's handy guide to what complex numbers are all about. We'll just briefly describe the actions of those primitive APL2 functions that may not be obvious when used with complex numbers. In what follows, to save space R and I refer to the real and imaginary parts of a complex number RJI, with Z the result of some primitive function. Functions not shown can be expected to follow the same rules with both real and complex numbers.

	⌊ and ⌈	rounds R and I
	+	negates the imaginary part
monadic	×	Z has magnitude 1 with same phase as RJI
functions	|	Z is $((R*2)+I*2)*.5$
	−	negates R and I
	÷	takes reciprocal of R and I
	8○	Z is $-(\,{}^{-}1-RJI*2)*.5$
	¯8○	Z is $(\,{}^{-}1-RJI*2)*.5$
	9○	returns R
	¯9○	returns RJI
	11○	returns I
	¯11○	Z is $0J1 × RJI$

$$\begin{array}{ll} ^-120 & Z \text{ is phase } R \\ ^-120 & Z \text{ is } \star 0J1 \times RJI \\ ^-40, ^-80, 80 & \text{holds only for complex numbers in first quadrant} \\ \lfloor, \lceil, <, \leq, >, \geq & RJI \text{ must be within system fuzz of a real number to avoid} \\ & DOMAIN\ ERROR \\ \star & \text{for multiple roots, } Z \text{ is the root with the least nonnegative angle in the} \\ & \text{complex plane.} \end{array}$$

Fortunately or unfortunately, depending on your point of view, operations in APL2 which result in complex numbers, even from real input (e.g., 1*.5) will return a complex result instead of the usual *DOMAIN ERROR* found on most systems. If this bothers you, you will have to bypass it with appropriate program instructions, since there is no way to 'turn it off' at the keyboard.

PROBLEMS

1. Use □*AI* **A** to pass through only those users whose sign-ons are in the vector *NUMBERS*, and **B** to quit a function if the elapsed time is greater than, say, 100 seconds.

2. Write an expression to create a dollar sign character if your system doesn't have one.

3. A company records billing dates and order numbers of its bills rendered in a numeric matrix *BILLS* in the form

```
12345    10     5    1982
14872    11    13    1982
15112     1    30    1983
```

the first column being the order numbers. Use □*TS* to determine which bills are overdue (same date of month following above billing date).

4. Write an expression to convert a vector *V* of positive integers into a logical matrix with one row for each integer *I* in the vector and *I* leading 1's.

5. Define a function *DISTRDS* to do distributive rounding to some decimal position *DEC*, i.e., make sure that the sum of the rounded values equals the rounded sum of the unrounded values.

6. Just to test your alertness: what happened to the space in the following sequence?

```
      □WA
125840
      SMASH
      □WA
132
      )FNS
SMASH
```

7. Devise a scrambling scheme which keys the account number to the random link to encrypt any array.

8. How do you decrypt the results of problem 7?

9. Using □*TS*, construct a niladic function *TIME* that will result in the current time expressed as, for example, 4:47:22 *PM EASTERN*. Truncate to seconds.

10. Define an APL function that will generate today's date as *MM/DD/YEAR*.

11. Define a niladic function that will, when executed, display a message for only those whose user numbers have been incorporated in the function.

12. Assign *A*←9.222222222222222 and *B*←9.222222222222227 and execute *A*=*B*, *A*∈*B* and *A*−*B*. Repeat after setting □*CT*←0. Account for the responses.

13. Why is the expression $A[\iota N]$ independent of the index origin?

14. Execute $\iota 0$ and $\iota 1$ after setting $\Box IO\leftarrow0$. Are they vectors? Of what size?

15. Define a function to identify whether it is morning, afternoon or evening and print an appropriate message.

16. Use $\Box DL$ to write a function that executes $DICE$ (page 58) N times, with a built-in delay of D seconds between repetitions.

17. Modify the multiplication drill function of problem 1, Chapter 23 to include a statement which gives the time required to get the correct solution.

18. Use $\Box LX$ to automatically display one message for authorized users 1500 and 1600, and another for all others when the workspace is loaded. Assume the messages are lines of a two-row matrix M.

19. Write a program to execute an APL statement and report how much time and space are used.

Answers to problems

Some of the problems will have more than one solution given. This will generally occur when there is more than one sound approach to the solution. The proposed solutions, because they are keyed to the operations presented up to that point in the text, will not always be the most concise or elegant possible, with the drill problems occasionally returning error messages. For this reason, an occasional solution will have forward references to simplify the task of defining the expressions needed to solve the problem.

Answers for Chapter 1

1.
```
        6 8 2 4+3 9 1 1
9 17 3 5
        1 0 9 8 - 4 2 2 3
¯3 ¯2 7 5
        3-¯1 ¯56.7 0 ¯.19
4 59.7 3 3.19
        5 4 3×6
30 24 18
        10÷10 5 2 1
1 2 5 10
        3 4 ×1 2 3
LENGTH ERROR
        3 4 × 1 2 3
              ^
        1 2 8÷1 2 0
DOMAIN ERROR
        1 2 8 ÷ 1 2 0
                  ^
        ¯2 0 .81+15 6 ¯5
13 6 ¯4.19
        2 ¯ 3
SYNTAX ERROR
        2 ¯   3
            ^
```
Reminder: the negative sign is a mark of punctuation, not a function.

3.
```
        155 89 45×1.25 .50 .25
193.75 44.5 11.25
```

4.
```
        59.50 79.88 83.00÷1263 1997 3028
0.04711005542 0.04 0.02741083223
```

5.
```
        .05×47 18 68 10
2.35 0.9 3.4 0.5
```

6.
```
        45201 64677 52468 68893 + 15000
46701 66177 53968 70393
```

7.
```
        356 205 189 322 257÷400
0.89 0.5125 0.4725 0.805 0.6425
```

8. The answer is the same as 3+2, or 5. −overstruck with + still looks like +. This exercise emphasizes again that in APL what you see is what you get.

Answers for Chapter 2

1. $\quad A \leftarrow 3 \ 4 \ 5 \ 6 \ 7$
    $\quad B \leftarrow 2 \times A$

2. $SPACEMAN$ and $\Delta 3X$ are valid. The others are invalid because they contain special characters
    (blank, +, −) or begin with a digit.

3. $\quad M \leftarrow 5 \ 3\rho 7$
    $Q \leftarrow 5 \ 3\rho 4 \ 9 \ 11$

4. $\quad N \leftarrow M \div 7$
    $\quad N \leftarrow M - 6$
    $\quad N \leftarrow 8 - M$

5. $\quad S \leftarrow 2 \ 3\rho 8 \ 15 \ 7 \ 12 \ 4 \ 0$
    $\quad P \leftarrow 2 \ 3\rho 3.10 \ 2.00 \ 4.17 \ 3.50 \ 2.75 \ 4.35$
    $\quad TOTSALES \leftarrow S \times P$

6. $\quad HRS \leftarrow 40 \ 55 \ 46 \ 40 \ 40$
    $\quad OT \leftarrow HRS - 40$
    $\quad OTPAY \leftarrow OT \times 1.5 \times 4.5$
    $\quad REGPAY \leftarrow 40 \times 4.5$
    $\quad GROSSPAY \leftarrow REGPAY + OTPAY$

    After you learn how APL handles multiple instructions in a single line (Chapter 6), you'll be able to
    write the answer as $GROSSPAY \leftarrow (4.5 \times 40) + 4.5 \times 1.5 \times HRS - 40$.

7. A $\quad AGE \leftarrow YR - BIRTH$
    B $\quad RET \leftarrow BIRTH + 65$
    C $\quad REMYRS \leftarrow RET - YR$

8. $\quad YES \leftarrow 356 \ 205 \ 189 \ 322 \ 257$
    $\quad NO \leftarrow 400 - YES$
    $\quad FRNO \leftarrow NO \div 400$

9. $\quad ST \leftarrow SALES \times TAX$
    $\quad CHARGES \leftarrow SALES + ST + PH$

Answers for Chapter 3

1. $\quad \ ^-2 * .5$
    $DOMAIN \ ERROR$
    $\quad \ ^-2 * 0.5$
    $\qquad \ \wedge$
    $\quad \ 3 * 4 \ 2 \ 1 \ 0$
    $81 \ 27 \ 9 \ 3 \ 1$
    $\quad \ 21.268E1 + 4.56E^-2$
    212.7256
    $\quad \ ^-5 \ 0 \ ^-22 \ 15 \lceil 3 \ 7 \ ^-10.8 \ 2$
    $5 \ 7 \ ^-10.8 \ 15$
    $\quad \ 2 \ 3 \ 4 \ 5 \circledast 2$
    $1 \ 0.6309297536 \ 0.5 \ 0.4306765581$
    $\quad \ 1 \ 10 \circledast 1$
    $1 \ 0$
    $\quad \ 2 * .5 \ .333 \ .25$
    $1.414213562 \ 1.25962998 \ 1.189207115$
    $\quad \ 1 * 0 \ 1 \ 10 \ 100 \ 1000$
    $1 \ 1 \ 1 \ 1 \ 1$
    $\quad \ 8.3E0 \times 7.9E^-3 \ 56$
    $0.06557 \ 464.8$
    $\quad \ ^-2 \circledast 25$
    $DOMAIN \ ERROR$
    $\quad \ ^-2 \circledast 25$
    $\qquad \ \wedge$
    $\quad \ 1 \circledast 0$
    $DOMAIN \ ERROR$
    $\quad \ 1 \circledast 0$
    $\qquad \ \wedge$

    Both arguments must be greater than 0. If the left argument is 1, the right argument must be 1
    also.
    $\quad \ ^-1 \ 9 \ ^-5 \ ^-2 \lfloor 0 \ 6 \ 4 \ 3$
    $0 \ 6 \ ^-5 \ ^-2$

```
      ¯8*.33333333333
DOMAIN_ERROR
      ¯8*0.33333333333
         ^
```

Why the *DOMAIN ERROR* in this example and the first above? Try adding a few more 3's on the right and reexecuting.

```
      ¯7.11E4+9.45E¯3
¯7523809.524
      346×2E3.7
SYNTAX ERROR
      346×2000 . 7
              ^
```

2.
```
      1E0
1
      1E1
10
      1E6
1000000
      1E9
1000000000
      1E10
1E10
      1E¯1
0.1
      1E¯2
0.01
      1E¯4
0.0001
      1E¯5
1E¯5
      1E¯6
1E¯6
```

3.
```
      L←3 7 15 2.7
      F←L*2
      AREA←6×F
      AREA
54 294 1350 43.74
```

4.
```
      A←1 2 3 4
      D←3×A
      A∘.×D
 3  6  9 12
 6 12 18 24
 9 18 27 36
12 24 36 48
      D∘.*A
 3     9    27     81
 6    36   216   1296
 9    81   729   6561
12   144  1728  20736
```

5.
```
      1 2 3 4 5∘.*2 .5
 1             1
 4             1.414213562
 9             1.732050808
16             2
25             2.236067977
```

6. There are 86400 seconds in a day.
```
      86400×365
31536000
```
(which is $3.1536E7$ seconds per year)

7.
```
      5280×24
126720
      12÷126720
9.46969697E¯5
```
(miles per hour)

8. The *DOMAIN ERROR* results because there is no real number that gives ¯8 when squared. APL2 gives an answer in the complex domain.

9.
```
      1.5E9÷9.3E7
16.12903226
```

10.   `15 20 32 29⌊18 20 10 49`
       `15 20 10 49`
11.   `10⍟1÷C`
    This is a bit ahead of the game in that we haven't said anything yet about order of execution, where multiple operations occur in a single expression. See Chapter 6 for more details. You can, of course, always write this as two steps, `D←1÷C`, followed by `10⍟D`.
12.   `C←A⌊B`
13.   A   `RATE←.08÷12`
              `RN←(1+RATE)*126`
              `1000×RN`
       B   `RATE1←.079÷360`
              `RN1←(1+RATE1)*3780`
              `1000×RN1`
14.   A kilometer is equivalent to 1000 meters or 1000×100 (100000) cm. Each fold doubles the thickness. The problem (in conventional notation) can be stated as $.01 \times 2^x = 100000$. Take the log of both sides and solve for X: `X←(10⍟100000÷.01)÷10⍟2` which is a little more than 23 folds.
15.   `1.15⍟1E3`
    (The problem is simplified by using 1.15 as the base for taking logarithms. With APL there's no need to use base 10.)
16.   `MEN←7*0`
           `WIVES←7*1`
           `SACKS←7*2`
           `CATS←7*3`
    or, more compactly, `7*0 1 2 3` for the number of men, wives, sacks and cats respectively.

17.   `GROWTH←1.00 1.02 1.04 1.06 1.08 1.10`
           `FUTVAL←GROWTH∘.*1 2 3 4 5 6 7 8 9 10`
18.   `.9⍟.25`
    (see comment at end of problem 15.)

Answers for Chapter 4

1.   `1 9 8⌊3 4 6`
       `0 4 6`
               `0 1 2 3 4!3 4 5 6 7`
       `1 4 10 20 35`
               `3|¯3 ¯1 0 1 2 3`
       `0 1 0 1 2 0`
               `0 0 1 1∨0 1 0 1`
       `0 1 1 1`
               `1 0 1 0∧1 0 0 1`
       `1 0 0 0`
               `2 4 7 ¯2>6 ¯1 0 4`
       `0 1 1 0`
               `4 ¯5 ¯1 ¯6.8≥4 1 ¯1 2`
       `1 0 1 0`
               `8 7 6 5 4 3 2 1≤1 2 3 4 5 6 7 8`
       `0 0 0 0 1 1 1 1`
               `1|3.4 ¯2.2 .019`
       `0.4 0.8 0.019`
               `0|1 2 3`
       `1 2 3`
               `¯2 4 ¯5|8 13 3.78`
       `0 1 ¯1.22`
               `2 3 0<5 ¯1 4`
       `1 0 1`
               `3 1 2≠1 2 3`
       `1 1 1`
               `0 1 2 3=0 1 3 2`
       `1 1 0 0`
               `0 0 1 1⍱0 1 0 1`
       `1 0 0 0`
               `1 0 1 0⍲1 0 0 1`
       `0 1 1 1`

2. The factors of an integer N are those integers which divide N. Hence, set $0 = 1\ \ 2\ \ 3\ \ \dots\ N\,|\,N$.

3. $A \geq 0$ or $0 \leq A$ yields a logical vector with 1's in those positions corresponding to the accounts not overdrawn.

4. Let $C \leftarrow 0 = B$. Then $A \vee C$ works if either or both conditions hold, while $A \neq C$ works when only one of the conditions holds, but not both. Later, when the logical negation function ($\sim$) is introduced, $A \vee \sim B$ will also be a possible solution.

5. EXCLUSIVE NOR or NEXCLUSIVE OR.

6. **A** $Z \leftarrow S \times 0$ $\quad Z \leftarrow S - S$ $\quad Z \leftarrow S \neq S$ $\quad Z \leftarrow S\,|\,S$ $\quad Z \leftarrow S > S$ $\quad Z \leftarrow 0 * S$ $\quad Z \leftarrow 0 \lfloor S$

    B $W \leftarrow S * 0$ $\quad W \leftarrow S = S$ $\quad W \leftarrow S \leq S$ $\quad W \leftarrow S \div S$ $\quad W \leftarrow S \circledast S$ $\quad W \leftarrow 0\,!\,S$ $\quad W \leftarrow S\,!\,S$

7.
```
B←2|A
C←0=B
```

8.
```
0 1∘.=0 1
0 1∘.>0 1
0 1∘.<0 1
0 1∘.≥0 1
0 1∘.≤0 1
```

9. $\times$ and $\lfloor$ are equivalent to $\wedge$, $\lceil$ to $\vee$, $*$ to $\geq$, $|$ to $<$ and $!$ to $\leq$.

10. If the result of $B\,|\,A$ is zero, then A is divisible by B.

11. Hours: $H - 1\,|\,H$; minutes: $60\,|\,H \times 60$. This last solution should be tried for typical values of H. You will see that H is multiplied by 60 first, and then $60\,|\,H$ is obtained.

12. $4\,!\,30$

13. $N - 1\,|\,N$ (this works only for nonnegative values of N)

14. $1\,|\,{}^{-}1 \times N$ or $1 - 1\,|\,N$

15. **A** $RESP1 \wedge RESP2$

    B $RESP1 \neq RESP2$

16. $I \leftarrow I + 1$. The left arrow is used in APL to store information, while =, like the other relationals, simply reports on the equality of the two arguments. In arithmetic the expression X=2 asserts that X is *assigned* the value 2, and is equivalent to $X \leftarrow 2$ in APL. Unfortunately, = in arithmetic is another concept that may assert equivalency, as in $^{1}/_{2} = {}^{2}/_{4}$. This ambiguity is absent in the APL notation.

Answers for Chapter 5

1.
```
       +/3 7 ¯10 15 22
37
       ÷/3 5 2
1.2
       ∧/1 1 1
1
       =/3 2 2
0
       ⌈/1 ¯14.7 22 6
22
       −/2 4 6 8 10
6
       */3 2 1
9
       ∨/0 1 0 1
1
       >/1 ¯2 ¯4
0
       ×\3 2 7 9
3 6 42 378
       ×/2 4 6 8 10
3840
       ∧/1 0 1 1
0
       ∨/0 0 0
0
       ⌊/¯2 4 0 ¯8
¯8
       ⌈\4 12 7 14
4 12 12 14
```

2. ∧/ returns a 1 if and only if all the elements are 1, 0 otherwise.
   ∨/ returns a 0 if and only if all the elements are 0, 1 otherwise.
   =/ (applied to a logical vector) returns 0 if there is an odd number of 0's, 1 otherwise.

3. `+/3×AV`
   6 9 (which is the same as $3×+/AV$)

4. `⌈/Q←1 7 ¯2 ¯3`

5. `S←.5×+/L`
   `A2←S-L`
   `Q←×/A2`
   `R←S×Q`
   `AREA←R*.5`

   After the rules of execution order are introduced in Chapter 6, this can be done more compactly as
   `S←.5×+/L`
   `AREA←(S××/S-L)*.5`

6. Since the X-coordinate of a point is customarily written first, it is not enough to take ÷/Q−P since this results in the difference in the X-coordinates divided by the difference in the Y-coordinates, which is the reciprocal of the slope, according to the definition given. Hence, $A←÷/Q-P$ and $SLOPE←1÷A$, or more compactly, $SLOPE←1÷÷/Q-P$ (see note to problem 5).

7. `SR←+\S`

8. `∧\LV` makes every element a 0 after the first 0.
   `<\LV` makes every element a 0 after the first 1.
   `∨\LV` makes every element a 1 after the first 1.

9. A   `TRANS←ρSALES`
   B   `⌈/SALES` and `⌊/SALES`
   C   `TOTSALES←+/SALES`
   D   `1.04×SALES`
   E   `AVGSALE←TOTSALES÷TRANS`

10. `V←6 2 1 8 4 3`
    A   `TOT←+/V`
    B   `TOT-11`
    C   `6300÷TOT`
    D   `TOT×75`

11. `T←10ρ1`
    `+\T`
    1 2 3 4 5 6 7 8 9 10

    When the interval function is introduced (Chapter 12), you will have a much faster way to generate this sequence.

Answers for Chapter 6

1.
```
      4*3⌈3*4
5.846006549E48
      (4*3)⌈3*4
81
      5*3×5
3.051757813E10
      1÷2+¯5 6 0 8 ¯6
¯0.3333333333 0.125 0.5 0.1 ¯0.25
      76÷+/2+3×1 2 3 4
2
      6÷2-4*3
¯0.09677419355
```

2. The first, second and fourth expressions are equivalent.

3. A   `(3÷4)+(5÷6)-7÷8` or better, `+/3 5 ¯7÷4 6 8`
   B   `(-/9 8÷7 10)÷-/1 2÷3 5`

4. `(×/X)*1÷ρX`
   6.386118449

5. B will be compared with B+A for equality, with A added to that result. The expression works only when A is 0. More generally, parentheses are needed around A+B.

6. Brute force solution: `(0≠4000|Y)∧(0=4|Y)∧(0=400|Y)=0=100|Y`
   Better solution:
   `2|+/0=4 100 400 4000|Y`
   Still better solution: `-/0=4 100 400 4000|Y`

7. The minus sign in front of the middle term acts on everything to the right of it. The correct version is $(X*2)+(\bar{}2\times X\times \underline{Y})+Y*2$ or $(X*2)+(Y*2)-2\times X\times Y$

8. $\bar{}8+X\times X\times 2+\bar{}3\times X*2$

9. $((+/X*2)\div\rho X)*.5$

10. Jack proposes if 1) he has the ring, 2) the weather is favorable, 3) Jill is younger than Jack and 4) Jack isn't over the age limit for Jill's beaux.

11. Annual: $P\times(1+.01\times R)*T$
    Quarterly: $P\times(1+.01\times R\div 4)*T\times 4$

12. $C\leftarrow 5\times(A>B)+4\times A<B$
    $C\leftarrow 8+2\times(A>B)\wedge D<E$

13. $2+2\quad 2+2$
    6 6
    Shame on you if you said the answer was 4 4.

14.
    A ρV
    B $+/V\div\rho V$
    C $+/V<0$
    D $+/V=0$
    E $\lceil/V$
    F $100\times(+/V>100)\div\rho V$
    G $+/(V\leq 200)\wedge V\geq 100$
    H $+/0=100|V\times V>0$

15. $A\times A>B$

16. $.25\times 16.5\times 16.5\times 160\times 144$ or $\times/.25\ 16.5\ 16.5\ 160\ 144$
    1568160

17. $(7.2\times 9\times 5)+4\times 235+39\times 3$
    1732

18. The results of these instructions are dependent on your implementation of APL. You cannot tell *when* the system evaluates an expression in parentheses. Hence, you should avoid writing commands like those shown in this problem.

19. $+/COMM\times\div/FUND$

20. $\lceil/5\ 4.5\ 7.25\div 2.75\ 1.8\ 3$

21. $\wedge/\wedge/A=A=1$

22. $BILLS\leftarrow BILLS\times 1+0.015\times 30<TODAY-DATE$

23. $YR\leftarrow 75\ 81\ 80$
    $PRICE\leftarrow 5200\ 8100\ 9500$
    $GAS\leftarrow 9660\ 8556\ 3080$
    $MILES\leftarrow 98730\ 84000\ 28000$
    $COST\leftarrow 1.35\ 1.30\ 1.47$
    A $GALLONS\leftarrow GAS\div COST$ and $TGAL\leftarrow+/GALLONS$
    B $TAX\leftarrow.04\times PRICE$ and $TTAX\leftarrow+/TAX$
    C $AVMIL\leftarrow MILES\div 80-YR$
    D $MPG\leftarrow MILES\div GALLONS$
    E $GASYR\leftarrow GAS\div 80-YR$
    F $GASPM\leftarrow GAS\div MILES$ and $TGASPM\leftarrow(+/GAS)\div+/MILES$
    Why is this different from $(+/GASPM)\div 3$?
    G $+/GAS$
    H $+/MILES$
    I $(+/MILES)\div+/80-YR$

24. $GROSSPAY\leftarrow R\times H$
    $NETPAY\leftarrow GROSSPAY-GROSSPAY\times.01\times S+I1+I2$

25.
    A $6\leq+/SALES$
    1 (quota exceeded or made)
    B $50\times SALES$
    100 200 0 50 150 (weekly earnings)
    C $((\bar{}50+600)\times+/SALES)-5\times 75$
    4575 (net revenue)

26. $WT\leftarrow 10\times.3\ .15\ .1\ .1\ .05\ .35$
    $COST\leftarrow 2\ 2\ 1.50\ 1.25\ 1.80\ .40$
    $SPRICE\leftarrow 1+.1\times+/WT\times COST$

27. $2.50+.10\times 0\lceil WORDS-15$

28. $(M=1)\wedge(S=0)\wedge(A<55)\wedge L>50000$ or $M\wedge(S=0)\wedge(A<55)\wedge L>50000$

Answers for Chapter 7

1.
```
        L¯2.7|¯15
¯2
        *3 4.7 ¯1.5
20.08553692 109.9471725 0.2231301601
        ⌈¯1.8 0 ¯21 5.6
¯1 0 ¯21 6
        ?3 4 5
1 4 3
        ÷3.5 ¯10 ¯.287
0.2857142857 ¯0.05 ¯3.484320557
        O1÷180
0.01745329252
        |3.1 0 ¯5.6 ¯8
3.1 0 5.6 8
        !3 5 7 4
6 120 5040 24
        L5.5 6.8 ¯9.1 ¯.12
5 6 ¯10 ¯1
        ?¯1.2 ¯6.7 .52 19.5
DOMAIN ERROR
        ? ¯1.2 ¯6.7 0.52 19.5
        ∧
        4×⌈5.8×¯31.046
¯720
        4O1 2 3
1.414213562 2.236067977 3.16227766
        ?10 10 10 10
6 3 1 7    (your random numbers may be different from those shown)
        ⊕14.1 86 .108
2.646174797 4.454347296 ¯2.225624052
        ×¯5.6 0 42
¯1 0 1
        ~0 1 1 0
1 0 0 1
        1OO1 2
1.743934249E¯16 ¯3.487868498E¯16
See comparison tolerance, page 295, for why these are not exactly zero.
        ¯1 ¯2O1 1O.5
0.5 1.070796327
```

2. Floor: $X-1|X$
   Ceiling: $X+1\lfloor -X$ (these expressions work for all real X)

3.
```
        A1←(¯1+A*3)÷2
        *2+A1
3269017.372
        ~(2≤A)∧∨/3=B
0
        C←((A*2)+(A+1)*2)*.5
        C≠LC
0
```

4. $0=(\lfloor N÷10)|N$ or $0=1|N÷\lfloor N÷10$

5.
```
A←Y-1969
LY←L.25×A
B←1+7|3+A+LY or, on one line:
B←1+7|3+A+L.25×A←Y-1969
```

6. A $10>|V$ or $0=\lfloor 10⊕|V$
   B $10≤|V$ or $\sim0=\lfloor 10⊕|V$

7.
```
        M←84.6129999993
        M
84.613
        1E5×M
8461300
        L1E5×M
8461299
```

8. $(\lfloor X×10*-(\lfloor 1+10⊛X)-N)= \lfloor Y×10*-(\lfloor 1+10⊛Y)-N$

9. **A** $D÷B$

     B $\lceil D÷B$

10. **A** $(10*-D)× \lfloor .5+N×10*D$

     B $(10*D)× \lfloor .5+N×10*-D$

11. $(\lfloor X+.5)-0=2 | X-.5$ or $(\lceil X-.5)+~×2 | X+.5$

12. $(~A)∨~B$

       1 1 1 0

     $A∨C∧B$

       1 1 0 1

     $(A∧~B)∧A∨C$

       0 1 0 0

     $(~B)∨A∨~C$

       0 1 1 1

13. $(202×⍳5)=((2⍳⍳5)*2)-(1⍳⍳5)*2$

       1 1 1 1 1

For X a scalar, try this:

     $0=-/(2\ \ 2\ \ 1⍟2\ \ 1\ \ 1×X)*1\ \ 2\ \ 2$

Can you explain why it doesn't work consistently for all X?

14. $1=+/(1\ \ 2○X)*2$

This version works only for scalar X. For X a vector we can use the outer product as follows:

     $∧/1=+⌿(1\ \ 2∘.○X)*2$

15. $?4\ \ 4ρ100$ or $4\ \ 4ρ?16ρ100$

16. The hard way: $(((|N)*.5)×N>0)+(N*2)×N<0$

     Much better: $N*.5**×N$

17. **A** $S∧~T$

     B $T∨~J$

     C $(T∧S)∨J$ or $T∧S∨J$

This ambiguous problem points out that it is more difficult to be precise in English than in APL.

18. $~(V1∧V2)$

       1 0 1 0 1 0

     $(~V1)∨(~V2)$

       1 0 1 0 1 0

     $~(V1∨V2)$

       0 0 0 0 1 0

     $(~V1)∧(~V2)$

       0 0 0 0 1 0

These two equivalences are known in logic as De Morgan's rules.

19. $BETTERGRADES←NEWGRADES \lceil 100 \lfloor \lfloor 1.2×GRADES$

20. $DED←100\ \ 250\ \ 500$

     $POL←608\ \ 1277\ \ 942$

     $PAY←.02\ \ .035\ \ .05$

     $OWNPAY←+/DED× \lfloor POL×PAY$

21. $DIV←.25×SHARES$

     $SHAREDIV← \lfloor DIV$

     $CASH←.01× \lfloor .5+100×16.50×1 | DIV$

22. $\lfloor (DATES+1000000×10000 | DATES)÷10000$

23. $\lfloor 10 | (| NUMBERS)×10*-POSITION$

24. $20+ \lceil (11×3412+175)÷144$

25. $(×X)× \lfloor .5+ | X$

     Note that the alternate algorithm $\lceil X-.5$, which rounds down numbers ending in $.5$, works in all cases.

Answers for Chapter 8

We haven't explained how to correct typographical errors in defined functions (Chapter 10), so for now you'll have to be very careful entering these exercises. If you do make mistakes, $)CLEAR$ and reenter. Most of the exercises don't depend on any other, so you can usually $)CLEAR$ before each exercise. On some systems you can't even $)CLEAR$ while in function definition, so you may have to enter a $∇$ (to close function definition) before you can $)CLEAR$.

1.
```
       ∇Z←EQ X
[1]    Z←0=×/X-2 3 ∇
```
or
```
       ∇Z←EQ1 X
[1]    Z←××/X-2 3 ∇
```
2.
```
       ∇R←H BB AB
[1]    R←H÷AB ∇
```
3.
```
       ∇T←HERO L
[1]    S←.5×+/L
[2]    T←(S××/S-L)*.5 ∇
```
4.
```
       ∇RESULT←REFUND BUCKS
[1]    R1←BUCKS⌊200
[2]    R2←.5×BUCKS-200
[3]    R3←0⌈R2
[4]    R4←R1+R3
[5]    RESULT←R4⌊350 ∇
```
Note the four extra intermediate variables used here. They clutter up the workspace. In Chapter 9 we'll see how to keep this kind of clutter down. Now for a more elegant solution:
```
       ∇RESULT←REFUND1 E
[1]    RESULT←+/.5×E⌊500 200 ∇
```
5.
```
       ∇RT←PR M
[1]    RT←+/÷÷M ∇
```
6.
```
       ∇R←SD X
[1]    R←AVG X
[2]    R←R-X
[3]    R←R*2
[4]    R←(AVG R)*.5 ∇
```
or
```
       ∇R←SD1 X
[1]    R←(AVG(X-AVG X)*2)*.5 ∇
```
7.
```
       ∇M←MR REL V
[1]    M←MR÷(1-(V*2)÷9E16)*.5 ∇
```
8.
```
       ∇Z←X PLUS Y
[1]    Z←X+Y ∇
       ∇Z←X MINUS Y
[1]    Z←X-Y ∇
       ∇Z←X TIMES Y
[1]    Z←X×Y ∇
       ∇Z←X DIVIDEDBY Y
[1]    Z×X÷Y ∇
```
9.
```
       ∇R←A HYPOT B
[1]    R←A×4○B÷A ∇
```
10.
```
       ∇Z←NUM DIVZ DEN
[1]    Z←DEN≠0
[2]    Z←Z×NUM÷DEN+~Z ∇
```
11.
```
       ∇Y←RULEOF72 INT
[1]    Y←⌈72÷INT ∇
```
12. A
```
       ∇Z←EXPENSE UNITS
[1]    Z←50000+(UNITS×20)+5×0⌈UNITS-5000 ∇
```
B
```
       ∇R←SALES PROFIT PRICES
[1]    R←(SALES×PRICES)-EXPENSE SALES ∇
```

Answers for Chapter 9

1.
```
       ∇FICA←P TAX IN
[1]    FICA←.01×P×MAX⌊IN ∇
```
This problem illustrates how a simple APL expression can replace a lot of fuzzy language in the tax code.
2.
```
       ∇A SQDIF B
[1]    T←(A-B)*2 ∇
```
3.
```
       ∇R←FERMAT N
[1]    R←1+2*2*N ∇
```

4.   ∇*COMP*
[1]   (0=*A*|*B*)∨0=*B*|*A* ∇
or
∇*COMP*1
[1]   0=(*A*|*B*)×*B*|*A* ∇

5. **A**   ∇*CHANGEA V*
[1]   *NV*←*NV*+ρ*V* ∇
B   ∇*CHANGEB V*
[1]   *SV*←*SV*++/*V* ∇
C   ∇*CHANGEC V*
[1]   *SVSQ*←*SVSQ*++/*V*∗2 ∇

6.   ∇*Z*←*SD*
[1]   *Z*←((*SVSQ*-(*SV*∗2)÷*NV*)÷ ⁻1+*NV*)∗.5 ∇

7. *A SQA B*   lacks the opening ∇
∇ *Z*←*B HYP*   monadic arguments must be on the right.
∇ *A* 1*FIB B*   illegal function name.
∇ *A HYP B C*   most APL systems can't handle more than two arguments.
∇ *A HYP B;B;C*   same argument appears twice in the header.

8.   **(3 HYP 4) HYP 3 HYP 1**
5.916079783
4+3 HYP 4−3
7.16227766
(4+3)HYP 4−3
7.071067812

9.   **)LOAD 1 CLASS**
SAVED 15.02.39 02/15/83
∇R←ARG1 D ARG2
DEFN ERROR
∇ *R*←*ARG*1 *D ARG*2
                    ∧
D is a variable in 1 *CLASS*. (Execute)*VARS D* to check.) The system will not let you have two objects with the same name in the same place at the same time.

10.   ∇*R*←*PLACE ROUND N*
[1]   *N*←*N*÷*PLACE*
[2]   *R*←⌊.5+*N*
[3]   *R*←*PLACE*×*R* ∇

11.   **)LOAD 1 CLASS**
SAVED 15.02.39 02/15/83
CLR←52 78 90
SYNTAX ERROR
CLR←52 78 90
∧
There is already a defined function by the name *CLR* in this workspace, as can be seen by executing)*FNS C*.

12.   **A←1+B←3**
T←F+7
VALUE ERROR
T←*F*+7
      ∧
T←Z+7
T
12
F is a function name and has no value. When executed, *Z* receives a value as a global variable.

13.   **PERIM1**
R
14
B
2
C
5
M
7
S
1

```
            S←M PERIM2 R
            R
    3
            B
    2
            C
    5
            M
    7
            S
    20
            S←PERIM3 R
            R
    3
            B
    2
            C
    5
            M
    7
            S
    10
```

This exercise is designed to give you practice in distinguishing among local, dummy and global variables. To reset the values after each execution, define a function like the following:

```
        ∇SETUP
[1]     S←1 ◇ B←2 ◇ C←5 ◇ M←7 ◇ R←3 ∇
```

14.
```
        ∇M←MARGIN P;S;C
[1]     S←40000-5000×P
[2]     C←35000+2×S
[3]     M←(P×S)-C ∇
```

15.
```
        ∇Z←NTAX COST TAX
[1]     Z←(+/NTAX)+1.05×+/TAX ∇
```

The taxable part of the line could also be written as $+/TAX+TAX×.05$ or $+/1.05×TAX$. These are less efficient than the answer given. Why?

Answers for Chapter 10

```
            )LOAD 1 CLASS
    SAVED   14.45.33 02/20/83
            ∇STD N
[1]     R←AVG N
[2]     R←R-N
[3]     R←AVG R*2
[4]     ANS←R*.5 ∇
```
1.
```
            ∇STD[□]
        ∇ STD N
[1]     R←AVG N
[2]     R←R-N
[3]     R←AVG R*2
[4]     ANS←R*0.5
        ∇
[5]     [4□7]
```
2.
```
[4]     ANS←R*0.5
        ///1
[4]     R←R*0.5
```
3.
```
[5]     [0□5]
[0]     STD N
        5
[0]     R←    STD N
```
4.
```
[1]     [Δ2]
```

```
 5.      [5]     [☐]
                 ∇  R←STD  N
         [1]     R←AVG  N
         [3]     R←AVG  R*2
         [4]     R←R*0.5
                 ∇
 6.      [5]     [3]
         [3]     R←AVG  (R-N)*2
 7.      [4]     [☐3]
         [3]     R←AVG(R-N)*2
         [4]     R←R*0.5
                 ∇
 8.      [5]     ∇
 9.              ∇STD[1.5]R←R-N
10.      [1.6]   [3☐10]
         [3]     R←R*0.5
                 /5
         [3]     ANS    ←R*0.5
         [4]     [.6]
11.      [0.6]   ρN
         [0.7]   ∇
12.              )ERASE  STD
13.              ∇STD[☐]  ∇
         DEFN  ERROR
                 ∇STD
                    ∧
```

Answers for Chapter 11

```
 1.              ∇FN1  S
         [1]     S*10  ∇
                 ∇X  FN2  V
         [1]     2⊛V≤X  ∇
                 VAR1←÷1  2  3  4  5  6
                 VAR2←⌈/VAR1
                 )SAVE  WORK1
            17.54.51  03/12/83
                 )CLEAR
         CLEAR  WS
                 ∇FN3  T
         [1]     ×T  ∇
                 VAR3←*1  2  3  4  5
                 )SAVE  WORK2
            17.56.04  03/12/83
                 )CLEAR
         CLEAR  WS
                 ∇A  FN4  B
         [1]     A-B*2  ∇
                 VAR4←4  6  8  9
                 )SAVE  WORK3
            17.56.42  03/12/83
                 VAR5←-3  7  10  78
                 )SAVE  WORK4
         NOT  SAVED,  WS  QUOTA  USED  UP
                 )LIB
         WORK1
         WORK2
         WORK3
                 )DROP  WORK1
            17.57.32  03/12/83
                 )LIB
         WORK2
         WORK3
```

```
        )LOAD WORK3
SAVED  17.56.42 03/12/83
        )FNS
FN4
        )VARS
VAR4
        ∇C FN5 D
[1]     (+C≤?D)×4 ∇
        VAR6←1 0 7 ¯6 ¯8
        )SAVE WORK2
NOT SAVED, THIS WS IS WORK3
        )WSID WORK2
WAS WORK3
        )SAVE
   17.58.19 03/12/83 WORK2
        )CLEAR
CLEAR WS
        )LOAD WORK2
SAVED  17.58.19 03/12/83
        )FNS
FN4     FN5
        )VARS
VAR4    VAR6
        )ERASE FN4 VAR4
        )SAVE
   17.58.42 03/12/83 WORK2
        )LIB
WORK2
WORK3
        )FNS
FN5
        )VARS
VAR6
```

Note that when you load one of your own workspaces and then try to save it with a different name,
the system won't let you if a workspace with that name already exists, or if your workspace quota
is used up. However, if you execute)WSID SOMENAME prior to saving, any existing version of
SOMENAME is overridden. Also, when)SAVE is executed the material will be saved under
whatever name the active workspace had prior to saving. The save doesn't take place, however, if
the active workspace was not given a name previously.

```
        )LIB 1
ADVANCEDEX
AIDRILL
CLASS
DPDEMO
FILEAID
FORMAT
NEWS
SHAPE
TYPEDRILL
        )LOAD 1 ADVANCEDEX
SAVED   9.40.34 02/10/71
        )FNS
AH       ASSOC    BIN      COMB
DESCRIBE          DTH      ENTER
F        FC       GC       GCD
GCV      HILB     HTD      IN
INV      INVP     IN1      LFC
LOOKUP   PALL     PER      PERM
PO       POL      POLY     POLYB
RESET    TIME     TRUTH    ZERO
```

```
        )VARS
DAH       DASSOC  DBIN      DCOMB
DDTH      DENTER  DESC      DF
DFC       DGC     DGCD      DGCV
DHILB     DHTD    DIN       DINV
DINVP     DIN1    DLFC      DLOOKUP
DPALL     DPER    DPERM     DPO
DPOL      DPOLY   DPOLYB    DTIME
DTRUTH    DZERO   J         M
N         NEW     R         TIMER
X         Z
        DESCRIBE
```

EACH OF THE VARIABLES OF THIS WORKSPACE WHICH BEGINS WITH THE
LETTER D IS THE DESCRIPTION OF THE FUNCTION WHOSE NAME IS
OBTAINED BY REMOVING THE D.

```
        )WSID
IS  1 ADVANCEDEX
        ∇L RECT W
[1]     L×W ∇
        )COPY 1 CLASS RECT
SAVED   14.45.33 02/20/83
        ∇RECT[☐] ∇
    ∇  L RECT H
[1]     2×L+H
[2]     L HYP H
[3]     L×H
    ∇
```

The original *RECT* is replaced by the version in 1 *CLASS*.

```
        )ERASE RECT
        ∇L RECT W
[1]     L×W ∇
        )PCOPY 1 CLASS RECT
SAVED   14.45.33 02/20/83
NOT COPIED: RECT
```

This command copies a global object in the same way as *COPY* only if one doesn't exist with the
   same name in the active workspace.

```
        ∇RECT[☐] ∇
    ∇  L RECT W
[1]     L×W
    ∇
        )SAVE JONES
   12.23.04 03/13/83
        )WSID SMITH
WAS JONES
        )DROP WORK2
   12.23.10 03/13/83
        )SAVE
   12.23.13 03/13/83 SMITH
        )CLEAR
CLEAR WS
        )LOAD 1 ADVANCEDEX
SAVED    9.40.34 02/10/71
        )SAVE 1 ADVANCEDEX
IMPROPER LIBRARY REFERENCE
```

The ordinary user can't save into a common library unless he put it in there originally.

```
        )CONTINUE HOLD
```

(after signing on again)

```
CONTINUE SAVED   12.24.46 03/13/83
        )LIB
CONTINUE
WORK3
JONES
SMITH
```

```
        )FNS
AH        ASSOC      BIN        COMB
DESCRIBE             DTH        ENTER
F         FC         GC         GCD
GCV       HILB       HTD        IN
INV       INVP       IN1        LFC
LOOKUP    PALL       PER        PERM
PO        POL        POLY       POLYB
RESET     TIME       TRUTH      ZERO
        )VARS
DAH       DASSOC     DBIN       DCOMB
DDTH      DENTER     DESC       DF
DFC       DGC        DGCD       DGCV
DHILB     DHTD       DIN        DINV
DINVP     DIN1       DLFC       DLOOKUP
DPALL     DPER       DPERM      DPO
DPOL      DPOLY      DPOLYB     DTIME
DTRUTH    DZERO      J          M
N         NEW        R          TIMER
X         Z
```

The command $CONTINUE$ $HOLD$ saves the active workspace in $CONTINUE$ and briefly holds open the phone line. The workspace is available to the user when he signs on again.

3.
```
        )SAVE CONTINUE
        )LOAD GOOD
        )COPY CONTINUE OK
        )SAVE
```

4.
```
        )LOAD 1 CLASS
SAVED   14.45.33 02/20/83
        )GROUP A TAB0 TAB1 TAB2 TAB3
        )GROUP B AVG1 AVG2 AVG3 AVG4 AVG5
        )GROUP A A PI
        )GRPS
A         B
        )GRP A
TAB0      TAB1      TAB2      TAB3      PI
        )GROUP A
        )GRPS
B
```

Answers for Chapter 12

1.
```
        A←0 8 ¯3 4 6 10
        M←2 4ρι8
        V←3 3ρι9
        ρA
6
        ρρA
1
        ρρρA
1
        A⌈0.8×ι6
0.8 8 2.4 4 6 10
        ρM
2 4
        (¯2) 1 2
SYNTAX ERROR
        (¯2) 1 2
           ∧
        ι10
1 2 3 4 5 6 7 8 9 10
        (ι5)+3
4 5 6 7 8
        ¯7×ι1
¯7
```

```
        ι⌈/A
1 2 3 4 5 6 7 8 9 10
        ¯2,1 2
¯2 1 2
        +/ι15
120
        ÷ι5
1 0.5 0.3333333333 0.25 0.2
        ι28÷3+1
1 2 3 4 5 6 7
        ρρV
2
        V,M
LENGTH ERROR
        V,M
        ∧
```

Why the error message?

2.
```
        A←0 8 ¯3 4 6 10
        ρA=6
6
        6=ρA
1
```
The first expression tells us how many elements A has, and the second tells us whether A has 6 elements.

3.
```
        )LOAD 1 CLASS
SAVED  14.45.33 02/20/83
        ×/ρTAB0
1
        ×/ρTAB1
4
        ×/ρTAB2
12
        ×/ρTAB3
24
```
The instructions tell us how many elements are in each of the arrays.

4.
```
        A←0 8 ¯3 4 6 10
        ιρA
1 2 3 4 5 6
        ριρA
6
```
The first expression gives us a vector of indices for the elements in A, while the second is equivalent to ρA. Compare $\rho \iota \rho A$ with $\lceil / \iota \rho A$. How do they differ? (Don't be too hasty in your answer.)

5. **A**
```
        ∇R←A1 N
[1]     R←+/(ιN)*.5 ∇
```
    B
```
        ∇R←B2 N
[1]     R←(+/ιN)*.5 ∇
```
    C
```
        ∇R←C3 N
[1]     R←(×/ιN)*÷N ∇
```

6.
```
        ¯1+2×ι8
1 3 5 7 9 11 13 15    .
        ¯12+5×ι5
¯7 ¯2 3 8 13
        .3+.3×ι6
0 0.3 0.6 0.9 1.2 1.5
        ¯350+100×ι6
¯250 ¯150 ¯50 50 150 250
        6-ι5
5 4 3 2 1
        2|ι6
1 0 1 0 1 0
```

7.  ```
         ι3*ι3
    RANK ERROR
         ι3*ι3
         ∧
    ```
    The order of execution is such that ι3 will be generated first and used as powers for 3, resulting in a vector for the right argument of ι on the left. Since interval requires a single element as its argument, the error message appears.

8.  ```
         51≠ι50
    50ρ1
         (ι50)=ι50
    ```

9.  ```
         ¯1+2×-/ι5
    5
         +/¯1+ι5
    10
         +/5=1+ι5
    1
         +/0=6=ι5
    5
         or
         +/~6=ι5
    5
    ```

10. A
    ```
         ∇R←SERIES1 N
    [1]  R←-/÷ιN ∇
    ```
    B
    ```
         ∇R←X SERIES2 N;T
    [1]  T←¯1+ιN
    [2]  R←+/(X*T)÷!T ∇
    ```

11. ```
         0=ρρA
    ```

12. ```
         A←3 4 5
         B←ι8
         ρA,ρB
    4
         (ρA),ρB
    3 8
    ```
    The first expression is equivalent to 1+ρA, while the second is the vector consisting of the lengths of A and B.

13. If E were a 'yadic function, we would have to write 6 E 8 to execute it. Spaces or other delimiters (e.g., parentheses) are required around a function name.

14. ```
         S←S,ι0 or S←(ι0),S or S←1ρS
    ```

15. ```
         11 1ρ1000,.05×ι10
         0
    0.156434465
    0.3090169944
    0.4539904997
    0.5877852523
    0.7071067812
    0.8090169944
    0.8910065242
    0.9510565163
    0.9876883406
         1
    ```
    This expression generates the values required by the problem, but without identification as to the magnitude (in radians) of the associated angles. With the transpose (Chapter 15) such information can be included: ⍉2 1 1ρ(○A),100A←(¯1+ι11)÷20. The table can also be generated with the outer product. Do you see how?

16. ```
         +/(ιN)×0=2|ιN or +/2×ι⌊N÷2
    ```
    Looking ahead a bit, once compression is introduced in Chapter 14, a more elegant solution will be +/(Nρ0 1)/ιN.

17. ```
         0 5ρι0
    ```

18. ```
         A←(321400÷27.8*.5)-17÷6.5E¯4
         B←5⍟÷(6.8E¯6)*.25
         C←32200*2÷9
         A
    34803.13833
         B
    1.848252091
         C
    10.04027826
    ```

```
                  ⌊/A,B,C
      1.848252091
```
19.
```
                  -/÷1,2×⍳29
```
20.
```
                  ((⍳N)∘.=⍳N)×(N,N)⍴V
```
21.
```
                  (⍳4)∘.+4⍴0
```
22. The sum scan shows that the following series converges fairly rapidly. Try it with some large value of *N*, say 20:
```
                  N←20
                  10000×+\÷2*0,⍳N
      10000 15000 17500 18750 19375 19687.5
            19843.75 19921.875 19960.9375
            19980.46875 19990.23438 19995.11719
            19997.55859 19998.7793 19999.38965
            19999.69482 19999.84741 19999.92371
            19999.96185 19999.98093 19999.99046
```
23. A
```
                  R≥⍳L
```
   B
```
                  (L-R)<⍳L
```
   When the function ↑ is introduced in Chapter 14, these expressions can also be written as $L \uparrow R \rho 1$ and $(-L) \uparrow R \rho 1$.

Answers for Chapter 13

1.
```
                  X←'MISSISSIPPI'
                  Y←'RIVER'
                  'ABCDE'='BBXDO'
      0 1 0 1 0
                  ⍴V←'3172'
      4
                  (⍴V)⍴V
      3172
                  3172=V
      0 0 0 0
                  X,Y
      MISSISSIPPIRIVER
                  1 2<'MP'
      DOMAIN ERROR
                  1 2 <'MP'
                    ∧
                  Y∈X
      0 1 0 0 0
                  +/X='S'
      4
                  +/X≠'S'
      7
                  X,' ',Y
      MISSISSIPPI RIVER
                  ⍴⍴AL←3 3⍴'ABCDEFGHI'
      2
                  X='S'
      0 0 1 1 0 1 1 0 0 0 0
                  +/'P'=X
      2
                  +/(X,' ',Y)≠'S'
      13
                  ∨/X='R'
      0
```
2. *D* is a character vector consisting of 15 blanks.
3.
```
                  ∇F A
      [1]         'THE SHAPE OF A IS ',⍕⍴A
      [2]         'THE RANK IS ',⍕⍴⍴A
      [3]         'THE NUMBER OF ELEMENTS IS ',⍕×/⍴A ∇
```
4.
```
                  (10>I)⍴' ',⍕I
```
   This is a formatting problem. Further details in Chapter 17.

5.
```
      )COPY 1 CLASS GEO3 HYP
SAVED  14.45.33 02/20/83
      ∇GEO3[.5]
[0.5] ⍝ THE LITERAL MESSAGES IN THIS FUNCTION
[0.6] ⍝ ARE KEYED TO THE ARGUMENTS USED
[0.7] ∇
      ∇GEO3[☐] ∇
   ∇ L GEO3 H;X;FLAG
[1]   ⍝ THE LITERAL MESSAGES IN THIS FUNCTION
[2]   ⍝ ARE KEYED TO THE ARGUMENTS USED
[3]   FLAG←((ρ,L)>1)∨(ρ,H)>1
[4]   X←((4×~FLAG)ρ' IS:'),(6×FLAG)ρ'S ARE:'
[5]   'PERIMETER',X
[6]   2×L+H
[7]   'AREA',X
[8]   L×H
[9]   'DIAGONAL',X
[10]  L HYP H
   ∇
      3 4 GEO3 5 6
PERIMETERS ARE:
16 20
AREAS ARE:
15 24
DIAGONALS ARE:
5.830951895 7.211102551
```
Comments introduced in this manner don't affect execution of the function, although they do take up space in storage. Note also that in entering the comment the closing del was placed on the next line rather than at the end of the comment. Do you see why?

6.
```
      ∇GPA;GR;CR;M
[1]   M←5 25ρ(25ρ4),(25ρ3),(25ρ2),(25ρ1),(25ρ0)
[2]   GR←M×CR←(3×GR3)+(2×GR2)+GR1
[3]   'STUDENT GRADE POINT AVERAGES ARE ',⍕(+/GR)÷+/CR
[4]   'THE CLASS AVERAGE IS ',⍕(+/+/GR)÷+/+/CR ∇
```

7.
```
      +/∧≠'AEIOU'∘.≠CHAR or
      (ρCHAR)-+/,'AEIOU'∘.=CHAR  or
      +/~CHAR∊'AEIOU'
```

Answers for Chapter 14

1.
```
      A←0 ¯5 ¯8 6.2 15 ¯2 25
      B←1 0 0 1 0 1 1
      C←'ABCDEFGHIJKLMNOPQRSTUVWXYZ ?'
      M←3 4ρ⍳12
      (2<⍳5)/⍳5
3 4 5
      B/A
0 6.2 ¯2 25
      A[ρA],B[¯2+ρB]
25 0
      A[3 6]←2E5 4E¯4
      A
0 ¯5 200000 6.2 15 0.0004 25
```
Note that A is respecified in this fourth drill problem. This will affect the remaining problems.
```
      'ABD'∊C
1 1 1
      4↑A
0 ¯5 200000 6.2
      2 3ρM
 1 2 3
 4 5 6
```

```
        M[2;3 1]
7 5
        1 1 0 1\'TWO'
TW O
        A[8]
INDEX ERROR
        A[8]
        ^
        AιΓ/A
3
        2 10 15εM
1 1 0
        ¯3↓C
ABCDEFGHIJKLMNOPQRSTUVWXY
        3 3 ρ1,3ρ0
   1 0 0
   0 1 0
   0 0 1
        1 0 1↑M
   1   2   3   4
   9  10  11  12
        A[1]+A[2 3 4]×A[7]
¯125 5000000 155
        1 0 0 1 1 1\M
   1   0   0   2   3   4
   5   0   0   6   7   8
   9   0   0  10  11  12
        B\2 3 4 5
2 0 0 3 0 4 5
        0 2↓M
   3   4
   7   8
  11  12
        1 3↑M
   1  2  3
        10ρ100
100 100 100 100 100 100 100 100 100 100
```
2. A
```
        D←¯2.1 4 1.9 0 ¯1 ¯4 ¯1.4 .7 2.5 2
        (D<.5)/D
¯2.1 0 ¯1 ¯4 ¯1.4
```
   B
```
        (D>0)/D
4 1.9 0.7 2.5 2
```
   C
```
        (4=|D)/D
4 ¯4
```
   D
```
        ((D<0)∧D>¯1)/D
```
   E
```
        (D=2)/D
2
```
   F
```
        ((D<1)∧D≥¯2)/D
0 ¯1 ¯1.4 0.7
```
3.
```
        ∇Z←INSERT1 V
[1]     Z←((2×ρV)ρ1 0)\V
[2]     Z[2×ι¯1+ρV]←'∘' ∇
```
When laminate is introduced in Chapter 19, this can be done more easily by
```
        ∇Z←CHAR INSERT2 V
[1]     Z←¯1↓,V,[1.2]CHAR ∇
```
4.
```
        ∇Z←INCR V
[1]     Z←1↓V-0,¯1↓V ∇
```
5.
```
        ∇Z←F X
[1]     Z←3×X*2 ∇
        ∇Z←I AREA X
[1]     Z←+/I×F X[1]+I×ιL|(-/X)÷I ∇
```
6.
```
        ∇Z←W WITHIN R
[1]     Z←(R≥|W-+/W÷ρW)/W ∇
```
7.
```
(R=LR)/R
```

8.
$\quad\nabla R \leftarrow A\ IN\ INT$
[1] $R \leftarrow (+/INT[2] > |A-INT[1]) \times 100 \div \rho A\ \nabla$
INT is defined here as the vector B,C.

9. $(\lceil/V) > (+/V) - \lceil/V$ or $(\lceil/V) > +/(V \neq \lceil/V)/V$

10. $Y[2 \times \iota \lfloor (\rho Y) \div 2]$ or $(2|1+\iota\rho Y)/Y$ or $(\sim 2|\iota\rho Y)/Y$

11.
$\quad\nabla R \leftarrow S\ INS\ X$
[1] $R \leftarrow ((S \geq X)/X), S, (S < X)/X\ \nabla$

12.
$\quad\nabla Z \leftarrow DELE\ V$
[1] $Z \leftarrow ((\iota\rho V) = V \iota V)/V\ \nabla$

13.
$\quad\nabla R \leftarrow X\ SELECT\ Y$
[1] $R \leftarrow X[Y \iota \lceil/Y]\ \nabla$

14.   The indices as given start with 0, which will result in an index error.

15. $(W = \lceil/W)/\iota\rho W$ or $W \iota \lceil/W$

16.   A $(V < 0)/V$
B $+/(V < 0)/V$
C $(V > 0)/\iota\rho V$
D $(V = \lceil/V)/\iota\rho V$
E $+/V[2\ 3\ \rho\ 1\ 5\ 6\ 2\ 4\ 8]$

17. $+/Q[\iota 8 \lfloor \rho Q]$ or $+/Q \times 8 \geq \iota\rho Q$

18. $^-1\ ^-1 \downarrow 1\ 1 \downarrow M$

19.   A $((^-1 + \rho V, V) \rho 1\ 0)\backslash V$
B $((\lfloor 1.5 \times \rho V) \rho 1\ 0\ 1)\backslash V$
C   Same as **B** provided we don't want a zero on the right end when ρV is odd.

20.
$\quad\nabla R \leftarrow FACTORS\ N$
[1] $R \leftarrow (0 = (\iota N)|N)/\iota N\ \nabla$
or
$\quad\nabla R \leftarrow FACTORS1\ N$
[1] $R \leftarrow (\sim \times 1|N \div \iota N)/\iota N\ \nabla$

21.
$\quad\nabla R \leftarrow LONGEST\ X; J; M; N; P$
[1] $J \leftarrow (X = '\ ')/\iota\rho X$
[2] $P \leftarrow J, 1+\rho X\ \diamond\ N \leftarrow ^-1 + P - 0, J\ \diamond\ M \leftarrow \lceil/N$
[3] $R \leftarrow X[(P[N \iota M] + \iota M) - 1 + \rho \iota M]\ \nabla$
In this solution J locates the blanks in X. N is a vector of word lengths, with M the largest. Line 3 generates the indices needed to pick it out of X.

22.
$\quad\nabla R \leftarrow A\ COMFACT\ B$
[1] $R \leftarrow (0 = (\iota A)|A)/\iota A$
[2] $R \leftarrow (0 = R|B)/R\ \nabla$

23. $(\sim(\iota\rho V) \in I)/V$

24.   The second is a 1 1 matrix, while the first is a scalar. Try ρ of each to check.

25. $W \leftarrow (W \neq 'A')/W$

26.   A $((0 = 2|X) \lceil (0 = 3|X))/X$ ($\vee$ may be substituted for $\lceil$)
B $((0 = 2|X) \vee (0 = 3|X))/X$

27.
$\quad\nabla Z \leftarrow CLOSEST\ A; M$
[1] $M \leftarrow (1000 \times (\iota\rho A)\circ. = \iota\rho A) + |A \circ. - A$
[2] $M \leftarrow , M = \lfloor/, M$
[3] $Z \leftarrow A[\lceil (M/\iota\rho M) \div \rho A]\ \nabla$
After looking at the matrix $A \circ. - A$, you should be able to figure out for yourself why the rest of line 1 was necessary. Also compare with the solution given in problem 4.

28.   A $M[\iota 3;]$
B $M[1\ 2;1\ 2]$
C $M[;4\ 5]$
D $M[1\ 5;1\ 5]$
With the take function, these can be expressed as
A $3\ 5 \uparrow M$
B $2\ 2 \uparrow M$
C $5\ ^-2 \uparrow M$
D $1\ 1 \uparrow M$ $^-1\ 1 \uparrow M$ $^-1\ ^-1 \uparrow M$ $^-1\ 1 \uparrow M$

29.   A $GALLONS \leftarrow +/INFO[;3\ 5]$ and $TGAL \leftarrow +/GALLONS$
     B $TAX \leftarrow .04 \times INFO[;2]$ and $TTAX \leftarrow +/TAX$
     C $AVMIL \leftarrow INFO[;4] \div 1980 - INFO[;1]$
     D $MPG \leftarrow INFO[;4] \div GALLONS$
     E $GASYR \leftarrow INFO[;3] \div 1980 - INFO[;1]$
     F $GASPM \leftarrow \div /INFO[;3\ 4]$ and $TGASPM \leftarrow \div /+\backslash +/INFO[;3\ 4]$
     G $+/INFO[;3]$
     H $+/INFO[;4]$
     I $\div /(+/INFO[;4]),+/1980 - INFO[;1]$

30. $N \leftarrow \iota 50$
         $COST \leftarrow (.08 \times N) + 10.24 \div N*.5$ (cost)
         $(COST = \lfloor /COST)/N$ (number of items sampled)

31. $\nabla Z \leftarrow T\ CENTER$
   [1] $Z \leftarrow (-1 \uparrow \rho R) - \rho T$
   [2] $Z \leftarrow ((\lceil .5 \times R) \rho '\ '),T\ \nabla$

32. $(^-1 \downarrow (\iota \times 1 \uparrow \rho M) \rho 1\ 0) \neq M$

33. $\nabla Z \leftarrow W\ FWIDTH\ V;L$
   [1] $L \leftarrow ((W=V)/ \iota \rho V),1+\rho V$
   [2] $Z \leftarrow ^-1 \uparrow L - 0, ^-1 \downarrow L\ \nabla$

34. $100 \times (+/ANS) \div 1 \uparrow \rho ANS$

35. $\nabla HI;A$
   [1] $A \leftarrow (4\ 2 \rho 0\ 8\ 8\ 11\ 19\ 17\ 36\ 17)[?4;]$
   [2] $A[2] \uparrow A[1] \downarrow V\ \nabla$

36.   A $?(?8\ 8) \rho 150$
     B $?(?8\ 8) \rho ?299$

37. $((|V) \in 0, \iota 9)/V$

38. $\wedge /(S1 \in S2),S2 \in S1$ or $\sim 0 \in (S1 \in S2),S2 \in S1$

39. $+/S \in 'ABCDEFGHIJKL'$

40. $C[('X'=C)/ \iota \rho C] \leftarrow 'Y'$

41. $(5 < \iota 8)/X$ and $^-3 \uparrow X$

42. $(,M)[N? \rho,M]$

43. $M \leftarrow M + (\rho M) \rho (1 \uparrow \rho M) \rho 0,N$

44. ∇AR
   [1] $M \leftarrow 5\ 15 \rho V1,V2,V3,V4,V5$
   [2] $'TOTALS\ BY\ CATEGORY\ ARE\ ', \bar\Phi +/M$
   [3] $'TOTALS\ BY\ CUSTOMER\ ARE\ ', \bar\Phi +/M$
   [4] $'THE\ TOTAL\ OF\ ALL\ ACCOUNTS\ RECEIVABLE\ IS\ ', \bar\Phi +/+/M$
   [5] $'CUSTOMERS\ WITH\ OVERDUE\ INVOICES:\ ', \bar\Phi (\vee / 0 \neq ^-3\ 15 \uparrow M)/ \iota 15\ \nabla$

45. $^-3 \uparrow 5 \uparrow V$ and $2 \downarrow ^-6 \downarrow V$

46. $P \leftarrow 6.99 + .01 \times \iota 51$
         $Q \leftarrow 600 - 3.7 \times P*2$
         $TR \leftarrow P \times Q$
    Price: $P[TR \iota \lceil /TR]$
    Production: $Q[TR \iota \lceil /TR]$

47. $A \leftarrow 50?100$
         $B \leftarrow 50?100\ \Diamond\ B \in A$

48.   A $(V1 \in V2)/V1$
    If there are duplicate elements in either $V1$ or $V2$, this expression is *not* symmetric with respect to $V1$ and $V2$, i.e., the above would not then be the same as $(V2 \in V1)/V2$.
     B $V1,(\sim V2 \in V1)/V2$
     C $(\sim V1 \in V2)/V1$
    You may recognize these expressions as corresponding to the intersection, union and difference of two vectors.

49. $M1 \leftarrow (((R-1),1 \downarrow \rho M) \uparrow M),[1](R,0) \downarrow M$ or $M1 \leftarrow (R \neq \iota 1 \uparrow \rho M) \neq M$

50. $((,V) \iota S) \uparrow,V$

51. $MAT[I;]$ is a 1 by n matrix, not a vector or scalar. Try instead $(,MAT[I;]) \iota VECTOR$.

52. $ORDERSN \leftarrow ORDERS$
         $ORDERSN[;2] \leftarrow 1.15 \times ORDERSN[;2]$
         $PRICESN \leftarrow PRICES$
         $PRICESN[;2] \leftarrow .9 \times PRICES[;2]$
         $(+/,ORDERSN \times PRICESN) \div +/,ORDERS \times PRICES$

53. $LOWSALES \leftarrow ORDERS < 10000$
         $HIPRICES \leftarrow PRICES > 20$
     A $LOWSALES \wedge HIPRICES$
     B $+/,LOWSALES \wedge HIPRICES$
     C $+/,PRICES \times ORDERS \times LOWSALES \wedge HIPRICES$

Answers for Chapter 15

1.
```
        A←3 2 0 ‾1 5 ‾8
        M←3 4ρι12
        N←4 3ρ9 7 1 2 3 5 6 9 15 22 1
        3⌽A
‾1 5 ‾8 3 2 0
        2⌽A[ι4]
0 ‾1 3 2
        ⊖A
2 3 4 5 1 6
        2↑‾3⌽A
‾1 5
        ‾2 1 3⌽M
   3   4   1   2
   6   7   8   5
  12   9  10  11
        ⌽0,ι3
3 2 1 0
        2⌽⌽ι7
5 4 3 2 1 7 6
        ⌽⊖N
   9   1  22
  15   9   6
   5   3   2
   1   7   9
        A[⍋A]
5 ‾1 0 2 ‾8 3
        M[⍋M[;1];]
   1   2   3   4
   5   6   7   8
   9  10  11  12
        A[⍒0 1 0 1 0 1]
2 ‾1 ‾8 3 0 5
        2⌽1⊖M
   7   8   5   6
  11  12   9  10
   3   4   1   2
        (⌽ι6)ιM
  6 5 4 3
  2 1 7 7
  7 7 7 7
        (ι6)=⍋A[⍋A]
1 1 1 1 1 1
        ⍉N
   9   2   6  22
   7   3   9   1
   1   5  15   9
```

2.
```
        ALF←'ABCDEFGHIJKLMNOPQRSTUVWXYZ '
        S←'THE QUICK BROWN FOX JUMPS OVER THE LAZY DOG'
        S[⍋ALFιS]
ABCDEEEFGHHIJKLMNOOOPQRRSTTUUVWXYZ
```

3.   `⍉4 3ρ0 1 2 3`
4.   `(V,V1)[⍋V,V1]`
5.   `∧/V[⍋V]=ιN   or   ∧/(V∈ιN),(ιN)∈V`
6.   `∇R←MED X`
   `[1]    R←.5×+/X[(⍋X)[⌈⌊‾.5 .5×1+ρX]] ∇`
7.   `∇R←ELIM V`
   `[1]    R←V=S`
   `[2]    R←((1↑R)↓R≠1⌽R)/V ∇`
8. **A**   `×/LENGTHS`
    B   `+/2×LENGTHS×1⌽LENGTHS`
9.   `∇Z←STRAIGHTLINE X`
   `[1]    Z←⌽X[3]+X[3]×(‾/X[1 3])÷X[2]×ιX[2] ∇`

10. $V[\Psi V>10]$

11. $\nabla Z \leftarrow MS \ N;Q$
[1] $Z \leftarrow (N,N)\rho \iota N \star 2$
[2] $Q \leftarrow (-\lceil .5 \times N + \iota N$
[3] $Z \leftarrow Q \ominus Q \phi Z \ \nabla$

12. A $HAND[;\Psi'CDHS' \iota HAND[2;]]$
     B $HAND[;DEN \leftarrow \Psi' 23456789TJQKA' \iota HAND[1;]]$
     C $HAND[;DEN[\Psi'CDHS' \iota HAND[2;DEN]]]$

13. $\nabla Z \leftarrow SORTR \ M;A$
[1] $Z \leftarrow \rho M$
[2] $M \leftarrow ,M$
[3] $A \leftarrow \spadesuit M$
[4] $Z \leftarrow Z \rho M[A[\spadesuit \lceil A \div 1 \downarrow Z]] \ \nabla$

If this solution seems a bit weird, it is. It is one which is uniquely APL. Perhaps a more natural
approach is to sort one row at a time. This requires that we know how to loop or iterate (Chapter
16). Below is a more conventional branching solution a la Fortran or PL/1, which for arrays with
many rows is much slower than $SORTR$:
     $\nabla Z \leftarrow SORTR1 \ M;I$
[1] $I \leftarrow 1 \uparrow \rho M$
[2] $Z \leftarrow M$
[3] $L:Z[I;] \leftarrow M[I;\spadesuit M[I;]]$
[4] $\rightarrow L \times \times I \leftarrow I-1 \ \nabla$

14. $\nabla R \leftarrow V \ LOC \ W$
[1] $R \leftarrow (\wedge \neq (\bar{\ } 1 + \iota \rho W) \phi W \circ . = V)/ \iota \rho V \ \nabla$

15. $\bar{\ } 2 \uparrow G[\spadesuit G]$ or $2 \uparrow G[\Psi G]$

16. A $(+/\wedge \backslash ' ' = M) \phi M$
     B $(-+/\wedge \backslash ' ' = \phi M) \phi M$

17. $\nabla Z \leftarrow CENT \ MAT;A$
[1] $Z \leftarrow ' '=MAT$
[2] $A \leftarrow +/\wedge \backslash Z$
[3] $Z \leftarrow (\lceil .5 \times A-+/\wedge \backslash \phi Z) \phi MAT \ \nabla$

18. $1 \uparrow \downarrow (.5 \times +/S) > +\backslash S[\Psi S]$

19. $(+/V[4 \downarrow \spadesuit V]) \div \bar{\ } 4 + \rho V$

20. $|/ \spadesuit V$

This expression is dependent on the index origin (see page 294). The authors concede that this is a
dirty problem.

21. $+/\vee \backslash \phi 0 \neq V$

22. $\nabla Z \leftarrow SCORES \ PRINT \ NAMES;ORDER$
[1] $ORDER \leftarrow \Psi SCORES$
[2] $'TOURNAMENT \ RANKING:'$
[3] $' '$
[4] $Z \leftarrow NAMES[ORDER;], \Phi((\rho SCORES),1)\rho SCORES[ORDER] \ \nabla$

23. $(1 + \rho V2)-(\phi V2) \iota V1$ or $+/\vee \backslash V1 \circ .= \phi V2$

24. A $((V \neq S) \iota 1) \downarrow V$ or $(\vee \backslash V \neq S)/V$
     B $((S \neq \phi V) \iota 1) \downarrow V$ or $(\phi V \backslash S \neq \phi V)/V$

25. $\nabla TRIANGLE \ N;SIDE$
[1] $SIDE \leftarrow (N,N)\rho' \circ ', N\rho' '$
[2] $SIDE \leftarrow (\ominus SIDE),SIDE$
[3] $(2 \times N)\rho' \circ ' \ \nabla$

26. $\nabla C \leftarrow SUBST \ M;ALF;P$
[1] $ALF \leftarrow 'ABCDEFGHIJKLMNOPQRSTUVWXYZ'$
[2] $P \leftarrow 26?26$
[3] ALF
[4] $ALF[P]$
[5] $' '$
[6] M
[7] $C \leftarrow ALF[P[ALF \iota M]] \ \nabla$

Grade up can be used to improve on the letter substitution by transposing the letters:
     $\nabla C \leftarrow SUBST1 \ M;ALF;P$
[1] $ALF \leftarrow 'ABCDEFGHIJKLMNOPQRSTUVWXYZ'$
[2] $P \leftarrow \spadesuit(\rho M)\rho 26?26$
[3] M
[4] $C \leftarrow M[P] \ \nabla$

27.
```
        ∇Z← K VIG M;C;D
[1]     ALF←'ABCDEFGHIJKLMNOPQRSTUVWXYZ'
[2]     C←ALFιM
[3]     M
[4]     D←1+26|C+(ρC)ρK
[5]     ALF[(ρC)ρK]
[6]     (ρM)ρ'-'
[7]     Z←ALF[D] ∇
```
Try $K←1\ 2\ 3$ for a test encoding of some message.

28.
```
        ∇R←DECODE C
[1]     R←ALF[PιALFιC] ∇
```
It is assumed that ALF and P are known to the decoder.

29.   The result shows that $A×B$ is a maximum when $A=B$, a conclusion well known to calculus students who have worked since time immemorial on problems like the following: show that a square is the rectangle with the greatest area for a given perimeter.

Answers for Chapter 16

1.   **A** If $5<W$, go to step 3; if $5>W$, go to 2; if $5=W$, go to the next step. W is assumed to be a scalar or vector of length 1.

   B Go to step 3 if $A=8$, otherwise drop through to the next step.

   C Go to END if $Y>1$, otherwise branch out of the program. At the same time R is reshaped as a 1 1 matrix containing a 1.

   D Go to step 7 if any element of B is a member of C, otherwise drop through to the next step.

   E If $A≤C$ go to 5, otherwise branch out of the program.

   F Go to step 3.

   G Go to step 8 if $0≠J$, otherwise go to the next step. At the same time J is decreased by 1.

   H If the absolute value of X is greater than or equal to I, go to step 4, otherwise leave the program. I is also incremented by 1.

   I Go to $AGAIN$ if $N=10$, otherwise execute the next line. R is reshaped as a 2 4 matrix.

2.
```
        ∇V←REMT;I
[1]     I←1
[2]     L:→(I≥ρT)/0
[3]     V←(T[I]≠V)/V
[4]     I←I+1
[5]     →L ∇
```
This function, which involves branching, solves the problem by brute force. You'll appreciate the power of APL from the following:
```
        ∇V←REM1 T
[1]     V←(~V∈T)/V ∇
```

3.
```
        ∇A←CMPX B
[1]     →BIGGER IF A>B
[2]     →SMALLER IF A<B
[3]     'EQUAL'
[4]     →0
[5]     BIGGER:'GREATER'
[6]     →0
[7]     SMALLER:'LESS' ∇
```

4.
```
        ∇R←MED N
[1]     N←N[♠N]
[2]     →(R=⌊R←.5×ρN)/ST
[3]     R←N[⌈R]
[4]     →0
[5]     ST:R←.5×N[R]+N[R+1] ∇
```
or
```
        ∇R←MED1 N
[1]     N←N[♠N]
[2]     R←N[⌈.5×ρN]
[3]     →L×~2|ρN
[4]     L:R←.5×R+N[1+.5×ρN] ∇
```

5.
```
        ∇R←N DUPL V
[1]     →0×ιρR←(N=V)/ιρV
[2]     'SCALAR NOT PRESENT' ∇
```

6.
```
        ∇Z←ROOT S
[1]     →(0≠ρρS)/0
[2]     Z←S*.5 ∇
```
7.
```
        ∇R←SORT TEXT
[1]     ALF←'ABCDEFGHIJKLMNOPQRSTUVWXYZ'
[2]     R←''
[3]     L:→0×ι0=ρTEXT
[4]     R←R,(TEXT=1↑ALF)/TEXT
[5]     TEXT←(TEXT≠1↑ALF)/TEXT
[6]     ALF←1↓ALF
[7]     →L ∇
```
or, without branching
```
        ∇R←SORT1 TEXT
[1]     TEXT←((ALFιTEXT)≤ρALF)/TEXT
[2]     R←ALF[R[↑R←ALFιTEXT]] ∇
```
8.
```
        ∇R←MODE N;V
[1]     V←R←ι0
[2]     AT:V←V,+/N[1]=N
[3]     R←R,N[1]
[4]     →(0≠ρN←(N[1]≠N)/N)/AT
[5]     R←R[(V=⌈/V)/ιρV] ∇
```
9.
```
        ∇R←FIB N
[1]     R←1 1
[2]     END:→(N>ρR←R,+/¯2↑R)/END ∇
```
10.
```
        ∇HISTOG A;I
[1]     I←⌈/A
[2]     L:I≤A
[3]     →L××I←I-1 ∇
```
To 'clean up' the histogram, change line 2 to $L:'$ $*'[1+I≤A]$. This function produces a vertical histogram. For a horizontal histogram try the following:
```
        ∇HISTOG1 A
[1]     A[1]ρ'*'
[2]     →×ρA←1↓A ∇
```
The outer product further simplifies the construction of histograms:
```
        ∇HISTOG2 A
[1]     ' .□'[1+A∘.≥ι⌈/A] ∇
```
11.
```
        ∇R INT P;IN;I
[1]     'YR PRIN INT'
[2]     ''
[3]     I←1
[4]     L:IN←.01×⌊.5+100×P×R[1]
[5]     I,P,IN
[6]     P←P+IN
[7]     →((I←I+1)≤R[2])/L ∇
```
Here $R[1]$ is the yearly interest rate in decimal form and $R[2]$ the number of years to be evaluated. As in problem 10, the outer product will greatly simplify the job of generating the table. Your table probably will not be formatted properly. If this bothers you, use the formatting operator to be introduced in Chapter 17.

12.
```
        ∇R←ODDS N;A;I
[1]     I←1+R←0
[2]     L:A←5?52
[3]     R←R+3≤+/A≤13
[4]     I←I+1
[5]     →(N≥I)/L
[6]     R←4×R÷N ∇
```
Note that the odds are figured for only one suit (random numbers 1 to 13) on line 3, and the result is multiplied by 4 on line 6, assuming each suit to be equally probable.

13.
```
        (ι4)□TRACE 'ACK'
        2 ACK 1
ACK[1]  →2
ACK[1]  →3
ACK[1]  →2
ACK[1]  →3
ACK[1]  →4
ACK[4]  2
ACK[3]  →0
ACK[1]  →4
ACK[4]  3
ACK[2]  →0
ACK[3]  →0
ACK[1]  →2
ACK[1]  →2
ACK[1]  →2
ACK[1]  →3
ACK[1]  →4
ACK[4]  2
ACK[3]  →0
ACK[1]  →4
ACK[4]  3
ACK[2]  →0
ACK[1]  →4
ACK[4]  4
ACK[2]  →0
ACK[1]  →4
ACK[4]  5
ACK[2]  →0
ACK[2]  →0
5
```

14.
```
        ∇R←A EQUAL B
[1]     R←(ρρA)=ρρB
[2]     →S×R
[3]     S:R←∧/(ρA)=ρB
[4]     →E×R
[5]     E:R←~0∈A=B  ∇
```

This function tests for equality of rank (line 1), shape (line 3) and elements (line 5). It will distinguish
between characters and numerics, e.g., '1' is not equal to 1, and simulates the match function
found in APL2.

15.
```
        ∇COND PRINT MESSAGE
[1]     →(~COND)/0
[2]     MESSAGE  ∇
```

16.
```
        ∇R←M DELE NAME;A;D;J
[1]     J←0
[2]     L:→(J≥D←1↑ρM)/END
[3]     J←J+1
[4]     →(~∧/((1↓ρM)↑NAME)=M[J;])/L
[5]     R←(J≠ιD)⌿M
[6]     'DONE'
[7]     →0
[8]     END:'NAME NOT FOUND'  ∇
```

When the inner product is introduced in Chapter 20, the function can be rewritten as
```
        ∇R←M DELE1 NAME;T
[1]     T←M∧.=(1↓ρM)↑NAME
[2]     →(∨/T)/END
[3]     R←(~T)⌿M
[4]     'DONE'
[5]     →0
[6]     END:'NAME NOT FOUND'  ∇
```

*DELE*1 is more general since it will handle multiple occurrences of *NAME* in *M*.

17.
```
        ∇R←GRADE2 M;A
[1]     R←ι1↑ρM
[2]     A←¯1↑ρM
[3]     L:R←R[⍋M[R;A]]
[4]     →L××A←A-1 ∇
```

18.
```
        ∇R←X FINDROW STRING;HOLD;I
[1]     R←ιI←0
[2]     STRING←(¯1↑ρX)↑STRING
[3]     LOOP:I←I+1
[4]     →(I>1↑ρX)/OUT
[5]     HOLD←X[I;]
[6]     →(~∧/HOLD=STRING)/LOOP
[7]     R←R,I
[8]     →LOOP
[9]     OUT:→(0≠ρR)/0
[10]    'NAME NOT FOUND' ∇
```
Or, replace lines 4 6 and 9 as follows:
```
[4]     →OUT⌈ιI>1↑ρX
[6]     →LOOP⌈ι~∧HOLD=STRING
[9]     →0⌈ι0≠ρR
```
The combinations ⌈ι and ×ι, which can be read as 'if,' are less general than compression. Their right arguments *must* be a nonnegative scalar or vector of length one.

19.
```
        ∇Z←CARDSORT MAT;D;ALF
[1]     D←¯1↑ρMAT
[2]     ALF←' ABCDEFGHIJKLMNOPQRSTUVWXYZ0123456789'
[3]     MAT←MAT[⍋ALFιMAT[;,D];]
[4]     L1:→(0=D)/L2
[5]     D←D-1
[6]     →L1
[7]     L2:Z←MAT ∇
```

20.
```
        ∇R←N FIB1 A
[1]     R←A
[2]     →(N=2)/0
[3]     R←(N-1) FIB1 R
[4]     R←R,¯1↑R+(¯1⌽R) ∇
```

Answers for Chapter 17

1. **A**   `10 4⍕TABLE`
        B   `10 ¯3⍕TABLE`
        C   `0 3⍕TABLE`
        D   `(8 3 10 5 6 3,(2ρ10 5))⍕TABLE`

2.   `(⍕Q)[;2×ι(ρQ)[2]] or 1 0⍕Q`

3.
```
        ∇INC SAL RANGE;A;B;W
[1]     A←1+(|-/RANGE)÷INC
[2]     W←(A,1)ρRANGE[1]+INC×¯1+ιA
[3]     B←52×W
[4]     '     WEEK     MONTH     ANNUAL'
[5]     ''
[6]     10 2⍕W,(B÷12),B ∇
```

```
4.                  ∇NAMES REPORT ACTIVITY;ACT;NO;OD;BAL100;HIBAL;LOBAL
        [1]         OD←(0>ACT←+/ACTIVITY)/NO←ι1↑ρNAMES
        [2]         BAL100←(100<ACT)/NO
        [3]         LOWBAL←⌊/+\ACTIVITY
        [4]         HIBAL←⌈/+\ACTIVITY
        [5]         ''
        [6]         '    CURRENT ACTIVITY REPORT'
        [7]         ''
        [8]         'THE FOLLOWING ARE OVERDRAWN:'
        [9]         ''
        [10]        ' NAME          BALANCE'
        [11]        NAMES[OD;],20 2⍕ACT[,OD;]
        [12]        ''
        [13]        'THE FOLLOWING HAVE BALANCES OVER 100 DOLLARS:'
        [14]        ''
        [15]        ' NAME          BALANCE'
        [16]        NAMES[BAL100;],20 2⍕ACT[,BAL100;]
        [17]        ''
        [18]        'FOLLOWING ARE THE LOW/HIGH BALANCES FOR THE MONTH:'
        [19]        ''
        [20]        ' NAME         LOW        HIGH'
        [21]        NAMES,20 2⍕LOWBAL, (NO,1)ρHIGHBAL ∇
5.                  ∇R←LITCHK X;Y
        [1]         R←2=ρ⍕Y←ιρ1↑,X ∇
6.                  ∇REPORT DAT;FLAG;REORD;NO
        [1]         REORD←DAT[;5]>+/DAT[;2 3])/NO←ι1↑ρDAT
        [2]         FLAG←(NO,6)ρ' '
        [3]         FLAG[REORD;2+ι4]←'*'
        [4]         ' PART NO  IN STOCK  ON ORDER  UNIT COST  REORDER  FLAG'
        [5]         ''
        [6]         (8 0 11 0 10 0 11 2 9 0⍕DAT),FLAG ∇
7.                  ∇INSUR BILL;INS
        [1]         'BILL IS ',(⍕BILL),' DOLLARS'
        [2]         'INSURANCE PAYS ',(⍕INS←(15<BILL)×.6×BILL-15),' DOLLARS'
        [3]         'YOUR COST IS ',(⍕BILL-INS),' DOLLARS' ∇
8.                  DATE←⁻1↓,(3 2ρ⍕DATE),'/'
```

Chapter 18 contains features that will simplify formatting expressions like this.

```
9.                  ∇Z←W FORM M;U;R
        [1]         R←ρM
        [2]         Z←(U←M≠0)/M←,M
        [3]         Z←W⍕((ρM),1)ρZ
        [4]         Z←(R×1,W[1])ρZ←U\Z ∇
10.                 ∇R←SPEC COLHEAD HDGS
        [1]         R←(SPEC[1]ρ' '),,((ρHDGS)[1],-SPEC[2])↑HDGS ∇
```

Answers for Chapter 19

```
1.                  U←2 3 4ρι24
                    C←2 4 3ρ'ABCDEFGHI'
                    ⌈/⌈/⌈/U
        24
                    ⌈/,U
        24
                    ×/U
           13   28   45   64
           85  108  133  160
          189  220  253  288
                    +/[2]U
           15  18  21  24
           51  54  57  60
                    +/U[;2;3]
        26
```

```
      ¯1 1 2↓C
F
I
C
      (2 4⍴⍳3)⌽C
BCA
FDE
GHI
BCA

FDE
GHI
BCA
FDE
      +/U[;1;3]
18
      ⍉C
AD
DG
GA
AD

BE
EH
HB
BE

CF
FI
IC
CF
      1 0 1 0/[2]C
ABC
GHI

DEF
ABC
      0 2 2 ↓U
  11 12

  23 24
      ⊖C
DEF
GHI
ABC
DEF

ABC
DEF
GHI
ABC
```

```
              3 1 2⍉C
AD
BE
CF

DG
EH
FI

GA
HB
IC

AD
BE
CF
              1 2 2⍉U
         1   6  11
        13  18  23
```

2.   `U[1;1;]←U[2;3;]`

3.   `R←M[;M]`   Reminder: the indices themselves may have rank >1.

4.   `∇Z←LIST N`
  `[1]`   `Z←⍉(3,N)ρ(⍳N),(!⍳N),÷⍳N ∇`

5. **A**   `+/+/[2]BUDG[;;4 10]`
   B   `BUDG[;3;6]` (per month) or
       `+/BUDG[;3;6]` (per year)
   C   `+/+/[2]BUDG`
   D   `10|Z1←(,Z)⍳⌊/,Z←BUDG[;2;]`(identifies account)
       `⌈/Z1÷12` (identifies month)
   E   `BUDG[;4 5;1 3]`
   F   `∇FORMAT;M`
  `[1]`   `'ACC',6 0 ⍕⍳10`
  `[2]`   `(3ρ'‾'),(54ρ' ‾'),' ‾‾'`
  `[3]`   `M←12 3ρ'JANFEBMARAPRMAYJUNJULAUGSEPOCTNOVDEC'`
  `[4]`   `M,6 0 ⍕+/[2] BUDG ∇`
   G   `C←BUDG[6+⍳6;;]`
       `D←BUDG[⍳6;;]`
       `BUDG←D,[1](+/D),[1]C,[1]+/C`

6.   `,V,[1.5]';'`

7.   `∇WINNER;A;B;B1`
  `[1]`   `A←⌈/B←+/MAGSALES`
  `[2]`   `B1←B=A∘.+25ρ0`
  `[3]`   `CAL,MAGNAMES[⌈/B1×(12ρ0)∘.+⍳25;] ∇`

8.   `∇Z←UNDER V`
  `[1]`   `Z←V,[.5](V≠' ')\'‾' ∇`
    `UNDER 'TEST  CASE'`
  `TEST  CASE`
  `‾‾‾‾  ‾‾‾‾`

    `ρUNDER 'TEST  CASE'`
   `2 10`

9. **A**   `+/,SALES[2;;]`
   B   `+/[2]SALES[3 4;;]`
   C   `+/−/SALES[5 3;;]`
   D   `SP[1 2;1 3;2]×SALES[1 2;1 3;2]`
   E   `+/,SP[5;;]×SALES[5;;]`
   F   `SP←SP,[1]1.2×SP[5;;]`

10. **A**   `TEMP←+/SALES[3;;2 4]`
       `100×(−/TEMP)÷TEMP[2]`
   B   `A←+/SALES[4 5;;]`
       `A×50000<A` (0 for those models selling less than 50,000)

11.
```
        ∇REPORT HWR;RH;RPT;CH
[1]     RH←'NAILS' ON 'TACKS' ON 'SCREWS' ON 'TOTAL'
[2]     HWR←(HWR,[1]+/HWR),+/HWR
[3]     RPT←RH,(4 9ρ' '),⍕HWR
[4]     'HARDWARE PURCHASES' CENTER RPT
[5]     ''
[6]     UNDER '  1Q   2Q   3Q   4Q   TOTALS'
[7]     RPT ∇
```
(*UNDER* is the utility developed in problem 8).

12.
```
        ∇Z←NUMBER LIST;S
[1]     S←1↑ρLIST
[2]     Z←(⍕(S,1)ριS),((S,3)ρ'.  '),LIST ∇
```

13.
```
        ∇R←TABLE M;A
[1]     A←2×∨/(,M)≠⌊,M
[2]     R←A⍕((×/ρM),1)ρM
[3]     R←R,'|'
[4]     R←((1↑ρM),(×/ρR)÷1↑ρM)ρR
[5]     R←'|',R
[6]     R←'_',[1]R,[1]'‾' ∇
```

14.
```
        ∇A←SIDE WITH MATRIX
[1]     A←(' ';[1]' ',[1]SIDE),MATRIX ∇
        ∇R←TOP ABOVE DATA
[1]     R←(,((1↑ρTOP),‾15)↑TOP),[1]' ',[1]15 2⍕DATA ∇
```
ABOVE may have to be adjusted for very wide column headings.

15.
```
        ∇Z←MAT1 BESIDE MAT2;M
[1]     M←(1↑ρMAT1)⌈1↑ρMAT2
[2]     Z←((M,1↓ρMAT1)↑MAT1),(M,1↓ρMAT2)↑MAT2 ∇
```

16.
```
        A,(A,[1]M,[1]A),A
```

17.
```
        ROWHEAD←(5 5ρ'STORE'),⍕ι5
        COLHEAD←9+ι5
        SALES1←(' ',[1]ROWHEAD),(1⌽10 0⍕COLHEAD),[1]10 1⍕SALES
```

18.
```
        1 1 2⍉V∘.+M
```
This procedure is overkill, since the result of the outer product can be a very large array, only a portion of which is really needed. Better is $M+(ρM)ρV$ which is more direct and economical.

19.
```
        1 1 ⍉⌽M or 1 1 ⍉2 0 1 ⌽M
```

Answers for Chapter 21

1.
```
        A←ι4  ◇  B←2 3ρ'ABCDEF'
        C←'ABD'  ◇  D←3 1ρι3
        E←3 4 5  ◇  F←4 3ρι10
        G←3 4ρ⌽ι7
        C∘.=B
     1 0 0
     0 0 0

     0 1 0
     0 0 0

     0 0 0
     1 0 0
        D∘.×A
     1  2  3  4

     2  4  6  8

     3  6  9 12
```

```
      1  3  9○.>D
 0
 0
 0

 1
 1
 0

 1
 1
 1
      E+.=E
3
      F×.-G
 ¯18    0   ¯4    0
   0   ¯6   ¯8    0
   0   24   70   18
  24   12    0   36
      F∨.<G
 1  1  1  1
 1  1  1  1
 0  0  0  0
 1  1  1  1
      A○.+3×D
  4
  7
 10

  5
  8
 11

  6
  9
 12

  7
 10
 13
      D○.÷A
 1    0.5      0.3333333333    0.25
 2    1        0.6666666667    0.5
 3    1.5      1               0.75
      B○.≠C
 0  1  1
 1  0  1
 1  1  1

 1  1  0
 1  1  1
 1  1  1
      E∧.>G
0  0  0  0
      E∨.≠F
LENGTH ERROR
      E∨.≠F
      ∧
      3+.×F
66  48  60
```

```
        ~(A∘.=A)∘.∧1 0 0 1
  0 1 1 0
  1 1 1 1
  1 1 1 1
  1 1 1 1

  1 1 1 1
  0 1 1 0
  1 1 1 1
  1 1 1 1

  1 1 1 1
  1 1 1 1
  0 1 1 0
  1 1 1 1

  1 1 1 1
  1 1 1 1
  1 1 1 1
  0 1 1 0
        ⍉D∘.*A
  1   2   3

  1   4   9

  1   8  27

  1  16  81
        A∘.⌈¯1 3 2 4
  1 3 2 4
  2 3 2 4
  3 3 3 4
  4 4 4 4
        F×.=E
0 0 0 0
        G|.-F
  0 0 2
  1 0 ¯3
  0 2 0
        (⍉G)⌈.+E
11 10 9 11
```

2.   4 2 2 or 2 2 4

3.
```
      ∇R←DIST L
[1]   R←⌊.5+(((L[;1]∘.-L[;1])*2)+(L[;2]∘.-L[;2])*2)*.5 ∇
```
or
```
      ∇R←DIST1 L
[1]   R←⌊.5+(+/1 3 2 3⍉(L∘.-L)*2)*.5 ∇
```

4.   +/'ABCDEFG'∘.='CABBAGE'

5.
```
      SUM←B|C+D
      CARRY←B≤C+D
      ∇ADDTAB B;T
[1]   INT←¯1+⍳B
[2]   T←INT∘.+INT
[3]   (B|T)+10×B≤T ∇
```

6.
```
      ∇Z←C1 MULT C2
[1]   Z←+⌿(1-⍳ρC1)⌽C1∘.×C2,0×1↓C1 ∇
```

7.   A
$$X \leftarrow {}^-5+\iota 9$$
$$F \leftarrow (\phi X)\circ .=|X$$
GRAPH

```
  o           +           o
    o         +         o
      o       +       o
        o   +   o
  +   +   +   +   o   +   +   +   +
              +
              +
              +
              +
```

   B
$$F \leftarrow (\phi X)\circ .={}^-5+X\star 2$$
GRAPH

```
    o           +           o
                +
                +
                +
  +   +   +   +   +   +   +   +   +
      o         +         o
                +
                +
      o         +         o
```

   C
$$F \leftarrow (\phi X)\circ .\le X+1$$
GRAPH

```
              +           o   o
              +       o   o   o
              +   o   o   o   o
              o   o   o   o   o
  +   +   +   o   o   o   o   o   o
          o   o   o   o   o   o   o
      o   o   o   o   o   o   o   o
  o   o   o   o   o   o   o   o   o
  o   o   o   o   o   o   o   o   o
```

   D
$$F \leftarrow (\phi X)\circ .\le 3|X$$
GRAPH

```
              +
              +
  o           o   +           o
  o       o   o   +   o   o       o
  o   o   o   o   o   o   o   o   o
  o   o   o   o   o   o   o   o   o
  o   o   o   o   o   o   o   o   o
  o   o   o   o   o   o   o   o   o
  o   o   o   o   o   o   o   o   o
```

   E
$$F \leftarrow ((\phi X)\circ .\le X+1)\wedge (\phi X)\circ .\ge 3-|X$$
GRAPH

```
              +           o   o
              +       o   o   o
              +   o   o   o   o
              +       o   o   o
  +   +   +   +   +   +   +   o   o
              +               o
              +
              +
              +
```

8.
$$X \leftarrow {}^{-}13 + \iota 20$$
$$Y \leftarrow \phi X$$
$$(0 = ({}^{-}3 \times Y) \circ . + (2 \times X) - 2) \vee 0 = (2 \times Y) \circ . + X - 8$$

```
0 0 0 0 0 0 [1] 0 0 0 0 0 0 0 0 0 0 0 0 0
0 0 0 0 0 0 0 0 [1] 0 0 0 0 0 0 0 0 0 0 0
0 0 0 0 0 0 0 0 0 0 [1] 0 0 0 0 0 0 0 0 0
0 0 0 0 0 0 0 0 0 0 0 0 [1] 0 0 0 0 0 0 [1]
0 0 0 0 0 0 0 0 0 0 0 0 0 0 [1] 0 0 0 0 0
0 0 0 0 0 0 0 0 0 0 0 0 0 0 0 0 [1] 0 0 0
0 0 0 0 0 0 0 0 0 0 0 0 0 0 0 0 0 0 [1] 0
0 0 0 0 0 0 0 0 0 0 0 0 0 [1] 0 0 0 0 0 0
0 0 0 0 0 0 0 0 0 0 0 0 0 0 0 0 0 0 0 0
0 0 0 0 0 0 0 0 0 [1] 0 0 0 0 0 0 0 0 0 0
0 0 0 0 0 0 0 0 0 0 0 0 0 0 0 0 0 0 0 0
0 0 0 0 0 0 [1] 0 0 0 0 0 0 0 0 0 0 0 0 0
0 0 0 0 0 0 0 0 0 0 0 0 0 0 0 0 0 0 0 0
0 0 0 0 [1] 0 0 0 0 0 0 0 0 0 0 0 0 0 0 0
0 0 0 0 0 0 0 0 0 0 0 0 0 0 0 0 0 0 0 0
0 [1] 0 0 0 0 0 0 0 0 0 0 0 0 0 0 0 0 0 0
0 0 0 0 0 0 0 0 0 0 0 0 0 0 0 0 0 0 0 0
0 0 0 0 0 0 0 0 0 0 0 0 0 0 0 0 0 0 0 0
0 0 0 0 0 0 0 0 0 0 0 0 0 0 0 0 0 0 0 0
0 0 0 0 0 0 0 0 0 0 0 0 0 0 0 0 0 0 0 0
```

The 1's correspond to integer number pairs satisfying the simultaneous linear equations 3Y=2X-2 and 2Y=8-X (conventional notation). The point of intersection (4,2) is the common solution of both equations.

9.   Change X to $X \leftarrow \lfloor . 5 \times X \div S$

10.
$$RET \leftarrow PRIN \circ . \times (1 + RATE) \circ . * TIME$$

11.   A
$$X \leftarrow \iota 20$$
$$Y \leftarrow X \neq 2$$
$$Z \leftarrow 2 \times X * 2$$
20 60 PLOT X VS Y

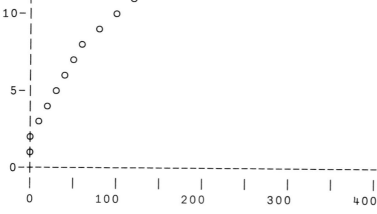

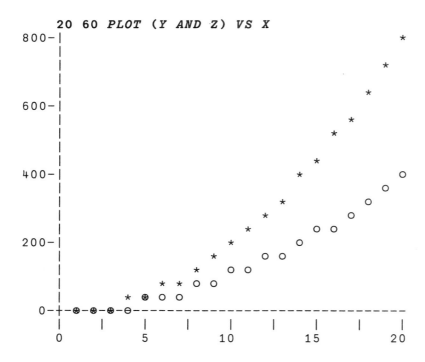

This last plot looks like something the cat dragged in. If we use only one symbol for each 'curve', we are constrained in the fineness of the plot by the 'size' of the print position (1/6 inch vertical by 1/10 inch horizontal). Many APL systems have other plotting routines that take advantage of features of particular terminals, such as the ability to place dots very close together. Your *DESCRIBE* or *HOWPLOT* may contain information on how this may be done. Here is the previous example, using the Tektronix 4015 display terminal:

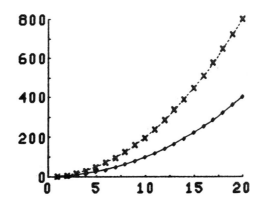

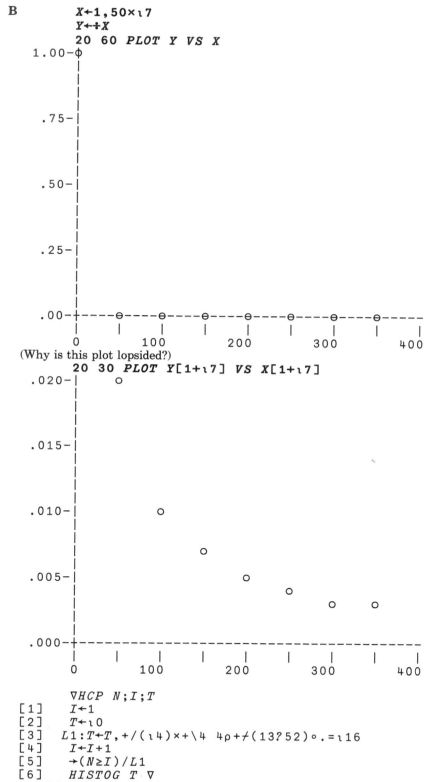

B
```
      X←1,50×ι7
      Y←÷X
      20 60 PLOT Y VS X
```

(Why is this plot lopsided?)
```
      20 30 PLOT Y[1+ι7] VS X[1+ι7]
```

12.
```
      ∇HCP N;I;T
[1]   I←1
[2]   T←ι0
[3]   L1:T←T,+/(ι4)×+\4 4ρ+/(13?52)∘.=ι16
[4]   I←I+1
[5]   →(N≥I)/L1
[6]   HISTOG T ∇
```
Line 3 is the key to this function. Since the numbers in the matrix generated by 13?52 are arbitrary and random, line 3 assumes 1 2 3 4 to be Jacks, 5 6 7 8 to be Queens, etc.

13.
```
        ∇W FIND1 T;A
[1]     A←∧≠(¯1+ιρW)ϕW∘.=T
[2]     T
[3]     A\'↑' ∇
```

14. **A** $A∧.=B$ results in a 1 if A and B are identical, 0 otherwise.

$M∧.=B$ yields a logical vector with a 1 for each row of M which is identical to B.

$A+.≠B$ gives the number of pairs of corresponding dissimilar elements in A and B.

$(M=0)∧.≥U$ produces a logical matrix which reproduces the initial 1's in each row of $M=0$ and fills the rest of the row with 0's, e.g.,

```
            M
    0  0  0  3  2  0  0  0
    0  0  1  7  9  2  8  0
    6  4  0  0  0  1  6  0
            M=0
    1  1  1  0  0  1  1  1
    1  1  0  0  0  0  0  1
    0  0  1  1  1  0  0  1
            (M=0)∧.≥(ι8)∘.≤ι8
    1  1  1  0  0  0  0  0
    1  1  0  0  0  0  0  0
    0  0  0  0  0  0  0  0
```

It may be considered a simulation of the 'and-scan' $∧\M=0$.

$A×.*B$ is equivalent to the times reduction of A raised to the B power. One possible use could be in getting a number from its prime decomposition. Here is an example of this latter use:

```
        2 3 5 7×.*2 1 0 1
84
```

Still another use may be seen in the expression $B×.*B<100$. This is the product of all $B<100$.

B $R[I;J]$ is 1 if and only if the Ith row and the Jth column of N have at least one 1 in the same location. It is used to represent two-stage connections, as in pecking orders or circuitry. (See the defined function RUN in this chapter.)

C For $R←C+.=D$, $R[I;J]$ is the number of matching pairs of elements of $C[I;]$ and $D[;J]$. For $R←C⌈.⌊D$, $R[I;J]$ is the largest of the smaller of $C[I;]$ and $D[;J]$ taken pairwise.

15.
```
        ∇R←X POLY C
[1]     R←C+.×X∘.*¯1+ιρ,C ∇
```

16.
```
        ∇Z←EXP A
[1]     Z←.21 .15 .10+.×(100⌊A),(50⌊0⌈A-100),0⌈A-150 ∇
```
or
```
        ∇Z←EXP1 A
[1]     Z←.01×6 5 10+.×(100 50,L/ι0)∘.⌊A ∇
```
which will handle both vector and scalar arguments. $⌊/ι0$ is the so-called *identity element* for the dyadic operation $⌊$. It yields $7.237005577E75$, the largest number generated by the APL system. The reason it is called an identity element is that when paired with any other number N with $⌊$, it yields N. (Try $+/ι0$, $-/ι0$, $×/ι0$, $*/ι0$, $⌈/ι0$, etc.)

17. **A**
```
        R←0≠.=4 100 400 4000∘.|Y
```
B
```
        ∇REFUND1 E
[1]     .5×20 500+.⌊1 1∘.×E ∇
```
This version can handle plural arguments, which the old version could not.

C
```
        ∇R←N DUPL1 V
[1]     R←'SCALAR NOT PRESENT'
[2]     →0×ι0=N∨.=V
[3]     R←(N=V)/ιρV ∇
```

18.
```
        ORDERS←300 500 200 1000
        PARTS←4 5ρ1 2 0 5 2 0 3 0 1 5 1 1 4 2 2 1 2 4 5 5
        PRICES←32 9.75 3.2 .78 7.2
        PARTORDERS←ORDERS+.×PARTS
        PARTORDERS
1500 4300 4800 7400 8500
        COSTOFALLPARTS←ORDERS+.×PARTS+.×PRICES
        COSTOFALLPARTS
172257
        COSTFOREACHMODEL←PARTS+.×PRICES
        COSTFOREACHMODEL
69.8 66.03 70.51 104.2
```

19.
```
        WDL.+DS
```
20.
```
        A←3 1 8 9
        A<.≥1⌽A
0

        A←1 3 8 9
        A<.≥1⌽A
1
```
This expression indicates whether A is in strictly ascending order. It is equivalent to $(\rho A) \le 1 + + / (1 \downarrow A) > (^{-}1 \downarrow A)$.

21. A
```
        UCOST+.×QUANT
```
B
```
        +/QUANT
```
C
```
        +/QUANT
```
D
```
        UCOST×+/QUANT
```
E
```
        UCOST+.×+/QUANT or +/UCOST+.×QUANT
```
F
```
        UCOST⌈.×QUANT
```
G
```
        (UCOST+.×+/QUANT)÷+/+/QUANT
```
H
```
        ROW←(FRUIT∧.=(^{-}1↑FRUIT)↑'GRAPES')/ι1↑ρFRUIT
```

```
        UCOST[ROW]+.×QUANT[ROW;]
```

22. It compares each row of M with every other row of M and returns 1 for each row which is smaller than the one being compared, 0 otherwise. The trailing zero is necessary to handle properly the case where a row has leading zeroes. Note that if the columns of the result are summed and graded, the resulting indices applied to M will sort the matrix. It is, however, very slow if there are a large number of rows.

23.
```
        ∇R←VECTOR SEARCH TABLE
[1]     R←(TABLE∧.=VECTOR)ι1 ∇
```

24. In general execute ⊞$(N,N)\rho 1,N\rho 0$. A specific example might be
```
        ⊞3 3ρ1 0 0 0
1 0 0
0 1 0
0 0 1
```
from which it should be evident that the identity matrix is its own inverse.

25.
```
        10 13 3⊞3 3ρ2 13 4 3 ^{-}1 2 1 ^{-}4
3.5 2.220446049E^{-}16 1
```

26.
```
        ∇LIN W;G
[1]     G←(W[1]×W[5])-W[4]×W[2]
[2]     →(0=G)/L1
[3]     'X IS ',⍕((W[5]×W[3])-W[2]×W[6])÷G
[4]     'Y IS ',⍕((W[1]×W[6])-W[4]×W[3])÷G
[5]     →0
[6]     L1:'NO UNIQUE SOLUTION' ∇


        ∇ABC SOLVE DEF
[1]     ⍝ ABC IS A 3-ELEMENT VECTOR A,B,C
[2]     ⍝ DEF IS A 3-ELEMENT VECTOR D,E,F
[3]     →(0≠-/×/(ABC,DEF)[2 2ρ1 5 2 4])/OK
[4]     'NO UNIQUE SOLUTION'
[5]     →0
[6]     OK:(ABC,DEF)[3 6]⊞(ABC,DEF)[2 2ρ1 2 4 5] ∇
```

27.
```
        ∇R←F X
[1]     R←X×300+^{-}2×X ∇
        1E^{-}6 SLOPE 0 100 200
299.999998 ^{-}100.000002 ^{-}500.0000001
        1E^{-}6 SLOPE 0 20 40 60 80
299.999998 219.9999972 139.9999974 59.99999757 ^{-}20.00000222
        1E^{-}6 SLOPE 60 65 70 75
59.99999757 39.99999717 19.99999768 ^{-}2.728484105E^{-}6
```
The sides of the rectangle are each about 75 feet long.

28.
```
        YR←84+ι7
        SALES←38 52 64 82 98 128 156
        SALES⌹YR∘.*0 1
¯1608.857143 19.28571429
```
The linear equation best fitting the data is $SALES←¯1608.86+19.28×YR$.

29. To solve for R:

R+UR=I

IR+UR=I

(I+U)R=I

(I+U)⁻¹(I+U)R=(I+U)⁻¹I where (I+U)⁻¹ is the inverse of I+U

IR=(I+U)⁻¹I

R=(I+U)⁻¹

Therefore the APL solution is
```
        ⌹((ι1↑ρU)∘.=ι1↑ρU)−U
  1  0  0  0  0  0  0  0  0
  0  1  0  0  0  0  0  0  0
  0  0  1  0  0  0  0  0  0
  1  2  0  1  0  0  0  0  0
  0  1  1  0  1  0  0  0  0
  1  3  3  1  1  1  0  0  0
  3 10  8  3  4  2  1  0  0
  6 12  8  3  4  2  1  1  0
 10 33 27 10 13  7  3  0  1
```
30.
```
        W←2000 2200 2500 2750 3000 3500 4000 4500 5000 5500
        C←4.14 4.67 5.35 5.61 6.77 7.39 9.29 10.45 10.95 12.16
        C⌹W∘.*0 1
1.929687474 0.001734030928
```
The equation is $C←1.93+.001734×W$. In these days of energy conservation, what can you deduce from these results?

Answers for Chapter 22

1.
```
        (3ρ40)⊥8 7 2
13082
        1 ¯4.1 .8⊥1 2 3
1.32
2 0
1 1 0 2 0
¯8190
68
585
0 2 0
0 1 3
81 117 153 189 225
0
1 1 0 2 0
1 3 3
```
```
        3 3⊤5217
        (5ρ3)⊤5217
        (4ρ8)⊥¯14
        2⊥5 1 9 6
        7 8 9⊥7 8 9
        3 3 3⊤5217
        1 4 6⊤345
        1 4 7⊥3 5ρι15
        3⊤5217
        (5ρ3)⊤5217
        2 4 5⊤78
```

2. A   `0 4 2⌊2 8 1`

     B   `0 2000 16⌊3 568 13`

3. A   `8⌊2 1 7 7`

     B   `2⌊1 0 1 1 0 1`

     C   `(10ρ3)⊤8933`

     D   `(10ρ5)⊤4791`

4.   `X⊤X⊥Y` and `X⊥X⊤Y`

    More generally, `X⊥X⊤Y` is the same as `(×/X)|Y`

5.   `∇P←CONV D`

    `[1]`   `P←10⊥⁻1+'0123456789'ι(D≠',')/D ∇`

6.   `N=+/(10 10 10⊤N)*3`

7. A converts M into a vector of digits.

     B converts M into the corresponding scalar.

     C same as B. The *execute* function (Chapter 24) will duplicate the effect of B or C more succinctly:

         `5+⍎M`

   `1234588`

8.   `0=11|⁻/((1+10⊛N)ρ10)⊤N`

9.   `∇TRICK N;D1`

    `[1]`   `D1←|N-10⊥φ(3ρ10)⊤N`

    `[2]`   `D1+10⊥φ(3ρ10)⊤D1 ∇`

10. A same as `+/V`

     B same as `⁻1↑V`

     C same as `-/V`

     D separates integer and decimal parts of N.

11.   `∇Z←C EVAL X`

    `[1]`   `Z←X⊥C ∇`

    (put 0's in for missing powers of X.)

12.   `∇Z←REP ENCODE N`

    `[1]`   `Z←((1+⌈REP⊛N)ρREP)⊤N ∇`

    The key here is the use of the characteristic of the log (`⌈REP⊛N`) to determine the positions needed.

13.   feet: `(0 3 12,÷12)⊥3 0 1 0`

    yards: `(0 3 12,÷36)⊥3 0 1 0`

    or `((÷12 3),1)⊥φ3 0 1`

    and for completeness:

    inches: `(0 3 12,÷1)⊥3 0 1 0`

    which is the same as `0 3 12⊥3 0 1`

14. A   `((V≠S)ι1)↓V` or

          `(∨\V≠S)/V` or

          `(((S=φV)⊥1)-1)↓V`

     B   `((S≠φV)ι1)↑V` or

          `(φV\S≠φV)/V` or

          `(1-(V=S)⊥1)↓V`

15.   `0 20 12⊤0 20 12⊥+⌿C`

    Jefferson was correct.

16.   `∇R←DIAG M`

    `[1]`   `R←10⊥1 1⍉M ∇`

17.   `(+/V)÷ρV`   `+/V÷ρV`   `+/V÷+/V=V`

    `(0⌈+\V)÷ρV`   `V+.÷ρV`   `1+.×V÷V+.*0`

    `V⊞((ρV),1)ρ1`   `V⊞V÷V`   `1⊥V÷1⊥V÷V`

18.   The result is `3521`. This suggests that in general decode can be simulated by `W+.×V`, where W is the weighting vector and V is the vector to be decoded, since the weighting vector `1000 100 10 1` is obtained by raising the radix vector `10 10 10 10` to the powers `3 2 1 0`.

Answers for Chapter 23

1.
```
        ∇MULT1 N;X
[1]     START:X←?N,N
[2]     (⍕1↑X),'×',⍕1↓X
[3]     L1:→(□=STOP,×/X)/0,CORRECT
[4]     'TRY AGAIN'
[5]     →L1
[6]     CORRECT:'CORRECT'
[7]     →START ∇
```

2.
```
        ∇MULT2 N;X
[1]     START:X←?N,N×I←1
[2]     (⍕1↑X),'×',⍕1↓X
[3]     L1:→(□=STOP,×/X)/0,CORRECT
[4]     I←I+1
[5]     →(4=I)/ANS
[6]     'TRY AGAIN'
[7]     →L1
[8]     ANS:'ANSWER IS ',⍕×/X
[9]     →START
[10]    CORRECT:'CORRECT'
[11]    →START ∇
```

3.
```
        ∇MULT3 N;X;I
[1]     START:X←?N,N×I←1
[2]     (⍕1↑X),'×',⍕1↓X
[3]     L1:→(□=HELP,STOP,×/X)/AID,0,CORRECT
[4]     I←I+1
[5]     →(4=I)/ANS
[6]     RETRY:'TRY AGAIN'
[7]     →L1
[8]     ANS:'ANSWER IS ',⍕×/X
[9]     →START
[10]    CORRECT:'CORRECT'
[11]    →START
[12]    AID:'COUNT THE STARS FOR THE ANSWER:'
[13]    Xρ'*'
[14]    →RETRY ∇
```

4.
```
        ∇MULT4 N;X;I;J;K;A
[1]     K←J←0
[2]     START:X←?N,N×I←1
[3]     J←J+1
[4]     (⍕1↑X),'×',⍕1↓X
[5]     L1:→(□=STOP,×/X)/END,CORRECT
[6]     I←I+1
[7]     →(4=I)/ANS
[8]     'TRY AGAIN'
[9]     →L1
[10]    CORRECT:'CORRECT'
[11]    K←K+1
[12]    →L2
[13]    ANS:'ANSWER IS ',⍕×/X
[14]    L2:→START
[15]    END:'YOUR SCORE IS ',(⍕⌈100×K÷J-1),' PERCENT RIGHT' ∇
```

5.
```
        ∇Z←LITPROMPT
[1]     Z←⍞←'           ',0/□←'⍞:'
[2]     Z←7↓⍞ ∇
```

6.
```
        ∇SPELL[6] 'THE CORRECT SPELLING IS ',SPL[N+1;] ∇
```

```
7.                    ∇R←ENTER;A
      [1]     R←''
      [2]     L1:A←,⍞
      [3]     →(0=ρA)/DONE
      [4]     R←R,20↑A
      [5]     →L1
      [6]     DONE:R←(1+,0 20⊤¯1+ρR)ρR ∇
```

ENTER1 is more general. It pads out the list each time to the width of the widest entry:

```
                     ∇R←ENTER1;Z;MAX
      [1]     R←0 0ρ''
      [2]     NEXT:Z←,⍞
      [3]     →(0=ρZ)/0
      [4]     MAX←⌈/(ρZ),1↓ρR
      [5]     R←((1↑ρR),MAX)↑R
      [6]     Z←MAX↑Z
      [7]     R←R,Z
      [8]     →NEXT ∇
```

```
8.                    ∇R←N LIST L;I
      [1]     R←ρI←1
      [2]     L1:R←R,L↑⍞
      [3]     I←I+1
      [4]     →(N≥I)/L1
      [5]     R←(N,L)ρR ∇
```

```
9.                    ∇LOOKUP L;M;NAME
      [1]     'ENTER NAME'
      [2]     NAME←⍞
      [3]     NAME←(¯1↑ρL)↑NAME
      [4]     M←(L∧.=NAME)/ι1↑ρL
      [5]     →(0=ρM)/NOGO
      [6]     'NAME IS ON ROW(S) ',(⍕M),' IN THE LIST'
      [7]     →0
      [8]     NOGO:'NAME NOT FOUND' ∇
```

```
10.                   ∇BALANCE;OPB;TRANS;R
      [1]     ⍞←R←'OPENING BALANCE: '
      [2]     OPB←(ρR)↓⍞
      [3]     ⍞←'TRANSACTIONS: '
      [4]     TRANS←⍎⍞
      [5]     ''
      [6]     R,OPB
      [7]     'TOTAL DEPOSITS: ',⍕+/(TRANS>0)/TRANS
      [8]     'TOTAL WITHDRAWALS: ',⍕|+/(TRANS<0)/TRANS
      [9]     'CLOSING BALANCE: ',⍕(+/TRANS)+⍎OPB ∇
```

```
11.                   ∇Z←MAT INS N;LINE;L
      [1]     ⍞←L←'ENTER LINE TO BE INSERTED: '
      [2]     LINE←(1↓ρMAT)↑(ρL)↓⍞
      [3]     Z←(N≠¯1+ι1+1↑ρMAT)⌿MAT
      [4]     Z[N+1;]←LINE ∇
```

INS solves the problem by brute force, actually expanding MAT to make room for the new line.
    INS1 below avoids expansion and uses a sneaky sort on line numbers to rearrange the rows:

```
                     ∇Z←MAT INS1 N;LINE;L
      [1]     ⍞←L←'ENTER LINE TO BE INSERTED: '
      [2]     LINE←(1↓ρMAT)↑(ρL)↓⍞
      [3]     Z←(MAT,[1]LINE)[⍋(ι1↑ρMAT),N+.1;] ∇
```

```
12.                   ∇R←MONTHLYINPUT;A
      [1]     'ENTER INPUT'
      [2]     L1:R←¯1↓A←⎕
      [3]     →(12=ρR)/L2
      [4]     'WRONG NUMBER OF ENTRIES'
      [5]     →L1
      [6]     L2:→((+/R)=¯1↑A)/0
      [7]     'CONTROL TOTAL DOESN''T CHECK OUT.  REENTER NUMBERS'
      [8]     →L1 ∇
```

Answers for Chapter 24

1.
```
       ∇ARITH DATA;A
[1]    A←1↑DATA
[2]    ⍕(A=15)/'ADD DATA'
[3]    ⍕(A=25)/'SUB DATA'
[4]    ⍕(A=35)/'BAL DATA'
[5]    ⍕(~A∊15 25 35)/'ERR DATA' ∇
```
better:
```
       ∇ARITH1 DATA
[1]    ⍕(4 3ρ'ADDSUBBALERR')[''ρ15 25 35⍳1↑DATA;],' DATA' ∇
```
`''ρ` is needed to make the expression in brackets a scalar rather than a 1-element vector. Why?

2. **A**   `⍕'X',' ←DAT'` or `⍕'X←DAT'`

    B   `⍕'NAM',(⍕I),' ←D'` where $I = 1,2,...$

3.
```
       ∇DECOM FN;M
[1]    ⍝FN IS A CHARACTER VECTOR HOLDING NAME OF FUNCTION
[2]    M←⎕CR FN
[3]    M←(M[;1]='⍝')⌿M
[4]    ⎕FX M ∇
```
This program works only where the comment symbol ⍝ is at the beginning of the line. Where a comment is imbedded elsewhere, more of a challenge is presented. Try to generalize $DECOM$.

4.
```
       ∇Z←FACTEX N
[1]    ⍕3 ¯14[1+N≠0]↑'Z←1 Z←N×FACTEX N-1' ∇
```

5.
```
       ⍕'M[',((¯1+ρρM)ρ';'),'I]'
```
which is equivalent to $M[;I]$ or $M[;;I]$

6.
```
       ⍕'L←''SOMEINSTRUCTION ◇ I←I+1 ◇ ⍕(N≥I)/L'
```
which is equivalent to the line
```
       L:SOMEINSTRUCTION ◇ I←I+1 ◇ →(N≥I)/L
```

7.
```
       ∇ERASEALLBUT M;ERASEALLBUT;A
[1]    A←(11+0 1+.×ρM)↑'M←⎕EX ⎕NL 3'
[2]    ⍕⎕FX('ERASEALLBUT',,';',M),[.5]A ∇
```
This function works equally well for other arguments of $⎕NL$. It is an ingenious use of a local variable to shield globals. On line 1 the $+.×$ calculates the number of spaces needed in the header for the names in M, including the semicolons, and adds 11 for the width of `'ERASEALLBUT'` to pad out the second line of the canonical representation. When $⎕EX$ is executed, those names listed in the header will not show in the result of $⎕NL$ 3 and therefore will not be erased.

8. Catenates contents of ⍞ to A or passes if only RETURN is entered.

9.
```
       ∇Z←REPRES MATRIX;A
[1]    A←',⍝',⍕MATRIX
[2]    Z←⎕FX 'TEMP' ON A ∇
```
```
       ∇Z←RESTORE TEMP;A
[1]    Z←1 1↓⎕CR TEMP
[2]    A←⎕EX TEMP ∇
```
$REPRES$ assigns a temporary name $TEMP$ to the matrix in function form (why the ⍝ symbols?). $TEMP$ may be edited as a function and recreated as a (character) matrix with $RESTORE$.

10.
```
       ∇REPORT;NAME;PROMPT
[1]    'HERE IS THE REPORT MENU:'
[2]    RPTS
[3]    ⍞←PROMPT←'ENTER THE REPORT DESIRED: '
[4]    NAME←(ρPROMPT)↓⍞
[5]    ⍕NAME ∇
```

11.
```
       ∇OMIT;A;B;NAM;OMT
[1]    A←ρ⍞←'ARRAY NAME? '
[2]    B←⍕NAM←A↓⍞
[3]    L:A←ρ⍞←'OMIT WHICH ROWS? '
[4]    OMT←⍕A↓⍞
[5]    →(∨/OMT>1↑ρB)/ERR
[6]    B←(~(⍳1↑ρB)∊OMT)⌿B
[7]    ⍕NAM,'←B'
[8]    →0
[9]    ERR:'INVALID ROW NUMBER'
[10]   →L ∇
```

12.
```
        )LOAD 1 CLASS
SAVED 14.45.33 02/20/83
        ∇DRILL
[1]     'ENTER YOUR CHOICE OF DRILL EXERCISES'
[2]     'SUB, ADD OR SPELL'
[3]     ⍎⍞  ∇
```

13.
```
        FALSE←'FALSE'
        TRUE←'TRUE'
        ∇A CHECK B
[1]     ⍎5 ‾4[1+A>B]↑'FALSE  TRUE' ∇
        3 CHECK 4
FALSE
        6 CHECK 3
TRUE
```
This illustrates the use of ⍎ to execute only that expression determined by the stated condition. Although in this example the expressions selected are literal, had they instead been instructions requiring considerable computation, some savings could result from avoiding unncessary calculations. Note that ⍎ isn't really necessary in this function; it is used only to make a point.

14.
```
        ∇A CMP B
[1]     ((A>B)/'GREATER'),((A=B)/'EQUAL'),(A<B)/'LESS' ∇


        R←⎕CR 'CMP'
        R
A CMP B
((A>B)/'GREATER'),((A=B)/'EQUAL'),(A<B)/'LESS'
        R[2;8+⍳7]←'MORE   '
        ⎕FX R
CMP
        ∇CMP[⎕] ∇
    ∇ A CMP B
[1]     ((A>B)/'MORE   '),((A=B)/'EQUAL'),(A<B)/'LESS'
    ∇
```

15.
```
        )CLEAR
CLEAR WS
        )COPY 1 CLASS HYP RECT
SAVED  14.45.33 02/20/83
        D←⎕CR 'HYP'
        ⎕EX 'HYP'
        ∇RECT[0⎕0]
[0]     L RECT H;HYP
[1]     [2]
[2]     ⍎'L ',(⎕FX D),' H' ∇
        ∇RECT[⎕] ∇
    ∇ L RECT H;HYP
[1]     2×L+H
[2]     ⍎'L ',(⎕FX D),' H'
[3]     L×H
    ∇
        )FNS
RECT
        3 RECT 4
14
5
12
```

16.
```
        ∇DISP;R;L;M
[1]     'WHAT LETTER(S)?'
[2]     L←⍞
[3]     'LABELS (1), VARIABLES (2), OR FUNCTIONS (3)?'
[4]     R←⎕
[5]     ⎕←M←L ⎕NL R
[6]     I←1
[7]     LP:⎕CR M[I;]
[8]     I←I+1
[9]     →(I≤1↑⍴M)/LP ∇
```

17.
```
[1]    →(7<ρ⎕LC)/EXIT
[2]    ⍝ NORMAL ROUTE HERE
[3]    EXIT:→
```
Don't forget that the first element of ⎕LC in a function is the current line being executed.

18.
```
       ∇LIST;A;B;I;⎕IO
[1]    ⎕IO←1
[2]    A←⎕NL 3
[3]    I←1↑ρA
[4]    →(0∧.=ρA)/0
[5]    ⎕←B←10ρ' '
[6]    L1:⎕CR,A[I̅;]
[7]    B
[8]    I←I-1
[9]    →(0≠I)/L1 ∇
```

20.
```
       ∇Z←F OPROD A
[1]    Z←⍕'(⍳1↑A)∘.',F,'⍳1↓A' ∇
```
Note that the left argument must be enclosed in quotes when executed.

Answers for Chapter 25

1.
```
3 4 5 simple
(,3) (,4) (,5) nested
(3) (4) (5) simple
3 4 'A' simple
3 (4 'A') nested
((3) (4) (5)) simple
(,3),(,4),(,5) nested
3 4 'AB' nested
'ABC' 'XYZ' nested
'ABC','XYZ' simple
'A' 'B' 'C' simple
'A' ('B' 'C') nested
```

2.

	depth	rank	shape
⊃A 1	0	0	⍳0
⊂A 1 2 3 4 5 6	2	0	⍳0

⊂⊂A
  1 2 3
  4 5 6
	3	0	⍳0

⊂⊃A 1	0	0	⍳0
(⊂A),(⊂B),(⊂C) 1 2 3 99 APL 4 5 6	2	1	3
⊃⊃A 1	0	0	⍳0
⊃A B 1 2 3 4 5 6	1	2	2 3

3 4ρA B C
1 2 3   99   APL   1 2 3
4 5 6   4 5 6
 	
  99   APL   1 2 3   99
            4 5 6
 	
APL   1 2 3   99   APL
       4 5 6
	2	2	3 4

2 3ρC APL APL	1	2	2 3

```
      2 3ρ⊂C                        2      2      2 3
APL APL APL
APL APL APL
      B B B                         1      1        3
99 99 99
      ⊂A B C                        3      0      ι0
   1 2 3    99 APL
   4 5 6

                                  depth   shape
                                    2       3
      D
   1 2 3    99 APL
   4 5 6
      D[1]                           2      ι0
   1 2 3
   4 5 6
      ⊃D[1]                          1      2 3
 1 2 3
 4 5 6
      ⊃⊃D[1]                         0      ι0
 1
      D[2]                           0      ι0
99
      ⊃D[2]                          0      ι0
99
      D[1],D[2]                      2       2
   1 2 3    99
   4 5 6
      D[1 2]                         2       2
   1 2 3    99
   4 5 6
      (⊃D[1]),D[2]                   1      2 4
1 2 3 99
4 5 6 99
      B                             0      ι0
99
      ⊂B                            0      ι0
99
      ⊂⊂B                           0      ι0
99
      ⊃B                            0      ι0
99
      ⊃⊃B                           0      ι0
99
      C,¨B                          2       3
 A 99   P 99   L 99
      A,¨B                          2      2 3
 1 99   2 99   3 99
 4 99   5 99   6 99
      ⊃¨D                           1       3
1 99 A
      ,¨D                           2       3
 1 2 3 4 5 6   99   APL
      ρ¨D                           2       3
 2 3     3
      ρ¨ρ¨D                         2       3
 2 0   1
      ⊃¨ρ¨ρ¨D                       1       3
 2 0 1
      +/¯1↓D                        2      ι0
100 101 102
103 104 105
      (⊂A),¨C                       2       3
 1 2 3 A    1 2 3 P    1 2 3 L
 4 5 6 A    4 5 6 P    4 5 6 L
```

3.

```
              A,¨⊂C                                    2        2 3
        1 APL    2 APL    3 APL
        4 APL    5 APL    6 APL
```

4. `1≥=A` tests if `A` is a simple array, and `⎕CR¨⊂[2]⎕NL 3` gives a vector of the `⎕CR`'s of all defined functions.

5. ` 1↓∪' ',¨VECTOR`

6. ` ((' '=VECTOR)/VECTOR)←⊂''' '''`
    ` ⍎'''',(∪VECTOR),'''' H0`

7. ` ⍎(1≥=A)/'A←⊂A'`

8. ` (⍳⊃⍴M),M`

9. ` (' ',ROWS),COLS,[1]DATA`

10.
```
        ∇Z←SHAPES A
   [1]    ⍝ SHAPES OF ALL SIMPLE ARRAYS CONTAINED IN ARGUMENT
   [2]    Z←⊂⍴A
   [3]    →(0∈⍴A)/0
   [4]    →(1≥=A)/0
   [5]    Z←(SHAPES ⊃A),SHAPES 1↓,A ∇
```

11. `A` is reformatted to be of rank ≥2. After enclosure it becomes a nested scalar, which, when formatted, is always a matrix regardless of its original rank.

12. ` X Y Z`

    (This identity is known in some quarters as the 'chipmunk' idiom.)

13. ` ⍎(1+X>Y)⊃L2 L1`

14. ` A B (A+.×B)`
```
        1  2  3  4    10 20      500   600
        5  6  7  8    30 40     1140  1400
        9 10 11 12    50 60     1780  2200
                      70 80
```

15. First define a function `TP` to make `TEXT` into a vector of words (see problem 6):
```
          ∇R←TP STRING
   [1]    R←(1+''''=STRING)/STRING ⍝REPLACE ' WITH ''
   [2]    ((' '=R)/R)←⊂''' ''' ⍝ REPLACE BLANKS WITH ' '
   [3]    R←⍎'''',(∪R),'''' ⍝EXECUTE WITH QUOTES AT BEGINNING AND END
   [4]    ⍝R IS NOW A VECTOR OF WORDS
   [5]    ∇
```
   A Sort `TEXT` and count the unique items:
```
          TEXT1←TP TEXT
          SORTTEXT←(⍋TEXT1)/TEXT1
          COUNT←+/SORTTEXT∘.(≡¨)TEXT1
```
   B ` ∨/∧/0 1⊖TEXT1∘.(=¨)'AN' 'EXAMPLE'`
   C ` (TEXT1~REFERENCE)`

16. A ` +/¨ACCOUNTS`
    B ` -/¨+/¨ACCOUNTS`

Answers for Chapter 28

1. A ` →CONTINUE×(1↑⎕AI)∈NUMBERS`
    B ` T←⎕AI[3]`
    .
    .
    .
    ` →(100≤⎕AI[3]-T)/QUIT`

2. ` 'S',⎕TC[2],'/'`

3.
```
        ∇R←DUE BILLS;BILLS1;CHECK
   [1]    BILLS1←BILLS
   [2]    BILLS1[;2]←12|BILLS1[;2]
   [3]    BILLS1←10⊥⍉BILLS[;4 2 3]
   [4]    CHECK←(10⊥⎕TS[⍳3])≥BILLS1
   [5]    R←CHECK/BILLS[;1] ∇
```

4. ` V∘.≥⍳⌈/V`

    This converts integers (4 bytes) to bit representation (1/8 byte), saving considerable space.

5.
```
      ∇Z←DEC DISTRD VALUES;B;C;□CT;□IO
[1]   □CT←□IO←0
[2]   VALUES←VALUES÷DEC
[3]   B←(⌊.5++/VALUES)-+/⌊VALUES
[4]   C←▲▼1|VALUES
[5]   Z←DEC×(⌊VALUES)+B>C ∇
```
The expression 1|VALUES contains the error if each element were represented by its floor. B is the total number of additional 1's needed in the vector. C ranks the elements according to the accuracy of their representation, with the least accurate element having C equal to 0.

6.
```
      ∇SMASH;BLANKS
[1]   BLANKS←(□WA-32)ρ' ' ∇
```

7.
```
      ∇Z←RLACC M;□RL;□IO;R
[1]   □IO←0
[2]   □RL←□AI[0]
[3]   R←ρM
[4]   →(0=ρR)/0
[5]   Z←×/R
[6]   Z←Rρ(,M)[Z?Z] ∇
```

8.
```
      ∇Z←DRLACC M;□RL;□IO;R
[1]   □IO←0
[2]   □RL←□AI[0]
[3]   R←ρM
[4]   →(0=ρR)/0
[5]   Z←×/R
[6]   Z←Rρ(,M)[▲Z?Z] ∇
```

9.
```
      ∇R←TIME;T;W
[1]   W←3↑3↓□TS
[2]   T←(12|1↑W),1↓W
[3]   T←((0=1↑T)/12),((0≠1↑T)/1↑T),1↓T
[4]   R←▼T
[5]   R[(R=' ')/ιρR]←':'
[6]   R←R,' ',('AP')[1+12≤1↑W],'M EASTERN' ∇
```

10.
```
      ∇DATE;S
[1]   S←3↑□TS
[2]   S[ι3]←S[2 3 1]
[3]   S←▼S
[4]   S[(S=' ')/ιρS]←'/'
[5]   S ∇
```

11.
```
      ▼FORYOUONLY
[1]   →(1421≠□AI[1])/0
[2]   'THIS IS THE MESSAGE' ∇
```

12.
```
      A←9.22222222222222
      B←9.22222222222227
      A=B
1
      A∈B
1
      A-B
¯4.884981308E¯15
      □CT←0
      A=B
0
      A∈B
0
      A-B
¯4.884981308E¯15
```

13. Because both bracket indexing and interval are affected in the same way by the change of origin.

14.
```
      □IO←0
      ι0

      ι1
0
      ρι0
0
```

```
                ρι1
           1
15.             ∇TIMEOFDAY;T
      [1]       T←4 9ρ(18ρ'MORNING   '),'AFTERNOONEVENING
      [2]       'GOOD ',T[1+⌊⎕TS[4]÷6;] ∇
16.             ∇N CRAPS D;I
      [1]       I←0
      [2]       L1:DICE
      [3]       ⎕DL D
      [4]       I←I+1
      [5]       →(N>I)/L1 ∇
17.             ∇MULTTIME N;X;I;A
      [1]       START:X←?N,N×I←1
      [2]       (⍕1↑X),'×',⍕1↓X
      [3]       A←⎕AI[3]
      [4]       L1:→(⎕=STOP,×/X)/0,CORRECT
      [5]       I←I+1
      [6]       →(4=I)/ANS
      [7]       'TRY AGAIN'
      [8]       →L1
      [9]       CORRECT:'CORRECT'
      [10]      →L2
      [11]      ANS:'ANSWER IS ',⍕×/X
      [12]      L2:A←2↑ 60 60 1000 ⊤⎕AI[3]-A
      [13]      'YOU HAVE USED ',(⍕1↑A),' MINUTES AND ',(⍕1↓A),' SECONDS'
      [14]      →START ∇
18.             ⎕LX←'M[1+(1↑⎕AI)∊1500 1600;]'
19.             ∇USAGE EXPR;A;Z
      [1]       A←((ρEXPR)↑'Z'),[.5]EXPR
      [2]       A←⎕FX A
      [3]       A←(1↑1↓⎕AI),⎕WA
      [4]       Z
      [5]       TS←(⍕⁻6+(1↑1↓⎕AI)-1↑A),' MILLISECONDS, AND '
      [6]       TS,(⍕(⁻1↑A)-144+⎕WA),' BYTES' ∇
```

The 'fudge' factors ⁻6 and 144 are needed to compensate for extra time and space required as a result of imbedding the expression in a defined function. They will vary with the system and should be adjusted to give zero time and space with a null expression.

Symbol index

Top row

¨ *dyadic* each, 265

‾ negative numbers, 6 47

< *dyadic* less than, 28; □*FMT* delimiter, 175

≤ *dyadic* less than or equal, 28

= *dyadic* equal, 28

≥ *dyadic* not greater than, 28

> *dyadic* greater than, 28; □*FMT* delimiter, 175

≠ *dyadic* not equal, 28; ≠ /, 39

∨ *dyadic* or, 29; ∨ /, 36; (.), 195; ∨ \, 39

∧ *dyadic* and, 29; ∧ /, 39; ∧ . =, 196; ∧ \, 39

− *monadic* arithmetic negation, 47; *dyadic* subtract, 6; − /, 37

÷ *monadic* reciprocal, 48; *dyadic* divide, 6; ÷ /, 38

0 1 2 3 4 5 6 7 8 9 digits used in ⍕, 167

9 in □*FMT* G code, 171

+ *dyadic* addition, 6; + /, 34; + \, 38; matrix multiply + . ×, 192

× *monadic* direction, 51; *dyadic* multiplication, 6; × /, 38

⍫ function lock, 81 252

⍒ *monadic* grade down, 139 142; *dyadic* grade down, 142

⍋ *monadic* grade up, 139 142; *dyadic* grade up, 142

⌽ *monadic* reverse, 135; *dyadic* rotate, 136

⍉ *monadic* transpose, 137; *dyadic* transpose, 184

⊖ *monadic* reverse, 135; *dyadic* rotate, 136

⍟ *monadic* natural log, 48; *dyadic* general log, 21

⍱ *dyadic* nor, 29

⍲ *dyadic* nand, 29

! *monadic* factorial or gamma, 148; *dyadic* combinations or beta, 26

⌹ *monadic* matrix inverse, 191; *dyadic* matrix divide, 199

Second row

? *monadic* random roll, 50 295; *dyadic* random deal, 144 295

∈ *monadic* type, 257; *dyadic* membership, 119

ρ *monadic* shape, 105; *dyadic* reshape, 14 110; ρ ρ for rank, 106

~ *monadic* not (logical negation), 49; *dyadic* without, 126; for intersection, 126

↑ *monadic* mix, 261; *dyadic* take, 127

↓ *monadic* split, 260; *dyadic* drop, 127

ι *monadic* interval or count, 103; *dyadic* ranking or index of, 118; empty vector ι 0, 104

○ *monadic* pi, 51; *dyadic* circular, trigonometric and hyperbolic, 52

* *monadic* exponential, 47; *dyadic* power or raise, 19; in state indicator, 152; □*FMT* overflow, 174

Q □*FMT* positive right decoration, 173

E in scientific notation, 21; □*FMT* scaled code, 170

R □*FMT* filler decoration, 170

T □*FMT* tab control, 174

I □*FMT* integer format, 169

O □*FMT* zero decoration, 173

P □*FMT* left positive decoration, 173

← assignment, 11; nested array assignment, 261; selective assignment, 262

→ branch, 149; naked branch, 153

ω in direct definition, 298

⎕ character input, 231; bare output, 233

Third row

α in direct definition, 298

⌈ *monadic* ceiling, 49; *dyadic* maximum, 22; ⌈/, 36

⌊ *monadic* floor, 49; *dyadic* minimum, 22; ⌊/, 36

_ underlined letters, 12 13

∇ function definition, 56

Δ *T*Δ trace designator, 150; *S*Δ stop designator, 151; character for names, 12

∘ outer product, 203

' character strings, 113 115; empty vector '', 120

☐ evaluated input, 234; system functions and variables, 100 280 292

(in APL expressions, 41; in operating system commands, 289; in strand notation, 262

) in APL expressions, 41; system commands, 13 87 100

A ☐*FMT* character format, 171

S ☐*FMT* character substitution, 175

F ☐*FMT* fixed point format, 169

G ☐*FMT* picture format, 171

J complex number notation, 302

K ☐*FMT* scale factor, 172

L ☐*FMT* left justify qualifier, 172

[ ] indexing or subscripting, 121 178; axis operator, 178 211; scatter indexing or choose, 264

◇ statement separator, 44

⍕ *monadic* execute, 254

⍕ *monadic* format, 161; *dyadic* format, 162 166

Bottom row

⊂ *monadic* enclose, 258 260

⊃ *monadic* pick, 262; *dyadic* first or disclose, 260 261

∩ *monadic* unique, 130

∪ *monadic* unite, 263

⊥ *dyadic* base or decode, 217

⊤ *dyadic* represent or encode, 221

| *monadic* residue, 27; *dyadic* magnitude or absolute value, 48

; in function headers, 73; in indexing, 122; in ☐*FMT* lists, 170

: for labels, 150; for passwords, 4 95

\ *monadic* scan, 38 209; *dyadic* expand, 126

Z ☐*FMT* zero fill qualifier, 171

X ☐*FMT* skip specification, 174

C ☐*FMT* comma qualifier, 172

B ☐*FMT* blank qualifier, 172

N ☐*FMT* right negative decoration, 173

M ☐*FMT* left negative decoration, 173

, *monadic* ravel, 108; *dyadic* catenate, 108 113 180; *dyadic* laminate, 183; in ☐*FC*, 166; in ☐*FMT* left argument, 169

. decimal point, 5; inner product, 191; outer product, 203; in ☐*FC*, 166

/ *monadic* reduce, 33 34 178; *dyadic* compress and replicate, 123 125

Δ character for names, 12

⍝ comment, 10 44

⍀ *monadic* scan, 38 209; *dyadic* expand, 126

⌿ *monadic* reduce, 33 34 178; *dyadic* compress and replicate, 123 125

= *monadic* depth, 258; *dyadic* match, 144

∊ *dyadic* find, 129

ι *dyadic* find index, 130

⍳ *dyadic* indexing with axis, 264

358

Index

Q

S

Postscript

All of the functions displayed in the text have been collected together for your convenience into a single workspace, *CLASS*, which may be purchased at a nominal cost on a diskette suitable for most personal computers, or on magnetic tape for VSAPL or APL2. Besides *CLASS*, other workspaces available are:

AIDRILL, which contains *TEACH* and *EASYDRILL*
EASYPLOT, which produced most of the plots in Chapter 20
TYPEDRILL, a typing drill practice
EASYSCREEN, simple full screen management for the IBM PC
TABULATE, a simple but effective utility for casual report preparation.

To order any of these workspaces, please send a check or money order to Allen Rose Associates, Box 58, Captain Cook, Hawaii 96704. For disk orders, the first workspace is $35, others are $25 each (in the same order). For tape, the first workspace is $75, others are $40 each. Postage and handling charges are included. To avoid delays, be sure to include information about which hardware and APL software you are using.

Additional materials, including the text-processing programs used in the production of this book, are also available. Please write for further details, or just to exchange ideas.